OCT - 9 2015

Man-Eaters of the World

D1548118

Man-Eaters of the World

True Accounts of Predators Hunting Humans

Alex MacCormick

A Herman Graf Book

Skyhorse Publishing

First published in 2003 in the UK as *The Mammoth Book of Maneaters*
by Robinson, an imprint of Constable & Robinson Ltd

This paperback edition published in 2014 by Skyhorse Publishing

Skyhorse publishing books may be purchased in bulk at special discounts
for sales promotion, corporate gifts, fund-raising, or educational
purposes. Special editions can also be created to specifications. For
details, contact the Special Sales Department, Skyhorse Publishing,
307 West 36th Street, 11th Floor, New York, New York 10018
or info@skyhorsepublishing.com

www.skyhorsepublishing.com

10 9 8 7 6 5 4 3 2 1

Library of Congress Cataloging-in-Publication Data is available on file

ISBN: 978-1-62914-675-1

Printed and bound in the UK by CPI Group (UK) Ltd, Croydon, CR0 4YY

Contents

Introduction

From aardvarks to zebras, from big cats to sharks, from dingoes to our fellow human beings – it sometimes seems that, given half a chance, maneaters of one kind or another are ever ready to sink their teeth into our flesh.

For most of us the fear of being attacked and eaten alive by an unseen monster that appears out of nowhere is a deep-seated one, but we try to dismiss such thoughts as irrational. "It couldn't happen to me," we say to ourselves. But, as you will see from the stories in this book, sometimes it *does* happen to people like us.

"When we opened up the croc, we found Olsen's legs, intact from the knees up, still joined together at the pelvis. We found his head, crushed into small chunks, a barely recognizable mass of hair and flesh," recalled a witness.

"We made eye contact. As the huge mass of white fur, claws and teeth charged, I knew I was seconds from death," said the teacher leading a group of students on a trip to the Arctic.

"When I reached Rod, I saw a shark had bitten into his left thigh and was tearing violently at his flesh. Clouds of blood mixed in with the air bubbles. Then a second shark appeared and made a blinding strike, ripping into his calf," recalled the diver working in the Caribbean.

"The rhino whipped round in his tracks like a cat and came for me in a beeline," said the badly gored safari tourist.

Paul Templer got a whiff of doom when a 4,000-pound hippo snatched him from a canoe and swallowed his head – "I went straight down his throat and it smelled like death."

The two fishermen who bled to death after piranha-like fish bit off their penises, the swimmer who suffocated after being paralysed by one of the fifty known species of venomous sea snake, the little girl who never woke up after being left home alone with a giant python, the railway workers devoured by a lion, the surfer who pleaded to be allowed to die after losing an arm to a shark, the little girl dragged from her home by a pack of wolves – none of these people expected to die. As a witness to one such horror remarked: "They say it's like a bullet – you never see the one that gets you."

However, that isn't *always* the case.

"Seeking young, well-built male 18–30 years old for slaughtering" read an internet advertisement in 2002. Would you have replied to it? Well, several young men did, and one – a computer technician by the name of Brandes – shared a dish of his own flambéed penis with his killer before allowing the Internet Cannibal to eat him alive.

Though less perverted, the outcome was not so very different in the old days for shipwrecked sailors and passengers: all too frequently they faced what became known as "the custom of the sea." Take, for example, the seven English sailors who, in the seventeenth century, set out on a voyage planned to last only a few hours but, instead, got blown off course and were lost at sea for seventeen days. When their meagre supplies of food and water ran out, hunger and thirst drove them nearly insane. Out of desperation one of the crew suggested they draw lots to decide which of them should die to feed the rest and who should act as the executioner. By a quirk of fate, the man who came up with this idea drew the short straw: he was killed, his blood drunk and his body eaten.

In the pages which follow you will find hundreds of true, often first-hand accounts of nightmare situations in which men, women and children lose their lives or parts of their bodies to creatures with teeth, fangs, tentacles, claws and beaks. The stories are grouped into five sections by type of location: low-lying areas such as grasslands, islands, and deserts; woods, forests and jungles; rivers, lakes and seas; in and around villages, towns and cities; and, finally, hills and mountains. No matter where in the world **you** live, there is a maneater not far away.

Some pieces are extracted from books by famous authors, some are by heroic explorers, some are from newspapers and other types of media; they come from all over the world. Many are horrifying to read, some are moving, a few are weird, and a very few are incredibly funny.

This book is, of course, meant to be a "good read", but I hope you will also find parts of it enlightening even if you only learn which type of bear you must stand up to, and which type you "play dead" with. However, this does not pretend to be a "Teach Yourself How to

Survive an Attack by a Maneater" guide, and nor is it an encyclopaedia. What you are about to read, though, is a huge, amazing collection of true accounts of bloodthirsty attacks by maneaters past and present.

Alex MacCormick

Natural Born Killer Instinct

We are so far from nature that we have forgotten the sheer viciousness of the animal world. Reducing wildlife to cute domesticity has its dangers, believes Stuart Wavell, who wrote the essay below in 1994.

The polar bear was intent on premeditated murder. Its victim was an adult male walrus basking on an ice-pan sunning area which the Inuit call *uglit*. Normally, the great white predator of the Arctic would be deterred by the sheer bulk of a walrus more than twice the bear's weight and the deadly tusks protruding from its lower jaw, but on this occasion the polar bear possessed the opportunity and the means.

Inuit who witnessed the incident, on the north coast of Baffin Island, were astonished to see the bear using its teeth and claws to fashion a large ball of ice. Walruses have poorly developed sight, relying on smell and hearing to detect danger, so the victim did not notice the bear's antics several hundred yards downwind. The bear was inching forward on its belly, pushing the ice ball in front of it. The Inuit observers recognized their own hunting technique of advancing behind white screens to within rifle range. Had their ancestors copied bears, or *vice versa*, they wondered. Their musings were cut short when, a few yards from its victim, the bear reared up to its full height and brought the ice block slamming down on the walrus's small skull.

There is something distinctly unsettling about such a degree of calculation. It is utterly out of kilter with the image we have of such noble, majestic creatures. It is of a different order from, say, the humble thrush using a pebble to crack a snail. Frankly, it is not cricket. Animals are supposed to kill their prey in a programmed way, as they appear to do in David Attenborough's and other wildlife programmes on television.

Technically, it was not murder, although a section of western society would have been eager to convene a court. The victim, after all, was not human. But polar bears do kill humans, sometimes without provocation. The two species of predators are in competition for seals. Bears occasionally kill men, and men occasionally kill bears. But polar bears are an endangered species, aren't they? No. There are some 2,500 polar bears in the north Baffin area alone, where they outnumber the Inuit.

These facts are calculated to generate frustration bordering on anger. For we have constructed a set of rules and assumptions about the natural world that are dangerously erroneous. We in the West are mostly so distanced from wildlife that we are deluding ourselves about the nature of the world we live in. In losing that link, we lose the opportunity to understand ourselves. In some cases we have undermined the best guarantors of wilderness and its creatures. Worse, we are engaging in a second Faustian bargain which proclaims nature redundant.

A revealing insight into our confused beliefs was provided when a Siberian tiger killed a keeper recently at John Aspinall's wildlife park near Canterbury, in England. There was an immediate expectation that the cat would be put down, as if it was a pet which had become dangerous rather than the greatest of the land predators. Aspinall let the cat out of the bag when he stated that tigers "see us as honorary tigers". No more keepers for Balkash, the 500-pound male tiger, he ruled, in punishment for "letting his species down".

This was straight out of Kipling's *The Jungle Book*. The Law of the Jungle was quite specific in forbidding "every beast to eat Man except when he is killing to show his children how to kill, and then he must hunt outside the hunting-grounds of his pack or tribe". Shere Khan, the tiger, broke this rule to hunt Mowgli, with the excuse that he had families dotted around the British Empire that were in a position to distinguish fact from fable. It is not his fault that his human-like bestiary was seized on by Disney to propagate its curious anthropomorphist message. Nor could Kipling guess that Shere Khan would become the classic stereotype for the mankiller.

Among the world's greatest concentration of tigers, in the 3,800-square-mile Sunderbans mangrove forest straddling Bangladesh and India, there seems to be little perception of man being an honorary tiger or, indeed, any appreciation of the above nostrums. Between 1956 and 1983, tigers killed 1,554 people, despite an abundance of axis deer and wild boar, their natural prey. In nearly every case, the victim was the last in a line of woodcutters or others entering the forest. Casualties were almost totally eliminated by the practice of wearing a boldly painted mask on the back of the head.

The notion that some animals kill for any motive other than necessity is unacceptable to the mythology we in the West have created. We have drawn the teeth from beasts that terrified our ancestors. A vigorous rehabilitation campaign asserts that wolves have been misrepresented. Yet most aboriginal hamlets in Canada's sub-Arctic or Arctic have accounts of wolf attacks on hunters. It is not uncommon to see wolves attacking caribou, apparently for the hell of it, chewing bits from them while they run and then breaking off to target another victim.

No more impressive somersault has been performed in the public mind than that of Orca, the killer whale. Today, crowds are captivated by killer whales' obliging antics and winning smiles. Most people have forgotten that in 1962, when killer whales were first considered for display in aquariums, the general reaction was horror. Orca was considered so rapacious that fisheries patrol boats were instructed to shoot killer whales on sight. Killer whales split boats in half and ripped nets. Their apparent idea of fun was and continues to be working in pairs to pulverize other whales.

This is not to characterize wild animals as bad, murderous or cruel, which are human values. They are simply wild and, notwithstanding intensive study, mysterious. They deserve our sense of awe and wonder, but they are not as cuddly, cute and predictable as we insist on depicting them. Lacking any serious predators in Britain and in other regions in the West, we envelop wild animals with the sentiments we accord to pets. Even our household animals are schizophrenic: most cats, under the cloying attentions of their owners, mentally revert to kittenhood until a bird triggers a violent personality swing to predator.

But what possible damage can be caused by our delusions about pets? Plenty. In the 1970s a pressure crack opened up between two sets of fundamental attitudes to nature. On one side were the native hunters of northern Canada, acknowledged as supreme environmentalists who had not hunted one single species to extinction. On the other was Western society, with a less illustrious record but now committed to an ordered world in which the lion lay down with the lamb. The consequences of that clash – alcoholism, welfare dependency and loss of identity – are still rippling through some Canadian settlements. Why should we care? Because they are the only successful custodians of wildlife in millions of square miles.

The detonator was a picture in 1977 of Brigitte Bardot cuddling a baby harp seal to draw attention to the seal-pup hunt off the coast of Newfoundland. The image was irresistible. The clamour to salve our consciences was undeniable whatever the cost. We fell for a pair of appealing eyes. Someone forgot to mention that seals are predators in competition with man: according to one estimate, Canadian seals consume as much fish as the total catch available to humans in the North Atlantic. Urban populations and the media, following the lead given by the influential London-based press, lined up behind Greenpeace's call for a ban on seal skins. The Inuit found themselves in the dock beside the main culprits.

It was a dialogue of the deaf. No matter that Newfoundland was a long way from the North-west Territories of Canada, where native peoples did not hunt seal pups. In vain it was pointed out that seal skins were a by-product of the Inuit's staple diet and that the meagre revenue from skin sales barely covered the overheads of Arctic travel. Adult seals would continue to be hunted in large numbers for subsistence. But the loss of income would exacerbate the problems of traditional hunters still adjusting from a nomadic lifestyle.

It was the same story when Greenpeace launched its anti-fur campaign in the 1980s. The main targets were weekend trappers in America, and subsequently fur ranchers. In Britain, remote from the action but skilled in class warfare, most opprobrium was directed against those who bought fur at Harrods. This time, the ecological blunderbuss caught Canada's Indians as well as the Inuit. The ultimatum they faced was as unreasoning as if we were asked to give up cars overnight. In 1986 Greenpeace abandoned its campaign, but the damage was done.

There were sound arguments on both sides, but some things could not be said. How could older Inuit hunters explain that their world is governed by two personages, Sila, who controls the weather, and Sedna, who gives or withholds animals from hunters? (You can hear the guffaws.) Or that, with one unseasonal flurry of rain, Sila can start a chain reaction which causes animal population crashes of such magnitude that the good work of environmentalists is wiped out overnight?

Most hunter-gatherer societies do not seek to escape the moral dilemma of killing animals. Our own attitudes are muddled. In part they reflect the Puritans' objection to bear-baiting: not that it gave pain to the bear, but that it gave pleasure to the spectators. But throughout Europe in the Middle Ages, scores of animals were tried for witchcraft in official courts, the last execution occurring in Switzerland in 1906.

Giordano Bruno was burned in 1600 for suggesting that humans were like other animals. A prevailing view, argued René Descartes in his *Discourses*, was that animals did not even feel pain. He was ringingly endorsed by Pope Pius XII, who proclaimed that cries from an abattoir should not arouse unreasonable compassion "any more than do red-hot metals undergoing the blow of the hammer".

European concern about unnecessary cruelty to animals emerged from the humanitarian movement in the nineteenth century. Inevitably, the focus was on household pets and farm animals. In Western Europe and America quite rational people are to be seen addressing the latter as if they are children. The campaign in Britain against blood sports has blurred further our view of animals in the wild and their relationship to man.

However, our fits of moral indignation are subordinate to a more powerful instinct. In Western Europe a unique conviction developed that it was our destiny to subdue and dominate nature for our own needs. The belief that we alone possessed souls separated us from the rest of creation. Darwin's theory of natural selection set us above the other animals. "Man chewed his habitat while secreting theories to justify his acts," Professor Jean Dorst noted drily in *Before Nature Dies*.

Some believe that we have already killed nature, or that world which was here before we arrived. "We as a race turn out to be stronger than we suspected, much stronger. In a sense we turn out to be God's equal or at least his rival able to destroy creation," Bill McKibben wrote in *The End Of Nature* (1990). In genetic engineering, we have gone one better, with serious implications for wild animals. By "picking the locks" which nature installed as definite limits on cross-breeding, we can build our own nursery of cuddly animals. Fulfilling man's dynamic towards moulding nature in his own image, many of the new creatures will have human characteristics. The question "Man or mouse?" was first resolved by a professor at the University of Pennsylvania who inserted human growth genes into a mouse foetus. When born, it grew to twice the size of any mouse in history.

As we narrow our vision to the mysteries of microbiology, the natural world becomes increasingly an abstraction. We have changed the climate with higher carbon dioxide levels, and acknowledge with sadness and shame that some things are now almost irreversible. As urban dwellers, we may not have much contact with nature, but at least we have it in the can. There is something deeply reassuring about the wildlife films played on television. Is it possible that videos will be all we have left?

There is a disturbingly prophetic scene in the otherwise undistinguished science fiction film *Soylent Green* (1973), set on an over-populated and dying earth where euthanasia is compulsory. The old are given one last vision before being turned into biscuits. To heavenly strains of music, they gaze at the video image of a beautiful glade, in which a fawn shimmers. It is implicit that all wildlife on the planet is dead.

Thirty years on, we have more of nature in the can. We have the promise of being able to reconstruct tigers from their genes. So will it really matter if they die out in the wild? We can fix up their natural habitats later. After all, there are twice as many Siberian tigers in zoos as in their normal surroundings. Nor will it matter when our distaste for imprisoned animals closes down all the zoos.

Our obstinate belief that we are entities distinct from the biological world points down this road. Perhaps we need a reconciliation with the primitive, whose beliefs and wilderness are deemed retrograde. Or we could discover an alternative option which few suspect.

The Bible's Genesis story, with its emphasis on Man's dominion, has been blamed for legitimizing Man's impulse to tame nature, but a very different picture emerges in the Book of Job. Job was a good man whose faith was sorely tested by God. Eventually God spoke from a whirlwind, glorying in those parts of creation *not* occupied by man. The message, a radical departure from our most deeply instilled beliefs, seems to be that we are not the centre of the universe, but some kind of experiment.

If so, one day there might be a smile on the face of the tiger.

Part 1

Predators Among the Trees

TRAVELS IN WEST AFRICA

Mary Kingsley (1862–1900) was a remarkable English traveller who, disregarding the conventions of her time, journeyed through western and equatorial Africa and became the first European to enter parts of Gabon.

A niece of the author Charles Kingsley, she led a secluded life until she was about thirty, when she decided to go to West Africa to study African religion and law, with a view to completing a book left unfinished by her deceased father. During 1873 and 1874 she visited Cabinda, the coastal enclave of Angola lying today between Zaire and the Congo; Old Calabar in south-east Nigeria; and the island of Fernando Po, now part of Equatorial Guinea, near the Cameroon coast. Around the lower Congo River she collected specimens of beetles and freshwater fishes for the British Museum.

Returning to Africa in December 1894, she visited the French Congo and, in Gabon, ascended the Ogooué River through the country of the Fang (whom she calls Fan), a tribe with a reputation for cannibalism. On this journey she had many harrowing adventures and narrow escapes. She then visited Corisco Island off Gabon and also climbed Mt Cameroon.

After returning to England with valuable natural history collections, she lectured widely about her travels. She died while nursing sick prisoners during the Boer War in South Africa. Mary Kingsley was not only very brave but also had a keen, often self-deprecatory sense of humour, both evident in her writings, which express her strong sympathies for black Africans. The following is extracted from Travels in West Africa, *which she wrote in 1897.*

My main aim in going to Congo Français was to get up above the tide line of the Ogowé [Ogooué] River and there collect fishes; for my object on this voyage was to collect fish from a river north of the Congo . . . But before I enter into a detailed description of this wonderful bit of West Africa, I must give you a brief notice of the manners, habits and customs of West Coast rivers in general, to make the thing more intelligible.

There is an uniformity in the habits of West Coast rivers, from the Volta to the Coanza, which is, when you get used to it, very taking. Excepting the Congo, every really great river comes out to sea with as much mystery as possible lounging lazily along among its mangrove swamps in a what's-it-matter when-one-comes-out and where's-the-hurry style, through quantities of channels inter-communicating with each other. Each channel, at first sight as like the other as peas in a pod, is bordered on either side by green-black walls of mangroves, which Captain Lugard graphically described as seeming "as if they had lost all count of the vegetable proprieties, and were standing on stilts with their branches tucked up out of the wet leaving their gaunt roots exposed in mid-air."

High-tide or low-tide, there is little difference in the water; the river, be it broad or narrow, deep or shallow, looks like a pathway of polished metal; for it is as heavy weighted with sinking mud as water e'er can be, ebb or flow, year out and year in. But the difference in the banks, though an unending alternation between two appearances, is weird.

At high-water you do not see the mangroves displaying their ankles in the way that shocked Captain Lugard. They look most respectable, their foliage rising densely in a wall irregularly striped here and there by the white line of an aerial root, coming straight down into the water from some upper branch as straight as a plummet, in the strange, knowing way an aerial root of a mangrove does, keeping the hard straight line until it gets some two feet above water-level, and then spreading out into blunt fingers with which to dip into the water and grasp the mud. Banks indeed at high-water can hardly be said to exist, the water stretching away in the mangrove swamps for miles and miles, and you can then go in a suitable small canoe, away among these swamps as far as you please.

This is a fascinating pursuit. For people who like that sort of thing it is just the sort of thing they like, as the art critic of a provincial town wisely observed anent an impressionist picture recently acquired for the municipal gallery. But it is a pleasure to be indulged in with caution; for one thing, you are certain to come across crocodiles.

Now a crocodile drifting down in deep water, or lying asleep with its jaws open on a sand-bank in the sun, is a picturesque adornment to the landscape when you are on the deck of a steamer, and you can write home about it and frighten your relations on your behalf; but when you are away among the swamps in a small dug-out canoe, and that crocodile and his relations are awake – a thing he makes a point of being at flood tide because of fish coming along – and when he has got his foot upon his native heath – that is to say, his tail within holding reach of his native mud – he is highly interesting, and you may not be able to write home about him – and you get frightened on your own behalf. For crocodiles can, and often do, in such places, grab at people in small canoes.

I have known of several natives losing their lives in this way; some native villages are approachable from the main river by a short cut, as it were, through the mangrove swamps, and the inhabitants of such villages will now and then go across this way with small canoes instead of by the constant channel to the village, which is almost always winding.

In addition to this unpleasantness you are liable – until you realize the danger from experience, or have native advice on the point – to get tide-trapped away in the swamps, the water falling round you when you are away in some deep pool or lagoon, and you find you cannot get back to the main river. For you cannot get out and drag your canoe across the stretches of mud that separate you from it, because the mud is of too unstable a nature and too deep, and sinking into it means staying in it, at any rate until some geologist of the remote future may come across you, in a fossilized state when that mangrove swamp shall have become dry land.

Of course if you really want a truly safe investment in Fame, and really care about Posterity, and Posterity's Science, you will jump over into the black batter-like, stinking slime, cheered by the thought of the terrific sensation you will produce 20,000 years hence, and the care you will be taken of then by your fellow-creatures, in a museum. But if you are a mere ordinary person of a retiring nature, like me, you stop in your lagoon until the tide rises again; most of your attention is directed to dealing with an "at home" to crocodiles and mangrove flies, and with the fearful stench of the slime round you.

What little time you have over you will employ in wondering why you came to West Africa, and why, after having reached this point of absurdity, you need have gone and painted the lily and adorned the rose, by being such a colossal ass as to come fooling about in mangrove swamps. Twice this chatty little incident, as Lady MacDonald would call it, has happened to me, but never again if I can help it. On one occasion, the last, a mighty Silurian [crocodile], as the *Daily*

Telegraph would call him, chose to get his front paws over the stern of my canoe, and endeavoured to improve our acquaintance. I had to retire to the bows, to keep the balance right – it is no use saying because I was frightened, for this miserably understates the case – and fetch him a clip on the snout with a paddle, when he withdrew, and I paddled into the very middle of the lagoon, hoping the water there was too deep for him or any of his friends to repeat the performance. Presumably it was, for no one did it again. I should think that crocodile was eight feet long; but don't go and say I measured him, or that this is my outside measurement for crocodiles. I have measured them when they have been killed by other people, fifteen, eighteen, and twenty-one feet odd. This was only a pushing young creature who had not learnt manners.

Still, even if your own peculiar tastes and avocations do not take you in small dug-out canoes into the heart of the swamps, you can observe the difference in the local scenery made by the flowing of the tide when you are on a vessel stuck on a sand-bank, in the Rio del Rey for example. Moreover, as you will have little else to attend to, save mosquitoes and mangrove flies, when in such a situation, you may as well pursue the study. At the ebb gradually the foliage of the lower branches of the mangroves grows wet and muddy, until there is a great black band about three feet deep above the surface of the water in all directions; gradually a network of gray-white roots rises up, and below this again, gradually, a slope of smooth and lead-brown slime. The effect is not in the least as if the water had fallen, but as if the mangroves had, with one accord, risen up out of it, and into it again they seem silently to sink when the flood comes . . .

I got my tea about seven, and then turned out to hurry my band out of Egaja. This I did not succeed in doing until past ten. One row succeeded another with my men; but I was determined to get them out of that town as quickly as possible, for I had heard so much from perfectly reliable and experienced people regarding the treacherousness of the Fan. I feared too that more cases still would be brought up against Kiva, from the *résumé* of his criminal career I had had last night, and I knew it was very doubtful whether my other three Fans were any better than he. There was his grace's little murder affair only languishing for want of evidence owing to the witnesses for the prosecution being out elephant-hunting not very far away; and Wiki was pleading an alibi, and a twin brother, in a bad wife palaver in this town.

I really hope for the sake of Fan morals at large that I did engage the three worst villains in M'fetta, and that M'fetta is the worst town in all Fan land; inconvenient as this arrangement was to me personally. Anyhow, I felt sure my Pappenheimers would take a lot of beating for good solid crime, among any tribe anywhere. Moreover, the Ajumba wanted meat, and the Fans, they said, offered them human.

I saw no human meat at Egaja, but the Ajumba seem to think the Fans eat nothing else, which is a silly prejudice of theirs, because the Fans do. I think in this case the Ajumba thought a lot of smoked flesh offered was human. It may have been; it was in neat pieces; and again, as the Captain of the late SS *Sparrow* would say, "it mayn't". But the Ajumba have a horror of cannibalism, and I honestly believe never practise it, even for fetish affairs, which is a rare thing in a West African tribe where sacrificial and ceremonial cannibalism is nearly universal. Anyhow the Ajumba loudly declared the Fans were "bad men too much", which was impolitic under existing circumstances, and in excusable, because it by no means arose from a courageous defiance of them but the West African! Well! "he's a devil and an ostrich and an orphan child in one."

The chief was very anxious for me to stay and rest, but as his mother was doing wonderfully well, and the other women seemed quite to understand my directions regarding her, I did not feel inclined to risk it. The old lady's farewell of me was peculiar: she took my hand in her two, turned it palm upwards, and spat on it. I do not know whether this is a constant form of greeting among the Fan; I fancy not. Dr Nassau, who explained it to me when I saw him again down at Baraka, said the spitting was merely an accidental by-product of the performance, which consisted in blowing a blessing; and as I happened on this custom twice afterwards, I feel sure from observation he is right.

The two chiefs saw us courteously out of the town as far as where the river crosses the out-going path again, and the blue-hatted one gave me some charms "to keep my foot in path", and the mourning chief lent us his son to see us through the lines of fortification of the plantation. I gave them an equal dash and, in answer to their question as to whether I had found Egaja a thief town, I said that to call Egaja a thief town was rank perjury, for I had not lost a thing while in it and we parted with mutual expression of esteem and hopes for another meeting at an early date . . .

I have never had to shoot, and hope never to have to; because in such a situation, one white with no troops to back him means a clean finish. But this would not discourage me if I had to start, only it makes me more inclined to walk round the obstacle, than to become a mere blood splotch against it, if this can be done without losing your self-respect, which is the mainspring of your power in West Africa.

As for flourishing about a revolver and threatening to fire, I hold it utter idiocy. I have never tried it, however, so I speak from prejudice which arises from the feeling that there is something cowardly in it. Always have your revolver ready loaded in good order, and have your hand on it when things are getting warm, and in addition have an exceedingly good bowie knife, not a hinge knife because with a hinge knife you have got to get it open – hard work in a country where all things go rusty in the joints – and hinge knives are liable to close on your own fingers. The best form of knife is the bowie, with a shallow half moon cut out of the back at the point end, and this depression sharpened to a cutting edge. A knife is essential, because after wading neck deep in a swamp your revolver is neither use nor ornament until you have had time to clean it. But the chances are you may go across Africa, or live years in it, and require neither. It is just the case of the gentleman who asked if one required a revolver in Carolina? and was answered, "You may be here one year, and you may be here two and never want it; but, when you do want it, you'll want it very bad."

The cannibalism of the Fans, although a prevalent habit, is no danger, I think, to white people, except as regards the bother it gives one in preventing one's black companions from getting eaten. The Fan is not a cannibal from sacrificial motives like the negro. He does it in his commonsense way. Man's flesh, he says, is good to eat, very good, and he wishes you would try it. Oh dear no, he never eats it himself, but the next door town does. He is always very much abused for eating his relations, but he really does not do this. He will eat his next door neighbour's relations and sell his own deceased to his next door neighbour in return – but he does not buy slaves and fatten them up for his table as some of the Middle Congo tribes I know of do. He has no slaves, no prisoners of war, no cemeteries, so you must draw your own conclusions. No, my friend, I will not tell you any cannibal stories. I have heard how good M. du Chaillu fared after telling you some beauties, and now you come away from the Fan village and down the Rembwé river . . .

I cannot close this brief notice of native ideas without mentioning the secret societies; but to go fully into this branch of the subject would require volumes, for every tribe has its secret society. The Poorah of Sierra Leone, the Oru of Lagos, the Egbo of Calabar [Nigeria], the Yasi of the Igalwa, the Ukuku of the M'pongwe, the Ikun of the Bakele, and the Lukuku of the Bachilangi, Baluba, are some of the most powerful secret societies on the West African Coast

These secret societies are not essentially religious; their action is mainly judicial, and their particular presiding spirit is not a god or devil in our sense of the word. The ritual differs for each in its detail, but there are broad lines of agreement between them. There are societies both for men and for women, but no mixed societies for both sexes. Those that I have mentioned above are all male, and women are utterly forbidden to participate in the rites or become acquainted with their secrets, for one of the chief duties of these societies is to keep the women in order; and besides this reason it is undoubtedly held that women are bad for certain forms of ju-ju, even when these forms are not directly connected, as far as I can find out, with the secret society. For example, the other day a chief up the Mungo River deliberately destroyed his ju-ju by showing it to his women. It was a great ju-ju, but expensive to keep up, requiring sacrifices of slaves and goats so what with trade being bad, the fall in the price of oil and ivory and so on, he felt he could not afford that ju-ju, and so destroyed its power, so as to prevent its harming him when he neglected it. Probably the destructive action of women is not only the idea of their inferiority – for had inferiority been the point, that chief would have laid his ju-ju with dogs, or pigs – but arises from the undoubted fact that women are notably deficient in real reverence for authority, as is demonstrated by the way they continually treat that of their husbands . . .

I believe that these secret societies are always distinct from the leopard societies. I have pretty nearly enough evidence to prove that it is so in some districts, but not in all. So far my evidence only goes to prove the distinction of the two among the negroes, not among the Bantu, and in all cases you will find some men belonging to both. Some men in fact, go in for all the societies in their district, but not all the men; and in all districts, if you look close, you will find several societies apart from the regular youth-initiating one.

These other societies are practically murder societies, and their practices usually include cannibalism, which is not an essential part of the rites of the great tribal societies, Yasi or Egbo. In the Calabar district [Nigeria], I was informed by natives that there was a society of which the last entered member has to provide, for the entertainment of the other members, the body of a relative of his own, and sacrificial cannibalism is always breaking out, or perhaps I should say being discovered, by the white authorities in the Niger Delta. There was the great outburst of it at Brass, early last year, and the one chronicled in the *Liverpool Mercury* for 13 August 1895, as occurring at Sierra Leone. This account is worth quoting. It describes the hanging by the authorities of three murderers, and states the incidents, which took place in the Imperi country behind Free Town [capital of Sierra Leone].

One of the chief murderers was a man named Jowe, who had formerly been a Sunday-school teacher in Sierra Leone. He pleaded in extenuation of his offence that he had been compelled to join the society. The others said they committed the murders in order to obtain certain parts of the body for ju-ju purposes, the leg, the hand, the heart, *etc*. The *Mercury* goes on to give the statement of the Reverend Father Bomy of the Roman Catholic Mission. "He said he was at Bromtu, where the St Joseph Mission has a station, when a man was brought down from the Imperi country in a boat. The poor fellow was in a dreadful state, and was brought to the station for medical treatment. He said he was working on his farm, when he was suddenly pounced upon from behind. A number of sharp instruments were driven into the back of his neck. He presented a fearful sight, having wounds all over his body supposed to have been inflicted by the claws of the leopard, but in reality they were stabs from sharp-pointed knives. The native, who was a powerfully built man, called out, and his cries attracting the attention of his relations, the leopards made off. The poor fellow died at Bromtu from the injuries. It was only his splendid physique that kept him alive until his arrival at the Mission."

The *Mercury* goes on to quote from the *Pall Mall,* and I too go on quoting to show that these things are known and acknowledged to have taken place in a colony like Sierra Leone, which has had unequalled opportunities of becoming christianized for more than one hundred years, and now has more than one hundred and thirty places of Christian worship in it.

"Some twenty years ago there was a war between this tribe Taima and the Paramas. The Paramas sent some of their war boys to be ambushed in the intervening country, the Imperi, but the Imperi delivered these war boys to the enemy. In revenge, the Paramas sent the Fetish Boofima into the Imperi country. This Fetish had up to that time been kept active and working by the sacrifice of goats, but the medicine men of the Paramas who introduced it into the Imperi country decreed at the same time that human sacrifices would be required to keep it alive, thereby working their vengeance on the Imperi by leading them to exterminate themselves in sacrifice to the Fetish.

"The country for years has been terrorized by this secret worship of Boofima and at one time the Imperi started the Tonga dances, at which the medicine men pointed out the supposed worshippers of Boofima – the so-called Human Leopards, because when seizing their victims for sacrifice they covered themselves with leopard skins, and imitating the roars of the leopard, they sprang upon their victim, plunging at the same time two three-pronged forks into each side of the throat. The Government some years ago forbade the Tonga dances and are now striving to suppress the human leopards.

"There are also human alligators who, disguized as alligators, swim in the creeks upon the canoes and carry off the crew. Some of them have been brought for trial but no complete case has been made out against them!"

In comment upon this account, which is evidently written by someone well versed in the affair, I will only remark that sometimes, instead of the three-pronged forks, there are fixed in the paws of the leopard skin sharp-pointed cutting knives, the skin being made into a sort of glove into which the hand of the human leopard fits. In one skin I saw down south this was most ingeniously done. The knives were shaped like the leopard's claws, curved, sharp-pointed, and with cutting edges underneath, and I am told the American Mendi Mission, which works in the Sierra Leone districts, have got a similar skin in their possession.

In Calabar [Nigeria] and Libreville [Gabon], these murders used to be very common right in close to the white settlements but in Calabar white jurisdiction is now too much feared for them to be carried on near it, and in Libreville the making of the "Boulevard" between that town and Glass has cleared the custom out from its great haunt along by the swamp path that was formerly there. But before the existence of the Boulevard, when the narrow track was intercepted by patches of swamp, and ran between dense bush, it was notoriously unsafe even for a white man to go along it after dark. In the districts I know where leopardism occurs (from Bonny in Nigeria to the Belgian Congo) the victims are killed to provide human flesh for certain secret societies who eat it as one of their rites. Sometimes it is used by a man playing a lone hand to kill an enemy.

The human alligator mentioned, is our old friend the witch crocodile – the spirit of the man in the crocodile. I never myself came across a case of a man in his corporeal body swimming about in a crocodile skin, and I doubt whether any native would chance himself inside a crocodile skin and swim about in the river among the genuine articles for fear of their penetrating his disguize mentally and physically.

In Calabar witch crocodiles are still flourishing. There is an immense old brute that sporting Vice-Consuls periodically go after, which is known to contain the spirit of a Duke Town chief who shall be nameless, because they are getting on at such a pace just round Duke Town that haply I might be had up for libel. When I was in Calabar once, a peculiarly energetic officer had hit that crocodile and the chief was forthwith laid up by a wound in his leg. He said a dog had bit him. They, the chief and the crocodile, are quite well again now, and I will say this in favour of that chief that nothing on earth would persuade me to believe that he went fooling about in the Calabar River in his corporeal body, either in his own skin or a crocodile's.

The introduction of the Fetish Boofima into the country of the Imperi is an interesting point as it shows that these different tribes have the same big ju-ju. Similarly, Calabar Egbo can go into Okÿon, and will be respected in some of the New Calabar districts, but not at Brass, where the secret society is a distinct cult. Often a neighbouring district will send into Calabar, or Brass, where the big ju-ju is, and ask to have one sent up into their district to keep order, but Egbo will occasionally be sent into a district without that district in the least wanting it; but, as in the Imperi case, when it is there it is supreme. But say, for example, you were to send Egbo round from Calabar to Cameroon. Cameroon might be barely civil to it, but would pay it no homage, for Cameroon has got no end of a ju-ju of its own. It can rise up as high as the Peak, 13,760 feet. I never saw the Cameroon ju-ju do this, but I saw it start up from four feet to quite twelve feet in the twinkling of an eye, and I was assured that it was only modest reticence on its part that made it leave the other 13,748 feet out of the performance.

Cameroon also has its murder societies, but I have never been resident sufficiently long in Cameroon River to speak with any authority regarding them, but when I was in there in May 1895 the natives of Bell Town were in a state of great anxiety about their children. A week before, two little girls and a boy belonging to one family had gone down among a host of other children to the river-beach by Bell Town, to fill the pots and calabashes for the evening. It was broad daylight at the time, and the place they went to is not a lonely place but right on the beach before the town and plenty of people about in all directions.

The children filled the pots and then, after playing about as is usual, the little girls went home with their vessels of water, with a nice piece of palm leaf put on the top of the water to prevent it splashing as they went up the hill side of the bluff on which the town stands.

"Where is your brother?" said the mother, and they said they did not know; they thought he was playing with the other children. As the dusk came down and he did not return, the mother went down to the riverside and found all the other children had gone home. She made inquiries, but no one knew of him save that he had been playing on the beach.

A thorough search was started, but it was five long days before the boy was found, and then his body, decorated with palm leaves, suddenly appeared lying on the beach. It was slit all over longitudinally with long cuts on the face, head, legs, and arms. The crime could not be traced by means convincing to white man's law, but had the witch doctors had the affair in their hands a near relative of the dead boy would have been killed. Those natives who did not share the opinion of this man's guilt said it was the people in the water who had done the thing. These people in the water are much thought of in Cameroon. "They are just the same as people on land, only they live in water."

Doctor Nassau seems to think that the tribal society of the Corisco regions is identical with the leopard societies. He has had considerable experience of the workings of the Ukuku, particularly when he was pioneering in the Benito regions, when it came very near killing him. I will not quote the grand account he gave me of his adventures with it, because I should wish every one to read for themselves the biography he wrote of his first wife, *Crowned in Palm Land*, for they will find there a series of graphic descriptions of what life really is in the Corisco region, and certainly one of the most powerful and tragic bits of writing in any literature – the description of his wife's death in an open boat out at sea when he was trying to take her to Gabon for medical aid.

In reference to Ukuku, he says the name signifies a departed spirit. "It is a secret society into which all the males are initiated at puberty, whose procedure may not be seen by females, nor its laws disobeyed by any one under pain of death, a penalty which is sometimes commuted to a fine, a heavy fine. Its discussions are uttered as an oracle from any secluded spot by some man appointed for the purpose.

"On trivial occasions any initiated man may personate Ukuku or issue commands for the family. On other occasions, as in Shiku, to raise prices, the society lays its commands on foreign traders."

Some cases of Ukuku proceedings against white traders have come under my own observation. A friend of mine, a trader in the Batanga district, in some way incurred the animosity of the society's local branch. He had, as is usual in the South-West Coast trade, several sub-factories in the bush. He found himself under taboo; no native came in to his yard to buy or sell at the store, not even to sell food.

He took no notice and awaited developments. One evening when he was sitting on his verandah, smoking and reading, he thought he heard someone singing softly under the house, this, like most European buildings hereabouts, being elevated just above the earth. He was attracted to the song and listened: it was evidently one of the natives singing, not one of his own Kruboys, and so, knowing the language, and having nothing else particular to do, he attended to the affair.

It was the same thing sung softly over and over again, so softly that he could hardly make out the words. But at last, catching his native name among them, he listened more intently than ever, down at a knot-hole in the wooden floor. The song was – "They are going to attack your factory at . . . tomorrow. They are going to attack your factory at . . . tomorrow." over and over again, until it ceased; and then he thought he saw something darker than the darkness round it creep across the yard and disappear in the bush. Very early in the morning he, with his Kuboys and some guns, went and established themselves in that threatened factory in force. The Ukuku Society turned up in the evening, and reconnoitred the situation, and, finding there was more in it than they had expected, withdrew.

In the course of the next twenty-four hours he succeeded in talking the palaver successfully with them. He never knew who his singing friend was, but suspected it was a man whom he had known to be grateful for some kindness he had done him. Indeed there were, and are, many natives who have cause to be grateful to him, for he is deservedly popular among his local tribes, but the man who sang to him that night deserves much honour, for he did it at a terrific risk.

Sometimes representatives of the Ukuku fraternity from several tribes meet together and discuss intertribal difficulties thereby avoiding war.

Dr Nassau distinctly says that the Bantu region leopard society is identical with the Ukuku, and he says that, although the leopards are not very numerous here, they are very daring, made so by immunity from punishment by man. "The superstition is that on any man who kills a leopard will fall a curse or evil disease, curable only by ruinously expensive process of three weeks' duration under the direction of Ukuku. So the natives allow the greatest depredations and ravages until their sheep, goats, and dogs are swept away, and are roused to self-defence only when a human being becomes the victim of the daring beast.

"With this superstition is united another similar to the werewolf of Germany, viz., a belief in the power of human metamorphosis into a leopard. A person so metamorphosed is called 'Uvengwa.' At one time in Benito an intense excitement prevailed in the community. Doors and shutters were rattled at the dead of night, marks of leopard claws were scratched on door-posts. Then tracks lay on every path. Women and children in lonely places saw their flitting forms, or in the dusk were knocked down by their spring, or heard their growl in the thickets. It is difficult to 'decide in many of these reports whether it is a real leopard or only an Uvengwa – to native fears they are practically the same – we were certain this time the Uvengwa was the thief disguised in leopard's skin, as theft is always heard of about such times."

When I was in Gabon in September 1895, there was great Ukuku excitement in a district just across the other side of the estuary, mainly at a village that enjoyed the spacious and resounding name of Rumpochembo, from a celebrated chief, and all these phenomena were rife there.

Again, when I was in a village up the Calabar there were fourteen goats and five slaves killed in eight days by leopards, the genuine things, I am sure, in this case; but here, as down South, there was a strong objection to proceed against the leopard, and no action was being taken save making the goat-houses stronger.

In Okÿon, when a leopard is killed, its body is treated with great respect and brought into the killer's village. Messages are then sent to the neighbouring villages, and they send representatives to the village and the gall-bladder is most carefully removed from the leopard and burnt *coram publico*, each person whipping their hands down their arms to disavow any guilt in the affair. This burning of the gall, however, is not ju-ju; it is done merely to destroy it, and to demonstrate to all men that it is destroyed, because it is believed to be a deadly poison, and if any is found in a man's possession the punishment is death, unless he is a great chief – a few of these are allowed to keep leopards' gall in their possession. John Bailey tells me that if a great chief commits a great crime and is adjudged by a conclave of his fellow chiefs to die, it is not considered right he should die in a common way, and he is given leopards' gall. A precisely similar idea regarding the poisonous quality of crocodiles' gall holds good down South.

The ju-ju parts of the leopard are the whiskers. You cannot get a skin from a native with them on, and gay, reckless young hunters wear them stuck in their hair and swagger tremendously while the elders shake their heads and keep a keen eye on their subsequent conduct.

I must say the African leopard is an audacious animal, although it is ungrateful of me to say a word against him, after the way he has let me off personally, and I will speak of his extreme beauty as compensation for my ingratitude. I really think, taken as a whole, he is the most lovely animal I have ever seen, only seeing him, in the one way you can gain a full idea of his beauty, namely in his native forest, is not an unmixed joy to a person, like myself, of a nervous disposition.

I may remark that my nervousness regarding the big game of Africa is of a rather peculiar kind. I can confidently say I am not afraid of any wild animal – until I see it – and then – well I will yield to nobody in terror. Fortunately, as I say, my terror is a special variety; fortunately because no one can manage their own terror. You can suppress alarm, excitement, fear, fright, and all those small-fry emotions, but the real terror is as dependent on the inner make of you as the colour of your eyes, or the shape of your nose and when terror ascends its throne in my mind I become preternaturally artful, and intelligent to an extent utterly foreign to my true nature, and save, in the case of close quarters with bad big animals, a feeling of rage against some unknown person that such things as leopards, elephants, crocodiles, *etc.*, should be allowed out loose in that disgracefully dangerous way, I do not think much about it at the time.

Whenever I have come across an awful animal in the forest and I know it has seen me I take Jerome's advice, and, instead of relying on the power of the human eye, rely upon that of the human leg and effect a masterly retreat in the face of the enemy. If I know it has not seen me, I sink in my tracks and keep an eye on it, hoping that it will go away soon.

Thus I once came upon a leopard. I had got caught in a tornado in a dense forest. The massive, mighty trees were waving like a wheat-field in an autumn gale in England, and I dare say a field mouse in a wheat-field in a gale would have heard much the same uproar. The tornado shrieked like ten thousand vengeful demons. The great trees creaked and groaned and strained against it and their bush-rope cables groaned and smacked like whips, and ever and anon a thundering crash with snaps like pistol shots told that they and their mighty tree had strained and struggled in vain. The fierce rain came in a roar, tearing to shreds the leaves and blossoms and deluging everything.

I was making bad weather of it, and climbing up over a lot of rocks out of a gully bottom where I had been half drowned in a stream, and on getting my head to the level of a block of rock I observed right in front of my eyes, broadside on, maybe a yard off, certainly not more, a big leopard. He was crouching on the ground, with his magnificent head thrown back and his eyes shut. His fore-paws were spread out in front of him and he lashed the ground with his tail, and I grieve to say, in face of that awful danger – I don't mean me, but the tornado – that depraved creature swore, softly, but repeatedly and profoundly.

I did not get all these facts up in one glance, for no sooner did I see him than I ducked under the rocks, and remembered thankfully that leopards are said to have no power of smell. But I heard his observation on the weather, and the flip-flap of his tail on the ground. Every now and then I cautiously took a look at him with one eye round a rock-edge, and he remained in the same position. My feelings tell me he remained there twelve months, but my calmer judgment puts the time down at twenty minutes; and at last, on taking another cautious peep, I saw he was gone.

At the time I wished I knew exactly where, but I do not care about that detail now, for I saw no more of him. He had moved off in one of those weird lulls which you get in a tornado, when for a few seconds the wild herd of hurrying winds seem to have lost themselves, and wander round crying and wailing like lost souls, until their common rage seizes them again and they rush back to their work of destruction.

It was an immense pleasure to have seen the great creature like that. He was so evidently enraged and baffled by the uproar and dazzled by the floods of lightning that swept down into the deepest recesses of the forest, showing at one second every detail of twig, leaf, branch, and stone round you, and then leaving you in a sort of swirling dark until the next flash came; this, and the great conglomerate roar of the wind, rain and thunder, was enough to bewilder any living thing.

I have never hurt a leopard intentionally; I am habitually kind to animals, and besides I do not think it is ladylike to go shooting things with a gun. Twice, however, I have been in collision with them. On one occasion a big leopard had attacked a dog, who, with her family, was occupying a broken-down hut next to mine. The dog was a half-bred boarhound, and a savage brute on her own account. I, being roused by the uproar, rushed out into the feeble moonlight, thinking she was having one of her habitual turns-up with other dogs, and I saw a whirling mass of animal matter within a yard of me. I fired two mushroom-shaped native stools in rapid succession into the brown of it and the meeting broke up into a leopard and a dog.

The leopard crouched, I think to spring on me. I can see its great, beautiful, lambent eyes still, and I seized an earthen water-cooler and flung it straight at them. It was a noble shot; it burst on the leopard's head like a shell and the leopard went for bush one time.

Twenty minutes after people began to drop in cautiously and inquire if anything was the matter, and I civilly asked them to go and ask the leopard in the bush, but they firmly refused. We found the dog had got her shoulder slit open as if by a blow from a cutlass, and the leopard had evidently seized the dog by the scruff of her neck, but, owing to the loose folds of skin, no bones were broken and she got round all right after much ointment from me, which she paid me for with several bites.

Do not mistake this for a sporting adventure. I no more thought it was a leopard than that it was a lotus when I joined the fight. My other leopard was also after a dog. Leopards always come after dogs, because once upon a time the leopard and the dog were great friends, and the leopard went out one day and left her whelps in charge of the dog, and the dog went out flirting, and a snake came and killed the whelps, so there is ill-feeling to this day between the two.

For the benefit of sporting readers whose interest may have been cxcited by the mention of big game, I may remark that the largest leopard skin I ever measured myself was, tail included, 9 feet 7 inches. It was a dried skin, and every man who saw it said, "It was the largest skin he had ever seen, except one that he had seen somewhere else."

The largest crocodile I ever measured was 22 feet 3 inches, the largest gorilla 5 feet 7 inches. I am assured by the missionaries in Calabar that there was a python brought into Creek Town in the Rev. Mr Goldie's time that extended the whole length of the Creek Town mission-house verandah and to spare. This python must have been over 40 feet. I have not a shadow of doubt it was. Stay-at-home people will always discredit great measurements, but experienced bushmen do not, and after all, if it amuses the stay-at-homes to do so, by all means let them; they have dull lives of it and it don't hurt you, for you know how exceedingly difficult it is to preserve really big things to bring home, and how, half the time, they fall into the hands of people who would not bother their heads to preserve them in a rotting climate like West Africa.

The largest python skin I ever measured was a damaged one, which was 26 feet. There is an immense one hung in front of a house in San Paul de Loanda, which you can go and measure yourself with comparative safety any day, and which is I think, over 20 feet. I never measured this one. The common run of pythons is 10–15 feet, or rather I should say this is about the sized one you find with painful frequency in your chicken-house.

Of the Lubuku secret society I can speak with no personal knowledge. I had a great deal of curious information regarding it from a Bakele woman, who had her information second-hand, but it bears out what Captain Latrobe Bateman says about it in his most excellent book *The First Ascent of the Kasai* (George Phillip, 1889), and to his account in Note J of the Appendix, I beg to refer the ethnologist. My information also went to show what he calls "a dark inference as to its true nature", a nature not universally common by any means to the African tribal secret society.

In addition to the secret society and the leopard society, there are in the Delta some ju-jus held only by a few great chiefs. The one in Bonny has a complete language to itself, and there is one in Duke Town so powerful that should you desire the death of any person you have only to go and name him before it. "These ju-jus are very swift and sure." I would rather drink than fight with any of them – yes, far.

A DEVILISH CUNNING PANTHER

A maneating tiger is supremely bad; but a maneating panther, hardened in sin, is superlatively worse. The tiger waits by the wayside to gather up what the gods of the jungle may send him. He will pull down an unfortunate charcoal-burner as he passes on his lawful occasions along a jungle road in India. A villager's luck fails him as he returns home one evening; and the next morning a shrill wailing in the village, and possibly a cloud of vultures hovering over one particular spot in the jungle, announce that the maneater has found another meal. A scared herdsman will bolt in with the news that the "shere" has carried off his companion as they were driving out the communal cattle in broad daylight; for the maneating tiger loses the habits of the more reputable of his kind, and seeks his prey at any hour of the twenty-four.

A maneating panther does all these things, and more. He is more cunning than the tiger, and that is saying a very great deal. But what chiefly makes him so terrible a scourge is his almost incredible boldness. He has no respect for nor fear of human beings or human habitations. He will cheerfully enter a house where half a dozen people are sleeping, and, quite unperturbed by the alarm raised by the others, will seize and drag out a child, or even a woman, to devour at his leisure. Indeed, on occasion, if he can find no other way in, he will effect an entrance by tearing through the thatched roof. Nor at times can he be held guiltless of killing for the sake of killing. A really bad maneating panther has been known to make his way into a hut and deliberately kill every one of the inmates on exactly the same principle as a fox in a chicken-run. Finally, the beast will teach his progeny to follow in his own wicked ways; and unless the whole line is extirpated, a district may continue indefinitely to suffer wholesale depredations, involving the loss of hundreds of lives.

My own experience of the blatant contempt of a maneating panther for the human race occurred in a native state to the south of the Central Provinces of India. I had received a permit to shoot in State territory, and an urgent request came along from the rajah to see what I could do towards ridding the land of one of these evil-doers, which was terrorizing something like two hundred square miles of country. It had an evil record, this beast, dating back over a couple of years or so, in the course of which it had claimed some 150 victims. Latterly its depredations had become – there is no other word for it – appalling.

Accordingly I went into camp on the outskirts of a largish village, where the local *thana* or police-station formed a convenient centre for the collection of information regarding the movements of the maneater. Every two or three days news came in of a woman or child having been killed and eaten. The beast rarely, if ever, touched a man or, if it did, I never heard of it. All these kills, however, were reported from villages some fifteen or twenty miles from where I was, and successive reports would come from places perhaps twenty or thirty miles apart. The brute was ranging over a big beat, and it was little use going after him. The only thing to do was to possess my soul in patience until such time as the mountain came to Mahomet, or, at any rate, within reasonable distance of him.

The outlook was anything but the hopeful one which I, in my innocence, had at first imagined it would be. But there was nothing to be done but wait. In the meantime the whole countryside was scared thoroughly stiff. By day or night no one moved abroad alone. Now and again I used to meet parties of ten or fifteen, all armed with axes, making their way from one place to another, and keeping a wary eye on both sides of the road as they went. As these people were Gonds, this state of affairs meant a great deal. To begin with, the Gond is an eminently plucky individual in himself. Then he has the contempt born of the familiarity of a lifetime with the beasts of the jungle. And if a panther can throw the Gond inhabitants of some 200 square miles of territory into a state of abject fright, it must be a very evil beast indeed.

After I had been in camp some ten days I had my first brush with the maneater, and he took all the honours of the round. One morning an unkempt individual was brought into my camp who announced that the *"shaitan"* had visited his house the previous night and attempted to carry off a small girl. Would the sahib give the matter his urgent and personal attention, and bring some medicine for the injured child? The sahib would, and as we went I heard the story of the attack.

It appeared that the girl was asleep in the middle of the hut, directly between the two doors. Near one door there was a group of three or four men sitting talking. Near the other, in the opposite wall of the hut, there was a single man whittling a stick for use as an axe-helve. Suddenly the panther bounded in through one door, past the group of conversationalists, picked up the child, and proceeded to walk out of the hut with her through the other door. The single man near the other door pluckily attacked the brute with the stick he was shaping. He managed to bring this unsatisfactory weapon hard down across the beast's hind-quarters, startling it into dropping its prey, and vanishing through the door into the night, to the accompaniment of a series of disappointed snarls. When we arrived at the village a mile away, I proceeded, so far as I could, to check the story. After a careful examination of the tracks, I came to the definite conclusion that it was correct in every detail.The panther had walked quietly up to the hut, and the scratches of its claws showed where it had made its bound through the front door. Other marks showed how it had picked up the child bodily, the drag of her heels along the ground alone being visible, and how it had dropped her when attacked by the man with the stick. The girl was torn about the throat, but not very badly. I dressed her wounds with carbolic, and up to the time I left that camp a fortnight or so later, she was doing well, and, I have no doubt, ultimately recovered.

The reputation of the panther left room for little hope that it would remain near the village. Accordingly I returned to my camp after a fruitless attempt to track the beast to its lying-up place, leaving word that any further developments were to be reported at once. As I expected, there were none, and two days later a kill was announced from a village miles away.

At the end of three weeks in that camp I was getting thoroughly tired of it. Day after day I scoured the neighbouring jungles for game, with a conspicuous lack of succcess. In the meantime reports of the maneater's activities continued to come in, but they were all from different and widely separated villages. Already the better part of a month of my hard-earned leave had been spent. The place where I was camping was undoubtedly convenient so far as getting the necessary *khubbar* of the panther was concerned. On the other hand, game was so scarce as to be to all intents and purposes nonexistent. Keen though I was to shoot the maneater, I could not spend the whole of my leave doing nothing in this way on the offchance of getting it, and as the days went on my hopes sank lower and lower.

One day I returned thoroughly disgusted from my customarily

unsuccessful morning round. While I was waiting for breakfast, the wish to move on elsewhere deepened into a fixed determination, and I decided to start getting ready to shift camp as soon as the meal was over. But the powers that be had decreed otherwise. I was in the middle of breakfast when a thoroughly scared urchin bolted in with the news that a panther had killed one of his companions as they were driving out the village cattle a couple of hours earlier. His shivering limbs and dirty grey colour were sufficient *prima facie* evidence of the truth of his story. He and three other small boys, he said, were driving out the cattle, when a panther suddenly bounded out of the jungle, seized one of the boys and dragged him off. The body was lying in the jungle, and would not be removed until I had arrived and inspected it.

I promptly set out for the scene of the tragedy four miles away. When I arrived at the village I was met by the headman and the father of the dead boy. The corpse was exactly as it had been found, they told me, so I went down to reconnoitre. The kill had taken place on the edge of a strip of jungle bordering a widish *nullah*. On the other side of the *nullah* was a similar strip, and neither was more than twenty or thirty yards wide. The body of the dead boy, who must have been about nine or ten years old, was lying in the middle of one strip under a mass of creeper forming a sort of tent about six feet square. As in the previous case of the girl, the panther had seized its victim by the throat, and, as far as I could judge, death must have been practically instantaneous.

It remained now to settle with the murderer – I hoped once and for all. Beating was out of the question. Apart altogether from the likelihood of its attacking the beaters, the devilish cunning of the panther and the fact that it might be lying up anywhere in either of the strips of jungle made any prospect of getting a shot at it by beating extremely remote. If I was to have any reckoning with the slayer, it meant sitting up over the body of the slain. It was very far from being a pleasant idea, but it had to be faced. The first thing to do was to persuade the father. He wanted to remove the body at once for decent cremation. After a lot of argument, however, he allowed it to remain, and I set about making what preparations I could for my vigil.

Now the body was lying under this mass of creeper, and close to it was the only decent-sized tree there was within reasonable distance. Accordingly I had a *charpoy* hoisted into its branches, whence I thought I could get a good view of the corpse just below me, and, taking my rifle and a kukri, established myself for the wait. It was about two o'clock in the afternoon when I got settled down. I did not expect an extended vigil. The panther, however, thought otherwise, and it was practically dark by the time he arrived. I just saw a shape glide in under the mass of creeper without giving me the chance of a shot, and the sound of rending flesh indicated that he had started his meal.

Then my troubles began. The corpse was lying under that mass of creeper with the panther tearing at it, and in the darkness I could see neither. There was no moon and, even if there had been, the opaque shadow of the creeper would still have been there. I waited for a long time, every minute expecting the beast to come out into the open, where I might get a chance at him. But he continued tearing at the body in a way that demonstrated very clearly that he was ravenous and had no intention of being interrupted until his hunger had been satisfied. Something had obviously to be done. Otherwise we might have remained as we were until morning. Eventually I decided to throw something down, in the hope that it might startle the maneater into showing himself outside the shadow of the creeper. The only thing I could think of was my bunch of keys. Down they went, and I gripped my rifle steady for the expected shot; but not a bit of it. The panther growled, walked once or twice round the corpse, still keeping under the creeper, and calmly returned to his meal.

This came as a revelation to me of the fearlessness of a hungry man-eating panther. But there were many more revelations to come that night. The fact that a bunch of keys dropping out of the sky with a metallic jingle close to the beast's head was insufficient to disturb him was astonishing enough. Accordingly I cast about for something more drastic, and decided to try clapping my hands. The first time or two the panther growled his acknowledgments, and did his little circum-ambulation. Then he got bored, and did not deign to pay any attention at all to my efforts. So I tried shouting at him, with equally unsuccessful results. Occasionally he growled back; generally he did not bother to do that, even when I bawled at him with the full strength of my lungs.

Now consider the ludicrousness of the position. Here, on the *machan*, was a man armed with a heavy rifle, and there below him, at a distance to be measured in feet, was the animal to shoot on which he had expended so much time and trouble. But so far as getting a shot was concerned, those few feet might have been as many miles. If only the panther would show himself outside that six-feet-square patch of creeper – but it remained "if only". I was getting desperate by this time. Hacking off a branch with my kukri, I cut it up and hurled the pieces into the darkness below. The maneater hardly troubled to growl back.

Only one thing remained. I lifted my rifle and let drive into the middle of that infernal creeper, ripping another cartridge into the chamber as fast as I could work the bolt. The noise the shot made in the quiet jungle was extraordinary. My rifle was a .400 full-cordite, magazine one, and the seeming loudness of the report startled even me, used as I was to the weapon. But it did not disturb that panther – at least, not to the extent anyone would have expected. He gave a blood-curdling snarl or two, and I heard him walk around the body, keeping as always under the creeper. Then the noise of his feeding began again. Three more shots I fired, hurling down the empty cartridge-cases after each shot to the accompaniment of my shouted objurgations. Then I stopped abruptly. Never expecting anything of this nature, I had only brought ten rounds with me, and the realization came very forcibly that I could not afford to waste any more of them on an entirely fruitless attempt to move a beast which had no intention of being moved.

I began to feel decidedly creepy. At the best the whole business had a very gruesome flavour about it; and when this amazing behaviour on the part of the panther came on top of everything else, all the local stories of the supernatural attributes credited to him began to come to mind. Cold clammy fingers began to tickle gently up and down my spine. In fact, not to put too nice a point on it, I was not very far from being in a state of what is commonly known as "mortal funk". It came as an immense relief, therefore, to hear human voices hailing me from the edge of the jungle. The villagers, hearing the shots, had come to the conclusion that the panther must be dead, and had come down in a body to hear all about it. I shouted back that the panther was very far from being dead, and that they had better clear out at once, advice which they lost no time in following.

The visit of the villagers had a soothing effect on nerves which, as I have said, were becoming more than a trifle strained. After they had departed, I dozed off, and the doze deepened into sleep. Just after one o'clock I snapped into sudden and complete wakefulness, and the realization that the maneater was clawing at the foot of my tree. I looked over the edge of the *machan*, but, though the moon had risen, he was in the shadow and was invisible to me. I felt profoundly uncomfortable.

The earlier behaviour of the brute had already instilled in my mind an intense respect for his uncanny contempt of my efforts to terminate his existence, not untinged, I admit, with a touch of superstitious awe. It may sound curious – to use no stronger term – that a man, armed with a rifle and perched on a *machan* some ten feet from the ground, should be scared by a large cat clawing at the foot of the tree in which he was situated. But this was no ordinary panther. It was so many cubic feet of concentrated activity, cunning, courage, deadly viciousness and utter contempt for the human race. Moreover, the whole circumstances of the vigil had been of a gruesomeness calculated to tax the strongest of nerves.

I grabbed my kukri and made ready to smite as soon as the panther should make its appearance over the edge of the *machan*, which I expected every moment. However, after a few minutes, and very much to my relief, it moved off. Looking back on things, I have come to the conclusion that the panther was only cleaning its claws by scraping them up and down the bark of the tree. Still, at the time I was very far from realizing that, and the sound of the animal's retreating footsteps was one of the things in my life for which I have felt most devoutly grateful. Another thing which I have often wondered, is whether the choice of my tree for those manicuring operations was not a deliberate act on the part of the panther to show his contempt for me. He knew well enough that I was in that tree. He must have realized that I had designs on his life. And he cared not one atom, except insofar as he consistently declined to come out into the open and to give me the chance of a shot at him.

I remained very much on the alert for the rest of the night, expecting him back at any moment. It was nearly four o'clock, however, before I heard him again. Keeping in the shadow the whole way, he slid in under the patch of creeper, and for ten minutes or so the sound of his feeding went on. Then he left again, this time, as it turned out, for good.

I was not feeling too happy. In the first place, the night had been an unholy one. But what was worse was the knowledge that I had to face the father of the dead boy in the morning. That, I think, was the least pleasing part of a wholly unpleasant business. At dawn I heard the villagers coming down, and stiffly descended from my *machan*. The sight was a horrible one. Only the hands and feet of the corpse remained. The rest was a litter of broken bones and fragments of flesh. The boy's father said never a word. He cast one look of unutterable reproach at me, gathered up the hands and feet, and walked quietly away, looking neither to the right nor to the left. It was a bad moment, and the memory of it has given me many bad moments since.

We made an attempt to track the panther in case he might be lying up in the neighbourhood. So far as we could gather, however, he seemed to have gone clean off across country, and after a mile or so of difficult tracking we had to give it up. There was obviously no prospect of seeing him again in that village, for the time being at any rate.

I came to the definite conclusion after this that the panther was not fated to die by my hand, and a day or two later I moved my camp to another village some ten miles away, where there was a chance of getting some of the shooting I had come for and hitherto had not got. Just before dawn on the second night after my arrival I was awakened by something bumping into my tent just behind my head as I lay in bed. I slept very lightly in those days: the presence in the district of the maneater did not encourage heavy slumber, any more than it encouraged me to go to bed without my rifle and kukri ready to hand. There was a gentle scratching just outside the tent, and then two long sniffs.

The hair started to bristle up at the back of my neck, and the palms of my hands became suddenly very cold and clammy. There was no mistaking the identity of the animal outside. It was a panther all right and, in the circumstances, it could only be the maneater. I grabbed my rifle and the kukri determined to sell my life as dearly as possible, and awaited developments.

Just then there was a shout outside. With the approaching dawn my camp was awakening into life, and one of my entourage was calling to the *bhisti* in the village to bring water for the preparation of my *chota hazri*. The scratching ceased, and I heard the intruder moving off. There was no undignified hurry about his retreat. Judging from the sound, his attitude was that he was leaving because he wanted to, and not because he was frightened into doing so.

After a discreet interval I got up and, as soon as it was light enough, examined carefully the ground around my tent. The whole position was very soon cleared up. The nocturnal visitor was the maneater, sure enough. He had prowled once or twice around the tent, evidently trying to make up his mind what it was. A tentative scratch or two in the ground just outside showed where he had tried a closer investigation of the queer object which obviously contained a desirable meal, but which might at the same time have been a trap. My followers mercifully opportune shout had apparently decided him that the chances of running into danger were too great to make an entrance worthwhile, and he had accordingly moved off with dignity.

To this day I am firmly convinced that the maneater was suspicious that the tent was a trap of some sort. If it had not been for that, he would certainly have come in, and the chances of my being alive at the present time would not have been worth considering. Even now the memory of those two long sniffs induces a rather creepy feeling around my spine.

The sands of the maneater's existence were, however, rapidly running out. Three days later a Gond villager turned up at my camp with an old Tower musket and the skin of a fine panther which he had shot in his compound the previous night. As I prefer to shoot my own trophies, I was not at first interested in the prospective deal; but, when he produced two things which he found in the animal's stomach, my attitude changed. The things he showed me were a black ball, which on closer inspection proved to consist of human hair, and a silver anklet. There was no mistaking the identity of the panther after that. This was the skin of the maneater which had taken all the honours of our three encounters, and incidentally given me some of the worst moments I have had in a fairly extended experience of big game shooting in India.

Glad as I was that the land had been rid of the pest, the manner of its death was rather a blow to my pride. After making an arrant fool of a sahib armed with modern weapons of destruction, who had devoted more than a month to an effort to compass its end, the maneater had fallen to a charge of nondescript missiles fired by a simple savage from a gas-pipe, which from its appearance threatened greater danger to its user than to the intended victim. But that was just one of the practical jokes which the gods of the jungle delight in playing as an antidote to sinful human pride.

The way in which the work of destruction had been accomplished was too beautifully simple. The Gond told me that a panther had come into his compound and killed one of his goats. He had frightened the animal away and ensconced himself in the door of his hut, waiting for its return. It had duly returned, to be dropped dead by an assorted mixture of slugs, nails and heaven knows what besides, fired from the old muzzle-loader at a range of five yards. Had this stalwart realized the identity of the beast he had sat up for, I have little doubt that he would never have waited for it as he did. All the characteristic pluck of the Gond notwithstanding, the maneater had established its reign of terror far too firmly throughout the country for any of the local inhabitants to tackle it single-handed in this way. But the villager did not realize what he was doing, and the result was that one of the most cunning and most ruthless of all the beasts in the Indian jungle had walked up to its death like any ordinary goat-killer.

The whole thing was astonishing enough; but what has always puzzled me most of all is the way in which the panther consented to be driven off its kill. It had no fear of human beings, and its record showed that it preferred them for edible purposes to the normal food of its kind. Yet the maneater, which had declined to be frightened off its kill by my missiles, shouted objurgations and rifle-shots, permitted itself to be driven off from a goat by the voice of an unarmed villager.

I bought the skin as a memento, and the Gond was delighted with the ten rupees he received for it. The panther was a large male, and, so far as it was possible to judge from the skin, in fine condition. One might have expected to find that the beast was an old and mangy one, but it was not. The skin was a beauty, and the claws did not suggest that their late possessor was in any way getting on in years. Nor were there any signs of a previous injury which might have accounted for the animal's original embarkation on its extended career of human destruction. To my lasting regret, I did not get the skull. It is possible that defective teeth may have accounted for its horrible proclivities. Failing that, the only explanation which suggests itself to me is that the panther acquired the taste for human flesh at an early age, having been educated to it by one of its parents which had been a maneater before it.

As there was the possibility of a reward being forthcoming for the destruction of the panther, I wrote to the State Durbar giving the name of the man who had killed it, the circumstances of the shooting and details of the evidence that the dead animal was the dreaded maneater. Whether the villager got his reward I never discovered. I certainly heard nothing more so far as that side of the matter was concerned. Long after, however, I learned that the panther's depredations had come to a sudden end at a time which coincided with the bringing of the skin to me. That removed any possible doubt there may have been that the skin I bought then, and still have, at one time belonged to one of the worst pests with which that particular part of India has ever been cursed.

HEADHUNTING
The practice of removing and preserving human heads

Headhunting arises in some cultures from a belief in the existence of a more or less material soul matter on which all life depends. In the case of human beings, this soul matter is believed to be particularly located in the head, and removal of the head is believed to capture the soul matter within and add it to the general stock of soul matter belonging to the community, wherein it contributes to the fertility of the human population, livestock and crops.

Headhunting has thus been associated with three things: with ideas regarding the head as the seat of the soul; with some forms of cannibalism in which the body or part of the body is consumed in order to transfer to the eater the soul matter of the victim; and with phallic cults and fertility rites intended to imbue the soil with productivity. It may thus develop into human sacrifice, a practice that has been generally associated with agricultural societies.

Headhunting has been practised worldwide and may go back to Paleolithic times. In deposits of the Late Paleolithic Azilian culture found at Ofnet in Bavaria, southern Germany and Austria, carefully decapitated heads were buried separately from the bodies, indicating beliefs in the special sanctity or importance of the head.

In Europe the practice survived until the early twentieth century in the Balkan Peninsula, where the taking of the head implied the transfer of the soul matter of the decapitated person to the decapitator. The complete head was taken by Montenegrins as late as 1912, being carried by a lock of hair worn allegedly for that purpose. In the Balkan War of 1912–13, nose taking was substituted, and it was the practice to cut off the nose and upper lip with the moustache (by which it was carried). In the British Isles the practice of head taking continued approximately to the end of the Middle Ages in Ireland and the Scottish marches.

Herodotus mentions Asian headhunters, and, on a bas-relief from Nineveh in the British Museum, Assyrians are depicted as cutting off and carrying away the heads of the slain during a battle.

In Africa headhunting was known in Nigeria (amongst other places), where, as in Indonesia, it was associated with the fertility of the crops, with marriage, and with the victim's obligation as a servant in the next world.

In Kafiristan (now Nurestan) in eastern Afghanistan, headhunting was practised until about the end of the nineteenth century, with women showering wheat upon men returning with heads from a successful raid.

In the north-east of India, Assam was famous for headhunting, and indeed all the peoples living south of the Brahmaputra River – Garos, Khasis, Nagas and Kukis – formerly were headhunters. Headhunting in Assam was normally carried out by parties of raiders who depended on surprise tactics to achieve their ends.

In Burma several groups followed customs similar to those of the headhunting tribes of India. The Wa people observed a definite head-hunting season, when the fertilizing soul matter was required for the growing crop, and wayfarers moved about at their peril.

In Borneo, most of Indonesia, the Philippines, and Taiwan, similar methods of headhunting were practised. The practice was reported in the Philippines by Martin de Rada in 1577 and was abandoned formally by the Igorot and Kalinga of Luzon only at the beginning of the twentieth century. In Indonesia it extended through Ceram, where the Alfurs were headhunters, and to New Guinea, where headhunting was practised by the Motu. In several areas of Indonesia, as in the Batak country and in the Tanimbar Islands, it seems to have been replaced by cannibalism.

Throughout Oceania headhunting tended to be obscured by canni-balism, but in many islands the importance attached to the head was unmistakable. In parts of Micronesia the head of the slain enemy was paraded about with dancing, which served as an excuse for raising a fee for the chief to defray public expenditure; later the head would be lent to another chief for the same purpose.

In Melanesia the head was often mummified and preserved, and sometimes worn as a mask in order that the wearer might acquire the soul of the dead man. Similarly, it was reported that Aboriginal Australians believed that the spirit of a slain enemy entered the slayer.

In New Zealand the heads of enemies were dried and preserved so that tattoo marks and the facial features were recognizable; this practice led to a development of headhunting when tattooed heads became desirable curios and the demand in Europe for Maori trophies caused "pickled heads" to become a regular article of ships' manifests.

In South America the heads were often preserved, as by the Jivaro, by removing the skull and packing the skin with hot sand, thus shrinking it to the size of the head of a small monkey, but preserving the features intact. There again headhunting was probably associated with cannibalism in a ceremonial form.

Despite the prohibition of headhunting activities, scattered reports of such practices continued well into the mid-twentieth century.

AMONG NEW GUINEA'S HEADHUNTERS

Travelling [in the early 1920s] by water from the inland swamps fed by the drainage from the Owen Stanley ranges we reached the junction of the Aramia and the mighty Bamu rivers with but one incident. While anchored off the communal house of Bimaramio, a floating archipelago of grass islets came sweeping down the stream and fouled the vessel. In the darkness and rain it was impossible to free the debris which began rapidly accumulating. All night we stood by expecting the anchor to drag or the cable to snap, and the vessel go drifting helplessly down the flood. The early morning found our craft the nucleus of a miniature island with grass, trees and debris firmly locked around the hull. The natives ashore observed our dilemma and came out in their canoes to assist. By laboriously removing the flotsam from the outer edge we were slowly disentangled and freed.

But still another peril menaced us. Being the time of spring tides, the navigation of the Bamu is rendered hazardous through the dangerous bore waters that sweep upstream leaving destruction in their wake. We had scarcely turned the bend into the Bamu when the lookout warned me that the bore was rushing up river. We had barely time to reach a sheltering point and run out both anchors when the seethe of waters was around us. A great tidal wave of mud went tearing up channel, churning in fury across the shallows over which we had just passed. The force of the wave was expended on the friendly point and we only experienced a violent rocking. The ride was now rapidly setting up river too swift to fight against, so we remained at anchor until the outflow when once more we reached the open sea and headed out across the shallow banks of the Turama.

The depth of water on the bar was only nine feet and, with the outrushing current and incoming tide, a dangerous sea was running. I was astonished at the amazing angles to which our shallow draught vessel rolled and how ill most of the party became after their long sojourn on peaceful rivers.

So it was with thankful hearts and stomachs that later in the evening we drew into the sheltered waters of Kerewa, behind the Island of Goaribari.

Scarcely had we dropped anchor before a canoe load of natives came alongside and informed us that all the people from the neighbouring villages were gathered at Kerewa, and that a great dance was going to be held that night. We were invited to join in, but feeling too weary, we declined the honour in favour of sleep. Of sleep there was none: the ceaseless tomtom of drums and chants made pandemonium of the night and, judging by female shrieks and wailing dogs, it was more a massacre than a festivity.

When morning broke I was grieved to observe that the dancers of the previous night were leaving the village in canoes and returning to their homes over the water. They were intensely pictorial in their feathery plumes and paint, even more so at a distance. Close inspection displayed grease, soiled feathers and much raddle [mud], charcoal and filth – not to mention the strongly pungent and repugnant smell of unwashed natives. The Goaribaries are conspicuous by the amount of ornate trappings which they wear, chiefly made from shells. No Goaribari is dressed without his leggings which fit the calf tightly and are adorned up the front by two rows of small cowrie shells. The women load their arms with the highly valued armlet shells and adorn the breasts with shapely crescents cut from the mother-o'-pearl shell. This treasured ornament, which can only be afforded by the well-to-do, is suspended by a string round the neck, and resembles a small breastplate. Then the ladies wear many-rowed necklaces of beads and band their shaven crowns in a manner that must be a sore encumbrance.

The men are of medium build, well proportioned and look as though food were abundant. The women are not as ugly as those of the Fly delta and a few might be regarded as comely – but a very few. Perhaps, if they wore a little more clothing, they might be more attractive, for apart from a grass belt and very narrow strip of fibre – they are unclothed. The men wear more: a large cumbersome section cut from the bailer shell, a very ornate belt of carved bark and a strange bundle of teased fibre or grass that falls behind like a bushy tail, conveying the impression of a richly caparisoned draught horse.

Numbers of the guests rowed off to pay their respects and barter their ornaments for Papuan currency-tobacco. While trade was actively progressing, a very amusing incident happened. Bell, the engineer, brought up on deck a rat in a spring trap and casually threw the rodent over the side. Instantly there was an undignified scramble among the canoes for the prize, which I learned is esteemed as a great delicacy. It was merely torn to pieces and devoured, the fur being spat out like pips!

From the vessel, an admirable view was presented of the long house, which extends along the river bank for no less than five hundred feet! This great structure was well and solidly constructed from lashed mangrove saplings and thatched with the leaf of the sago palm. The edifice stands some five feet off the ground on a jungle of piles, and was, excepting in height, the largest house that we saw in Papua. The flat space between the river and the house was abustle with the departing guests, while the river was animated with canoes returning to their villages. The hour was yet too early to use the cinema to advantage, but as soon as the opportunity presented itself I went ashore.

The first objects that attracted our attention were small groups of skulls impaled on posts facing the river. The gruesome relics were tastefully decorated by a ruffle of palm leaves rolled into scrolls at the end, which maintained a shivering movement in the breeze. The skulls were provided with very long noses, more like long beaks, and the eye sockets were filled with clay and eyes made from small red seeds. They were painted with raddle and were indeed grinning caricatures of death.

We were extremely fortunate in observing this display, for such treasured belongings are hidden in the fastnesses of the long house and are only brought out on ceremonial occasions or to display to visitors the valour of the village. They appeared to me to present rather a warning to guests than hospitality.

For a while we became the centre of attraction, which rather pleased me as it gave me an opportunity of studying the spectators. They were as savage a collection as we had encountered, made more so by the wildness of their garb and painting.

It will be observed that the raised road of sticks follows parallel to the entire length of the long house and that on its other side are arranged numerous irregular groups of houses, similar in external construction to the long house itself. These are the abodes of the women. As we passed by, a few coyly left the small porticoed verandah in front to peer through cracks and crevices, but most remained where they were to smile and gossip among themselves. It appears from numerous inquiries that the wives of all the male members of a family dwell in the one house and that family life as we understand it does not exist.

Seeking and gaining the permission of one of the men who chanced to be visiting his wife's apartment, we entered one of the houses to satisfy our curiosity.

We found so much impedimenta dangling from the roof that it was necessary to proceed bowed double. The houses are rarely more than thirty or forty feet long and from the small door a narrow hallway leads the length to an exit at the opposite end. On either side small cubicles are arranged, similar to those in the long house; but, in place of indolence, here is activity. The fires burn smokily, choking the acrid atmosphere, so that we could barely see or breathe.

The women were busy kneading sago, mixing it with mashed bananas and rolling the mixture into sausages with outer coverings of leaf. These they laid on the embers and baked. I could not bring myself to sample the staple diet which smelt much like burnt glue.

On the walls hung fish traps and nets, while from the roof pended inverted cornucopia-like receptacles woven from fibre, which I was informed were for holding and parcelling up of sago. The women here are ever busy. They are bought like merchandize and become slaves to the indolent males. When the food was cooked, the women carried it to the long house where the hungry lords awaited. We visited several of these hives of industry and always did we find the women busy, and leading what we would regard as lives of slavery – to them the only lives they know.

We left Kerewa with few regrets. Our next stopping place was Dopima, a village conspicuous because of the missionaries, Chalmers and Tomkins, who while endeavouring to proselytize the people were killed and eaten. We did not go ashore (although the people are now peaceful enough), owing to the vast expanse of low-tide mud which forms an extensive morass of the most loathsome nature. With the change of tides, we proceeded, and on the following day came suddenly upon a long house facing, not a mudflat this time, but a fine beach of hard dark sand. The village, we learned, was known as Babai and the long house had been recently built and was in a fine condition. The construction was identical with that of Goaribari and the inmates similar in most respects, excepting that we noticed the women also moving about the long house and squatting by the fire with the males. This we did not observe at Kerewa, except to bear in the food.

The long house had more of convenience for entering and leaving than Kerewa, there being well-notched steps cut in a heavy timber leading up from the ground to the floor level. The smell of new timbers and thatch more than overpowered the smell of the tenants, giving to the atmosphere the perfume of a sawmill, which to me is as the breath of the forest.

The inmates were all idling, excepting a few old men making arrow-heads. This process was extremely interesting as the points were being shaped and barbed by the use of a mollusc shell. The deftness in the use of this crude knife raises it in effectiveness above a steel blade, and it is notable that the instrument which nature has cast up on the beaches in vast profusion should still be preferred in these villages.

There was a particularly fine skull shrine near the entrance to this long house and I tried every possible ruse to secure it precisely as it stood. I offered two pounds money plus one hundred sticks of tobacco, rice, armshells, knives, axes or whatever the owner might desire. I was put off by being informed that the owner was away making sago. As I saw many interesting items here for the cinema, I asked the people to send for the owner and I would trade with him. The son of the owner arrived late in the afternoon and I displayed the purchase price before him – one axe, one hundred sticks of tobacco, twenty pounds of rice, five ramis, five strings of beads, five white cowre shells, five bidi-bidi (head of cone shells), one large knife, two large armshells; but all these enticements availed not.

The son of the owner informed me that, if he disposed of these things, his father would be annoyed on his return and also that the sorcerers would kill him by puripuri!

To test the truth, I placed a large and tempting bundle of armshells with the rest of my offerings. This was too much for the young fellow, who, without hesitation, acquiesced.

After a brief, but profitable few hours spent in Babai, we continued towards Urama. Our coxswain aptly said: "By-me-by you and me go halong bush and we come out colose hup."

The waterways with their narrow banks grown with mangroves and nipa palms are indeed like roadways through the jungle. They have, however, the unfortunate habit of meandering the longest way round.

Thinking the "bush roadway" shorter than going out to sea and navigating among the maze of sandbanks, I assented. To my disgust, I found ourselves wandering in an amazing and wasteful fashion, turning into creeks, then through great rivers and finally becoming stuck on a silt flat. With the incoming tide we floated off, but I put to sea at the first opening and ranted soundly the coxswain for "bushing" us.

At lunch time the following day we "went bush" again, following the course of a narrow water track that resembled a glass road winding through dense mangrove jungles. Countless waterways branched off in every direction, which filled me with qualms as the constant expressions of my dubious pilot – "Last time I bin go along bush, he altogether not the same; bush he different" – suggested we were likely to be bushed for some days. It was a deep relief when the waterway widened into a broad expanse and the Urama villages came into view on a salient point.

As usual the rattling out of the anchor was the signal for a flotilla of canoes to put off from the shore. They seemed to dart from nowhere and yet come from everywhere; from the mangroves that overhung the waters, from unseen creeks, down slimy mudbanks, tobogganing as they poled ahead over the slime. It was, indeed, a carnival of the queerest craft I have ever seen. The impression conveyed from a short distance was that the people were walking on the water. As the canoes came closer they resolved themselves into hollowed out grooves, ten feet long and wide enough for a single figure to stand in. The hull was half round, devoid of outrigger, keel or stabilizing device of any kind except the rower who stood upright and propelled the extraordinary craft with long sweeps of a broad paddle. So deftly are these canoes handled and balanced that they seem to become part of the paddler himself, the balance being maintained instinctively much as a bird on the wing. As the canoes had but three to four inches of freeboard each wavelet broke "aboard". This did not perturb the paddlers who solved the bailing out problem by standing on one leg while vigorously kicking the water out astern with the other.

The waters swarm with hungry crocodiles, a fact which suggested a parallel of a starving man refusing a banquet.

The environment of these people is water and ooze, and, as their only means of moving about is by canoe, they are literally born with canoes on their feet: to them canoeing is as natural a process as walking. I purchased the finest of the canoes for the Australian Museum paying one axe, twenty-four sticks of tobacco, one mirror and several yards of cloth! Evidently the purchase price was highly satisfactory, for the owner took his vessel ashore and redecorated it, whilst the entire fleet crowded round to auction their vessels at half the price! Whilst the hubbub was in progress a large canoe paddled by a crew of ten came out and, as it drew alongside, the smaller fry made passage and became silent. In the canoe were two elderly men plainly decorated but of a dignified presence that at once evinced authority. My interpreter informed me, that these were, "Two big fella man stop along village bin come, makem frien' halong me and you." This was the polite way of informing me the village Chiefs were making their official call.

"This fella heye all same hawk, teeth all same crocodile, he Gormier. He very big man along fight. Other feller, he Coir all same you. He talk halong people – all same you talk halong boat – he tell village people do somesing – he do all same boy along boat – he savvy too much!"

In other words Gormier was the War Chief and Coir the Village Chief who attended to village welfare and social affairs. I invited the dignitaries aboard – quite an unprecedented honour – and gave them presents of axes, tobacco and armshells, which at once put us on good terms and made an impression on the crowd standing about the vessel – on the water. We received a return invitation to visit the village, which we did without delay. Gormier and Coir transferred their large canoe and crew to us for the remainder of our stay, our dinghy being quite useless amid the muddy shallows surrounding the village. We secured a short staff to the stern of the canoe, from which fluttered the ensign of the Australian Commonwealth, and heavily necklaced ourselves with beads.

McCulloch and self cautiously stepped down into the wobbly craft and, squatting low to prevent it from overturning, rakishly put off for the shore. Soon we were on the threshold of the village, which owing to the falling tide was surrounded by mudflats several hundred yards wide. Without more ado the crew put down their paddles, jumped overboard knee deep into the ooze and, to our great surprise and amusement, sledged the canoe along a mud groove up to the village.

As we glided over the mud we scared myriads of tiny hopping fishes which apparently abhorred swimming about in the water to the luxurious pleasures of wallowing and jumping about on the tepid mud. McCulloch informed me of their name – a typical anomaly of scientific nomenclature that magnifies diminutive objects with colossal names, and colossal objects with diminutive ones – adding that, as these fish spend most of their time out of the water, the gills have become useless for breathing; nature has compensated by providing their tails with innumerable microscopic blood vessels which they keep in the moisture and through which the dissolved oxygen is absorbed; literally speaking these fish breathe through their tails, as incongruous as the fishes living out of water! Still this is a land of surprises and another awaited us as we glided up alongside the village and stepped ashore.

Coir loudly announced our arrival in the village, a ceremony which proved an order for the women and children to flee to their homes and for the men to welcome us at the waterfront.

It was not through fear of molestation that Coir ordered the women away; he was merely conforming with tribal etiquette. We immediately won amiable relations with the men by bestowing lavish presents of tobacco and forthwith Coir led us around the village with the whole tribal horde close on our heels.

I at once noticed the freedom from the hideous sipuma, a scaly skin disease which I had observed universally elsewhere, and, on inquiring the reason, was shown many huge scars where the disease had been stopped in its incipient stages. This is done by cauterizing the affected spot with a glowing stick, a painfully drastic treatment yet obviously efficacious. They were a wild looking motley famed on account of their warlike and independent nature and the failure of the authorities until recently to subdue them. Even now the villages will have naught to do with missionaries, traders or labour recruiters, which pleases me greatly, for so soon as the missionaries and civilization encroach upon a village the whole tribal sociology is subverted. I found the ethical and social laws of Urama remarkably adapted to the existing culture of the people and it impressed me as being unwise and almost foolish to attempt to thrust them under the control of a civilization and religion thousands of years in advance.

Certain of the missionaries influence the natives to abandon dances and customs allegedly evil. They are only evil by comparison, and basically such customs have some subtly wise inception. What is given in return for the banishment of age-old customs? A spiritual teaching that has little compensation and lesser consolation for the natives. If the missions would combine more physical application with their teachings, the native would develop into something more than a spiritual idler. Before the mission tampers with native customs or traditions it should be subject to the carefully considered intimate deliberations of the Administration.

While I meditated over these things we were squelching up a rise to the village beneath the glorious foliage of the huge Ilima trees that formed a canopy overhead of leafy lacery and blue sky. Right up to the extremities, the trunks and branches were covered with vines and orchids, and at their base peaceful and quiet, as though in recumbent slumber lay the village huts. I was much mystified to account for the high land on which we stood, for all around stretched the interminable swamp. A close analysis revealed the fact that the mound was of man's making, grown into height through the age-old accumulations of shells, coconut husks and canoe chippings – veritable refuse heaps!

Coir led the way through the village, which seemed deserted, but I heard feminine whisperings and titterings as we passed close to the huts, which convinced me that civilization has not changed this trait of feminine nature. The huts resembled those of oilier delta villages and internally, perhaps, they were less filthy and malodorous. Coir stopped before a house which differed only from the others through having a large tassel of teased fibre dangling from the apex of its porch-like entrance. Coir spoke a few words to my interpreter which were translated into "House belong him," and then raising his voice called "Yarib! Yarib!"

Immediately a not uncomely woman coyly appeared at the entrance, with two big brown-eyed infants. She wore, pending from her neck, the conventional pearl shell crescent; a few strands of grass completed an embarrassing attire. I noticed her hands were scored with hard labours and her feet were characteristically large, a natural evolution inherited from generations of mudwalkers. Coir conversed with Madam Yarib whilst I entertained the children with lollypops, much to the amusement of the chuckling entourage and the delighted father.

Mrs Yarib Coir cast a not unkindly eye on the rows of beads around my neck and McCulloch's immaculate white legs. Accordingly I handed my interpreter several of the necklaces which were the cause of the covetous glance and asked him to present them to Mrs Yarib Coir from "Woman belong me." The brown lady became appreciably coquettish and disappeared into her house. Soon she returned with a tuft of at least a score of long grass strands and expressing herself to my interpreter handed it to him. In turn the raiment was presented to me with the translation "Woman belong Coir – make present Woman belong you."

I was much touched by this thought and graciously accepted the chic mode which was the height of Urama negligée. I am inclined to believe that this prehistoric creation would be a very fashionable deshabille for these ultra modern times.

By now we had trudged to the far end of the village, which was bounded by a very oozy creek. On the far side rose several colossal temples – the Dubu Daimas or club houses of the men, which could only be reached by a frail bridge of doubtful construction, a bridge over which women were not permitted to pass. Coir's authority terminated by this moat; he was only concerned with village affairs, a lord mayor of a mud capital. Beyond the bridge lay Gormier's province and all laws and things concerned with the Dubu Daimas and war came under his jurisdiction.

The two characters were quite dissimilar. Coir, garrulous and flippant, made a display of his authority. Gormier was even sullen, but also given to acting; when he spoke he uttered wisdom. I took a liking to Gormier, as indeed I had reason to do: he rendered me unlimited and faithful assistance, and stood out a dominant figure above all the natives with whom I came in contact. As he took the lead to guide us across the bridge he much reminded me of Charon crossing the Styx into a metropolis of the underworld.

As McCulloch and I carefully picked our way over the rotten slippery sticks, our tribal escort followed close on our heels, causing the bridge to sway and creak ominously. There were shouts of warning from Gormier, which kept the crowd back until we were almost over. But the oncoming file was too much for the bridge: it rocked and cracked and before the crowd could rush back to safety collapsed amid wild yells. We had just landed on the far side and, looking back, observed half a dozen natives stuck thigh deep in the mud and others wallowing out amid roars of laughter and, I doubt not, good-humoured banter.

Climbing up a crude ladderway, we stood on the threshold of a great arched porch that rose fifty feet above us. From the apex, dangled a weird collection of amulets carved from wood: human effigies, small crocodiles, lizards and other symbolic objects, which were to protect the house against the evil spirits of which they live in eternal dread.

Bending low, we passed through a ridiculously small doorway into the eerie gloom of an immense hall – a veritable place of death. As the concourse of warriors filed in behind me a hushed silence was observed, all speaking in subdued tones as though in the sacred precincts of a sanctuary.

In the semi-darkness we stood in a large vestibule, from which a wide hall extended the length of the temple to a door at the far end. This vestibule was evidently the general assembly chamber. The walls were hung with gigantic masks, shields, weapons and ceremonial garb. On either side of the hall entrance were two large racks filled with human skulls; beneath these racks pended "Gope" plaques with wondrously carved faces no two of which were alike. These represented the ancestral spirits of the tribe. Below these again and resting on the floor were rows of boar and crocodile skulls, probably trophies offered to the ancestral spirits. As we passed down the gloomy hall I noticed on either side small cubicles, each with its own skull shrine and ancestral spirit plaques, dark dens over which the very shadow of death seemed to brood.

At the far end the passage opened into another vestibule, on the opposite walls of which were large skull racks and enormous Kaiva-Ku-Ku masks. Gormier indicated that this was his *lavara* or cubicle. By exhaustive interpretation I gathered that the skulls were those of enemies that had been killed and eaten. According to the number of skulls won in combat, so was the warrior's status in the tribal hierarchy; and he was given a cubicle in the temple commensurate with the dignity of his rank. Gormier, having the greatest number, was supreme.

It appears that the religion of the tribes is a combination of Manes or Ancestor worship and skull cult. Gormier informed my interpreter that, so long as the ancestral plaques were attached to the enemies' skulls, the latters' spirits were enslaved to the ancestral spirits in the next life, and that the more enemies they killed in this life the more slaves they would have in the next. Later I inquired from Coir if this were so. He displayed surprise at my knowledge and assented.

A short distance from the warriors' Dubu were three smaller dubus, which I learned were the compounds of the unmarried novitiates. On reaching puberty, they are transferred to isolation and spend their adolescence rigorously acquiring the tribal tenets and proving their manhood by ordeal. If a man is physically unable to endure the training, he is ineligible for marriage. Something of this kind might well be introduced into present-day eugenics . . .

On the following day the canoe with my picked crew and interpreter Bormi came alongside at breakfast and, as the weather inclined to the gloomy, I decided to spend the day flashlighting the interior of the Dubu and opening negotiations for what I was reticent about mentioning previously to the people – skulls. It has been my ardent desire to secure a number of skulls, and re-establish them in the Museum, an exact replica of the skull racks in the Dubu.

When the flashlighting was over, I made council in the remote end of the Dubu and started preliminary negotiations for the purchase of a complete skull rack of twenty-four skulls, the Gope shields pending beneath it and the pig skulls which were arranged in a long row at the bottom.

I must admit that this was an unprecedented overture to make and I was not surprised at the astonishment of the good Gormier. By patient interpretation, which lasted a couple of hours, I opened the discussion by saying that we white men were travelling over the length and breadth of New Guinea, learning the customs and ways of its people, collecting their arts, crafts and all things appertaining to their life. That beyond New Guinea and the sunrise was a great world where the white people came from. I spoke of their great villages and of the enormous Dubus made of stone that the great cities owned, wherein all things belonging to the native people all over the world were kept. That white people came day after day to look at the things and learn of other people. That all things were kept there for all time. That when Gormier was dead and his people dead and new people came, the trophies which we would collect would live on, and memories of them would never be forgotten. We had collected from everywhere and now wanted the people of Urama to help us.

The price, I said, they could fix themselves. I intimated that I realized fully what these trophies meant to them. Each one was a record of a deed of valour, each Gope a tablet to a dead brother – each pig skull a treasured souvenir of the chase. If it was against the laws of the Dubu Daima, then I must go without, for I did not wish to impose upon nor digress from what might be their religion.

Gormier was obviously relieved by my last remarks and also understood quickly that we were not going to make playthings of the most treasured of all possessions. He asked shrewd, intelligent questions about the Museum and was satisfied that we were genuine. I said I should like to take the whole partition from the Dubu, skull rack and all. I had photographed it and would erect it exactly as it stood in the Great Dubu of the Whitemen.

The old fellow left us and went down to talk with his clansmen who were seated smoking in the vestibule. A short while after he returned and said that the laws of the Dubu did not allow of any part of its structure being removed. If the partition were cut out, a new Dubu would have to be built entirely. He had spoken with his brothers about the heads and other things, and they had all agreed to do as he desired to do. He could not give me his rack of skulls – they were the inheritance of his children and must be passed on, but he would help me.

The old man then rose and took from the rack one of his best skulls. He pondered affectionately over the terrible object, then untied one of the Gope from its setting and selected one of the largest pig skulls. These he collected in a small pile and placed them beside me. Gormier then called the names of the warriors individually. They entered their small cubicles and did as he did and desired.

It might seem strange that I felt rather sad about the whole affair. To secure a head from a headhunter might sound a permissible action to most people; but when it is understood that many of those skulls were relics passed down by ancestors – fine old warriors – heads won in fair combat, by strength of arms and valour, and objects of religious reverence, it is natural that they must have felt a deep pang at parting with them. One young man spent fully ten minutes in allowing his eye to roam over the thirty-six skulls which his brave father had won. He must part from one of these heirlooms to the stranger: which one must it be? The expression was downcast, sad and tearful. What volumes of tragic story these racks could tell! What awful sights the eyeless things had seen! Awful to us who regard with horror the eating of human flesh; but infinitely worse are we who murder by the millions.

I had great esteem for these men who parted with their belongings – things that ordinarily could not be bought; for I am convinced that no tobacco nor trade objects could have purchased them. Elsewhere I had striven to purchase skulls at fanciful prices, and had failed. Henceforth each rack will have a vacant hole. Perhaps it will remind them of the strangers who passed their way, but I am sure it will ever be a space of regret.

The little bundles were all brought and laid down on the floor of Gormier's cubicle. On each I placed a knife, twenty-two sticks of tobacco, six bidi-bidi and one armshell. I asked Gormier if the purchase money was satisfactory. He assented. Then the same question was asked of each. They all assented and the transaction – surely one of the strangest of trading incidents – was closed. Nor did the interest of the people wane here. They tore fibre from the Dubu decorations and helped to pack the skulls and tie up the Gope. I expressed a wish to have a rack made exactly similar as to that of Gormier's. The old men went away and late in the evening the rack was brought out complete in infinite detail, even to the crude little decorations of queer figures and totemic symbols. This is the first occasion that I have experienced such punctuality and contract-keeping by the natives.

Daybreak and a full tide enabled us to pass over the shallow bank by the village and take a shorter route by way of Port Romilly to the open sea. While it was still scarcely light our friends collected along the waterfront, and a kindly thought sent one of their canoes ahead to guide us through the intricate passage. I had many regrets on leaving these wild, untamed, kindly people, for they had helped us with alacrity and the payment which I gave them never caused a demur. As we turned into the daybreak stillness of a jungle waterway the last farewells died from my ears – "Ba-ma-huta! Ba-ma-huta!" . . .

The Styx Promenade, as I have named the main thoroughfare of Kaimari, is a raised roadway of mangrove sticks that runs the length of the village and spans creeks and slime in rickety rottenness. From it, pathways ramify to the domiciles, and so the inhabitants are able to move about without sinking thigh-deep in filth. The *Eureka* and "Seagull" are moored close inshore at the southern end of the village, and a large crowd of males of all ages, collect there from dawn till dark to gossip over the strange craft that came to them through the skies. A low fence extends around the waterfront which keeps the crocodiles without and the pigs within – sometimes.

On the mud flat before the fence lie stranded large numbers of the characteristic Purari canoes. These strange craft are simply excavated logs varying in length up to forty-five feet. Eccentric features in design are noticeable in the bow and stern. The former is cut so low that, when heavily laden, a small boy squats there and is caulked in with mud. Little "stick-in-the-mud" keeps out the bow wave, whilst a narrow barrier of mud seals off the wake astern. That indispensable tenacious slime – mud!

Kaimari mud has a thousand uses. It is the playground where the pigs and children revel and wallow. It is the field where the staple foods, crabs and sago, thrive. In fact the whole place is an odoriferous quagmire, from which the populace seem moulded. I have no doubt that the quality of this mud is responsible for the reek of the people . . .

McCulloch and myself will guide my readers through a tour of this city. Step lightly along the Styx way, in single file extended. The sticks are decayed, and six feet below awaits the slimy pit. McCulloch is a great "hit" in the village: his extra short shorts display an ivory lankiness that is the admiration of the fair dusky ones. On either side the bungalows face the road, and gossip and giggles greet us.

But Lang and myself have our share of triumphs. Lang has a plate of false teeth which, by clever manipulation, he causes to disappear and reappear to the astonishment of the natives who stand about him in a circle shouting with mirth. As for me, since childhood I have been able to move my scalp and wriggle my ears. This extraordinary accomplishment has been no less successful in collecting a crowd. They surround us on all sides – men, women and children – delighted with their strange white visitors.

As regards looks, the Kaimari ladies are the most unbeautiful creatures I have seen. Their dress, microscopically speaking, is customary rather than effective. The hair is shorn close, leaving a narrow ridge down the centre, and two rings above the ears resemble tufts of astrakan. Fashions in coiffure are variable, and the design might riot to a knob fore and aft, or a ridge athwart the cranium. In others the hair covers the scalp in small sprouts as if sown. Eyes are unusually goo-goo (probably on account of the eyebrows having been plucked out), and as scandalous as the broad nose with its pierced septum and six-inch nasal decoration. Lips thick and framing a mighty red orifice displaying two rows of black teeth – discoloured by the habitual chewing of betel nut and lime. No, my lady, you are an ugly gargoyle! Methinks the Potter's hand must have shaken badly, or perhaps it is the Kaimari mud from which He moulded you.

A few straggling coconuts struggle for existence in the less submerged mud areas, but nothing else does well about the village but mangroves, death and decay. Hunched up by her doorway sits an old woman plastered in mud from head to toe. Her shrivelled body is encumbered with skeins and cables of native cords. Her limbs are bound with ligatures until the flesh stands out. She mourns her husband and does penance for his death.

On another verandah squats a group of garrulous freaks – females that resemble moving mud casts. They are all in mourning, someone or something died. Perhaps a distant relative or a dog. These people are never so happy as when they appear miserably sad. Their life appears to have absorbed the inexpressible gloom that permeates even the weeping skies; for rain it does, and each evening as darkness falls the lightning plays and the thunder growls about these hapless people of gloom and storm.

As we advance there gathers behind a trail of boys and men. They follow to a colossal building whither the Styx path leads and ends. Across the imposing entrance stretches a barrier of woven palm leaf, with a flap obscuring the door. We tarry to regard in awe the majesty or the great arch that culminates seventy feet above us. It seems as if the warning, "All hope abandon ye who enter here," is inscribed on the portals. We will lift the screen and go in.

We stood on the threshold of a great hall that extended like a vast cavern to a remote gloom. On the floor some forty or fifty sleeping forms snored their afternoon siesta. From roof and walls pended an amazing collection of fantastic masks in various stages of construction.

The hubbub behind us awakened the sleepers, who viewed us with resentment until a few sticks of trade tobacco induced them to cheerfulness. A particularly repulsive old gentleman, much decorated with dog's teeth and evidently the chief, assigned himself to showing us around, which he did with great ostentation and jabber. A crowd of men followed us through the Ravi, for such is the name of these great Purari ran clubhouses, sullenly looking on as we noted and examined everything.

For three hundred feet we walked along an aisle, with the heavy constructional poles on either side. These poles, as well as supporting the roof, marked the limits of *lavara* or cubicles which contained numbers of remarkably carved plaques, probably representing ancestral spirits. Beneath these "Kwoi" plaques were heaps of crocodile, pig and occasional human skulls, doubtless heirlooms and trophies. We then came to a partition that barred further progress. At the last *lavara* before this barrier, the followers halted and only the chief and we two white men proceeded.

Squeezing through a narrow opening, we were blinded for the moment by the darkness, but obviously we had scared great numbers of bats and vermin. As our eyes penetrated the gloom we discovered that we were in an apartment some fifty feet in length by fifteen in width; the roof had tapered from the entrance and was now only ten feet high. Grouped closely together were seventeen wild and eerie effigies, the sacred and dread Kopiravi. These grotesque objects were reminiscent caricatures of crocodiles yawning heartily. They stood on four legs of cassowary design and had an opening in the belly so that a man might stand erect therein and carry them about. Until recently the mangled bodies of victims were thrust into the gaping jaws of these implacable gods as offerings; in the morning the bodies were removed and cut up for the ghoulish feast. Beneath each was placed a carefully sealed package, which made us exceedingly curious.

McCulloch was very anxious to procure one of those packages for the Museum, and I had made up my mind to secure photographic records of this den at all costs. On emerging from the chamber of horrors, the old chief truculently demanded "Ku-Ku" (tobacco) and intimated that, unless we gave and appeased the wrath of the Kopiravi, a serious calamity or sickness would befall us; so we gave. Attractive overtures to purchase and for permission to photograph availed us not, so I spoke to my native coxswain Vaieki of our desires, and that wily rascal formulated a plan. The old men are an astute lot of impostors and hypocrites, and I suspected that the motive of the Kopiravi is to terrorize the young men, women and children so that they might be worked to gratify the desires of these old drones, in order that the choicest of foodstuffs might be offered to the Kopiravi and fall to their lot.

So Vaieki waylaid the old men of the Ravi, and it was suggested by them that a package might disappear in the night, if a large knife took its place. This was done, but it so happened that the contents of the mystic packet belonged to twenty various people; and, on the very brink of achievement, the owners learned of the dark deed, the package was rescued, and after much altercation was returned to the Ravi. After much watching and waiting an opportunity arrived at last. Death called the villagers to a house of mourning to cry their grief, so we found the Ravi deserted and unguarded.

Without hesitation we made our way to the Holy of Holies and demolished and re-erected the barrier so that I might have room to operate. Numerous flashlights which nearly set fire to the Ravi enabled several exposures to be made. We even went so far as to desecrate the sanctity by removing the Kopiravi and arranging them to our satisfaction and advantage.

McCulloch, with trembling fingers, opened one of the mysterious packages and found it to contain twenty "bull-roarers" of diverse shapes and sizes. These were thin tapering pieces of wood varying from eight to sixteen inches in length, and with a small loop at one end to attach a cord. When whirled around the head a gruff sound is produced, varying in pitch according to the size of the "bull-roarer". This blood-curdling noise is the voice of the Kopiravi which strikes consternation and terror throughout the village.

Scarcely had we finished when the savages began to file into the Ravi, but so far we were unseen. When all were seated and drowsy I arranged a diversion so that we might escape unnoticed. I gave to McCulloch a packet of firecrackers, and he quietly left our hiding and mingled with the natives, gaining at once their attention and approbation by distributing a few sticks of "Trade". A yell from the sanctum (mine) caused the necessary diversion to allow McCulloch to light the crackers unseen. The ruse was successful beyond hopes. Bang-bang, helter skelter, shouts and shrieks and a confused rabble rushed the entrance and made a terrified exit.

During the bubbub, Vaieki and I hurriedly replaced the barrier, and, by the time the natives had composed themselves and returned, we were seated complacently on our belongings, breaking up small presents of Ku-Ku. We again made overtures to purchase one of the bundles. Some were for it, but the majority were unwilling. However, as my friend McCulloch says, "No hide, no Christmas box"; so we prevailed by a great display of presents and bluff. The outcome was that we might extract one bull-roarer from each packet in return for twenty sticks of tobacco and a bag of rice.

With the chief keeper of the Kopiravi, McCulloch entered the sanctum and began making his selection. No one ventured near the barrier. Nor would the high priest touch any of the packages. In the darkness McCulloch's job was unenviable, for as he opened each packet spiders, lizards, scorpions and centipedes crawled out. The impatience of the waiters was relieved by occasional Ku-Ku gifts.

At last the selection was made and wrapped up in palm leaf. None would venture near, nor would they allow the parcel to leave the Ravi until it was rolled in numerous sleeping mats and McCulloch's singlet wound around the outside. As we passed along the Styx Promenade not a soul was to be seen in the village, for should any but the initiated old men gaze upon these things they would either die or else become violently ill. We were only saved from being stricken by the generous presents which we made to the old men of the Ravi . . .

I decided not to enter the lake by night, knowing nought of its uncharted waters and having been previously informed as to the treachery of the natives. The watch was doubled and a keen look-out maintained against surprise.

Deferred realization retarded the night, which was rendered painfully harassing by myriads of mosquitoes and by numberless swarms of diminutive Mayflies. These came from the swamps in dense clouds and, attracted by the light, found their way into our food, eyes, nostrils and mouths, making breathing well-nigh impossible, so perforce we had to dispense with a light . . .

The zephyrs from the south were sweet-laden with the fragrance of flowers, and the starlit dome of heaven strewed the mirror-like waters with scintillation. Across the waters of the lake came the tom-tom of drums, the frogs chorused an anthem from the swamps, and the eerie cry of night-birds made the air pregnant with mystery and enchantment.

While dawn was kindling the east, all were a-bustle. The anchor was heaved up and the rhythmic cough of our engine stirred the fowl from the marshes and the crocodiles from their lairs. These infested the waters in large numbers, attaining a great length and conjuring in my imagination scenes of primordial days when the mammoth Brontosaurus and Dinosaurus wallowed in the tepid slime of such a lake.

As the curtain of dawn was raised, from the masthead a wondrous scene unfolded. The pink-flushed river led on to an expansive sheet of gold. Our hopes and dreams were realized, for the goal of our ambitions lay before us. The banks were clothed with vast fields of giant lotus in full bloom, from which flocks of ibis, duck and cormorants took wing. Beyond eye-reach extended verdant flats of marshland, resembling a field of young wheat, swamped by flood waters. It was from these immense beds of lotus that the sweet perfume of last evening exhaled. In the delicate beams of sunrise the whole scene was hospitable and inviting. Our bows were now entering the portals of the lake, and on the very threshold above the surrounding flats rose a low isolated hill, rudely planted, cultivated with coconuts, bananas and sugar cane.

As we drew near, the fantastic outlines of a great house came into view – before us stood the citadel of the headhunters. The anchor chain rattled out and we came to rest, crying, "Sambio! Sambio! Sambio!" the sole word which we knew of the lake-dwellers' language. "Sambio", the "sesame" that sheathes the arrow and kindles the calumet. But the only answer to our "Sambios" was the echo that travelled through the deserted house and "came out by the same door as in it went".

What had become of the people? It was hardly rational to surmize that they had vanished without leaving pickets to spy on our movements or maybe they were hiding in ambush until we came ashore. We remained inert, but for occasional salvos of "Sambios" and flutterings of gaudy-coloured fabrics and axes.

I can only attribute the failure of our golden lure to the exhaust of our engine, which pops away a merry *feu-de-joie*, like a miniature *mitrailleuse*. I have no doubt that the natives regarded us as offensive invaders, equipped with deadly armament and were naturally reticent about accepting our "Sambios" and presents merely on their sound and face values. As nothing appeared to be stirring, the *Eureka* was nosed in-shore, as depth allowed, and, accompanied by McCulloch and four of the most trusty of my native crew, I went ashore in the dinghy to make our official call. My nervy native bodyguard was well armed, though I candidly must admit the quivering barrels behind us two white men presented more of a menace than a flight of arrows.

However, we had made up our minds, and pushed on up the narrow track that led between the tall reeds, expecting momentarily what never happened, until further progress was barred by arrows thrust in the ground and a skull impaled on a pole. This we could scarcely interpret as a hospitable welcome, but as Lake Murray skulls were urgently needed for the Australian Museum collection, McCulloch annexed them, whilst I substituted a green bough, red calico and presents, emblematic of peace. The native guardsmen were placed at strong points to command the village paths whilst we investigated.

The village comprised a single immense house, three hundred feet long, fifty feet wide and thirty-five feet high to the apex of the arched entrance. This building reminded me very much of similar colossal "ravis" of the Purari Delta, with the roof projecting in a tapering snout, symbolizing a crocodile couchant with jaws a-yawn. The ridge-pole projected an additional twelve feet and was split at the end, beak-like, and a human thigh-bone thrust in transversely suggesting the armorial bearings of the tribe.

This informal decoration we greatly admired, so we added it to our bone bag. Apart from the main entrance there were eleven small openings on either side, which led to small cubicles. The entire edifice resembled a ramshackle shearing shed with a sheepy atmosphere of unwashed humanity. The main porch in front of the building was apparently reserved exclusively for the fighting men, whilst the women and children occupied the smaller cubicles.

This amazing communal house was built on a strongly strategic site: the front porch commanding a prospect over the entire lake, while in the event of surprise or defeat the entire community could melt away into the shadows of the surrounding bamboo thickets, exactly as they had done during our approach.

Instructing the guard to maintain a vigilant patrol and to acquaint us at the first danger sign, we entered and passed within the gloom of the headhunters' citadel.

The floor of the main portico was divided into rectangles merely by laying down and lashing transversely heavy saplings. Each space was apparently allotted to the fighting males of a family, who slept on the bare ground, coiled close to the smouldering embers to avoid mosquitoes or squatted on the saplings during the day, grinding their stone axes, fashioning arrowheads from bones with flint gouges, and chewing betel nut. At convenient points hooked uprights were placed where the bows, arrows, and stone clubs were hung in constant readiness. From the rafters pended gruesome war trophies of human skulls and souvenirs of the chase. Truly it was a model dwelling out of the Stone Age.

The family section was partitioned off from the warriors den by a high partition made from sago frond stems cunningly lashed together. Climbing up on to the top of this partition, we looked down the gloom of this Augean hall, and in the faint light made out the outlines of two rows of dismal pens fenced off by low barriers. Each was provided with a raised platform for sleeping and a small doorway into the open.

Everything was inexpressibly crude and primitive. We had entered the Stygian home of prehistoric swamp-dwellers living by the shores of a primeval sea. In the pens warm embers still remained; the belongings hung from the rafters in countless bags, and, though feeling compunction for our actions, we ransacked them. In the cause of science, McCulloch allows that even an unfair exchange is no robbery; so we collected and exchanged, to the great advantage of the owners and to our supreme satisfaction.

Skulls, human bits, and tit-bits filled our bone-bag, whilst axes, knives and fabrics were substituted. Surely, indeed, Father Christmas had visited the house! Iron and steel replaced bone and stone, and a million years was bridged in a day! To record all the things we found in the bags would be as impossible as listing the countless little treasures and mysteries of my lady's ditty bag.

The grass bag contains a full dress. It is the height of prehistoric fashion – a chic grass mode that begins at the waist and ends at the knees; perhaps in the near future your silk bag will carry a wardrobe, for it seems today that the ultra-modern is reverting to the prehistoric! The grass ditty contains less of golden wealth and poverty, and, I doubt not, less of worries, troubles and anxieties that a million years has thrust upon us. But, as my friend Mancer would say, we digress, and we will peer into just a few more bags, for we are just as curious, but perhaps less nervous, than you, dead ladies. Here is baby's cradle. Mother just places him within the knitted bag, and suspends him to rock from the nearest pole while she turns a fish in the embers for the evening meal. This large bag – it swarms with earwigs, scorpions, cockroaches, and spiders – contains lots of small grass-plaited pouches.

In each reposes the blade of the Stone Age – a stone axe-head. Hanging beside are the handles. Near by, carefully wrapped in leaf, Paradise bird plumes – a headhunter's head-dress! Then there are bags of empty mussel shells, used for knives and scrapers; red and yellow ochre, for decorative purposes; stabbing daggers of keen-edged bamboo, and terrible arrow points, barbed and cut in murderous fashion. Some bags contain grass skirts, others bits of wood, charms, seeds, and bush herbs – the purposes of which we know not.

Thus we went the round of the bags, carefully selecting our choices, and always replacing the theft with presents of axes and knives and articles likely to be of perpetual use.

From a dim alcove I gave a yell of delight! We had discovered treasures beyond bonanza! Human heads! Stuffed heads! What luck!

Skulls painted and decorated had grinned from every niche, but heads – stuffed heads! Glorious beyond words! Had we raided a bank and carried off the bullion we could scarcely have been more pleased than with such desirable objects.

This is, of course, scientifically speaking, for I can scarcely conceive anything so gruesome as these hideous human trophies of the head-hunters. The heads had been severed from the victims, preserving the neck as long as possible; the skin had been slit up the back of the neck to the cranium, and the brain and all fleshy parts extracted by mascer-ating in water and scraping with a bamboo knife. The skin had been replaced on the skull and stuffed with coconut fibre. The native taxi-dermist then sewed it up at the back. The stuffing process distorted the face longitudinally, whilst the mouth which was forced open exces-sively was stopped with a ball of clay. The eyes were likewise treated and decorated with red seeds. The whole gruesome object had evidently been subjected to a lengthy smoke-curing process which mummified it and stopped decay. Finally the trophy was decorated with iconic designs executed in red and yellow ochre and a large seed was found in the brain cavity – which evidently caused much grim amusement when shaken as a rattle during their death dances.

I have never seen objects more ghastly and horrible than these grim trophies.

What sort of people could these be that so callously made toys of their victims? Infinitely barbarous, ferocious, and cruel, with no feeling nor thought for human agony and suffering, and I shuddered to think of the ghastly scenes that had taken place in the small clearing by the gloomy bamboos.

THE ROGUE ELEPHANT OF
ABERDARE FOREST

Two natives were returning to their village one evening when they saw a great black mass standing motionless in the shadows of the huts. The men shouted to scare the thing away. At once the mass left the shadows and charged them at fearful speed. Then the men saw it was a huge bull elephant.

They ran for their lives, each going in a different direction. One man was wearing a red blanket and that blanket was his death warrant, for the elephant followed him. The villagers cowering in their huts listened to the chase, powerless to help their friend They heard the man's screams as the elephant caught him. The great brute put one foot on his victim and pulled him to pieces with his trunk. Then he stamped the body into the ground and went away.

I was guiding two Canadian sportsmen through the Aberdare Forest in British Fast Africa when runners arrived from the chief of the murdered man's village to ask my help in killing the elephant. The natives in Kenya knew me well, for I had lived there many years [in the 1930s] as a white hunter – taking out sportsmen, to shoot big game and killing dangerous animals at the request of the government. The chief sent me word that this bull was a rogue elephant that had been destroying farms and terrorizing the district for many months. If the animal were not destroyed, he was sure to kill someone else sooner or later.

I was under contract to my two sportsmen. They were brothers, Allen and Duncan McMartin, and we had been in the bush many weeks looking for bongo, a rare antelope not easily come by. If I took off time to track down the rogue, it would lessen the brothers' chances of getting a good trophy. Still, the McMartins told me to go ahead. I have seen other sportsmen who would not have been so generous. I started back at once with the runners, taking Saseeta, my Wakamba gunbearer who had been with me many years.

When we arrived at the village, I was met by the chief. His name was Ngiri and we were old friends. But we had little time to talk of past adventures for the village was in a panic. The natives were afraid to venture into the *shambas*, as, their maize fields are called, and many of them would not even leave their huts although the wattle shacks would have been little enough protection against a rogue elephant. Ngiri told me the rogue moved from village to village, destroying the maize fields as he went, and unless he was killed the villagers would be in dire straits indeed.

With Saseeta, I went out to look for the body of the dead native. We picked up his tracks on the edge of the village where he had first seen the elephant and followed them through the bush. It was a sad sight to see how he had zigzagged and doubled, trying to throw off his pursuer. Well do I know how he felt, for I have often been chased by elephants. It is like running in a nightmare, for the wait-a-bit thorns hold you back and the creepers pull at your legs while the elephant goes crashing after you like a terrier after a rat. Not a second goes by but you expect to feel that snakey trunk close about your neck, yet you dare not look back for you must keep your eyes on the brush ahead.

We found what was left of the body, but there was no sign of the red blanket that the man had been wearing. The elephant had no doubt carried it off with him. This was not the first time I had heard of a native dressed in red being attacked by an elephaut and I believe the colour must attract them.

I was ready to start at once on the rogue's spoor, but Ngiri told me to wait. The bull was sure to despoil another village that evening and runners would bring in word during the night. Then I could start out on the fresh spoor in the morning and save a day or more of hard tracking. Ngiri was right. I could only wait and hope that the rogue would ruin a shamba and not take another life.

A few hours before dawn, a runner arrived all breathless from a village in the uplands some five miles away. The rogue had entered the village in the evening but, instead of going straight to the fields, had wandered up and down among the huts. He stopped in front of one hut and stood there so long that he dropped a great mass of dung not six feet from the door. One can imagine the feelings of the wretched natives who were huddled together under the flimsy thatch roof while outside stood the rogue elephant, unafraid and forbidding in the darkness. After a time that must have seemed to the natives like an eternity, they heard the great beast move off in the direction of their shamba and listened despairingly while he destroyed the crop – their little all, the fruits of their sweat and labour. When he had gorged himself, he moved away into the bush to digest his feast and sleep during the day.

As soon as dawn broke, Saseeta and I started out for the village. We had a stiff, uphill climb of nine thousand feet and the going was hard on the lungs. In the village we picked up the bull's spoor at a trodden gap in the thorn-bush barricade around the shamba. The trail led us toward the deepest part of the great Aberdare Forest.

After the bright light of the open country, the forest seemed like a great building with a green roof and tree trunks for pillars. There was an eerie stillness about the place for the thick foliage deadened sounds. We walked noiselessly among the boles of the vast trees. I was glad there was little undergrowth. I could see twenty yards ahead; as much as one might ask or want.

I smelt the pungent odour of elephant droppings and saw ahead of us a pile of these unsightly dollops, surrounded by myriads of small forest flies. Saseeta kicked the heap and pointed to the kernels of undigested maize. The droppings were fresh. The bull was only a few hours ahead of us.

I had hoped to come up with the bull in this semi-open part of the forest. But he was cunning and had gone into the thicket to take his daytime rest. The tracks led us into a belt of dense bamboo, inter-growing with a tall plant like forest nettle that was anything but desir-able to hunt in. We put up troops of Colibi and Sykes monkeys that bounded away through the trees and I prayed the rogue wouldn't hear their startled crashing. In any case, the rotting bamboo underfoot made it impossible to walk quietly. I tried to step in the deep impressions made by the bull but his great stride dwarfed the efforts of mere man. Every time a red-legged francolin or tiny duiker antelope burst out of the cover, my heart gave a jump and I clutched my rifle. This kind of work is very different from trophy hunting, where you can locate a herd in open bush and pick your bull. If it hadn't been for my promise to Chief Ngiri, I would have turned back and tried again when the bull was in better country.

The bamboo opened out and we came on a spot where natives had been cutting wood. I swore to myself when I saw how the bull had shied away from the hated man smell and knocked the bamboos aside as he raced off through the grove. An elephant that has no fear of human scent at night in shanibas will often grow panicky when he smells man in the jungle. So far the bull had been moving slowly, grazing as he went. Now he was trying to put as many miles as possible between him and the woodcutters' camp.

Saseeta and I looked at each other. He shrugged. It was hunting luck. Doggedly we set out on the great spoor, which took us up an almost unbelievably steep slope to a high ridge. Here the tracks went through a tangle of wild briars and stinging nettles as if the rogue were deter-mined to find the foulest cover in the whole Aberdare. The snarl was so bad we had to crawl under it on our hands and knees, a time-consuming business and hard on the back. Wriggling along, I suddenly came out into a place where the elephant had stopped to rest. I was most grateful to him for having moved on. Coming unexpectedly on a rogue when you are flat on your belly under a briar tangle is not pleasant.

Suddenly a distinct crackling sound came from ahead. Saseeta and I lay still. The noise came again. The bull was feeding in a grove of bamboo only a few feet ahead of us.

We crawled forward. Once in the bamboo, we could stand upright – a great relief. We moved toward the noises, stepping carefully on the ground already flattened by the bull's great imprints. The wind was uncertain. Cross drafts in the bamboo tossed it about in all directions. There was no way we could be sure of keeping downwind of the elephant and the growth was so thick we could move only by staying in his tracks. I knew we must be almost up with him but I could see little through the tall stalks of bamboo hemming us in on every side.

Saseeta stopped and pointed with his lips toward our left. I could still see nothing, but I slowly raised my rifle. I was using a .475 Jeffery #2, double-barrel express – a reliable gun that has never failed me or I wouldn't be writing these notes. The crashing sounded again only a few feet away. I held my breath, waiting for a shot.

Suddenly the noises ceased. There was absolute silence. Saseeta and I stood motionless and I wished I could stop the noise of my heart. It sounded to me like a drum. Then we heard the bamboos crack and sway as the bull turned and ran through the grove at full speed. That accursed breeze had given him our scent.

Saseeta and I looked at each other. Poor fellow, there is no profanity in his language, but I was more fortunate and swore for us both. But I did so silently, for even though the elephant was now far away, we never spoke in the bush unless absolutely necessary.

The sun was beginning to drop and I knew it must be about five o'clock. We had been going since dawn through very hard country, and the elephant was now definitely alarmed. He might go for miles before he stopped. A wise man would have given up and returned to camp, but I have never been very wise as far as hunting is concerned and I motioned to Saseeta that we'd continue to track.

Light in the undergrowth was already failing, but we had no trouble following the bull. He had trampled down the tough bamboos like so much grass in his fright. As we pressed on, the rotting surface of the ground became worse than ever. My shoes plunged through it, producing sounds that not even an unwary elephant would have stood for.

After an hour's tracking, Saseeta gave a low, bird-like whistle – the recognized bush signal for "attention". We stopped and listened. I could hear the bull moving through the bamboo to our left. He was going downwind, trying to pick up our scent. Then the sounds stopped and I knew he had paused to listen. Instead of our stalking the elephant, he was now stalking us, and in my experience an elephant is a better stalker than a man.

I again considered turning back, but I hated to break my promise to old Ngiri. My chances of getting a shot at the rogue were now very slim, but Saseeta and I kept on. He could not have caught our scent as yet for we didn't hear him crashing away. He was still standing there, probably testing the air with his raised trunk. If he waited a few more minutes, we would be up to him. My eyes ached from the constant strain of peering ahead through the greenish yellow bamboo poles.

Suddenly I saw an indistinct, shadowy shape through the bamboo. I stopped dead and slowly raised my rifle. In the thick cover I could not tell head from tail. There was no gleam of white or yellow ivory to guide me. I held my breath until I nearly strangled to avoid the slightest noise and I knew Saseeta behind me was doing the same. I wanted badly to fire, but was afraid of only wounding him. If he moved a few feet one way or the other I could tell where to shoot.

Then a sudden breeze swept through the bamboo. In an instant the bull got our scent and was gone

I felt a sickly feeling. If I had fired I might have brought him down. But if I had only injured him, he might have killed us both in the thick cover or raced off with the pain of the wound driving him for miles before he stopped. A wounded elephant is a terrible creature and I never like to shoot unless I can be sure of a kill.

There was no use in going on. Evening was falling and the camp many miles away. Saseeta and I slowly toiled back over the long route. In the village everyone was bitterly disappointed at my failure. Hardly a word was spoken. Supper was served in complete silence.

After I had eaten and lit my pipe, I could regard this whole business more philosophically. The failures make hunting worth while. If you won every time, there would be no thrill to it. I hoped the natives whose shambas the rogue was destroying that night could view the affair equally impartially.

I went to bed and lay awake listening to the herd calls of the hyrax, a curious beast that looks like an overgrown guinea pig, and the steady beat of native drums in the village. I knew they were keeping up their courage by gulping quantities of homemade brew and I wished I could join them, but I needed a clear head for hunting in the morning. Then came the haunting grunt of a lion. The sound of the drums quickly petered out as the natives hurried to their huts. I heard the lion drinking at the stream a few feet from my camp and move off again. Then there was silence except for the occasional distant chatter of disturbed monkeys and the twitter of a drowsy bird. I fell asleep.

The next morning a heavy fog covered the forest. The grass was heavy with dew and the air was distinctly chilly. While I was drinking my hot tea, a half-naked runner rushed into camp. During the night the bull had raided a shamba three miles away and destroyed the crop. The rogue was so cunning that he never raided the same village twice in succession and this made hunting him far more difficult.

Saseeta and I started off at once. When we reached the raided village, some of the natives volunteered to go along as guides. We picked up the bull's trail. By now, I knew every toenail in his huge feet and was beginning to hate the sight of them. We followed him as fast as we could go. He was headed toward the hills and our guides assured me that the country was more open there. I hoped they were right.

The slopes were steep and I had to stop constantly for rests. I envied the local natives their remarkable staying power. Still, the brush was open and we made fair time. But this was too good to last. By noon we entered some of the most damnable cover it has ever fallen my lot to hunt in. Bamboo shoots and fallen stems were woven into a virtual mat. Boles of dead trees lay across the trail, some four feet high. They were hard to climb over and worse to crawl under. The elephant had taken all these obstructions in his stride, but we were not so fortunate. Moving quietly was impossible. I scowled at Saseeta for making an unnecessary noise and a moment later made a much louder noise myself.

We came on a spot where the bull had lain down at full length to sleep. I could see the imprint of his hide on the soft earth. This was encouraging, for if he had kept going, we never would have caught up with him. At the same time, I hoped we would not meet him in this thick stuff. We were in a secondary growth of bamboo, the stalks barely half as high as the long poles we had struggled through the previous day, and their tufted tops made it impossible to see beyond muzzle range.

Gusts of wind began to spring up making the long bamboos clank together. We moved forward with the greatest caution as it is difficult to tell whether wind-borne noises are caused by stems or by beast. This was the last place I wanted to meet the rogue, for when an elephant charges in bamboo, he knocks down the long, springy stems in front of him and you may be pinned under them before getting a chance to shoot. Even Saseeta, generally afraid of nothing, made an ugly grimace when I looked back as if to say, "This is a sticky business."

Suddenly we heard a movement in the bamboo ahead of us. Saseeta and I both stopped dead and I raised my rifle, waiting for the charge. Instead of the elephant, a magnificent male bongo broke out of the cover and stood in front of us. This was the very trophy the McMartins and I had been after for many long weeks. Yet I could not shoot for fear of alarming the rogue. Often it happens you see the best trophies when you can't collect them.

We passed the fern-clad banks of a mountain stream and saw where the bull had been pulling tip bracken with his tusks to get at the roots. The roots of the bracken seem to possess a medicinal quality that serves to keep the great beasts healthy. We knew the bull must be just ahead of us now for the turned-over earth was still moist.

While we were checking the signs, one of our native guides darted back to say he heard a noise in the bamboo ahead of us. This might mean much or little. Saseeta and I moved forward as quietly as possible. The wind was steady now and in our favour. We moved slowly through the high stalks. Then we heard the ripping noise of bamboo being torn apart. The bull was right ahead of us. He could not hear us above the noise of his own feeding, and, if the wind held, we had him.

I saw his trunk appear above the stalks and pull a particularly succulent tip down to him. I crept along, trying to see through the stalks ahead and at the same time watch where I put my feet. Saseeta kept behind me, constantly testing the breeze with a small forest fungi puff. When shaken, these little puffballs give off a fine white powder almost like smoke and you can tell every shift of the wind by watching it. As we went deeper into the bamboo, the heavy growth cut off the breeze and the puffball dust hung motionless around Saseeta's hand. Then I saw the bull not fifteen yards from me.

I could hear him munching bamboo shoots as the line conveying elevator of his trunk hoisted them into his mouth. Between us was a network of bamboo poles through which I dared not shoot lest the bullet be deflected by one of the tough stems. Another of those terrible decisions. Should I take the chance and shoot? Or should I wait a few minutes and hope the bull would shift his position slightly and give me a shoulder shot? I would have to make up my miud quickly for we were so close that our smell would permeate to him in the absence of wind.

Suddenly the bull saw us. He did not run as he had the day before. Without the slightest hesitation or warning, he spun around and charged.

Almost before I could raise the rifle he was on top of us. His great ears were folded back close to his head and his trunk was held tight against the brisket. He was screaming with rage – a series of throaty *"urrs"* is the nearest I can describe the sound. I aimed the right barrel for the centre of his skull, a point three inches higher than an imaginary line drawn from eye to eye, and fired. For an instant after the shot the bull seemed to hang in the air above me. Then he came down with a crash. He lay partly hidden by the bamboo, giving off high-pitched cries and low, gurgling sounds. I fired the second barrel through the centre of his neck. Instantly the whole body relaxed, the hind legs stretched to their fullest. So ended the raider that had brought death and terror to Chief Ngiri's people.

Our local scouts had wisely vanished when the shooting started. Now they began to appear as if out of the earth. They gathered around the dead rogue and stood looking at him, so overjoyed that they could not speak. It must have seemed to them almost too good to be true that they could now work their fields in peace and security.

I sat down on one of the dead rogue's legs to fill my pipe. Everyone wanted to do something to express his gratitude, although all the poor fellows could do was to offer me a drink of cool water. Some of the sectional parts of the bamboo stems showed tiny openings bored by insects. The natives, selecting these sections, cut them down and pressed them on me. Each section contained a few mouthfuls of clean, cold water.

When I had finished my pipe, I examined the dead rogue's carcass. The ivory was very poor. The tusks were only about forty pounds each, whereas a really good bull will carry ivory weighing three times that much. Forest vegtation seems to lack calcium, for the forest elephants never have as good tusks as the bush dwellers. While examining the tusks, I found an old bullet hole at the base of the right hand tusk. With my knife I dug out a musket bullet, probably fired by an Arab ivory hunter years before. The bullet was embedded in the nerve centre of the tusk and the pain must have been terrible. The constant suffering had driven the old bull mad and that was why he had become a rogue. No doubt the Arab who had fired the shot was now living comfortably with never a thought for the suffering he had caused to both man and beast.

We headed back toward camp. Everyone was in high spirits and elated with success. The leading scouts cut a path for us through the tangle with their knives, shouting and laughing as we progressed, a noisy contrast to the deathly stillness with which we had crept along that same trail a few hours before. As we came out into open country, I could see the hill slopes dotted with black figures who had heard the sound of the rifle shots and come hurrying to meet us. Our scouts yelled some guttural sounds across the valley. Native voices carry a surprising distance and I could see the black dots stop and then go scurrying back to the village with the good news.

Back in camp, a great welcome was given Saseeta and me. Even the old and sick tottered out of their huts to thank us. The white man had not failed them. I sent word to Chief Ngiri that the raider was dead and then sat down to a well-earned supper.

That evening, sitting in front of my campfire and smoking my pipe, I thought back over the many years I'd spent in Africa as a hunter. When I first came to Kenya, the game covered the plains as far as a man could see. I hunted lions where towns now stand, and shot elephants from the engine of the first railroad to cross the country. In the span of one man's lifetime, I have seen jungle turn into farmland and cannibal tribes become factory workers. I have had a little to do with this change myself, for the government employed me to clear dangerous beasts out of areas that were being opened to cultivation. I hold a world's record for rhino, possibly another record for lion (although we kept no exact record of the numbers shot in those early days) and I have shot more than fourteen hundred elephant. I certainly do not tell of these records with pride. The work had to be done and I happened to be the man who did it. But, strange as it may seem to the armchair conservationist, I have a deep affection for the animals I had to kill. I spent long years studying their habits, not only in order to kill them, but because I was honestly interested in them.

Yet it is true I have always been a sportsman. Firearms have been my ruling passion in life and I would rather hear the crack of a rifle or the bang of a shotgun than listen to the finest orchestra. I cannot say that I did not enjoy hunting, but looking back I truly believe that in most cases the big game had as much chance to kill me as I had to kill them.

I am one of the last of the old-time hunters. The events I saw can never be relived. Both the game and the native tribes, as I knew them, are gone. No one will ever see again the great elephant herds led by old bulls carrying 150 pounds of ivory in each tusk. No one will ever again hear the yodelling war cries of the Masai as their spearmen swept the bush after cattle-killing lions. Few, indeed, will be able to say that they have broken into country never before seen by a white man. No, the old Africa has passed and I saw it go.

THE WILY TIGER OF MUNDACHIPALLAM

I shall now tell just two of the many adventures we have experienced together, namely that of the bears of Talvadi, in which Byra so nobly offered his life for mine, and the story of the maneating tiger of Mundachipallam.

Talvadi is the name given to the wide valley through the centre of which trickles the mountain stream known by the same name. It is situated some eleven miles north of the spot where I first met Byra, and is quite one of the wildest spots of the Salem North Forest Division [in the state of Tamil Nadu, in southern India].

The Talvadi river takes its rise in the forest plateau of Aiyur, whence it dips sharply into a mountainous gorge, locally known as Toluvabetta gorge, but rechristened by me as "Spider Valley", because of the species of enormous red and yellow spiders that weave their monstrous webs across the narrow jungle trail. These webs are somewhat oval in shape and sometimes reach a width of over twenty feet. In the centre hangs the spider itself, often nine inches from leg-tip to leg-tip. Despite its size, it is a very agile creature and extremely ferocious, and its prey – the large night moths and beautiful butterflies and insects of the forest – stand no chance of escape once they become entangled in the huge web.

These spiders are equally cannibalistic and will not tolerate the presence of another member of their tribe within their own web. I have sometimes amused myself by transporting one of these fierce creatures at the end of a stick to the web of another of its kind, when a battle royal immediately ensues, often lasting half an hour, but always ending in the death of one or other creature, whose blood is then thoroughly sucked by the victor, till the loathsome insect is so gorged that it can only just crawl back to the centre of its web.

The Talvadi stream passes down this gorge and then bifurcates, the lesser portion flowing southwards, bordered by the towering peak of Mount Gutherrain and the small hamlet of Kempekarai, to join the Chinar river in the stream of Annaibiddahalla. This area was once the stamping ground of the notorious rogue elephant of Kempekarai, which killed seven humans, two or three cattle, smashed half a dozen bullock carts and overturned a three-ton lorry loaded with cut bamboos. However, that is another story. The main portion of the stream flows westwards for some miles and, bordering the forest block of Manchi, then turns south-westwards, crossing the forest road leading from Anchetty to Muthur and Pennagram in the aforementioned valley of Talvadi.

As may be imagined, all this area is densely wooded, clothed on its higher reaches by miles upon miles of towering bamboo, and towards the lower levels by primeval forest, interspersed with rocky stretches, till it finally flows into the Cauvery river near the fishing village of Biligundlu. The whole area, from source to estuary, forms the home of herds of wild elephant, a few bison, and invariably a tiger or two, which use the line of the stream as a regular beat. The Talvadi Valley itself, abounding in rocks and very long grass, is the habitat of large panthers, many bear, and wild pig, sambar, barking deer, and more pea-fowl than I have met anywhere else.

My story begins at the time when Byra had sent word to me, in a letter written by the postmaster of Pennagram, that a panther of exceptional size had taken up its abode in the valley and was regularly killing cattle all along the Muthur–Anchetty road from the 11th to the 15th milestone. The letter asserted that the panther was of enormous proportions, "much bigger than ordinary tiger".

Having some five days to spare, I motored by the shortcut road through the forest from Denkanikota to Anchetty and past Talvadi Valley to Muthur, where I met Byra. From there we returned to the 15th milestone, which was right in the valley itself. The road was really execrable, with many streams to be crossed, ruts made by cartwheels, and interspersed with boulders galore, taxing the car and its springs severely. After pitching camp, we went down to the nearest cattle-patti, some three-quarters of a mile distant, where I was able to hear for myself about the depredations of this panther. The story told was that it generally attacked the herds on their homeward journey to the pens about 5.30 p.m., and that it would select the largest cow among the stragglers for its victim. Several herdsmen had actually seen the animal and attempted to drive it from its kills, only to be met with snarls and a show of ferocity quite exceptional for a panther. The animal was not known to live in any particular spot, but, as I have said, ranged for about four miles along the road.

It was difficult to persuade these herdsmen to sell me live baits, as although they realized the slaying of the panther would benefit them directly, their caste and religious obsessions were such as to oppose absolutely the practice of deliberately sacrificing a life in this way. Albeit, by various methods I finally succeeded in purchasing two three-quarter grown animals, one of which I secured on the bank of the river itself, about a mile downstream from the road, and the second not far from the 14th milestone.

There was now nothing to be done but wait, and as I did not deem it wise to disturb the countryside by shooting the pea-fowl and jungle-fowl that abounded, I contented myself by strolling in the forest in other directions, both morning and evening, in the hope of accidentally meeting the panther or perhaps a wandering tiger from the Cauvery.

As luck would have it, I received news at about 7 p.m. on the third day that the panther had that very evening killed a cow belonging to another cattle-patti three miles away, as the herd was returning home. A runner had been sent to inform me as soon as the loss was discovered, which had accounted for the passage of time.

Grabbing rifle, torch and overcoat, Byra and I hastened to the spot, and, when still some furlongs away, I extinguished my torch, creeping forward in the wake of the herdsman who had brought us the news, Byra following at my rear. A half-moon was just raising its silver crescent above the ragged line of jungle hills that formed the eastern horizon, when we turned a sharp bend in the cattle-track and came upon a panther crouched behind the dead bullock that lay across the track.

I had armed myself with my .12 shotgun for work at close quarters, while Byra, behind me, carried the Winchester, but, before I could raise the gun, the panther bounded off the carcase and into the undergrowth beyond.

Hastily whispering to Byra and the herdsman to return slowly the way we had come, talking to each other in a normal tone to give the panther the impression we had departed, I dived behind a wild plum bush that grew some twenty paces away, hoping the animal would return.

The panther did not take long to advertise its presence, for within a few minutes I heard its sawing call from the forest before me. The sound gradually receded in the direction Byra and the herdsman had taken, by which I interpreted that it was following them at a distance, probably to ensure that they had really departed. Afterwards there was tense silence, unbroken by any sound for perhaps the best part of an hour. And then, as if from nowhere, and unheralded by even the faintest rustle of dried leaves or crackle of broken twig, appeared an enormous panther, standing over its kill, but still looking suspiciously down the track we had just traversed.

Aiming behind the shoulder as best I could in the half-light, the roar of the gun was followed by the panther leaping almost a yard into the air. Without touching earth again it convulsed itself into a spring and was gone before I could fire the second barrel. Its departure was heralded by the unmistakably low, rasping grunts of a wounded panther. Waiting for a few minutes, till the sound died away, and realizing that nothing further could be accomplished that night, I retraced my steps to the cattle-patti and to camp.

By dawn next morning Byra and I were at the place of my encounter. Casting about where the animal had disappeared, it did not take long for Byra to detect a blood-trail on the leaves of the undergrowth through which the animal had dashed away. Heartened by the fact that at least some of my L.G. pellets had found their mark, I took the lead, this time armed with the rifle, Byra following close behind and guiding me on the trail. In this formation, it was my business to keep a sharp lookout for the animal, and deal with it should it charge, while Byra, in the slightly safer position behind me, could concentrate on his tracking.

Within the first 100 yards we came to a spot where the animal had lain down, as revealed by the crimson stain that covered the grass and the unmistakable outline of the body. From here the animal had slithered down the banks of a narrow nullah, densely overgrown with bushes on both sides, where following up became trebly difficult and hazardous.

As we tip-toed forward, with many a halt to listen, I scanned each bush before me, striving to penetrate its recesses for a glimmer of the spotted hide, alive or dead now, we did not know. I strove to pierce with my eyes the rank undergrowth of jungle-grass that grew between the bushes, and to look behind the boles of trees and rocks that fortunately were few in number just there.

We had advanced a comparatively few paces in this way when suddenly, from out of a hole in the ground before me, rose a shaggy black shape, a smaller similar shape tumbling off beside it. We had stumbled upon a mother bear with her young, asleep in the hole she had dug overnight in the bed of the nullah, in her assiduous search for roots!

I could see the white V mark on her chest distinctly as she half-rose to her feet, surprise and then fury showing in her beady, black eyes. Down she went on all fours again, to come straight at us. Thrusting the muzzle of the Winchester almost into her mouth, I pressed the trigger. Then occurred that all-important moment, which balances the life or ignominious death of the hunter: a misfire!

The she-bear closed her jaws on the muzzle, and with one sweep of her long-toed forepaw wrested the weapon from my grasp, so that it hung ludicrously from her mouth for a moment before she dropped it to the ground. Involuntarily I had stumbled backwards, and as the bear rose to her feet to attack my face – which is the part of a human anatomy always first bitten by these animals – Byra attempted the supreme sacrifice.

Nimbly throwing himself between me and the infuriated beast, he shouted at the top of his lungs in a last-minute attempt to divert its further onslaught. He was successful only to the extent that it turned its attention upon him, seemingly to forget my existence for the moment.

As he ducked his head in the very nick of time, the bear buried its fangs in Byra's right shoulder, while the long talons of its forefeet tore at his chest, sides and back. Byra went down with the bear on top of him. I sprang for the fallen rifle. Working the under-lever to eject the misfired cartridge, I found to my horror that, with the force of its fall, the action of the rifle had jammed. All this took only a few seconds.

Byra screamed in agony, while the bear growled savagely. Stumbling forward and using the rifle as a cudgel, I smote with the butt-end with all my might at the back of the animal's head. Fortunately my aim was true, for the bear released Byra and like lightning grabbed the rifle in its mouth, this time by the butt, again tearing the weapon from my grasp. It then started to bite the stock savagely.

By an act of Providence the cub, which during all this time had remained in the background, a surprised and obviously terrified witness, at this juncture let out a series of frightened whimpers and yelps. As if by magic the attention of the irascible mother became focused on her baby, for she dropped the rifle and ran to its side. There she sniffed it over to assure herself that all was well, and as suddenly as this unwelcome pair had appeared on the scene they disappeared, a few last whimperings from the now reassured youngster forming the last notes to that unforgettable scene of horror, from which it took me days to recover.

Byra was on his hands and knees, streaming with blood and evidently in great pain. Going across to him, I removed my coat and shirt, tearing the latter into strips and attempting to bind up the more serious of his wounds and to stem the bleeding. Then, hoisting him on my back and carrying my damaged rifle, I staggered back to the cattle-patti, where I placed him on a charpoy. Four herdsmen carried him to my camp, where I poured raw iodine into the wounds. Camp was struck and in a few moments my car was jolting the fifteen miles to the village of Pennagram, where at the dispensary rough first aid was rendered. By this time the poor man was faint with the loss of blood and almost unconscious. Replacing him in the car, I covered the sixty-one miles to the town of Salem, where there was a first-class hospital, in almost record time.

Penicillin was unknown in those far off days, and the first week that Byra spent in hospital, hovering between life and death, with me at his side, was an anxious time. But his sturdy constitution won through and after the first few days the doctors definitely pronounced him out of danger.

I returned to Pennagram, where Byra's wife and children had come and were anxiously awaiting news. Giving them some financial help, I also received a surprise when I was presented with the worm-eaten skin of the panther, which I had quite forgotten in the excitement and pressure of subsequent events. It appeared that the sight of vultures on a carcase had attracted some of the herdsmen of the cattle-patti at Talvadi, who had found the body of the animal within 200 yards of where the adventure with the bear had occurred. It was stated to have been an outsize specimen but, as I have said, the skin was worm-eaten and beyond preserving.

Returning to Salem, I left sufficient money to cover Byra's treatment, expenses and final return to his native haunts at Muthur, but it was over two months before he could go back to his family with a slight permanent limp in his right leg due to the shortening of a damaged muscle, and with many permanent scars on his body as reminder of the incident.

My rifle needed a new stock, and to this day, six inches from the muzzle, it bears the marks of the she-bear's teeth. Thus ended the adventure which formed the blood brotherhood, so to speak, between Byra and myself, founded on his attempted cheerful sacrifice and almost literal fulfilment of the words "greater love than this hath no man than that he should lay down his life for another".

Many years passed after this occurrence to the occasion of my next story, that of the maneating tiger of Mundachipallam.

Mundachipallam, or to give it its literal Tamil translation, the "hollow" or "stream" of Mundachi, is nothing more than a rivulet skirting the base of the Ghat section, halfway between the 2,000-foot-high plateau occupied by the village of Pennagram and the bed of the Cauvery river, only some 700 feet above sea-level. This stream crosses the Ghat Road, which drops steeply from Pennagram to the Cauvery river at a point just about four miles from the destination of the road where stands the fishing hamlet of Ootaimalai above the famed water-falls of Hogenaikal. The Forest Department has constructed a well on the banks of Mundachipallam, beside the road, to facilitate the watering of cattle, especially buffaloes and bullocks, drawing heavily-laden carts of timber and bamboo, before they begin the remaining six miles of steep ascent to Pennagram.

This little well, surrounded as it is by dense jungle, except for the narrow ribbon of road and the small width of Mundachipallam, which cross at right angles, is the spot where my story begins and, strangely enough, ends, though only after many deaths, and the narrow escape of Ranga, my shikari.

It was early morning, about 7.30 a.m., and droplets of dew twinkled on the grass like myriads of diamonds cast far and wide, as they met, scintillated, and reflected the rays, of the newly risen sun, filtering through the leafy branches of the giant "muthee" trees and the tall, straight stems of the wild cotton trees that bordered the shallow banks of Mundachipallam.

One man and two women, carrying round bamboo baskets, laden with river fish netted during the night on the Cauvery river, approached the well and laid down their heavy burdens on the low parapet wall that encircles it. The man unwound a thin fibre rope coiled around his waist and, slipping one end of it over the narrow neck of a rounded brass *lotah*, carried by one of the women, let the receptacle down the well, from which he presently withdrew a supply of cold, fresh water. In accordance with the normal village custom, where a man comes before a woman, he began to pour the contents down his throat in a steady silvery stream, not allowing his lips to touch the mouth of the vessel, for to do so was considered unhygienic.

The fish were being taken to market at Pennagram, and this was the last water available before tackling the stiff climb to their destination. After drinking his fill, the man returned the *lotah* to the well and twice refilled it, for the benefit of the two maidens who accompanied him. They were in their twenties and wore nothing above their waists beyond the last fold of their graceful sarees, which passed diagonally across one shoulder. Their smooth dark skins glistened with sweat despite the coolness of early morning, due to the heavy load of fish they had carried for four miles from the big river.

After drinking, the party sat down for a few minutes, each member producing a small cloth bag, from which were taken some *betel* leaves, broken sections of areca-nut and semi-liquid *chunam* or lime of paste-like consistency. Some sections of nut were placed in an open leaf, which was liberally smeared with the chunam, and then chewed with evident relish. In a few minutes the mouths of all the members exuded blood-red saliva, which was freely expectorated thereafter in all directions.

Just then, rustling and crackling was heard from the undergrowth bordering the well. These sounds ceased and began again at intervals. There was no other sound.

The trio conjectured among themselves as to the cause of these sounds and reached the conclusion that it was some member of the deer family, probably injured by gunshot wounds or wild dogs or some other animal, and struggling to get to its feet. Urged on by the hope of obtaining easy meat and undoubtedly in order to impress the females of the party, the man got up and, with a stone in his hand, walked into the jungle.

The noise had momentarily ceased, and he penetrated further to try to find the cause of the disturbance. Rounding a Babul tree that grew in the midst of a clump of bushes, he was petrified when he almost walked into a pair of tigers, probably engaged in the act of mating.

Now a normal tiger is a beast with which very wide liberties may be taken. When once out fishing, I was surprised by a tiger that broke cover hardly fifteen paces away; it was difficult to tell which of us was more alarmed by the presence of the other at the time. Anyhow, that tiger simply sheered off the way he had come. Although unarmed at the time, curiosity and natural excitement urged me to follow it, to ascertain if possible the presence of a kill. But it just kept running before me like any village cur, till I eventually lost it among the many bushes that grew around.

But there are with tigers certain moments when even they demand privacy. Or it may have been the urge to show off to the female of the species, an urge which I have known affect otherwise quiet men in a very surprising manner. Anyhow, this tiger definitely resented the intrusion and with a short roar he was upon the unfortunate fish-seller, burying his fangs through the back of his neck and almost severing the spinal column. Not a sound escaped the man as he fell to earth, the tiger still growling over him. The two women had heard the short roar and, recognizing the sound as that of a tiger, fled the way they had come to Ootaimalai. The victim was not eaten on this occasion, the effort having been but a gesture of annoyance at being disturbed at the wrong moment, but it had taught that particular tiger the obvious helplessness of a human being.

Some weeks later, a wood-cutter, carrying his burden from the forest, encountered the same tiger on turning a bend in the path. Again that short roar, followed by the deadly spring, and another man lay dead, killed for no reason at all. Again the tiger did not eat.

Two months passed, and a party of women had gone into the forest to gather the fruit of wild tamarind trees that grew in profusion throughout the valley. One of them had strayed a little away from the rest. She had stooped down to lift the basket to her head, when, looking up, she met the glaring eyes of the great cat. A single shrill scream escaped her before that short roar sounded for the third time and the cruel fangs buried themselves in her throat. This time the jugular was severed and the salty blood spouted into the tiger's mouth; thus was born the maneating tiger of Mundachipallam. The woman was dragged away to some bushes and there devoured, except for her skull, the palms of her hands, and the soles of her feet.

Three more deliberate kills followed in quick succession, one at the 7th milestone of the road itself, the other by the banks of the Chinar river near to its confluence with the Cauvery, and the third but a mile from the village of Ootaimalai itself. In all three cases the victims were eaten, or partly eaten.

It was this last kill that caused the greatest consternation, leading the villagers of Ootaimalai to come in deputation to Pennagram to beg the authorities to take some action to rid them of the menace that now threatened their very village. Ranga, my shikari, was there at the time and promised them that he would persuade me to help, and, having made the promise, travelled the hundred odd miles to Bangalore by bus, arriving late in the evening to present his report.

Now a few words about Ranga will not be amiss at this stage. Strangely enough, I had also met him at Muthur, where I had met Byra some years earlier. Ranga was the hired driver of a buffalo-cart, used to haul cut bamboo from the forest to Pennagram. He had initiative, however, and in his spare time was given to poaching, like Byra, with a matchlock that he hired for the occasion. He was a very different man from Byra, however, in both physical and personal attributes, for he was tall and powerful compared with Byra's somewhat puny build, and showed a forceful and distinctly positive character in all his under-takings. He had spent a year in jail for the attempted murder of his first wife, whom he had stabbed in the neck in a jealous quarrel. After returning from jail he had married again, and at the time I first met him had three children. Not being content, he later took one more wife and now had a dozen children in all, and was a grandfather besides.

He had better organizing capacity than Byra and got things done when required. I have known him to thrash a recalcitrant native thoroughly for not obeying instructions. He has also a lucrative side to his character – trade in liquor illicitly distilled in the forest from Babul bark and other ingredients. I have sampled some of his produce and can tell you it is the nearest approach to liquid fire that I have known. Lastly, he is a far more dishonest man than Byra and given to petty pilfering, especially of .12 bore cartridges. He despises Byra, whom he looks down upon as a semi-savage. Secretly, I think he is jealous of my affection for the little Poojaree. But Ranga is a brave man, staunch and reliable in the face of danger, who certainly fears no jungle animal or forest spook, as do the vast majority of other native shikaris.

Unfortunately, Ranga came at a time when I was very busy and could not possibly leave the station for another fortnight. So I sent him back to Pennagram with a number of addressed envelopes and instruc-tions to write to me every second day, regardless of events.

My inability to answer Ranga's first summons was perhaps indi-rectly responsible for two fresh tragedies that occurred before I was able at last to pick Ranga up in my car at Pennagram, motor down to Muthur for Byra, and arrive at Ootaimalai, where I was joined by a third henchman, an old associate named Sowree.

This Sowree, like Ranga, was quite a versatile fellow, and had himself spent three months in jail for shooting and killing a wild elephant with his muzzle-loader while on a poaching trip. The elephant was a half-grown cow and had approached the hide in which Sowree lay concealed. Fearing that it might really tread upon him, Sowree had aimed his musket behind its left ear. The solid ball had only too effectively done its work,. and the elephant dropped in its tracks. Unfortunately for him, he was caught red-handed. I had been shooting on the Coimbatore bank at the time, and had seen and photographed the elephant, which incidentally was how I met Sowree.

I was extremely fortunate in being able to obtain the services of these three men, as in their varied spheres and capabilities they presented a vast store of jungle experience and ability. Byra at once volunteered to scout around the neighbouring forest, and along the Coimbatore bank, in an effort to ascertain the immediate whereabouts of the tiger. This I emphatically forbade him to do, as being suicidal. We finally compromised by agreeing that he should be accompanied by Sowree, armed with my .12 bore gun, and another man who very surprisingly, bore the name of Lucas and was a "watcher" in the employ of the Government Fisheries Department.

Ranga was given the job of obtaining three baits and tying them out in likely spots. The usual difficulty in obtaining animals was met, but the resourceful Ranga quickly overcame it by threats and other expedients, of which I was not supposed to know.

The first of the three baits was tied a mile up the Chinar river from where it joined the Cauvery and the second some three miles further on, where Mundachipallam met the Chinar. The third was tethered within 100 yards of the well where the first tragedy had occurred. On alternate days Byra and his party would scour the forests on one bank of the Cauvery, while I, with a local guide, combed the opposite bank. Ranga, as I have said, attended to the feeding and watering of the baits.

In this way we spent four days, while nothing happened. Tiger pugs were discovered at several localities, but they were not fresh, and nobody could tell with certainty whether they belonged to the maneater or some other animal.

There was no possibility of driving the mankiller to cattle-killing to avoid starvation, by prohibiting the villagers from entering the forests or using the road to Pennagram. To begin with, considerable traffic existed along this road, as it formed a main artery to the many hamlets lying on the opposite bank of the Cauvery. In addition, the forests, particularly on the Coimbatore side, were plentifully stocked with game, to which the tiger could always turn in necessity.

In the meantime I endeavoured by every possible means to spread the news of my presence and purpose to all surrounding hamlets, in order that I might hear of any fresh kill with the least possible delay. There was then some hope; with Byra's expert help, of being able to track the animal to where it was lying up or perhaps even to its lair. Beating was out of the question, even if there had been volunteers for the task, of which there were none, as we were dealing with a very bold and clever animal who would as likely as not add one more victim to his list from among the beaters themselves.

Early in the morning of the fifth day, I received news that a man had been killed at Panapatti cattle-pen, some four miles away, late that previous evening. He had gone out of his hut for 100 yards to call his dog, which was missing, and had not been heard of again. We hurried to the spot and Byra was successful in discovering the spot at which the man had been attacked: the great splayed-out pugs of the tiger were soon clearly visible across the sandy bed of the Chinar river as he had dragged his victim across and through the intervening reeds to the borders of the sloping bamboo forest beyond. Here we discovered the remains, almost totally devoured.

No trees were available, except for a mighty clump of bamboo that grew some thirty feet from the remains. Inside this I instructed Byra to make me a suitable hide by the simple expedient of removing some eight or nine of the stout bamboo stems, cutting through them about four feet from the ground and again at the ground level, and then taking out the intervening four-foot lengths. The upper parts of the bamboo stems, being in the centre of the clump, would not fall to earth so entangled were the tops with the fronds of neighbouring stems and those of other clumps.

After completing his work, Byra had succeeded in making a sort of hollow cave for me in the midst of the clump. Seated in the middle of this I knew I would be quite safe from attack by the tiger, either from behind or from either side, as he could not get at me owing to the numerous intervening stems. The only way he could reach me was from in front, and this I felt quite capable of countering provided I kept myself awake throughout the night.

The faithful Poojaree persisted in his wish to sit with me, till I was compelled to order him peremptorily to go. I would, indeed, have been glad of his company, but the space we had cleared in the midst of the bamboo clump offered only restricted accommodation to one individual. To cut more stems to increase this space meant that we were reaching the outskirts of the clump and the unsupported bamboo stems would then fall to earth, not only causing much disturbance by the crash, but littering the surroundings with debris, which might quite possibly frighten the tiger away.

The night would be dark, with no moon, so I took the precaution of clamping my spare shooting light to my shotgun, which I carried into the hide with me, in addition to the Winchester, with its own lighting arrangement. Being in the midst of the bamboo, I knew I was almost completely sheltered from the dew and the cold jungle air, and fairly safe from snakes – or so I thought.

I was in position by 1 p.m., and sent my followers away – Byra still protesting – with instructions to call to me from the bed of the Chinar next morning before approaching. With their departure I was left to my own devices for the next seventeen hours.

You will appreciate that from my position in the midst of the bamboo clump my view was entirely restricted on all sides except for the narrow lane of jungle right in front of me, with the human cadaver in the foreground. Much as I would have preferred a wider range of vision, I knew I would be thankful once the hours of darkness fell, as the more I could see by day the more I would be exposed to the maneater after dark, when the tables would be turned and he could see while I could not.

The human remains, being hidden from the sky by the canopy of overhanging bamboos, were not troubled by vultures. Flies, however, covered it in hordes and the stench soon began to get painfully noticeable.

I will not burden you with descriptions of the sounds of a jungle evening and the close of a jungle day beyond mentioning that they were practically all present on that occasion and offered sweet accord to my jungle-loving ears.

Nothing happened before darkness set in, which it did both earnestly and rapidly, till I was left in stygian blackness, intensified by the additional shadows cast by the towering bamboo stems above me. It was so dark that I could not see my own hands as they rested on my lap; I would have to feel for the trigger and the torch switch, and, indeed, everything. All that was visible was the luminous dial of my wrist-watch showing that it was a quarter to eight. Ten long hours before daylight came.

I knew that during this time I would have to strain myself to the utmost in pitting my poor, human and town-bred skill against that of the king of the jungles, at which he was a past-master, with decades of skilful ancestors behind him, namely, at listening and hearing. For I could not see an inch before me, while he could see clearly. Nor could I smell him at all, but neither could he smell me.

For success I would have to depend entirely on my hearing the sound of his soft approach, and I well knew from long experience how sound-less the approach of a cautious tiger can be. I would have to remain absolutely silent myself; worse, the slightest movement or sound from me would betray my presence to those ever-acute ears, and once he knew I was there, only one of two possible things could happen. Either his courage would fail him and he would desert the kill, or he would attack me by a sudden pounce through the opening in front of me, before I was aware of his coming. I certainly had no wish to become the next item on his menu.

Therefore, I could do nothing but sit absolutely and completely still. Mosquitoes found their way even inside that clump, and tortured me acutely. Once some cold creeping thing passed across my lap. It had length but no legs and was undoubtedly a snake. Movement at that time meant a bite and, if it was a poisonous snake, possibly death. With extreme difficulty I controlled my twitching nerves, and the snake glided away. I could just sense its rustle as it slipped between the inter-vening bamboo stems and was gone.

By and by my throat began to tickle and I had an overpowering desire to cough. I counted sheep to divert my thoughts from this urge till it eventually died away.

At 10.25 p.m. I heard a distinct sound in the jungle behind me. A faint rustle, then all was still. The minutes dragged by. Then it came again, on my right and in line with the very clump where I was sitting. Heavy breathing was clearly audible. A very faint grunt, silence, another grunt, and then the quick rush of a heavy soft body before me. Was it on the kill or was it staring me in the face from the inky darkness, perhaps even at that instant drawing the powerful hind-legs below the supple belly to catapult itself upon me? And I could not see even the end of my own nose.

I had already cocked my rifle, and had slowly raised the muzzle, finger on trigger, to meet the coming onslaught at point-blank range. The perspiration poured down my face in sheer terror, and my whole body trembled with nervous suppression.

I depressed the torch switch and the brilliant beam blazed out upon a large hyena, standing above the kill, growling to find out it was a dead man that lay there. He stared blankly at the light for seconds and was gone. I could have laughed aloud with relief and the thought that I was safe once more – at least for the present.

Anyhow, my position had been temporarily revealed and I could only hope the maneater was not in the vicinity to become aware of it. Hastily I took advantage of the disturbance to swallow a mouthful of hot, refreshing tea from the flask I had brought, and quickly move my cramped limbs before resettling myself for the remainder of my vigil. I was in stygian darkness again, but considerably refreshed and relieved of the morbid nervous tension that had threatened to overcome me a few minutes before.

At ten minutes to twelve I heard the moan of a tiger in the distance. This was repeated again at intervals of five to ten minutes, the last being at twelve-twenty, and from a spot I judged to be a quarter of a mile away. It was difficult to gauge the exact distance of sound in this densely wooded locality, but I thanked Providence and my lucky stars that the tiger had decided on making a noisy approach rather than the silent one I had dreaded.

A quarter of an hour slipped by without further sign. In the meantime the usual midnightly jungle breeze had sprung up to cause the bamboo stems to groan and creek against each other weirdly. This aroused a fresh and ominous thought in my mind. Supposing one of the several cut bamboo stems, balancing upright above my head, was to become dislodged and slip downwards under its own weight. The cut end would impale me to the ground, like some rare beetle in a collector's box. The thought was not very pleasant and for a moment it eclipsed even the thought of the maneater and its proximity.

And then I heard the crack of a bone on the cadaver lying in the darkness before me. Slowly I lifted the rifle to shoulder level, steadied it and depressed the torch-switch for the second time that night. But nothing happened. I depressed the switch again and again, but still nothing happened. Undoubtedly the bulb had burnt out or some connection had come loose. I had now the choice of sitting very still till the tiger fed and departed, or changing my rifle for the smooth bore and attempting a shot. I quickly decided to use the gun. Ever so gently I lowered the rifle to ground level and then groped silently in the dark for the .12 bore. Finding it, I drew it towards me and then began manoeuvring the weapon to shoulder level. I could only hope that the tiger was looking away from me or was too engrossed in his meal to notice all the movement that was going on in the midst of the bamboo clump. And then misfortune befell me. Slightly, but quite distinctly, the muzzle of the gun came into contact with a bamboo stem and there was an audible knock.

The sounds of feeding stopped abruptly, followed by a deep-chested and rumbling growl. Hastily I got the gun into position and pressed the switch of a new torch. Luckily it did not fail, and the beam burst forth to show clearly a huge striped form as it sprang off the cadaver and behind the bamboo clump next to mine. From there a succession of earth-shaking roars rent the silence, as the maneater demonstrated in no uncertain manner his displeasure at being disturbed, and his discovery of a human being in the near vicinity

Keeping the torch alight and a sharp lookout for his sudden attack, with one hand I groped for the spare bulb I always carried in my pocket. I extracted it and kept it on my lap. Still working with one hand, I unscrewed the cover of the torch on my rifle, extracted the faulty bulb and substituted the new one. Fortunately, the torch was one of those focused by adjustment from the rear and not the front end, and as the rifle torch was now functioning again, I extinguished that on the smooth bore, though I kept the gun ready across my knees for any further eventuality.

The tiger was still demonstrating, but had moved to a position in my rear. I knew I was safe enough, except from a frontal attack. To guard against this I would have to keep the torch alight continuously, but as over five hours still remained till daylight, there was the certainty the batteries would run low, even on both torches, if burned incessantly. So I switched off the light and relied on my hearing. When things became too silent for a long stretch, I would switch on the beam, expecting to see the creeping form of the tiger approaching me. But this did not happen and he kept his distance, demonstrating frequently till past 2.30 a.m., when I heard his growls receding in the distance. No doubt he was disgusted, but by this time I welcomed his disgust.

You may be certain I kept a sharp lookout for the rest of the night against the tiger's return, for the habits of a maneater are often unpredictable; but the chill hours of early morning crept past without event, till at last the cheery cry of the silver-hackled jungle-cock made me grateful for the dawn and the light of another day, which on more than one occasion during the terrible hours that had just dragged by I had not thought of seeing.

Soon the halloa of my followers from the bed of the Chinar river fell like music on my tired ears, and I shouted back for them to advance as the coast was clear. With their arrival I staggered forth from my night-long cramped position to finish the tea that remained in my flask and to smoke a long-overdue pipe, while relating the events of the night.

All three of the men knew me most intimately, but, although they did not say as much, it was clearly evident they were surprised to see me alive, for the roars and demonstrations of the frustrated maneater had been clearly audible to them where they had spent the night with the shivering herdsmen of Panapatti.

Byra now said that he would like to take a quick walk up the Chinar to Muthur, just four miles away, and fetch his hunting dog, which he felt would be of considerable help in following the trail of the tiger. This dog was a very nondescript white and brown village cur, answering to the most unusual name of Kush-Kush-Kariya. How it happened to possess this strange name I had never been able to fathom. In calling the animal, Byra used the first two syllables in a normal tone, but would accentuate the third into a weird rising cry resembling that of a night heron. I had never been able to emulate him in this, and had contented myself in the past with Kush-Kush alone, which the dog would obey without hesitation.

Insisting that he at least took Sowree as company. I returned with Ranga to Ootaimalai and had a hot breakfast and a bath in the Cauvery, followed by a long-overdue sleep. I awoke at 2 p.m. with the return of Byra, Sowree and the much-prized Kush-Kush-Kariya, who wagged his tail at me in joyful recognition and nuzzled his cold snout against my shoulder.

Swallowing a hasty lunch and plenty of hot tea, we returned to the spot of my night's adventure, accompanied by the relatives of the dead man, who yearned to bring away his remains but were far too afraid to visit the spot unprotected.

As may be imagined, the corpse was by this time smelling to high heaven, so they decided to carry it only as far as the Chinar river and bury the remains on the bank. With their departure, poor Kush-Kush made a brave attempt to follow the cold trail of the tiger but was not very successful in going even 100 yards. Probably the stench that still pervaded the atmosphere and lingered on the quiet evening air had overpowered all faint smell that might have remained in the tiger's tracks over the hard ground. We returned to camp just before nightfall a very disappointed group.

The following day nothing happened, but on the morning of the day after Ranga nearly met his end.

Each day, as I have already said, Byra, Sowree and I scoured the forest in opposite directions in the hope of locating the tiger, while it was Ranga's duty to feed and water our three baits, none of which had been killed up to that time. He had made an early start that morning, with another villager for company, and had already visited the bait at the well on Mundachipallam, which was found untouched, as expected. After depositing some of the straw carried by his companion, Ranga watered the animal and then the two men moved down Mundachipallam itself, to look to the second bait tied at its confluence with the Chinar river. The villager was leading, Ranga bringing up the rear. They had come about a mile from the road when, standing fifty yards from them in the middle of the dry stream, was the tiger.

The villager dropped his bundle of straw and shinned up the only tree at hand. For the few seconds it took him to climb a reasonable height, he blocked Ranga's progress, and within those few seconds the maneater had reached the base of the tree, reared up on its hind legs, and with a raking sweep of its forepaw removed the loin-cloth around Ranga's waist, the end of which had hung downwards, while he climbed. The tiger halted momentarily to worry the cloth, while Ranga, minus his loin-cloth, climbed energetically, overhauling and almost knocking his companion off the tree, in his efforts to reach the higher terraces and safety. The disappointed tiger remained below, looking upwards and growling savagely, while Ranga and his companion shouted loudly for help, telling the world at large that they were being killed and eaten.

Fortunately, a party of people, travelling in large numbers for safety's sake, happened to be coming from Pennagram and were at that time in the vicinity of the well, from where they heard the shouts and recognized its message. At the double the whole group, men, women and children of all ages, covered the remaining four miles to reach me at Ootamalai with the news.

Not knowing it was Ranga who had been attacked, and Byra and Sowree not having yet returned, I jog-trotted the distance alone, arriving at the well in record time. From here I could plainly hear the shouting myself. By this time the tiger had left the foot of the tree and vanished into the forest, but the two men were afraid to descend, for fear it might be in hiding and rush forth on them. Hoping to surprise the maneater, I refrained from answering them while hastening forward as swiftly as caution permitted.

When I reached the tree, however, it was only Ranga and his companion who were surprised at seeing me, till I explained the circumstances. We then attempted to follow the tiger, but no signs of him were evident on the hard ground; so we desisted and turned back to visit the remaining baits. I accompanied the men, and we found both animals unscathed. It was past midday when we returned to Ootaimalai with the despairing knowledge that the leery tiger we were after apparently was not going to kill any of our baits. Nor, with the experience I had had with him, was he ever likely to return to a kill again. To say I was exceedingly crestfallen and despondent would be putting it too mildly. The wily maneater of Mundachipallam looked like being one of those tigers that would stay put for a long time to come, if it did not go away of its own accord to continue its depredations elsewhere.

And then, about 7 a.m. two days later, came the event that brings this story to an end. As I have mentioned, in coincidence it remarkably resembled the events with which the tale started.

Again a group of persons, except that they were ten in number for the sake of safety, had placed their baskets, laden with fish for Pennagram, on the ground, to water at the well beside Mundachipallam and to rest awhile.

Women being in the party, one of the men stepped behind the nearest tree to ease himself. There was a short roar, an elongated golden body with black stripes hurled itself as if from nowhere, and the squatter had disappeared. By good fortune, Byra, Ranga, Sowree and myself had set forth in company to visit our baits and were hardly a mile behind the party of ten. Soon we met the nine who were returning with the sad news of the one who was not. Running forward as fast as we could, we reached the well, where I whispered to Ranga and Sowree to climb up adjacent trees and await my further need. Byra and I crept forward and, behind the tree chosen by the unfortunate man to answer the call of nature, we picked up the trail of his blood as it had ebbed away in the jaws of the tiger.

With Byra tracking, and closely in his wake with rifle to shoulder and scanning every bush, we had penetrated only a short hundred yards when we heard the sharp snap of a bone in the mouth of the feeding tiger. The sound had come from a half-left direction ahead of us. Laying a restraining hand on Byra, I motioned him to remain where he was, while I crept cautiously forward, knowing well that under such circumstances a companion becomes an additional life to care for.

The forest was still and breathless, and the sound of gnawing and crunching could now be heard more clearly. Very carefully and silently edging closer, with downcast eyes watching each footstep, for fear I should rustle a leaf, snap a twig, or overturn a loose stone, it took me a considerable time to advance a mere fifteen yards. From there I thought I could see the slayer, crouched on the ground. A few paces nearer, and suddenly he arose and faced me, a dripping human arm, torn off at the shoulder, held across his mouth. The wicked eyes gazed at me with blank surprise, then a snarl began to contort the giant face, rendered more awful by the gruesome remains it carried.

The soft-nosed Winchester bullet penetrated correctly into the base of the massive neck. The human arm dropped into the grass with a plop. The animal lurched forward with a gurgling grunt. Quick working of the under-lever of the old, trusted rifle, and a second missile buried itself in that wicked heart. It beat no more. The maneating tiger of Mundachipallam lurched forward to his end in almost the same spot where he had begun his wicked career months before. A large male, he was without blemish. Undoubtedly a wicked tiger by nature, he had evidently turned maneater through an unlucky chance. On such trivial circumstances often hang the threads of fate . . .

THE SPOTTED DEVIL OF GUMMALAPUR

The leopard is common to practically all tropical jungles, and, unlike the tiger, indigenous to the forests of India; for whereas it has been established that the tiger is a comparatively recent newcomer from regions in the colder north, records and remains have shown that the leopard – or panther, as it is better known in India – has lived in the peninsula from the earliest times.

Because of its smaller size and decidedly lesser strength, together with its innate fear of mankind, the panther is often treated with some derision, sometimes coupled with truly astonishing carelessness, two factors that have resulted in the maulings and occasional deaths of otherwise intrepid but cautious tiger-hunters. Even when attacking a human being, the panther rarely kills, but confines itself to a series of quick bites and quicker raking scratches with its small but sharp claws; on the other hand, few persons live to tell that they have been attacked by a tiger.

This general rule has one fearful exception, however, and that is the panther that has turned maneater. Although examples of such animals are comparatively rare, when they do occur they depict the panther as an engine of destruction quite equal to his far larger cousin, the tiger. Because of his smaller size he can conceal himself in places impossible to a tiger, his need for water is far less, and in veritable demoniac cunning and daring, coupled with the uncanny sense of self-preservation and stealthy disappearance when danger threatens, he has no equal.

Such an animal was the maneating leopard of Gummalapur in Tamil Nadu state. This leopard had established a record of some forty-two human killings and a reputation for veritable cunning that almost exceeded human intelligence. Some fearful stories of diabolical craftiness had been attributed to him, but certain it was that the panther was held in awe throughout an area of some 250 square miles over which it held undisputable sway.

Before sundown the door of each hut in every one of the villages within this area was fastened shut, some being reinforced by piles of boxes or large stones, kept for the purpose. Not until the sun was well up in the heavens next morning did the timid inhabitants venture to expose themselves. This state of affairs rapidly told on the sanitary condition of the houses, the majority of which were not equipped with latrines of any sort, the adjacent wasteland being used for the purpose.

Finding that its human meals were increasingly difficult to obtain, the panther became correspondingly bolder, and in two instances burrowed its way in through the thatched walls of the smaller huts, dragging its screaming victim out the same way, while the whole village lay awake, trembling behind closed doors, listening to the shrieks of the victim as he was carried away. In one case the panther, frustrated from burrowing its way in through the walls, which had been boarded up with rough planks, resorted to the novel method of entering through the thatched roof. In this instance it found itself unable to carry its prey back through the hole it had made, so in a paroxym of fury had killed all four inhabitants of the hut – a man, his wife and two children – before clawing its way back to the darkness outside and to safety.

Only during the day did the villagers enjoy any respite. Even then they moved about in large, armed groups, but so far no instance had occurred of the leopard attacking in daylight, although it had been very frequently seen at dawn within the precincts of a village.

Such was the position when I arrived at Gummalapur, in response to an invitation from Jepson, the District Magistrate, to rid his area of this scourge. Preliminary conversation with some of the inhabitants revealed that they appeared dejected beyond hope, and with true eastern fatalism had decided to resign themselves to the fact that this *shaitan*, from whom they believed deliverance to be impossible, had come to stay, till each one of them had been devoured or had fled the district as the only alternative.

It was soon apparent that I would get little or no cooperation from the villagers, many of whom openly stated that if they dared to assist me the shaitan would come to hear of it and would hasten their end. Indeed, they spoke in whispers as if afraid that loud talking would be overheard by the panther, who would single them out for revenge.

That night, I sat in a chair in the midst of the village, with my back to the only house that possessed a twelve-foot wall, having taken the precaution to cover the roof with a deep layer of thorns and brambles, in case I should be attacked from behind by the leopard leaping down on me. It was a moonless night, but the clear sky promised to provide sufficient illumination from its myriad stars to enable me to see the panther should it approach.

The evening, at six o'clock, found the inhabitants behind locked doors, while I sat alone on my chair, with my rifle across my lap, loaded and cocked. a flask of hot tea nearby, a blanket, a water bottle, some biscuits, a torch at hand, and of course my pipe, tobacco and matches as my only consolation during the long vigil till daylight returned.

With the going down of the sun a period of acute anxiety began, for the stars were as yet not brilliant enough to light the scene even dimly. Moreover, immediately to westward of the village lay two abrupt hills which hastened the dusky uncertainty that might otherwise have been lessened by some reflection from the recently set sun.

I gripped my rifle and stared around me, my eyes darting in all directions and from end to end of the deserted village street. At that moment I would have welcomed the jungle, where by their cries of alarm I could rely on the animals and birds to warn me of the approach of the panther. Here all was deathly silent, and the whole village might have been entirely deserted, for not a sound escaped from the many inhabitants whom I knew lay listening behind closed doors, and listening for the scream that would herald my death and another victim for the panther.

Time passed, and one by one the stars became visible, till by 7.15 p.m. they shed a sufficiently diffused glow to enable me to see along the whole village street, although somewhat indistinctly. My confidence returned, and I began to think of some way to draw the leopard towards me, should he be in the vicinity. I forced myself to cough loudly at intervals and then began to talk to myself, hoping that my voice would be heard by the panther and bring him to me quickly.

I do not know if any of my readers have ever tried talking to themselves loudly for any reason, whether to attract a maneating leopard or not. I suppose they must be few, for I realize what reputation the man who talks to himself acquires. I am sure I acquired that reputation with the villagers, who from behind their closed doors listened to me that night as I talked to myself. But believe me, it is no easy task to talk loudly to yourself for hours on end, while watching intently for the stealthy approach of a killer.

By 9 p.m. I got tired of it, and considered taking a walk around the streets of the village. After some deliberation I did this, still talking to myself as I moved cautiously up one lane and down the next, frequently glancing back over my shoulder. I soon realized, however, that I was exposing myself to extreme danger, as the panther might pounce on me from any corner, from behind any pile of garbage, or from the rooftops of any of the huts. Ceasing my talking abruptly, I returned to my chair, thankful to get back alive.

Time dragged by very slowly and monotonously, the hours seeming to pass on leaden wheels. Midnight came and I found myself feeling cold, due to a sharp breeze that had set in from the direction of the adjacent forest, which began beyond the two hillocks. I drew the blanket closely around me, while consuming tobacco far in excess of what was good for me. By 2 a.m. I found I was growing sleepy. Hot tea and some biscuits, followed by icy water from the bottle dashed into my face, and a quick raising and lowering of my body from the chair half-a-dozen times, revived me a little, and I fell to talking to myself again, as a means of keeping awake thereafter.

At 3.30 a.m. came an event which caused me untold discomfort for the next two hours. With the sharp wind banks of heavy cloud were carried along, and these soon covered the heavens and obscured the stars, making the darkness intense, and it would have been quite impossible to see the panther a yard away. I had undoubtedly placed myself in an awkward position, and entirely at the mercy of the beast, should it choose to attack me now.

I fell to flashing my torch every half-minute from end to end of the street, a proceeding which was very necessary if I hoped to remain alive with the panther anywhere near, although I felt I was ruining my chances of shooting the beast, as the bright torch-beams would probably scare it away. Still, there was the possibility that it might not be frightened by the light, and that I might be able to see it and bring off a lucky shot, a circumstance that did not materialize, as morning found me still shining the torch after a night-long and futile vigil.

I snatched a few hours' sleep and at noon fell to questioning the villagers again. Having found me still alive that morning – quite obviously contrary to their expectations – and possibly crediting me with the power to communicate with spirits because they had heard me walking around their village talking, they were considerably more communicative and gave me a few more particulars about the beast. Apparently the leopard wandered about its domain a great deal, killing erratically and at places widely distant from one another, and as I had already found out, never in succession at the same village. As no human had been killed at Gummalapur within the past three weeks, it seemed that there was much to be said in favour of staying where I was, rather than moving around in a haphazard fashion, hoping to come up with the panther. Another factor against wandering about was that this beast was rarely visible in the daytime, and there was therefore practically no chance of my meeting it, as might have been the case with a maneating tiger. It was reported that the animal had been wounded in its right forefoot, since it had the habit of placing the pad sidewards, a fact which I was later able to confirm when I actually came across the tracks of the animal.

After lunch, I conceived a fresh plan for that night, which would certainly save me from the great personal discomforts I had experienced the night before. This was to leave a door of one of the huts ajar, and to rig up inside it a very life-like dummy of a human being; meanwhile, I would remain in a corner of the same hut behind a barricade of boxes. This would provide an opportunity to slay the beast as he became visible in the partially-opened doorway, or even as he attacked the dummy, while I myself would be comparatively safe and warm behind my barricade.

I explained the plan to the villagers, who, to my surprise, entered into it with some enthusiasm. A hut was placed at my disposal immediately next to that through the roof of which the leopard had once entered and killed the four inmates. A very life-like dummy was rigged up, made of straw, an old pillow, a jacket, and a saree. This was placed within the doorway of the hut in a sitting position, the door itself being kept half-open. I sat myself behind a low parapet of boxes, placed diagonally across the opposite end of the small hut, the floor of which measured about 12 feet by 10 feet. At this short range, I was confident of accounting for the panther as soon as it made itself visible in the doorway. Furthermore, should it attempt to enter by the roof, or through the thatched walls, I would have ample time to deal with it. To make matters even more realistic, I instructed the inhabitants of both the adjacent huts, especially the women folk, to endeavour to talk in low tones as far into the night as was possible, in order to attract the killer to that vicinity.

An objection was immediately raised, that the leopard might be led to enter one of their huts, instead of attacking the dummy in the doorway of the hut in which I was sitting. This fear was only overcome by promising to come to their aid should they hear the animal attempting an entry. The signal was to be a normal call for help, with which experience had shown the panther to be perfectly familiar, and of which he took no notice. This plan also assured me that the inhabitants would themselves keep awake and continue their low conversation in snatches, in accordance with my instructions.

Everything was in position by 6 p.m., at which time all doors in the village were secured, except that of the hut where I sat. The usual uncertain dusk was followed by bright starlight that threw the open doorway and the crouched figure of the draped dummy into clear relief. Now and again I could hear the low hum of conversation from the two neighbouring huts.

The hours dragged by in dreadful monotony. Suddenly the silence was disturbed by a rustle in the thatched roof which brought me to full alertness. But it was only a rat, which scampered across and then dropped with a thud to the floor nearby, from where it ran along the tops of the boxes before me, becoming clearly visible as it passed across the comparatively light patch of the open doorway. As the early hours of the morning approached, I noticed that the conversation from my neighbours died down and finally ceased, showing that they had fallen asleep, regardless of maneating panther, or anything else that might threaten them.

I kept awake, occasionally smoking my pipe, or sipping hot tea from the flask, but nothing happened beyond the noises made by the tireless rats, which chased each other about and around the room, and even across me, till daylight finally dawned, and I lay back to fall asleep after another tiring vigil.

The following night, for want of a better plan, and feeling that sooner or later the maneater would appear, I decided to repeat the performance with the dummy, and met with an adventure which will remain indelibly impressed on my memory till my dying day.

I was in position again by six o'clock, and the first part of the night was but a repetition of the night before. The usual noise of scurrying rats, broken now and again by the low-voiced speakers in the neighbouring huts, were the only sounds to mar the stillness of the night. Shortly after 1 a.m. a sharp wind sprang up, and I could hear the breeze rustling through the thatched roof. This rapidly increased in strength, till it was blowing quite a gale. The rectangular patch of light from the partly open doorway practically disappeared as the sky became overcast with storm clouds, and soon the steady rhythmic patter of raindrops, which increased to a regular downpour, made me feel that the leopard, who like all his family are not over-fond of water, would not venture out on this stormy night, and that I would draw a blank once more.

By now the murmuring voices from the neighbouring huts had

ceased or become inaudible, drowned in the swish of the rain. I strained my eyes to see the scarcely perceptible doorway, while the crouched figure of the dummy could not be seen at all, and while I looked I evidently fell asleep, tired out by my vigil of the two previous nights.

How long I slept I cannot tell, but it must have been for some considerable time. I awoke abruptly with a start, and a feeling that all was not well. The ordinary person in awaking takes some time to collect his faculties, but my jungle training and long years spent in dangerous places enabled me to remember where I was and in what circumstances, as soon as I awoke.

The rain had ceased and the sky had cleared a little, for the oblong patch of open doorway was more visible now, with the crouched figure of the dummy seated at its base. Then, as I watched, a strange thing happened. The dummy seemed to move, and as I looked more intently it suddenly disappeared to the accompaniment of a snarling growl. I realized that the panther had come, seen the crouched figure of the dummy in the doorway which it had mistaken for a human being, and then proceeded to stalk it, creeping in at the opening on its belly, and so low to the ground that its form had not been outlined in the faint light as I had hoped. The growl I had heard was at the panther's realization that the thing it had attacked was not human after all.

Switching on my torch and springing to my feet, I hurdled the barricade of boxes and sprang to the open doorway, to dash outside and almost trip over the dummy which lay across my path. I shone the beam of torchlight in both directions, but nothing could be seen. Hoping that the panther might still be lurking nearby and shining my torch-beam into every corner, I walked slowly down the village street, cautiously negotiated the bend at its end and walked back up the next street, in fear and trembling of a sudden attack. But although the light lit up every corner, every rooftop and every likely hiding-place in the street there was no sign of my enemy anywhere.

Then only did I realize the true significance of the reputation this animal had acquired of possessing diabolical cunning. Just as my own sixth sense had wakened me from sleep at a time of danger, a similar sixth sense had warned the leopard that here was no ordinary human being, but one that was bent upon its destruction. Perhaps it was the bright beam of torchlight that had unnerved it at the last moment; but, whatever the cause, the maneater had silently, completely and effectively disappeared, for although I searched for it through all the streets of Gummalapur that night, it had vanished as mysteriously as it had come.

Disappointment, and annoyance with myself at having fallen asleep, were overcome with a grim determination to get even with this beast at any cost.

Next morning the tracks of the leopard were clearly visible at the spot it had entered the village and crossed a muddy drain, where for the first time I saw the pug-marks of the slayer and the peculiar indentation of its right forefoot, the paw of which was not visible as a pug-mark, but remained a blur, due to this animal's habit of placing it on edge. Thus it was clear to me that the panther had at some time received an injury to its foot which had turned it into a maneater. Later I was able to view the injured foot for myself, and I was probably wrong in my deductions as to the cause of its maneating propensities; for I came to learn that the animal had acquired the habit of eating the corpses which the people of that area, after a cholera epidemic within the last year, had by custom carried into the forest and left to the vultures. These easily procured meals had given the panther a taste for human flesh, and the injury to its foot, which made normal hunting and swift movement difficult, had been the concluding factor in turning it into that worst of all menaces to an Indian village – a maneating panther.

I also realized that, granting the panther was equipped with an almost-human power of deduction, it would not appear in Gummalapur again for a long time after the fright I had given it the night before in following it with my torchlight.

It was, therefore, obvious that I would have to change my scene of operations and so, after considerable thought, I decided to move on to the village of Devarabetta, diagonally across an intervening range of forest hills and some eighteen miles away, where the panther had already secured five victims, though it had not been visited for a month.

Therefore, I set out before 11 a.m. that very day, after an early lunch. The going was difficult, as the path led across two hills. Along the valley that lay between them ran a small jungle stream, and beside it I noted the fresh pugs of a big male tiger that had followed the watercourse for some 200 yards before crossing to the other side. It had evidently passed early that morning, as was apparent from the minute trickles of moisture that had seeped into the pug marks through the river sand, but had not had time to evaporate in the morning sun.

Holding steadfastly to the job in hand, however, I did not follow the tiger and arrived at Devarabetta just after 5 p.m.

The inhabitants were preparing to shut themselves into their huts when I appeared, and scarcely had the time nor inclination to talk to me. However, I gathered that they agreed that a visit from the maneater was likely any day, for a full month had elapsed since his last visit and he had never been known to stay away for so long.

Time being short, I hastily looked around for the hut with the highest wall, before which I seated myself as on my first night at Gummalapur, having hastily arranged some dried thorny bushes across its roof as protection against attack from my rear and above. These thorns had been brought from the hedge of a field bordering the village itself, and I had had to escort the men who carried them with my rifle; so afraid they were of the maneater's early appearance.

Devarabetta was a far smaller village than Gummalapur, and situated much closer to the forest, a fact which I welcomed for the reason that I would be able to obtain information as to the movements of carnivore by the warning notes that the beasts and birds of the jungle would utter, provided I was within hearing.

The night fell with surprising rapidity, though this time a thin sickle of new-moon was showing in the sky. The occasional call of a roosting jungle cock, and the plaintive call of pea-fowl, answering one another. from the nearby forest, told me that all was still well. And then it was night, the faint starlight rendering hardly visible, and as if in a dream, the tortuously winding and filthy lane that formed the main street of Devarabett.

At 8.30 p.m. a sambar hind belled from the forest, following her original sharp note with a series of warning cries in steady succession. Undoubtedly a beast of prey was afoot and had been seen by the watchful deer, who was telling the other jungle-folk to look out for their lives. Was it the panther or one of the larger carnivore? Time alone would tell, but at least I had been warned.

The hind ceased her belling, and some fifteen minutes later, from the direction in which she had first sounded her alarm, I heard the low moan of a tiger, to be repeated twice in succession, before all became silent again. It was not a mating call that I had heard, but the call of the King of the Jungle in his normal search for food, reminding the inhabitants of the forest that their master was on the move in search of prey, and that one of them must die that night to appease his voracious appetite.

Time passed, and then down the lane I caught sight of some movement. Raising my cocked rifle, I covered the object, which slowly approached me, walking in the middle of the street. Was this the panther after all, and would it walk thus openly, and in the middle of the lane, without any attempt at concealment? It was now about thirty yards away and still it came on boldly, without any attempt to take cover or to creep along the edges of objects in the usual manner of a leopard when stalking its prey. Moreover, it seemed a frail and slender animal, as I could see it fairly clearly now. Twenty yards and I pressed the button of my torch, which this night I had clamped to my rifle.

As the powerful beam threw across the intervening space it lighted a village cur, commonly known to us in India as a "pariah dog". Starving and lonely, it had sought out human company; it stared blankly into the bright beam of light, feebly wagging a skinny tail in unmistakable signs of friendliness.

Welcoming a companion, if only a lonely cur, I switched off the light and called it to my side by a series of flicks of thumb and finger. It approached cringingly, still wagging its ridiculous tail. I fed it with some biscuits and a sandwich, and in the dull light of the starlit sky its eyes looked back at me in dumb gratitude for the little food I had given it, perhaps the first to enter its stomach for the past two days. Then it curled up at my feet and fell asleep.

Time passed and midnight came. A great horned owl hooted dismally from the edge of the forest, its prolonged mysterious cry of *"Whooo-whooo"* seeming to sound a death-knell, or a precursor to that haunting part of the night when the souls of those not at rest return to the scenes of their earthly activities, to live over and over again the deeds that bind them to the earth.

One o'clock, two and then three o'clock passed in dragging monotony, while I strained my tired and aching eyes and ears for movement or sound. Fortunately it had remained a cloudless night and visibility was comparatively good by the radiance of the myriad stars that spangled the heavens in glorious array, a sight that cannot be seen in any of our dusty towns or cities.

And then, abruptly, the alarmed cry of a plover, or "Did-you-do-it" bird, as it is known in India, sounded from the nearby muddy tank on the immediate outskirts of the' village. *"Did-you-do-it, Did-you-do-it, Did-you-do-it, Did-you-do-it"*, it called in rapid regularity. No doubt the bird was excited and had been disturbed, or it had seen something.

The cur at my feet stirred, raised its head, then sank down again, as if without a care in the world.

The minutes passed, and then suddenly the dog became fully awake. Its ears, that had been drooping in dejection, were standing on end, it trembled violently against my legs, while a low prolonged growl came from its throat. I noticed that it was looking down the lane that led into the village from the vicinity of the tank.

I stared intently in that direction. For a long time I could see nothing, and then it seemed that a shadow moved at a corner of a building some distance away and on the same side of the lane. I focused my eyes on this spot, and after a few seconds again noticed a furtive movement, but this time a little closer.

Placing my left thumb on the switch which would actuate the torch, I waited in breathless silence. A few minutes passed, five or ten at the most, and then I saw an elongated body spring swiftly and noiselessly on to the roof of a hut some twenty yards away. As it happened, all the huts adjoined each other at this spot, and I guessed the panther had decided to walk along the roofs of these adjoining huts and spring upon me from the rear, rather than continue stalking me in full view.

I got to my feet quickly and placed my back against the wall. In this position the eave of the roof above my head passed over me and on to the road where I had been sitting, for about eighteen inches. The rifle I kept ready, finger on trigger, with my left thumb on the torch switch, pressed to my side and pointing upwards.

A few seconds later I heard a faint rustling as the leopard endeavoured to negotiate the thorns which I had taken the precaution of placing on the roof. He evidently failed in this, for there was silence again. Now I had no means of knowing where he was.

The next fifteen mjnutes passed in terrible anxiety, with me glancing in all directions in the attempt to locate the leopard before he sprang, while thanking Providence that the night remained clear. And then the cur, that had been restless and whining at my feet, shot out into the middle of the street, faced the corner of the hut against which I was sheltering and began to bark lustily.

This warning saved my life, for within five seconds the panther charged around the corner and sprang at me. I had just time to press the torch switch and fire from my hip, full into the blazing eyes that showed above the wide opened, snarling mouth. The .405 bullet struck squarely, but the impetus of the charge carried the animal on to me. I jumped nimbly to one side and, as the panther crashed against the wall of the hut, emptied two more rounds from the magazine into the evil, spotted body.

It collapsed and was still, except for the spasmodic jerking of the still-opened jaws and long, extended tail. And then my friend the cur, staunch in faithfulness to his newfound master, rushed in and fixed his feeble teeth in the throat of the dead monster.

And so passed the "Spotted Devil of Gummalapur", a panther of whose malignant craftiness I had never heard the like before and hope never to have to meet again.

When skinning the animal next morning, I found that the injury to the right paw had not been caused, as I had surmized, by a previous bullet wound, but by two porcupine quills that had penetrated between the toes within an inch of each other and then broken off short. This must have happened quite a while before, as a gristly formation between the bones inside the foot had covered the quills. No doubt it had hurt the animal to place his paw on the ground in the normal way, and he had acquired the habit of walking on its edge.

I took the cur home; washed and fed it, and named it "Nipper". Nipper has been with me many years since then, and never have I had reason to regret giving him the few biscuits and sandwich that won his staunch little heart, and caused him to repay that small debt within a couple of hours, by saving my life.

VIETNAM TIGERS

During the Vietnam War in the 1960s tiger attacks on humans increased due, in part at least, to the frequency with which bodies lay unburied. Despite claims to the contrary, tigers will scavenge and feed at old kills, be they their own or someone else's. Having developed a taste for human flesh, they would then attack soldiers quite readily and did so quite often. What follows is but one example.

A maneating tiger was killed by members of a small recon patrol when the 400-pound cat attacked a 3rd Reconnaissance Battalion marine in the north-western corner of [what was then] South Vietnam.

The six-man recon team was on an observation mission near Fire Support Base Alpine, about six miles east of the border with Laos, when the incident occurred. The team had completed its assignment and was waiting to be lifted by helicopter from the area. Bad weather conditions had prevented their immediate extraction and the team had posted a two-man radio watch while the others settled down to sleep.

The tiger struck swiftly and silently.

"Suddenly I heard somebody scream," said PFC Thomas E. Shainline. "Then somebody else was yelling, 'It's a tiger, it's a tiger!'"

PFC Roy Regan, who had been sleeping next to the victim, recalled, "I jumped up and saw the tiger with his mouth around my partner. All I could think about was to get the tiger away from him. I jumped at the tiger and the cat jerked his head and jumped into a bomb crater about ten metres away, still holding his prey."

The marines quickly followed the tiger to the crater and opened fire on the beast. They could not be sure which of them actually killed the tiger, since they all fired at it. Once hit, the tiger released his prey and the man staggered out of the bomb crater.

"He looked dazed and he asked what happened," recalled PFC Maurice M. Howell.

The injured marine was given first aid treatment and a marine CH-46 helicopter arrived to pick up the victim, the rest of the team and the dead tiger. The injured man was rushed to the 3rd Medical Battalion Hospital at Quang Tri, suffering from lacerations and bite wounds on the neck. His identification was withheld for family reasons.

Meanwhile, the tiger, measuring nine feet from head to end of tail, was transported to the 3rd Reconnaissance Battalion headquarters.

The incident took place about ten miles south of the demilitarized zone, near a spot where a young marine was slain by a maneating tiger on 12 November 1967. Military authorities had sent out a marine contingent and two professional South Vietnamese tiger hunters three weeks before the attack on the recon team to find the killer tiger and three others believed to be in the area, but the hunt failed.

CANNABALISM IN LATIN AMERICA

There is no doubt that some Indian tribes of Latin America practised cannibalism in one form or another well into the twentieth century. Because it was abhorrent to Europeans, cannibalism became a pretext for attacking Indians, who soon became wary of talking about it, and the custom has been gradually disappearing. It was reported most frequently in the tropical lowlands of South America and in the Circum-Caribbean region, but was not confined to these areas. Human sacrifice and cannibalism were widely practised in Colombia before the Conquest.

The word "cannibal" has a Latin American origin. It came from Columbus hearing the Carib Indians called "Cariba". The Carib were feared cannibal warriors of the Antilles in his time. The use of "cannibal" in literature may have been heightened by its similarity to "can", meaning "dog" in Spanish.

There were two types of cannibalism in Latin America: exocannibalism, eating members of an enemy group, and endocannibalism, eating members of one's own group.

The former was a celebration of victory over an enemy. The symbolic treatment of the enemy as a game animal was an extreme form of racism that served to heighten enthusiasm for warfare. In the times just after Brazil was colonized, the Tupinamba would go on raids against other Indian villages. If they were successful in killing the enemy, they would butcher the bodies, and feast on them in the jungle before returning home. If they captured live male prisoners, they took them back to the Tupinamba village, where they allowed the prisoners to live for a time, sometimes for many years. After a ritual "escape", they would sacrifice, roast and eat a prisoner.

Many cannibal people have expressed a taste for human flesh. From this, some observers have drawn the conclusion that human flesh was an important part of the diet; however, these gustatory expressions were highly symbolic. Desiring to eat the enemy was an expression of fierceness that elevated the status of the warrior and struck fear into his enemies.

Endocannibalism symbolized very different things: reverence for the dead, an incorporation of the spirit of the dead into living descendants, or a means of insuring the separation of the soul from the body. A Mayoruna man once expressed a wish to remain in his village and be eaten by his children after his death rather than be consumed by worms in the white man's cemetery.

In recent times the Panoan, Yanomamö and other lowland groups have consumed the ground-up bones and ashes of cremated kinsmen in an act of mourning. This still is classified as endocannibalism, although, strictly speaking, "flesh" is not eaten. The Yanomamö mix the bones and ashes with plantain soup before consuming the mixture.

Theories that a lack of protein in the South American tropical forest environment stimulated cannibalism have not received support from recent studies showing that tropical forest tribes have a more than adequate protein intake and are successful hunters despite environmental limitations. The theory that the Aztecs depended on the consumption of sacrificial victims for food lacks convincing data on the extent of this consumption. Some Aztecs consumed parts of some victims; however, most estimates of the number of victims eaten represent figures lower than what would have provided critical protein. Evidence points to Latin American exocannibalism as a symbolic expression of the domination of an enemy in warfare rather than as a significant source of protein.

THE BLACK BEAR OF MYSORE

The story I am now about to relate concerns an Indian sloth bear. Quite a big, black and bad bear.

All bears, as I have had occasion to remark, are excitable, unreliable and bad-tempered animals. They have a reputation for attacking people without apparent reason, provided that person happens to pass too close, either while the bear is asleep or feeding, or just ambling along. So the natives give bears a wide birth; together with the elephant, they command the greatest respect of the jungle-dwelling folk.

This particular bear was exceptional among his kind for his unwarranted and exceptionally bad temper and aggressiveness. He would go out of his way to attack people, even when he saw them a long distance away.

The reason for his unusual conduct was difficult to explain. There were many stories about him, which were as varied as they were extraordinary. The most unpretentious was that he was quite mad. Other stories have it that he was a "she" who had been robbed of her cubs and had sworn a vendetta against the human race. I think that the bear had been wounded or injured at some time by some human being. Perhaps the most fantastic of the stories was to the effect that this bear, almost a year previously, had kidnapped an Indian girl as a mate, while she was grazing a flock of goats on the hill where he lived. The story went on to say that the whole village had turned out, *en masse,* to rescue the girl, which they had finally succeeded in doing, much to the bear's annoyance; he had then taken to attacking human beings in retaliation.

Whatever the reason, this bear had quite a long list of victims to his credit; I was told that some twelve persons had been killed, and two dozen others injured.

Like all bears, he invariably attacked the face of the victim, which he commenced to tear apart with his tremendously long and powerful claws, in addition to biting viciously with deliberate intent to ensure the success of his handiwork. Quite half the injured had lost one or both eyes; some had lost their noses, while others had had their cheeks bitten through. Those who had been killed had died with their faces almost torn from their heads. Local rumours had it that the bear had also taken to eating his victims, the last three of whom had been partly devoured.

I had no opportunity to verify the truth of these rumours, but felt that they might be true to some extent, as the Indian sloth bear is a known devourer of carrion at times, although generally he is entirely vegetarian, restricting himself to roots, fruit, honey, white ants and similar delicacies. So fresh meat, even human meat, might not be unwelcome.

This bear originally lived in the Nagvara Hills, which lie to the east of the large town of Arsikere, some 105 miles north-west of Bangalore, and in Mysore State.

It was on these hills that he had perpetrated his earliest offences. Then, as he lost his fear of mankind and grew bolder, for no apparent reason he came down to the plains and commenced to harass people in their fields at dawn and dusk. He would come out from one or other of the numerous small boulder-strewn hillocks that were dotted here and there, to forage for food.

I had been hearing occasional stories of this animal for about a year, but had not paid much attention to them, as I felt that, like nearly all the stories one hears in India of maulings and killings by wild animals, they were greatly exaggerated. Furthermore, as I think I have mentioned somewhere else, Bruin is quite an old friend of mine, against whom I have no antipathy. I was therefore most disinclined to go after him.

But there came an incident that made me do so. I have an old friend, an aged Muslim named Alam Bux, who is the guardian of a Mohammedan shrine situated on the main road which leads past Arsikere and on to Shimoga. This shrine is the burial place of a

Mohammedan saint who lived some fifty years ago and, like hundreds of similar shrines scattered over the length and breadth of India, is preserved and held sacred by the Muslim community. Each shrine has its own guardian or caretaker, invariably some old man who is quartered at the shrine itself to keep it clean and care for it. One of his particular duties is to light a lamp over the shrine, which is kept burning all night, to signify that the memory of the saint burns ever brightly in the bosoms of the faithful.

I first met Alam Bux on a dark night while motoring from Bangalore to Shimoga on my way to a tiger-hunt. The rear wheel of my Studebaker flew off, and the back brake-drum hit the road with a terrific jolt. I happened to be alone at the time and, stepping out of the car, viewed the situation with considerable disgust and annoyance. Fortunately for me, the incident had taken place almost opposite the shrine, and old Alam Bux, waking up at the noise made by the brake-drum striking and dragging along the road, came out to see what it was all about.

Seeing my predicament, the old man volunteered to help me, which he did to a very considerable extent by bringing a lantern from his abode, gathering stones to serve as "packing" while I raised the axle of the car, and last, but by no means least, by serving me with a bowl of hot tea. I thanked the old man, after I had replaced the truant wheel, and promised that I would look him up whenever I happened to pass his little hut again. This promise I had faithfully kept, and I never failed to bring the old man something by way of supplies on any occasion that I happened to pass.

Some four hundred yards beyond the shrine is a small knoll of heaped boulders, among which grew the usual lantana shrub. All around this knoll, and right up to the shrine and adjacent roadway, were fields in which the villagers grew groundnuts after the monsoon rains. Now, bears are very fond of groundnuts and our big bad black bear was no exception to this rule. The boulder-covered hillock offered a convenient lodging, and the groundnut fields were a great attraction. So he took up residence among the rocks.

He made his abode in a deep recess beneath an overhanging boulder. Hungry by sunset, he could be seen coming forth from this cave, and, as twilight deepened into nightfall, he would amble down the knoll and come out on to the groundnut fields. Here he would spend a busy night, eating, uprooting, and generally snuffling about over a wide area throughout the hours of darkness. Early dawn would find him replete, with his belly full of roots and nuts, white ants, grubs and other miscellaneous fodder which he had come across during the hours of his foraging. Leisurely he would climb back to his abode, there to spend the hot hours of the day in deep and bearly slumber. I forgot to mention that a small "tank", which is the Indian colloquial name for a natural lake, was conveniently situated on the other side of the hillock, so that our friend, this bad bear, wanted for nothing.

About this time the fig trees that bordered the main road which ran past the little shrine came into season, and their clusters of ripe red fruit filled the branches, spilling on to the ground beneath, carpeting the earth in a soft, red, spongy mass. Hundreds of birds of all varieties fed on the figs during the day. At night scores of flying fox, the large Indian fruit bat resembling in size and appearance the far-famed "vampire" bat, would come in their numbers, flapping about with leathern wings, screeching, clawing and fighting among themselves as they gourmandized the ripe fruit.

These numerous visitors, both by day and night, would knock down twice the number of figs they ate, which added to the profusion of fruit already lying scattered on the ground, blown down by the wind and often falling of their own weight. All this offered additional attraction to the bear, which now found a pleasing change to his menu. It was there in abundance, just waiting to be eaten.

So from the fields he would visit the fig trees, and thus his foraging brought him into the precincts of the shrine. That is how the trouble began.

Alam Bux had a son, a lad aged about twenty-two years, who, together with the guardian's aged wife and younger sister, lived at the shrine. One night the family had their meal at about nine, and were preparing to go to bed, when the boy for some reason went outside. It happened to be a dark night, and the bear also happened to be eating figs in the vicinity. Seeing the human figure suddenly appear, he felt that this was an unwarranted intrusion and immediately attacked the youth; more by accident than deliberately, the bear bit through the youth's throat and not the face, which was his usual first objective. The boy tried to scream. and had kicked and fought. The bear bit him again, this time through the nose and one eye, and clawed him severely across his chest, shoulders and back. Then it let him go and loped away into the darkness.

The boy staggered back to his parents streaming with blood. His jugular vein had been punctured and, although they had tried to staunch the bleeding with such rags as were available, they failed in their attempt to save his life, which ebbed away in the darkness, as cloth after cloth, and rag after rag, became soaked in his blood.

The false dawn witnessed the youth's passing, while the old bear, replete with figs and groundnuts, climbed back to his cave among the boulders.

Alam Bux was a poor man and could not afford the money to send me a telegram, nor even his fare to Bangalore either by train or by bus. But he sent me a postcard on which was scrawled the sad story; it was written in pencil, in shaky Urdu script. It was stained with the tears of his sorrow. The postcard arrived two days later, and I left for Asikere within three hours.

I had anticipated that the shooting of this bear would be an easy matter and that it would take an hour or two at the most. Therefore, I did not go prepared for a long trip. I carried just my torch, .405 Winchester rifle, and a single change of clothing. I reached Alam Bux shortly after five in the evening and it did not take him long to tell me his story.

There was no moonlight at this time. Nevertheless the plan to be followed seemed a simple one: namely, to wait till it grew quite dark and then set forth to search for the bear with the aid of my torch.

With the procedure in view, Alam Bux allowed me inside his abode by sunset, and closed the door to give the appearance that all was quiet. In the dingy little room we chatted in the flickering light of a small oil lamp, while he repeatedly lamented the death of his son. In fact, within a few minutes the whole family were weeping and wailing. I had, perforce, to listen to this continuously till eight, when I could stand it no longer and decided to go out in search of the bear.

Loading my rifle, and seeing that the torch was functioning properly, I stepped outside, Alam Bux closing and bolting his door behind me. The darkness was intense, and as I pressed the switch of the torch fixed near the muzzle of the rifle, its bright beams shone forth over the groundnut fields to my left, and the dense aisle of fig trees bordering the road to my right.

The bear was nowhere in sight and so I started to look for him, beginning with the fig trees. These trees grew on both sides of the road, so I judged the best thing to do would be to walk along the road itself, swinging my rifle from one side of the road to the other. I walked in this fashion away from Asikere for about a mile and a half, but saw no signs of the bear. I then walked back to the shrine and continued in the opposite direction for another mile and a half, but there were still no signs of the bear. So I came back to the shrine, and started to search the groundnut fields.

Bright glimmers of various pairs of eyes glared back at me, reflected by the torch beam. But they proved to be those of rabbits and three or four jackals. I circumvented the hillock and walked along the margin of the tank on the other side, where I put up a small sounder of wild pigs wallowing in the mud. But still no sign of the old bear was to be seen. I then walked closer to the foot of the knoll, and around it two or three times, shining my light upwards and in all directions. It was tiring work, and the old bear did not put in his appearance.

On the third occasion I almost stepped upon a very large Russell's Viper that was coiled between two rocks in my direct path. Engaged as I was, looking for the reflecting gleam of the bear's eyes, I did not watch the ground before me. My foot was within a few inches of the viper when he inflated his body with a loud, rasping hiss, preparatory to striking. Instinctively I heeded his warning not to come any nearer and leapt backwards, at the same time shining the torch directly upon the snake, which lunged forth with jaws apart to bite the spot where, just a moment before, my legs had been. It was a narrow shave, and for the moment I felt like shooting the viper. But that would have caused a tremendous disturbance and might frighten away the bear, in addition to wasting a valuable cartridge. After all, the snake had been good enough to warn me, and so, in return, I threw a small stone at it, which caused it to slither away beneath the rocks.

By this time it was evident that the bear had either gone out earlier in the evening and wandered far away, or else he was not hungry and was still in his cave. I returned to Alam Bux's shack and decided to make another tour in a couple of hours.

This I did, and made two further tours after that, making four in all, but the bear was not to be seen, and the false dawn found me still vainly circling the hillock in search of the enemy.

With daylight, I told Alam Bux that I would return to Bangalore, but he begged me to stay for the day and to climb the hill and search the cave for the bear. In the meantime his wife had prepared some hot *chapaties* – round flat cakes made from wheat flour – and a dish of steaming tea, both of which I consumed with relish. Then I fell asleep. At about noon Alam Bux woke me, to say that his wife had prepared special "pillao rice" in my honour. Thanking him for this, I tucked into it too, and in a very short time polished off the lot. Mrs Alam Bux appeared highly gratified that I so relished her cooking. The sun was now at its meridian and shone mercilessly on the rocks which blazed and shimmered in the noonday heat. It would be a good time to look for the bear, I knew, assuming he was at home, as he would be fast asleep.

Alam Bux came with me up the hill and from a distance of fifty yards pointed out the shelving rock beneath which the bear had its cave. I clambered upwards on tiptoe, the rubber soles of my shoes making no sound on the rocks. But against this advantage I was soon to feel a greater disadvantage, as the heat from the sun-baked stone penetrated the rubber and began to burn the soles of my feet.

Coming up to the entrance of the cave, I squatted on my haunches and listened attentively.

Now a sleeping bear invariably snores, often as loud as does a human being. If the bear was fast asleep, as I hoped he would be, I counted upon hearing that telltale sound. But no sound greeted my ears, and after sitting thus for almost ten minutes, the sun began making itself felt through the back of my shirt. Some pebbles lay at hand and, picking up a few, I began to throw them into the cave.

Now such a procedure is calculated to make any sleeping bear very angry. But I could still hear nothing. So I went closer to the entrance and threw the stones right inside. Still nothing happened. I threw more stones, but again with negative results. The bear was not in his cave.

Descending the hill, I told Alam Bux the news and announced my intention to return to Bangalore, asking him to send me a telegram if the bear put in a further appearance. I gave him some money, both for the cost of the telegram and to tide him over immediate expenses. Then I left for Bangalore. A month elapsed, and I heard nothing more.

About twenty miles across country, and in a north-westerly direction from where the shrine is situated, the forest of Chikmagalur, in the Kadur district of Mysore, begins. About halfway between Chikmagalur and Kadur stands the small town of Sakrepatna, surrounded by the jungle.

The next news that came to me was that a bear had seriously mauled two wood-cutters near Sakrepatna, one of whom had later died. The District Forest Officer of Chikmagaiur wrote to me, asking if I would come and shoot this bear.

I concluded that it was the same bear that had been the cause of the death of Alam Bux's son, but to look for one particuiar bear in the wide range of forest was something like searching for the proverbial needle in a haystack, and so I wrote back to the D.F.O. to try and get more exact information as to the whereabouts of the animal.

After ten days he replied that the bear was said to be living in a cave on a hillock some three miles from the town, near the footpath leading to a large lake known as the "Ionkere"; also that it had since mauled the Forest Guard, who had been walking along this path on his regular beat.

So I motored to Chikmagalur, picked up the D.F.O., and proceeded to the town of Sakrepatna, where there is a small rest house owned by the Mysore Forest Department. Here I set up my headquarters for the next few days.

As luck would have it – or bad luck, if you call it that – the very next afternoon a man came running to the bungalow, to tell us that a cattle grazier – his brother, in fact – had been grazing his cattle in the vicinity of the very hill where the bear was supposed to be living, when he had been attacked by the animal. He had screamed for help, and his cries had been mingled with the growls of the bear. His brother, who was lower down the hill and nearer the footpath, hearing the sounds had waited no longer, but had fled back to the bungalow to bring us the news.

Now bears are essentially nocturnal animals, never moving about during daylight. At most, they may be met with at dusk or early dawn, but certainly not in the afternoon. Probably the unfortunate grazier had strayed too close to some spot where the bear had been sleeping, causing it to attack him at that unusual time. That could be the only explanation for this strange attack.

It was nearing 4.30 p.m. when he brought us this news, and I set forth with my rifle and torch and three or four helpers to try to rescue the grazier who had been attacked. We soon found that the distance to the spot was much greater than we had been told by the unfortunate man's brother. I figured I had walked nearly six miles into the jungle before we came to the foot of a hill that was densely covered with scrub, including clumps of bamboo. It was then nearly six and, being winter, it was getting dark.

The men I had brought along refused to come farther, and said that they would return to Sakrepatna, advising me to accompany them and suggesting that we should go back next morning to continue our search. The brother of the missing man volunteered to wait where we stood, but was too fearful to come farther into the jungle. The most he could do to help me in finding his missing relative was vaguely to indicate, with a wave of his arm, the general area where the attack had occurred.

I went forward in that direction, calling loudly the name of the man who had been mauled. There was no answer to my shouts, and I advanced deeper and deeper into the scrub. By this time it was almost dark, but I did not feel perturbed, as I had brought my torch and began to flash it about as I sought a way through the undergrowth.

Soon it became so dense that I could make no further progress, and was on the point of turning back, when I thought I heard a faint moan, away in the distance. The ground at this point sloped downwards into a sort of valley that lay between two ridges of the hill, and the moan seemed to come from somewhere in the recesses of this valley.

The missing man's name was Thimma, and, cupping both hands to my mouth, I shouted this name lustily, waiting every now and then to listen for a reply. Yes! There, undoubtedly, it was again! A moaning cry, feeble, but nevertheless audible. It definitely came to me from the valley.

Forcing my way through the thickets, I struggled down the decline, slipping on rocks and loose stones, catching myself every now and then on the thorns. After a couple of hundred yards of such progress, I called again. After some time I heard a moaning answer, somewhere to my right. I proceeded in this fashion, following the cry till I eventually found Thimma, lying at the foot of a tree in a puddle of his own blood. His face was a mass of raw flesh and broken bones, and the only way of distinguishing that he was breathing was by the bubbles of air that forced themselves through the clotting blood. In addition, the bear had raked him across the stomach with its claws, tearing open the outer flesh, so that a loop of intestine protruded. He was hardly conscious when I found him, and I soon realized that what I had taken to be a moaning reply to my calls were just the groans he kept making, every now and then, in his delirium.

The situation was critical, and after examination I saw that another night's exposure would cause him to die by morning. There was therefore no alternative but to carry him back to the spot where I had left his brother. Lifting him on to my shoulder was a tricky business, in the terrible state that he was in. To make matters worse, he was a heavily built man, equal to myself in weight. But I managed to lift him and, using my rifle butt as a prop, began to struggle upwards the way I had come.

I never wish to experience again so terrible a journey. I had almost gained the ridge down which I had lately come when the accident occurred. My left foot slipped and came down heavily between two boulders. There was a sharp, shooting, wrenching pain as I collapsed on the rock with Thimma on top of me, while the rifle clattered to the ground.

I had sprained my ankle, and was now myself unable to walk. From where we lay, I began to shout to the brother; but after nearly an hour I realized he either could not or would not hear me. There was no alternative but to spend the night with the dying man.

Desiring to make the torch batteries last the night, if that were possible, I refrained from using them more than was necessary. The early hours of morning became bitterly cold and Thimma's groans became more and more feeble, till eventually they turned into a gurgle. I realized he was dying. At about 5 a.m. he died, and there I sat beside him till daylight eventually came, shortly after six.

I then made a determined effort to drag myself to my feet, but found my leg would not support my weight. I tried to crawl, but the thorns formed an impenetrable barrier. They tore my hands, my face and my clothing to shreds. I soon gave it up and became reconciled to the fact that I would have to wait till a rescue party came to search for us.

It was well past noon before the Forest Department people, accompanied by Thimma's brother and a dozen villagers, came anywhere near the scene. Eventually, guided by my shouts, they located us, and that evening I was back at Sakrepatna forest bungalow, lying on the cot with an immensely swollen ankle. The D.F.O. turned up at about nine o'clock and drove me in my car to Chikmagalur, where I went to the local hospital for treatment. It was a week before I managed to hobble around. You may guess that by this time I was extremely angry with myself at the delay, and more so with the big, bad, black bear that had caused all the trouble. I was determined that I would get him at any cost, just as soon as I could walk.

In the meantime he had not been idle, but had mauled two more men who had been walking along the path to the Ionkere Lake.

Four days later saw me back at Sakrepatna, just about able to walk, although not for long distances. Here I was told that the bear had taken to visiting some fields about a mile from the village, bordered by boram trees, the fruit of which was just then coming into season. At 5 p.m. I reached the trees in question and, selecting the largest, which had the most fruit, decided to spend the night at its foot, hoping that the bear showed up. I sat on the ground with my back to the trunk, my rifle across my knees.

Shortly after eleven I heard the grunting, grumbling sound of an approaching bear. He stopped frequently, no doubt to pick up some morsel, and as he came closer I heard the scratching sounds he made in digging for roots. He took nearly an hour to reach the boram tree, by which time I was amply prepared. Finally, he broke cover and ambled into the open, a black blob silhouetted in the faint glimmer of the stars.

I pressed the torch switch and the beams fell on him. He rose on his hind legs to regard me with surprise, and I planted my bullet in his chest between the arms of the white V-mark that showed clearly in the torchlight. And that was the end of that really bad bear.

Bears, as a rule, are excitable but generally harmless creatures. This particular bear carried the mark of Cain, in that he had become the wanton and deliberate murrderer of several men, whom he had done to death in most terrible fashion, without provocation.

THE ROSTOV RIPPER

April 1992

Andrei Chikatilo was haunted by the knowledge that a cousin was eaten during the Ukrainian famine of 1934 and tortured by the humiliation he suffered as the son of a "traitor" – a prisoner returned from the Second World War only to be interned as an "enemy of the people".

But to most people, 56-year-old Chikatilo was an innocuous grandfather, a little eccentric perhaps, but with a university degree in literature. No one – not even the wife who hen-pecked him – suspected that the former teacher was becoming one of this century's most sadistic and prolific mass murderers, stalking a succession of young victims before killing and mutilating their bodies.

In the unprecedented hunt for the murderer who has been dubbed Pussia's Hannibal the Cannibal and the "Rostov Ripper", half a million people were investigated by the demoralized and underpaid local police force. The fact that the disappearance of many of the victims went unreported by their parents made the task even more difficult.

Chikatilo, who has admitted fifty-five murders, was twice arrested, but managed to convince detectives he was innocent until he was finally apprehended in 1990. It was only then that the police discovered many of the experts had been wrong. The man who had eluded them for years was not a devil-worshipper, nor a deranged doctor carrying out mad experiments, nor an individual obsessed by the secrets of life and death.

He had his little peculiarities. At home, Chikatilo moved the cast-iron bathtub into the kitchen and slept in the bathroom. He enjoyed horror films and wrote letters to President Gorbachev complaining of the neighbours' plans to build a toilet and garages next to his flat.

However, in Court No 5 of Rostov's courthouse last week – Chikatilo – who bears a striking resemblance to Anthony Hopkins in *The Silence of the Lambs* – cut a terrifying figure. His head shaved and his eyebrows barely visible, he was held in a cage – to protect him from the hysterical crowd that included many relatives of his victims. Chikatilo appeared to pay no attention to the proceedings, lost in his own world and rocking his head from side to side. Yet as the trial opened, he unexpectedly sprang into action, producing a poster of a naked pin-up girl and a bloodied corpse and waving it at the judges' bench. "Greetings to you, gentlemen," it mocked.

The impression he made on his fifty-five victims, most of them young boys or girls, was anything but menacing. Tempted by the bespectacled stranger's promise of a gift or his kindly manner, they followed him into the undergrowth and to their deaths. Victims were raped, blinded, mutilated and sometimes disembowelled. Parts of corpses were missing, cut out or bitten off. Sexual organs were eaten.

Lieutenant-Colonel Viktor Burakov, the detective who led the hunt, said: "In our search for the criminal we just couldn't imagine what sort of person we were dealing with. This was the height of sadism, the like of which we had never seen."

The investigation was getting nowhere. Eleven bodies were discovered in 1984 alone, but the police were spending more time trying to establish their identities than actually tracking down the killer. Burakov turned to a local psychiatrist, Dr Alexander Bukhanovsky, for advice. The portrait he painted of the killer's psychological make-up – a middle-aged, self-pitying misfit heterosexual but impotent – proved to be remarkably accurate. With only the victims' remains and the circumstances of their deaths to work on, Dr Bukhanovsky, head of the Phoenix centre in Rostov, made an approximate guess as to the killer's profession: possibly supplies supervisor at a factory. He was right again.

"His internal world is a thousand times richer than the surface expression of that world," said Dr Bukhanovsky. His brain was a playground for the most depraved perversions. But it was blessed with an exceptional memory which knew the lives and biographies of every American president and the exact circumstances of each of his murders years afterwards. A model pupil at school, an example to the other boys and girls, he was in later life a frequent theatre-goer who wept at plays.

On one level Chikatilo, a committed Communist convinced himself that he was purging society. Even before admitting his guilt he told investigators: "Vagrants . . . they beg, demand and seize things. From the stations they take off in different directions on the commuter trains. I saw scenes of these vagrants' sex lives and I remembered my humiliation, that I could not prove myself as a real man. The question arose – do these rootless elements have the right to life?"

Even boys and girls as young as eight or nine qualified as candidates for Chikatilo to destroy. What were they doing roaming the streets? Would not they too grow up into "rootless elements"?

"As they walked through the forest together there was a refrain playing in his head: 'Some higher force has brought us together, the victim and myself'," Dr Bukhanovsky said. This was the other level at which Chikatilo's mind worked. His fetish was the immature body, of either sex. Terrified of the victim's gaze he would make ritual incisions to the eye-sockets and beg in his orgy of dismemberment and cannibalism.

Chikatllo is said to be so impressed with the analysis of the psychiatrist-sleuth that he has asked Dr Bukhanovsky to be with him before the execution that will doubtless be his sentence.

A frequent business traveller, Chikatilo killed in regions as remote as St Petersburg in the north-west and Tashkent in Uzbekistan. But most of his victims were local. One can follow in some of their footsteps to this day – from the crowded bus-stops on Voroshilov Avenue, across the bridge and into the forest on the left bank of the Don.

An important part of any Russian criminal investigation is the "experiment" during which the accused demonstrates to camera exactly how he committed the crime. "He showed no remorse whatsoever. He chatted and made rather heavy-handed jokes about Gorbachev," said Burakov. But the gruesome details of the murders have proved too much for Chikatilo's wife and two grown-up children, who have fled the town and gone into hiding.

At the height of the manhunt, policemen in camouflaged hides kept watch through binoculars in the woods around Rostov. But the final arrest was a testimony to more old fashioned methods. After the body of Chikatilo's final victim was discovered, police collected evidence from the site of the killing and cross-checked it with a card-index containing 25,000 possible suspects. The trail led to Chikatilo. He was tailed and, when he approached teenagers on the streets again, the police pounced.

Chikatilo's arrest, at the end of 1990, was not the first time he had come to the police's attention. He was suspected of the very first murder he committed, in 1978. But the trail went cold when another man was arrested, wrongly convicted and then executed.

In 1984 Chikatilo was stopped again after police spotted him trying to strike up conversations with girls on the street. In his briefcase was a sharp knife, a jar of petroleum jelly and a length of cord. Again he slipped the net.

On closer inspection of his personal history it transpired that the suspect had been dismissed from the boarding school he taught at for molesting pupils. But after a conviction for a petty larceny the investigators once again lost interest. Besides, his blood group was not the same as that released by experts.

As the Chikatilo trial continues, police in nearby Taganrog on the Black Sea coast are hunting another serial killer who has raped and murdered eight women, leaving their bodies naked except for their black tights. The lessons of the Chikatilo case have been learnt but far from being a triumph for the forces of law and order, the whole grisly story looks more like their indictment

October 1992

Andrei Chikatilo, alias the "Rostov Ripper", the Russian serial killer who tortured, cannibalized and murdered at least 52 people, was sentenced to death in Rostov-on-Don yesterday [14 October 1992]. The packed courtroom erupted in applause as Judge Leonid Abubzhanov pronounced the sentence on Chikatilo, aged fifiy-seven. No mass murderer has ever been tried for more killings.

From behind his iron cage, Chikatilo, a former teacher and Communist Party member, jumped up when the sentence was announced and shouted at the judge: "You're a crook. You're a crook." As he was restrained by guards, relatives of his victims tried to push through a cordon of police, crying, "Kill the beast."

In the course of twelve years Chikatilo tempted young women and children into forest walks with him around Rostov, 500 miles south of Moscow, before carrying out sadistic sexual and cannibalistic acts on his victims.

As the trial reached its climax, order in the court broke down. With the judge demanding quiet and police trying to keep at bay a large crowd outside the court, grandmothers jostled students to stand on courtroom chairs to gape at Chikatilo.

"They'll use electricity, won't they?" asked a *babushka* in a tattered fur coat.

"No, no. They'll use a bullet to kill him," replied another elderly woman.

In fact, the murderer will be killed by a single bullet in the back of the head – probably by the end of next month, if the planned appeal on the grounds of insanity fails.

Chikatilo may well be the last Russian murderer to be executed. In the past six months a presidential commission has commuted forty-five death sentences and backed only one for a multiple killer and rapist.

The trial, the first criminal case to receive Western-style media attention, has shocked a nation not given to reading sordid details of murder cases. Chikatilo often dismembered his victims and, as his lust for killing developed, he began to eats parts of them.

The case has done little to encourage public confidence in the police. Accusations of bungling by the Soviet militia, whose presence has always been overwhelming apart from when crimes were being committed, came from all quarters, including the judge. One man has already been executed for one of the murders to which Chikatilo has since confessed.

Only in 1982 was the decision made to treat the child killings in and round Rostov as the work of one man. Chikatilo had already been questioned once by then. He was arrested again in 1984 and taken in for questioning. He was released after being discounted as a suspect because of a rare discrepancy between his blood and sperm types. He went on to murder twenty-two more times after his release in 1985.

The judge remarked that the root of the police's failure to find Chikatilo lay not only in their inability to act effectively but also in the state of Soviet society: "Children were taught to do whatever adults wanted them to. There were no independent-minded children who might have challenged or doubted him."

Chikatilo killed twenty-one boys aged between 8 and 16, fourteen girls aged between 9 and 17, and seventeen women. He buried most in woodland.

"He tortured his victims by biting out their tongues, tearing away their sexual organs and cutting their bellies open," the judge said.

The emotional scenes that marked the trial proceedings earlier in the year were repeated in the courtroom yesterday. "I can't breathe the same air as him, live on the same earth as him!" a woman in a black mourning dress screamed from the public gallery. "Execution by firing squad isn't enough for him. Let me tear him apart with my own hands!"

Chikatilo terrorized southern Russia, Ukraine and Uzbekistan. He was arrested in November 1990 after he made advances to a boy. Police made dramatic mistakes as they tried to catch the killer. They arrested three men on suspicion of committing some of the crimes. One committed suicide, another tried to hang himself, and the third was executed for the first of Chikatilo's murders.

"In all those years he did not leave a single trace, with the exception of his own sperm, which he left on the victims intentionally," the judge said. The rare discrepancy between Chikatilo's sperm and blood groups prevented police from identifying him as the killer much earlier. He was detained on one occasion emerging from a wood with blood on his hands and carrying a rope, but he was released for lack of evidence. Once he was arrested, Chikatilo confessed to twenty-one more murders than the original thirty-three he was charged with.

"Colleagues at work considered him a robot unable to take independent decisions. Even his children treated him with contempt," the judge said. "By killing defenceless victims he not only satisfied his sexual demands but also affirmed his power."

WOLVES IN UTTAR PRADESH

Hunters aiming to destroy packs of wolves which are alleged to have killed five children and mauled four others in northern India are being hindered by superstition and wildlife laws.

Armed with radio transmitters, they were keeping vigil near nine villages where wolves had been sighted. They said they were confident of ridding the area of maneating wolves "soon". But illiterate villagers in the Rae Bareli district of Uttar Pradesh believe that the "wrath of God" will descend on them if the wolves are killed. They chase them away into the thick undergrowth.

The villagers believe wolves have supernatural powers and near-human intelligence.

Forest officials and paramilitary personnel combing the region around the Lone river and its three tributaries for the maneating wolves cannot shoot any wolf they see because the animal is protected under a Wildlife Act. They are only allowed to shoot wolves which are proven maneaters.

SECRET SOCIETIES IN WEST AFRICA

For one week in each year the towns of Yorubaland in Nigeria reverberate to the sound of drums as troupes of colourfully garbed musicians and dancers throng their narrow streets during the festival of Ogun. Vehicles are not permitted to pass through towns during the night and may only pass through by day when bedecked with palm fronds. In years gone by strangers have been killed when innocently trangressing this law and I narrowly escaped a similar fate in my early years in Africa. Driving through an apparently deserted town at dead o'night, I came under fire from a veritable fusillade of stones. The fist-sized stones rained down on my Landrover from all quarters, whanging tinnily on the bonnet and roof and sides as I reversed frantically back out of town and into the safety of the surrounding bush.

In the bad old days, Ogun was propitiated by human sacrifice. Things have changed now at least inasmuch as the casual observer is permitted to know.

Many years ago I worked among the beautiful, cool forests of maple-leaved obeche skirting the craggy bluffs of Ondo Province. It was festival time, and I was delighted to be invited to a soirée being held at one of the picturesque little villages scattered around the ancient town of Ondo. Darkness had fallen by the time I arrived and already the huge tropic moon had edged her way up over the black silhouettes of the crags that stood sentinel around us.

The night air vibrated to the rhythm of drums and the musical tinkling of tiny "calabash pianos". Dancing girls, naked from the waist up, shimmied around in the dust of the compound, their ebony bodies gleaming with perspiration in the silvery, spectral moonlight. Gourds of palm wine and bottles of the traditional illicit "gin" were much in evidence. The old chief grinned tipsily at me from the shadows. I sat down beside him and accepted the customary offering of gin and kolanut. The gin was raw and evil smelling. The kolanut was dry and bitter as gall.

Much, much later I found myself tucking into a bowl of thin and very peppery stew. It was quite good, though, and I asked the chief what sort of meat it contained. "'Dog," he said briefly

Maybe it was, indeed, dog. But to this day I sometimes wonder. I cannot help recalling that he had a wicked glint in his eye as he spoke, and it is a fact that he and a collection of minor chiefs were arrested later that year for the suspected ritual murders of children . . .

Pagan mythology has not always been the instigator of happy malarkey. More often than not, tribal tenets are carried from generation to generation on undercurrents of sheer terror – fear of enemies, known and unknown, and of the malignant spirits that haunt the dark corners of the forest by night and by day. Greatest of all, though, is the dread of the secret societies that ply their evil trade along the Coast from Sierra Leone to the Congo. They are all-powerful, and they have a terrible hold over the lives of those in whose domain they fester. They rule entirely by fear, and the stench of blood is never too far from the nostrils wherever they gather to practice their odious rites.

Colonial governments did their best to eradicate the more barbaric practices of the societies. They never managed to stamp them out completely but they were successful in curbing some of their more public excesses. Mostly, though, the cults – secretive enough before – were simply driven underground. They became even more clandestine in their activities. Fishermen all along the Gulf of Guinea now had to exercise extreme care when the time came to smother newborn babies in the mud of their shores to propitiate their gods. Likewise, deep in the forests of the Ivory Coast the hunters of the little bush elephant had to keep a good lookout while stuffing infants into the bellies of their newly slaughtered prey. Those who flouted the colonial laws soon found out that a Christian death by hanging was just as final as – if less protracted than – death by ritual sacrifice.

Nothing much changed in Liberia. In this quasi-American colony – the self-styled "Land of the Free" – the secret societies flourished. Unfettered by the irksome restraints imposed by the administrators of French and British territories, the Liberian cults ran riot. Indeed, there were times when they virtually ruled the nation. It is no coincidence that in recent times this country has had to endure a succession of the most corrupt and brutally repressive regimes in the turbulent history of West Africa.

In my time [1950s and 1960s], cannibalism certainly existed on the Coast. It probably still does in remote areas. But wherever it did occur, I never knew it to be anything more than ritual cannnibalism. I have met those who claimed to have eaten human flesh, but never as a gastronomic preference. It has never been too hard to find proof of this – the mangrove swamps and sluggish estuaries of the Coast have always provided a handy repository for what was left of cadavers after the societies have finished with them. From time to time along that lonely shoreline, bits and pieces of what had once been human beings would be washed ashore and the same grim rumours would be recycled on the bush telegraph. The cults were back in business.

The Leopard Society was a particular menace. The cool nights of the harmattan at the end of the year would invariably herald a renewal of its activities. Workers on rubber and tea plantations trembled in their huts at night, afraid to venture out for fear of attack. Women living in remote areas were particularly vulnerable when collecting firewood or going down to the river at sunset. The body would be left where it dropped, with deep lacerations on the back and neck to simulate leopard attack. The human involvement was usually evidenced by the fact that the heart would be missing – excised neatly from the body and carried off into the forest for the macabre rituals.

After their annual orgies, the members of this most elusive of all African cults seemed to vanish into thin air. But not always into complete anonymity, for few secrets can remain hidden in the forests of the White Man's Grave. For a time, I had a Leopard Man working for me – not that I was aware of this fact when I employed him. Indeed, I did not become aware of it until after he died.

I had hired him as a humble trace-cutter for my survey gang and the thing most immediately noticeable about him was his heavily cicatriced face, which gave him the appearance of an ornately decorated black pot. The other memorable thing about him was his veritable jaw-breaker of a name – Mgbemezirinnandi Obi.

Apart from his quite startling facial markings, though, he was just about the most nondescript human being I had ever seen in my life. He was little more than pygmy-sized, as thin as a stick-insect, and he had the furtive, browbeaten air of the archetypal henpecked husband. But he had no wives that I ever heard of nor – unusually for an African – did he show the slightest desire for the company of either women or men. He was the complete loner, to the extent that even his fellow workers shunned him. Perhaps this alone should have sounded warning bells for me, for the average African is a carefree, gregarious sort of person, not given to long, introspective silences. But he was a reliable worker, going about his allotted tasks quietly and efficiently enough, albeit with a sort of obsequious resignation. When, towards the end of the year, he asked for a couple of weeks off work to return to his home-land far to the east as his father was dying, I readily acquiesced. I never saw him again.

I suppose that he would have faded forever from my memory but for the way in which his life ended. Some months later I was summoned to my headquarters, a sprawling timber port several hundred miles away on the Niger Delta. Awaiting my arrival was an English colonial police officer with whom I was already acquainted and whom I knew to be one of the country's most senior murder investigators. He quizzed me for a time about my erstwhile employee and I gave him what little information I had on the man. In the end, unable to contain my curiosity I asked him why he should be so interested in such a nonentity "Because," he replied in a matter of fact tone, "I have just shot him."

His was an interesting story. A spate of murders on the little farms bordering the Great River had been virtually ignored by the powers-that-be until the slaying of an eminent black politician's daughter. She had been struck down on her father's cocoa farm as she returned to her hut in the evening with a pan of water on her head. Like the other victims, she had been mutilated, her neck and shoulders ripped open by razor-sharp claws. Her heart had been removed.

The wheels of justice, hitherto so leaden of movement when the victims had been simple peasants, now went into overdrive. Armed police were drafted in from all over the region for surveillance duties. My friend was in charge of them. Sitting on a log by the edge of a plantation one moonlight night with a double-barrelled shotgun cradled on his knee, he saw a shadowy figure emerge from the bush about fifteen yards away. He flicked on his torch. Caught in the sudden glare of light, the figure paused, startled, then dived like a rabbit for the cover of the trees. Without hesitation, the policeman fired.

Mgbemezirinnandi Obi was stone dead when his executioner reached him, riddled through and through by the heavy buckshot. On his body were the terrible tools of his trade: the leopard skin tied securely around his head and shoulders, the deadly claws of iron strapped to his fingers, and the long, thin-bladed knife for butchering his victims.

Small, obsequious men fill me with disquiet to this day, and the Biblical exhortation that the meek shall inherit the earth no longer has the salutary effect upon me that it used to have.

FLY RIVER, NEW GUINEA

Daumori. It faces the Fly River island of Adulu, an island overgrown with jungle where, I'm told, the Magic Fire Spirits live. The spirits can be seen at night, riding the Fly River in their dugout canoes, fire trailing behind them. These spirits also live in the sky, up by the stars, and visit their brothers on earth by riding down on a path of fire. Their job is to seek out bad people. Few are safe; the spirits' justice is fierce and irreversible. When they come to you and touch you, their fire goes out and you will rot and die. The body will wither. The inner flame dies.

The children of Daumori tell me these stories, their eyes wide. They truly believe in the Magic Fire Spirits, telling me that the spirits turn invisible when they land on earth and that, as soon as they touch the unsuspecting bad people, the sinners begin to rot. A marvellous idea! I picture the world's tyrants decaying away, skin peeling, extremities falling off. At last, reduced to a mere skeleton of their former selves, the bad men stare in perplexed awe at the night sky . . .

The kids tuck their knees inside their T-shirts, shivering from the cold. Cold! I can't believe it, the days and nights in New Guinea are always so sultry. I sit with them on the bank of the wide river; my legs dangling over the edge of the shore. The Fly's pale water creeps past, the wind creating tiny waves. I tell them the stories I'd heard about Tahitian ghosts; they can appreciate the tales of animal spirits following lone travellers into the night. They want more and more stories, and the night seems to grow thicker around us. Only the flames of the huts' cooking fires intrude on the darkness.

In the distance, some village men beat on enormous, hollowed-out logs – *garamut* drums – and sing. Their songs are droning, mesmerizing tunes, while the surrounding immensity of water and jungle have me feeling as small and inconsequential as the most distant of the stars. The children keep my reveries company, ignoring the reprimands of the older kids and touching my hair every chance they get.

Above us, the stars reign. I study them. For some reason, everything ceases to matter whenever I look at the stars. I've always known this. Yet, I so seldom looked at them back home. City life prevented it. But so did all the daily concerns which had come to consume my life – school job, responsibility. Here in New Guinea, the brightness of the night sky overpowers us all in the village; it is an imperious presence we pay homage to. Our own lights could never hope to drown it out.

"I wish some moments would never end," I whisper. "Why do they have to end?"

A couple of children start to braid my hair. All around, the jungle sits in weighted silence.

When the stories run out, and the children grow tired, I reluctantly call it a night. I head back to the hut where I'm staying, and am caught by the sight of a bush that looks bewitched. Thousands of white lights swirl around it, diving and flashing and rising up into the starry sky. I imagine that it is here, in this very place, that the gods of the universe create the stars and send them up into the heavens. I cautiously step toward the bush, discovering the cause: fireflies. A bush alight with them. Thousands and thousands. On the branches, they scramble upon each other. Hundreds swarm about me while a few intrepid ones fly off into the night.

This evening the Old Ones want to tell me about when the missionaries came to Daumori.

Their voices sound like low murmurs. The dim kerosene lamp reflects off of their blind eyes – glimmering blue cataract eyes which don't move, yet possess an unsettling omniscience. The woman is supposedly 95 years old, the man 93. They sit quietly in the corner of the hut with the kerosene lamp's light catching on their white hair and the dustiness of their skin. I sit near them, and a man from the village, Salle ("Sal-lay"), acts as translator.

They were children when the mission men had come. The mission men wore black clothes, carried strange objects with many leaves inside. (Salle laughs. "A book!" he says to me.) The Old Ones had heard of such things, and had seen such strange creatures before, so they weren't scared. But maybe the mission men were, because they never stayed long in Daumori. However, one man finally stayed behind. "He showed pictures of a *waitman* with long hair which is Jeesis."

The men of the village did not like this mission man, so one night they hit him over the head and killed him. Then they made a big fire to cook him. They ate his book with the leaves, and his clothes and his body. They ate everything except the tough skin he wore on his feet. ("His shoes," Salle explains.) That part tasted terrible, and couldn't be easily cut, so they had to throw it to the pigs. After that, they didn't see a mission man for a long time. They didn't see his Jeesis for a long time, either.

SIERRA LEONE EATING HABITS

10 May 2000

Sitting in the shade of a mango tree in Vice-President of Sierra Leone Foday Sankoh's hometown of Bo, Francis told me about "rebel stew". Shaking with terror at the recollection, casting nervous glances over his shoulder – and at the psychologist who had been deprogramming this boy soldier – he said he had been press ganged into an army infantry unit as a sort of servant when it overran a position held by Sankoh's Revolutionary United Front (RUF).

"We were starving," Francis whispered, tears in his eyes, pleading for a form of compassion he could not find for himself. "The huts all around were burning. A few of the rebels were killed and the rest ran away, vanished into the bush. We were so hungry, so hungry. We saw that they had left a pot of food on their fire, there was hot tea too, we were so hungry," he sighed. "It was good food. I had not eaten like that for months, not since I was taken from my home and made to join the army. It was really good. I dug down for more meat with my knife. When I pulled it up, a hand hung from it – a human hand."

At that point, Francis collapsed forward, shivering as if he had suddenly been seized by a bout of malaria. Around us flies buzzed in the stunned silence.

This was in 1995, four years after Sankoh had launched his "revolution" in the name of agrarian reform and for the peasants who were not getting their share of Sierra Leone's fantastic mineral resources. In just four years of bush warfare Sankoh had taken a grip on the heart of darkness. He had harnessed the deepest human fears and distorted traditional animistic belief into a voodoo that made the muggy air which hangs over Sierra Leone's interior seem misty with rot, blood and terror.

After reaching corporal in Sierra Leone's colonial army, Sankoh became a photographer and video cameraman in Bo. In the 1960s and 1970s he made a decent living, taking wedding snaps for the mainly Lebanese diamond dealers who worked closely with government officials to bypass taxes. In Bo he learned that he who controls Sierra Leone's diamonds owns the country.

The gems, whose prices are guaranteed by De Beers' Central Selling Organization, were an instant cash producer requiring no more than a shovel and some elbow grease to mine. The alluvial stones, highly prized by jewellers, are dug from pits a few feet deep. Last year the diamond areas under his control produced, officially, only $30 million. But another $300 million was shipped out through Liberia, which has almost no diamonds. The fields around Bo, Kono and Koidu, in eastern Sierra Leone, are pockmarked with individual digs, making the countryside look like a First World War battlefield.

In the late 1960s and early 1970s Sankoh spent a few years in jail for plotting one of the country's many coups. There he developed a taste for power and the "agrarian" revolutionary theory; this, apparently, singled out the Krio, a Creole race of returned Caribbean slaves who founded Sierra Leone at the turn of the century, for particular contempt. Later his aim seems to have been to destroy the Krio and return his country to "truly black" rule. Instead, most of his victims were – and remain – the rural poor.

Sankoh learned at the feet of Africa's other master of despotism, Charles Taylor, now President of Liberia, where he was based in

1990–1991. Both countries have a tradition of secret societies, a sort of pre-medieval masonry. These societies meet most often at night; their participants wear masks symbolic of spirits and ancestors sent to guide them, or wild animals and other fetishes. In times of trouble they served to hold communities together and as a means of distributing scarce resources without argument.

Myth has it that, very occasionally, blood sacrifices would extend to include the killing of a human being. Human boy parts are much prized in witchcraft all over Africa for their potency (only last week a Johannesburg witchdoctor was arrested after the body of a child was found under his shop floor). But in Sierra Leone no anthropologist had ever proved the existence of human sacrifice, much less the cannibalism that was said to follow.

That is, not until Sankoh's "revolution" got into full swing. Like his Liberian mentor, he discovered that the most effective way to keep his rebel army tightly knit, fast moving and, above all, obedient was by ritualistic indoctrination. The belief that eating the body of a vanquished warrior gives great strength is an ancient one. Sankoh appears to have encouraged this horrific idea and, if there was going to be any cannibalism, there would be no bystanders at the rituals. One former rebel explained that it became easy after a while, and people would fight over what they thought were the "best bits".

Sankoh added layer upon layer to his theory of leadership by terror. One of his most "brilliant" appointments was Sam "Mosquito" Bokarie, who had joined the RUF while waiting for a bus to take him to the discothèque where he worked as a dancer in Abidjan, the capital of Ivory Coast. Bokarie was inspired by the songs of young RUF recruits returning to their home country. He leapt aboard a passing truck, which took him to infamy.

He has claimed that he is called "Mosquito" not because he is a bloodsucker, but "because of my fighting style, I'm always moving, always striking". In Bokarie, Sankoh found the perfect lieutenant, a man who relished his job, who loved to kill. Together they swarmed across the countryside, terrifying young boys into joining their ranks.

Their method was a bastardization of the Jesuits' boast that, given a child before he was seven, they would make him a devout Catholic for life. The RUF targeted pre-teens – "pre-moral" – boys, who would be forced to kill or rape, then be given drugs to dull the pain that followed.

Soon these prepubescent boys became ideal killing machines. They knew nothing other than violence, and no other way to survive.

Last year, when Sankoh launched "Operation No Living Thing" against Freetown, his army of child soldiers had little trouble interpreting their orders. They killed indiscriminately, burnt the eastern third to the ground and enjoyed an orgy of mutilations that amounted to slow murder. The question "long sleeve or short sleeve?" asked by a boy of maybe a dozen years means simply: "'Do you want me to chop off your arm at the bicep or at the wrist?" It makes little difference to Sierra Leoneans. The loss of both hands means the end of a farmer's life and is a death sentence to his young children, too.

Sometimes an entire family of double amputees, the white of their newly exposed bones glinting in the tropical sunshine, would arrive at Freetown's Connaught Hospital and stand silently in line waiting for treatment.

"Even suicide is a struggle when you've got no hands," said an old man. A former schoolteacher, he was crouched on the floor of the operating theatre, laughing drily. "Someone has kindly popped some painkillers in my shirt pocket. How do I get them out again?" he asked.

Sankoh forced his way into a power-sharing deal with Johnny Paul Koroma, an officer who deposed the democratically elected Ahmed Tejan Kabbah soon after he was elected in 1996. In 1998, when his RUF forces were driven out by Nigerian and other West African soldiers, he was arrested, tried, and sentenced to death for treason and murder. In jail, he drove other prisoners to distraction with his nocturnal ravings.

"That bastard howls like a wolf. He jabbers to himself all night, and then gets up and says he feels fine. We've had to move him out of earshot," said a Nigerian officer guarding his prison.

By that time Sankoh appeared unhinged, but his men remained loyal to his movement and managed to infiltrate Freetown – just as they were reported to be doing again this week. In January last year they came close to driving out the Nigerians and sacking the entire city. Sankoh sat in his prison while the Nigerians and President Kabbah ignored advisers who told them to carry out the death sentence – instead, he was rehabilitated by a British- and American-sponsored, United Nations-backed peace accord.

He emerged, blinking, from jail with the title of Vice-President and the minerals portfolio. Almost immediately he insisted that the diamond industry should be "cleaned up" – which meant driving the Lebanese traders out and securing the lion's share of gems for himself.

It was clear that peace could not last. The camps set up to demobilize fighters became conflict flash points. His men handed over only 4,000 rifles, although his boy soldiers numbered at least 15,000. At that time Chief Sam Hinga Norman, who controlled the Kamajors, a militia that had remained loyal to the Government, said: "You can't make deals with a man possessed by demons."

Recent history has proved the chief right in many respects. And Sankoh has shown no sign that he has the remotest purchase on reality. Not long ago he told the Freetown *Concord Times* that he does not need to eat: "I am fed by some supernatural force," he explained. On why he had launched yet another offensive, he was no less stable: "I heard a voice that commanded me to liberate my people," he insisted.

21 May 2000

When today Sankoh, Sierra Leone's captured rebel leader, was asked why he had his wife and three children murdered, the reply was chilling and direct: "I will get another when the war is over, so what does it matter?"

Her sin? He suspected her of treachery. There were others, too. In a purge carried out on their village in the east of the country, up to 1,000 people were butchered; some were tied up with ropes before having hot palm oil poured over their naked bodies. For a man whose rebel movement is believed to have dismembered 50,000 men, women and children, and who is reputed to have fifteen wives, such brazen savagery was second nature. In almost a decade of civil war, his followers in the RUF, burned, looted, maimed, killed and ate their enemies in ritual cannibalistic practices.

Last week his reign came to an end. As he peered from the back of a car on his way to prison, Sankoh no longer resembled the murderous psychopath whose name had inspired terror. Arrested last Wednesday morning, a stone's throw from his house in the capital, Freetown, he was exhausted, hungry and subdued after nine days on the run. Suddenly he had shrunk into the pathetic wedding photographer he once was. Stripped, beaten and wounded, Sankoh was nearly lynched and had to be put into the hands of the SAS for his own safety. He was whisked away in a British special forces helicopter, and today he is in

Sierra Leonean custody, his whereabouts a secret known only to senior British and United Nations officials.

Although details of the atrocities committed by Sankoh and his henchmen are now emerging, mystery remains about how a farmer's son turned into one of Africa's most powerful psychopaths. There was little sign of Sankoh's festering evil in his childhood. He was born sixty-four years ago into a poor farming family in the north of the country. Like many locals, he joined the Poro, a secret society that initiated boys into manhood. "He was shy and talked slowly. He did not read books and did no sport," says Abu Conteh, a childhood friend.

Sankoh's recollection of his youth is somewhat different. In an interview with *West African* magazine, he paints a picture of a tough upbringing in which he set traps for wild animals, fought with his brothers and staged ambushes for children from other villages. "We used to fight them and my group was always on top. They used to call me the warrior," he boasted, showing the scar that he still bore from one encounter.

He disregarded his father's advice and joined the army in 1956 after being enlisted by a British colonial officer. There was no hint of passionate rebellion in him – the seeds of revolt would be sown after the British had given Sierra Leone independence in 1961. In the following years, self-rule plunged the country into a cycle of corruption, deepening poverty and incompetence. Sankoh was not alone in resenting this collapse. After being jailed for seven years for his part in an abortive coup, he told Conteh, who was also imprisoned: "I will wait, I will take my revenge."

Nobody believed him. He was only a former corporal of moderate intellect. But he was deadly serious about building up an underground movement from scratch. When he came out of jail, he moved to Bo, Sierra Leone's second city and the home of Lebanese diamond dealers, and started recruiting. It is believed he masterminded the murder of two gem traders, found robbed with their throats cut, to obtain the funds he needed to embark on his campaign to seize power.

It was his passion for photography, which he had learnt in Britain while in the army several years before, that provided Sankoh with the perfect cover. Sent for training at the School of Infantry in Hythe, Kent, he completed a twelve-week signals instructor's course. He did not excel and left with a low grade. At the end of the training, he went to the army's Kinema Corporation at nearby Shorecliff for a cinematography course. This, he says, would later prove crucial in putting together his revolutionary organization.

"The government looks down on cameramen. What can a cameraman do?" he said in his *West African* magazine interview. In the innocent guise of a photographer, he toured villages up and down the country, politicizing students and villagers while snapping portraits.

Sankoh has always shied away from discussing his Libyan connections, but his followers say he was trained there in the early 1980s, together with a group of radical students expelled from Sierra Leone's university because of their connections with a Gadaffi study group. The meddlesome Libyan leader was obsessed with expanding Libyan influence into West Africa and attracted a following from disaffected youth across the region.

Sankoh is believed to have spent many months in Libya, where many in Sierra Leone believe he trained with Charles Taylor, currently president of neighbouring Liberia. Taylor was then a rebel, destined to play a sinister role in Sierra Leone's own civil war when it erupted in 1991 after Sankoh, operating from Liberia, gave the military government ninety days to democratize. With Taylor's help, Sankoh's men took over the eastern diamond mines. Sankoh used the money from the gems to buy weapons and fund his rebellion.

Taylor also profited and provided him with many Liberian fighters from the maneating Geo tribe. Ritual cannibalism – eating parts of the human body to take on extra powers – is part of the culture. Dried pieces of human meat are occasionally found in remote jungle markets and relatives have had to guard the graves of dead family members to ensure their corpses were not dug up and eaten.

There is no evidence that Sankoh was a practitioner, but it was taken up with gusto by his fighters. Corinne Dufka, who spent a year in Sierra Leone until this spring for Human Rights Watch, said she had been told of numerous cases of cannibalism, although it was as prevalent among the pro-government Kamajor militiamen. Witnesses describe people being roasted and having their hearts cut out in the heat of battle. At the same time, many fighters were decapitated.

"There was one demobilized child soldier who gave me a detailed description of how they caught Ecomog soldiers (West African peace-keepers) during the January 1999 offensive, tying them up and cutting out their livers and describing how they cooked them. I've heard it from enough people that I tend to believe it," said Dufka.

According to witnesses, everyone present had to participate. One former rebel said that, after a while, it became easy and people would fight over the "best bits".

A government soldier – part of a force that overran an RUF position – told how, after weeks without adequate food, they started eating stew from a pot. "It was really good," he said. "I dug down for more meat with my knife. When I pulled it up, a hand hung from it, a human hand."

Indeed, under Sankoh, the RUF committed some of the worst atrocities Africa has seen. They included amputations by machetes of hands, arms, legs, ears and buttocks, the gouging out of eyes, rape, injections with acid, burning victims alive and beatings. Sankoh made killing machines out of his raw recruits, many of whom were illiterate children kidnapped from villages. To control them he let them take drugs. Deprived of their own will, they came to believe that the plump, bearded leader they knew as "Papa" had magical powers that enabled him to appear and disappear at will.

He and his RUF thugs are believed to have hacked off the hands, arms, legs and even lips of men, women and children alike. Boy soldiers as young as twelve have asked their victims: "Long sleeve or short sleeve?" giving them, the choice of having their arm amputated at the shoulder or the wrist. The youngest known victim was a twenty-month-old baby. Girls held as sex slaves by the rebels have wandered into hospitals with arms missing.

Sankoh sometimes gave conflicting messages, followers said. Once he issued orders that anyone caught raping should be executed. One of his lieutenants, Rashid Mansaray, also Libyan-trained, shot two rebels who had raped villagers. Yet Sankoh had him put in prison. Later, he had Rashid and other henchmen killed in a bloody purge.

The two biggest constants in his drive for power have always been diamonds and women. He enjoyed both in abundance as leader of a force that controlled Sierra Leone's diamond mines and, therefore, most of the country's wealth. His generosity, lavish spending and womanizing are well known and he has several mistresses. The Libyans provided Sankoh with $500,000, which he carried in a brief-case, but it lasted just six months and was spent on sybaritic pleasures. He once gave $6,000 to a mistress who needed appeasing, a former aide recalled last week.

The rebel leader has never shown any compassion for the human suffering he caused. He was fond of quoting the saying: "When a lion and an elephant are fighting, the grass is going to suffer."

His capture last week was a humiliating end for a man known and feared throughout Sierra Leone as the "Lion". His outwardly gentle demeanour took a lot of people in, but Deen Jalloh, a former RUF member who knew him, said he was interested in only one thing – personal power.

"He claimed to be influenced by Gadaffi and Mao Tse-tung and to want genuine reform, but it was nonsense," Jalloh said. "I thought he had ideas. I once suggested I prepare a manifesto for a shadow government. "Don't worry about that. Let the guns talk," Sankoh said. "He was not interested in reading. We would write beautiful speeches for him to present to the people, but he did not care and read them badly. He would not allow anyone who had soft hands to guide him."

May 2000

Sia was 11 when her elder sister was killed in front of her. She did not have time to weep. She was abducted by an RUF rebel soldier, taken to his commander and made a "bush wife" – a sex slave who is kept in a command post and raped repeatedly by soldiers.

When they were bored, the rebels sent her into villages they planned to attack on "missions" – to sleep with Nigerian Ecomog soldiers to find out information. "I was a spy," she says. "I gave them sex and they gave me information. Then we would kill them."

Before long the RUF realized her value. They made her a captain. She went through an initiation rite which included carrying out her first killing, eating the victim's heart and liver, being cut all over her own body and injecting her wounds with drugs. Sia, who is now 18, still has the scars, deep angry marks which run down her arms and neck. At first she is embarrassed to admit what they are.

Sia spent seven years with RUF before the UN found her in the bush and brought her to St Michael's Lodge, a rehabilitation camp run by two tireless Xavieran priests, which shelters 152 former child soldiers. Sia has been at the centre for more than one year.

"I'm tired of killing," she says. "I'm not taking drugs, so I don't feel the need to go out and kill." Now she is training as a hairdresser.

An estimated 5,400 children have been forced into combat in the Sierra Leone conflicts. The initiation is brutal – beatings, indoctrination, torture and drugs. According to one Unicef report last year, children often make better killers because their conscience is not yet fully developed.

Sia recalls: "They knew I would be a good soldier, so they began training me – weapon training, manoeuvres, how to kill close up with a pistol. They gave me two pistols for close range. I always saw the people before I killed them. I checked if they were dead, then I gave them another shot in the head if they weren't." She says that she was stoned when she did this. She snorted "brown-brown" (cocaine), took "red tablets" and "white tablets" (believed to be amphetamines or crack), "blueboats" (crack and was injected with "medicine" (cocaine or speed) that "made me strong and made me want to go out and kill".

She was so good at killing and cutting off limbs that she began to train younger children – captured five- six- and seven-year-olds. "She was a good teacher," says Anthony, now 11. "Sia told us to kill or she would kill us. So we killed."

Alhough Sia will talk willingly about the killings, she is embarrassed by amputations, which she calls "cuttings". She says that one of her other children would hold down the victims while she brought down the axe on their elbow or wrist. "I cut people big and small, big and small. I couldn't kill everybody, so the ones I didn't kill, I cut."

Sia now plans to move into her own house in Freetown with her boyfriend, another child soldier, whose *nom de guerre* in the bush was "Killer".

From the outside, St Michael's looks like a rundown holiday camp in the middle of the bush. Outside the window of the bungalows where the boys live, the Atlantic Ocean breaks on an idyllic beach. The boys, drawn from all the militia factions, swim on Sunday after Mass where many now sing gospel in the choir. The two priests, one Spanish, one Italian, spend months, sometimes years, trying to enable the boys to function in the real world. There is a glazed look in many of their eyes. When they talk of their experiences, some become aggressive.

Momoh, 17, spent five years as a soldier for the Sierra Leone Army (SLA). His dark eyes grow hostile when he recalls the cannibalism he committed, the murders and the rape.

"When he first got here, he used to complain that he needed to eat a human liver," says Father Chema, a young, bearded priest who has long hair and wears shorts, a T-shirt and sandals. "Some of the other boys, when I try to break up fights, scream at me: 'You can't tell me what to do! I drank human blood!' They are not lying – all of the children speak of cannabilism and eating the organs of their first victim."

It takes three months for them to trust the priests. "We first make them feel safe and secure, then we talk to them all the time," says Father Chema. One boy, Prince, aged nine, is so traumatized that he clings to the priest's legs and is unable to talk about his experiences at all. Going inside the mind of a child killer is a disturbing prospect, but the priests approach it with patience, faith and good humour.

The boys, many of whom lived like kings in the bush with sex slaves, drugs and looted goods, now live in poverty.

"When they arrive, we first have to get them off drugs, which is hard," says Father Chema. "And then we have to break the chain of command that they established in the bush. Then we talk to them, talk to them, talk to them. They scream at night for a long time."

Alhough all the militias forced children into combat, the RUF has a particularly nasty reputation: they called their looting "Operation Pay Yourself" and the killing sprees "Operation No Living Thing".

Even if these children are taken out of the bush and rehabilitated, they still are not safe. "If the town people recognize them as the former rebels and killers, they want to kill them," says Father Berton. "So I tell them, make friends, make friends. Your friends will protect you. ID cards and documents mean nothing."

Because part of the initiation rite can involve killing a relative – either a parent or an uncle – or amputations on family members, many can never go home. Because of the tension and the threat of the rebel invasion of Freetown, most of the boys are afraid to go to town where they might be recognized by some of their victims or their families, or by their former commanders. Father Chema admits, in a weary voice, that their re-integration into society is a long and delicated process.

"We do not hold them, they are free to go," says Father Berton. "I tell them that to be a noble soldier, you need to be eighteen and in the right mind. The fact that not one of them went back to join their militias is a sign that they are trying to change."

Part 2

Blood on the Lowlands

ISSEDONES AND INDIANS

Born around 490 BC in Halicarnassus on the south-west coast of what is now Turkey, Herodotus wrote the first masterpiece of European prose: Histories *is built around the great struggle between Greek freedom and oriental despotism.*

While this historical epic forms the main theme of Herodotus's narrative, he fleshes out the text with dozens of digressions. He describes, for example, the monuments, crocodile-hunters and natural wonders of Egypt, the warriors of the Sudan, various Indian sects, and the tribes of Europe and the Near East.

To the north and east lives another Scythian tribe, which moved into these parts after revolting from the Royal Scythians to which it originally belonged. As far as this, the country I have been describing is a level plain with good deep soil, but further on it becomes rugged and stony; beyond this region, which is of great extent, one comes to the foothills of a lofty mountain chain, and a nation of bald men. They are said to be bald from birth, women and men alike, and to have snub noses and long chins; they speak a peculiar language, dress in the Scythian fashion, and live on the fruit of a tree called ponticum – a kind of cherry – which is about the size of a fig tree and produces a stoned fruit as large as a bean. They strain the ripe fruit through cloths and get from it a thick dark-coloured juice which they call *aschy*. They lap the juice up with their tongues, or mix it with milk for a drink, and make cakes out of the thick sediment which it leaves. They have but few sheep, as the grazing is poor. Every man lives under his ponticum tree, which he protects in winter with bands of thick white felt, taking them off in the summer. These people are supposed to be protected by a mysterious sort of sanctity; they carry no arms and nobody offers them violence; they settle disputes amongst their neighbours, and anybody who seeks asylum amongst them is left in peace. They are called Argippaei.

As for the bald men, a great deal is known of the country and of the people to the south and west from the reports, which are easy enough to come by, of Scythians who visit them, and of Greeks who frequent the trading port on the Dnieper and other ports along the Black Sea coast. The Scythians who penetrate as far as this do their business through seven interpreters in seven languages. Beyond the Argippaei, however, lies a region of which no one can give an accurate account, for further progress is barred by a lofty and impassable range of mountains. The bald men themselves tell the tale (which I do not believe) that the mountains are inhabited by a goat-footed race, beyond which, still further north, are men who sleep for six months in the year – which to my mind is utterly incredible. East of the Argippaei, however, the country is definitely known to be inhabited by the Issedones; but the region north of those two nations is unknown, apart from the stories they themselves tell of it.

Some knowledge of the customs of the Issedones has come through to us: when a man's father dies, his kinsmen bring sheep to his house as a sacrifidal offering; the sheep and the body of the dead man are cut into joints and sliced up, and the two sorts of meat, mixed together, are served and eaten. The dead man's head, however, they gild, after stripping off the hair and cleaning out the inside, and then preserve it as a sort of sacred image, to which they offer sacrifice. Son does this to father, just as the Greeks observe ancestral commemoration.

In other respects the Issedones appear to have a sound sense of justice and among them men and women have equal authority . . .

The whole region I have been describing has excessively hard winters; for eight months in the year the cold is intolerable; the ground is frozen iron-hard, so that to turn earth into mud requires not water but fire. The sea freezes over, and the whole of the Cimmerian Bosphorus; and the Scythians, who live outside the trench which I mentioned previously, make war upon the ice, and drive waggons across it to the country of the Sindi. Even apart from the eight months' winter, the remaining four months are cold; and a further point of difference between the winters here and in all other parts of the world is that here, in Scythia, no rain worth mentioning falls during the season when one would naturally expect it, whereas throughout the summer it never stops. There are no thunderstorms during what is the usual season for them elsewhere, but only in the summer, when they are very violent; a winter thunderstorm is looked upon as a prodigy, as are earthquakes whether in summer or winter. Horses stand the winter well, but mules and donkeys cannot stand it at all; this is unusual, for elsewhere mules and donkeys bear cold easily, but horses kept standing during hard weather, are subject to frostbite. I think the cold may explain the fact that the cattle in this part of the world have no horns . . .

There are many tribes of Indians, speaking different languages, some pastoral and nomadic, others not. Some live in the marsh-country by the river and eat raw fish, which they catch from boats made of reeds – each boat made from a single joint. The people of this tribe make their clothes from a sort of rush which grows in the river, gathering it and beating it out, and then weaving it into a kind of matting which they wear to cover their chests, like a breastplate.

Another tribe further to the east is nomadic, known as the Padaei; they live on raw meat. Among their customs, it is said that when a man falls sick, his closest companions kill him, because, as they put it, their meat would be spoilt if he were allowed to waste away with disease. The invalid, in these circumstances, protests that there is nothing the matter with him – but to no purpose. His friends refuse to accept his protestations, kill him and hold a banquet. Should the sufferer be a woman, her woman friends deal with her in the same way. If anyone is lucky enough to live to an advanced age, he is offered in sacrifice before the banquet – this, however, rarely happens; because most of them will have had some disease or other before they get old, and will consequently have been killed by their friends.

There is another tribe which behaves very differently: they will not take life in any form; they sow no seed, and have no houses and live on a vegetable diet. There is a plant which grows wild in their country, and has seeds in a pod about the size of millet seeds; they gather this, and boil and eat it, pod and all. In this tribe, a sick man will leave his friends and go away to some deserted spot to die – and nobody gives a thought either to his illness or death . . .

CELTS IN ENGLAND

Archaeologists from Bristol University have uncovered evidence for the most recent cannibalism in the British Isles in a cave at Alveston, South Gloucestershire.

Dr Mark Horton, Reader in Archaeology, has been working with a local caving group who made the discovery of numerous bones, some ten metres below ground. Radiocarbon dating of the bones from the cave suggests that they were buried around 2,000 years ago, at the very end of the Iron Age or the beginning of the Roman occupation.

Last September the full horror of the cave's grisly contents came to light.

About five per cent of the bone deposit has so far been excavated, and the remains of at least seven individuals have been discovered. At least one had been murdered, as the rear of the skull was first pole-axed and then smashed inwards; another bone showed evidence of a deformity, and a third showed traces of Paget's Disease. But the most interesting find was an adult human femur, which had been split longitudinally and the bone marrow scraped out. This practice, which cannot happen accidentally, is considered to be very good evidence of cannibalistic activity.

The clue as to why these bones were placed in the cave comes from the other finds. These included numerous dog bones, as well as the occasional cattle bone, and a possible vertebra of a bear, as well as wooden twigs.

Dr Horton said: "This was a highly structured deposit that can only have got there as a result of some form of ritual activity. This region was an important centre for underworld cults during the later Iron Age, some of which survived into the Roman period; in particular the Celtic Hound God, Cunomaglus, was represented as a dog guarding the underworld in local temple sculpture."

Archaeologists have suspected Iron Age cannibalism for some time, from bones found in rubbish pits, but this is the first time that strong evidence has been found for the practice. Roman sources describe human sacrifice among the Celts, but do not mention cannibalism. The sheer scale of cave deposits, and the identical radiocarbon dates from the bones might suggest a single great massacre and feast, perhaps involving over fifty individuals, whose remains were then placed in the cave.

THE FIRST CRUSADE

On Thursday [15 July 1999] hundreds of Christians will enter Jerusalem on a "Pilgrimage of Apology". The men, women and children on the pilgrimage, which is organized from offices in Harpenden in Hertfordshire, will walk to the site of the Temple of

Solomon, and then solemnly apologize to Muslim and Jewish leaders. For what?

Not for abandoning the Muslims in Bosnia to murder and massacre by the Orthodox Serbs, as the nominally Christian Western powers did six years ago [in 1993]; not for frustrating attempts to rescue small numbers of European Jews from extermination by Hitler in the Second World War, as Britain and America both did. No, the apology will in fact be for an event which took place on 15 July 1099: the sack of Jerusalem by the knights and foot soldiers of the First Crusade.

The predominantly evangelical Protestants who make up the "Pilgrimage of Apology" are not the only Christians who feel that apology is the most appropriate response to an event which took place 900 years ago. The Pope will publish a document next year which will also include an apology for the Crusades. Mgr Bruno Forte, a theologian on the Pope's Theological Commission, insists that the Crusades were part of a history of 'episodes of violence perpetrated by Christians . . . contrary to the commandment of Christ and therefore sinful.'

Why, nine centuries after the event do the Crusades generate such pangs of guilt? After all, the history of medieval Christendom is full of appalling massacres, tortures, rapes and murders. Come to that, so is the history of modern Christendom. The Crusades are not even unique in the way that they mixed horrific violence with professions of devout Christian piety: the conquests of Mexico and Peru four centuries later exhibited precisely the same combination of prayer and murder, as did the wars, sanctioned by the Catholic Church, against sects of Christians in south-west France condemned as heretical.

Still, the First Crusade was, even by medieval standards. exceptionally bloody. When Pope Urban II first urged Christians to "take the road to the Holy Sepulchre, rescue that land from a dreadful race and rule over it yourselves," he seemed to have no idea that thousands would take him at his word.

The Pope was himself responding to a plea by Alexius Comnenus, the Emperor of Byzantium, for reinforcements in his battle against Muslim forces which had gobbled up large parts of his empire.

Alexius was astonished and deeply alarmed when, instead of a few mercenaries, three whole armies of "barbarians" turned up. The most reliable estimates suggest a total of about 35,000 crusaders: 4,500 knights with horses, the rest foot soldiers. Alexius wanted to get rid of them as fast as possible. The crusaders – Alexius called them Franks – were known to be big, strong. extremely violent and totally untrustworthy. His daughter Anna described one of them, the Norman general Bohemond: "His stature was such that he towered over the tallest men . . . There was a certain charm about him, but it was dimmed by the alarm his person inspired. There was a hard, savage quality to his whole aspect. Even his laugh sounded like a threat."

And Bohemond was one of the more civilized of the crusaders. Among the army there were a number of survivors from the People's Crusade, an unofficial movement made up of perhaps 20,000 people, many of them women and children, fleeing famine and hardship in their own lands. Most of them, having massacred Jews wherever they found them on the way, were themselves enslaved or massacred in Bulgaria or in the doomed attempt to take the city of Nicea in Turkey.

A few survived to join the main crusading armies. According to Guibert of Nogent one of the crusaders who could write and who left an account of what he saw on the First Crusade, these men "marched barefoot, baring no arms, and had no money at all. Entirely filthy in nakedness and want, they lived on the roots of plants." Or on the flesh of Muslims: the "Tafurs" as they were known, developed a taste for human meat. They revelled in their reputation as maneaters.

"In full view of the enemy," Guibert explains, "they roasted the bruised body of a Turk for eating."

The crusading army had to resort to cannibalism several times on the trek to Jerusalem. During the siege of Ma'arra (a city near Antioch in Syria), for instance, Fulcher of Chartres, who was there, describes how "our people were so frenzied by hunger that they tore the flesh from the Saracens who had died there, which they chewed and devoured, even," he adds in outrage, "though it had been insufficiently cooked."

Despite famine, disease, battles and sieges, the Crusaders managed to hold together and to repel enemies, or at least terrify them into moving out of the way. But by the time it finally arrived outside the Holy City, on the evening of Tuesday, 7 June 1099, nearly three years after the original expedition had begun, the Crusading army was down to about one third of its original strength: 10,000 foot soldiers and about 1,000 knights.

They could not surround the whole city: they did not have enough men. Their most urgent need was water, but the garrison in Jerusalem had poisoned the wells. The Crusaders also needed wood, to build siege engines and scaling ladders, but the Muslims had also taken the precaution of cutting down all the trees. That did not put off the faithful. One of the many "holy men" travelling with the Crusading army said they should attack the city immediately. When it was pointed out to him they had no ladders with which to scale the walls, he said it did not matter: their faith would give them victory. So next day, 12 June, the army attacked. The assault was a fiasco. The soldiers were stuck at the foot of the walls. unable to climb them, and were deluged by boiling oil, burning rocks and giant boulders hurled at them by the defenders.

After that, the leaders of the Crusade – Godfrey of Bouillon. Raymond of Toulouse, Robert of Flanders and Robert of Normandy – decided to build ladders and siege-engines. They foraged for wood. They were helped by the arrival of some Genoese traders who donated their ships. But the army continued to suffer from an acute shortage of water. The nearest unpolluted supply was six miles away.

By 10 July, the Crusaders had built several giant wooden towers. It was decided to begin the assault on the night of 14 July. They had little choice: a force of Muslims from Egypt was coming to relieve the city and they knew it. During the day, the army prepared itself for the final battle with fasting and a solemn barefoot procession around the walls. In an attempt to show their contempt for their besiegers, the Muslim defenders of the city (recorded William of Tyre) "spat on crosses, and subjected them to still greater shames, outrages of which it is not decent to speak". It had the effect of sending the Crusaders into a frenzy of fury.

On the evening of the 14th, Raymond of Toulouse wheeled his tower against the walls of Jerusalem, but his men made no headway against the defenders: they could not breach the wall. "We were all numb with astonishment," noted one eyewitness, "and very frightened." Next morning, Godfrey of Bouillon moved his tower to the north wall of Jerusalem. There was a ferocious hand-to-hand battle. Two Flemish knights managed to gain a foothold on the wall. then to push the defenders from a small section of it. Hundreds of Crusaders poured in through the breach.

What happened next was dreadful. With the exception of the garrison commander and his bodyguards. who managed to buy their lives, every inhabitant of the city – man, woman and child – was killed. An army of 11,000 Crusaders massacred around 40,000 Muslims and

6,000 Jews in thirty-six hours. It is a rate of killing of unarmed non-combatants which would not be matched until the Nazi *Einsatzgruppen* in the Second World War. "Our squires and footmen," wrote Fulcher of Chartres, "split open the bellies of those they had just slain in order to extract from the intestines the gold coins which the Saracens had gulped down into their loathsome throats while alive . . . Our men ran through the city, not sparing anyone, even those who begged for mercy."

In the area by the Temple of Solomon, where the killing was most intense, the Crusaders waded up to their ankles in blood (according to one account), up to their knees in blood (according to another) or up to their horses' bridles in blood (according to a third).

The next day, the leaders ordered that all the dead should be removed "on account of the terrible stench". The Saracens who were still alive dragged the dead out in front of the gates and made piles as big as houses out of the corpses – before themselves being killed.

When the orgy of death was over, even some of the Crusaders felt it had been excessive. "The city," wrote William of Tyre – admittedly nearly a century after the massacre – "offered such a spectacle of slaughter, such a profusion of bloodshed that even the victors themselves could not help but be struck with horror and disgust." But there were no apologies. Most of the Crusaders agreed with Fulcher of Chartres, who felt the massacre was "a deed before all other deeds" which had "cleansed Jerusalem from the contagion of pagans". Soldiers in the age of faith had few doubts that in fighting and killing Muslims they were doing Christ's work. Jesus's one bellicose aphorism – "I come not to bring peace, but to give you a sword" – was very dear to the Crusaders.

It is a long way from the sentiments of Harpenden and the Pilgrimage of Apology. It is a testament to the enduring power of what happened on that day in Jerusalem 900 years ago that some Christians feel the need to ask forgiveness for it. Whether it will be understood in those terms is more debatable. Many of the Muslims and Jews of Jerusalem seem to think it is just one more attempt to convert them to Christianity. Seen in that light, the "pilgrims of forgiveness" have something in common with the men who sacked Jerusalem. The conversion of Jews and Muslims was, after all, one goal of the original Crusade.

SHERIFF BROTH

It is not often that you find a property where cannibalism has taken place, but this is the case with the Rockhall fishing station at St Cyrus, Kincardineshire.

In *Portrait of a Parish*, Duncan Fraser writes of an old castle within the grounds of the station:

> The castle was built in the early 15th century by a courtier to King James I, James Barclay, who detested the local sheriff. The King apparently told them to "go and make soup of the sheriff and sup him". Barclay and the lairds took him literally, toppled the sheriff into a boiling cauldron and one by one "had a sup of the broth".

The salmon fishing station, which was built in the mid-nineteenth century, is dilapidated. Planning permission has been obtained for it to be converted to residential or commercial use; plans suggest a four-bedroom house.

EUROPEAN "STEAK"

Scotland, as wild and lawless as the most secret heart of continental Europe until well into the sixteenth century, still has a proprietorial affection for some of her more picturesque reprobates.

As far back as AD 367, the Roman province of Britain was invaded by Picts, Scots, Saxons and Franks, reinforced by the Attacotti, a cannibal tribe from Argyllshire who later turned respectable and signed on in the Roman army. A thousand years after, there were still some who clung to the old ways, including a family that inhabited a cave near St Vigean's in Angus and lived, literally, off passing travellers. The descriptively named Christie o' the Cleek was much addicted to human flesh, and as famous for the fearsome hooked axe (the cleek) with which he hauled his victims from their ponies as he was for his gastronomic tastes. And the moss troopers of the Borders, clinging to the ancient traditions, are said to have eaten the flesh and drunk the blood of their enemies, and are reputed to have boiled a certain Lord Soulis alive and then quaffed the broth.

Best known of all, however – having been immortalized by Captain Johnson, the best-selling eighteenth-century anthologist – is Sawney (Sandy) Beane. Born not far from Edinburgh towards the end of the fourteenth century, he wandered away with a local girl and finally settled in a cave on the lonely coast of Galloway in the south-west corner of Scotland. Cattle rearing was not an occupation for an impoverished (and possibly idle) peasant, while cattle rustling was one of the most dangerous occupations imaginable at the time. Sawney and his wife made do with people.

Sallying forth from their vast and well-hidden cavern, they waylaid travellers, slaughtered them, and took them home for supper. As the family increased over the next twenty-five years – Sawney and his wife raised eight sons and six daughters, and they in turn produced (presumably incestuously) eighteen grandsons and fourteen granddaughters – the whole tribe went hunting together. People began to shun the coast road on which so many travellers mysteriously disappeared and where severed limbs were often cast up by the tide "to the Astonishment and Terror of all the Beholders". The Beanes, first and last, were estimated to have disposed of more than a thousand victims.

They were caught in the end when, one day, a party of horsemen rode into sight as the Beanes were dismembering a woman they had just killed. The Beanes fled, but were traced with the aid of bloodhounds. When the pursuers found their way into the secret recesses of the cave, they were met by the sight of arms, legs and haunches hanging from the roof as neatly as in a butcher's shop. That Mrs Beane was a thrifty housewife was proved by the discovery of other choice cuts preserved in brine. The law, however, wasted no time on compliments and the whole Beane clan was dragged back to Leith, there to be summarily and painfully exterminated in the year 1435.

At the other end of Europe and the other end of the social scale, there flourished in the second half of the same century Vlad V of Wallachia, reputedly the original of Bram Stoker's Dracula (although being a vampire does not, in fact, appear to have been one of Vlad's failings).

Vlad the Impaler, as he was affectionately known to his contemporaries, ruled the principalities of Wallachia from 1456 until 1462 and again for a short period in 1475–6, doing what he could to strengthen the central power and curb that of the *boyars*, the feudal barons, while at the same time promising improvement to the peasantry and damnation to the Turks. His methods were crude but effective.

When he heard of a plot to depose him, "he robbed the St Jacob church and set fire to the outskirts of the town [Kronstadt, in Transylvania]. And early next day he had women and men, young and old. . . impaled and had a table put in their midst and partook of breakfast with great appetite."

Some *boyars* who especially offended him were beheaded; their heads were then fed to crabs and the crabs served up at a feast attended by the relatives and friends of the victims. Mothers were thus forced, if indirectly, to eat their children, husbands their wives. When three hundred wandering Tartars rode into Wallachian territory, Vlad took the three stoutest of them "and had them fried. The others had to eat them, and he said unto them, 'You will have to eat each other in the same manner unless you go to fight the Turks'." They went.

The exploits of Vlad the Impaler, thanks to the contemporary development of movable type, became almost as popular with horror fans in the late fifteenth century as those of his reincarnation, Count Dracula, were to be with the *frisson*-seekers of the nineteenth and twentieth.

Vlad's approach to cannibalism was exploitative; he seems to have been something of a psychologist ahead of his time. But it would have needed a very professional psychiatrist indeed to handle some of the other cases that stud the pages of cannibal history.

There was the fourteen-year-old French girl who had a compulsive thirst for blood; there was the Italian brigand Gaetano Mammone, who habitually drank the blood of his captives; there were the cave dwellers on the Côte d'Azur who strangled and violated a twelve-year-old girl and then drank her blood and devoured her flesh.

MEXICAN MEALS

Historical descriptions of Aztec sacrifice and cannibalism were all made or compiled by Europeans in the sixteenth century during and after the Spanish conquest of 1521. Despite some inevitable ethnocentric exaggeration and bias, the consensus academic view does grant the accounts a core of accuracy.

The longest, most reliable and most respected ethno-historical records for Aztec society in central Mexico were compiled by Fray Bernardino de Sahagún, a Franciscan priest who first arrived in Mexico in 1529. He learned the native language, Nahuatl, and spent the rest of his life compiling a kind of encyclopedia of Aztec culture called the *General History of the Things of New Spain*. His work covers virtually all aspects of Aztec society, including detailed accounts of religion, botany, folk medidne and economics. He collected descriptions in words and pictures from Nahuatl-speaking informants and translated them into Spanish.

In Sahagún's descriptions of the Aztecs' religious ceremonies over their eighteen-month year were many sacrificial rituals when victims were dedicated to the gods. During the second month:

> Captives were killed by scalping them, taking the scalp off the top of their head . . . When the masters of these captives took their slaves to the temple where they were to be killed, they dragged them by the hair. As they pulled them up the steps of the Cu [temple], some of these captives would faint, so their owners had to drag them by their hair as far as the block where they were to die . . . After thus having torn their hearts out, and after pouring their blood into a jacara [bowl], which was given to the master of the dead slave, the body was thrown down the temple steps. From there it was taken by certain old men called Quaquaquilti, and carried to their calpul [chapel] and cut to pieces, and distributed among them to be eaten. Before cutting them up they would flay the bodies of the captives; others would dress in their skins and fight sham battles with other men.

Human sacrifice occurred in slightly different forms in honour of several deities within the Aztec pantheon. Tlaloc, god of rain and fertility identified with mountaintop shrines, had children sacrificed to him at particular ceremonies in the year, as did the feathered serpent, Quetzatcoatl, god of winds and storms. As well as sacrifice, cannibalism featured in rituals in honour of Xipe Totec, god of seeds and crops, and Huitrilopochtli, god of war, to whom the two temples on top of the great pyramid in the Aztec capital of Tenochtitlan were dedicated.

A major purpose of Aztec warfare was the procurement of enemy prisoners who would be taken back to Tenochtitlan and sacrificed in the manner described by Sahagún. This could happen on a terrifyingly large scale. Another Nahuatt-speaking monk who came to Mexico shortly after the conquest began was Fray Diego Duran, and he discussed the scale of sacrifice and cannibalism:

> I am not exaggerating; there were days in which 2,000, 3,000, 5,000 or 8,000 men were sacrificed. Their flesh was eaten and a banquet was prepared with it after the hearts had been offered to the devil.

The pioneering Mexican archaeologist Carmen Maria Pijoan Aguade has examined a number of assemblages of damaged human skeletal remains excavated around temple complexes in Tenochtitlan, over which now stands Mexico City. She analysed a series of dismembered body parts of 153 individuals excavated in 1961 by Francisco Gonzalez Rul. The remains were found near a structure called Templo Redondo that had been built between 1400 and 1420 and the burial occurred between 1418 and 1427. The majority of the skeletons had their sternum bones cut in half above the heart so were clearly sacrificial victims of the kind described by Sahagún. The analysis of Pijoan and her colleagues showed a strong pattern of cut marks on the various elements. The pattern indicated dismemberment and the removal of flesh. Young men, women and children had all been processed as part of this event.

Duran also described a colossal rack of human skulls in the central square of Tenochtitlan, clearly a form of trophy display. In 1963 excavations by Gonzalez, to the north-west of the main pyramid of Tlatelolco in Tenochtitlan, found an orderly mass of 170 skulls in front of a low platform with west-facing stairs. In 1989 three Mexican archaeologists analysed a hundred of the skull and found that only one of them didn't have either cut marks or holes on the side through which a rack pole would have been inserted. The rack holes were generally circular, having been punched through the bone by a sharp pointed punch or chisel. Their diameter varied from five to ten centimetres. The majority of the skulk had cut marks consistent with severing the head and then removing attached skin and muscle tissue . . .

Other lines of evidence also support the claims of the early writers concerning the violent rituals of the Aztecs and their attendant paraphernalia. Some of the Aztec codices, the indigenous religious and historical texts, have survived, and a number of them include drawings of body parts either being feasted on or jammed in cooking pots. One codex, currently housed in Florence, shows food offerings to a deity, which include a human arm, as well as a feasting scene that has various pots containing body parts.

After the conquest the Catholic Church had some difficulty in eradicating the indigenous customs of human sacrifice and cannibalism. On 23 June 1523 Spanish Law prohibited, among other activities, "to eat human meat, even if it be of prisoners and war dead". In 1537 the Bishop of Mexico, Don Juan de Zumarraga, wrote that everywhere he looked he saw "heinous practices, at one time suppressed, coming back stronger than ever; human sacrifice and cannibalism were almost common again".

Other ethno-historical accounts indicate that the link between cannibalism, human sacrifice and warfare was a common one throughout Mesoamerica. In 1932 the American anthropologist Ralph Beals published an ethno-historical study of northern Mexico before 1750 and surveyed the violent rituals associated with warfare in northern and central Mexico:

Human sacrifice rarely occurs in Mexico without an association of cannibalism. Cannibalism in much of our area [of northern Mexico] was ceremonial in nature, even where not associated with human sacrifice . . . In practically all cases it was connected with the celebration of war victories, and in many cases with the preservation of the bones and skulls of enemies. Among the Acaxee, where cannibalism was most highly developed in our area, the bones and skulls were presented to an idol or deity on certain occasions, and the first portion of human flesh prepared for eating was placed on the altar . . . [Among the Aztecs] the sacrifices were in most cases associated with ceremonial cannibalism, and the heart of the victim was usually "fed" to the god. There exists, then, a roughly continuous series starting on the one hand with the human sacrifice of Mexico, with the heart and other foods fed to the gods (a rather direct manifestation of the widespread idea of food offerings to the supernatural), and cannibalism. Next is the ceremonial cannibalism of the Acaxee (the first portion given to the god, the second to the slayer of the enemy being eaten) and the preservation of bones and skulls. Finally there are the less specialized methods of the Sinaloans and the peoples of Nuevo Leon and elsewhere, and the apparently simple ceremonial cannibalism of the Yavapai.

NATIVE AMERICAN CANNIBALISM

From the very outset of European contact, the view of native populations of the Americas was coloured by dark talk of cannibalism. Columbus arrived in this hemisphere at a time when the local people of the Lesser Antilles islands, the Arawaks, a society of village agriculturalists with complex social ranking, had been preyed upon and largely driven out by people from the mainland of South America – the Caribs. These were a loosely organized society of hunters and seafaring warriors who raided the Arawaks for women and food. The Arawaks name for the Caribs gave us the word "cannibal". That the Carib warriors were reputed by their victims to be cannibals helped justify the subsequent Spanish enslavement and extermination of Caribs in the islands of that sea to which they also had their name attached.

No reliable evidence exists that the Caribs were, in fact, cannibals, but it was commonplace in much of the world for one group of people to explain to European explorers and conquerors that the next tribe over was of sufficiently low character to eat people. This apparently roused the moral ire of the conquerors to the point that the enemy tribe might suffer most at their hands. Apparently more than half of the tribes of California, for example, told stories of cannibalism on the part of others but, again, evidence is lacking. Lesser forms of such bad-mouthing – or at least indirection – are also common. After the Spaniard Coronado reached and brutalized the Zuni in his great *entrada* into the present United States, seeking the seven fabled cities of gold, the Zuni with wonderful disingenuousness sent the Spanish on to the Hopi villages far to the west.

European reports of cannibalism among various groups of American Indians would accompany virtually all of the movements of Europeans into Indian territory, and the subject is (as can be imagined) one of the most emotionally laden in their history and, of course, one of the most painful to discuss in any context.

For many Indian people today, such accusations smack of colonialist put-downs motivated, at the very best unconsciously, by racist attitudes which the European-American mind simply cannot get over even now, whether dealing with the native peoples of the Americas, Fiji, New Guinea or Africa. Anthropologists have been roundly chastized even from within their own ranks for uncritically accepting ethnographic accounts of cannibalism as true; as early as 1937, Ashley Montagu said flatly, "In fact, cannibalism is a pure traveller's myth." And, in 1979, William Arens, an anthropologist at the State University of New York, decried his profession's uncritical support of "the collective representations and thinly disguized prejudices of western culture about others". Having reviewed the worldwide literature on cannibalism and having found the evidence at best merely anecdotal, or what could be called hearsay, Arens said, "The idea of 'others' as cannibals, rather than the act, is the universal phenomenon."

Many Indian people today are not overly fond of anthropologists as a profession, and anthropology, to boot, is among those disciplines most given to internecine squabbles, but controversy also is heard equally in the realm of ethnohistory, which is essentially the study of the earliest (European) records of the nature of Indian life, a sub-discipline lying athwart the frontier of history and ethnography in the odd compartmentalization of the scholarly world.

Reports of cannibalism were not infrequent among what came to be called "captivity stories", accounts by Europeans who were captured by and lived with Indians for various periods of time. Captivity tales, indeed, would become a highly popular literary genre both in the USA and abroad for three hundred years as the frontier moved westward, and many were not unlike the titillating and at best exaggerated material regularly sold to today's tabloids. Seen as such, captivity tales have tended to be dismissed as highly untrustworthy given their source, almost surely riddled with the perfervid inventions of someone looking to make a name for himself and some money, and someone also blinded by cultural preconceptions. But here it is useful to be careful. To say that every reporter tends to see another culture through the lens of his own is, by now, a truism, and not an especially useful one, given the fact that it is universally applicable. But to claim that all observers from an alien culture are incapable of reporting facts and events about another is to commit, in historian James Axtel's words, a "genetic fallacy". More precisely put, it is racist.

Many who wrote of their experiences as captives of Indians wrote long after the fact, and in the relatively straightforward voice of someone not seeking to embellish events for sensational effect. One of these was Alexander Henry, a British trader on the Michigan frontier in the 1760s who found himself witness to an attack by the Chippewa on an English-held fort at the height of a widespread revolt led by the great Ottawa leader, Pontiac, and in the midst of the nearly continuous warfare between the French and English with whom the tribes variously aligned themselves depending on what they saw as their interests. The Chippewa entered the fort by feigning to play a game of beggataway (the forerunner of lacrosse), chasing an errant ball into the confines of the walls and then setting upon the British there. Henry witnessed the killing of numerous countrymen, noting that, "From the bodies of some, ripped open, their butchers were drinking the blood, scooped up in the hollow of joined hands, and quaffed amid shouts of rage and victory." This is an example of *ritual* cannibalism, often based on taking into oneself the courage or other desirable attributes of the victim.

Henry himself avoided death by the intervention of a Chippewa named Wawatam who took in the Englishman less as a captive than as a member of his family. At one point, after some white prisoners were killed, Henry evidently observed the Indians cut up the bodies of "the fattest" and put them into kettles hung over fires:

> . . . A message came to our lodge for Wawatam to take part in the feast . . . Wawatam obeyed the summons, taking with him his dish and spoon. After about an hour he returned, bringing in his dish a human hand and a large piece of flesh. He did not appear to relish the repast, but told me it always had been the custom, among all the Indian nations when returning from war, to make a war feast from among the slain. This, he said, inspired the warriors with courage in attack.

For about a year, Henry lived with this family, hunting, fishing and otherwise involved in its normal affairs, they taking on the responsibility of keeping him out of the hands of Indians hostile to the English. At one point, as part of a hunting party, Henry shot a female bear.

> All, but particularly my old mother (as I used to call her), took the animal's head in their hands and stroked and kissed it several times, calling her their relation and grandmother. They begged a thousand pardons of the bear for taking away her life . . . The pipes

were now lit and Wawatam blew tobacco smoke into the nostrils of the bear, telling me to do the same and thus appease the anger of the bear on account of my having killed her . . . At length the feast was ready. Wawatam commenced a speech [in which] he deplored the necessity of men to kill *their friends* thus. He represented, however that the misfortune was unavoidable, since without doing so they could not live.

In due course, Henry had the chance to leave safely and the family agreed he should go:

I did not leave the lodge without the most grateful sense of the many acts of goodness I had experienced in it, nor without the sincere respect for the virtues of its members. All the family accompanied me to the beach, and the canoe had no sooner put off than Wawatam commenced an address to the Great Spirit, beseeching him to take care of me, his brother, till we should next meet.

These hardly seem the words of a totally culture-bound racist bent on sensationalism.

NAPOLEON'S RETREAT FROM MOSCOW

The first tragic saga of the nineteenth century was the retreat of Napoleon's Grande Armée from Moscow, an army that at one stage numbered more than half a million men, but was reduced in the end to less than one third of its original strength.

As the long columns of hungry, exhausted, undisciplined French, Germans, Italians and Poles plodded homeward across the snowy plains of northern Russia, followed on a parallel route by the army of the Tsar and attacked at every opportunity by bands of guerrilla fighters, the men began by hacking slices from the haunches of their cold-numbed horses.

When the horses died, they finished off the carcasses, and when there were no more horses they turned to the corpses of their fellow soldiers. Even before Smolensk, when the weather by Russian standards was still comparatively mild, the Russian General Kreitz reported discovering some Frenchmen in a wood, eating the flesh of a dead comrade.

"Hunger has compelled them to eat horses' carcasses, and many of us have seen them roasting the flesh of their compatriots . . . The Smolensk road is covered, at every step, with dead men and horses," wrote another Russian from Elna in November, and by December witnesses such as the Muravievs were reporting that "they had often met Frenchmen in some barn, sitting round a fire on the bodies of their dead comrades, from which they had cut the best parts to satisfy their hunger. Later, they grew weaker and weaker, and fell dead only to be eaten in turn by other comrades."

There was an obvious element of propaganda in the Russian reports, but also an element of truth. Before Vilna, twelve thousand men of a French corps numbering fifteen thousand are believed to have perished of cold and hunger in just three days. No one who lived through the last weeks of the retreat, who dragged himself over that final two hundred miles from the Berezina river to Kovno on the Polish frontier, seems ever to have succeeded in describing the experience. Always, accounts break off with the statement that no words were adequate to express the horrors of those days.

A FEROCIOUS FRENCH WOLF

On the 30th January 1838, about 10 o'clock at night, the peasants of the village of Avers, near Grenoble in France, were awakened by the noise of the church bells, which announced a farm on fire.

Men and women from all quarters instantly hurried to the somewhat distant spot, forgetting the perils that beset their path, in the middle of the night, at a season the severity of which had driven all the famished wolves of the mountains to prowl in the plains, and even around the villages.

A father and son of the name of Joseph, and another of the name of Alloard, having set out before the others, and being separated by a short distance from the others, had nearly reached the bridge of Vareille, on the river Eyburon, when a furious she-wolf rushed from the wooded part of the road on old Joseph, threw him down, and devoured his face and tore his clothes in tatters.

The unfortunate man had no defence against the ferocious animal, and his two companions could do nothing but join their cries of despair to his. Nevertheless, the wolf abandoned its prey, and disappeared for some time in the thickness of the wood; but soon after it came back more ardent, more formidable than ever.

At this instant many other inhabitants ran to the cries of Joseph and his two friends, and were going to transport the wounded man to the next village, when the returning wolf rushed on the group, consisting of from sixteen to seventeen individuals, tearing them one after the other. Surprised, without arms, and in the extreme of fright, the unfortunate peasants had no other resource that the obscurity of the night to escape the attacks of the famished beast; many of them, horribly wounded, lay in the snow, whilst the others tried to save themselves by flight.

The scene of carnage and frightful desolation had lasted no less than a quarter of an hour, when a young man, called Correard, reached the spot with a hatchet, which he had taken when going to the fire. Without hesitating, the courageous peasant attacked the furious wolf, who, seeing this new enemy, abandoned the other victims for him, but Correard was fortunate enough to lay the furious animal dead at his feet. A great number of the peasants were brought home in a dreadful state of mutilation. It is to be hoped that the wolf was not mad.

THE FRANKLIN ARCTIC EXPEDITION

They were described by Charles Dickens as the "flower of the trained English Navy"; their fate was to become cannibals.

The Franklin Expedition, comprising two ships and 133 men, set off in 1845 into the Arctic Circle in search of the final section of the elusive North-West Passage. Nine years later Inuit told Dr John Rae and fellow would-be rescuers that the ships had been trapped by ice for two years. Those Franklin Expedition members still alive had finally gone ashore in the hope of reaching Fort Reliance, in Canada, 930 miles away. None made it.

"British sailors would never do such a thing!" was the response of Rae upon his homecoming to England in 1854. He had just returned from the Canadian Arctic with the first evidence of the demise of the crew of the Franklin Expedition. He brought with him spoons, knives, forks and trays which had been purchased from an Inuit at Pelly Bay.

The aspect of the tragedy which most repulsed the British public was the story of cannibalism related to Rae by the Inuit. Despite his public declaration, in his report to the Admiralty in October 1854 Rae wrote: "From the mutilated state of many of the corpses and the contents of the [cooking] kettles, it is evident that our wretched countrymen had been driven to the last recourse – cannibalism – as a means of prolonging existence."

The British public and the Admiralty refused to believe such a story based entirely on the testimony of natives. Many found it inconceivable that anyone would resort to an act as abhorent as consuming the remains of another human being and also felt that military discipline would have prevented such an act occurring on the expedition.

Rumours of cannibalism had, however, been linked to Franklin's first overland expedition of 1819–22; and the Greely Expedition of 1881–4 had hard evidence of cannibalism: six men survived to tell their story.

Until recently there was no pathological evidence that cannibalism occurred on the second, ill-fated Franklin Expedition. It was not until 1981 that the first evidence surfaced, when Dr Owen Beattie discovered cut marks on a femur recovered from a Franklin site on King William Island. Despite this, there were still those who chose to explain the marks as resulting either from surgery to remove frost-bitten limbs or from wounds inflicted during an attack by local natives. Neither of these suggestions holds water, however. Surgery for frost-bite would scarcely occur on bones such as a pelvis, collar bone and neck vertebra. Equally implausible is the attack theory since the few small Inuit families who came across the Franklin men actually risked their own lives by assisting them with food and anyway the crews were trained in armed combat, with the best weapons of the time.

Convincing pathological evidence finally appeared in 1992 with the discovery of a major new site located on an islet in Erebus Bay on King William Island. Surrounded by mud, it is approximately the size of a soccer field.

In 1993 a team of seven, let by archaeologist Margaret Bertulli and anthropologist Anne Keenleyside, arrived on the site to conduct an investigation. The following information and quotations are by kind permission of Anne Keenleyside*.

*"The Final Days of the Franklin Expedition: New Skeletal Evidence', Anne Keenleyside, Margaret Bertulli and Henry C. Fricke, *Arctic*, vol. 50, No 1, March 1997, pp 36–46.

More than 200 artefacts were recovered from the site, including copper and iron nails, buttons, shoe leather, cloth samples, a broken clay pipe, a buckle, a comb, glass, wire gauze and percussion caps. Wood fragments, probably from a lifeboat, were scattered over a 10 metre x 15 metre surface area. Nearly 400 human bones and bone fragments were recovered from the site.

Morphological observations (based on the presence of 8 mandibles) indicated that the remains represented a minimum of 8 individuals, while X-ray fluorescence revealed the presence of at least 11 individuals . . . Age estimates indicated that all of the individuals were under the age of 50 at the time of death. One individual was initially estimated to have been 12 to 15 years of age on the basis of the stage of dental calcification of the third molars.

This leads to the speculation that the latter may have been one of the four cabin boys on the trip. The minimum age for members of the expedition was believed to be eigthteen, but baptism records cannot be found to confirm this and it was not unusual for enlisting youths to lie about their age.

The most noteworthy aspect of the analyses was the discovery of cut marks on 92 bones, or approximately one quarter of the total number of bones. Most of the affected elements were recovered from the western end of the site, where the densest concentration of bones and artefacts was found. The cut marks, which ranged in length from 2 mm to 27 mm, were easily distinguished from animal tooth marks by their sharper borders, narrower width and wider spacing. In contrast to cuts typically made by stone tools, the observed cuts, examined under a scanning electron microscope, exhibited features characteristic of cuts made by blades, namely straight edges, a V-shaped cross-section and a high depth to width ratio.

Cut marks were noted on most types of elements, including the clavicles, scapulae, humeri, radii, pelvic bones, ribs, vertebrae, femora, tibiae, metacarpals, tarsals, metatarsals, and proximal, middle and distal phalanges. Of those elements with cut marks, the pelvic bones were the most frequently affected elements (64%), with a minimum of four individuals being involved. The

5 crania, 2 patellae and 3 carpal bones recovered from the site showed no cut marks. While 45% of the affected bones had single cuts, 55% had multiple cuts, which tended to occur in clusters.

Particularly revealing is the distribution of cut marks on the remains. Approximately one quarter of the cut marks are located in close proximity to articular surfaces, a pattern consistent with intentional disarticulation. Affected areas include the articular and spinous processes of the vertebrae, the glenoid fossa and coracoid process of the scapulae, the distal articular surface of the radius, the margin of the greater sciatic notch of the pelvic bones, and the condyles of the femora and tibiae. The location of the cut marks is also consistent with defleshing or removal of muscle tissue. Evidence for decapitation is suggestive, but not conclusive.

In spite of overwhelming evidence of cannibalism, some people still refuse to accept that it occurred. Perhaps they fear that the reputation of the British Navy will be irredeemably tarnished and perhaps, too, there is a fear that the brave accomplishments of the expedition members will be diminished. However, nothing can take away from the amazing achievements of these men. The weather was too cold and rescue came years too late. They endured unbelievable privations and hardships, and no one should blame them for having made absolutely every effort to survive.

ANTIPODEAN CANNIBALISM

As the nineteenth-century scramble for empire intensified, the number "new-caught, sullen peoples" increased, and colonial administrators and diplomats, travellers and traders, began to vie with the missionaries in pouring out gruesome tales for the delectation of the reading public. Every continent except Europe and every chain of islands produced its crop of ritual cannibals.

In Samoa, it was usually only enemies who were eaten (roasted), as an expression of revenge, which meant that the worst insult that could be paid to a Samoan was to talk of roasting him. (This seems to have had the happy effect of damping down the hellfire in missionary sermons.) In the Marquesas islands, north-east of Tahiti, revenge was also the primary motive for cannibalism, although when it was later suppressed one doctor complained that the effect had been to depopulate the islands, because the people had been deprived of an important source of protein. In the islands of the New Hebrides, the tribes also ate their enemies with relish, but usually arranged a swap in the case of friends – a typical expression of exophagy, of avoiding eating members of one's own tribe.

The aborigines of Australia – who maintained their ancient way of life until well into the twentieth century – ate human flesh for any one of a number of reasons. It was a sacrificial ritual, it was good magic, a symbol of revenge, a sign of respect for the dead; it gave strength and courage, and some tribes are said to have believed that it was what led women to conceive. The life essence of the dead man passed into the woman's body from which it was restored again to the tribe.

Sensitive, emotional, inclined to be gentle, the Australian aborigine differed greatly from the Maori of New Zealand, whose wars and cannibalism were marked by the same jaunty ferociousness as those of the Fijians (to whom, of course, they were related). Absorbing an enemy's strength was again the primary motive for people-eating, although one authority went so far as to suggest that the Maoris' basically vegetarian diet must undoubtedly have encouraged the despatch of raiding parties in search of stray humans to liven up the menu.

Certainly, one Maori chief who was imported to London in 1818 and remained there for some years is said to have confessed that what he missed most about home cooking was "the feast of human flesh, the feast of victory. He was weary of eating English beef . . . The flesh of women and children was to him and his fellow-countrymen the most delicious, while certain Maoris prefer that of a man of fifty, and that of a black rather than that of a white. His countrymen, Touai said, never ate the flesh raw, and preserved the fat of the rump for the purpose of dressing their sweet potatoes." Touai also assured his interviewer that missionaries who feared they might be popped in the cooking pot really had very little to worry about. A hungry man would be more likely to go to a neighbouring tribe for his dinner, since black men had a far more agreeable flavour than white.

Even so, the Maoris did manage to force a white man down occasionally. When they killed the unfortunate Captain Grant during the course of "Heke's war", they dried and ate his flesh with the object of reducing the *mana,* or supernatural power, of the rest of his force.

In Sumatra, ritual cannibalism was part not so much of the religious as of the judicial system. The Batak tribe formally dined on anyone who had committed adultery with one of their sovereign's wives, or who was a traitor, a spy, a deserter, or a member of an attacking war party, and the victim's relatives were required to supply salt and lime for dressing the carcass. They thus became party to the punishment, which ruled out any possibility of a subsequent vendetta.

FIJI CANNIBALS

Men and Brethren, To your sympathy this Appeal is made, and your help is implored on behalf of a most interesting but deeply depraved people, the inhabitants of the group of islands called FEEGEE, little known to the civilized world except for the extreme danger to which vessels touching at them are exposed, from the murderous propensities of the islanders, and for the horrid CANNIBALISM to which they are addicted.

In FEEGEE, cannibalism is not an occasional but a constant practice; not indulged in from a species of horrid revenge, but from an absolute preference for human flesh over all other food.

It is on behalf of this cannibal race that we appeal to you. Let all the horrors of a CANNIBAL FEAST be present to your minds while you read . . . Pity CANNIBAL FEEGEE, and do so quickiy. Come, then, ye Christians, and teach the poor, idolatrous, war-loving, man-devouring FEEGEEANS better things.

We spare you the details of a cannibal feast: the previous murders, the mode of cooking human beings, the assembled crowd of all ranks, all ages, both sexes, Chiefs and people, men, women, and children, anticipating the feast with horrid glee. The actual feast. The attendants bringing into the circle BAKED HUMAN BEINGS – not one, not two, nor ten but twenty, thirty, forty, fifty at a single feast! . . . The writer of this APPEAL has himself conversed with persons who have seen forty and fifty eaten at a single sitting – eaten without anything like disgust; eaten indeed with a high relish!

CANNIBALISM IN NEW ZEALAND

On 19 December 1821 and following Hongi's expedition to the South, three of the war canoes returned from the Thames and arrived at Kenkeri. They had upwards of 100 prisoners with them, who were easily distinguished by their sorrowful appearance. Some of them were weeping bitterly and, in particular, one woman, before whom they had with savage cruelty placed the head of her brother stuck upon a pole. She sat upon the ground before it, the tears streaming down her cheeks. These canoes brought the news of the death of Tete, son-in-law to Hongi, who was slain in a fight. He was one of the most civilized and best behaved of the natives. His brother Pu, a fine young man, was also among the slain. This created great grief in the family.

Tete's wife and Matuka, his brother, were watched to prevent them from putting an end to their lives. Pu's wife hanged herself on hearing the news, and Hongi's wife killed a slave, which was a customary act on such occasions.

The next day Hongi and his people arrived with the dead bodies of Tete and Pu. Messrs. Francis Hall and Kemp went to see the ceremony of their landing, but were very sorry that their curiosity had led them to witness such a scene of horror. A small canoe with the dead bodies first approached the shore. The war canoes, about forty in number, lay at a short distance. Soon after, a party of young men landed to perform the war dance and "pihe", song over the bodies of the slain. They yelled and jumped, brandishing their weapons, and threw up human heads in the air in a shocking manner; but this was only a prelude to the horrid work which was about to follow.

An awful pause ensued. At length the canoes moved slowly and touched the shore, when the widow of Tete and other women rushed down upon the beach in a frenzy of rage, and beat in pieces the carved work at the head of the canoes with poles. They proceeded to pull out three prisoners into the water and beat them to death. The frantic widow then went to another canoe and killed a female prisoner. The missionaries retired from the distressing scene, as no interference of theirs could avail; and they were told that, after they went away, Hongi killed five more with his own hand. In the whole nine persons were murdered that evening and were afterwards eaten.

The prisoners were very numerous, men, women, and children, but chiefly the latter. They were said to amount to about two thousand, and were distributed chiefly among the tribes of the Bay of Islands. The people were now more bloodthirsty than ever and talked of going again soon, meaning to devastate the whole island. In this expedition they had done all the mischief they had threatened. Poor Hinaki, the chief to whom Hongi had given warning a short time before, was killed and eaten.

The next day Hongi was busily employed in making an enclosure with pieces of canoe, decorated with feathers and carved work, in which to deposit the bodies of the two brothers, Tete and Pu. Part of the remains of the people killed the day before were toasting in the fire at a little distance, and some human flesh, ready cooked, lay in baskets on the ground. Hongi had the audacity to ask Mr Kemp to eat some, and said it was better than pork. A part of one of the poor women killed the day before by the natives was cooked on the side of the hill at the back of Mr Kemp's house. The head they cut off and rolled down the hill, and several of them amused themselves with throwing large stones at it, until they had dashed it to pieces. Among the slaves who were taken to Waimate on the preceding day, one of them, a woman, becoming tired or lame, could not keep up with the rest and was, therefore, killed.

A few days later it was reported that Hongi and his people had killed more of the prisoners, making the number eighteen who had been murdered in cold blood since their return. Several heads were stuck upon poles near the mission dwellings, and the tattooed skin of a man's thigh was nailed to a board to dry, in order to be made into the covering of a cartridge box.

It did not occur to this people that their relatives had fallen in fair fight, or rather that they had brought upon themselves a well-merited death by going to attack those who, by comparison, were defenceless, and perhaps, too, had given no sufficient cause for hostilities. Neither did they bear in mind how much larger a number of the enemy had fallen than the few over whom they were grieving. They had lost their nearest relatives, and they knew of no other way of moderating their grief for this than by the indulgence of brutal revenge . . .

Within a few months these incidents were repeated again, when another large force was assembled to revenge the deaths of Tete and Pu upon the natives of Waikato.

ABORIGINE RECIPE

A detailed description of aboriginal principles and processes in preparing dead bodies has been given by the Reverend Dr Lang in his book *Cooksland* (1842). Lang had most of his facts from "Durrambhoi" Davies, an escaped convict who lived for seventeen years among the Australian aborigines.

"When the dead body of a person who has either fallen in battle or had died a natural death is to be subjected to this horrid process, it is stretched out on its back and a fire lighted on each side of it. Firebrands are then passed carefully over the whole body, till its entire surface is thoroughly scorched. The cuticle, consisting of the epidermis or scarf-skin, and the *reticulum mucosum* or mucous membrane of Malpighi, in which the colouring matter of the skin is contained, is then peeled off, sometimes with pointed sticks, sometimes with mussel shells, and sometimes even with the finger nails, and then placed in a basket or dilly to be preserved. And as the *cutis vera* or true skin is, in all varieties of the human family, perfectly white, the corpse then appears of that colour all over; and I have no doubt whatever, that it is this peculiar and ghastly appearance which the dead body of a black man uniformly assumes under this singular treatment, and with which the aborigines must be quite familiar wherever the practice obtains, that has suggested to them the idea that white men are merely their fore-fathers returned to live again; the supposition that particular white men are particular deceased natives, known to the Aborigines when alive, being merely this idea carried out to its natural result, under the influence of a heated imagination. There is reason also to believe, *e converso*, that wherever this idea prevails, the practice in which it has originated – that of peeling off the cuticle previous to the other parts of the process to be described hereafter – is still prevalent also, or has been so, at least, very recently.

"After the dead body has been subjected to the process of scorching with firebrands, it becomes so very stiff as almost to be capable of standing upright of itself. If the subject happens to be a male, the subsequent part of the process is performed by females, but if a female, it is performed by males. The body is then extended upon its face and certain parties, who have been hitherto sitting apart in solemn silence (for the whole affair is conducted with the stillness of a funeral solemnity), step forward, and with a red pigment, which shows very strongly upon the white ground, draw lines down the back and along the arms from each shoulder down to the wrist. These parties then retire, and others who have previously been sitting apart in solemn silence step forward in, like manner, and with sharp shells cut through the *cutis vera* or true skin along these lines. The entire skin of the body is then stripped off in one piece, including the ears and the finger nails, with the scalp, but not the skin of the face, which is cut off. This whole process is performed with incredible expedition, and the skin is then stretched out on two spears to dry, the process being sometimes hastened by lighting a fire under the skin. Previous to this operation, however, the skin is restored to its natural colour, by being anointed all over with a mixture of grease and charcoal.

"When the body has thus been completely flayed, the dissectors step forward and cut it up. The legs are first cut off at the thighs, then each arm at the shoulder, and last of all the head; not a drop of blood appearing during the process. The larger sections are then subdivided and portioned out among the expectant multitude, each of whom takes his portion to one or other of the fires and, when half-roasted, devours it with great apparent relish. The flesh of the natives in the northern country generally is very fat, and that of children, which are never skinned like adults, particularly so. Davies has often seen a black fellow holding his portion of his fellow creature's dead body to the fire in one hand, on a branch or piece of wood stuck through it like a fork or skewer, with a shell or hollow piece of bark under it in the other, to receive the melted fat that dropped from it, and drinking it up when he had caught a sufficient quantity to form a draught with the greatest gusto. In this way the body disappears with incredible rapidity, the bones being very soon cleaned of every particle of flesh.

"The bones are then carefully collected, and placed in a dilly or basket, and forwarded by a trusty person to all the neighbouring tribes, in each of which they are mourned over successively, for a time, by those to whom the deceased was known. They are then returned to the tribe to which the deceased belonged, and carried about by his relatives for months, or even years, till at length they are deposited permanently in a hollow tree, from which it is esteemed unpardonable sacrilege to remove it."

FIJI FANCIES

Feejee as we are told lies three days' sail from Tongabatoo in the direction north-west by west. It was described to us as a large, but very fruitful island; abounding with hogs, dogs, fowls and all kinds of fruits and roots . . . Feejee and Tongabatoo frequently make war upon each other. And it appeared from several circumstances that the inhabitants of the latter are much afraid of this enemy . . . And it is no wonder that they should be under dread; for these of Feejee are formidable on account of the dexterity with which they use their bows and slings, but much more so on account of the savage practice to which they are addicted . . . of eating their enemies whom they kill in battle. We were surprised that this was not a misrepresentation. For we met several Feejee people at Tongabatoo and, on inquiry of them, they did not deny the charge.

Captain Cook, October 1773

To comprehend cannibalism in Fiji, you have to understand its people's ancient belief system, founded on the worship of ancestor spirits, which is antithetical to Judaeo-Christian notions of God and self, and was tragically destroyed by the advent of Christianity.

Europeans were shocked and disgusted when they witnessed cannibalism and other strange customs, such as elderly parents being voluntarily strangled by their offspring and widows being killed when their husbands died. But all these were part of an underlying cultural logic that was obscure to all but the most observant and persistent Westerners. Fijians were not the bloodthirsty savages celebrated in much generalized fiction about the South Seas, Like Defoe's *Robinson Crusoe*. As William Lockerby, a Scottish seaman stranded in Fiji in 1808, wrote:

In war they are fearless and savage to the utmost degree, but in peace their disposition is mild and generous towards their friends, and the affection they bear towards their relatives is seldom found among Europeans.

It is important to keep in mind that cannibalism was still a terrifying act for Fijians, albeit one that was a distinct part of their behavioural repertoire in a way unfamiliar to Europeans. That isn't to say there weren't many atrocities associated with Fijian warfare and cannibalism, because there were, just as there is with 'civilized' warfare in its various guises. But Fijian cannibalism itself was not an atrocity but a perfectly logical, religiously and socially sanctioned practice. As the missionary Thomas Williams, perhaps the most diligent of all the early observers of Fijian life, wrote:

> Cannibalism among this people is one of their institutions; it is interwoven in the elements of society; it forms one of their pursuits, and is regarded by the mass as a refinement.

Cannibalism was always a special event, and bodies were always eaten as part of a religious ceremony. Consumption of a body was the critical act in the process of human sacrifice. Generally, those eaten were enemies killed in war, but other categories of people (conquered peoples, slaves) could also be legitimately killed to acquire a bakola at any time. This was necessary because certain regular events required human sacrifice: the construction of temples, chiefs' houses and sacred canoes, or the installation rites of a chief, for example. The paramount chief had special assassins (sometimes Europeans) who would procure these victims, generally by ambush.

Europeans often found the religious basis hard to believe, considering the scale on which cannibalism occurred in Fiji. The missionary Reverend Hunt estimated that over a five-year period in the 1840s approximately five hundred people had been eaten within fifteen miles of his residence at Viwa. Massacres of more than three hundred people were known to follow successful attacks on large towns. Ra Udreudre of Rakiraki, an infamous chief, built a line of stones, each marking an eaten enemy. Reverend Lyth, shown them by Udreudre's son in 1848, counted a total of 872.

These may sound like exaggerated numbers, but warfare in old Fiji sometimes did occur on a grand scale . . .

Many visitors to the Fiji Islands, sceptical about tales of cannibalism, were in for a profound shock. In July 1840 the US Navy Exploring Expedition had what was literally an 'eyewitness' encounter with cannibalism off Vitu Levu in the aftermath of a local battle. Commodore Charles Wilkes recorded what happened in the official account of the four-year voyage:

Shortly afterwards a canoe came alongside, bringing the skull yet warm from the fire, much scorched, and marked with the teeth of those who had eaten of it. The brain had been roasted and taken out, as well as the eyes and teeth. Another canoe came alongside with some roasted flesh in it.

While Mr Spieden and others were agreeing with the natives for the purchase of the skull for a fathom of cloth, a native stood near him holding something in his right hand, which he soon applied to his mouth, and began to eat. To their utter astonishment they discovered it to be the eye of the dead man, which the native had plucked from the skull a few moments before. So revolting and unexpected a sight produced a feeling of sickness in many; this ocular proof of their cannibal propensities fully satisfied them. The native was eating it, and exclaiming at the same time, "Vinaka, Vinaka" ("Good, Good"). Another was seen eating the last of the flesh from the thighbone. This was witnessed by several of the officers and men, who all testify to the same facts.

Previous to this occurrence, no one in the squadron could say that he had been an eyewitness to cannibalism, though few doubted its practice, but the above transaction placed it beyond all doubt, and we have now the very skull, which was bought from those who were picking and eating it, among our collections.

The Fijians believed that the spirit of a body clung to the corpse for four days after death. Sacrificing and eating the body in wartime annihilated the spirit and prevented it from ascending to the spirit world and becoming a source of power and guidance to your enemies. If you could kill an enemy, especially a chief or great warrior, and eat him, then by annihilating his spirit you were scoring a tremendous additional blow against your opponents. As William Endicott, a mate on the ship *Glide*, reported:

Little credit is given to the warrior who kills his enemies if he does not obtain their bodies; much more is thought of the savage who kills one man and carries him home than of the individual who may kill a hundred and let their dead bodies fall into the hand of the enemy. The chief glory consists not so much in killing as in eating their enemies.

Destroying a great chief meant the destruction of the power of his Land. It was the worst fate that could befall a clan. A kinsman eaten, particularly a chief, was a devastating blow.

Victorious warriors would consume some enemies on the battlefield but would always ensue that some bodies were taken back to their town or village . . . transported sitting up in the prow of a canoe. As John Jackson wrote in 1840:

They were set up in quite formal array in two rows along the spacious decks, on their hindquarters with their knees cocked up and their hands lashed together over their knees so as to leave a space in the hind part of the bend of the same, to admit a long pole . . . each body supporting the other, as the whole row of bodies were in contact with each other.

Often this notion of having the bodies look as lifelike as possible would be carried further, and they would be painted and decorated as warriors looked in life. If the [bodies] were being transported overland, they were, as Endicott described:

lashed on poles in a singular manner. They were bound . . . by bringing the upper and lower parts of the legs together and binding them to the body, and the arms in a similar manner by bringing the elbows to rest on the knees, and their hands tied upon each side of the neck. Their backs were confined to poles, which were about twelve feet long. One was lashed on each pole, with six men, three at each end, to carry it.

On reaching the outskirts of town . . . before the temple, the bodies would be flung at the feet of the paramount chief, and the priests would dedicate them to the war god.

The heads of the bodies would then be dashed open against the braining stone column in the ground outside the temple – sacrificing the brain to the appetite of the god.

With these rituals concluded, the sanctified pit ovens in the temple compound were prepared and lit, and the bodies were taken away to be washed in the sea, in a stream or on a large flat dissecting stone.

The butchering and cooking process itself varied by region. Captain Richard Siddins, a sandalwood trader in Fiji in 1808 and

1809, described the treatment of the body of a chief of Navaika at Bua Bay:

> The multitude then went down to their dead enemy, and with pieces of wood or bamboo, made very sharp, cut off his hands at the wrists, his feet at the ankles, his legs at the knees, and his thighs near the middle . . . the head was cut off very low towards the breast; and they placed it on some hot ashes that had previously been prepared in a hole dug out for the purpose; and when it had remained there a sufficient time, they rubbed off the hair with shells, and replaced it with the other parts of the body in the hole, surrounding it on all sides with stones that had been made very hot. They then covered it up till it was completely roasted.

The body was sometimes cut up into smaller pieces, as witnessed by Dr R. B. Lyth, himself a surgeon, in 1840. After being singed and scraped of hair, the body parts were "further cut and divided into a great number of small parcels. The instrument employed was the bamboo, which was used with great dexterity, every now and then taking a fresh piece of bamboo, or tearing a piece with the teeth to have a new edge." The meat, once cooked, was often then scraped off the bone and "made into parcels using the banana leaf for a bag".

EASTER ISLANDERS

Every Easter Islander knows that his ancestors were *kai-tangata*, "maneaters". Some make jokes about it, others take offence at any allusion to this custom which has become in their eyes barbarous and shameful.

Acording to Father Roussel, cannibalism did not disappear until after the introduction of Christianity. Shortly before this, the natives are said to have eaten a number of men, including two Peruvian traders. Cannibal feasts were held in secluded spots, and women and children were rarely admitted. The natives told Father Zumbohm that the fingers and toes were the choicest morsels.

The captives destined to be eaten were shut up in huts in front of the sanctuaries. There they were kept until the moment when they were sacrificed to the gods.

The Easter Islanders' cannibalism was not exclusively a religious rite or the expression of an urge for revenge: it was also induced by a simple liking for human flesh that could impel a man to kill for no other reason than his desire for fresh meat. (Man was the only large mammal whose flesh was available.) Women and children were the principal victims of these inveterate cannibals.

The reprisals that followed such crimes were all the more violent because an act of cannibalism committed against the member of a family was a terrible insult to the whole family. As among the ancient Maoris, those who had taken part in the meal were entitled to show their teeth to the relatives of the victim and say, "Your flesh has stuck between my teeth." Such remarks were capable of rousing those to whom they were addressed to a murderous rage not very different from the Malay *amok*."

HORROR IN THE SAHARA

The narrative of the last days of the Flatters mission contains in its terribly dry detail a suggestion of horror almost unprecedented.

Most of the victims were *spahis* belonging to the race of the desert's children; but they had long been accustomed to the comparatively civilized life of Algeria or the Senegal colonies, and their last struggle took place in a region known only to the wildest and fiercest of all nomad Arabs, who sweep through it on their way to carry off a sable booty of slaves from the black cities of the Niger, leaving behind them on their return a track marked with skeletons.

In these latitudes time has stood still for uncounted thousands of years, naught has been changed since the primeval sea dried up. It is all a dead and ruined world like the Moon.

Occasionally a caravan passes, with traders armed to the teeth, prepared to fight every yard of the way against the Touareg. To be robbed in the desert is death; for, without camels, travelling is impossible. Vast distances separate the green islands in this yellow ocean of sand, where the mouths of the wells are still guarded against the drift with great stones, as in the days when Jacob served seven years for Rachel.

Between these halting places the sand is burning enough to blister the skin of the feet; the thermometer registers an incredible temperature; the least portion of the features exposed is scorched as by fire; and travelling is possible only with veiled face. Then there are sandstorms, sand pillars reaching from earth to sky, and the wrecks of camel skeletons bleaching to the whiteness of chalk.

In this ghastly desolation the last fragment of the [Flatters] exploring mission finds itself reduced to such misery that, even with the certainty of water a few miles off, the men cannot summon enough strength to advance. There is only one camel; it is their ship, their engine, their forlorn hope – the riches of a thousand kingdoms would be as nothing in their eyes at such ajuncture in exchange for one day, one hour, of that camel's life. There is a single native French officer alive – the quartermaster. He is trusted by the Moslem *spahis* to go forward with the camel to the well, procure water and send back the animal with a supply of well-filled skins. But within a few hundred yards of the well his strength fails him. The Arab soldier accompanying him volunteers to obtain water, but rewards himself for his pains by stealing the camel! The frightful despair of the survivors may be imagined. Without their camel, to carry water with them is impossible.

For days subsequently that little band of human skeletons struggle vainly to leave the well – compelled by infernal thirst and heat to return after having marched a few miles under the sun; lizards and sand insects are eaten alive; reason weakens and looses its grasp upon the reins of passion. An Arab sent out for assistance is shot and eaten by his comrades. Two more are subsequently murdered. The survivors devour the bodies; and a new phase of horror commences. Those who had marched on in advance return upon hearing the shots; they partake of the repast; they even kill another of the weaker ones and eat his flesh.

After this the wreck of the expedition supports itself by cannibalism – as a pack of wolves devour each other in the madness of hunger. There is little flesh on those starving bodies – the bones are crushed and devoured.

Discipline is, of course, forgotten; the French officer is killed and eaten. Then appears the most horrible phase of the long tragedy – the sufferers conceive a hideous dread of each other. They separate; they fear at night to sleep; the man who yields to slumber in spite of himself may never awake.

Carrying with them a provision of human flesh, they continue to struggle backward and forward between two oases, dreading each other more than death – fearing the sunset, the flesh-coloured sunset of the desert, fearing the tepidness of night tempting the weary to close their eyes, fearing the furnace-glow of dawn heralding another day of horrors. In the glare of his comrade's eyes, in the fleshlessness of his comrade's face, each sees a menace and mockery of death, each keeps his finger upon the trigger of his revolver. Only when nearly one half of the survivors have been devoured by the rest does the remnant of the expedition succeed in reaching a nomad camp, whose friendly sheik affords them true Arab hospitality.

Strangely enough, these wretched survivors still feel the most intense hatred towards one of their number who had been left behind at Hassi Hadjadj, "the Pilgrim's Well", and who had repeatedly fled from those who sought to kill and devour him. They design to return and kill him, and beg that camels be lent to them. But the Arab host suspects something: he insists upon accompanying them and beholds sights that would have sickened the fiercest even of Touareg. By his coming, the life of the *spahi* is saved, but his fear of his old comrades is such that he refuses to accept aid until they have themselves departed another way. At last a troop of friendly horsemen escort the victims to Ouargla – the Tunis of the desert – whence it is generally possible to obtain an escort to the last of the French military outposts, Tuggarth. But even Ouargla is remote from the civilized world proper, and the French flag could never be maintained there except under the protection of an expeditionary column.

When the reader pictures to his mind the unutterable misery of that march through a waste fantastically desolate as a lunar landscape – under a sky whose very clouds are flying sand, under a perpendicular sun, whose beams scorch like molten iron, against a wind whose heat flays the face, excoriates the hands, shrivels even the waterskins upon the backs of the dromedaries – and when he imagines that silent struggle about the oasis – the murder of sleepers at the well, the frenzy of mutual hatred inspired by cannibalism, the emaciation that rendered it almost impossible to obtain three days' food from nearly twelve adult bodies, the crunching of bones when starvation had consumed the muscles of the victim, the thirst that blackens the lips and makes the tongue crack open and stifles speech in the throat – it is indeed difficult to conceive how men can pass through such experience and remain sane! The most pitiful case of all seems that of the poor *spahi* left alone for nearly a week at the well, who took to flight whenever his ghoulish companions came back for water and returned by stealth in the night to gnaw the bones of the dead.

ANASAZI MAN CORN

It is one of the great prehistoric puzzles: what caused the Anasazi people, who had one of the most sophisticated civilizations in North America, to abandon their beautiful stone dwellings in the mid-twelfth century? What made families walk away, seemingly in great haste, leaving behind food cooking over fires and sandals hanging on pegs?

In Chaco Canyon, a stark landscape in North-west New Mexico presided over by brooding red mesas, clues lie buried within a nest of hundreds of rooms strewn among the remnants of distinctive Cibola pottery and exquisite jewellery: bones. Chopped-up human bones with marks indicating systematic cutting and scraping, suggesting that groups of people were killed and butchered, the meat carefully cut away at the tendons and roasted. Long bones halved and boiled to extract the marrow. Skulls, their tops removed like lids, placed on hearths and cooked. Brains removed.

Scientists have long puzzled over the meaning of these artefacts. Now, at least one chilling explanation has come forth from physical anthropologist Christy Turner. With the publication [1999] of *Man Corn: Cannibalism and Violence in the Prehistoric American Southwest*, which he wrote with his late wife, anthropologist Jacqueline Turner, he has managed to anger Native Americans, rile scientists, horrify New Agers and provide a fascinating theoretical glimpse into the collapse of a great civilization.

"I'm the guy who brought down the Anasazi," Turner said wryly.

The book debunks the traditional view of the Anasazi as peaceful agriculturists, whose modern-day descendants are the highly spiritual Hopi, Zuni and Pueblo peoples. Previously, the bone heaps have been variously explained as the handiwork of warring clans, remnants of the killing of witches and/or part of ritual mortuary practices.

But Turner contends that a "band of thugs" – Toltecs, for whom cannibalism was part of religious practice – made their way to Chaco Canyon from central Mexico. These invaders used cannibalism to overwhelm the unsuspecting Anasazi and terrorize the populace into submission over a period of 200 years.

Turner says the culture's carefully constructed social fabric began to tear. Finally, the Anasazi fled the oppressive cultists and sought haven deep in remote canyons. The next time any part of the culture appeared, these Pueblo people were found to have constructed elaborate dwellings adhered to the sheer sides of cliffs. Generations of scientists have postulated that such suspended villages – located far from water – represented a fear of a great foe. Turner suggests the Anasazi took up these defensive positions against a horrible enemy – the evil that had infiltrated their own people.

Turner's theory has been attacked by American Indians and by scientists who say he has shoehorned a disparate collection of findings into one convenient theory. While respected in his field, Turner's explanation for the cannibalism has been met mostly with scepticism. But even with his provocative hypothesis, Turner admits he hasn't solved all of the Chaco puzzle: who built these grand edifices, what were they used for, and where did all the people go?

Turner, a professor of anthropology at Arizona State University, had established an international reputation in forensic dentation long before taking up the cannibalism issue.

He was sifting through a box of human remains in 1967 taken from Polacca Wash, on what is now the Hopi Indian Reservation in Northeast Arizona, when something struck him as odd. He thought they resembled the remains of a meal. The unassuming box led to a paper, "A Massacre at Hopi", written with Nancy Morris. Turner's presentation and the reaction were harbingers of thirty years of controversy and scorn.

In presenting his original paper, Turner said that the box contained the remains of thirty people who had been "violently mutilated" and whose heads showed signs of defleshing and roasting. The response from his peers, Turner said, "wasn't so much a reaction as silence".

He concluded that Polacca Wash could be shown to be the site of what Hopi legend called the Death Mound. According to anthropologists, the people in a particular village were known to practice forbidden witchcraft. Nearby villages attacked the renegade group, burning most of the men and capturing the women and children. In the chaos that followed, the women and children were tortured and dismembered.

Apart from the scientific doubts about Turner's conclusions, the notion that the Hopi – revered in scholarship as wise and gentle astronomers who lived in an enlightened society – would be capable of killing and eating members of their own clan stunned the scientists. Anthropologists acknowledge that any theory that seems to portray Pueblo Indians in a negative light would be hard to sell.

"Our understanding of the Anasazi is exactly parallel to what was thought of the Maya years ago – this advanced society responsible for beautiful things, that now we realize was not a peaceful place," said David Wilcox, curator of the Museum of Northern Arizona. "We are in a period where everything Native American is (seen as) spiritual, sensitive and wonderful. We would like to believe that all of the nasty stuff was introduced by the Europeans, and before that it was all truth, beauty and love. Sorry, that's just not so. These were complex societies. We are all capable of doing those things."

Turner has refined his cannibalism theory over the years, even pointing to seven identifying characteristics that must be present in bone assemblages before cannibalism can be established. These include cut marks that indicate flesh was meticulously cleaned from bones, and bones broken into smaller pieces that show signs of "pot polish", with the ends worn smooth by being stirred in a pot.

In his book, he claims to have identified at least thirty-eight Anasazi sites where cannibalism took place. The cannibalism was, he says, a means of political control within Chaco and a scare tactic to ward off potential attackers. The book's title, *Man Corn*, is a translation of an Aztec word meaning a sacred meal of human meat cooked with corn.

Debra Martin, a professor of biological anthropology at Hampshire College in Massachusetts, agrees that there were horrifically violent episodes in the prehistoric South-west, but argues that Turner's conclusions are flawed.

"Why does Christy think that if bones are cut and flesh cooked that it means cannibalism?" she said. "Why can't it also indicate the killing of witches? Why can't it be ritual mortuary practice?"

The crux of any debate about cannibalism is how to prove, absent first-person testimony, that human flesh was ingested. Now, there may be a method. Seven years ago a team of archaeologists working at Sleeping Ute Mountain in Colorado excavated an Anasazi site. Led by Brian Biliman, the scientists discovered several of Turner's cannibalism signs. Near the remains of five people whose bodies appeared to have been cooked was a stone tool kit, of the kind used to butcher game animals. Later, laboratory tests found human blood on the implements.

Billman discovered one other significant item, a coprolite – a pile of preserved human fecal matter – in the centre of a fireplace. He concluded that after the fire had died, someone had squatted over the hearth and defecated. The coprolite has become a key part of the cannibalism puzzle. It has been analyzed for the presence of human protein, which would prove the ingestion of human flesh. The results are expected to be published shortly [see below].

As for the big question – why the Anasazi in Chaco Canyon disappeared – scientists seem to have rejected at least one explanation, found in Hopi belief. In this explanation, there is no mystery to the abandoning of Chaco: like Christians who believe they will be whisked away in the Rapture, Hopi believe that, when the spirit called, the Anasazi simply left this world.

Turner, asked point-blank if his theory has solved the mystery of the Anasazi, betrayed the first sign of ambivalence. "The Anasazi puzzle, in my mind, is as far along as I can take it," he said.

Scientists say they have found the first indisputable evidence of cannibalism among ancient peoples. The sensational discovery, made by analysing faeces more than eight centuries old, appears to resolve one of the most contentious issues in anthropology.

The sample of human waste, known as coprolite, was found in a hearth at a site called Cowboy Wash in southern Colorado; the settlement appears to have been abandoned in 1150. The coprolite contained traces of a human muscle protein called myoglobin. The protein occurs only in heart and skeletal muscle; none is found normally in the intestines or in blood. The only way the traces could have cropped up there, says Richard Marlar, the University of Colorado biochemist who did the study, was through the eating of human flesh.

The biochemical evidence that people ate people is bolstered by grisly circumstantial pointers – the site contained butchered and burnt human bones, stone tools stained with human blood and a ceramic cooking pot lined with the remains of human tissue. The bones appeared to belong to seven people, among them women and children. The finding is reported in *Nature* magazine, September 2000. There are a dozen similar sites in the American South-west; the inference is that cannibalism was not rare.

Trying to find evidence of "customary cannibalism", or the consumption of human flesh as a social practice rather than a desperate anti-starvation measure, has been a thankless task. Folklore suggests it has been a common activity in, for example, Papua New Guinea. It has long been suspected that ancient Native Americans occasionally ate dead relatives or defeated enemies – there have been many finds of human bones that appear to bear distinctive butcher's marks more often found on animal bones, and of bloodstained knives and pots.

However, descendants of the tribes most often accused of the practice are unhappy at their ancestors being labelled cannibals. There are also anthropologists who feel that such accusations stray into racism. That is why Marlar has spent years analysing and re-analysing the remains. (Refining the chemical tests involved boiling in saucepans human flesh harvested during surgical operations.) He said he had "no doubts" about what the data pointed to.

The finding adds a gruesome dimension to the events of 850 years ago, when Cowboy Wash was abandoned. It is thought to have been a time of drought, which may have prompted social chaos. According to Brian Billman, an archaeologist at the University of North Carolina and a co-author of the *Nature* paper, the community of 70 to 125 people possibly died during one episode. The perpetrators could have been starving raiders, hoping to scare people away and keep the failing harvests for themselves. What better way to terrify people than feasting on one's foes?

SOUTH SEA SAVAGES

When the Victorian adventurer H. W. Walker eventually returned home after spending nearly twenty years travelling around the islands of the South and West Pacific, including the Philippines and New Guinea, he put together his memoirs based upon letters written to his family and friends.

Walker's travels took him to many then remote areas, where few, if any, white men had ventured before. One particular visit, to a village in one of the Fijian islands, seems to have made him rather more nervous than usual.

"On my return to the village I had a most interesting interview with these ex-cannibals, one old and two middle-aged men, thanks to Masirewa, my interpreter.

"He first asked them how they liked human flesh, and they all shouted, 'Venaka, venaka!' (good). Like the natives of New Guinea, they said it was far better than pig. They also declared that the legs, arms and palms of the hands were the greatest delicacies, and that women and children tasted best. The brains and eyes were especially good. They would never eat a man who had died a natural death.

"They had eaten 'white man'. He was salty and fat, but he was good, though not so good as 'Fiji man'. One of them had tasted a certain Mr—, and the meat on his legs was very fat. They chopped his feet off above the boots, which they thought were part of him, and they boiled his feet and boots for a day, but they did not like the taste of the boots . . .

"Lastly, I asked if they would still like to eat a man if they got the chance and they were not afraid of being punished, and there was no hesitation in their reply of 'I' (yes), uttered with one voice like the yelp of a hungry wolf, and it seemed to me that their eyes sparkled. They were certainly a very obliging lot of cannibals."

RUSSIA 1918

Following the commencement in 1918 of civil war in Russia between Bolsheviks and Mensheviks, there occurred a period of brutality which rivalled the excesses of earlier periods. Captured communists were given short shrift by the peasantry for whom the overthrown Tsar still represented the nation's "little father":

They would open a prisoner's belly, take out the small intestine and, nailing it to a tree or telegraph pole, they drove the man around the tree with blows, watching the intestine unwind through the wound. Stripping a captured officer naked, they tore strip's of skin from his shoulders in the form of shoulder straps and knocked in nails in place of pips; they would pull off the skin along the lines of the sword belt and trouser stripes – this operation became known as "to dress in uniform".

AFRICAN LIONS WITH AN APPETITE

Lions *(Panthera leo)* are big and powerful cats, and their tendency to hunt co-operatively in a pride makes them formidable predators, well able to pull down animals much bigger than themselves. In the wild, they rarely grow larger than nine feet (2.7 m) long and weigh 550 1b (249 kg), although there was a huge lion shot near Hectorspruit in the eastern Transvaal of South Africa in 1936 that scaled 690 1b (313 kg). While game, such as antelope, wild pigs and buffalo, makes up most of a lion's diet, occasionally people are taken as well.

One of the earliest records of a maneating lion appears to be an Assyrian ivory panel from Nimrud, dating from the eighth century BC. It depicts a man being grabbed by the throat by a lion. The panel is exhibited at the British Museum in London.

One of the most successful group of maneating lions must have been a pride of seventeen lions that lived in a game reserve at the northern end of Lake Nyasa in Tanzania. The pride and its offspring went on a fifteen-year rampage that accounted for about 1,000 to 1,500 human deaths. Records were not kept so nobody is certain of the final toll. The pride was known as the "'Njombe Man-eaters".

In 1925, two lions were reported to have devoured 124 people in Ankole in Uganda, and another pride, consisting of five sub-adult lions, accounted for twenty human deaths in the Lindi district during 1935. Previously in the same area, lions killed and ate 140 people in the course of a few months.

During the Second World War, reports emerged describing how 153 people were eaten by two prides of lions – one group of five and the other of eight – in the sub-chiefdom of Wangingombe, in Uganda.

These bouts of maneating seemed to coincide either with a reduction in the numbers of game animals or with inclement weather. In 1904, for example, maneating lions were prevalent in Rutshuru in eastern Congo, their newly acquired eating habits coinciding with a marked reduction in the herds of topi and kob.

In the main, though, humans seem to fall foul of solitary or "exiled" lions without a pride and old or infirm individuals who are incapable of running down a meal. In 1977 a rogue lion, which attacked twelve people and killed eight in Tanzania, was found to have only three legs.

People, particularly anybody walking alone in the bush, present an easy feeding option for lions, that is, after the initial fear of man is overcome. But once a lion has tasted human flesh it seems to seek more. There is, for example, the case of a rogue lion taking fourteen people in Malawi during the course of just one month. Another in the Numgari District of what was Portuguese West Africa accounted for twenty-two local village folk in eight weeks. It was shot in September 1938. And in October 1943, a rogue lion was shot after it had killed and eaten forty people in Kasama District of what was Northern Rhodesia.

At the Lake Manyara National Park in Tanzania, a lion took an interest in a village rubbish dump where it came into contact with human smells, and lost its fear of people. One night a drunken man staggered about in the road and the lion grabbed and ate him. Having acquired the taste of human flesh, it despatched another two villagers before it was isolated and killed.

Further to the south, in South Africa, the stories are legend. The Landdrost, Joseph Sterreberg Kupt, for example, was looking to buy some oxen for the Dutch East India Company and arrived at a kraal and pitched camp. During the night the horses and cattle were restless, and the entire camp left their tents, guns in hand, to investigate the disturbance. About 100 yards (100 m) from the tents they could see a lion standing. When it saw the people assembling, the lion moved about thirty yards (30m) further on. It stopped behind a small thorn bush at the bottom of a steep hill where Kupt thought it had hidden a young ox. The men fired about sixty shots, hoping to kill the beast. The moon shone brightly and so they could see clearly that there was no movement from the vicinity of the bush.

Kupt's people settled the cattle, but then noticed that a sentry – Jan Smit from Antwerp – was missing. They called for him, but there was no reply. They then thought that the body the lion had behind the bush was that of Jan Smit. A group of men moved cautiously towards the bush, but the lion was still alive and stood up and roared. They all retreated rapidly, but not before they spotted the cocked musket of the sentry. The men fired another barrage of 100 shots at the bush. All was still, and so a marksman worked his way forward. Again, the lion roared and leapt at the man. He threw a thunderflash, and the others fired a fusillade of ten more shots. The lion hid again behind the bush.

As dawn came up, the lion climbed the hill with the sentry's body in his mouth. Another forty shots were loosed, but the lion escaped with his victim. In order to retrieve the body fifty armed Hottentots were despatched. They found the lion a few miles further on. It began to run away, but they gave chase. The lion then turned and ran straight towards its pursuers. One of the group was attacked, but the head of the kraal put himself between the lion and the man, and stabbed it with an assegai. The rest of the Hottentots drew their weapons and speared the lion until it resembled a porcupine, but the lion was still full of life. Eventually, the marksman put a ball in the lion's eye, which caused him to fall. Others shot him dead. The lion was recognized as one which had taken one of the Hottentots from the kraal and eaten him only a few days before Kupt's visit . . .

STALIN'S TERROR FAMINE

Seventy years after the events, Ukrainian Bishop Alexander Bykovetz vividly recalled the horrors of Stalin's "terror famine", which occurred in the Ukraine and elsewhere in the Soviet Union in the 1930s:

"I remember well the events of 1932–3, even though I was only a small boy . . . I have first-hand information from my grandfather, who came to us begging for help and then described in detail the terrible problems in the villages . . .

"People started to eat their animals, then pets like cats and dogs. They were wandering around the village and its outskirts looking for dead horses and cows and then consumed them raw. Then, when there were no more animals to eat, people started to die by the hundreds. Finally, when there was nothing at all to eat and no one to turn to for help, some women, in a fever of hunger and out of their minds, even started to eat their own babies . . ."

HE WAS A GOOD LION

When I was a little girl I spent all my days with the Nandi Murani, hunting barefooted, in the Rongai Valley, or in the cedar forests of the Mau Escarpment, Kenya.

At first I was not permitted to carry a spear, but the Murani depended on nothing else.

You cannot hunt an animal with such a weapon unless you know the way of his life. You must know the things he loves, the things he fears, the paths he will follow. You must be sure of the quality of his speed and the measure of his courage. He will know as much about you, and at times make better use of it.

But my Murani friends were patient with me.

"Amin yut!" one would, say. "What but a *dik-dik* will run like that? Your eyes are filled with clouds today, *lakweit!*"

That day my eyes were filled with clouds, but they were young enough eyes and they soon cleared. There were other days and other *dik-dik*. There were so many things.

There were *dik-dik* and leopard, *kongoni* and wart-hog, lion, and the "hare that jumps". There were many thousands of the hare that jumps.

And there were wildebeest and antelope. There was the snake that crawls and the snake that climbs. There were birds, and young men like whips of leather, like rainshafts in the sun, like spears before a *singiri*.

"Amin yut!" the young men would *say*. "That is no buffalo spoor, *lakweit*. Here! Bend down and look. Bend down and look at this mark. See how this leaf is crushed. Feel the wetness of this dung. Bend down and look so that you may learn!"

And so, in time, I learned. But somethings I learned alone.

There was a place called Elkington's Farm by Kabete Station. It was near Nairobi on the edge of the Kikuyu Reserve, and my father and I used to ride from town on horses or in a buggy, and on the way my father woud tell me things about Africa.

Sometimes he would tell me stories about the tribal wars – wars between the Masai and the Kikuyu (which the Masai always won), or between the Masai and the Nandi (which neither of them ever won), and about their great leaders and their wild way of life which, to me, seemed much greater fun than our own. He would tell me of Lenana, the brilliant Masai *ol-oiboni*, who prophesied the coming of the White Man, and of Lenana's tricks and stratagems and victories, and about how this people were unconquerable and unconquered – until, in retaliation for the refusal of the Masai warriors to join the King's Africa Rifles, the British marched upon the native villages; how, inadvertently, a Masai woman was killed, and how two Hindu shopkeepers were murdered in reprisal by the Murani. And, thus, why it was that the thin red line of Empire had grown slightly redder.

He would tell me old legends sometimes about Mount Kenya, or about the Menegai Crater, called the Mountain of God, or about Kilimanjaro. He would tell me these things and I would ride alongside and ask endlesss questions, or we would sit together in the jolting buggy and just think about what he had said.

One day, when we were riding to Elkington's, my father spoke about lions.

"Lions are more intelligent than some men," he said, "and more courageous than most. A lion will fight for what he has and for what he needs; he is contemptuous of cowards and wary of his equals. But he is not afraid. You can always trust a lion to be exactly what he is – and never anything else."

"Except", he added, looking more paternally concerned than usual, "that damned lion of Elkington's!"

The Elkington Lion was famous within a radius of twelve miles from the farm, because, if you happened to be anywhere inside that circle, you could hear him roar when he was hungry, when he was sad, or when he just felt like roaring. If, in the night, you lay sleepless on your bed and listened to an intermittent sound that began like the bellow of a banchee trapped in the bowels of Kilimanjaro and ended like the sound of that same banshee suddenly at large and arrived at the foot of your bed, you knew (because you had been told) that this was the song of Paddy.

Two or three of the settlers in East Africa at that time had caught lion cubs and raised them in cages. But Paddy, the Elkington lion, had never seen a cage.

He had grown to full size, tawny, black-maned and muscular, without a worry or a care. He lived on fresh meat, not of his own killing. He spent his waking hours (which coincided with every body else's sleeping hours) wandering through Elkington's fields and pastures like an affable, if apostrophic, emperor, a-stroll in the gardens of his court.

He throve in solitude. He had no mate, but pretended indifference and walked alone, not toying too much with imaginings of the unattainable. There were no physical barriers to his freedom, but the lions of the plains do not accept into their respected fraternity an individual bearing in his coat the smell of men. So Paddy ate, slept and roared, and perhaps he sometimes dreamed, but he never left Elkington's. He was a tame lion, Paddy was. He was deaf to the call of the wild.

"I'm always careful of that lion," I told my father, "but he's really harmless. I have seen Mrs Elkington stroke him."

"Which proves nothing," said my father. "A domesticated lion is only an unnatural lion – and whatever is unnatural is untrustworthy."

Whenever my father made an observation as deeply philosophical as that one, and as inclusive, I knew there was nothing more to be said.

I nudged my horse, and we broke into a canter covering the remaining distance to Elkington's.

It wasn't a big farm as farms went in Africa before the First World War, but it had a very nice house with a large veranda on which my father, Jim Elkington, Mrs Elkington, and one or two other settlers sat and talked with what to my mind was always unreasonable solemnity.

There were drinks, but beyond that there was a tea-table lavishly spread, as only the English can spread them. I have sometimes thought since of the Elkington's tea table – round, capacious, and white, standing with sturdy legs against the green vines of the garden, a thousand miles of Africa receding from its edge.

It was a mark of sanity, I suppose, less than of luxury. It was evidence of the double debt England still owes to ancient China for her two gifts that made expansion possible – tea and gunpowder.

But cakes and muffins were no fit bribery for me. I had pleasures of my own then, or constant expectations. I made what niggardly salutations I could bring forth from a disinterested memory and left the house at a gait rather faster than a trot.

As I scampered past the square hay-shed a hundred yards or so behind the Elkington house I caught sight of Bishon Singh, whom my father had sent ahead to tend our horses.

I think the Sikh must have been less than forty years old then, but his face was never any indication of his age. On some days he looked thirty and on others he looked fifty – it all depended on the weather, the time of day, his mood, or the tilt of his turban. If he had ever disengaged his beard from his hair and shaved the one and clipped the other he might have astonished us all by looking like one of Kipling's elephant boys, but he never did either, and so, to me at least, he remained a man of mystery, without age or youth, but burdened with experience, like the Wandering Jew.

He raised his arm and greeted me in Swahili as I ran through the Elkington farmyard and out towards the open country.

Why I ran at all or with what purpose in mind is beyond my

answering, but when I had no specific destination I always ran as fast as I could in the hope of finding one – and I always found it.

I was within twenty yards of the Elkington lion before I saw him. He lay sprawled in the morning sun, huge, black-maned, and gleaming with life. His tail moved slowly, stroking the rough grass like a knotted rope end. His body was sleek and easy, making a mould where he lay, a cool mould, that would be there when he had gone. He was not asleep; he was only idle. He was rusty-red, and soft, like a strokable cat.

I stopped, and he lifted his head with magnificent ease and stared at me out of my yellow eyes.

I stood there staring back, scuffling my bare toes in the dust, pursing my lips to make a noiseless whistle – a very small girl who knew about lions.

Paddy raised himself then, emitting a little sigh, and began to contemplate me with a kind of quiet premeditation like that of a slow-witted man fondling an unaccustomed thought.

I cannot say that there was any menace in his eyes; because there wasn't, or that his "frightful jowls" were drooling, because they were handsome jowls and very tidy. He did sniff the air, though, with what impressed me as being close to audible satisfaction. And he did not lie down again.

I remembered the rules that one remembers. I did not run. I walked very slowly, and I begin to sing a defiant song.

"Kali coma Simba sisi," I sang, *"Asikari yoti ni udari!"* ("Fierce like the lion are we, Askari all are brave!")

I went in a straight line past Paddy while I sang it, seeing his eyes shine in the thick grass, watching his tail beat time to the metre of my ditty.

"Twendi, twendi – ku pagana – piga aduoi – piga sana!" ("Let us go, let us go – to right – beat down the enemy! Beat hard, beat hard!")

What lion would be unimpressed with the marching song of the King's African Rifles?

Singing it still, I took up my trot towards the rim of the low hill which might, if I were lucky, have Cape gooseberry bushes on its slopes.

The country was grey-green and dry, and the sun lay on it closely, making the ground hot under my bare feet. There was no sound and no wind.

Even Paddy made no sound, coming up swiftly behind me.

What I remember most clearly of the moment that followed are three thing – a scream that was barely a whisper, a blow that struck me to the ground, and as I buried my face in my arms and felt Paddy's teeth close on the flesh of my leg, a fantastically bobbing turban, that was Bishon Singh's turban, appear over the edge of the hill.

I remained conscious, but I closed my eyes and tried not to be. It was not so much the pain as the sound.

The sound of Paddy's roar in my ears will only be duplicated, I think, when the doors of hell slip their wobbly hinges one day, and give voice and authenticity to the whole panorama of Dante's poetic nightmares. It was an immense roar that encompassed the world and dissolved me in it.

I shut my eyes very tight and lay still under the weight of Paddy's paws.

Bishon Singh said afterwards that he did nothing. He said he had remained by the hay-shed for a few minutes after I ran past him, and then, for no explainable reason, had begun to follow me. He admitted, though, that, a little while before, he had seen Paddy go in the direction I had taken.

The Sikh called for help, of course, when he saw the lion meant to attack, and half a dozen of Elkington's sices had come running from the house. Along with them had come Jim Elkington with a rawhide whip.

Jim Elkington, even without a rawhide whip, was very impressive. He was one of those enormous men whose girths alone seem to preclude any possibility of normal movement, much less of speed. But Jim had speed – not to be loosely compared with lightning, but rather like the speed of something spherical and smooth and relatively irresistible, like the cannon balls of the Napoleonic Wars. Jim was, without question, a man of considerable courage, but in the case of my Rescue from the Lion it was, I am told, his momentum rather than his bravery for which I must ever be grateful

It happened like this – as Bishon Singh told it:

"I am resting against the walls of the place where hay is kept, and first the large lion and then you, Beru, pass me, going towards the open field, and a thought comes to me that a lion and a young girl are strange company, so I follow. I follow to the place where the hill goes up becomes the hill that goes down, and where it goes down deepest I see thta you are running without much thought in your head and the lion is running behind you with many thoughts in his head, and I scream for everybody to come very fast.

"Everybody comes very first; but the large lion is faster than anybody, and he jumps on your back and I see you scream, but I hear no scream. I only hear the lion, and I begin to run with everybody, and this includes Bwana Elkington who is saying a great many words I do not know and is carrying a long *kiboko* which he holds in his hand and is meant for beating the lion.

"Bwana Eikington goes past me the way a man with lighter legs and fewer inches around his stomach might go past me, and he is waving the long *kiboko* so that it whistles over all of our heads like a very sharp wind, but when we get close to the lion it comes to my mind that that lion is not of the mood to accept a *kiboko*.

"He is standing with the front of himself on your back, Beru, and you are bleeding in three or five places, and he is roaring. I do not believe Bwana Elkington could have thought that that lion at that moment would consent to being beaten, because the lion was not looking the way he had ever looked before when it was necessary for him to be beaten. He was looking as if he did not wish to be disturbed by a *kiboko*, or the Bwana of the sices, or Bishon Singh, and he was saying so in a very large voice.

"I believe that Bwana Elkington understood this voice when he was still more than several feet from the lion, and I believe the Bwana considered in his mind that it would be the best thing not to beat the lion just then, but the Bwana when he runs very fast is like the trunk of a great baobob tree rolling down a slope, and it seems that because of this it was not possible for him to explain the thought of his mind to the soles of his feet in a sufficient quickness of time to prevent him from rushing much closer to the lion than in his heart he wished to be.

"And it was this circumstance, as I am telling it," said Bishon Singh, "which in my considered opinion made it possible for you to be alive, Beru."

"Bwana Elkington rushed at the lion then, Bishop Singh?"

"The lion, as of the contrary, rushed at Bwana Elkington," said Bishon Singh. "The lion deserted you for the Bwana, Beru. The lion was of the opinion that his master was not in any honest way deserving of a portion of what he, the lion, had accomplished in the matter of fresh meat through no effort by anybody except himself."

Bishon Singh offered this extremely reasonable interpretation with impressive gravity, as if he were expounding the Case for Lion to a chosen jury of Paddy's peers.

"Fresh meat . . ." I repeated dreamily, and crossed my fingers. "So then what happened . . . ?"

The Sikh lifted his shoulders and let them drop again. "What could happen, Beru? The lion rushed for Bwana Elkington, who in his turn rushed from the lion, and in so rushing did not keep in his hand the long *kiboko,* but allowed it to fall upon the ground, and in accomplishing this the Bwana was free to ascend a very fortunate tree, which he did."

"And you picked me up, Bishon Singh?"

He made a little dip with his massive turban. "I was happy with the duty of carrying you back to this very bed, Beru, and of advising your father, who had gone to observe some of Bwana Elkington's horses, that you had been moderately eaten by the large lion. Your father returned very fast, and Bwana Elkington some time later returned very fast, but the large lion has not returned at all."

The large lion had not returned at all. That night he killed a horse, and the next night he killed a yearling bullock, and after that a cow fresh for milking.

In the end he was caught and finally caged, but brought to no rendezvous with the firing squad at sunrise. He remained for years in his cage, which, had he managed to live in freedom from his inhibitions, he might never have seen at all.

It seems characteristic of the mind of man that the repression of what is natural to humans must be abhorred, but that what is natural to an infinitely more natural animal must be confined within the bounds of a reason peculiar only to men – more peculiar than seems reasonable at all.

Paddy lived, people stared at him and he stared back, and this went on until he was an old, old lion. Jim Elkington died, and Mrs Elkington, who really loved Paddy, was forced, because of circumstances beyond her control or Paddy's, to have him shot by Boy Long, the manager of Lord Delamere's estates.

This choice of executioners was, in itself, a tribute to Paddy, for no one loved animals more or understood them better, or could shoot more cleanly than Boy Long.

But the result was the same to Paddy. He had lived and died in ways not of his choosing. He was a good lion. He had done what he could about being a tame lion. Who thinks it just to be judged by a single error?

I still have the scars of his teeth and claws, but they are very small now and almost forgotten, and I cannot begrudge him his moment.

SPOTTED HYENAS HUNT IN PACKS

It was at Olorgesailie that I saw my first striped hyena by daylight. While driving at night I had from time to time glimpsed striped hyenas crossing the road in the glare of the headlights, but on this occasion Mary and I were exploring a small side gully in the cliffs about a mile to the south of the camp when, suddenly, our long-haired Dalmatian, Sally, rushed into a clump of bushes and drove a pair of striped hyenas out into broad daylight, where we could see them clearly. These are the true hyenas, known scientifically as *Hyena hyena*. They have a wide geographical distribution, ranging from India through the Near East and all along the North African coast as well as most of Africa south of the Sahara. They seldom occur in forested areas, except in a small corner of the eastern Congo. Striped hyenas were known to science long before spotted hyenas and earned themselves the reputation, in North Africa and in India, of being cowardly scavengers, who would venture into villages at night and steal whatever refuse they could find but run away at the first sight of man.

As exploration in Africa increased, the much larger spotted hyena, known to science by a different generic name, *Crocuta,* became confused by laymen with the striped hyena and, consequently, earned the same reputation as a cowardly scavenger and thief. When I was a boy, this view was widespread among Europeans. But it was mistaken. My Kikuyu friends used to warn me against the dangers of being attacked by the spotted hyena, which they called *hiti,* while the striped hyena, known as *kibubui,* was not feared at all. Spotted hyenas often hunt in packs. Recent scientific studies undertaken by Dr Hans Kruuk and the van Lawicks have revealed that they quite frequently kill large animals, like wildebeest and zebra. On occasion, they will even attack lions on a kill or a baby rhinoceros that is being defended by its mother.

I vividly remember three incidents in my childhood days involving attacks by spotted hyenas. In the first, a big bull accidentally left out at night on Gray Leakey's farm near Nyeri, on the slopes of Mount Kenya, was found and killed by a pack of spotted hyenas.

The second attack involved a young girl of about fifteen near my home at Kabete. Fortunately, her screams were heard, and the villagers rushed out and drove off the hyenas, but she suffered a severe bite in the buttocks. Although it healed eventually, she was left with a permanent hollow where the flesh had been torn out.

On the third occasion, also near Kabete, two bullocks that had been left in a paddock by my friend Miss Olive Collier were killed and eaten by spotted hyenas . . .

As I have recounted in my earlier book, *White African*, Ndekei, my driver, and I were once attacked on the Balbal, near Olduvai, by a clan of about seventeen of these animals and managed to escape only by driving them off with shotguns and killing two of them. These two were then eaten by the rest of the pack. Such cannibalism is rare among spotted hyenas; these must have been very hungry indeed.

Unlike the spotted hyena, which has been the subject of at least two detailed studies and is likely to be studied again, we still know extraordinarily little about the habits of the striped hyena, partly because it is so completely nocturnal that it is seldom seen.

WHITE FURY ON THE BARRENS

The weather-beaten trading schooner *Venture*, forty-three long and auxiliary powered with an ancient diesel engine, dropped anchor in Long Island Sound on the evening of 22 July 1937. Not the Long Island Sound you have heard about. This one is a narrow channel of the sea lying between another Long Island and the east shore of Hudson Bay, about thirty-five miles north of Cape Jones, where the huge funnel of that bay narrows into James Bay, which forms its spout.

For an Arctic trading schooner, the *Venture* carried strange cargo, including eighteen humans. Nine of us were clients, sportsmen from the States, the first such party ever to cruise up the Quebec shore of James Bay and Hudson Bay to fish, hunt, photograph and see the country.

Lloyd Melville, from Rydal Bank, Ontario, who had organized the trip and chartered the *Venture* for it, planned to conduct similar guided tours into and fabulously wild country each year from then on, but the plan fell through, and ours was the last as well as the first group to undertake it.

Melville's crew consisted of three guides and a cook. The *Venture* was skippered by Jack Palmquist, the only free trader then operating on James Bay in competition with the Hudson's Bay Company. He had a small trading post at Old Factory, on the coast about half way between the Eastmain and Fort George rivers. Married to a mission-educated Cree girl, and speaking Cree as readily as English, he had an inside track with the Indians and was doing all right.

He had a crew of three aboard the *Venture*. Alagkok, the little Eskimo engineer, spoke no English but understood the workings of the throbbing old diesel as a man understands a well-loved wife – and gave it the same affectionate care. The deckhand was a Cree, equally innocent of English, whose name time has erased from my memory. And, because no charts existed for the treacherous island-girt passages along that coast, and no white skipper of that day would have dreamed of sailing them without a Cree pilot aboard (and probably wouldn't even today), at Eastmain we had taken on an aged and leather-faced Indian, Boson Kagaback, as pilot.

Only the Crees knew those waters well enough, from a lifetime of canoe travel, to recall the endless landmarks along the bleak coast, follow the channels and avoid the reefs. Kagaback, who had piloted for years for the Hudson's Bay Company, saw us safely north to Fort George. There we exchanged him for Tommy Lameboy, equally weathered, who knew the coast the rest of the way.

We had left the end of steel on the T & NO Railroad at Moosonee on 12 July, when the *Venture* moved down the Moose River into the open waters of James Bay and pointed her nose north. When the wind favoured us, we ran under sail. When it didn't, the wheezing diesel pushed us along at a lumbering six knots.

We were headed into a region that only a handful of whites – the men of the Hudson's Bay Company, an occasional free trader, missionaries, Mounties, and now and then a roving prospector – had ever seen. Not a foot of road lay between us and the Arctic ice, not even a blazed trail save for the portages the Crees had cut around the rapids on the big rivers they travelled. If you went into that bleak Land of Midnight Twilight, you went by canoe or ship in summer, by dog team in winter.

Below decks the *Venture* carried our duffle and luggage, tents and camping equipment. Lashed to the rails were four big freight canoes that would carry us to the fishing pools of the barrenland rivers, and also would serve to ferry the clients and guides ashore each night to make camp. There was not room aboard the old forty-three footer for eighteen to sleep.

I have roamed the back country of this continent for almost fifty years, from the Great Smokies and the diamondback-infested flatwoods of Florida to the Aleutian Islands of Alaska, but that treeless and empty subarctic land was the most fascinating place I have ever seen.

At Moose Factory, at Fastmain and at Fort George we found big camps of the Crees, down to the posts for the summer from their trapping and hunting grounds along the big rivers of the interior, a few of them living in tents, but the great majority in wigwams, as they had lived long before the first white men saw them. The wigwams were big and comfortable, and clean, too.

Consisting of a circular frame of poles, twelve to twenty feet across, they were covered with canvas, sealskins, whatever was available. The floor was carpeted deep with green spruce twigs, a ring of stones in the centre contained the fire, and a small opening at the top carried the smoke out. On poles outside hung gear of all kinds, snowshoes, dog harness, frames for drying pelts, and bundles of sphagnum moss that would be used for baby diapers and sanitary napkins, the all-around absorbent cotton of the North. And tied to stakes in front of every wigwam were the gaunt, hungry sled dogs, half-wild, furtive-eyed, crafty thieves, great workers but vicious fighters, ever on the lookout for trouble. Snowshoes and every scrap of harness had to be hung beyond their reach.

On Cape Hope Island, only 125 miles north of the mouth of the Moose, we dropped anchor one morning in front of a drab and cheerless cluster of low-roofed houses, some built of logs, some of rough, unpainted lumber whipsawed by hand from driftwood. This was the home of the Cape Hope Eskimo band, the southernmost of their race on the North American continent, headed by a wise old patriarch named Weteltik.

The smell of seal oil hung over the place, rancid and all-pervading. Whale and seal harpoons were racked by the doors, canoes and boats rested on high pole frames or, if they contained no leather, were drawn up on shore, and big surly dogs ranged the camp.

We went ashore, avoiding the dogs, and were met with a welcome so friendly that I have never forgotten it. We couldn't buy anything, for money had no value there, but we gave away cigarettes and traded tennis shoes and knives, soap, tea, sugar and jam, for whale harpoons, mukluks, ivory carvings and snowshoes. The trading was done through two interpreters. Weteltik understood Cree. Palmquist told him in that language what we wanted, and he passed the word on to his people in Eskimo. That morning was one I'll remember all my life.

But of that whole fascinating month, nothing stands forth in my mind more clearly than the trout fishing we found in the wonderful, tumbling rivers of the rocky moors, north of the limit of trees. (We were in that kind of country for more than a week, carrying our tent poles along from camp to camp, and combing the rocky beaches for driftwood to feed our camp and cooking fires.)

The fish were squaretails, the big speckled trout of northern Canada (we caught a few Arctic char too), but they were different in some ways from any of their kind I had ever encountered. They were untutored, uneducated and unwise.

They came of generations that had had no dealing with flies, spinners or any man-made device of treachery save the nets the roaming Crees set at the mouths of the rivers.

They took whatever was offered, swiftly and recklessly. They rose to flies, wet or dry, they smashed at spinners or the throat latch of another trout. They were no more canny than bluegills in a millpond, and no harder to catch.

One morning, without much hope of getting a response, I tore a narrow strip from a red bandanna handkerchief, knotted it around the shank of my hook, and fed it into a chute of green water at the foot of a pool. A sixteen-inch fish struck like forked lightning.

The trout ran from fifteen to twenty inches in length, heavy-bodied and fat. Many of them weighed three pounds, and they were as rugged in battle as any fish I have ever taken. It was no trick for three or four rods to catch in a morning all the party of eighteen needed for a day. Many times two flies on a leader took doubles, and frequently we landed six or eight trout from one pool before the action slacked off. I have never seen any other fishing to match it.

In the summer camp of the Crees at the Fort George Post, where 500 Indians were living in wigwams and tents scattered over a long, level meadow below the red-and-white buildings of the Hudson's Bay Company, we were introduced in a small way to the thing I was chiefly interested in, a polar bear hunt.

One of the Crees brought three white bearskins out of his wigwam and spread them on the grass. He wanted to trade.

They were the pelts of an adult and two fair-sized cubs. When we asked him, through Palmquist, where and how he had killed them, he had quite a story to tell.

Coming down the east coast of Hudson Bay and around Cape Jones in the spring, he said, he had blundered into the sow and her yearling youngsters. He had run his canoe ashore for the night and his woman was lugging the tent and other gear up to a little hollow above the beach. The Indian himself was still fooling around the canoe when the three bears walked into sight over a low ridge only thirty or forty yards away.

The female reared up to look things over and didn't like what she saw. She began to growl and swing her head. One of the cubs walked on a few feet, got a noseful of Cree, and squalled in alarm. That did it. The sow let go a hair-lifting bellow of rage and charged.

Luckily for the Indian, he had been watching for seals that afternoon and his rifle still lay in the bottom of the canoe, loaded and uncased. He scrambled for it while the bear was making up her mind, and when she started her rush he was ready for her. He knocked her off her feet with the first shot, finished her with the second, and then killed the cubs.

Those three pelts were the first polar bearskins I had ever seen outside a zoo. Thickly furred, ivory white and lustrous, they whetted my appetite for an ice-bear rug of my own as nothing else had done.

At the end of his recital, the Indian ventured a sentence in English. "Plenty bear this year!" he grunted.

To this day I don't know whether he meant that he had had his fill of them for the time being, or that they were abundant and our chances would he good.

There was no open hunting season for sportsmen on polar bears on that coast then. All game was kept for the natives. If an ice bear was taken by a white man, it had to be under a permit issued to a museum or scientific institution and the bear, or at least its skull, must go for scientific purposes. That did not prevent the hunter from keeping the pelt, however.

Two of us had the coveted permits, calling for two bears apiece. Howard Cooper of Kalamazoo, a friend and hunting partner of mine who died many years ago, would try to collect his bears for a museum in his home city. My permit had been issued to the Cranbrook Institute of Science at Bloomfield Hills, Michigan.

The great white bear of the north (the Eskimos call him Nanook, the Crees Wahb'-es-co) is not always an animal of sea and ice floe. In the brief arctic summer he ranges along the coast and the rocky islands of the polar sea as well, I suppose feeding on mice and lemmings, birds' eggs, berries, and fish and seals, like all bears.

The Crees and Eskimos had told us that bears summered regularly on the islands in Hudson Bay and at the northern end of James Bay, but, because twenty to forty miles of open ocean lay in their way, they rarely hunted them, although the law allowed them to kill any they could.

We found ample proof of what they said on some of the islands, too. Bear tracks crossed the beaches, holes had been dug in gravel banks for shelter from the summer sun, grass flattened where the animals had bedded, rocks overturned, and other sign was there in abundance. One of the islands – the Crees called it Niska or Grey Goose – had been literally torn up by bears.

A few days after we saw the three pelts at Fort George and heard the Indian's story of how he took them, we reached Long Island Sound, the bleakest and most desolate region we had seen. Treeless islands, rocky shores, moss and arctic willow. We were in polar bear country at last.

The first evening Eskimos paddled out to the *Venture* to trade fresh caught char for canned peaches. Through two interpreters, Alagkok and our skipper, they told us there were many bears on a place they called Bear Island, fifteen to thirty miles offshore. It did not show on our maps, and even now I am not sure of its correct name.

Cooper and I headed for it the next morning with Palmquist and the crew, leaving the rest of the party camped on Long Island.

When we reached the island the Eskimos had talked about, it proved to be a bleak, rolling tabletop of rock and moss, some two miles long and half as wide, rising steeply in a series of cliffs at the southern end, sloping to the north and ending in a long reef running out into the ocean.

We came in under it in a north-west gale, with a black squall sweeping down on us, and the rocky bottom would not hold the *Venture*'s anchors. We looked in vain for an opening in the ragged, surf-fringed beach, and when none appeared we ran for a smaller island a mile away.

There we found a snug little harbour, covered with a black raft of ducks. We went ashore to have a look at the bigger island with binoculars, and almost at once Howard Cooper spotted what we were hoping to see, a white bear at the foot of the cliffs, alternately lying down and pawing rocks around as if hunting for mice.

The storm and raging seas held us in that harbour for four hours. All that time the bear wandered around in plain sight, either below the cliffs or on the rocky tundra above them. At last our patience was exhausted. If we did not go after him before dark, Tommy Lameboy and Palmquist agreed, he would be likely to leave the island and take to the sea during the night.

There was no hope of crossing to Bear Island in a canoe. We'd have to run the *Venture* out in plain view and risk spooking him.

He saw or heard us as soon as we cleared our little harbour and, while we beat our slow way across the churning channel, he stood near the top of the cliffs and watched us, the only thing on all that bleak island or in the smoking sea, a bear carved from old ivory, the most unforgettable animal my eyes have ever rested on.

When we were within 300 yards of shore he climbed deliberately up the cliff and galloped off, stopping now and then to look back our way.

Lameboy had the *Venture*'s wheel. At Palmquist's sharp order he ran the schooner within fifty yards of the jagged rocks where the surf was smoking, then turned parallel to the beach. A canoe was trailing at the stern. Tommy and Cooper and I tumbled into it, and somehow we got through the surf and scrambled out on shore, and dragged the freight canoe up beyond reach of the sea. Then we followed the bear up the cliff.

Cooper and I were carrying .300 Savage rifles. At the time we thought them adequate. I wouldn't think so today, not for a bear of that size. But at least we were better off than the old Cree. He had no gun at all.

The bear was out of sight behind the low backbone of the island, and we went after him at a run. But the running was wretchedly hard, over soft moss, around shallow pools and between huge rocks, and before we reached the crest of the ridge I dropped out. Sweat was streaming down my face despite the bitter ice-field wind, and I couldn't get enough air into my lungs. I'd be in no condition to shoot if we met the bear, I concluded. I swung back toward the sea cliffs, thinking he might have turned that way.

I was at the top of the cliff when I heard distant rifle fire. Whirling around, I could see Cooper almost at the far side of the island, alternately shooting and then running a few steps. Another shot thudded and to my total astonishment the slug sang above my head. It had ricocheted off a rock, and the realization hit me that the bear must be somewhere between Cooper and me, or he would not be shooting in my direction.

I swung my head, and sure enough there was the bear, out of Cooper's range now, coming straight for me at a lumbering run.

He did not know I was there. Directly behind me a ravine led down the face of the cliff to the sea, forming a natural bear trail. It was for that he was headed.

I went down on the moss to get out of sight and watched him lope toward me, and I had mixed feelings. I wanted him to come on. This was the thing I had come north for, and the hunt was all in my hands now. We'd be face to face in another minute or two. Unless I stopped him cleanly and in his tracks, there'd be a very one-sided bear-and-man fight.

He was the first game I had ever faced more dangerous than a white-tail deer. I was no expert rifleman, no crack shot, and I couldn't help some small misgivings as to whether I was up to my part of what was coming. Events were to prove I wasn't.

He went out of sight in a shallow dip, and I got to my feet and started after him, afraid he'd turn off and get away. Then he came up on my side of the hollow, and I suddenly realized that a running bear is neither slow nor clumsy. This one was covering ground like a racehorse.

I dropped to one knee, and when I thought he was close enough I threw my first shot. It had no effect and I tried again, with no better result.

The third one stopped him. He stood, whipping his head from side to side, lashing and hitting at his own shoulders. When it was all over I learned that my 180-grain softnose had cut across his back under the skin and fat, just too high to break the spine or put him down. It was probably a painful wound, and it turned him into a bundle of explosive white fury, but it did nothing to disable him.

I thought he was badly wounded, and I scrambled erect to finish him. But, just as I shot the next time, he lurched ahead, and that one missed. Then, for the first time, he saw me.

The whole character of the hunt changed in a fraction of a second. I was no longer hunting the bear. He was hunting me. He dropped his head and came like an overgrown farm dog rushing out of a driveway at a passing car, and I did some desperately fast mental arithmetic.

I had started with five shells in the Savage. I had shot four times. I did the problem in subtraction with the speed of a computer, and did it over again. The answer was the same each time. There was one shell left in the chamber of the gun and there would be no time for reloading.

Instinct told me to drop the rifle and run, but my conscious mind knew better. Everything rested now on that single shell, and I still remember thinking I couldn't possibly kill him in time.

I cannot recall aiming or firing, but at the shot his head went down between his forelegs and he skidded to a stop, rolled up as tight as a shrimp. The bullet had struck him between the eyes, just below the bulge of the forehead, and had expanded so effectively that there was not a piece of unbroken bone bigger than a silver dollar left in his skull. A lightning bolt could not have killed more instantly.

I backed away while I fed five fresh hulls into the rifle. I waited two or three minutes then, feeling a whole lot better. When he did not move or twitch, I walked in with the safety off and prodded him around the head with the muzzle of the Savage. He was as lifeless as the rock he had fallen beside.

The next thing I did was walk back and find the empty cases I had levered out. From them to the bear I paced off exactly seventeen steps, fifty-one feet.

Someone asked me long afterward whether I had actually shot at his head the last time. "Hell, no," I said. "I just shot at the bear." And I guess that was the truth.

I had my white bearskin. I also had nightmares for weeks afterward.

It happened thirty-three years ago. I have done much hunting since, some with a gun, some with a camera. But I have never again put myself in a situation of that kind, and as long as I live I don't intend to.

TIGERS IN THE SUNDERBANS

Field workers in the Sunderbans, the 3,000-square-mile delta of the Ganges and Brahmaputra rivers straddling India and Bangladesh in the Bay of Bengal, have devised a range of human dummies wired to car batteries in an attempt to shock tigers out of their maneating habits.

Tigers are protected in the region, and the population of between 600 and 700 was thought in 1984 to be the largest in the world. Although few people live in the unhealthy landscape of mangrove forests, islets and mud flats, fishermen, woodcutters and honey collectors visit regularly and are picked off by the tigers at the rate of about fifty a year.

According to Earthscan, a London-based environment and development information agency, the experimental dummies have been devised to supplement a number of other defence techniques. Fireworks, for example, are provided free by the authorities, and other defences include body armour or helmets. Tribes have resisted the protective gear, however, as signifying a lack of faith in local sorcerers' abilities to protect against tigers.

It is thought that relatively few of the deaths in the Sunderbans are caused by maneaters; but the tiger population as a whole is noticeably more aggressive than most, and merely surprising a tiger can be fatal.

Unusually for tigers, the Sunderbans population have become good swimmers and include fish, crabs and monitor lizards among their prey. Drinking the predominantly brackish water in their environment may account for their exceptional ferocity, some scientists think, and artificial ponds are being built to trap fresh rainwater.

The dummies are linked to a twelve-volt battery through a transformer with an output of 240 volts. The current is very low, 0.001 amperes, and a fuse blows when the wires are touched. Individual tigers seem to have learned their lesson once they have been shocked, but it is still too early to tell whether the electrified "fishermen" will make any long-term difference to the casualty toll.

VAMPIRE BITES

A man aged 65 and his 11-year-old grandson have died after vampire bat bites which gave them rabies. Brazilian health officials are to start an anti-bat campaign.

"Bats usually attack animals, but attacks in Minas Gerais and Sao Paulo districts may be explained by a scarcity of livestock due to drought," said a local government officer.

A DINGO TOOK THE BABY

Twelve years after her ordeal began – three of them spent in jail – Lindy Chamberlain, the victim of what has been dubbed Australia's worst miscarriage of justice, won $Aus900,000 (£375,000) in compensation on 25 May 1992. Her estranged husband, Michael, was awarded $Aus400,000 (£166,000).

The case began in 1980 when Azaria, the Chamberlain's baby daughter, disappeared from her bed one night while the family was camping beneath Ayers Rock, the giant red monolith in the central Australian desert. The baby's disappearance and what followed became both the subject of a Hollywood film and arguably the most bizarre and bitter affair in Australian legal history.

Mrs Chamberlain's famous cry that "a dingo took the baby" became a catchphrase that divided Australia between those who believed her and those who did not. Dingo jokes in dubious taste are still told today, and the case, its facts and fiction, continues to be fiercely debated.

Among the believers was Meryl Streep, who starred as Mrs Chamberlain in *A Cry in the Dark*, the film which went some way towards bringing the family's side of the story to the attention of a wider audience. But years of vilification in the media, and their shabby treatment by the Northern Territory police and courts, contributed to the Chamberlains' divorce before the case was finally resolved.

Ignoring vital forensic evidence, the Northern Territory legal system in 1982 convicted Mrs Chamberlain of murdering her nine-week-old daughter in 1980. She was sentenced to life imprisonment and served three years in Darwin's Berrimah Prison before being pardoned. Mr Chamberlain was sentenced to eighteen months suspended, as an accessory after the fact of murder.

Their sentences were quashed in 1988 after an enquiry by the Northern Territory court of criminal appeal. Yesterday Daryl Manzie, the Northern Territory's attorney-general, settled their claims for compensation by making *ex gratia* payments totalling £Aus1.3million. The settlement was assessed independently by Judge Trevor Morling on behalf of the government. The Chamberlains' campaign for justice and compensation was consistently supported by Bob Collins, the Northern Territory Labour senator who is now a cabinet minister in Paul Keating's Australian government.

"In so far as money can compensate anybody for what, without question, has been the grossest miscarriage of justice in this country's legal history, I'm personally satisfied that it is impossible to argue with the amount," Senator Collins said.

The Chamberlains remain hidden from sight. Speaking from his home in Christchurch, New Zealand, Michael Chamberlain's father, Ivan, 75, told reporters. "As far as Michael is concerned, he vaguely endeavours to keep his life together and I think we are grateful for that. If money could rectify the harm and distress that has been caused to all the family, including my wife and myself, it would need to be substantial."

Michael Chamberlain now lives with Greta, his new wife, in the precincts of the Seventh Day Adventist College near Newcastle, on the coast north of Sydney. They have little contact with Lindy Chamberlain, who lives in the same region at Cooranbong on the New South Wales central coast. Both have shunned the media, as has Stuart Tibble, their lawyer. But Harry Miller, the Chamberlains' publicist, said: "News of what has happened is to be digested by them – for them to discuss with their attorney." The appearance on the scene of Mr Miller, regarded as Australia's biggest showbiz agent, suggests that the last of the Chamberlain affair has not necessarily yet been heard.

POLAR BEAR INVADER

Donald Chaffin was relaxing in front of the television at a remote Air Force radar station in Alaska when he noticed a visitor peeking in the window.

A polar bear, standing eight feet tall, was peering inside, with its nose and paws pressed against the glass. Chaffin tried to shoo it away, swatting at the pane with a rolled-up newspaper or magazine.

It was a mistake.

The bear ducked, then crashed through the window about seven feet above the ground. As Chaffin and a co-worker fumbled with a jammed door, the immense animal attacked, mauling Chaffin's face, neck and chest before another man shot it to death.

"Everything that moves is food to a polar bear," station manager Tom Leddy said.

Chaffin, 55, a civilian mechanic from Wasilla, Alaska, was in a serious condition Wednesday at an Anchorage hospital. His injuries from the attack on Tuesday evening, 31 November 1993, included lacerations and a collapsed lung.

The bear was shot by Alex Polakoff, one of Chaffin's five co-workers at the Alaska Long Range Radar System site at Olitok Point, about thirty miles north-west of Prudhoe Bay.

"There was no way to protect Don," Leddy said. "He was just brutally attacked. [The bear] was just doing what bears do . . . It was just fortunate Alex had a gun."

Leddy, who didn't see the attack, said workers told him Chaffin and another man were relaxing in the lounge when the bear appeared at the window. When it broke inside and attacked, one worker tried to distract the bear by spraying it with a fire extinguisher while Polakoff got his gun, which he kept for protection while working outdoors.

US Fish and Wildlife Service spokesman Bruce Batten said a bear had been spotted recently in the area, apparently attracted to the radar site by whale meal stored by native hunters. Leddy said he had been concerned the meat would attract bears and had been trying on Tuesday to get it removed.

He said officials at the nearby Kuparuk oil field had told him on Tuesday that a polar bear sow and two cubs were headed towards the radar site. It wasn't clear if the sow was the bear that attacked Chaffin.

Batten said polar bears are naturally curious and come around inhabited sites fairly often. The large, fearless hunters have no natural enemies except man and can grow to 1,500 lbs. Alaska has between 3,500 and 5,000 polar bears. By law, the bears can only be hunted by Inuit for food and traditional crafts. Non-Indians may only kill them in defence of life and property.

Batten said an attack like Tuesday's is unusual. Three years ago an underweight polar bear killed and partially ate a 28-year-old man walking through a village.

"A polar bear crashing through someone's window is the worst nightmare of the Arctic." Batten added. The bear's carcass will be studied by Fish and Wildlife Service veterinarians and scientists to see whether the animal was undernourished or suffering from some other condition that prompted the unusual behaviour.

CHINA'S TRADITION OF CANNIBALISM

Cannibalism has played a central role in Chinese Life and culture for nearly four millennia. So integral was it that Chinese author Lu Xun in his famous short story *Diary of a Madman* wrote that "4,000 years of Chinese history is actually 4,000 years of cannibalism".

Yet today in China, cannibalism is a dirty word. Only in the safety of exile can dissident academics such as Liu Binyan of Princeton University in America talk about how cannibalism evolved in Chinese culture:

> Firstly, it was of course related to natural disasters in China. During times of famine, people had no other way out, so they resorted to cannibalism. They would even use the phrase "to exchange one's children to eat" ("yi zi er shi") and actually eat their own children. I heard about this when I was young. It was true. But starvation was only one reason for cannibalism. Another was vengeance between one race and another, or one faction and another. You can find this in the poetry of Yue Fei. "Manjianghong" is one of his famous poems. It describes drinking the barbarians' blood and eating the barbarians' flesh. That was a way of treating other races – or one's own. Another form was not an expression of hatred, but an expression of loyalty to an emperor, or filial piety to one's parents. People might cut off part of their flesh or even cut out their liver to give their parents. This used to happen quite a lot.

Ever since the third century BC, when Han Emperor Gao Zu issued an official edict permitting people to sell or eat their children to ward off starvation, cannibalism has emerged at frequent intervals in Chinese history.

During sieges of walled cities in the dynastic conflicts of the sixth century, when warring clans like the Chu and the Song were continually skirmishing for territory, the word would go out that it was permitted "to exchange children to eat". More often, in fact, children who couldn't be fed would be taken into town to be sold. From there, the fate of these poor unfortunates was in the lap of the gods. So ingrained was this idea on the Chinese psyche that the expression "exchanging children to eat" worked its way into the language and is still used figuratively at times of great hunger.

Unlike in Russia, cannibalism in China was not practised merely to ward off starvation. It was also thought to have a medical and nutritional purpose. Dating back to the Tang Dynasty of the seventh to ninth centuries, the practice of Ko Ku was based on the powerful spiritual tradition of filial piety. It was when a faithful son or daughter cut off a portion of thigh or arm to serve to an ailing relative as the final medicinal resort.

American academic Professor Christine Yu Chun-Fang of Rutgers University, New Brunswick, New Jersey, heard about this notion of filial piety from her grandmother and set out to discover its origins. Of the many cases reported, most were of daughters-in-law seeking to help a parent-in-law after all other remedies had been exhausted and death was perhaps close at hand.

Typically, the devoted daughter-in-law would tie her thigh or her arm very tightly with a piece of clothing. She would then use a very sharp knife to quickly slice off a piece from her upper arm or upper thigh. The flesh would immediately be mixed in with soup or gruel, which had been heated in preparation, and this would then be offered to the dying mother-in-law or father-in-law. According to folklore, there would then follow without exception a miraculous recovery.

In an eerie echo of this ancient practice, a young Taiwanese woman, Li Xiujin, cut off a piece of her thigh and fed it to her unsuspecting mother and father as recently as 1987. Though she was later diagnosed as being mentally unstable, her action nevertheless appeared to be some kind of throwback to the filial piety of Ko Ku . . .

It has been suggested that China's ambivalent attitude to cannibalism has much to do with what is considered edible in a country which – like Russia – has always struggled to feed itself, as Liu Binyan explains:

Chinese cuisine is among the best in the world. Chinese restaurants keep many millions of Chinese in business around the world. We should either thank or blame our ancestors for this, because eating has also caused many problems, including environmental destruction and poverty-induced eating of everything edible or inedible.

When it comes to cannibalism, we have discussed famine and other reasons for it. But I think another reason is this: why, in history, did a minister kill his son, cook him and give him to his emperor? Surely it must have tasted good? Isn't that right? At first I didn't know, but I'm told that human flesh tastes good. The emperor would eat it because it was delicious. Human eating is to do with man and nature – whether you eat, how much you eat. But this then related to the relations between people. People became something that could be eaten. This desire can grow and grow.

This is a problem in China now. People want to eat everything, whether or not it should be eaten. This is a problem very peculiar to China . . . Otherwise why do people still eat people? Twenty years later there are still occasionally people in Beijing and the south who eat human flesh. I suspect that they might have had this experience in the past and have never forgotten the good taste. They are also probably deranged, so they carry on eating human flesh.

But one of the main reasons for today's reticence about cannibalism in China can be put down neither to a broad moral ambivalence nor to gastronomic adventurism, but to the consequences of her tragic and bloodstained revolutionary history. First there was the great famine of 1958–60. As in Stalin's Russia, Mao forced the rapid collectivization of farms in the Great Leap Forward. Grain levies were based on hugely inflated boasts of production. More was demanded than had actually been produced, and the people in the countryside were left starving. Jasper Becker, author of a major study of the famine entitled *Hungry Ghosts*, who has perhaps read more accounts of the suffering of the Chinese at the time than any other specialist on modern China, has commented:

Officials went around the countryside searching people's homes and collecting all possible grain. And if they couldn't find grain they took livestock and anything as a substitute. And by the end of the winter of 1958 in many places in China, people were left with nothing to eat, although the granaries were actually full and there was plenty of food. People began to starve and there were protests. A number of senior leaders began to protest about this, but Mao refused to believe it. He thought the protests signified the remnant of the capitalist spirit, and that the peasants were being dishonest. So they renewed the great quotas. This went on for three years, by which time thirty million, forty million, nobody is quite sure, a great, great many people had died in the countryside in China. Later on they claimed that this was a result of natural disasters. But there were no particular natural disasters during those years, and in fact the weather in most parts of the country was unusually good. This was a purely man-made famine.

Figures for the numbers of dead in the great famine range from twenty million to forty million. It was a period when the phrase to exchange one's children to eat' ('yi zi er shi') once again entered the Chinese vernacular. Jasper Becker believes that this was far from a simple turn of phrase or gallows humour:

> Some of the children were reportedly eaten. It was also claimed that people went out at night and cut the flesh off corpses that were lying in their huts or in the fields and consumed that. And in doing this they said they fell back on the traditions of surviving famines which had been part of their heritage for several thousand years. When I heard these stories I was rather sceptical. It is hard to believe that in the middle of the twentieth century, in a country basically at peace, where there was no real reason for there to be a famine, that such things could happen. And I went to the countryside in Hunan and I stopped peasants by the side of the road and I eventually asked them straight out if they had resorted to cannibalism. And people frankly admitted that they had, they themselves had taken part in this . . .
>
> In the party archives in An Hui province, official documents specifically described cases of cannibalism, of people being arrested and shot, of the government issuing public notices forbidding cannibalism. So you have this documentary evidence in addition to the fact that the local people frankly admitted what they had done. And, you know, because there's not such a specific moral or religious taboo about this, they don't really feel particularly ashamed of it.

The Communist Party has never acknowledged that a major famine existed, let alone revealed accurate figures for the numbers of dead. Even now, ordinary people and officials alike refer to that period as

"The Three Years of Natural Disaster" or "The Three Years of Difficulties".

But there was an even greater shame than refusing to acknowledge the millions who died in the famine. In one particular period of Chinese history, respect for human dignity broke down altogether. The brutality of Mao Zedong's Cultural Revolution in the late 1960s has long been known, but only recently has it come to light that in extreme cases cannibalism became an act of revenge against the class enemy.

At great risk to his own life, the writer and former Red Guard Zheng Yi smuggled into America evidence and official documents about the atrocities committed during the militant phase of the Cultural Revolution from 1966 to 1968. For giving away the secrets of the "revolution" he is now in permanent exile and can never again set foot in China. He, like Liu Binyan, pursues his writing and research at Princeton University.

One of the most appalling events about which he collected evidence is believed to be the most prolific episode of aggressive cannibalism in post-war history – an episode in which up to 10,000 people are believed to have taken part and over 100 people are believed to have been eaten. Zheng Yi not only procured official documents on this horror but also compiled the results of his own private investigation into the incident, conducted before he made his escape from the mainland. He interviewed the ringleaders and secretly took photographs that reveal an extraordinary and terrifying story.

The beautiful landscape of the province of Guangxi belies the barbaric fighting that took place here between rival factions of Red Guards during the Cultural Revolution. At the middle school in Wuxuan County, at the height of what is known as the militant phase of the Cultural Revolution, fanatical students turned on their own teachers.

It was, says Zheng Yi, a time when just killing the class enemy was not enough to express class hatred. Normal human notions of kindness and compassion – and indeed all ethical principles – were completely turned upside down. No moral or ethical obstacles were left to deter people from killing and even eating other people.

VENOMOUS SNAKES

A number of years ago a story was circulated about a Boer farmer in South Africa who was ploughing with his team of oxen when his plough passed through the subterranean nest of a mamba. The aroused snake quickly glided up the furrow and set out after the farmer and his oxen. The gracefully curved body flowed rapidly over the ground, and the snake neatly nipped the farmer on the neck. It then proceeded to bite each ox on the flank, and as quickly returned to its lair. The hapless farmer and the oxen allegedly died almost immediately.

This tale strongly impressed on me the terribly aggressive nature and deadliness of the mamba. Later I read another story confirming these early impressions. In this story, a pair of the snakes were engaged in amorous pursuits when they were disturbed by a young couple on horseback. At the sight of the snakes, the couple galloped away from the spot. Although they urged the horses to their best efforts, the enraged male mamba swiftly overtook them and bit both horses and riders, all of whom died shortly after.

Another story has appeared about a young couple driving along a South African road in a small open sportscar. They ran over a large Black Mamba that was basking in the road. The impact merely annoyed the snake, which set out after the fleeing car, soon caught up with it, and bit both occupants fatally.

Each of these stories was presented at the time as a supposedly factual experience. In the light of present knowledge about this snake and its frequent role in fictitious or exaggerated stories of African adventure, however, it seems certain that none of the stories has much factual basis, and that the similarity among them is more than coincidental. A large number of stories – virtually all imaginary – feature the mamba as a real terror of the bush, THE great hazard of life and travel in Africa.

Few snakes have ever had such energetic press agents as the mamba. Its very name is symbolic of treacherous and sinister death. Such is the dreadful spell of this name that a best-selling novel by the African writer Stuart Cloete bears the single-word title, "Mamba". Is such an awe-inspiring and infamous reputation justified, or is it, like so many things about snakes, another exaggeration?

While the mamba is perhaps the best known symbol of serpentine aggression, all snakes are considered in the same light by some people, and a number of other species are widely believed to attack human beings on sight. We must, of course, consider what we mean by the terms "aggression" and "aggressive" before we examine some examples of snake behaviour considered to be aggressive. For the individual killed by a falling airplane, it is of no consequence whether the plane was guided intentionally by a lunatic or whether it fell out of control of the hands of an inept student. However, the difference is of considerable interest to the rest of mankind. Similarly it makes a difference whether a snake makes an unprovoked attack, or whether it simply conducts an active defence when *it* is attacked.

Venomous snakes do not attack human beings for food. Only the rare giants among the largest species are physically capable of coping with prey as large as a man or woman. In the few cases where human beings have been killed by such giant snakes, the snake was either attacked or injured. Other than the necessity to defend itself, none but the larger snakes have any reason to attack human beings. Still the belief persists. Usually it is attributed to an inherent viciousness in snakes; occasionally it is linked to a strong territorial sense in which the snake is said to vigorously defend its home or nest. This notion involves a stronger sense of territorial rights or parental devotion than is known for snakes.

One of the most common reports of this supposed type of aggression is the tale of the enraged snake who comes to its murdered mate, usually seeking revenge. When Huckleberry Finn and his friend Jim were rafting down the Mississippi River, they camped on an island where Huck killed a rattlesnake and curled it up on the foot of Jim's blanket, hoping to have some fun at Jim's surprise when he found it. Huck forgot about the snake by nightfall, and poor Jim was bitten by the snake's mate. Remorsefully Huck says, "That all comes of my being such a fool as not to remember that wherever you have a dead snake its mate always comes there and curls around it." The widespread nature of this belief is indicated by the remarks of one of Stuart Cloete's characters, "Because you know, and I know, that if you kill a mamba its mate will look for it."

When two snakes are found near each other, their presence is usually coincidental; they are just as often of the same sex as of opposite sexes – and neither is likely to be interested in making an attack on the intruding human being. During the mating season snakes, particularly males, are alert to all movements and are more curious and bolder than at other times of the year. In some species the males locate females by following their scent. During this brief time a male could locate and remain near a freshly-killed female, but it would have no way of identifying the killer of the snake. And it would be no more likely to attack an intruder at such a time than it would before it encountered the dead snake.

Many other yarns about snakes elaborate beliefs of their supposedly aggressive nature. The Hoop Snake of the southern United States is alleged to launch its attacks by taking its tail in its mouth and rolling along like a hoop after its intended victim. When within striking distance, it supposedly releases its tail and hurls its body, tail first, inflicting a deadly sting with the tip of its tail. This story is entirely fictitious. No snake can roll along like a hoop, and no snake has a stinger in its tail. The Coachwhip Snake is another vicious attacker in American folklore. This speedy snake is said to be able to outrun the fastest horse. Supposedly when it overtakes its human victim it wraps the fore part of its body around the man's legs so that further running is impossible, and then it flogs him mercilessly with its long whiplike tail. The debunking of this belief, far more prevalent in the South than elsewhere, is said to have resulted in a widespread rise in juvenile delinquency. There is a snake known as the Coachwhip Snake because of its resemblance to a slender braided whip. It is a fast traveller, but any able-bodied boy or girl can outrun it with ease, and it does not use its tail as a whip.

A distinction should be made between an unprovoked attack and what can be termed "active defence." Technically there probably is no such thing as an *unprovoked* attack. However, if a snake attempts to rush toward a person and to bite *without having been disturbed*, this is, practically speaking, an unprovoked attack, and therefore a case of aggression. Striking at, hitting, stepping on, or suddenly threatening a snake constitutes provocation, and a snake reacting vigorously to any of these does so defensively and not aggressively. If you suddenly step beside a snake, or accidentally put your hand on one or close to it, such acts represents a threat to its welfare, and the snake's response, if any, is defensive. Since none but the largest snakes might eat human beings, the only reason for aggression would be malevolent viciousness or an easily-excited defensive behaviour. The latter might be related to the defence of a territory against intruders, or the active guarding of a nest. All have been cited in relation to alleged attacks by snakes, but are definitely exceptional types of behaviour.

Most snakes – both harmless and venomous – protect themselves from human beings by quickly crawling away or remaining completely still and being overlooked. Trouble often arises when snakes are cornered and cannot escape, when they are come upon suddenly and do not have time to escape, or when the intruder stands between them and the usual place of shelter. Being cornered is the primary reason for aggressive displays by snakes in captivity. Given the opportunity, most of the supposedly aggressive snakes escape. If they cannot rely on this normal means of protection, they are forced to defend themselves. Therefore, consideration here will be given primarily to snakes in the wild.

Often any movement toward a person is interpreted as an attack. This is especially true if the person is afraid of snakes. The greater the fear, the less the movement required to qualify as aggression in the mind of the person. In some instances this interpretation may be completely wrong. Twice when I have been snake-hunting I have had snakes try to escape by coming straight toward me and crawling between my legs *without* any attempt to bite. Another time, while I was watching some lizards in Florida, I had a Black Racer follow me for almost a hundred feet. As soon as I made a move in its direction, it departed in haste. Many herpetologists have had similar experience.

Arthur Loveridge, a longtime student of African wildlife both in the field and the laboratory, has written: "One day, I was standing on a large mass of smooth, but highly sloping rock, on a boulder-strewn hill. Below, and to the left of me, was a gunbearer searching for a hyrax which I had just shot. Above, and behind me, a second native was descending after going to retrieve a lizard which I had shot.

"Apparently, in descending he disturbed a mamba, possibly six feet in length, certainly not an inch less than five feet. It was so quick in its rush that he never saw it. I felt something bump and brush against my shoe, as I half-turned the snake was already in mid-air, having shot off the rock with the impetus of its descent. It landed twenty feet below on a mass of scrub and thorn, never paused, slid straight over another huge slab in full view, then dived into a tangle of vegetation beyond this rock and was seen no more. The boy on the rocks to the left below me, exclaimed: "'Did you see that big snake go right between your legs?'"

"As a matter of fact it was not actually between; what happened was that it had side-slipped with the velocity with which it arrived on the rock, then carromed against my shoe. I was thankful that my back was not towards it, for had I been facing the other way I should doubtless have gone to swell the ranks of those who thought they had been attacked by a mamba."

The existence of one aggressive snake out of a thousand does not earn the designation "aggressive" for the entire species. However, if many individuals are truly aggressive, then the species can be considered generally aggressive.

Pride of place for aggression unquestionably goes to the mamba on the basis of its widespread infamy. There are four species of mambas, all living in Africa and found nowhere else. They are:

Black or Brown Mamba – found throughout a wide area of Africa south of the Sahara. It attains a maximum length of fourteen feet, and is the longest venomous in Africa.

Green Mamba – occurs in central, eastern, and southern Africa. It reaches a maximum length of nine feet.

West African Mamba – inhabits western Africa and attains a length of eight feet.

Jameson's Mamba – found in the forest and scrub areas of central Africa. It reaches a maximum length of eight feet.

A fifth form, called the Transvaal Mamba, is listed in some books, but it is a minor variant of the Black Mamba and should not be considered distinct from it.

All of these are long, slender, agile snakes are found on the ground, as well as in the bushes and trees. The average person could not distinguish among the different species of mambas, and generally would confuse all of them with several other long and slender snakes. For years many herpetologists confused the Black (really a dark gray or brown and not a black-coloured snake) and the Green Mambas because the young and half-grown individuals of the Black Mamba are green in colour. However, there are important differences in structure and temperament. Because of its large size and excitable disposition, the Black Mamba is the scourge of the group, and especially aggressive individuals of this species have been reported frequently from South Africa. The others are generally shy and retiring except when injured or touched. Most field accounts do not distinguish accurately between these forms, and even if Black Mamba is specified, the identity is not certain in many instances.

F.W. Fitzsimons, for many years Director of the Port Elizabeth Museum and Snake Park in South Africa, had considerable experience with Black and Green Mambas, and related many stories about both in his book, *Snakes*. He says that the Green Mamba is shy and timid in disposition, always retreating when disturbed. He does not know of a single instance in which a Green Mamba has attacked without provocation. He does report cases where individuals were bitten when they brushed against a Green Mamba that was resting in a bush or stepped on one lying on the ground. In contrast to the Green Mamba, the Black Maniba is cousidered by Fitzsimons as a very excitable snake that will "invariably flee when disturbed" if given the opportunity.

Other herpetologists also have a great respect for this large snake, but all agree that it is not aggressive and will flee when given the chance. Walter Rose, in his book, *Snakes – Mainly South African*, wrote as follows: "Deadly it certainly is, having long fangs well to the front of the mouth, and venom of a highly toxic character; and in activity few if any snakes can surpass it; but it cannot be regarded as ferocious, being indeed an extremely nervous creature. Since we expressed this opinion in an earlier book, we have received letters from several correspondents, who have lived for years in mamba country and who have caught dozens of them, entirely agreeing with it. All lay stress on its inoffensiveness *unless molested*, deliberately or inadvertently."

He went on to say that deaths from mamba bite "are rare outside the pages of fiction, and then generally following some ill-advised, semi-hysterical attempt to kill one."

Arthur Loveridge has had many personal encounters with both Black and Green Mambas. His experiences confirm the statements already cited, but indicate that mambas are sometimes a hazard simply by their presence in the area and the fear they inspire in the human population. This is true wherever they may occur in abundance near human habitation. Sometimes trails or roads are closed merely because large mambas are regularly been in a given location. In Nyasaland, Loveridge reports that mambas appear to be particularly troublesome in the vicinity of Mount Hora, a rocky hill beside the main road. A government agricultural officer driving in the neighbourhood once had a large mamba rear up and hit the windshield of his car. Another district officer had a similar experience when a snake struck the door of the open touring car in which he and his family were driving. Loveridge quotes the acting provincial commissioner, whom he had queried about these snakes, as stating that what he assumed to be Black Mambas were fairly common in the district. "When surprised it rears up about chest high. Bus drivers stop if they see one on the road for fear it may strike a passenger."

This habit of rearing the head is common among racer-like snakes when disturbed or when investigating some movement. Loveridge cites an instance of a surprised mamba rearing up for a look and then going on its way. The group's headman was hurrying along after Loveridge "when he encountered a big snake that came sliding down the eroded, rock-strewn hillside and out on to the footpath within six feet of him. The startled snake reared up (allegedly higher than Thomas' face, a statement that may be discounted – Loveridge) and faced him for a few seconds, then dropping to the ground, it continued on downhill to a bush-choked ravine.

Loveridge reports other somewhat similar encounters with large Black Mambas. C. J. P. Ionides, Senior Game Ranger of Tanganyika territory and an experienced herpetologist, once suddenly came upon a large Black Mamba at close quarters. The snake raised its head about a foot off the ground and spread a hood so large that Ionides took a good look to be sure it was not a cobra. Meanwhile he retreated to get a stick, but the snake crawled off before he could catch it. On another occasion Ionides surprised a large female of the same species. The snake darted off but when Ionides followed, the mamba turned, reared about two feet from the ground, and spread a hood. After remaining motionless for awhile, she slowly advanced towards a small patch of grass that lay between them. For a short time she continued to stare at him over the grass, then made for a termite hill. He took out after the snake and caught it. Ionides has given his opinion of the mamba: "I quite agree that the mamba is not an aggressive snake, being rather timid and anxious to avoid an encounter. If cornered, it will strike out in self defence, but prefers to get away if it can. I have caught scores during the last few years and consider them quite gentle but very nervous snakes."

How, then, do we explain the aforementioned reports of mambas striking cars? Probably the snakes raised their heads to see what was approaching, but the cars came on them so fast they didn't get out of the way in time, and either struck at, or were hit so hard their heads were jerked against, the cars. In either case, the action would be an unsettling and dangerous one to experience, but can scarcely be attributed to truly aggressive action by the snake.

Loveridge tells of another encounter with a mamba that might have ended quite differently, one hardly in keeping with the popular idea of standard behaviour for a mamba. The episode occurred on Manda Island off the coast of Kenya. Loveridge was leading his men along a trail through an acacia forest when he stooped and passed beneath a spreading bough, as he had done many times before on the trip. He was followed by a native carrying a small antelope in each hand. This man also stooped and moved on. Next came the gunbearer carrying a collecting gun in his right hand and with a rifle slung across his back, projecting above his left shoulder. He was a tall man, and did not stoop sufficiently, so the muzzle of the rifle became entangled in the branch. Without looking around he jerked his shoulder impatiently, but this failed to free the gun. Turning to see how he could best set it free, he found himself face to face with a large and surprised mamba, not more than six inches away! With a wild cry the man sprang forward, freeing the gun by his sudden, forceful movement. Loveridge rushed back to see what the commotion was about, and by the time he reached the spot the mamba was three trees away and travelling fast over the foliage at a height of twenty-five feet. He shot the snake and found it measured exactly nine feet, but a few inches were missing from the tail.

A somewhat similar instance was reported in Uganda in 1952 when a native policeman was retrieving a guinea fowl he had shot. He accidentally stepped on a mamba, which coiled around his foot and ankle, but which fled precipitously as soon as the officer realized his predicament and jumped back. R. M. Isemönger, experienced collector of snakes in South Africa, has related a Zululand encounter with a large Black Mamba in which he had a most frightening escape. In his book *Suakes and Snake-catching in Southern Africa* he wrote, "Whilst groping my way through thick brush, I noticed the tail-end of a snake nearby, but at first did not realize what species it was, only about twelve inches were in view. As it happened, the tail belonged to an enormous Black Mamba lying in a semi-circular position, so that its head, instead of being about twelve feet away, was, in fact, barely a few feet from where I was standing.

"As I moved closer to get a better view in order to confirm the identification, my intentions were interpreted as definitely hostile, whereupon the snake struck at once, hooking its fangs into the khaki fabric of my slacks. It released its grip immediately but remained motionless, staring at me, rather as if it were about to say: 'Your move next!' I was wise enough (or frightened enough) to stand quite still, and it gently lowered its head and slithered off towards a crevice at the base of the cliff.

"Mambas usually slip away before you get too close, but as I had probably come upon it suddenly and too near to its home, its reaction was pardonable, if a little disturbing. Amongst the many I have caught, this was the only time one had actually struck at me before having been grabbed."

So much for the mambas. Judged by the unemotional opinions of men who have had wide experience with these snakes, they are not aggressive and rarely bite unless provoked, but they may defend themselves actively if wounded, suddenly threatened, or startled. How different from the terrible attacking demons of fiction!

But what of the cobras, particularly the King Cobra? Is it, too, the victim of fearful exaggerations, or is it perhaps deserving of its awesome reputation? From the point of size alone the King Cobra is worthy of respect, for it is the longest, and perhaps the heaviest, venomous snake in the world, reaching a maximum length of eighteen feet four inches. It is equipped with a nerve-affecting venom powerful enough to knock out an elephant. In fact, there are records of elephants having been killed by King Cobras that bit them on the tip of the trunk – about the only place that such a snake could bite an elephant and penetrate its skin. Throughout south-eastern Asia where this Cobra dwells, it is a common belief that King Cobras attack human beings on sight. A few more sophisticated souls claim these fits of aggressive behaviour are indulged in only during the mating season or by females guarding their nests.

In 1903, in what was reported to be an unprovoked attack, a King Cobra feet ten feet one inch in length bit and killed a coolie woman while she was picking tea on an estate in Assam. The snake retained its grip on the woman's leg for eight minutes while she remained "absolutely paralyzed with fear, and apparently did nothing to free herself." The snake finally released its grip when a group of men arrived on the scene. The snake crawled away, but when pursued by the men, it turned and attacked them but was killed The woman died "about twenty minutes after being bitten."

This account has been cited on several occasions to prove that King Cobras occasionally attack without provocation and that they are extremely deadly snakes. However, it is quite unusual for death to occur in such a short time as the result of the effects of the venom. It seems more likely that the woman died as a result of a heart attack rather than from the venom, particularly since the story says she was so frightened. The snake was sent to authorities in Bombay for identification, and the sender was told it was "undoubtedly a Hamadryad or King Cobra". Hamadryad is another name for this snake, but the "undoubtedly" raises the possibility that the attacking snake was a harmless species, possibly the large Indian Rat Snake or Dhaman, which is a large, excitable snake.There also is the question of whether the attack *was* unprovoked. A woman picking tea would probably be concentrating on her work, and not watching where she was stepping. Thus she might approach close to or even step on a resting snake, which might be startled into biting. In any case, we cannot be certain this is a true account of an unprovoked attack by a King Cobra.

Colonel Frank Wall, a student of Asiatic snakes, collected a great deal of information on the King Cobra, and was convinced that it would "sometimes atttack without provocation, other than being confronted in its natural haunts." The only specific instance of an allegedly unprovoked attack that Wall cites, however, is the one referred to above. He remarks that the "female when disturbed in the process of brooding her eggs, seems to be especially sensitive, and usually attacks the intruder at sight. Several instances are recorded where a jungle path has become closed to the wayfarer, owing to a brooding female and her mate attacking anyone attempting to pass. When actually molested the snake frequently accepts the challenge, and attacks with great determination and ferocity."

Colonel Wall has reported an adventure of a Major Fraser and his wife, who were driving in the Nilgiri Hills when they saw a large snake in the road in front of them. The Major at first thought the snake was a python, and tried to run over it, aiming to cross the snake's tail. Instantly it reared up on the side of Mrs Fraser, who, seeing its head on a level with the door, threw herself across her husband on the opposite side of the car. Major Fraser stopped the car and got out to investigate further, armed only with a butterfly net. He found the snake in the middle of the road with its head raised and hood spread, turning right and left in a threatening manner. The Major hesitated, and the snake came down the road straight for him. He jumped back in the car, released the brake, rolled down the road for a hundred yards or so, and got out again. The snake was still in the middle of the road with head and hood raised. It remained in this position for a moment and then crawled away.

Colonel Wall's report also refers to the ferocity attributed to female King Cobras when guarding their nests. He does not cite any specific cases, although there are several reports of encounters with snakes on or in their nests. One of the earliest reports of a snake on its nest was made by George K. Wasey in 1892. He wrote, "Information was brought to me that a path into a village situated some three or four miles from here, was closed owing to a large and deadly snake having taken up his quarters close by the side of it. My informant also told me that the snake had made a chamber, upon the top of which it was sitting. This morning I went out to have a look at it, and sure enough within two yards of the path was a heap of dried leaves and on top of them the snake. The head seemed to be down in the leaves, but two coils were visible. After throwing a few stones at the heap, one of which hit the snake, it erected its head and on seeing us distended the hood, when I fired and killed it."

This snake was nine feet eight inches long and made no attempt to attack either before or after it was hit with the stone. The trail was closed, not because the snake was attacking the villagers, but rather to keep them from going too close to the snake and possibly disturbing it.

All of the reports of personal encounters with King Cobras made by naturalists bear out the conclusion of Colonel G. H. Evans of Rangoon, who said, "I am more than ever convinced that Hamadryads as a rule are as glad to escape as most other snakes." Evans quotes an officer of the Indian Forest Department who had had considerable experience with these snakes in the wild, and who was sceptical of its aggressiveness. He said that, unless molested, this snake sought retirement in preference to hostilities in nine cases out of ten.

Two additional encounters can be cited here as further evidence of the lack of aggressiveness in the King Cobra. Both are taken from the *Journal of the Bombay Natural History Society*.

R. N. Champion Jones reported, "I was in the office one afternoon and heard my clerk's dog making a fiendish yapping down at his quarters. On enquiring the cause thereof I was informed that it was fighting a big cobra. Although cobras have been captured on the lower lying estates in this district I had not previously seen one here and was somewhat sceptical as there are plenty of very large rat snakes about. However, when I had finished my work in the office, I went to investigate and found about four coolies standing round and the dog still keeping up its cacophony. Although at the first glance nothing was visible as the 'conflict' was in amongst some grown-up tea, but upon a closer approach I was able to discern a section of the snake about three feet off the ground between two bushes and it sent me hot foot back to the bungalow for my gun. I found I only had some old No. 8 shot cartridges and so took along my .380 revolver. On arriving back I thought I would see if I could see the head and to this end crawled on hands and knees under the tea and saw the dog barking only a few inches away from it. I drove it away and had four shots at the snake with the revolver but all missed – a lamentable occurrence. I then thought I would give it a shot with the gun and this did not have much effect other than to make it come down sluggishly to earth when I managed to hit it with a revolver bullet in the neck. One or two facts emerge from the hunt. Firstly the extreme sluggishness and apparent docility of the snake – I never saw its hood expanded once. Secondly the striking proof that a snake is deaf to ordinary sound; it never turned an inch at the four revolver shots fired a few feet away from its head, from which one presumes it neither heard the dog; and lastly the time it took to die, although the backbone was broken at the neck it took half an hour at least before it was dead. It taped 10 feet 4 inches before skinning and 11 feet 6 inches after and was a male. There were numerous ticks under its scales and a large leech was found adhering to it.

"I cannot account for the dog getting away with it as it did, as I was told the Hamadryad, which it proved to be, was in the open when the dog found it and the King Cobra is reputed to be the fiercest and most dangerous of Indian snakes. The bands on this snake were not well defined."

The account of H. C. Smith is of particular interest, since it involves a snake on its nest guarding eggs. "On 7th June 1936 I was walking through fairly open moist bamboo forest at about 2,000 foot elevation near Ahisakan (some 8 miles from Maymyo) in the Mandalay District, Burma. Noticing a rather curious looking heap of dead leaves close to the rough track I was following I thrust a small cane into the heap. Immediately a snake's head shot out from the top of the heap and, as quickly disappeared. Having no gun and being with a picnic party I decided to leave well alone for the time being.

"On 11th June 1936 I returned to the place accompanied by Mr T. S. Thompson, Divisional Forest Officer, Maymyo, and some followers. Mr. Thompson and I posted ourselves on one side of the heap whilst our men cautiously pushed a long bamboo into it from another quarter. The snake soon emerged from the top of the heap and we shot it. It was a hamadryad measuring 7 feet 5 inches.

"We then proceeded to examine the heap which was about 1 foot 9 inches in height and 3 feet 6 inches in diameter. Within this heap of dead leaves was the nest proper. It was placed on the ground and comprised a compact mass of dead bamboo and other leaves and a few small twigs and leaf stalks. Externally it measured about 1 foot 7 inches in diameter and 9 inches deep. It was a comparatively solid structure and could be lifted off the ground without its falling to pieces. In the centre was a cup about 8 inches in diameter and about 8 inches deep.

"Within the nest were twenty-seven eggs, white, soft-shelled and measuring about 55 mm by 27 mm. The eggs were comparatively fresh and in some cases stuck lightly together. Above the eggs there was a compact covering of dead bamboo leaves which filled in the cup of the nest flush with the edges. Upon this nest, though separated from the eggs the snake had evidently been lying coiled up. The leaves forming the mound covered the snake and nest and they were lying loosely as compared with the solid and almost woven nature of the nest proper.

"It is interesting to note that fourteen people accompanied by seven dogs twice passed at different times within two yards of the nest and yet the hamadryad failed to show itself and the nest remained undiscovered until I prodded the heap of leaves with a small cane."

From these and other similar reports the editors of the *Journal of the Bombay Natural History Society* concluded in 1936 that "while the King Cobra has a reputation for ferocity, for the making of immediate and unprovoked atttacks, the sum of recorded evidence, supported now by these notes indicates that normally, the snake behaves in the manner of all snakes and usually endeavours to escape.

Thus the King Cobra, like the mamba, loses some of its malevolent character when carefully studied. Both snakes should be respected as dangerous adversaries when disturbed, but neither species can be considered aggressive. Undoubtedly part of the erroneous notions about these snakes have come from observations of the species in captivity. Under these abnormal conditions, where escape is impossible and the snakes are usually in close confinement, they appear more aggressive than they are in the wild. Many snakes will defend themselves vigorously when cornered. The same snakes if given a chance to escape will do so rather than fight.

In 1953, three large King Cobras were received at the New York Zoological Park. The smallest, a male, measured eleven feet six inches, while the largest, also a male, taped fourteen feet four inches. For some time after they arrived at the Zoo, all three would rush the keeper as soon as the cage door was opened. These were large snakes confined in a relatively small area from which they could not escape when disturbed. Their only alternative was to fight, and in doing so they lunged toward the obvious threat to their peace, the keeper. When they were proffered a plastic shield against which they could strike without danger, they soon tired of such action and quietened down. The snakes are now [1958] so accustomed to captivity and human beings that they rarely erect their hoods. For three years the smaller male and the female have mated, and the female has made a large nest in which she has laid her eggs each year. Most of the eggs have been removed to be incubated under artificial conditions. From these have hatched the first King Cobras bred in captivity. When the female is moved off the nest in order to remove the eggs, she makes no show of belligerence, and watches the procedure with no outward signs of excitement. Which of these attitudes indicates the true nature of the King Cobra – the excitable individuals of the early days of adjustment to captivity, or the calm, indifferent snakes of later months?

Tall tales of Bushmasters stalking and attacking unsuspecting hunters and explorers are commonplace in northern South America and lower Central America. There seems to be even less justification for considering this snake aggressive than for so viewing the mamba and King Cobra. I recently asked a South American herpetologist which of his native snakes he considered the most dangerous. Without hesitation he replied, "Bushmaster! Because it is so aggressive." When asked what he meant by "aggressive," he replied that "it won't run away like the other snakes do." This hardly qualifies as truly aggressive behaviour, and indicates something of the varying connotations placed on the word.

Large size, a very high strike, and virtually no knowledge of its normal habits are responsible for the Bushmaster's sinister reputation. It is the longest venonous snake in the New World, attaining a length of more than twelve feet. When assuming a defensive position, the Bushmaster loops a large portion of the anterior part of its body into a series of S-shaped vertical coils. As a result, it has a long and high strike that makes it a dangerous adversary. In spite of its formidable size, its venom is not particularly potent in comparison to the venoms of some of its smaller relatives. Actually the Bushmaster appears to be a shy, retiring inhabitant of the upland tropical forests. Scientists and hunters who have frequently encountered this snake in the wild discount any aggressive tendencies on its part.

The Taipan of Australia is a large active snake attaining a length of ten or eleven feet, and the possessor of relatively long fangs and copious quantities of venom. Four recorded bites on human beings all proved fatal, and a Taipan in North Queensland is said to have killed a horse in five minutes. Another report states that there appear to be only two cases of recovery from its bite. The Taipan occurs on the Cape York Peninsula of Australia and in eastern New Guinea – both regions of sparse human habitation. Within these areas it is considered to be a rare snake, and few specimens have been preserved in museum collections. Like all large venomous snakes about which little knowledge is available, there is considerable legend about the ferocity and aggressiveness of the Taipan, but there are few firsthand accounts of encounters with this snake. One story that was widely circulated in Australian newspapers in 1957 related the death of Kevin Budden, a young snake collector from Sydney, who was bitten by a Taipan near Cairns. Budden was bitten after he had captured the snake and while he was putting it in a bag for safe carrying. Despite the fact that he had received what he knew was probably a fatal bite, he secured the snake and requested that it be sent to the Commonwealth Serum Laboratories in Melbourne where its venom could be studied.

Eric Worrell, Curator of the Ocean Beach Aquarium in Umina, is one of the few persons who have had personal experience with the Taipan in the wild. In his *Dangerous Snakes of Australia*, he said, "I saw several Taipan in the Cairns sugar-cane fields. We found Taipan to be extremely shy and surprisingly quick to vanish into heavy grass when we approached. We captured three, one of which was taken to Taronga Zoo (Sydney)."

The Australian naturalist David Fleay has also had personal experience with the Taipan both in the wild and in captivity. His opinion is that this snake, like all others, does not look for trouble and usually tries to get away. He says they characteristically "vanish in a flash, but, if suddenly encountered or provoked, the highly nervous creatures react with unequalled ferocity." It looks as if the Taipan also will have to be removed from its legendary role of a truly aggressive snake. What is true of these snakes is equally true of *all* species of venomous snakes; they seek to escape rather than to fight. No species of snake is aggressive in the sense that most or many individuals make unprovoked attacks on human beings.

While no species of snake can be considered generally aggressive, an occasional irascible individual does turn up. Just as there are occasionally diabolical human beings, so there are misfit snakes – fortunately more often encountered in harmless than in venomous species. In the United States, Racers and Whipsnakes are most frequently reported to show definite aggressive tendencies, especially in the spring. Many herpetologists have had experiences with aggressive individuals of these species. Whether such attacks are stimulated by some types of territorial defence, or simply result from over-excitement, is impossible to say. Certainly all cases of aberrant aggressiveness are not limited to sexually mature individuals. A Long Island woman once brought the Zoo a newly-born Eastern Garter Snake that was one of the most vicious snakes I have ever seen. As soon as the lid was taken off the small box in which it was carried, the tiny demon rushed at my finger, lunging vigorously with open mouth and advancing farther with each lunge. I placed it on the floor and backed away a distance of about four feet. Without hesitating, it started toward me, with a wonderful display of ferocity considering that my towering figure was many times larger than its eight-inch length.

Others have reported similar exceptional performances, outstanding because of their radical departure from the normal behaviour of the species. When E. Raymond Hall visited a large Rattlesnake den in eastern Nevada, he found most of the snakes sluggish and lethargic in disposition, but one of the many he saw was an exception. This grumpy individual was in the middle of the road when the party drove up, and he immediately struck at the car. Hall said, "On getting out of the car we found him coiled about 12 feet away. He almost instantly uncoiled and with surprising speed made directly for me with his head and about seven inches of his neck slightly raised off the ground. When two of us shifted our locations he changed his course and made directly for another person until stopped with a charge of dust shot."

Similar unusually aggressive behaviour has been reported in other Rattlesnakes in the vicinity of hibernating dens, usually when the human being was between the snake and the den hole. Wilfred T. Neill has reported the case of a surprisingly aggressive Cottonmouth Moccasin from Georgia. The moccasin is noted for its threatening behaviour, which includes a fearsome gaping of the white mouth and vibration of the tail. Despite this display, these snakes are frequently quick to slink away, and I had never heard of nor seen one make an effort to approach an intruder. Neill's mad moccasin was a real exception to the rule. Neill wrote, "On the opposite bank we spied a Cottonmouth of perhaps a yard in length, basking on some cypress roots. The snake was separated from us by a steep eight-foot bank overgrown with smilax and poison-ivy, and by a sluggish stream about 12 feet wide and four feet deep. Having already collected a good series from the area, we were preparing to leave the Moccasin undisturbed, when it shook its tail angrily for a moment and then lunged openmouthed in our direction. Its strike carried it into the stream, where it floated with uplifted head. Piqued by such belligerency, I seized a stick and scrambled down the bank into the stream. To my surprise, the Cottonmouth swam to meet me. I waved the stick over its head; it did not strike at it until touched on the anterior part of the body. It embedded its fangs in the wood for a moment and then swam toward my legs. With the stick I pitched the snake on to the bank near the spot where it was first noted and, wading across, pinned it to the ground. This is the only Cottonmouth in my experience that made an entirely unprovoked attack when every opportunity for escape was presented."

These few examples indicate that an occasional individual snake may put on an aggressive display or actually come toward a person. The probability of anyone getting bitten by such an aberrant snake is a highly unlikely occurrence. One has a far better chance of being hit by lightning – actually neither is likely enough to cause you much concern.

Furthermore, *no* snake can crawl as fast as a man can run. The terrible tales of speedy mambas are sheer exaggerations. Mambas are about as fast and agile as any snakes, but probably no faster than a number of slender, racer-like species. The speeds of only a very few snakes have been accurately clocked with a stopwatch, and many highly erroneous ideas are based on *estimates* of their speed. The long, slim body of a snake moving smoothly and rapidly over stones and sticks, through weeds and grass, past bushes and trees, gives a completely false impression of fast movement relative to the small objects of the habitat. Because of this relative movement, it is extremely difficult to judge the speed of such a snake with any degree of accuracy. In Florida, my wife and I demonstrated this false impression by releasing a Black Racer on rough terrain and asking a group of people to guess the best speed at which it moved. The estimates ran between 10 and 15 miles per hour, but the best speed measured with a stopwatch was 3.7 miles per hour – less than a good walking pace for a man.

Walter Mosauer measured the speed of several species of desert snakes in California. Using a stopwatch, the fastest speed he recorded was 3.6 miles per hour for the Colorado Desert Whipsnake. Most of the snakes travelled at a far slower speed. One of the fastest movements he measured was the sidewinding type of movement used by the Sidewinder Rattlesnake when on loose sand. When really warmed up, these Rattlesnakes can move at a clip of 2.04 miles per hour!

In discussing the speed of the mamba in his book, *A Guide to the Snakes of Uganda,* Captain Charles R. S. Pitman said, "One could only obtain a true estimate of the mamba's exceptional speed by practical test, though the writer can visualize no more suicidal form of amusement than that of deliberately provoking a large mamba in order to put it through its paces!" On at least one occasion this has been done, and a maximum speed of seven miles per hour was measured by stopwatch. The figure was published recently by Colonel R. Meinertzhagen in connection with speeds of other animals. When I asked him how and where he had obtained this record Colonel Meinertzhagen kindly sent me the following account, the only one I have been able to locate which gives an actual measurement of a mamba's speed.

"The record was taken on 23 April 1906 near Mbuyuni on the Serengeti Plains between Voi and Taveta in Kenya. The terrain was recently burned grass. I first saw the snake crossing my path about 20 yards distant so I got my men to surround it as I wished to photograph it. The snake turned to bay with about a quarter of the head-end raised. We baited it with clods of earth until it was really angry. It kept making small rushes at my men so I tried to measure its pace, having been told that mambas could travel at the pace of a trotting horse. I waited, gun in hand to shoot if necessary and eventually got the snake to chase one of my men over a measured distance of 47 yards when I shot it as my man tripped up and fell. Timed with a stop-watch. The snake had not been handled, only baited. It measured five feet seven inches."

Mambas are similar in build and disposition to the harmless racers and whipsnakes of North America. They are agile and fast, as snakes go. Herpetologists estimate that no mamba can go more than twice as fast as these snakes, or a top speed of 8 miles per hour. Meinertzhagen's figure comes within this estimated range of speed.

Incidentally, the estimated and observed speeds of the mamba are well below the top figure for both man and the horse, both of which can run at a top speed of better than twenty miles per hour for short distances. If Colonel Meinertzhagen hadn't been sure of this, his method of measuring the mamba's speed would have been dangerous indeed.

Some people believe a venomous snake cannot bite unless it is coiled, while others believe the snake can hurl itself through the air a distance several times greater than its length. Neither of these beliefs is correct. A snake can bite at any time, from any position and even under water. Biting is simply opening the mouth and inserting the fangs or teeth into any accessible object. In fact, the severed head of a venomous snake has inflicted a fatal bite as a result of the marked reflex action of these animals.

The tongue is often thought to be the snake's "stinger." Actually it is perfectly harmless. It is used to pick up odours or chemical substances which are carried to the sense organs in the roof of the mouth. For this reason snakes flick their tongues out rapidly when they are excited. In doing so the snakes are just investigating the disturbance or the environment.

A strike is the lunging out of the head and anterior body from a coiled or defensive position. Snakes can inflict a venomous wound *only* by means of the mouth – either through enlarged, hollow teeth in front of the upper jaw, as in cobras, rattlesnakes, mambas and vipers, or by means of enlarged, grooved teeth at the rear of the upper jaw, as in the rear-fanged snakes, such as the Boomslang. Pit vipers and true vipers normally strike from a coiled position, whereas cobras, mambas, and their relatives strike from an erect or drawn back position. These snakes usually strike more slowly than the vipers. For example, an Asiatic Cobra strikes about one-sixth as fast as a Timber Rattlesnake, or much slower than a man can punch with his fists. Skilled snake charmers can pat a cobra on the head in the middle of its strike without difficulty.

The speed of the strike of the Prairie Rattlesnake has been studied at length by Walker Van Riper by means of high-speed photography. He calculated the speed of this "fast" motion at an average of 8 feet per second. Van Riper concluded, "It is one of the slowest of the animal movements we ordinarily regard as being fast. The truth seems to be that we nearly always greatly over-estimate the speed of small animal movements nearby (they must be close to be seen at all clearly)."

Van Riper showed that a man of average ability could punch his fist out at a speed of 18 feet per second, or more than twice as fast as the rattler's strike. A golfer was shown to move his hands at 40.6 feet per second in a golf stroke. A trout swam at 7 feet per second; a bee flew at 8.3 feet per second; and a dragonfly went at 22.7 feet per second. This all makes the rattler look pretty slow – and other snakes even slower by comparison. Few venomous snakes have been calibrated for the speed of their strike, and it seems certain that some species will be found to strike much faster than the Prairie Rattler, but also many, particularly the relatives of the cobras and mambas, will be found to strike much slower than that. With photographic consultant Henry Lester, Staff Photographer Sam Dunton, and Curator of Publications William Bridges of the Bronx Zoo, I was once engaged in getting an ultra-highspeed coloured movie of a rattlesnake striking, for an educational film we produced. After six months of ironing out technical difficulties, we obtained several records of the strike of the Western Diamondback Rattlesnake, a notoriously irascible snake. Where we were able to compute the speed of the strike, we got a figure about twice that for the Prairie Rattlesnake. Our data were inadequate to demonstrate whether this was an average or a maximum figure, but they do suggest the possibility, which is recognized by virtually all herpetologists, that the speed of the strike varies from species to species.

In a popular article on his observations in *Animal Kingdom*, Van Riper related the exploits of W. C. Bradbury who "liked to start an argument about the speed of the Rattlesnake – which he could always do by maintaining that it was slow, not fast. If a snake could be produced, he would make a demonstration. Holding a sack or something of the sort in his left hand to attract the snake's attention, and a sharp bowie-knife in his right, he would clip off the head of the snake when it reared to strike."

On level ground snakes generally strike one-third to one-half of their length. A viperine snake, such as a Timber Rattlesnake or a Fer-de-lance in a circular coil, with the anterior part of its body drawn back in a horizontal S-shape, will strike about one-third its length. If the fore part of the body is raised into a partially vertical coil, as an aroused Western Diamondback Rattlesnake or a Bushmaster is prone to do, the snake will strike farther and higher. Similarly, if the snake is resting on a rock ledge, a log, or the bank of a stream, the increased altitude may give it extra range.

This is a constant concern to hunters and woodsmen in hilly areas. For example, in the Northern Range in Trinidad the trails, or traces as they are called, are cut deep in the side of the hills in places so that the upper bank of the trail is as high as or higher than a man's head. One night in the Arima Valley, my East Indian companion, Otar Lal, entertained me by relating some of his encounters with Bushmasters on the high, uphill bank. He said, "When you meets them thar and they get stirred up, they flies right over you. And when they misses, as please God they do, they shoots right on down the hill." I can't vouch for the truth of his remarks, but it would be exciting to catch a large Bushmaster in such a position.

Cobras rear the anterior part of the body in a vertical position, and in a striking lunge forward a distance slightly greater than the vertical height to which the head is raised. An aggravated snake will strike farther than one that is just aroused from rest. A Western Diamondback Rattlesnake or a greatly excited Fer-de-lance can – but rarely does – actually strike a distance equal to its own length, and may momentarily leave the ground in so doing. If one estimates the length of a snake and stays that distance from it, there is little chance of being bitten – especially since the estimate is likely to be far more than the snake's length, and the creature cannot strike anywhere near such a distance.

Some of the cobras and their relatives have evolved the ability to "spit" or eject their venom. The venom is ejected in the general direction of a man's head, and can produce blindness if it gets into the eyes and is not treated promptly. The exact distance to which these snakes can "spit" their venom is somewhat uncertain. Certainly they can eject the venom a distance of six feet with good accuracy and eight feet with fair results; beyond that distance an effective hit is probably fortuitous.

Charles M. Bogert, Chairman and Curator of the Department of Amphibians and Reptiles of the American Museum of Natural History, in his scholarly study of the "spitting" snakes, shows that they are able to eject their venom in this fashion because of special modifications of their fangs. The Black-necked Cobra of Africa and the Asiatic Cobra in the eastern part of its range are the two cobras that practice this method of defence. The South African Ringhals, a close ally of the cobras, also possesses the ability to "spit". This is a purely defensive weapon and is not used in securing prey. Many individuals with this ability fail to use it until thoroughly aroused, and "spitting cobras" have been captured under the mistaken notion they were another species.

So much for the defensive behaviour of snakes, which is sometimes so vigorous as to be mistaken for aggressive action. There is no scientific evidence to support the oft-cited, but erroneous, belief that any species of snake is habitually aggressive. Mambas, King Cobras, Bushmasters, and others do not indulge in unprovoked attacks on human beings. A rare, exceptional individual of any species *may* exhibit aggressive behavior and slowly approach a humnan being in a threatening manner, but this happens only in extraordinary instances, under highly unusual circumstances. In no instance can a snake crawl faster than an adult man or woman can run. Virtually all snakes will try to escape from an encounter with a human being if given the opportunity. When you walk through the countryside or forest, far more snakes see you than you see snakes. They are simply content to let you pass, or they silently crawl away.

BOBCAT ATTACK IN SOUTH GEORGIA

Two men in the South Georgia town of Ty Ty, near Tifton, were being treated for rabies after a rare bobcat attack on a farm owned by one of the men.

A rabid bobcat jumped out from under a building on Oren Burdett's farm on the afternoon of 13 February 1998, biting Ossie Chaney on his right leg. "Chaney hit the bobcat with a shovel, and the animal ran into a shed," said Burdett's wife Betty.

Burdett heard Chaney yell and ran to see what was wrong. "The next thing he knew, that thing was wrapped around his leg a-scratchin' and a-bitin'," Betty Burdett said.

"Burdett suffered scratches and gouges on his leg," she said. "When it finally turned him loose, it run back into the barnyard where Mr Chaney was, and Mr Chaney had picked up a two-by-four and he finally hit him in the head and killed him."

Nick Nicholson, a wildlife biologist with the Georgia Department of Natural Resources, said that, although bobcats are common in the state, people usually do not even see them because they are nocturnal and solitary animals. "Bobcat attacks on people are extremely rare, except in a case where they might be sick," Nicholson added.

"The bobcat, which later tested positive for rabies, probably attacked because it had the disease," said Larry Branch, a veterinarian in Tift County, where the attack occurred, about forty miles east of Albany.

Bob Chaney and Burdett immediately started getting shots for the potentially fatal disease and will need to continue the injections for the next three Sundays, Betty Burdett said.

CUBANS TURNED CANNIBAL

A group of Cuban exiles, who escaped alive from the Bay of Pigs fiasco in 1961, resorted to cannibalism while adrift at sea for sixteen days, one of them disclosed last night.

Julio Pestonit, fifty-seven, told Fox News Channel in New York that he ate the flesh and drank the blood of comrades who had died of starvation and dehydration.

Señor Pestonit, then twenty, was one of 1,500 ideologically driven exiles who launched an invasion of Cuba, backed by the CIA, in an attempt to topple the Communist regime of Fidel Castro. The attack was easily repulsed and about 200 men died.

The cannibalism happened on a flimsy sailing boat, carrying twenty-two exiles who had eluded capture. The group had neither food nor water and men soon began to die. Señor Pestonit said the group reluctantly ate a corpse. Señor Pestonit said: "I did eat some of the interior of the body that was extended to me. It was crazy. It was like being in hell." After sixteen days the survivors were rescued, but seven had died.

Señior Pestonit said he had broken a vow to keep the cannibalism secret out of anger at the Kennedy Administration, which failed to provide promised air support.

PLANE CRASH IN THE ARCTIC

While the Old Christians rugby team in their crashed plane confronted the issue of survival in the heights of the Andes, a solitary German-born bush pilot was facing the same decision in the wilds of the Canadian Arctic. Forty-seven-year-old Marten Hartwell had no one with whom to share the burden. He was also suffering from two broken ankles, a shattered kneecap and an injured hand.

On 8 November 1972, reluctantly and in contravention of at least two official flight rules, he had taken off from Cambridge Bay on a mercy mission to Yellowknife in the North-West Territory, with Judith Hill (an English nurse) and two critically ill Inuit patients as passengers. One of the patients was David Kootook, fourteen years old and thought to have acute appendicitis, the other his aunt, twenty-five-year-old Neemee Nuliiayok, eight months pregnant and suffering complications.

Hartwell was licensed for VFR flying, which meant he was permitted to fly only if he could see the ground at all times, but his Beechcraft 18 soon ran into low cloud, air icing and snow. Night was falling and his radio contact with ground beacons was faulty. The plane was almost two hundred miles off course when it crashed into a hillside.

Nurse Hill died instantly, Mrs Nulliayok a few hours later. Only David was uninjured (a pathologist later confirmed that he had been suffering not from appendicitis but a penetrating stomach ulcer). Under the crippled pilot's guidance, the boy constructed a shelter from sleeping bags and set up rabbit traps, and in the following days made several abortive attempts to reach a lake they believed to be only about three or four miles away, though it was actually twelve. The snow was waist deep, the traps produced nothing, and David and Hartwell had to fall back on the plane's emergency rations of six small cans of corned beef, four packets of dehydrated chicken noodle soup, a dozen Oxo cubes, a twelve-ounce packet of rice, a packet of powdered potato, some glucose pills and a few ounces of raisins.

By the twentieth day there was no food left. David said he could not eat the bodies of the nurse or his aunt, who had been good to him, and Hartwell deferred to his feelings. On 30 November, Hartwell noted, "Still alive. David is going to die tomorrow and I two or three days later. No food. My legs don't carry me." Next day, David Kootook was dead.

Alone now, Hartwell succeeded in dragging himself twelve yards to the nearest tree, hacked off the lichened lower branches, and struggled back to the tent. It took him two hours. He made a small fire and concocted a mouthful of soup from the lichens and melted snow, but there was no possibility of finding enough lichens to keep him going until his ankles mended sufficiently for him to reach the lake and try for fish.

"There was no way out but to eat human flesh and this I did," he said later. For the days between the final decision and his rescue on 9 December, Hartwell – normally a vegetarian – sustained himself on the flesh of the twenty-seven-year-old nurse.

The inquest jury returned a verdict of accidental death on the crash victims, and the nurse's family stated that they felt no "vindictiveness or malice" towards Hartwell for what he had done. Then they instituted a $100,000 lawsuit – not for cannibalism but for negligence – against the pilot and his employers. A lawyer acting for the Inuit Brotherhood also filed a suit for $215,000.

Hartwell continued as a bush pilot in the Arctic until he reached his mid-sixties, when he retired from flying.

TRAMPLING ELEPHANTS

Dr Thorley Sweetman, aged thirty-five, of Sheffield, a British geologist who has lectured at the University of Zimbabwe since 1989, was trampled to death by a herd of elephants on Sunday, 22 August 1991, while collecting rock samples in the Zambezi valley.

He failed to return to camp by sunset and was found by searchers the following morning.

A LEOPARD IN BOTSWANA

A drill operator who was attacked at a mineral exploration site in the Kalahari Desert by a leopard fought back against the animal and eventually strangled it.

Frik van Heerden, thirty-five, nursing painful bites and scratches at his home in Bothaville, in South Africa's Free State province, described the attack ten days ago deep in Botswana. He said he was walking the short distance from his caravan home to another trailer used as an office, "when I heard a noise and spun round. As I did so, the leopard pounced on me."

His shouts alerted his wife, Alta, and their two young sons, but they could do nothing to help as Mr van Heerden wrestled for his life.

"I punched and fought with it, but I could not get it off me," he said. "I did not know what I was doing, but I suppose the survival instinct took over. Somehow I managed to grab its throat and eventually I felt it go limp. I had strangled it."

Mrs van Heerden radioed for help and her husband was flown by helicopter to hospital in Gaborone, the Botswanan capital. He will be returning to work soon.

Leopards, known as silent killers, are solitary beasts and regarded as among the most dangerous by wildlife experts. They circle their prey and attack from behind. The animal that attacked Mr van Heerden probably was attracted to the family's camp by the smell of food.

DEATH BY WHITE RHINO

A British conservation worker was gored to death by a rhinoceros at an African wildlife reserve after climbing into its enclosure.

Daniel Lipscombe, twenty-two, from Guernsey, was helping the fully grown male to settle into its new surroundings when it charged. He died instantly at the Khama Rhino Sanctuary, near Serowe, in Botswana. A graduate of Bristol University, he was working as a volunteer, helping a breeding programme for the endangered white rhinoceros. His parents, John and Nadia Lipscombe, arrived at the sanctuary yesterday after flying from the Channel Islands.

The animal involved had just arrived at the reserve and Mr Lipscombe was moving it between large enclosures known as *bomas* where the animals are monitored for a few days before entering the main sanctuary. It was the first time he had carried out the monitoring work and colleagues said it was not standard practice to enter a *boma* with a rhinoceros.

Rachel Potasznik, the administrator of the sanctuary, said: "All rhinos are dangerous, but they are not normally aggressive. Mr Lipscombe was not carrying a weapon or stick," she said. "This was a tragic accident . . . We don't understand why he was inside the *boma*."

The rhinoceros, which is more than thirty years old, will not be destroyed. Miss Potasznik, an American, said: "Daniel would be horrified if we killed the animal. It cannot be blamed."

"Daniel was a gentle, caring, self-effacing man and we will all miss him," she added.

The white rhinoceros is one of five rhino species left in the world and is the commonest, mainly because of strict conservation policies in South Africa during the apartheid years.

KENYAN DEVIL WORSHIPPERS

"Kenyans are eating human flesh and drinking human blood as part of devil worship rituals," says a presidential commission of inquiry.

A government statement said the commission, set up by President Moi [in 1994] to look into allegations of satanic cults, had gained confessions from devil-worshippers around the country. It said human sacrifice, naked rituals, sexual abuse and rape of children and drug-taking were widely practised. Cults were often associated with an obsession with sex and homosexuality and the presence of snakes.

"After carefully considering reports from individuals with personal experience in the cults and evidence from self-confessed devil worshippers whose submissions were confirmed by credible independent sources, the commission found ample corroborative evidence of the existence of devil worship," the government statement said.

The commission was chaired by Roman Catholic Archbishop Nicodemus Kirima. An Anglican bishop and a theologian were among the other commission members. A senior Catholic Church official said the findings were "very true and very serious". He said most cult members were "rich, educated and powerful people".

The Government said it had studied carefully a number of

recommendations made by the commission after its findings. It warned the public against "abetting or getting involved in devil worship which is in its formative stages in our country".

The disclosures were greeted with scepticism by some Kenyans, who fear the report may be used by the government to act against dissidents.

BOKASSA OF THE CENTRAL AFRICAN REPUBLIC

I

The former self-styled Emperor of the Central African Republic, Jean-Bedel Bokassa, whose thirteen-year dictatorship was marked by delusions of grandeur, extravagance and cruelty on an epic scale, has died [November 1996]. He was seventy-five.

He had a heart attack on Sunday night at the main hospital in Bangui, capital of the impoverished nation he ruled until he was overthrown in a French-backed coup in 1979. The former leader had been suffering from kidney and cerebral problems and hypertension, and had a brain haemorrhage last year.

Hours after Bokassa's death was confirmed by Jean Charles Bokassa, one of his children, several thousand mourners assembled outside the hospital.

In 1966, six years after the country gained independence from France, Bokassa, a lieutenant-colonel risen from the ranks of the French colonial army, seized power. He established a regime that became more fantastic and capricious with every year as he declared himself, progressively, Life President, Father of the Nation and then Emperor Bokassa I of the Central African Empire.

Modelling himself on Napoleon Bonaparte and claiming descent from the pharaohs, Bokassa created a one-man cult of which he was the principal devotee.

Bokassa was once one of France's closest African allies, but politicians in Paris were noticeably silent yesterday on his death.

His "imperial coronation" in 1977 cost a quarter of the country's annual foreign exchange earnings and his diamond-studded crown and robes, fashioned by twenty-five Parisian seamstresses, were valued at £4 million.

France's interest in the lucrative uranium trade of its former colony ensured the support of Paris for much of Bokassa's rule. But the links between the nations brought scandal amid allegations that former President Giscard d'Estaing, a friend and sometime hunting partner of the African leader, had accepted a gift of diamonds from the dictator. The charges contributed to the French leader's election defeat in 1981.

As his despotism, avarice and butchery mounted, Bokassa's French backers came to see him as a serious liability. In 1979 more than 100 schoolchildren were massacred after they complained about the expense of their new and elaborate school uniforms, which were designed by Bokassa. Within months French troops moved in to reinstate the country's first President, David Dacko, Bokassa's nephew.

A recipient of the Legion d'Honneur and the Croix de Guerre, Bokassa spent seven years in quiet but unhappy exile in France and Ivory Coast until 1986, when he abruptly returned home, mistakenly expecting to be acclaimed by the populace. He was immediately put on trial for murder embezzlement, infanticide and cannibalism.

During the three-month trial prosecutors presented horrific evidence of his atrocities, including gruesome and doubtlessly exaggerated allegations of cannibalism.

Witnesses said that the body of a murdered schoolteacher was kept on a meat hook in the freezer of Bokassa's imperial palace. His former chef claimed that Bokassa ate cooked human flesh "with relish" and enjoyed watching foreign dignitaries consuming his political opponents in the belief that they were being served roast beef.

"I am not a cannibal," he told the court, in floods of tears.

The self-styled "Thirteenth Apostle of Christ" was finally acquitted of cannibalism, but condemned to death for murder. The sentence was first commuted to hard labour for life, then to twenty and finally to ten years in prison. He was freed after only six years, in September 1993, and was planning a political comeback.

II

. . . In October 1986, for reasons best known to himself Bokassa returned to the Central African Republic. He was put on trial for a catalogue of offences of which he was already convicted in his absence.

Despite the discovery of human corpses stuffed with rice in the presidential freezer, accusations of cannibalism were dismissed for lack of evidence, but there was proof enough to convict him of conspiracy to murder, illegal detention of people and embezzlement of state funds . . .

III

The emperor who ate his enemies for lunch . . . a cannibalistic lust for blood that struck terror into the dark heart of Africa . . . an unrepentant sadist whose sins knew no bounds . . . Thus the *Daily Mail*, salivating over the death of Emperor Bokassa last week.

It's a good tale to titillate a tabloid audience at breakfast. Perhaps we should just let it go at that: in tabloid parlance, it's too good a story to check, But suppose we look closer at the *grand guignol*? Suppose we ask whether it was in someone's interest to present Jean-Bedel Bokassa as a mad cannibal, so crazed that nothing he said would be taken seriously? Could it be that the French government worried about the scandal linking Bokassa, President Giscard d'Estaing and a supply of illegally-obtained diamonds, set the whole thing up in order to deflect everyone's attention?

No one invented the madness. One look at the coronation photograph in 1977 as Bokassa sat on his Indiana Jones throne, a Napoleonic crown of golden oak leaves around his brow, is enough to show that he was a loony capable of scoring straight sixes on the Gaddafi-Zhirinovsky scale.

No one invented the fact that he ordered his troops to shoot schoolchildren when they protested at having to buy school uniforms from Bokassa's own company. We are not talking liberal democracy here.

Equally, though, no one invented the relationship with Giscard: the letters from the Elysée Palace addressed to "*mon cher cousin*" the supply of diamonds which passed from the Central African Empire sometimes to Giscard and sometimes as part of a deal, never properly investigated, with Giscard's brother. And no one invented the fact that when Bokassa knocked Giscard's personal representative on the head with his silver cane in 1979, Giscard sent in troops to depose him.

Then the French put out their story. The star witness was his chef. He said the emperor had ordered his chief political opponent to be executed, cooked, stuffed with truffles, and kept in the deep freeze. When he felt peckish, Bokassa he would tell the chef to cut him off a slice.

The chef's testimony was everything the world's tabloids had always thought about Africa anyway.

In 1985 Bokassa left his exile in the Ivory Coast and settled into his chateau at Hardricourt, outside Paris. Giscard had lost the presidency four years earlier, thanks to the diamond scandal, but the Secret Service still looked after him. To make sure Bokassa wouldn't give his version of things, they dug up the road to Hardricourt and took away his driving licence for good measure.

By chance, my television crew and I [John Simpson] managed to get through to the château. The emperor opened the door to us himself, a wizened little character with several days' worth of silver stubble around his chin. As we stood awkwardly in the entrance hall we saw, with the effect of a powerful electric shock a six-foot deep freeze at the far end: big enough to hold say, a leader of the Opposition.

"Get him into the next room," I hissed to the producer. Like someone from a gothic horror novel, I opened the lid of the deep freeze with trembling hands – and saw a pile of frozen herrings and chops inside.

It was clear to us that Bokassa was barking mad. His house was full of paintings and busts of Napoleon, some bearing his own features. And yet he was calm and rational.

He told me of his diamond dealings with the Giscard brothers, and of how French commandos blew up his safe and took sixty-three big uncut diamonds from it. They were, they said, for the Elysée Palace. As for cannibalism, he assured me with tears in his eyes, that the very idea was abhorrent to him; and I believed him.

POLAR BEAR CHARGE

As the huge mass of white fur, claws and teeth charged, British explorer Marcus Barton knew he was a second from death. The crazed animal – almost twice the size of a man – was infuriated and bent on destruction.

Dr Barton pulled the trigger of his rifle and the polar bear stopped dead in its tracks, then crashed to the ground only a few feet away. As its corpse lay in the snow, it became clear it was an emaciated youngster, recently separated from its mother and in search of food.

Barton, thirty-two, described killing the bear as a horrendous experience which had a devastating effect on the other members of his group. It was the second time in thirty-six hours he had been forced to shoot a polar bear dead. The first animal had charged his colleague who fired a shot into his leg, before Dr Barton, armed with a 7.6 mm heavy calibre hunting rifle, finished the animal off within seconds.

Speaking of the terror of those moments, he said: if we had missed, the person that bear was charging would have died, along with several others in the party. These Irvine Sparks costume drama bears can kill very effectively."

Dr Barton, a recent dental graduate of Manchester University, was leading a seventeen-strong group of Durham University students, doctors, engineers and army reservists on an Arctic mountaineering and geological expedition.

They came under attack from the bears – each weighing twenty-one stone – on two consecutive days on the Norwegian Svalbard Islands. Dr Barton's team had tried to frighten off the two separate hungry beasts without success.

The first of the two animals, which can kill a man with a single blow, approached the remote camp on Saturday looking for food. Dr Barton said: "We did everything we could and went to incredible lengths to deter him. We used pyrotechnics, live ammunition fired into the ground, flares, thunder flashes, even banging mess tins together – nothing seemed to deter him. In the end, unfortunately, the bear charged my colleague, who fired a shot into his leg. And then very quickly, in the next five or six seconds, we killed the bear."

He was forced to do the same thing on Sunday, when a second bear entered the camp. "The second one was worse because it approached in a very straight line to our camp," he said.

The bear was provoked by the group making a noise in an attempt to scare it off and attacked.

"It charged the base of a mound just in front of us where it went out of sight, which was very unnerving. We had about forty seconds of wondering where this polar bear was, knowing it was probably only thirty metres away. In the end, it popped up over the centre of this mound. We both made eye contact and it charged. I shot it when it was about six metres from me. It was very traumatic. I would never in my worst nightmares anticipate having to kill a bear, let alone two bears."

The party had earlier come across about eight other bears without incident. Members of the group were interviewed by local police about the incident but Erik Nygaarb, a police inspector on the Svalbard

Islands, said they seemed to have acted "within the law". Polar bear hunting has been banned in the country since 1972, although Norwegian law allows killing in self-defence.

CANNIBALISM IN CAMBODIA

In the office of the United Nations centre for human rights in Phnom Penh [the capital of Cambodia], I am handed a colour snapshot of a decaying, half-naked corpse lying face down in the mud of a rice field. The eyes are missing, one side of the face has been smashed, the left ear has been severed, the fingers of both hands have been chopped off and the legs have been stripped of skin and flesh from the thigh to the toes.

It is a picture of Thong Sophal, forty-five, an electoral observer with Funcinpec, the royalist party and one of two main opposition groups contesting today's Cambodian elections.

"I have never seen a body like this before," said Christophe Peschoux, the centre's director. "There are two explanations: ritual cannibalism or ordinary cannibalism."

The photograph, one of many gruesome pictures that the centre has collected as evidence of political killings, overwhelms all who see it.

Sophal was a former village chief and the father of seven children, but, on 5 June, he enrolled as a Funcinpec observer. Three weeks later he was summoned to the village office run by the formerly communist Cambodian People's Party (CPP), the ruling party of Hun Sen, the Prime Minister, in his native Kandal province. Sophal emerged distressed and confided that he was "sad and worried". Two days later he disappeared. Pointing to a vial of cleaning fluid found near the corpse, the police have suggested that his death was suicide.

It is a risible conclusion. Sophal was tortured and killed. Quite why he was then partially eaten is unclear, though ritual cannibalism is not unheard of in the backward parts of Cambodia, even today. By eating an enemy's human flesh, it is believed, one incorporates his soul and courage, depriving him of any possibility of survival in the world after death.

Sophal is one of eighteen victims of political murder identified by the human rights centre during a short election campaign.

As Peschoux showed his grisly picture, Danh Teav, an Interior

Ministry employee and supporter of Funcinpec, was being beaten and tortured not far away. When an Amnesty International representative finally reached Teav, he was unable to stand without help. He had bruises and abrasions on his back and chest, and cuts around the wrists where he had been shackled. He was not allowed access to a lawyer, doctor or family member. Later, dressed in fresh clothes, but looking terrified, he appeared on the front page of one of the regime's most subservient newspapers, which reported that he had confessed to involvement in the attempted murder of a pro-Government newspaper editor.

What primeval energy produces such cruelty? Whatever the reasons, the security forces have been able to commit such violence against the regime's opponents in a climate of institutionalized impunity. There has been near-silence from Europe about the pre-election atrocities. With certain honourable exceptions, diplomats in Phnom Penh have hidden behind the idea that Cambodia is a violent society anyway; that political killings have always happened and so can be ignored. Europe is the single largest donor to today's polls. The European Union is funding them to the tune of $11.9m and consequently is not being as critical as it should be.

A rift has developed in the international community between the EU on one side and human rights groups supported by America on the other, who do not condemn the elections outright, but believe there should be a more honest assessment and a greater effort to confront the abuses . . .

These polls come five years after the United Nations helped Cambodia to take its first tottering steps towards democracy. Those elections [1993] were declared a success, but Hun Sen, the loser, threatened to plunge the country into civil war unless he shared power with Prince Norodom Ranariddh, the victor. The UN accepted the compromise and Hun Sen and Ranariddh governed in an uneasy alliance. This broke down when Hun Sen staged a coup in July [1997], using tanks and artillery to smash the power base of Funcinpec and Ranariddh. Dozens of royalists were hunted down and killed. It is clear that the CPP was seeking to break the back of the opposition to maximize its chances of victory in the polls, which Hun Sen needs to legitimize his rule.

Cambodians, however, may yet surprise us all. It is the first time they have been able to vote free from the shadow of the Khmer Rouge.

Cambodian peasants make up seventy per cent of the electorate. They have an instinct for survival honed from years of Khmer Rouge tyranny; the hope is that the intimidation will backfire and that, on the day, they will say what they think.

"The vote is secret and I will vote for a party that respects human rights and democracy," said one old farmer in Kompong Cham, northeast of Phnom Penh.

For the better part of three decades, Cambodia has known little but bloodshed. Superficially, now, it is up and running. In Phnom Penh there are banks and street lamps where there used to be misery and darkness; huge hotels where there were once squalid refugee camps. My former room at the top of Le Royal, which cost $5 a night in 1975, when it was vulnerable to rocket attacks, now costs $115. There are Internet cafes, casinos, even a Greek restaurant.

However, as another amputee scurries crab-like across a broken pavement, a child whines with hunger and the violence continues, it is obvious that it will take a lot more than a flawed election to fix this sad but beautiful little country.

KILLER LIONS OF ZIMBABWE

An Earl's grandson has been killed in an horrific attack by lions at a safari pork in Zimbabwe. Public schoolboy David Pleydell-Bouverie, nineteen, was sleeping inside a tent when they pounced late on Saturday night.

The teenager, who left Harrow last year, had been working as a cook at the Matusadona National Park when the attack happened. He had been due to return to Britain soon.

Last night his father Richard Pleydell-Bouverie, High Sheriff of Hertfordshire and the son of the late Earl of Radnor, said: "Yes it's true. my son has been killed – and that's all I know."

Muffled screams were heard coming from David's tent at around 2 a.m. and a guide was then called to the camp to track the lions.

"When they heard the noises, they came out of their tents to see what was going on, but by then it was all quiet and they could see nothing," said the guide, who gave his name only as Ozias. He said that he then followed the prints from the tent and discovered David's remains about twenty metres away.

"We, then got into our vehicles and tracked the lions and we came across a lioness, one of the oldest lionesses in the park, and shot her. We tracked the other lions for another six hours and found a big male, which we shot? "

In Britain, a friend of David's family said last night that staff on his father's large estate near Luton were shocked by the news. "David was enjoying his stay in Zimbabwe so much," said the friend. "He had got to know the rangers on the safari park very well. His family are utterly distraught."

David's parents, who have two other children – Bartholomew, seventeen, and fifteen-year-old Harriet – are now believed to be planning to fly to Zimbabwe. The tragedy happened on one of the largest islands on Lake Kariba, which is popular with tourists on safari.

Hotel worker Shame Veremu said: "Everyone in the party was deeply shocked by what had happened. They couldn't believe that the boy had been taken while they were all asleep. They think from the footprints that led from his tent that he was first attacked by two lions."

A source close to the British High Commission in Harare said: "There were a number of lions around, but nobody knows which ones attacked him or why?" Staff from the High Commission will travel to the safari park today to monitor the investigation into David's death.

Until this weekend, there has been no recent history of maneating lions at Matusadona. But the park is famed for having the highest concentration of wild lions in Africa. Its poor accessibility and inadequate road network have helped to keep it remote and unspoilt but make providing urgent medical attention difficult. The park covers 338,000 acres, yet visitors are told that the best way to experience the wildlife is on a "walking safari", to get as close to the animals as possible.

Many lions roam free across the park usually preying on the large herds of buffalo. Leopards, hyenas and cheetahs are other predators. Tour operators boast that rangers do their best to maximize your exposure to the "wilderness".

A Foreign Office spokesman said on 1 August 1999: "I cannot confirm the exact circumstances of Mr Pleydell-Bouverie's death, because a full investigation is under way."

David's father, Richard Pleydell-Bouverie who married his wife Victoria in 1978, is known for being outspoken on countryside issues.

He was praised for his part in a dramatic rescue in 1976, when a plane crashed close to the family's Georgian home, Lawrence End House, on the Lawrence End estate in Peter's Green, near Luton.

ELEPHANT SAFARI DEATH

Many of the 5,000 tourists who step into Zambia's Luangwa Park each year consider it the experience of a lifetime. There are few places on earth where the plains animals can be observed at such close quarters and the sights, sounds and smells of the gentle river valley blend into an intoxicating cocktail.

For Johnny Ambrose, a British guide, working in this paradise after graduating from Bristol University meant the fulfilment of a cherished ambition. But as a nature-lover he also knew the risks.

Last week Ambrose, twenty-three, was trampled and gored to death by an enraged female elephant. In a final act of heroism, he distracted the charging beast from his client, an American engineer, who had slipped and fallen to the ground.

"Johnny's actions saved his life," said Robin Pope, Ambrose's boss and one of Africa's most experienced walking guides. "His own injuries were such that it's clear he would not have suffered pain."

The death, one of the few recorded in what is considered one of Africa's safest wildlife destinations, has thrown the tightly knit local safari community into mourning.

Ambrose, who was educated at Sherborne School in Dorset, had been a qualified guide for just one month. Last Saturday he collected Godfrey Muyunda, his scout, and Kenny Karen, forty, the American client, and set off on a known route, weaving through a wooded savannah that contains more than sixty species of animal and 400 types of bird. It was on their way back, as the sun dipped towards the lazy waters of the Luangwa River, that Ambrose and his group noticed at least three elephants in thick bushes about sixty yards ahead of them. They sought shelter behind a sausage tree, characterized by its long, dangling gourds.

Crouching, Muyunda made a bush cry in an attempt to discourage the advancing elephants, and then fired a warning shot. Ambrose tried to lead Karen to the safety of some thick bushes ten yards from the tree. But, according to local police, the gunshot panicked the elephants. One peeled away and charged just as Ambrose and Karen were between the tree and bushes.

"They were just a few yards from the river and it seems the mother was anxious about her young," said Detective Constable Andrew Chola from the local Mfue police station. "She seemed to go for Karen, who fell over, and then went for Ambrose, who was trampled and gored."

Muyunda fired another desperate shot over the mother elephant, which fled. Chola said Ambrose died "very quickly".

Ambrose, who spent his infancy in Tanzania, had known his vocation from an early age. David Scott, his physical education teacher, remembered him declaring his passion for the great spaces of East Africa at thirteen. "He knew what he was going to do, which was to run safaris," Scott said. "He was always going to go back to Africa."

Ambrose left Bristol last year, his chances of first-class honours for his degree in zoology dashed by a bout of malaria. A powerfully built rugby player, he toured Sri Lanka with the university team in 1998. He was known for his humour and tales of Tanzania, where his parents, Belinda and Gerard Ambrose, still live, near Arusha in the shadows of Mount Meru and Kilimanjaro.

"Taz", as Ambrose was nicknamed, would talk of walks with his dog ending in confrontations with cobras or worse. Once, fascinated by the raw power of a crocodile, he lured the creature out of the water, using his body as bait. He timed his escape to perfection.

In a last e-mail to friends, dated 26 June 2000, Ambrose talked of the goal of running his own safari outfit. "The idea may go ahead, hopefully . . ." he wrote, before reverting to bush fables. "A baboon has just nicked a pineapple from the kitchen so have got to go and deal with the offending individual . . . A honey badger nicked a box of wine the other day . . . very serious offence, but I think he paid for it in terms of a fantastic hangover. He was found passed out behind the bar . . ."

Robin Pope Safaris has continued to operate in the belief that Ambrose would have expected it. He was, Pope said, "a person of great warmth, humour, compassion and a genuine love of the bush".

Margo Pfeiff, a travel writer and recent guest of the company, said she would have no hesitation going on such a safari again. "I felt completely safe," she said. "No guest has ever been injured by a beast in the park. With guides, it's another story."

Ambrose was buried on Friday, across the Rift valley from Zambia in the southern Tanzanian town of Iringa. It was where he had spent his gap year clearing the bush around an aunt's homestead. Ollie Green, a university friend who visited him there, said: "It was the place Taz loved most, where he was happiest and where he belonged."

CHANCES WITH WOLVES

Should we reintroduce wolves to the wilds of Scotland? Alone in a forest on a winter's night you hear wolves howling at the moon. It is a good time to ask yourself whether we British really want to have such efficient carnivores as our wild neighbours once more.

Wolves are charismatic creatures of legend, but also one of the most ruthless predators the world has ever seen. This harsh truth is easily forgotten when you see the crowds drawn to the irresistably cute wolf cubs Nadja and Mischka at the Wildwood Discovery Park near Canterbury in Kent, UK. Playful as puppies, the two cubs wag their tails, lick your hand and scoot around their pen with fluffy toys in their mouths. They are just like every friendly young dog you have ever known.

Recently born in captivity at Wildwood to parents imported from Romania and Germany, Nadja and Mischka can do a lot to reverse old misconceptions about a species man has previously reviled, poisoned, shot and generally persecuted off the planet for centuries.

Derek Gow, the conservation centre's manager, says: "Wolves are not only shy and retiring creatures by nature but, contrary to popular myth and legend, they have also never posed any real threat to people." Like many lupine enthusiasts, Gow also believes that the time is now right to set aside our "medieval attitudes" about wolves and seriously consider reintroducing them into the wild in Britain – where they once roamed in large numbers before being hunted to extinction in the eighteenth century.

Gow feels that his native Scotland would be the most practical place to start such a reintroduction, because of the space available and the abundance of natural prey for wolves – deer. Gow's vision is of the sheep-farming wastes of Scotland transformed back into medieval woodland, full of native creatures such as beaver and wolves, which would draw money-paying crowds.

"Farmers who are now making a loss out of sheep could then make a better living out of eco-tourism," he says. "In the case of wolves, I also feel there has to be some moral obligation involved. How can we justify going to other countries such as India to tell poor, terrified people that they must preserve their tigers – creatures you couldn't trust near your granny, let alone your livestock – and then say we can't tolerate living with one of our oldest indigenous species on our own shores?"

It is a timely and persuasive argument in an age in which it is fashionable to reflect on our past persecution of fellow species with guilt. But could living with wolves as our neighbours again really work?

In the United States – a country with more wilderness to spare than most – millions of dollars have been spent in recent years on projects to return wolves to territories they once occupied. One scheme transported wild Canadian wolf packs to Yellowstone National Park and another – begun in 1998 – reintroduced captive-bred Mexican wolves to the forests of Arizona and New Mexico.

Many lessons have been learnt from these schemes, and we should heed them before releasing packs of wolves into the hills a few miles north of Perth, Scotland.

The first lesson is that captive-bred wolves – such as the Mexican variety, which was eliminated from its original territories – fare far less well on release than animals that have known only a wild existence. In everything from hunting skills to knowing how to establish territory, how to relate to other wild wolves and avoid hazards such as cars and hunters, the captive-bred Mexican wolves displayed relative incompetence and already many have been killed.

Wolves also have the inconvenient habit of not staying where they are put. Around two years of age, youngsters will establish new territories and packs – and these are often hundreds of miles from their original families. They will also travel immense distances in search of prey – and along the way farm livestock are as likely to feature on their menu as their staple diet of deer and elk. The US Government and environmental agencies have already spent fortunes compensating farmers for the loss of cattle and other livestock to these reintroduced predators.

Another cost is the labour-intensive transportation of wolves back to their territories after they have strayed – as they frequently do – into areas of human habitation. This requires extreme care, not just because of the stress on the animals concerned but also because a wolf put in the territory of another pack is likely to be ripped apart by its rivals.

The US wolves also display an insensitive tendency to eat domestic dogs and livestock. There are reports of pet dogs being carried off by wolves, sometimes with chains and kennels still attached.

Such horror stories will test almost anyone's enthusiasm for living with such a predator on their doorstep.

Sue Hull, a British wolf behaviour expert, says: "If I really thought it could work, I'd be as keen as anyone else to see wolves re-established as a wild species in this country. Wolves are fascinating creatures, and many past beliefs about their true natures or characters might have been unjust, but at the same time they're also not the goodie-goodies some of their fans might have us believe. They can be ruthless hunting other animals and equally ruthless among themselves, with family members often killing each other to attain pack supremacy.

"During numerous talks I have given on wolves around this country, I always try to give people the downsides of the species as well as the upsides, but it's amazing how few people seem to take the downsides in. It's as if wolf enthusiasts over the years have done too good a job of rehabilitating their image with the public, to the point where they can no longer see what the dangers of living with a predator this size in their neighbourhood might be, because wolves will always be drawn towards where people and their animals live."

You understand what Hull means about the affinity with people when you see Nadja and Mischka at Wildwood. They have been hand-reared from birth. They will never run wild because it is unlikely they would ever develop the skills and instincts to survive. At the same time, they may never be reunited with their parents and former pack – kept in a separate large enclosure – for fear that they would be rejected and, as a result, seriously injured or killed.

Gow believes that mankind's fascination with wolves, as timeless, charismatic and intelligent predators, will never go away. Nor, he says, will his "dream of one day having them living wild among us again in this country".

It is easy to admire his enthusiasm for this "ultimate symbol of wilderness" from the right side of a safety fence. But maybe – as Americans are finding – the reality of living with one of your oldest adversaries on your doorstep is not as simple as some would like it to be.

OWL ATTACKS HUMAN LOVE RIVAL

A man was attacked by an owl after he interrupted it having sex.

Kirk Hall was taking a short cut to a pub in Oswestry, Shropshire, when he heard the bird making a noise. The tawny owl then flew into him and pecked at his head for around thirty seconds.

The tyre centre boss eventually fought the owl off and ran to the Highwayman pub, where landlady Denise Crofts dressed his cuts and gave him a whisky.

Bird expert Jay Brittain, who runs the Kington Owl Centre near Hereford, England, said: "Owl attacks are rare but are always in the mating season. It would have been a male that attacked him. The bird would have just paired up with a mate and seen him as a threat."

Mr Hall, forty-five, said: "It was absolutely terrifying. I could have lost an eye. I thought I'd been mugged at first because it felt like I'd been hit on the side of the head with a cricket bat. It looks like I wandered by just as the owl was about to get it together with a lady owl. My mates can't stop laughing about it."

ONE DARK NIGHT IN ETHIOPIA

The hyenas struck at night, as eleven-year-old Mehamed Muhammed slept alongside his parents and two of his brothers at a refugee camp in south-eastern Ethiopia.

The animals tore at his mother's abdomen and broke the skulls of both of his brothers. One hyena gripped Mehamed's face in its jaws and began dragging him along the ground. The boy's father lunged at the hyena in a desperate rescue attempt.

When the attack was over, Mehamed's mother and two brothers were dead. His father died later that night, possibly from a heart attack or a stroke; no one is sure.

Somehow, Mehamed survived, but the left side of his face was ripped off. His left eye was torn out of its crushed socket. His nose was severed, leaving a gaping hole into his sinus cavity. Now, Mehamed is rebuilding his life piece by piece. He's getting a prosthetic eye and a new nose. He's found a new family. And he's doing it all in suburban Atlanta, Georgia, USA, thanks to a local humanitarian group that provides medical services to children across the globe.

Mehamed laughs as he runs about the children's waiting room at the North Atlanta office of his plastic surgeon, Dr Joseph Williams. He's wearing a baseball cap pulled low across his forehead. The hat hides much of his face and covers two large bald patches on his head – areas where skin has been grafted to rebuild his nose. He feels more comfortable this way, partially hidden, when he's out in public

On this mid-October morning, Mehamed has a check-up in preparation for another round of surgery – his fifth since coming to Georgia last February, just days after the hyena attack. As he waits, Mehamed takes a crayon and draws a stick figure of a person. Beside it, he slowly writes "M-O-M". Unsure whether he spelled it correctly, he taps Kitty Gomez on the shoulder.

"Mom, Mom, is that right?" Mehamed asks.

Gomez smiles down at Mehamed. Soon, she hopes, he will indeed be her son. Kitty and her husband Al, an airline pilot, took Mehamed into their Peachtree City home last winter. It was only supposed to be a temporary placement until Mehamed completed his medical treatment. But the Gomez family immediately warmed to the boy, and Al and Kitty began to talk about adoption. The Gomezes plan to take Mehamed to Ethiopa in December 2000 to take legal custody.

Mehamed already acts like part of the Gomez family. He insists on being called Mehamed Gomez. Kitty and Al are "Mom" and "Dad". Velasco, twenty-six, Martina, twenty-four, Mariana, seventeen, and Vanessa, fifteen, are his "brother" and "sisters".

"He's a great addition to the family," Kitty Gomez said. "There's no doubt that he's ours."

"He just seemed to fit in our family from the start," Al Gomez said. "We couldn't stand the thought of him leaving us and going back to a difficult life in an orphanage and in that poverty. It wasn't a hard decision for us to make."

The Gomezes took in Mehamed after talking to their friends Pam and Kenneth Rundle, founders of Children's Cross Connection, an Atlanta-based international medical relief agency. The group brings seventy-five to 100 children a year to the United States for surgery, placing them with host families before returning them to their home countries. Last winter, when the Gomezes asked Pam Rundle whether she needed a host family, she told them she was looking for a place to put Mehamed.

Mehamed does not talk much about the attack or about his life in

Ethiopia. For many months, when Al and Kitty would ask him about the incident, he said he didn't remember. Only recently has he begun to provide sketchy details.

"All he remembers is that he was asleep, and that [the hyena] was dragging him across the ground to eat him," Al Gomez said.

Mehamed spent the first eleven years of his life wandering with his family across the Ogaden region in south-eastern Ethiopa, near Somalia. They were nomadic herders, travelling with a small flock of camels, goats and other animals. Mehamed never went to school and never learned to read.

The night of the hyena attack, Mehamed's family stopped at a refugee camp en route to a feeding station run by an international relief agency. A devastating drought in the area had led to a famine. Mehamed's family's animals had died, and the family had no food. Mehamed's oldest brother, twenty-one-year-old Ahmed, left the refugee camp to save a place in line at the feeding station. He is still living in Ethiopia.

Mehamed saw many people die during his years in Ethiopia, which may have helped him deal with the gruesome deaths of his parents and two of his older brothers.

"He pretty much perseveres," Al Gomez said. "Where he's from, people die so young and so often. People just die. He's just used to seeing that."

It will be a long time before Mehamed's face returns to something approaching normal. Two long vertical scars line each side of his face. His left eye is gone; it's covered with a flap of skin until a glass eye is put in. The bones around his right eye are damaged, but the eye itself is healthy. His right eye droops a half-inch or so, something that will be corrected in a future operation. Doctors have built a nose, using skin and blood vessels from his scalp. Cartilage was taken from one of Mehamed's ribs to form the bridge of the new nose. For now, the nose looks much too large for his face; because the nose won't grow, Mehamed has been given an adult-size nose that he'll grow into.

Still, Mehamed's physical transformation has been remarkable. At the doctor's office, nurses and physicians marvel at Mehamed's progress. Mehamed, who will turn twelve next month, is shy around strangers. When asked how he likes his new nose, he gives a one-word answer: "Good." He gives the same answer when asked about his new family and his new life in Peachtree City.

Mehamed's spoken English is a bit halting, but he understands nearly everything said to him. He is taking classes from a Fayette County public school teacher who visits the Gomez home twice a week. An interpreter makes frequent visits, but Mehamed often chooses to speak English instead of his native Somali. The Gomezes have put vocabulary words on coloured strips of paper throughout the house to help Mehamed's reading – the word "light" hangs from the light fixture over the kitchen table, "cabinet" is written on a card taped to a cabinet above the kitchen sink.

Mehamed has adapted quickly to life in America. He loves riding his BMX bicycle and watching Bugs Bunny cartoons. He has learned to swim and to send e-mail. His favourite food? McDonald's burgers. His favourite movie? *Home Alone*. But it's not always easy. Almost everything has been new to him – elevators, microwave ovens, computers, cheeseburgers. At a Fourth of July parade in Peachtree City, Mehamed saw fireworks for the first time.

Understandably, Mehamed is self-conscious about his injuries. He is reluctant to pose for pictures. When kids on the playground ask him about his face, he tells them he fell down.

Despite his injuries and the loss of his family, the Gomezes say Mehamed is never depressed. He doesn't talk about missing his Ethiopian family. "He's blocked out a lot," Al Gomez said. "In his mind, his life started when he came here."

FRASER ISLAND KOOKABURRAS

Rangers on Australia's Fraser Island have killed three kookaburras after a series of attacks on visitors.

The move to kill the large birds has been criticized by the Queensland Conservation Council as being an unacceptable drastic solution. Fraser Island was the focus of attention recently after dingoes were culled following the fatal mauling of a Brisbane boy.

A spokeswoman for Queensland Environment Minister Dean Wells said a number of people had been pecked on the hand by the birds and one person suffered a graze on the cheek.

Rangers tried to scare the birds with firecracker, but the three which were killed had not been frightened away.

The spokeswoman added human safety came first and urged people not to feed wildlife in any national park.

KENYAN KILLER ELEPHANT

A German tourist in Kenya has been trampled to death by an elephant as he tried to take its photograph.

The tourist, on an African Safari Club holiday, was walking with his wife and son when the attack happened. Wilfred Njiiri, manager of Tsavo Park Hotel, said the elephant was alone. He added park rules ban unsupervized walks.

The attack happened near the Voi River when the family had gone for an unsupervized walk from their campsite.

"They must have gone too close for the comfort of the elephant. The elephant attacked the man and killed him instantly," Mr Njiiri said in a letter to tour operators.

An official at the Kenya Wildlife Service confirmed the death on 10 August 2001, but would not release any additional information. The man has not been named.

Mr Njiiri has told tour operators that the hotel will take extra precautions to avoid a repeat of the death.

HONEY BEE HORROR

A nine-year-old boy has died after being attacked by hundreds of bees while riding his bike past a field of sunflowers, hospital officials in France said.

A passerby found the boy on a roadside covered with bees on 11 August 2001 and rushed him to the hospital in Poitiers.

The child had about 1,000 stingers removed from his body and suffered cardiac and breathing problems after the attack, a doctor who treated him said.

The boy died five days later.

According to Joseph Lame, an assistant to the mayor of Montils, where the boy lived, the bees came from hives that had been placed in a sunflower field to be harvested for honey.

ANGRY AFRICAN AARDVARK

A Scottish fundraiser has told how he survived an attack by a wild aardvark in Kenya. Stewart Douglas, from Newton Mearns, East Renfrewshire, suffered four broken ribs.

The ten-stone aardvark charged at him at an estimated twenty miles per hour. Mr Douglas, fifty-nine, was taking part in a cancer fundraiser in Samburu province.

He told relatives and friends: "I think the aardvark must have been startled by one of our camels. "It came charging out of the bushes and must have been travelling at about twenty miles an hour when it hit me."

Mr Stewart says doctors in Nairobi told him he was lucky to be alive after being thrown into the air when it hit.

He said: "After the aardvark hit me, one of our guides massaged my ribs with oil for about ten minutes. When I got to hospital two days later, the doctors said the guide had massaged my ribs back into place and had saved me from a punctured lung."

SCOTCH STEAK ON THE HOOF

A Stirlingshire woman is in intensive care after being attacked by a bull.

Christine Hamilton, a farmer's wife, suffered a broken jaw, cheekbone and ribs, a bruised lung and a dislocated shoulder. The animal hurled her against a fence.

She was airlifted to Southern General Hospital in Glasgow, where she is stable in intensive care, said a hospital spokesman on 17 October 2001. Mrs Hamilton, fifty-four, will be in hospital for several weeks.

Her son John,, said: "My mother is very lucky to be alive. If it wasn't for the air ambulance I doubt whether she would be here. She is going to be in hospital for quite a few weeks."

John, partner in the family farm at Wester Third, Gartmore, added: "We were running behind schedule and tried to catch up by bedding down the bulls. One of them charged her and threw her against a fence. It was one of the pure Ayrshire breeds. They are much more highly-strung than crossbreeds."

The fifteen-month-old bull had been due for slaughter in four months, but will now be killed next week. Experts said an Ayrshire bull of that age would normally weigh between 500 and 600 kilos.

MICHIGAN DEER DEVIL

A hunter in Michigan has wrestled a deer for forty-five minutes after it charged him. David Gutowski eventually strangled the animal with his belt, before clubbing it to death with a lump of wood.

He is now angry that wildlife officials won't let him eat his trophy. They want to analyse the animal to see what caused the attack in Manistee.

"I fought for my life with that deer and I think it should be mine," said the forty-one-year-old.

Mr Gutowski engaged in hand-to-hoof combat after the 200-pound deer ran at him and tried to spike him with its horns. The buck went for him while he was fishing on a riverbank. Alone and not knowing what to do, Gutowski said he grabbed the deer by its antlers and hung on.

"He was going to spear me in the guts if I didn't," Mr Gutowski said. "It was grunting and going crazy. I had my legs wrapped around its rib cage and I was squeezing for all I was worth. I was afraid to let go, for fear that it would kill me."

He managed to undo his belt and wrap it around the animal's neck. He choked the animal until it was too weak to move, then used a piece of railroad sleeper he found nearby to club it to death.

"I didn't kill him on purpose; I was scared for my life," he said. "I promise I will never get into a fight with a deer again."

VENOM VERSUS SEPTIC BITE

Venom makes its user a specialist. Whereas more primitive snakes simply swallow prey or else suffocate it by constriction, venomous snakes have the option of delivering a killing strike and then allowing their prey to die before moving in for a meal. This tactic spares them some of the danger involved in overpowering prey; living prey can bite and claw.

The venomous bite has evolved independently in many different animals, from octopi to shrews. It even evolved independently in different types of snakes. No one knows exactly how it came about in rattlesnakes, but some clues can be found in the behaviour of the monitor lizards.

The monitors constitute the lizard family most closely related to snakes. This relationship is not hard to spot once you've seen a large monitor move: it walks on legs, but with an ophidian essing of the body. In the largest monitor, the Komodo dragon, the males engage in courtship battles similar to those of rattlesnakes, rising into the air as they push against each other in a sort of sumo match. And, most snakelike of all, the Komodo dragon smells by constantly lashing the air with its forked, black tongue.

The big lizard (up to about ten feet and three hundred pounds) can find fresh carrion more than a mile away by scent. Its sense of smell is, in fact, more acute than that of a bloodhound, which itself can seem almost supernatural to us. But the dragon doesn't restrict its diet to carrion; it also actively hunts, and its predatory technique is strikingly similar to that of the rattlesnake. The dragon rushes the prey – which can be something as large as a pig, a deer, or a human child – and delivers a toothy bite. Then it allows the prey to escape, and tracks it by scent. The dragon has no venom; the tactic works because of the festering meat between the reptile's teeth, which makes the bite septic. In the hot, humid tropics, a septic bite can kill a big animal in a couple of hours.

The rattlesnake's venom may be a refinement of a septic-bite tactic, which both the monitors and the rattlesnake's ancestors might have developed to complement their extraordinary smelling abilities – an example of convergent evolution. Killing by septic bite is also a feline tactic. The lynx uses it on young caribou. Many people mauled by lions have died from wounds that should have been survivable: the meat caked under the attackers' claws and teeth injected the victims with disease, and they died in a gangrenous fever.

PANDA POWER

A Chinese court has ordered a school to pay damages to a student who was attacked by a giant panda while he was on a field trip.

Qi Ming was fourteen when he was bitten by one of the animals at a panda breeding park.

The court in Chengdu ordered Xindu School Number Four to pay the boy around £2,500. He suffered head and arm injuries. According to reports, the court ruled the school hadn't provided enough supervision.

In 1999 a worker was bitten on both legs when she slipped and fell into the animals' enclosure at the park.

ELEPHANTS IN SOUTH AFRICA

A twenty-eight-year-old illegal immigrant from Mozambique was killed in an encounter with five elephants near Giyani, outside the Kruger National Park on Wednesday, police said in South Africa on 24 January 2002.

Inspector Moatshe Ngoepe said three illegal immigrants from Mozambique had entered South Africa through the Kruger National Park. After making it though the park, they decided to sleep near Giyani.

On awaking, the men were confronted by five elephants, and fled in different directions. According to Ngoepe, the elephants pursued one of the men, Fernado Shishongi, and trampled him to death. The other two men alerted local residents who contacted the police

Ngoepe said rangers from the department of environmental affairs went on a search and found the mutilated body of Shishongi. Ngoepe said the rangers were searching for the five elephants.

William Mabasa of the Kruger National Park could not confirm whether the elephants were from the park itself.

Ngoepe said the two illegal immigrants were in police custody and were being questioned. Police would liaise with the department of home affairs on deporting them.

IN THE TIGERS' DEN

A thief escaping from a botched robbery at a game sanctuary near Johannesburg made a fatal mistake when he climbed a high fence and found himself in the tigers' den, police said Monday, 11 March 2002

"The tigers grabbed him and first played with him. He died of a broken neck and a fractured skull," police spokeswoman Milica Bezuidenhout said. The body was removed after the tigers, a male and a female, had been sedated, she said.

The twenty-eight-year-old victim, a South African, and an accomplice had held up the gate guard at the Rhino and Lion Reserve at Krugersdorp, west of Johannesburg, Saturday, but fled when staff and visitors became suspicious and chased them.

The accomplice and the driver of the getaway car were arrested and were to appear in court later Monday, Bezuidenhout said.

ENRAGED HIPPO IN SOUTH AFRICA

In an emergency air dash from Durban, South Africa, 12 April 2002, a thirty-five year-old Zululand man was airlifted to Ngwelezane Hospital in Empangeni after an enraged hippo virtually bit off his face, leaving him without a nose, one eye and massive internal injuries.

Doctors at Manguzi Hospital in the rural area of northern Zululand, where the "appallingly" injured man was first taken, managed to stabilize the victim until the air mercy services arrived. He was later transferred to the ICU at King Edward VIII Hospital for further long-term treatment, which will include extensive reconstructive surgery.

Fumukwiyo Mbonambi was walking home along a dirt road in the Black Rock area, one hour south of Kosi Bay, on Thursday night when he accidentally stumbled into a hippo in the darkness. The animal lunged at him, biting his face with such force that it removed most of his features including his nose, right eye and much of the flesh.

With blood pumping from massive wounds he somehow managed to escape the jaws of the hippo, crawl along the road and then stand long enough to flag down the first vehicle that came along.

"How he survived the attack, let alone the hour's journey to the hospital, is incredible," said Manguzi Hospital resident doctor Mark Blaylock. "He must be remarkably fit because it was adrenaline alone that got him through. The people who picked him up must have got the fright of their lives to see this blood-soaked man in their headlights. Thank goodness they kept their heads and brought him here as quickly as they did."

Hospital staff, who dubbed him "The Miracle Man", were astounded when the victim tried to tell them that his arm hurt, not realizing that most of his face was missing.

"We could hear the word 'hippo', but then we told him not to talk as it was endangering his life," said Blaylock, who inserted an endotracheal tube to "maintain" the man's airway. "We realized that his ribs were also crushed and that air was escaping from his lungs, resulting in a life-threatening bilateral pneumothorax – air trapped between wall of thorax and lungs causing the lungs to collapse."

Doctors and staff fought through the night to save him. But without an intensive care unit and specialist treatment, it was vital that the patient be transferred to a hospital that could deal with this type of injury.

A telephone fault in Manguzi meant that the first alert could only go out to the KwaZulu Natal provincial emergency medical rescue services (EMRS) early on Friday morning. Lynette Thomas of the South African Red Cross Air Mercy Service, which operates in association with the KZN department of health, coordinated the air transfer in a pressurized single-engined Pilatus PC12 with two paramedics and a doctor in attendance.

CANADIAN COUGARS POUNCE

An eight-year-old US girl recovered after being attacked and bitten by a cougar off northern Vancouver Island. The attack occurred Sunday, 23 June 2002, on Compton Island, a tiny island about twenty-four kilometres east of Port McNeill, British Columbia, and about 350 kilometres north-west of Victoria.

Rita Hilsabeck of Reno, Nevada, was on a kayaking trip with her parents and five other people when the cougar pounced on her just after the group had returned from a pre-dinner paddle on the first day of a six-day tour.

"It was odd, really, there were people all around her when it happened," her father, Chuck, fifty-two, said at Port McNeill and District Hospital. "She's got a lot of stitches and she's got soreness, but she's very tough and resilient and she's going to be okay. Rita's most serious wounds are deep gashes around her neck, where the cougar grabbed her," he said. She also had to have some stitches on her arm and lower back.

Three members of the group remained on Compton Island after the incident, along with Jason Doucet, a guide with Northern Lights Expeditions of Bellingham, Washington.

"Rita was just near the kayaks and the cougar came up and just picked her up on the beach and started dragging her up towards the woods," Mr Doucet said. The others raised enough of a commotion to startle the big cat into dropping the child.

But the cougar, a large male weighing about thirty kilograms, moved only a short distance away and found a perch a few metres up a spruce tree in the middle of the camp area. Mr Doucet said the animal was still in the tree when it was shot. It managed to move a few steps and then died in the middle of the camp's makeshift kitchen area.

Conservation officer Greg Kruger said the animal appeared healthy, but will be tested for rabies and several other conditions. It was instinct that led the animal to linger in a tree after being scared away from the person it had set upon, he said. "Once they're startled that's a natural defence mechanism, they go up a tree."

Just seconds before the attack, Charles Eisner, eleven, of Tucson, Arizona, and Rita had been playing together on the beach. They found a crab and were trying to decide what to name it "and then thirty seconds later, she was grabbed by the cougar," he said. "The attack was quick," he said. "It was way too fast."

Her mother, Barbara Atwood, said the experience was horrifying. "It happened so quickly, it was very hard to register in a circumstance like that," she said.

Ms Atwood said her family plans to continue with the six-day kayak trip. The attack was "very scary, but we know it's very rare and extremely unlikely anything else would happen like this," she said.

A wildlife official said it is rare for a cougar to attack a human. Cougars have killed eleven people in British Columbia, ten of them children, since 1900. Most cougar attacks occur on Vancouver Island, which has the highest concentration of British Columbia's cougars. There have been fifteen cougar attacks on Vancouver Island since 1970, including three deaths.

The last fatal attack occurred in August 1996, when a thirty-six-year-old woman died near Princeton, about 200 kilometres east of Vancouver, while fighting off a cougar that mauled her son.

Cindy Parolin, an experienced outdoorswoman, was killed by the twenty-seven-kilogram cougar when she rushed to defend her six-year-old son Steven. He was attacked by the big cat after it spooked his horse and he fell off. Ms Parolin, thirty-six, went at the cougar with a stick and it turned on her, allowing two of her other children to carry

Steven away and get help. The family had just started a horseback camping trip when the attack occurred.

HE ATE IT, DR LECTER

Alexander Pierce (also known as Edward Pearce) was the last survivor of a party of six runaways who had successively killed and eaten each other. Ths experience seems to have given him a taste for human flesh, for he absconded a second time with the following grisly results as quoted in the Appendix to Report from the Select Committee on Transportation (1838).

"Alexander Pierce and Thomas Cox absconded from Macquarie Harbour on 16 November 1823. On the 21 November, as the *Waterloo* was sailing down the harbour, some of the pilot's crew observed a man on the beach making a signal by smoke; Mr Lucas sent his boat ashore in consequence. The same signal was observed from the settlement from which a boat was also sent, both boats returned before dark, bringing with them Alexander Pierce, who had confessed having murdered his fellow-prisoner, Thomas Cox, two days before, and that he had lived upon his body ever since. A piece of human flesh, about half-a-pound, was found upon his person. Pierce told Lieutenant Cuthbertson all the particulars of the murder, and that he would point out the unfortunate Cox's remains.

"A boat was accordingly dispatched with Pierce early next morning for King's River, well guarded. After the party landed, and had walked about 400 yards by Pierce's dfrections, the body was found and brought to the settlement in a dreadfully mangled state, being cut right in two at the middle, the head off, the private parts torn off, all the flesh off the calves of the legs, back of the thighs and loins, also off the thick part of the arms, which the inhuman wretch declared was most delicious food; none of the intestines were found; he said that he threw them behind a tree, after having roasted and devoured the heart and a part of the liver; one of the hands was also missing.

"Pierce would not be in want of food when he committed this horrid deed, as he had been then only three days from the settlement, and had some flour with him when they absconded and further, when he was taken, there was found upon his person a piece of pork, some bread and a few fish, which he had plundered from a party of hunters two days before, but which he had not tasted, stating that human flesh was by far preferable.

"On being questioned why he murdered Cox, he said that they quarrelled about the route they were to pursue, and Cox being the strongest man, he was obliged to take up an axe, with which he knocked him down and killed him.

"His reason for giving himself up was, that he had no hope of ultimately escaping, and that he was so horror-truck at his own inhuman conduct, and that he did not know what he was about when he made the signal on the beach. He had on the murdered man's clothes when brought back to the settlement. He was sent to Hobart Town, per *Waterloo* 21 November 1823, tried for the murder, and executed."

In 1832 the convicts Edward Broughton and Mathew Maccavoy were hanged "for the wilful Murder of three of their Fellow Transports and eating them as Food".

Part 3

Death in the Water

BOLD AFRICAN CROCODILES

The wanderer William Bartram, never at a loss for a lurid description, tells us something of what it is like to be alone in a strange place surrounded by threatening saurians. In his *Travels* (1791), he tells how he happened on a place where many large alligators had gathered to feed on easily caught fish that crowded into a narrow channel:

> But ere I had halfway reached the place, I was attacked on all sides, several endeavouring to overset the canoe. My situation now became precarious to the last degree; two very large ones attacked me closely, at the same instant, rushing up with their heads and part of their bodies above the water, roaring terribly and belching floods of water over us. They struck their jaws together so close to my ears, as almost to stun me, and I expected every moment to be dragged out of the beat and instantly devoured. But I plied my weapons so effectually about me, though at random, that I was so successful as to beat them off a little. When, finding that they desired to renew the battle, I made for the shore . . .

Later, having run that gauntlet, he came upon yet another ominous situation:

> I began to tremble and keep a good lookout; when suddenly a huge alligator rushed out of the weeds, and with a tremendous roar came up and darted as swift as an arrow under my boat, emerging upright on my lee quarter with open jaws and belching water and smoke that fell upon me like rain in a hurricane. I laid soundly about his head with my club.

Men who go to unknown places tend to see things larger than life; reactions to strange phenomena are often exaggerated in the light of later encounters. Thus Bartram was probably describing what he really felt was happening, though we might nowadays think he was embellishing.

Bartram lived to regale us with his exploits. So did many African adventurers who often assumed it was incumbent upon them to have witnessed at least one fatal croc attack when the time came to write up their "diaries". Apart from such yarns there are many authentic eyewitness accounts which serve to illustrate the things that happen when crocs try to kill men. Attacks naturally occur most often when man takes to the water.

Nor should even a substantial boat be thought of as absolutely safe. "The boldness of crocodiles at times is inconceivable. Captain Ross lost the coxswain of one of his barges, who was taken in the act of micturition whilst crouching upon one of the barge's rudder pintles, and this whilst the steamer was under way in the Shire River."

Sitting or standing half in the water is just asking for an attack. About fifteen years ago a particularly gruesome croc attack took place in the Tsavo National Park. An Asian family were sitting on a raft moored to the bank at Mzima Springs, a pleasure spot where tourists can leave their cars and enjoy restful surroundings by the cool spring waters. Several members of the family were dangling their legs over the edge of the raft when suddenly a croc seized one of the men by his leg just above the knee. His family then grabbed him and a tug-of-war ensued which the family won by slowly drawing the victim's leg through the beast's clenched jaws. Seventy sharp teeth shredded his leg frightfully, and his screams and the copious blood so demoralized his fellows, that having freed him from the reptile's grasp, none of them thought to stop the bleeding. To the accompaniment of much weeping and wailing he died shortly after from shock and loss of blood – a pathetic accident caused by a mixture of ignorance and panic.

How quick the ponderous-looking crocodile is to exploit an opportunity is shown by a sinister attack that took place on the northern border of the Serengeti National Park some years ago. So dramatic was this incident that it lives on in the region's folklore. A notorious hunter named Kwehahura living in the area defiantly continued "poaching" despite regular arrests by the warden, Myles Turner. Surprised one day by a ranger patrol, Kwehahura took off like a springhare for the bush along the nearby Grumeti river, the haunt of many monstrous crocs. The patrol saw him reach the river and without pausing jump into a large pool, evidently meaning to swim across. Immediately following the splash they heard another, louder splash. Arriving at the brink of the pool they looked down, but saw only wide muddy swirls in the water, which gradually subsided and became still again. Kwehahura had crossed all right – this time to the "other side," to poach forever in the happy hunting ground. The place today is called Kirawira after him, and has been the scene of many other strange events.

Nor is it essential to be in or on the water to provoke an attack. A croc will come out after a suitably vulnerable man. The earliest recorded instance of a croc attack on Lake Rudolf was the bold taking on dry land of Arthur Neumann's cook, Shebane, at the north end of the lake in 1897. Neumann vividly describes the suddenness and finality of the attack, which obviously he himself barely escaped:

Having bathed and dried myself, I was sitting on my chair, after pulling on my clothes, by the water's edge, lacing up my boots. The sun was just about to set, its level rays shining full upon us, rendering usconspicuous from the water while preventing our seeing in that direction. Shebane had just gone a little way off along the brink and taken off his clothes to wash himself, a thing I had never known him to do before with me; but my attention being taken up with what I was doing, I took no notice of him. I was still looking down when I heard a cry of alarm, and, raising my head, got a glimpse of the most ghastly sight I ever witnessed. There was the head of a huge crocodile out of the water, just swinging over towards the deep with poor Shebane in its awful jaws, held across the middle of his body like a fish in the beak of a heron. He had ceased to cry out, and with one horrible wriggle, a swirl and a splash, all disappeared. One could do nothing. It was over: Shebane was gone. The dreadful incident had an insupportably depressing effect on me – a melancholy new year's day indeed.

Of all the characteristics that cause men to fear croc attacks, such as the animal's stealth (or boldness), ferocity, or strength, one in particular stands out – the unexpectedness. The concealment of water, the beast's cryptic looks and its hunting skill combine to make croc attacks sudden and therefore more terrifying.

Crocodiles . . . hide under willowes and greene hollow bankes, till some people come to the waters side to draw and fetch water, and then suddenly, or ever they be aware, they are taken, and drawne into the water. And also for this purpose, because he knoweth that he is not able to overtake a man in his course or chase, he taketh a great deale of water in his mouth, and casteth it in the path-waies, so that when they endeavour to run from the crocodile, they fall downe in the slippery path, and are overtaken and destroyed by him.

Men do not care to be caught unaware – even a stumble is blamed on the crocodile. It matters little if one's lack of vigilance is due to ignorance, carelessness, indifference or whatever; to be caught out is humiliating and unnerving.

Crocodile victims fall into three broad categories: the resigned (which includes the majority), that is, those like Kwehahura who for one reason or another consider the risk unavoidable. Secondly, the unaware, those who suffer real accidents of chance. Thirdly, the tantalized, men lured by some compelling aspect of a situation into exposing themselves to attack . . .

It was in the middle of our survey that we learned of a fatal croc attack that took place not far from Lake Rudolf, in south-west Ethiopia. It was typical of countless croc attacks, and its circumstances emphasize the stark reality of such accidents to those who, ignorant of the ways of the bush, do not believe or appreciate that such things actually do take place. As it happened, a professional hunter, Karl Luthy, was there to witness the incident. Luthy also took the trouble to record what took place, thus providing an unusually authentic and vivid description of the circumstances:

Shortly after noon on 13 April 1966, the DC 3 from Addis Ababa landed at Gambela in south-west Ethiopia. The plane brought six Americans of the Peace Corps, two girls and four boys, who had chosen to spend a short vacation visiting Gambela.

Through the village runs a slow, muddy river, the Baro, on the sandy banks of which I was working that day, building a pontoon on which to ferry my equipment across the river so that my client, an American named Dow, and I could resume our safari to the south. Hot and eager for a swim the Peace Corps came down to the river and I heard them discussing the prospect not far away. But their enquiries of the villagers elicited only a strong warning to stay out of the water on account of a large croc, which it was asserted, had only recently killed and eaten a native child, and later a woman, in the brazenest manner imaginable – by which I mean right in the middle of town, in plain view of a crowd! I, too, strongly warned them against swimming, and for a while they thought better of it.

Not long afterwards I heard a splash and looking up from my work saw one of the Peace Corps in the river striking out for the other bank. At this the others, abandoning all caution, also dived into the water and swam to the other side. For a while they splashed and cavorted in the shallows, maybe 150 yards from where I was working. It was naturally alarming, and very annoying to see them completely ignore my warnings and those of so many well-meaning and experienced people; but I did not wish to intervene again, it was no business of mine and in any case out of my control. Yet it was with considerable relief that I saw five of the six swim back to my side and climb out.

Bill Olsen remained behind, why, I never discovered. I recall seeing him on the far side of the river waist high in the water, his feet on a submerged rock. He was leaning into the current to keep his balance, a rippled vee of water trailing behind him; his arms were folded across his chest and he was staring ahead as if lost in thought. I continued working for a while and looked up again a few minutes later. Olsen had gone – vanished without a trace or a sound, and instinctively I glanced around, a prickle of apprehension spreading over me. But he was nowhere to be seen and I never saw him alive again, although we were to meet face to face much later when I fished his head out of the croc's belly.

Give or take half an hour the croc took Olsen at 3.30 p.m. After that events followed in quick succession. Although I knew instinctively what had happened I had, as yet, no definite proof. At this point the other Peace Corps volunteers came back to the river shouting for Olsen to join them, little knowing that he had in fact left them for ever. I continued to scan the river and eventually, a short distance downstream, a croc surfaced, with a large, white, partially submerged object in its jaws, whose identity was in no doubt.

About fifteen minutes had elapsed since Olsen disappeared. The croc then dived to resurface (still carrying the corpse) ten minutes later, now some distance downstream and difficult to see. The Peace Corps were at first incredulous at the news, stubbornly unwilling to believe what was obvious. Olsen had wandered off somewhere, they said, he would be back soon; they clutched at the silliest possibilities rather than accept the bitter facts. Eventually my binoculars arrived and they saw for themselves what was obviously the body of their companion in the jaws of a croc. They went to pieces then, crying, full of remorse and self-incrimination, and I confess that one of them received a sharp rebuke when he ran to me pleading for help.

"Help who?" I shouted. "Help him? He's dead! Help you? I should hit you!"

One does not care to see one's fellow men die such needless deaths, however ignorant they may be.

By this time a crowd of excited people had gathered on the river bank and the commotion caused my client, Colonel Dow, to come with his rifle demanding to know what was going on. On learning the story he wanted to try and shoot the croc then and there, but I persuaded him not to, pointing out that killing the animal now, in midstream, would surely result in Olsen's body being lost, possibly for good. I reasoned that the croc would behave like any other croc; that is, he would haul out of the river early next morning, not too far away, to rest in the morning sun for a while, after the activities of the night.

Sure enough, around seven the next morning, a breathless villager ran up to tell us that a large croc, undoubtedly *the* croc, was lying ashore across the river not fifty yards from where Olsen had been taken. I got my binoculars and located the beast. That this was our quarry was in no doubt, for hanging from his mouth in some macabre reminder of a recent banquet, was a large piece of pale coloured flesh.

We were determined to destroy this croc, not only because it was a menace to the people on the river but also because an undeniable vengeance was in us. This was no circumstantial accident, but a deliberate and vicious attack in our midst and a certain urge for revenge moved us. Dow wanted to be the one to kill the animal so off he went on a careful route which took him upstream on foot for some distance, then across the Baro in a canoe and back down the other side on a painstaking stalk until eventually he lay directly behind the beast. It was a difficult shot with the croc facing away from him so that its protruding back partially obscured its head. The Colonel shot too high and the bullet struck its neck, temporarily stunning the reptile, but causing only a flesh wound. He then fired four more shots, three of which were well placed, but despite this the croc crawled into the river and disappeared.

I watched all this through binoculars and feared at first that we'd lost the beast. I joined Dow and together we made for a sandbank in midstream, followed by a flotilla of dugouts, carrying the other Peace Corps and as many Amhara and Anuak villagers as could get in the canoes, all very noisy and excited. We stepped out on to the sandbank and began searching the river for some sign of the croc. Quite suddenly it surfaced not ten yards away and Dow, rather hastily shot and missed. But the animal, mortally wounded took no notice and he was able to fire again, this time hitting the head, sending the brute spinning crazily about its own axis. I rushed forward with several other men and we dragged the carcass from the water on to the sand.

There remained only the gruesome business of opening up the croc, and it was not long before Olsen's fate was established beyond all doubt. We found his legs, intact from the knees down, still joined together at the pelvis. We found his head, crushed into small chunks, a barely recognizable mass of hair and flesh; and we found other chunks of unidentifiable tissue. The croc had evidently torn him to pieces to feed and abandoned what he could not swallow.

The circumstances of Olsen's killing are of some interest in illuminating the way in which crocodiles set about taking their prey. First of all he disappeared without a sound which suggests that he was not standing on the rock at the final moment – I think he would have had time to scream if he was. It seems to me that he must have started swimming back and was simply pulled under without warning, and held under until he drowned. Secondly, there is the fact that no one saw any sign of the beast before the event although it was flagrantly bold afterwards, illustrating the stealth and cunning with which a crocodile hunts. The croc measured exactly thirteen feet and one inch long, by no means a monster but still powerful enough to catch a human like a fish.

THE SUFFERINGS OF THE
CREW OF THE *ESSEX*

Herman Melville's novel Moby Dick *was inspired by the dramatic events surrounding the sinking of the Nantucket whaleship* Essex *by an infuriated sperm whale in the middle of the Pacific in November 1820.*

As the ship began to sink beneath the waves the twenty crewmen, who were of mixed nationality and race, took to three boats. They tried to stick together, but a night-time storm drove the one commanded by Chase out of the sight of the other two. Thus the two boats under the command of Pollard and Hendricks set off on a different course. However, the crewmen in all three boats shared a particular kind of hell as they struggled for three months to reach the coast of South America.

On 20 January 1821, eight days after losing sight of Chase's boat, Pollard's and Hendricks's men were coming to the end of their provisions. That day, Lawson Thomas, one of the blacks on Hendricks's boat, died. With barely a pound of hardtack left to share among ten men, Hendricks and his crew dared speak of a subject that had been on all their minds: whether they should eat, instead of bury, the body.

For as long as men had been sailing the world's oceans, famished sailors had been sustaining themselves on the remains of dead shipmates. By the early nineteenth century, cannibalism at sea was so widespread that survivors often felt compelled to inform their rescuers if they had *not* resorted to it since, according to one historian, "suspicion of this practice among starving castaways was a routine reaction". One of the most thoroughly documented cases of cannibalism occurred in the winter of 1710, when the *Nottingham Galley*, a British trading vessel under the command of Captain John Dean, wrecked on Boon Island, a tiny outcropping of rock just off the coast of Maine.

One hundred and eleven years later, in the middle of the Pacific, ten men of the *Essex* reached a similar conclusion. Two months after deciding to spurn the Society Islands because, in Pollard's words, "we feared we should be devoured by cannibals", they were about to eat one of their own shipmates.

First they had to butcher the body. On Nantucket there was a slaughterhouse at the foot of Old North wharf where any island boy could watch a cow or sheep be transformed into marketable cuts of meat. On a whaleship it was the black members of the crew who prepared and cooked the food. In the case of the *Essex,* more than thirty hogs and dozens of tortoises had been butchered by the African American cook before the whale attack. And, of course, all twenty crew members had taken part in the cutting up of several dozen sperm whales. But this was not a whale or a hog or a tortoise. This was Lawson Thomas, a shipmate with whom they had shared two hellish months in an open boat. Whoever butchered Thomas's body had to contend not only with the cramped quarters of a twenty-five-foot beat but also with the chaos of his own emotions.

The crew of the *Nottingham Galley,* the ship that wrecked off Maine, had found it so difficult to begin the gruesome task of cutting up the carpenter's body that they pleaded with the reluctant Captain Dean to do it for them. Dean, like most sailors forced to resort to cannibalism, began by removing the most obvious signs of the corpse's humanity – the head, hands, feet, and skin – and consigned them to the sea.

If Hendricks and his men followed Dean's example, they next would have removed Thomas's heart, liver, and kidneys from the bloody basket of his ribs. Then they would have began to hack the meat from the backbone, ribs, and pelvis. In any case, Pollard reported that after lighting a fire on the flat stone at the bottom of the boat, they roasted the organs and meat and began to eat.

Instead of easing their hunger pangs, their first taste of meat only intensified their atavistic urge to eat. The saliva flowed in their mouths as their long-dormant stomachs gargled with digestive juices. And the more they ate, the hungrier they became.

Anthropologists and archaeologists studying the phenomenon of cannibalism have estimated that the average human adult would provide about sixty-six pounds of edible meat. But Lawson Thomas's body was not average. Autopsies of starvation victims have revealed a dramatic atrophy of muscle tissue and a complete absence of fat – replaced, in some instances, by a translucent gelatinous substance. Starvation and dehydration had also shrunk Thomas's internal organs, including the heart and liver. His body may have yielded as little as thirty pounds of lean, fibrous meat. On the following day, when the captain's store of bread ran out, Pollard and his men "were glad to partake of the wretched fare with the other crew".

Two days later, on 23 January – the sixty-third day since leaving the wreck – yet another member of Hendricks's crew died and was eaten. And like Lawson Thomas before him, Charles Shorter was black.

It was likely that the African Americans had suffered from an inferior diet prior to the sinking. But there may have been yet another factor at work. A recent scientific study comparing the percentage of body fat among different ethnic groups claims that American blacks tend to have less body fat than their Caucasian counterparts. Once a starving body exhausts its reserves of fat, it begins consuming muscle, a process that soon results in the deterioration of the internal organs and, eventually, death. The blacks' initially lower amount of body fat meant that they had begun living off muscle tissue before the whites.

Now that people had begun to die among the *Essex* crew, it was no accident that the first to go (with the exception of the sickly Matthew Joy, who, in Chase's words, "did not die of absolute starvation") were African American.

Of the whites, the *Essex*'s twenty-nine-year-old captain had an advantage. He was short, had a tendency toward corpulence prior to the ordeal, and being older had a lower metabolic rate. Of these twenty sailors, Pollard was the most likely to survive this ordeal of starvation. Yet, given the complex range of factor – psychological as well as physiological – influencing each man's health, it was impossible to predict with total precision who would live and who would die.

More than a hundred miles to the south, as their shipmates consumed their second body in four days, Owen Chase and his men drifted in a windless sea. A week of eating only one and a half ounces of bread a day had left them "hardly able to crawl around the boat, and possessing but strength enough to convey our scanty morsel to our mouths." Boils had begun to break out on their skin. On the morning of 24 January with another day of calms and broiling sun ahead of them, Chase was certain that some of his crew would not see nightfall. "[W]hat it was that buoyed me above all the terrors which surrounded us", Chase wrote, "God alone knows."

That night the first mate had a vivid dream. He had just sat down to a "splendid and rich repast, where there was everything that the most dainty appetite could desire". But just as he reached for his first taste of food, he "awoke to the cold realities of my miserable situation". Fired to a kind of madness by his dream, Chase began to gnaw on the leather sheathing of an oar only to find that he lacked the strength in his jaws to penetrate the stiff, salt-caked hide.

With the death of Peterson, Chase's crew had been whittled down to only three – Nantucketers Benjamin Lawrence and Thomas Nickerson, along with Isaac Cole from Rochester, Massachusetts. As their sufferings mounted, the men relied increasingly on the first mate. Chase reported that they "press[ed] me continually with questions upon the probability of our reaching land again. I kept constantly rallying my spirits to enable me to afford them comfort."

Chase had changed since the beginning of the ordeal. Instead of the harsh disciplinarian who had doled out rations with a gun by his side, he now spoke to the men in what Nickerson described as an almost cheerful voice. As their torments reached new heights, Chase recognized that it wasn't discipline his men needed but encouragement. For as they had all seen with Peterson, hope was all that stood between them and death . . .

Chase, at twenty-three had learned to move beyond the ruthless intensity of a fishy man and do everything in his power to lift his men from the depths of despair

Nickerson called the first mate a "remarkable man" and recognized Chase's genius for identifying hope in a seemingly hopeless situation. Having already endured so much, Chase reasoned, they owed it to one another to cling as tenaciously to life as possible: "I reasoned with them, and told them that we would not die sooner by keeping our hopes." But it was more than a question of loyalty to one another. As far as Chase was concerned, God was also involved in this struggle for survival. "[T]he dreadful sacrifices and privations we [had] endured were to preserve us from death," he assured them, "and were not to be put in competition with the price which we set upon our lives." In addition to saying it would be "unmanly to repine at what neither admitted of alleviation nor cure," Chase insisted that "it was our solemn duty to recognize in our calamities an overruling divinity, by whose mercy we might be suddenly snatched from peril, and to rely upon him alone, 'Who tempers the wind to the shorn lamb.'" Although they had seen little evidence of the Lord's mercy in the last two months, Chase insisted that they "bear up against all evils . . . and not weakly distrust the providence of the Almighty, by giving ourselves up to despair."

For the next three days the wind continued out of the east, forcing them farther and farther south. "[I]t was impossible to silence the rebellious repinings of our nature," Chase admitted. "It was our cruel lot not to have had one bright anticipation realized – not one wish of our thirsting souls gratified."

On 26 January, the sixty-sixth day since leaving the wreck, their noon observation indicated that they had sunk to latitude 36° south, more than 600 nautical miles south of Henderson Island and 1,800 miles due west of Valparaiso, Chile. That day the searing sun gave way to a bitterly cold rain. Starvation had lowered their body temperatures by several degrees, and with few clothes to warm their thin bodies, they were now in danger of dying of hypothermia. They had no choice but to try to head north, back toward the equator.

With the breeze out of the east, they were forced to tack, turning with the steering oar until the wind came from the starboard side of the boat. Prior to reaching Henderson, it had been a manoeuvre they had accomplished with ease. Now, even though the wind was quite light, they no longer had the strength to handle the steering oar or trim the sails. "[A]fter much labor, we got our boat about," Chase remembered, "and so great was the fatigue attending this small exertion of our bodies, that we all gave up for a moment and abandoned her to her own course."

With no one steering or adjusting the sails, the boat drifted aimlessly. The men lay helpless and shivering in the bilge as, Chase wrote, "the horrors of our situation came upon us with a despairing force and effect." After two hours, they finally marshalled enough strength to adjust the sails so that the boat was once again moving forward. But now they were sailing north, parallel to, but not toward, the coast of South America. Like Job before him, Chase could not help but ask, "[What] narrow hopes [still] bound us to life?"

As Chase's men lay immobilized by hunger in the bottom of their boat, yet another member of Hendricks's crew died. This time it was Isaiah Sheppard, who became the third African American to die and be eaten in only seven days. The next day, 28 January – the sixty-eighth day since leaving the wreck – Samuel Reed, the sole black member of Pollard's crew, died and was eaten. That left William Bond in Hendricks's boat as the last surviving black in the Essex's crew. There was little doubt who had become the tropic birds and who had become the hawks . . .

It is not uncommon for subgroups to develop as a collective form of defense against the remorseless march of horror, and it was here that the Nantucketers – their ties of kinship and religion stitching them together – had an overwhelming advantage. Since there would be no black survivors to contradict the testimonies of the whites, the possibility exists that the Nantucketers took a far more active role in insuring their own survival than has been otherwise suggested. Certainly the statistics raise suspicion – of the first four sailors to be eaten all were black. Short of murdering the black crew members, the Nantucketers could have refused to share meat with them.

However, except for the fact that the majority of the blacks were assigned to a whaleboat commanded by a sickly mate, there is no evidence of overt favouritism in the boats. Indeed, what appears to have distinguished the men of the *Essex* was the great discipline and human compunction they maintained throughout the whole ordeal. If necessity forced them to act like animals, they did so with the deepest regrets. There was a reason why William Bond in Hendricks's boat was the last African American left alive. Thanks to his position as steward in the officers' quarters, Bond had enjoyed a far more balanced and plentiful diet than his shipmates in the forecastle. But now that he was the only black among six whites, Bond had to wonder what the future held.

Given the cruel mathematics of survival cannibalism, each death not only provided the remaining men with food but reduced by one the number of people they had to share it with. By the time Samuel Reed died on 28 January, the seven survivors each received close to three thousand calories' worth of meat (up by almost a third since the death of Lawson Thomas). Unfortunately, even though this portion may have been roughly equivalent to each man's share of a Galapagos tortoise, it lacked the fat that the human body requires to digest me at. No matter how much meat they now had available to them, it was of limited nutritional value without a source of fat.

The following night, 29 January was darker than most. The two boat-crews were finding it difficult to keep track of each other; they also lacked the strength to manage the steering oars and sails. That night, Pollard and his men looked up to find that the whaleboat containing Obed Hendricks, William Bond, and Joseph West had disappeared.

Pollard's men were too weak to attempt to find the missing boat – either by raising a lantern or firing a pistol. That left George Pollard, Owen Coffin, Charles Ramsdell, and Barzillai Ray – all Nantucketers – alone for the first time since the sinking of the *Essex*. They were at latitude 35° south, longitude 100° west, 1,500 miles from the coast of South America, with only the half-eaten corpse of Samuel Reed to keep them alive.

But no matter how grim their prospects might seem, they were better than those of Hendricks's boat-crew. Without a compass or a quadrant, Hendricks and his men were now lost in an empty and limitless sea.

On 6 February, the four men on Pollard's boat, having consumed "the last morsel" of Samuel Reed, began to "[look] at each other with horrid thoughts in our minds," according to one survivor, "but we held our tongues." Then the youngest of them, sixteen-year-old Charles Ramsdell, uttered the unspeakable. They should cast lots, he said, to see who would be killed so that the rest could live.

The drawing of lots in a survival situation had long been an accepted custom of the sea. The earliest recorded instance dates back to the first half of the seventeenth century, when seven Englishmen sailing from the Caribbean island of St Kitts were driven out to sea in a storm. After seventeen days, one of the crew suggested that they cast lots. As it turned out, the lot fell to the man who had originally made the proposal, and after lots were cast again to see who should execute him, he was killed and eaten.

In 1765, several days after the crew of the disabled *Peggy* had eaten the remains of the black slave, lots were drawn to see who would be the next to serve as food. The lot fell to David Flatt, a foremastman and one of the most popular sailors in the crew. "The shock of the decision was great," wrote Captain Harrison, "and the preparations for execution dreadful." Flatt requested that he be given some time to prepare himself for death, and the crew agreed to postpone the execution until eleven the next morning. The dread of his death sentence proved too much for Flatt. By midnight he had become deaf; by morning he was delirious. Incredibly, a rescue ship was sighted at eight o'clock. But for David Flatt it was too late. Even after the *Peggy*'s crew had been delivered to England, Harrison reported that "the unhappy Flatt still continued out of his senses." . . .

Faced with similarly dire circumstances, other sailors made different decisions. In 1811, the 139-ton brig *Polly*; on her way from Boston to the Caribbean, was dismasted in a storm, and the crew drifted on the waterlogged hull for 191 days. Although some of the men died from hunger and exposure, their bodies were never used for food; instead, they were used as bait. Attaching pieces of their dead shipmate's bodies to a trolling line, the survivors managed to catch enough sharks to sustain themselves until their rescue. If the *Essex* crew had adopted this strategy with the death of Matthew Joy, they might never have reached the extreme that confronted them now.

When first presented with young Ramsdell's proposal, Captain Pollard "would not listen to it", according to an account related by Nickerson, "saying to the others, 'No, but if I die first you are welcome to subsist on my remains.'" Then Owen Coffin, Pollard's first cousin, the eighteen-year-old son of his aunt, joined Ramsdell in requesting that they cast lots.

Pollard studied his three young companions. Starvation had ringed their sunken eyes with a dark, smudge-like pigmentation. There was little doubt that they were all close to death. It was also clear that all of them, including Barzillai Ray, the orphaned son of a noted island cooper, were in favour of Ramsdell's proposal. As he had two times before – after the knockdown in the Gulf Stream and the sinking of the *Essex* – Pollard acquiesced to the majority. He agreed to cast lots. If suffering had turned Chase into a compassionate yet forceful leader, Pollard's confidence had been eroded even further by events that reduced him to the most desperate extreme a man can ever know.

They cut up a scrap of paper and placed the pieces in a hat. The lot fell to Owen Coffin. "My lad, my lad!" Pollard cried out. "[I]f you don't like your lot, I'll shoot the first man that touches you." Then the captain offered to take the lot himself. "Who can doubt but that Pollard would rather have met the death a thousand times," Nickerson wrote. "None that knew him, will ever doubt."

But Coffin had already resigned himself to his fate. "I like it as well as any other," he said softly.

Lots were drawn again to see who would shoot the boy. It fell to Coffin's friend, Charles Ramsdell.

Even though the lottery had originally been his idea, Ramsdell now refused to follow it through. "For a long time," Nickerson wrote, "he declared that he could never do it, but finally had to submit." Before he died, Coffin spoke a parting message to his mother, which Pollard promised to deliver if he should make it back to Nantucket. Then Coffin asked for a few moments of silence. After reassuring the others that "the lots had been fairly drawn," he lay his head down on the boat's gunwale. "He was soon dispatched," Pollard would later recall, "and nothing of him left."

Chase and his men lay in the bottom of their boat in a cold drizzle. All they had to shield them from the rain was a piece of battered, water-soaked canvas. "Even had it been dry," Nickerson wrote, "[it] would have been but a poor apology for covering."

On 28 January 1821 the breeze finally shifted into the west. But it brought them little comfort. "It had nearly become indifferent to us," Chase wrote, "from what quarter it blew." They now had too far to go and too few provisions to have any hope of reaching land. Their only chance was to be sighted by a ship. "[I]t was this narrow hope alone," Chase remembered, "that prevented me from lying down at once to die."

They had fourteen days of hardtack left, but that assumed they could live two more weeks on only an ounce and a half a day. "We were so feeble," Nickerson wrote, "that we could scarcely crawl about the boat upon our hands and knees." Chase realized that if he didn't increase their daily portion of bread, they all might be dead in as few as five days. It was time to abandon the strict rationing regime that had brought them this far and let the men eat "as pinching necessity demanded".

Success in a long-term survival situation requires that a person display an "active-passive" approach to the gradual and agonizing unfolding of events. "The key factor . . . [tis] the realization that passivity is itself a deliberate and 'active' act," the survival psychologist John Leach writes. "There is strength in passivity." After more than two months of regimenting every aspect of his men's lives, Chase intuitively understood this – that it was now time to give "ourselves wholly up to the guidance and disposal of our Creator". They would eat as much bread as they needed to stave off death and see where the westerly wind took them.

By 6 February they were still alive, but just barely. "Our sufferings were now drawing to a close," the first mate wrote. "[A] terrible death. appeared shortly to await us." The slight increase in food intake had brought a return to their hunger pangs, which were now "violent and outrageous." They found it difficult to talk and think clearly. Dreams of food and drink continued to torment them. "[O]ften did our fevered minds wander to the side of some richly supplied table," Nickerson remembered. His fantasies always ended the same way – with him "crying at the disappointment."

That night rain squalls forced them to shorten sail. The off-islander Isaac Cole was on watch and, rather than awaken his companions, he attempted to lower the jib himself, but it proved too much for him. Chase and Nickerson awoke the next morning to find Cole despondent in the bilge of the boat. He declared that "all was dark in his mind, not a single ray of hope was left for him to dwell upon." Like Richard Peterson before him, he had given up, asserting that "it was folly and madness to be struggling against what appeared so palpably to be our fixed and settled destiny".

Even though he barely had the strength to articulate the words, Chase did his best to change Cole's mind. "I remonstrated with him as effectually as the weakness both of my body and understanding would allow of." Suddenly Cole sat up and crawled to the bow and hoisted the jib he had lowered, at such cost, the night before. He cried out that he would not give up and that he would live as long as any of them. "[T]his effort was," Chase wrote, "but the hectic fever of the moment." Cole soon returned to the bottom of the boat, where he lay despairing for the rest of the day and through the night. But Cole would not be permitted the dignity of a quiet and peaceful death.

On the morning of 8 February the seventy-ninth day since leaving the *Essex*, Cole began to rant incoherently, presenting to his frightened crew members "a most miserable spectacle of madness". Twitching spasmodically, he sat up and called for a napkin and water, then fell down to the bottom of the boat as if struck dead, only to pop up again like a possessed jack-in-the-box. By ten o'clock he could no longer speak. Chase and the others placed him on a board they had laid across the seats and covered him with a few pieces of clothing.

For the next six hours Cole whimpered and moaned in pain, finally falling into "the most horrid and frightful convulsions" Chase had ever seen. In addition to dehydration and hypernatremia (an excess amount of salt), he may have been suffering from a lack of magnesium, a mineral deficiency that, when extreme, can cause bizarre and violent behaviour. By four o'clock in the afternoon, Isaac Cole was dead.

It had been forty-three days since they'd left Henderson Island, seventy-eight days since they'd last seen the *Essex*, but no one suggested – at least that afternoon – that they use Cole's body for food. All night the corpse lay beside them, each man keeping his thoughts to himself.

When the crew of the *Peggy* shot and killed a black slave in 1765, one of the men refused to wait for the meat to be cooked. "[B]eing ravenously impatient for food," the sailor plunged his hand into the slave's eviscerated body and plucked out the liver and ate it raw. "The unhappy man paid dear for such an extravagant impatience," Captain Harrison wrote, "for in three days after he died raving mad." Instead of eating that sailor's body, the crew, "being fearful of sharing his fate", threw it overboard. No one dared to consume the flesh of a man who had died insane.

The next morning, 9 February, Lawrence and Nickerson began making preparations for burying Cole's remains. Chase stopped them. All night he had wrestled with the question of what they should do. With only three days of hardtack left, he knew, it was quite possible that they might be reduced to casting lots. Better to eat a dead shipmate – even a tainted shipmate – than be forced to kill a man.

"I addressed them," Chase wrote, "on the painful subject of keeping the body for food." Lawrence and Nickerson raised no objections and, fearful that the meat had already begun to spoil, "[we] set to work as fast as we were able".

After separating the limbs from the body and removing the heart, they sewed up what remained of Cole's body "as decently" as they could, before they committed it to the sea. Then they began to eat. Even before lighting a fire, the men "eagerly devoured" the heart, then ate "sparingly of a few pieces of the flesh". They cut the rest of the meat into thin strips – some of which they roasted on the fire, while the others were laid out to dry in the sun.

Chase insisted that he had "no language to paint the anguish of our souls in this dreadful dilemma". Making it all the worse was the thought that any one of the remaining three men might be next. "We knew not then", the first mate wrote, "to whose lot it would fall next, either to die or be shot, and eaten like the poor wretch we had just dispatched."

The next morning they discovered that the strips of flesh had turned a rancid green. They immediately cooked the strips, which provided them with enough meat to last another six or seven days, allowing them to save what little bread they had left for what Chase called "the last moment of our trial".

In Captain Pollard's boat, on 11 February, only five days after the execution of Owen Coffin, Barziliai Ray died. Ray, whose biblical first name means "made of iron, most firm and true", was nineteen old. It was the seventh death George Pollard and Charles Ramsdell witnessed in the month and a half since departing Henderson Island.

Pollard and Ramsdell suffering from a double burden; not only had they seen seven of nine men die (and even killed one of them), but they had been forced to eat their bodies. Like Pip, the black sailor in *Moby-Dick* who loses his mind after several hours of treading water on a boundless sea, Pollard and Ramsdell had been "carried down alive to the wondrous depths, where strange shapes of the unwarped primal world glided to and fro." Now they were alone, with only the corpse of Barzillai Ray and the bones of Coffin and Reed to sustain them.

Three days later, on 14 February, the eighty-fifth day since leaving the wreck, Owen Chase, Benjamin Lawrence, and Thomas Nickerson ate the last of Isaac Cole. A week of living off human flesh, combined with their earlier decision to increase their daily ration of hardtack had strengthened them to the point where they could once again manage the steering oar. But if they were stronger, they were also in a great deal of pain. As if the boils that covered their skin weren't enough, their arms and legs started to swell shockingly. Known as edema, this disfiguring accumulation of fluid is a common symptom of starvation.

Several days of westerly winds had brought them to within three hundred miles of the islands of Masafuera and Juan Fernandez. If they averaged sixty miles a day, they might reach safety in another five days. Unfortunately, they had only three days of hardtack left.

"Matters were now with us at their height," Chase wrote. "[A]ll hope was cast upon the breeze; and we tremblingly and fearfully awaited its progress, and the dreadful development of our destiny." Surrendering all prospects, the men were convinced that after two and a half months of suffering they were about to die nearly within sight of salvation.

That night Owen Chase lay down to sleep, "almost indifferent whether I should ever see the light again". He dreamed he saw a ship, just a few miles away, and even though he "strained every nerve to get to her", she sailed off into the distance, never to return. Chase awoke "almost overpowered with the frenzy I had caught in my slumbers, and stung with the cruelties of a diseased and disappointed imagination."

The next afternoon, Chase saw a thick cloud to the north-east – a sure sign of land. It must be the island of Masafuera – at least that was what Chase told Lawrence and Nickerson. In two days, he assured them, they would be on dry land. At first, his companions were reluctant to believe him. Gradually, however, after "repeated assurances of the favourable appearances of things" on the part of Chase, "their spirits acquired even a degree of elasticity that was truly astonishing." The wind remained favourable all night, and with their sails trimmed perfectly and a man tending the steering oar, their little boat made the best time of the voyage.

The next morning the cloud still loomed ahead. The end of their ordeal was apparently only days away. But for fifteen-year-old Thomas Nickerson the strain of anticipation had become too much. After bailing out the boat, he lay down, drew the mildewed piece of canvas over him like a shroud and told his fellow crew members that "he wished to die immediately".

"I saw that he had given up," Chase wrote, "and I attempted to speak a few words of comfort and encouragement to him." But all the arguments that had served the first mate so well failed to penetrate Nickerson's inner gloom. "A fixed look of settled and forsaken despondency came over his face," Chase wrote. "[H]e lay for some time silent, sullen, and sorrowful – and I felt at once . . . that the coldness of death was fast gathering upon him."

It was obvious to Chase that some form of dementia had seized the boy. Having watched Isaac Cole slip into a similar madness, Chase could not help but wonder if all of them were about to succumb to the temptations of despair. "[T]here was a sudden and unaccountable earnestness in his manner", he wrote, "that alarmed me, and made me fear that I myself might unexpectedly be overtaken by a like weakness, or dizziness of nature, that would bereave me at once of both reason and life." Whether or not it had been communicated to him through Cole's diseased flesh, Chase also felt the stirrings of a death wish as dark and palpable as the pillarlike cloud ahead.

At seven o'clock the next morning, 18 February, Chase was sleeping in the bottom of the boat. Benjamin Lawrence was standing at the steering oar. Throughout the ordeal, the twenty-one-year-old boat-steerer had demonstrated remarkable fortitude. He was the one who, two months earlier, had volunteered to swim underneath the boat to repair a sprung plank. As Lawrence had watched Peterson, Cole, and now Nickerson lose their grip on life, he had clung, as best he could, to hope . . .

Safe in Lawrence's pocket was the piece of twine he had been working on ever since they'd left the wreck. It was now close to twelve inches long. He leaned into the steering oar and scanned the horizon.

"There's a sail!" he cried.

Chase immediately scrambled to his feet. Just visible over the horizon was the speck of pale brown that Lawrence had taken for a sail. Chase stared for several suspenseful moments, gradually realizing that, yes, it was a sail – the topgallant of a ship, about seven miles away.

"I do not believe it is possible", Chase wrote, "to form a just conception of the pure, strong feelings, and the unmingled emotions of joy and gratitude, that took possession of my mind on this occasion."

Soon even Nickerson was up on his feet and gazing excitedly ahead.

Now the question was whether they could catch up to the much larger vessel. The ship was several miles to leeward, which was an advantage for the smaller vessel, and heading slightly north of their position, which meant that it might intercept their line of sail. Could their whaleboat reach that crossing point at approximately the same time the ship did? Chase could only pray that his nightmare of the missed rescue ship would not prove true. "I felt at the moment", Chase wrote, "a violent and unaccountable impulse to fly directly towards her."

For the next three hours they were in a desperate race. Their battered old whaleboat skimmed lightly over the waves at between four and six knots in the north-easterly breeze. Up ahead, the ship continued to emerge from the distant horizon, revealing, with excruciating slowness, not only the topgallant sails but the topsails beneath and, finally, the mainsail and foresail. Yes, they assured themselves, they were catching up to the ship.

There was no lookout at the vessel's masthead, but eventually someone on deck saw them approaching to windward and behind. Chase and his men watched in tense fascination as the antlike figures bustled about the ship, shortening sail. Gradually the whaleboat closed the distance, and the hull of the merchantman rose up out of the sea, looming larger and larger ahead of them until Chase could read her quarterboard. She was the *Indian* from London.

Chase heard a shout and through glazed, reddened eyes saw a figure at the quarterdeck rail with a trumpet, a hailing device resembling a megaphone. It was an officer of the *Indian*, asking who they were. Chase summoned all his strength to make himself heard, but his desiccated tongue stumbled over the words: "*Essex* . . . whaleship . . . Nantucket."

When Chase, Lawrence, and Nickerson attempted to climb aboard, they discovered that they didn't have the strength. The three men stared up at the crew, their eyes wide and huge within the dark hollows of their skulls. Their raw, ulcerated skin hung from their skeletons like noxious rags. As he looked down from the quarterdeck, Captain William Crozier was moved to tears at what Chase called "the most deplorable and affecting picture of suffering and misery."

The English sailors lifted the men from their boat and carried them to the captain's cabin. Crozier ordered the cook to serve them their first taste of civilized food – tapioca pudding. Made from the root of the cassava plant, tapioca is a high-calorie, easy-to-digest food rich in the proteins and carbohydrates that their bodies craved.

Rescue came at latitude 33°45′ south, longitude 81°03′ west. It was the eighty-ninth day since Chase and his men had left the *Essex*, and at noon they came within sight of Masafuera. Chase had succeeded in navigating them across a 2,500-mile stretch of ocean with astonishing accuracy. Even though they had sometimes been so weak that they could not steer their boat, they had somehow managed to sail almost to within sight of their intended destination. In just a few days the *Indian* would be in the Chilean port of Valparaiso.

Three hundred miles to the south, Pollard and Ramsdell sailed on. For the next five days they pushed east, until by 23 February, the ninety-fourth day since leaving the wreck, they were approaching the island of St Mary's just off the Chilean coast. Over a year before this had been the *Essex*'s first landfall after rounding Cape Horn. Pollard and Ramsdell were on the verge of completing an irregular circle with a diameter of more than three thousand miles.

It had been twelve days since the death of Barzillai Ray. They had long since eaten the last scrap of his flesh. The two famished men now cracked open the bones of their shipmate – beating them against the stone on the bottom of the boat and smashing them with the boat's hatchet – and ate the marrow, which contained the fat their bodies so desperately needed.

Pollard would later remember these as "days of horror and despair". Both of them were so weak that they could barely lift their hands. They were drfting in and out of consciousness. It is not uncommon for cast-aways who have been many days at sea and suffered both physically and emotionally to lapse into what has been called "a sort of collective confabulation", in which the survivors exist in a shared fantasy world. Delusions may include comforting scenes from home – perhaps, in the case of Pollard and Ramsdell, a sunny June day on the Nantucket Commons during the sheepshearing festival. Survivors may find them-selves in conversation with deceased shipmates and family members as they lose all sense of time.

For Pollard and Ramsdell, it was the bone – gifts from the men they had known and loved – that became their obsession. They stuffed their pockets with finger bones; they sucked the sweet marrow from the splintered ribs and thighs. And they sailed on, the compass card wavering toward east.

Suddenly they heard a sound; men shouting and then silence as shadows fell across them and then the rustle of wind in sails and the creaking of spars and rigging. They looked up, and there were faces . . .

DREADFUL SHIPWRECK OF THE *GEORGE*

The brig *George*, Captain John McAlpin, sailed from Quebec with a cargo of timber for Greenock [Scotland] on the 12th of September last [1822] with a crew consisting of nine persons besides three passengers.

Early in the morning of the 6th of October, she was overtaken by a violent storm, which continued without intermission during the day. Towards sunset the gale increased and the vessel became quite unmanageable. At two o'clock the following morning a tremendous sea broke over the *George* and swept away three of her best hands, with the companion, binnacle, a cable and boom, and greatly damaged the hull.

All hands were then called to the pump, but only three were able to render any assistance. At six o'clock they found the vessel to be water-logged. Nothing then remained but to endeavour to gain the main-top, which with immense difficulty they accomplished, carrying with them one bag of bread, about eight pounds of cheese, two dozen of wine, with a small quantity of brandy and rum.

Before they had time to secure themselves in their perilous situation, the vessel fell on her beam ends; but within half an hour the hatches blew up and she again righted. Their scanty stores were now examined, when, to their utter dismay, all had been washed away except the bag of bread. At this period a distressing scene occurred in the midst of their afflictions. One of the passengers had his wife on board and a child fifteen months old, which he carried in his arms. The infant, however, he was compelled to abandon to the merciless waves in the view of its distracted mother!

The mainsail was now let down to screen them from the severity of the weather, which continued tempestuous until Friday the 11th when they were able once more to go upon the deck. Their thirst had now become excessive and nothing but salt water to be procured.

Having found the carpenter's axe, they cut a hole in the deck, near to where a water cask had been stowed. But, alas, the cask had been stove, and nothing was to be found either for support or convenience but an empty pump-can, which they carried with them to the main top.

That night the female passenger became insensible and next day, Saturday the 12th she died. This poor woman, whose name was Joyce Rae, came with her husband from between Belfast and Larne, in Ireland.

The unhappy survivors were now reduced by raging thirst to support nature by sucking the blood of their deceased companion, and, shocking to relate, the miserable husband was necessitated to partake of the unnatural and horrid beverage.

Their sufferings, however, met with little allay from this temporary but dreadful relief. They were now assailed by the most acute and ungovernable hunger, and were compelled to distribute the flesh of the deceased among the famishing survivors!

While in the acme of their sufferings, a ship hove in view, but this joyful sight was of short duration for, it being nearly dark, they remained unperceived by the vessel, which continued her own course and was soon out of their reach. This fresh misfortune threw them into greater despair than they had yet experienced. From this time to the 23rd the following died: John Lamont, a boy; John McKay, carpenter; George McDowell, passenger; Colin McKechnie, and the steward,

Gilbert McGilvray. Part of the flesh of these wretched sufferers was also devoured like that of the woman.

The whole number was now reduced to the Captain and one of the seamen, who, by the help of the mainsail and the can already mentioned, contrived to supply themselves with water till the 14th of November (having been thirty-eight days on the wreck), when they were providentially discovered by Captain Hudson of the *Saltom*, of Carlisle. But they were yet fated to suffer another shipwreck, though of minor importance.

On Tuesday, the 10th instant, this vessel, whilst riding off Beckfoot, on the Cumberland coast, it blowing a gale, broke her chain cable, when she drifted too near to Mayborough and was considerably damaged. But all hands were saved, including the two unfortunate sufferers, who arrived at Annan on Wednesday evening last and, what is very remarkable, apparently in good health.

MEN WHO RIVALLED JONAH

In *A Pilgrim Returns to Cape Cod* I told the Story of Peleg Nye, the whaler who fell from his ship's longboat directly into the mouth of a huge sperm whale in March 1863. Nye scrambled to escape the closing jaws, but felt himself caught just below the knees. When the whale sounded a short time later, Nye was taken far under the surface of the sea and soon lost consciousness. On board the whaling vessel his fellow crew members had decided that Peleg Nye was drowned. When Nye's body was seen floating in the water, they quickly rowed over and found him alive but unconscious. The whale, believed to have died with Nye still in his jaws, soon rose to the surface.

Nye lived to a ripe age after his miraculous escape and much to his delight, acquired the designation "the Jonah of Cape Cod."

An even more remarkable incident took place about twenty-eight years later – so remarkable, in fact, that the scientific editor of a Paris journal debated for four and one-half years whether to publish the facts in his possession. Every item was carefully checked and rechecked. Finally convinced of the truth of the story, Monsieur Henri de Parville of Paris authorized its publication in the *Journal des Debats* on 14 March 1896.

On the afternoon of 25 August 1891, the whaling vessel *Star of the*

East had come up with a great school of sperm whales. One of the whales, which had been wounded by a bomb-lance thrown from a whaleboat, seized the boat in his jaws and crushed it in two. The sailors leaped in all directions to escape. Steersman James Bartley jumped with the others, but, just as he leaped, the whale made a quick turn in the water, opening his mouth to catch the falling sailor. The other sailors saw the mighty jaws close over Bartley and, giving him up as lost, they sorrowfully rowed back to the *Star of the East*.

Later in the day a dead whale came to the surface of the ocean. For two days the men worked at removing its blubber. When they had finished, it occurred to one of the sailors that the whale they had been working on might possibly be the one that had swallowed Bartley. After much discussion, the other whalers finally agreed to open up the stomach and intestines of the immense animal. As they cut open the stomach, to their amazement and horror the outline of a man showed through the membranes. Carefully slicing the muscles away, they uncovered the missing sailor, unconscious but still alive.

Moving Bartley with care, the sailors placed him on the deck, rubbed his limbs and forced brandy down his throat. His entire body had turned purple, and he was smeared with the whale's blood. Working on him in relays, the men soon had Bartley washed and his circulation restored. Then he regained a partial consciousness. It was his hallucination that he was being consumed in a fiery furnace. Although the average temperature of a whale is 104 degrees, this does not account for the terrible sensation the sailor experienced. Possibly it was caused by the constant pressure of the whale's body against his own.

The returning voyage to England nearly restored his health, and after he had a complete rest, he made a statement about his experience which I quote verbatim:

I remember very well from the moment that I jumped from the boat and felt my feet strike some soft substance. I looked up and saw a big-ribbed canopy of light pink and white descending over me, and the next moment I felt myself drawn downward, feet first, and I realized that I was being swallowed by a whale. I was drawn lower and lower; a wall of flesh surrounded me and hemmed me in on every side, yet the pressure was not painful, and the flesh easily gave way like soft india-rubber before my slightest movement.

Suddenly I found myself in a sack much larger than my body, but completely dark. I felt about me; and my hand came in contact with several fishes, some of which seemed to be still alive, for they squirmed in my fingers, and slipped back to my feet. Soon I felt a great pain in my head, and my breathing became more and more difficult. At the same time I felt a terrible heat; it seemed to consume me, growing hotter and hotter. My eyes became coals of fire in my head, and I believed every moment that I was condemned to perish in the belly of a whale. It tormented me beyond all endurance, while at the same time the awful silence of the terrible prison weighed me down. I tried to rise, to move my arms and legs, to cry out. All action was now impossible, but my brain seemed abnormally clear; and with a full comprehension of my awful fate, I finally lost all consciousness.

So improbable did the story seem that the captain and the entire crew of the *Star of the East* thought it necessary to give testimony of the incident under oath.

Bartley was about thirty-five years of age, strong in build and constitution at the time. The only lasting effect of his terrible experience seems to have been a recurring nightmare in which he relived his sensations in the whale's stomach. Since Monsieur Henri de Parville did not publish his story until some years later and does not mention any further ill effects of the horrible experience, we can safely assume that Bartley completely recovered.

It might be well to review here what the *Bible* says about Jonah. It is not claimed that Jonah was in full possession of his faculties for the three days he was in the whale. We know that he prayed, and then he probably lost consciousness, just as James Bartley did centuries later. To Jonah and his associates, a miracle had occurred:

And the Lord spake unto the fish, and it vomited out Jonah upon the dry land.

So another name may be added to the list of those who have been in the jaws of a whale – Jonah, the son of Amittai; Peleg Nye of Cape Cod; and James Bartley of England.

THE BURNING OF THE *COSPATRICK*

On 8 September 1874 the *Cospatrick*, a teak-hulled sail-steam ship, left Gravesend, England bound for New Zealand *via* South Africa's Cape of Good Hope. She was carrying 433 passengers, mostly emigrants, including 127 children, plus forty-two crew. By the time the ship had crossed the equator and rounded the Cape, eight children had died and two babies had been born. On 18 November, shortly before 1 a.m., disaster struck. The following is taken from *The Times*, London, 31 December 1874 and subsequent issues.

On 31 December 1874 the Union Company's steamship *Nyanza* from the Cape, St Helena and Madeira arrived in Plymouth, Devon, bringing with her the three survivors of the ship *Cospatrick*. Mr MacDonald, the second officer, . . . gave the following statement, which he made at St Helena, on board [the *Nyanza*]:

Tuesday, 17th November, noon, latitude 37 15S, longitude 12 25 E, wind light from NNW, sea smooth. It was my watch on deck from 8 p.m. till midnight. Everything was quiet. I was relieved by the chief officer and went to bed. I had just dropped off to sleep when I was awakened by the alarm of fire. Jumping out of bed, I met the Captain at the cuddy door and he ordered me to go forward to see what was the matter.

I ran forward and saw smoke coming out of the fore hatch, all passengers rushing on deck and the chief officer getting the force pump at work.

I ran aft to report this to the Captain and to put my clothes on, as I had nothing on at that time.

When I went forward again they were playing the hose down the fore scuttle, as everybody said that the fire was in the boatswain's locker. I ran aft to put the ship before the wind and found the Captain endeavouring to do so, but in vain. He told me to get a few volunteers down the fore hatch to see where the fire came from, but this was impossible, as the flames were then coming up the fore hatch and the passengers were doing their best to keep the fire down.

The fire was rapidly gaining on us, the flames bursting out of the fore hatch, but we still continued our endeavours to extinguish it. The passengers rushed all about with loud screams for help, impeding us in our work. The ship came head to wind, which drove flames and a thick body of smoke aft, setting fire to the forward boats, and obliged us to recede.

I asked the Captain if we should lower away the remaining boats, but was told, "No," but to endeavour to extinguish the fire.

The passengers rushed to the two quarter boats which were hanging on the davits over the side and crowded them. I consider that no less than 80, mostly young women, got on and in the starboard boat, when the davits bent down with the weight and the boat's stern dipped under the sea. The boat filled and capsized, and there was only one who got out of her. All the rest were drowned. Although we flung hen coops and other floating things overboard to them, we could render no other assistance.

I had stationed some sailors by the port boat, giving strict orders not to lower away unless by order of the Captain, but the passengers made a rush for her and we could not prevent them from getting in.

By this time the foremast had fallen over the side and the flames were bursting out of the after hatch. I then heard the Captain, who was standing at the wheel, say to those around, "Now, everybody try for himself to save his own life," or words to that effect. His wife, son and the doctor were standing alongside of him.

The mate, boatswain, third officer and myself were trying to turn the large pinnace [longboat] over to launch her, but could get no assistance and, as her bow was catching fire, we left her. Some threw the Captain's gig over the side, but I saw no more of her. I ordered the port boat to be lowered and, when half down, I got in her. When we got clear of the ship's side, the chief officer jumped overboard and swam to the boat. We helped him in, also a female passenger. The boat was kept off the ship's side, being overloaded, 34 persons being in her.

The mainmast fell over the side, which must have killed a good many. The ship's stern blew out under the poop deck. One passenger told me subsequently he saw the Captain throw his wife overboard and jump after her, while the doctor jumped overboard with the Captain's boy in his arms, and that they were drowned. The mizenmast then fell overboard.

We lay by the burning ship till daylight. Some people hung to the spars alongside. We picked one man up who had been floating on a piece of plank all the time. We pulled towards some spars floating at a distance and met the starboard boat full of people, the boat having been righted by some sailors.

Not having an officer in the boat, they begged of me to take charge, which I willingly did, and, as their boat was not so full, I took one able seaman, one ordinary seaman and one male passenger along with me. Thomas Lewis went in first, I went second, Cotter third, and Mr Bentley, a passenger, next. They divided the passengers, leaving 30 in my boat and 32 in the chief mate's boat. We were deep loaded then.

We stopped by the ship until she sank, which was on the 19th, at 5 p.m. During that time we saw people clinging to her, but we were so full that we could not render them the slightest assistance. After the ship went down it was no good stopping any longer. She was burnt down to the copper, and the fire being of course out we were deprived of that which was before a signal to any vessels that might be passing.

We drifted all the night, and next morning divided oars – 1½ in my boat, no rudder; two oars and rudder in the mate's [port] boat.

We were without provisions or water; had neither masts nor sails, but I got a petticoat from an Irish girl in the mate's boat to use as a sail. We then shaped, as we thought, our course for the Cape of Good Hope [South Africa] and kept company all the 20th and 21st, when it commenced blowing. We got separated during the night. I whistled and shouted, but got no answer and, at daylight, the boat was nowhere to be seen.

My boat contained the baker, the emigrant's cook, three able seamen and one ordinary seaman, and 23 passengers, all males, and myself, in all 30 people. The other boat contained the Chief Mate Cunningham, Able Seaman Nicolls, Able Seaman Turvey and Able Seaman Ruske.

About 11 days out, Sunday, 22nd, weather dull and a heavy swell on. Thirst began to tell severely on us all. The passenger named Bentley fell overboard while steering and sank. Three men died, having first become mad in consequence of drinking salt water. We threw their bodies overboard.

Monday, 23rd – Blowing hard and a high sea running, which kept us continually baling out water. We tore seats and stern sheets out and made a drag [sea anchor], which caused the boat to lay easier; but it being only fastened with strands of a boat's painter, we lost it.

Four men died the same as the others, but we were that hungry and thirsty that we drank the blood and ate the livers of two of them.

We lost our only oar this day by the man steering falling asleep.

Tuesday, 24th – Strong gales, rigged another drag, fastened with braces and belts and clothing of the dead. Six more deaths today.

Wednesday, 25th – Light breeze and awfully hot; some more died and we were reduced to eight, three of these out of their minds. We all felt very bad that day.

Early on the morning of Thursday, the 26th, it not being daylight, a bark passed close to us, running, about 50 yards off. We hailed, but got no answer. Our opinion was that she saw us, which made us lose all hope. One more died. Light, fine weather.

We kept sucking the blood of those that had died.

Friday, 27th – Squally all around, with light showers, but we never caught a drop of water. Two more died that day. We threw one overboard, but were too weak to lift the other. We were five, two able seamen, one ordinary seaman, myself, and a passenger, who was mad and attempted to drown himself three times. We were all fearfully bad and had all drunk sea-water.

We were all dozing, when, being awakened by the madman biting my feet, I saw a vessel bearing down on us. The vessel proved to be the British ship *British Sceptre* of Liverpool, from Calcutta for Dundee. We were (five in all) taken on board and treated with every kindness, but two, Able Seaman Bob Hamilton and the passenger, name unknown, died; and Able Seaman Thomas Lewis, Ordinary Seaman Edward Cotter and myself were brought to St Helena and landed.

2 January 1875

The special train which left Plymouth . . . with the survivors from the *Cospatrick* . . . was met at Paddington Station, London, by Mr Petherbridge, an agent of the owners, who took charge of the men.

Charles Henry Macdonald, the second mate, is a tall and spare young man of dark complexion. His home is in Montrose, Scotland, and then his wife is to come to London at the owners' expense. He had a letter from her this afternoon.

Thomas Lewis, able seaman, is of middle height, a strong but weather-beaten man of forty-six. He is by birth a Welshman, of Anglesey, and his friends do not appear to have heard of his danger or of his wonderful escape, for they have not yet communicated with the owners. His sister is Catherine Williams, living in a little village called Bordone, or by some such name, and close to Bangor, on the Menai Strait. The others call him the "old man" and, because of his long service among Flemings [Belgians], "the foreigner". Such as he was, the mate called him his "right-hand man in the boat". Cotter said he was their salvation. He prevented Cotter and the mate from going to sleep and dying as others did in their sleep.

After the Welshman and the Scotsman comes Edward Cotter, ordinary seaman, an intelligent lad of eighteen, fair and thick set, born in London, but of Irish parents. To him in the afternoon came up a messenger from his mother, who was ill in bed, had heard of the loss of the *Cospatrick* and would not believe her son was saved till she saw him. The messenger was his elder brother, a labourer, and when the two young labouring men met after such an eventful separation they first grasped hands and then kissed each other on the lips . . .

Subsequent lengthy reports in *The Times* and elsewhere covered in detail the official investigation into the possible causes of the fire, its effects, the behaviour of the crew and why the lifeboats were ill equipped. Every aspect of the sinking and its aftermath was pored over – but, perhaps not surprisingly, there was no further mention of cannibalism.

MATAWAN CREEK SHARK ATTACKS

Captain Thomas Cottrell, a retired sailor, caught a glimpse of a dark gray shape swimming rapidly in the shallow waters of Matawan Creek this morning [12 July 1916] as he crossed the trolley drawbridge a few hundred yards from Town. So impressed was he, when he recalled the two swimmers killed by sharks on the New Jersey coast within two weeks, that he hurried back to town and spread the warning among the 2,000 residents that a shark had entered Matawan Creek.

Everywhere the Captain was laughed at. How could a shark get ten miles away from the ocean, swim through Raritan Bay, and enter the shallow creek with only seventeen feet of water at its deepest spot and nowhere more than thirty-five feet wide? So the townsfolk asked one another, and grown-ups and children flocked to the creek as usual for their daily dip.

But Captain Cottrell was right, and tonight the people are dynamiting the creek, hoping to bring to the surface the body of a small boy the shark dragged down. Elsewhere, in the Long Branch Memorial Hospital lies the body of a youth so terribly torn by the shark that he died of loss of blood, and in St Peter's Hospital in New Brunswick doctors are working late tonight to save the left leg of another lad whom the shark nipped as the big fish fled down the creek toward Raritan Bay.

The dynamiters hoped, when they brought their explosives to the creek, that, beside the body, they might bring up the shark where men, waiting with weapons, could kill it. Others hastened to the mouth of the creek where it empties into the bay a mile and a half from town and spread heavy wire netting.

The people of Matawan had been horrified by the tales of sharks which came to them from Spring Lake, Beach Haven, Asbury Park and the other coast resorts. They had been sympathetically affected by the reports of the death of Charles E. Vansant and Charles Bruder. But those places were far away and the tragedies had not touched them closely.

Tonight the whole town is stirred by a personal feeling, a feeling which makes men and women regard the fish as they might a human being who had taken the lives of a boy and a youth and badly, perhaps mortally, injured another youngster. The one purpose in which everybody shares is to get the shark, kill it and to see its body drawn up on the shore, where all may look and be assured it will destroy no more.

The death of the boy and youth, and the injury to the other youngster were due to the refusal of almost every one to believe that sharks could ever enter the shoal waters where clam-diggers work at low tide. As long ago as Sunday, Frank Slater saw the shark and told it everywhere. He stopped repeating the tale when every one laughed him to scorn.

Then today came Captain Cottrell's warning, and with that Lester Stilwell, twelve years old, might have been the only victim had it not been for the unfortunate coincidence that the boy suffered from fits. It was supposed that an attack in the water had caused him to sink, and rescuers, with no notion that a shark had dragged him down, entered the water fearlessly.

It was while trying to bring young Stilwell's body ashore that Stanley G. Fisher, son of Captain W. H. Fisher, retired Commodore of the Savannah Line fleet, lost his life. The third victim, Joseph Dunn, twelve years old, was caught as he tried to leave the water, the alarm caused by Fisher's death at last having convinced the town that a shark really was in the creek.

Stilwell was the first to die. With several other boys, he had gone swimming off a disused steamboat pier at the edge of the town. He was a strong swimmer and so swam further out than his companions.

So it was that none could follow him, but several boys, instead, raced through the town calling that Stilwell had had a fit in the water and had gone down. They said the boy rose once after his first disappearance. He was screaming and yelling, and waving his arms wildly. His body was swirling round and round in the water. Fisher was one of the first to hear and immediately started for the creek.

"Remember what Captain Cottrell said!" exclaimed Miss May Anderson, a teacher in the local school, as Fisher passed her. "It may have been a shark."

"A shark here!" exclaimed Fisher incredulously. "I don't care anyway. I'm going after that boy."

He hurried to the shore and donned bathing tights. By the time he was attired many others had reached the spot, among them Stilwell's parents. Fisher dived into the creek and swam to midstream, where he dived once or twice in search of Stilwell's body. At last he came up and cried to the throng ashore; "I've got it!"

He was nearer the opposite shore and struck out in that direction, while Arthur Smith and Joseph Deulew put out in a motor boat to bring him back. Fisher was almost on the shore and, touching bottom, had risen to his feet, when the onlookers heard him utter a cry and throw up his arms. Stilwell's body slipped back into the stream and, with another cry, Fisher was dragged after it.

"The shark! The shark!" cried the crowd ashore, and other men sprang into other motor boats and started for the spot where Fisher had disappeared. Smith and Deulew were in the lead, but, before they overtook him, Fisher had risen and dragged himself to the bank, where he collapsed.

Those who reached him found the young man's right leg stripped of flesh from above the hip at the waist line to a point below the knee. It was as though the limb had been raked with heavy, dull knives. He was senseless from shock and pain, but was resuscitated by Dr G. L. Reynolds after Recorder Arthur Van Buskirk had made a tourniquet of rope and staunched the flow of blood from Fisher's frightful wound.

Fisher said it was a shark that had grabbod him. He had felt the nip of its teeth on his leg, and had looked down and seen the fish clinging to him. Others ashore said they had seen the white belly of the shark as it turned when it seized Fisher. Fisher said he wasn't in more than three or four feet of water when the fish grabbed him, and he had had no notion of sharks until that instant. If he had thought of them at all, he said, he had felt himself safe when he got his feet on the bottom.

Fisher was carried across the river and hurried in a motor car to the railroad station, where he was put aboard the 5.06 train for Long Branch. There he was transferred to the hospital, but died before he could be carried to the operating table.

At the creek, meantime, dynamite had been procured from the store of Asher P. Woolley and arrangements were being made to set it off when a motor boat raced up to the steamboat pier. At the wheel was J. R. Lefferts and in the craft lay young Dunn. With his brother William and several others, he had been swimming off the New Jersey Clay Company brickyards at Cliffwood, half a mile below the spot where Stilwell and Fisher were attacked.

News of the accident had just reached the boys and they had hurried from the water. Dunn was the last to leave and, as he drew himself up on the brick company's pier, with only his left leg trailing in the water, the shark struck at that. Its teeth shut over the leg above and below the knee and much of the flesh was torn away.

Apparently, however, the fish had struck this time in fright, for it loosed its grip on the boy at once, and his companions dragged him, yelling, up on to the pier.

He was taken to the J. Fisher bag factory nearby, where Dr H. J. Cooley of Keyport dressed his wound, and then he was carried in a motor car to St Peter's Hospital in New Brunswick by E. H. Bomick. There it was said last night that the physicians hoped to save his leg if blood poisoning did not set in. The youngster steadfastly refused to tell where he lived, for, he said, he did not want his mother to worry about him. From his relatives, however, it was learned that his home is at 124 East 128th Street, New York. He and his brother had been visiting an aunt in Cliffwood.

Fisher was the son of Commodore Watson H. Fisher, who for more than fifty years commanded boats of the Savannah Line up and down the coast. He retired from active service a few years ago. About ten days ago the father and mother went to Minneapolis to visit a daughter there, and they had intended to remain for another week, but, when word was sent this evening of the death of their son, they sent a message that they would leave for home immediately.

News of the tragedies here spread rapidly through neighbouring towns, and from Morgan's Beach, a few miles away, came a report that two sharks had been killed there in the morning by lifeguards. One was said to be twelve feet long. Persons who saw the fish when it grabbed Fisher said they thought it was about nine feet long.

WHO'S WHO OF CROCODILIANS

Needless to say most crocodillians are best avoided and some are very aggresssive.

Class: Reptila
Sublass: Archosauria
Order: Crocodylia
Family: Crocodylidae

American Alligator – *Alligator mississippiensis*
Subfamily: Alligatorinae
- Diet: Insects, snakes, turtles, snails, slow-moving fish, small mammals and birds. Large adults may eat small calves and, rarely, people.
- Habitat: Marshes, swamps, rivers, lakes, tidal areas, and, rarely, the ocean.
- Distribution: South-eastern US.
- Conservation: Narrowly escaped extinction thanks to strict laws prohibiting hunting, but habitat destruction now poses a considerable threat.
- Size: Up to about thirteen feet.

- Croc bite: In the past, individuals of sixteen to twenty feet were reported.

Chinese Alligator – *Alligator sinensis*
Subfamily: Alligatorinae
- Diet: Snails, clams, rats and insects.
- Habitat: Marshlands, ponds and lakes. They use caves or burrows, especially in the cold and dry months.
- Distribution: The lower Yangtze River and its tributaries.
- Conservation: The world's most endangered crocodilian, due to habitat loss, wetland development, dam-building and flooding.
- Size: Usually about six-point five feet in length.
- Croc bite: Despite its timid nature, this species has historical associations with the mythical Chinese dragon.

Spectacled/Common Caiman – *Caiman crocodilus*
Subfamily: Alligatorinae
- Diet: Smaller caimans eat insects, crabs and other invertebrates; larger ones eat water snails and fish.
- Habitat: Almost all natural open wetland and riverine habitats.
- Distribution: Southern Mexico to northern Argentina.
- Conservation: Population has diminished from serious hunting that began about 1950, but populations remain in good standing.
- Size: Up to eight feet.
- Croc bite: Caiman most likely to be mistaken for a member of the Crocodylinae.

Broad-snouted Caiman – *Caiman latirostris*
Subfamily: Alligatorinae
- Diet: The young eat insects, crustaceans; adults eat snails, fish, mammals and birds.
- Habitat: Shallow freshwater swamps.
- Distribution: Argentina, Bolivia, Brazil, Paraguay, Uruguay.
- Conservation: Hunting and habitat destruction threaten this species, whose skin is in high demand for tanning purposes.
  Size: Males up to ten feet, females to six-point-five feet.
- Croc bite: This species can sometimes be found in cattle ponds and heavily polluted rivers near cities.

Yacare Caiman – *Caiman yacare*
Subfamily: Alligatorinae
- Diet: Aquatic invertebrates, particularly snails, and vertebrates such as fish
- Distribution: Argentina, Bolivia, Brazil, Paraguay.
- Conservation: Population low due to hunting.
- Size: Up to about ten feet.
- Croc bite: Now considered a separate species, it was previously thought to be a subspecies of the common caiman.

Black Caiman – *Melanosuchus niger*
Subfamily: Alligatorinae
- Diet: Small caiman eat invertebrates and fish. Larger caiman eat mostly fish; the largest ones consume mammals, reptiles, even other caiman.
- Habitat: Flooded forests around lakes and slow-moving rivers.
- Distribution: Bolivia, Brazil, Colombia, Ecuador, French Guiana, Guyana, Peru.
- Conservation: Population reduced by an estimated ninety-nine per cent in the last century. Illegal hunting and habitat destruction impede repopulation.
- Size: The largest predator in South America, it can grow to over twenty feet.
- Croc bite: The only caiman considered dangerous to humans and domestic livestock, though it rarely makes these its prey.

Cuvier's Dwarf Caiman – *Paleosuchus palpebrosus*
Subfamily: Alligatorinae
- Diet: Invertebrates and fish.
- Habitat: Rivers, streams, and forests around major lakes.
- Distribution: Bolivia, Brazil, Colombia, Ecuador, French Guiana, Guyana, Paraguay, Peru, Surinam, Venezuela.
- Conservation: Since its skin is not in high demand, its population is stable, but habitat destruction and pollution pose threats.
- Size: Males grow to about five feet, females to about four feet.
- Croc bite: No one knows why, but it has a dog-like skull. It passes much of the day in burrows and travels large distances overland at night.

Smooth-fronted Caiman/Schneider's Dwarf Caiman – *Paleosuchus trigonatus*
Subfamily: Alligatorinae
- Diet: Mammals such as porcupines and pacas (a rodent).
- Habitat: Mound nests along – small rainforest streams.
- Distribution: Bolivia, Brazil, Colombia, Ecuador, French Guiana, Guyana, Peru, Surinam, Venezuela.
- Conservation: Threats include habitat loss and pollution caused by gold mining.
- Size: Males grow up to five-point five feet, females to four-point-five feet.
- Croc bite: They walk, literally, with their heads held high.

American Crocodile – *Crocodylus acutus*
Subfamily: Crocodylinae
- Diet: Hatchlings eat aquatic and terrestrial insects; juveniles live on fish, frogs, turtles, birds, small mammals, and aquatic invertebrates; adults consume larger mammals and birds as well as the food groups eaten by their young.
- Habitat: Freshwater and brackish coastal waters.
- Distribution: Southern Florida, southern Central America, northern-most South America, and various Caribbean islands, including the Cayman Islands, Cuba, Hispaniola, Jamaica, Margarita, Martinique, and Trinidad.
- Conservation: Threatened by hunting for their high-quality skin and by habitat destruction.
- Size: twenty feet or more.
- Croc bite: They can be dangerous to humans, though there are few documented cases of attacks.

Slender-snouted Crocodile – *Crocodylus cataphractus*
Subfamily: Crocodylinae
- Diet: Crabs, shrimps, snakes, frogs, fish.
- Habitat: Freshwater habitats, sometimes coastal areas.
- Distribution: West and central Africa.
- Conservation: Populations seem to be declining in many areas and may be extinct in Gambia, Nigeria, Guinea-Bissau, Senegal, and Zambia.
- Size: ten to thirteen feet.

- Croc bite: This species' call has been described as "sounding like a truck exhaust backfiring."

Orinoco Crocodile – *Crocodylus intermedius*
Subfamily: Crocodylinae
- Diet: Fish, small mammals, amphibians, and reptiles.
- Habitat: Freshwater riverine habitats.
- Distribution: Colombia and Venezuela.
- Conservation: Intense illegal hunting and habitat loss pose the gravest threat
- Size: Up to twenty feet.
- Croc bite: Changes in the colour of their skin have been observed in captivity over long periods.

Australian Freshwater/Johnston's Crocodile – *Crocodylus johnstoni*
Subfamily: Crocodylinae
- Diet: Fish, crustaceans, insects, amphibians, reptiles, birds, small mammals.
- Habitat: Upstream freshwater habitats.
- Distribution: Northern Australia.
- Conservation: Populations depleted by hunting have largely recovered, though its habitat continues to disappear.
- Size: Up to ten feet.
- Croc bite: This species has demonstrated a distinct homing ability.

Philippine Crocodile – *Crocodylus mindorensis*
Subfamily: Crocodylinae
- Diet: Aquatic invertebrates and small vertebrates.
- Habitat: Freshwater areas such as small lakes, swampy depressions, marshes, and tributaries of large rivers.
- Distribution: Philippine islands.
- Conservation: Once found throughout the Philippines, this species has a dangerously low population.
- Size: Up to ten feet.
- Croc bite: Long thought to be a subspecies of the New Guinea croc, which it closely resembles.

Morelet's Crocodile – *Crocodylus moreletii*
Subfamily: Crocodylinae

- Diet: Snails, mud turtles, small mammals, catfish. Juveniles eat insects, snails, slugs, and other small animals.
- Habitat: Mostly freshwater areas sometimes brackish water around coastal areas.
- Distribution: Belize, Guatemala, and Mexico.
- Conservation: Hunters seeking their high-quality skin drastically depleted the population mid-century.
- Size: Ten to eleven-point-five feet.
- Croc bite: At hatching time, a female carries her eggs to the water, where she helps crack them open.

Nile Crocodile – *Crocodylus niloticus*
Subfamily: Crocodylinae
- Diet: Juveniles eat insects, spiders, frogs and probably snakes, lizards and other small vertebrates; adults eat fish, antelope, zebra, warthogs, large domestic animals, and occasionally humans.
- Habitat: Freshwater areas and some coastal habitats in Africa.
- Distribution: Tropical and southern Africa and Madagascar
- Conservation: Legal protection has helped diminishing populations recover from hunting, but the species still suffers in central and western countries.
- Size: Up to sixteen feet:
- Croc bite: Displays a hierarchy of feeding order, with dominant crocs getting more, even during cooperative feeding. The most famous of the crocodillian maneaters.

New Guinea Crocodile – *Crocodylus novaeguineae*
Subfamily: Crocodylinae
- Diet: Insects, amphibians, snakes, birds and fish.
- Habitat: Mainly freshwater habitats.
- Distribution: New Guinea.
- Conservation: Recently recovered from population depletion, today it benefits from low human population and large areas of wetland habitat.
- Size: Up to thirteen feet.
- Croc bite: Of two distinct populations: the Papuan nests in the wet season, the Northern in the dry season.

Mugger/Marsh Crocodile – *Crocodylus palustris*
Subfamily: Crocodylinae

- Diet: Juveniles eat insects and small vertebrates. Adults live on frogs, snakes, small mammals and birds; the largest ones dine on deer and buffalo.
- Habitat: Freshwater habitats.
- Distribution: Bangladesh, Iran, India, Myanmar, Nepal, Pakistan, Sri Lanka.
- Conservation: Threatened by habitat loss, with the Bangladesh and Myanmar populations possibly already extinct.
- Size: Reaching to over thirteen feet.
- Croc bite: With a snout wider than any other in the *Crocodylus* genus, it resembles an alligator.

Estuarine/Saltwater/Indopacific Crocodile – *Crocodylus porosus*
Subfamily: Crocodylinae
- Diet: Juveniles eat insects, crabs, shrimp, mudskippers, lizards, and snakes; adults dine on birds, fish, and mammals, including the occasional human.
- Habitat: Brackish and freshwater areas.
- Distribution: Most widely distributed of crocodilians, it lives throughout tropical regions of Asia and the Pacific.
- Conservation: Its hide is the most valuable of any crocodile.
- Habitat loss and hunting imperil some populations.
- Size: twenty-three feet or more. Some in captivity weigh up to 2,200 pounds.
- Croc bite: The largest reptile and most feared crocodile, it can travel long distances by sea; indeed, this species has been seen with barnacles attached to its scales.

Cuban Crocodile – *Crocodylus rhombifer*
Subfamily: Crocodylinae
- Diet: Fish, turtles, small mammals.
- Habitat: Freshwater swamps.
- Distribution: Cuba.
- Conservation: One of the most threatened New World crocodilian species, primarily because of its small distribution.
- Size: About eleven-point-five feet.
- Croc bite: 800-year-old fossils of this species have been found on Grand Cayman Island, where it is now extinct.

Siamese Crocodile – *Crocodylus siamensis*
Subfamily: Crocodylinae
- Diet: Mainly fish, but also amphibians, reptiles and perhaps small mammals.
- Habitat: Tropical freshwater lakes, rivers and marshlands.
- Distribution: South-east Asian tropical lowlands.
- Conservation: Possibly extinct in the wild
- Size: No longer than thirteen feet.
- Croc bite: Juveniles, which are yellow or tan with black markings, can be confused with the similarly coloured Indopacific crocodile.

Dwarf Crocodile – *Osteolaemus tetraspis*
Subfamily: Crocodylinae
- Diet: Crabs, frogs and fish.
- Habitat: Swamps and slow-moving freshwater in rain forests.
- Distribution: West and west-central Africa.
- Conservation: This widely distributed species is probably not threatened, though information on populations is scant.
- Size: Reaches six-point five feet.
- Croc bite: Mostly nocturnal, it does not bask in the sun for long stretches like most other crocodiles.

False Gharial/Gavial – *Tomistoma schiegelil*
Subfamily: Crocodylinae
- Diet: Small vertebrates and fish.
- Habitat: Freshwater habitats, swamps, lakes and rivers.
- Distribution: Thailand, Malaysia, Sumatra, Java, Borneo, and possibly Sulawesi.
- Conservation: According to the few studies done, population is very low.
- Size: Thirteen feet or more.
- Croc bite: Disagreement among biologists about whether this species belongs here or in the Gavialinae subfamily.

Gharial/Gavial – *Gavialis gangeticus*
Subfamily: Crocodylinae
- Diet: Fish (cannot eat large animals because its jaws are too slim).
- Habitat: Calmer stretches of deep, fast-moving rivers.
- Distribution: India, Pakistan, Bangladesh, Nepal, Bhutan, Myanmar.

- Conservation: Nearly extinct by the 1970s, it survives primarily in protected areas.
- Size: Up to twenty-one feet.
- Croc bite: Its name comes from the bump on the nose of adult males, which resembles the Indian pot or "ghara".

AROUND LAKE RUDOLF, AFRICA

South Island, of about thirty square miles, is the biggest island on the lake. In many ways it is also the most mysterious, for it has several secrets, two of which in particular will never be revealed. Although uninhabited, there are more than 500 feral goats on it – a living reminder of a past habitation by men. These goats were first seen in 1934 by Sir Vivian Fuchs' expedition, the first recorded visitors to the island. Fuchs found human bones and pottery shards, as well as the goats. Nobody knows who these people were or how they got to the island, or when. A band of aventurers of long ago, bent on discovery and new lives, perhaps.

Before Fuchs set off on his expedition he spoke of his plans to visit South Island to Ludwig von Höhnel, after whom the island was originally named. Von Höhnel, then seventy-seven, had not forgotten his terrible journey with Teleki in 1888. He considered Fuchs' plans madness, and said so:

> I fear that I have not warned you seriously enough that you must be very careful and not underrate the risk of the enterprize. If the weather conditions are anything like they were at our time then you would be senseless to try the venture. I do not think the lake at any time of the year is so calm as to be navigated with a small collapsible boat to justify any attempt to reach the island.

On 28 July, 1934, Fuchs left two members of his expedition, Martin and Dyson, on South Island to survey it. They were to return not later than 13 August. But they never did return, nor were they ever seen again. An aerial search of the island and neighbouring mainland revealed nothing. Attempts by Fuchs to reach the island in another boat were frustrated by bad weather. Two oars, two tins, and Dyson's hat were eventually found washed up on the west shore seventy miles north of the island.

While the circumstances of their death can only be surmized, there is one plausible explanation. Firstly, the objects washed ashore suggest that they were afloat at the time of the disaster, probably making their way back to the mainland. There had been no storms, and their boat was a seaworthy type with two four-gallon buoyancy tanks, which were never found. Had they simply holed the craft on an underwater object they could have done so only very close to the island, for a short distance offshore on all sides is deep, clear water. Such an accident would have left them within easy swimming distance of land. Had their engine stopped, or the vessel sprung a leak on the way back, they could, at the worst, have drifted to shore by clinging to the buoyancy tanks. There can be little doubt that they met a much more violent end.

There are two ways in which their boat and its tanks could have been destroyed and its occupants killed – attacks from either a hippo or a croc. Big male crocs in territorial mood will attack canoes as they would other crocs. Just how ferocious and destructive a big one can be was made frighteningly clear to two other scientists in 1962. They were sounding Lake Chishi in Zambia from a small rubber dinghy when, without warning, they were set upon by a crocodile. In its first assault it tore open the front compartment of the dinghy, collapsing it, and then began threshing about with the boat draped over its back. While the men were trying to shove themselves clear of the beast, one of them was seized by his foot. He managed to free himself, after which the croc renewed its demolition of the boat, clambering over the side, biting savagely at everything and rapidly shredding the rubber hull. It ignored their efforts to beat it off with an oar, and soon only the rear compartment remained intact. Since the croc was obviously committed to their total destruction, the two men took to the water, a desperate but as it happened, wise move. In the rough water they somehow managed to swim away unmolested. They saw no further sign of the croc (or their boat) and had to swim for two hours before they made land. Had they stayed with their boat the croc would undoubtedly have killed them.

P. B. M. Jackson, a biologist, records six attacks from as many crocs while he was in a boat on Mweru Marsh, near Lake Chishi. All were consistent with the territorial aggression described by Hugh Cott and Muiji Modha. Such attacks are most common in places where crocs are unharassed and therefore unafraid of man.

August is the beginning of the breeding season on Rudolf. It is highly probable that Martin and Dyson, ignorant and trusting of crocs, were attacked by an old black-backed male as they unwittingly infringed its territorial waters on their way back to the mainland. A half-ton croc could have crunched up their small canvas boat like a biscuit, leaving the explorers at its mercy in the lake.

An even more formidable aggressor would have been a hippo. They are actually more notorious than crocs for attacking boats (also for territorial reasons), and since a large male hippo weighs two or three tons the ease with which it can pulverize a small boat is obvious. A sudden, furious attack on the unsuspecting scientists and it would have been all over in a few minutes, with nothing surviving but a hat and a few pieces of debris. Von Höhnel's foreboding proved well grounded.

A CUNNING CROCODILE

From the early 1930s onwards the celebrated palaeontologist L. S. B. Leakey was working in Africa, searching for early primate fossils in Olduvai Gorge and around Lake Victoria, mainly in Kenya and Tanzania. The following is one of several encounters he had with crocodiles.

All round the shores of Lake Victoria and its islands, including Rusinga, one can always be sure of seeing fish eagles. In fact, almost every large tree in the area seems to boast at least one pair, and occasionally two, of these magnificent birds. Since these eagles are long-lived and have few natural enemies apart from man, one would expect them to suffer a fantastic population growth, but that is not the case. I think the explanation lies in the unusually high mortality rate among newly hatched chicks. I can give no reason why this should be so, but again and again over the years I have found small, fluffy, white baby fish eagles, about the size of a tennis ball, lying dead or dying on the ground.

Three such babies came into our hands one day shortly after we returned from Olduvai. They were very newly hatched, and Peter Bell and I decided to try to rear them. We fed them small scraps of fresh lake fish and were so successful that when the day came for us to pack up the Kanjera camp, early in October, all three were of adult size, although still retaining their juvenile plumage. They had never been kept in cages, and throughout their stay in camp they had been free to fly wherever they pleased. By the time we were ready to return to Nairobi they had started to fly down to the lake shore and catch their own fish in the shallow waters. We therefore had great hopes that they would remain happily in their own habitat when we left.

But this was not to be. The three fish eagles had become so accustomed to human company that when our convoy finally moved off, heading for Nairobi, they followed us on the wing. The first part of the track ran for about ten miles along the shore of the lake, and all the way the eagles flew behind us, landing every now and again on one or other of the vehicles. When, at length, we turned inland at Kendu Bay, we hoped that we had said good-bye to our faithful friends. That night, however, already halfway to Nairobi, we found that they were still with us and very hungry. We gave them a meal and resigned ourselves to the fact that they would probably escort us all the way to Nairobi – which is exactly what they did.

We were about to begin the second half of our season's work and planned to explore the side gorge at Olduvai. But since there was little water there, and certainly no fresh fish on which to feed the eagles, they could not possibly be allowed to follow us any longer. Fortunately, the curator of the Natural History Museum in Nairobi, Dr van Someren, had erected a large aviary behind the museum a few years earlier, and this was now empty. It was forty feet high and both longer and wider than that, providing plenty of room to house our three eagles for the time being. Accordingly, I decided to leave them in the aviary and promised Dr van Someren that I would pay for the fish he had to buy for them while I was at Olduvai.

Before we left Rusinga, however, I had a less friendly encounter with another specimen of the area's wildlife. All the water for use in the villages on the island was drawn from the lake, mainly by the women and children, who filled their earthenware pots and tin canisters and carried them on their heads to their huts. In the ordinary course of events, fetching water from the crocodile-inhabited lake was made safe by the building of an enclosure of stakes extending out into the water about five feet from the place on shore where the water was drawn. However, one crocodile had become very cunning. On several occasions it had come out of the water, crawled along the lake shore, and made its way through the grass behind the enclosure to carry off an unsuspecting woman or child, sometimes a goat or a sheep. This had been happening at intervals for nearly two years. When we arrived on Rusinga the island's chief asked for my help in getting rid of this scourge, and I promised that if the crocodile was located while we were there, I would do my best to dispose of it.

A few days later, when we were in the middle of lunch, a messenger rushed into camp to say that a crocodile was sunning itself on a small mud bank about half a mile off. I immediately went to the spot and managed to put a bullet into the back of the crocodile's neck just behind the head, thus killing it. This is a difficult shot to make, but the only effective one. If a crocodile is hit in any other part of its anatomy it disappears into the water, even though it may be mortally wounded, and is irrecoverable. In this instance, the local inhabitants particularly wished to cut the creature open to make sure that it was, in fact, the maneater.

The sound of the shot brought hundreds of people running down to the shore from all directions, and when they saw the dead crocodile there was great rejoicing, wild dancing, and shouting – though there were some who wept, remembering the loved ones they had lost. In a few minutes the crocodile was brought up from the mud bank on to the grass by the shore and laid stomach upwards to be cut open. It was a gruesome spectacle. The stomach contents included bracelets, beads, necklaces, and many other indisputable indications of the human meals that had been eaten. Many of the objects were identified by relatives of the victims. There was, therefore, no doubt whatsoever that the crocodile I had shot was indeed the one that had been terrorizing the people of the island for so long.

BULL SHARKS

The bull shark is number three in the league table of sharks known to kill people and is extremely aggressive, both in the sea and in rivers and lakes. Indeed, it is regarded by some shark experts to be the most dangerous of all sharks. It is thought to have been responsible for many attacks originally attributed to great whites, particularly in warmer waters. It is as catholic in its tastes as the tiger shark, but it has powerful jaws, wider in relationship to its body length. It has a blunt snout, small eyes, triangular-shaped teeth in the upper jaw with coarse serrations, and dagger-like teeth in the lower jaw. The upper surface of the body is grey, and the edges of the fins are dark in younger specimens. The shark is a first-class hunter, with refined senses including the ability to hear sounds in the 100–1500 Hertz range, the middle part of the spectrum of human hearing. It cruises relatively slowly but the muscles of its heavily built body can put on an extraordinary burst of speed when homing-in on a target.

The shark's habit of patrolling inshore waters also brings it into more frequent contact with people. Attacks in the Zambezi and Limpopo rivers, for example, have been attributed to bull sharks, and in the sacred Ganges the bull shark is thought to be responsible for attacks previously attributed to the very rare Ganges shark *(Glyphis gangeticus)*. It has been known to frequent the bathing ghats of Calcutta, feeding on partially cremated bodies and attacking religious bathers. In one year, as many as twenty pilgrims were attacked, half of whom were killed. In the estuary of the Devi, five people were killed and another thirty badly mauled during a period of two months in 1959. In the estuary of the Limpopo in Mozambique, three attacks on people occurred within a space of six months during 1961, all attributed to a single rogue bull shark. One attack was 150 miles (241 kilometres) from the sea.

During the Second World War a most unusual attack took place at Ahwaz in Iran, about ninety miles (145 kilometres) from the sea. A British soldier, intent on washing the mud from his ambulance, stepped down into no more than a foot of water in the Karun River (a tributary of the Tigris) and, as he was beginning to set to work, was seized on the leg by a shark. Caught off balance, he fell over and began to fight for his life in water no deeper than in a bathtub. Defending himself with arms and fists, the soldier was badly lacerated. His right arm was torn open, his hands slashed, and his leg badly gouged. He was one of twenty-seven people attacked by sharks between 1941 and 1949, the period when Allied military authorities kept records. All had been attacked in shallow water. Bull sharks were the likely culprits.

Local folklore has it that the sharks wait below date palms at Khorramshahr, downstream from Ahwaz. In the Tigris, they are supposed to head for Baghdad and its melons, 350 miles (563 kilometres) from the sea. Folklore aside, many rivers entering the Persian Gulf have been the sites of shark attacks. Danish biologist H. Blegvad, writing in a paper on the fish of the Persian Gulf, stated that many people, especially children who play in the rivers, were killed by sharks every year. He thought that with less food available in rivers than in the sea, sharks that enter freshwater were more liable to attack people. It would be interesting no know whether these types of shallow-water attacks still occur today in the rivers at the head of the Gulf.

Some Australian east coast rivers are known to be visited by sharks. The Brisbane River in Queensland and George's River, New South Wales, have been the locations of shark attacks. The stories are not recent but nevertheless relevant. In the Bulimba Reach of the Brisbane River in 1921, a man was carrying his young son on his back and wading to his dinghy, just thirty feet (9.1 kilometres) from the river bank. A shark seized his hip, and in the struggle the boy slipped off and into the water. The shark let go and the boy was taken, never to be seen again. At East Hills, about twenty miles (thirty-two kilometres) from the mouth of George's River a shark struck a fifteen-year-old boy swimming to fetch a tennis ball. The boy managed to get back to the river bank, only to turn around and find that the river was filled with sharks. Onlookers gazed in amazement. A year later, in 1935, another boy was swimming in a race with his companions, about two miles (3.2 kilometres) upstream from East Hills, when he was struck by a shark. He was dead before his rescuers got him to the river bank. On the same night, a further three miles (five kilometres) up river, a young girl playing in about four feet (1.2 kilometres) of water had both her hands bitten off by a shark. She survived by the prompt action of rescuers. In 1927, at Eden, New South Wales, a man on a horse were attacked by a shark in the Kiah River. The horse bucked and the man was thrown into the water. The commotion startled the shark and it swam away.

Whether these Australian attacks were by bull sharks must remain speculation, but the pattern of behaviour suggests this species is a likely candidate.

Central and South American lakes and seas are also haunts of the bull shark. In Lake Nicaragua, site of the first observations of freshwater sharks, it is a known killer, accounting for at least one human death and numerous dog deaths each year. In 1944, one shark attacked three people near Granada, the largest town on the lake. Two of them died. Of late, sightings of bull sharks in the lake have been few, the result of bounty hunting introduced by the authorities in Granada or by the silting-up of the San Juan River.

Like many sharks, the bull shark is quick to take advantage of changing circumstances and new feeding opportunities. Such was the case at beaches in Recife, north-west Brazil, when the ecology of the area was changed radically by human activity. On 28 October 1996 a surfer and body-boarder were attacked by a 8.2 feet (2.5 metres) bull shark. At 10.30 in the morning the two surfers were in murky water, about 329 feet (100 metres) from the beach at Barra de Jangada, close to the mouth of the Jaboatao River. One was seized on the knee and the other was badly bitten on the thigh when he went to help. Tourniquets made from the board-straps prevented them from losing too much blood and they both survived. A damaged tooth recovered from an injured leg was identified as from a bull shark.

These accidents represented the twenty-second shark attack, with six fatalities, since September 1993 on the same 6.2-mile (ten kilometre) stretch of beach where no attack had been recorded previously. It occurred despite a ban on surfing in the area since January 1995. The sharks came in a variety of sizes, 3.3-ten feet (one to three metres), and five were positively identified – four bull sharks and a tiger shark. An increase in shipping to and from a nearby port was coincident with the sudden spate of attacks. A shark workshop attended by experts in November 1995 identified several other factors: there was a definite increase in the number of surfers and bathers in the area; the by-catch from shrimp trawlers was dumped nearby; the near-shore river channel is a favourite spot for bull sharks; and climatic change with more southerly winds and less rain at the time of the attacks drove ocean currents from south to north, the water moving from the new port area to the beach south of Recife. Again, human activities and people's behaviour have more significance in shark attacks than the behaviour of the sharks themselves.

The carnage, however, has continued. In November 1998, a surfer was attacked and later died after a shark had bitten off his hands at the Praia da Boa Viagem beach of Recife. It was the second fatal attack during 1998 and the twenty-seventh shark attack in the area in two years. And, in May 1999, Boa Viagem was to feature again when two sharks, one an eight-foot (2.5 metres) long tiger shark, were thought to have attacked a twenty-one-year-old male surfer. The sharks attacked several times, biting into the man's thigh and hands, but he was able to fight back and was rescued eventually by three lifeguards . . .

SHARKS IN THE SHALLOWS

This selection of newspaper reports emphasizes the worrying fact
that the majority of unprovoked shark attacks occur in water less
than five feet deep.

Sydney, Australia, 1942

Zieta Steadman, twenty-eight, single, of Ashfield was killed by a shark while she was standing in shallow water in an upper part of Middle Harbour yesterday afternoon.

Miss Steadman was so shockingly mutilated that only the upper part of her body could be recovered. The remains were dragged from the jaws of the shark by Mr Frederick H. Bowes of Charlotte Street, Ashfield. Mr Bowes estimates that the shark was fourteen feet long.

Miss Steadman was a member a picnic party, the other members of which were Mr and Mrs Bowes and Mrs Reeve.

One of the boys grabbed an oar, with which he tried to drive off the shark. Other members of the party joined him, armed with sticks and stones. A few moments later Miss Burch appeared above water. She was taken ashore by her companions. She had suffered terrible injuries and she was dead before the party reached the shore. The body was taken to the Spit, and Sergeant van Wouwe and Constable C. Fenton of the Water Police met the party.

Mrs Burch and her two daughters were among those evacuated from Hong Kong about two years ago. Her husband, Mr R. J. Burch and their son are prisoners of war in the hands of the Japanese.

Sydney, Australia, 1955

A man was killed by a fourteen-foot tiger shark in Sugarloaf Bay, Castlecrag, yesterday afternoon.

The man, Bruno Aloysius Rautenberg, a twenty-five-year-old German migrant, was attacked twice in about fifteen feet of water between fifteen and twenty yards from the shore. The shark tore Rautenberg's legs to pieces. The flesh on the left leg was torn off between the knee and the foot. Large pieces of flesh were bitten on the right leg.

Yesterday's shark fatality, the second in Sydney in three weeks, occurred at about 2 p.m.

Rautenberg, a metalworker, boarded with Mr and Mrs K. Wood in

Edinburgh Road, Castlecrag. He was cleaning himself in the bay after helping to clean out the Woods' swimming pool when the shark attacked. The attack was in a lonely part of Sugarloaf Bay, at the bottom of a high, sloping cliff.

Mr Wood, thirty-seven said that after he and Rautenberg cleaned out the pool, which is built of rock, Rautenberg said he would wash the mud off himself in the bay. "I warned him not to go out far, but he said he would try and recover an anchor we lost a few days ago. Suddenly I heard him give a piercing scream. He was a very good swimmer, but I thought he was in difficulties. I ran to the bank near him. There was blood in the water all around him. The shark was right beside him. I saw the shark grab him by the leg, drag him under and hang on.

"I didn't think the shark would let his leg go. Neither my wife nor I can swim. We were the only people around. I grabbed a piece of water pipe about fifteen foot long and threw it at the shark to try and drive it off. By this time Rautenberg was so weak he couldn't do anything.

"When he came to the surface again I waded out a little way from the rock, grasped his body and carried him up the bank. He was dead when I got him ashore. My wife called the police and ambulance."

Mr Wood said the shark seemed to have a pointed nose. It was black along the back. "It had a high triangular fin on its back," he said. "It was more than twice as long as Rautenberg. After the attack the shark swam around for more than two hours and I saw it six times during that time.

"Rautenberg migrated to Australia from Germany and had been boarding with us for about two months. He worked at Alexandria. He never spoke much about himself, but he told my wife he had a little girl, aged five, in Germany. He wanted the child and her mother to come to Australia and had been saving up for their fare. As far as we know, they were not very keen on coming out here."

Central District Ambulance officers and Dr E. Manuel of Castlecrag hurried to the scene soon after the attack, but Rautenberg was dead. Police said they thought he died within about two minutes of the first attack because he lost so much blood.

Police and ambulance men had to make their way down hundreds of steps, through thick bush, to reach the scene. They said the arteries had been torn out of Rautenberg's legs and it would have been impossible to save his life.

Police said that the risk of shark attacks was high at present because the water temperature along the coast was about 74° F. They said this high temperature was bringing scores of sharks and big game fish into the harbour.

On 13 January Jolin Willis, thirteen, was killed by a twelve-foot grey nurse shark while spearfishing off Balmoral Beach. On 1 March last year a shark mauled a lifesaver swimming alone at The Entrance, near Gosford. The lifesaver died three days later. There have been more than thirty-two fatal shark attacks in New South Wales since 1919. Yesterday's fatality was the eighth in Sydney Harbour since that same year . . . Six species of sharks in New South Wales waters are regarded as maneaters: the tiger, grey nurse, blue pointer or mako, white shark, black or bronze whaler and the hammerhead.

Natal, South Africa, 1957

Doctors and nurses at Port Shepstone Hospital were still fighting early today to save the life of Julia Painting, a fourteen-year-old Bulawayo girl mauled by a shark as she bathed among hundreds of visitors at Margate yesterday. At midnight her condition was reported as "unchanged". Her left arm was torn off and flesh savaged from her body.

She murmured, "Let me die," as she was being taken to hospital. Julia was later reported to be still in a serious condition, but "there is a very slight improvement". She was operated on soon after the attack – the fourth since 19 December 1957 on the Natal South Coast. Her life hung in the balance when it was learnt that the hospital's blood bank was empty. Nurses and hospital staff immediately volunteered to be bled and, while two pints were being collected, an urgent call for ten pints of blood was sent to the hospital at Renishaw. It arrived in time.

The Margate Town Council banned all bathing off the beach until further notice at a special meeting held after the attack on Julia. Bathing will be allowed in the lagoon as soon as it has been deepened and the mouth sandbagged. The Council also decided to erect a shark net immediately.

A large crowd on the beach heard Julia's screams for help. They watched in horrified silence as the shark wrestled with her in clear, knee-deep water about thirty yards from the beach. Two men, Mr Paul Brokensha, thirty-six, of Fort Victoria, Rhodesia, and a Margate lifesaver, Mr Aubrey Cowan, fought to free Julia from the shark's jaws. Eventually the shark let go and swam away.

Julia was standing in unclouded water on the fringe of hundreds of other bathers when the shark made its savage attack, taking away her left arm and leaving lacerations on her chest. A dumbfounded crowd of more than 2,000 on the beach heard the first frantic warning screams of "shark" and watched as the flurried water became blood red.

Lifesavers jumped to action and sounded a warning siren. Only moments previously a spotter aircraft of the shark patrol had passed over the area before wheeling back towards St Michael's.

Julia, her fifteen-year-old nephew Laurie, an uncle, Mr Arthur Painting, and Mr Brokensha were having a final dip before leaving the surf. Julia was due to return home today. She had been on holiday with her uncle and aunt for a month.

Mr Brokensha described how, standing only a few yards from Julia, he saw, simultaneously with her, the shark moving in to the first attack. It went straight for her without turning on its side. With a savage thrust it hit her and immediately mauled her side, before wheeling around for a second attack.

Mr Brokensha caught the shark's tail and tried to drag Julia away, but her costume came away in his hands. He started raining blows on the shark's back, but, in his own words, 'It was like punching very solid leather and there was no 'give' at all."

The shark was so powerful that, with a flick of its tail, it threw him off. He immediately returned to the fray and hit the shark again. The shark let go, but not until it had severed the girl's arm at the shoulder and severely savaged her body.

The attack was so sudden and unexpected that the four lifesavers realized that a shark was in the water only when they heard horrified screams and saw the water churning beneath flaying fins. Mr Frank Shephard, the Durban fishing authority, said that, from the description, the shark was undoubtedly a ragged-tooth shark – one of the most dangerous, and a cunning and quiet scavenger which creeps along the bottom towards the shore.

Natal, South Africa, 1958

The increasing prevalence of attacks on human beings has led the Natal authorities to declare war on two kinds of pests – sharks and crocodiles.

The shark menace has grown alarmingly at bathing beaches at Natal South Coast resorts, where tens of thousands of visitors are now on summer holiday. In the past two weeks two youths have died after being attacked, another youth had a leg bitten off, and a fourteen-year-old girl is in a critical condition after her arm was torn off and other parts of her body mutilated. All these attacks occurred in shallow water near the beach in the presence of large numbers of other bathers. Helicopter and light aircraft have been engaged on a shark-spotting patrol on this stretch of the coast, and a South African naval minesweeper has now been ordered to the area to lay depth charges.

In the northern Natal territory of Zululand crocodiles have been making frequent attacks on human beings. The outcry against protection of these creatures reached a climax after the fourteen-year-old son of a Johannesburg doctor was killed while fishing on the bank of a lake. The provincial authorities have now decided to shoot out all crocodiles. Professional hunters and game wardens have been ordered to shoot crocodiles on sight, and local farmers have been asked to cooperate. Victims of crocodile attacks include both Europeans and Africans.

Natal, South Africa, 1958

As a wave of horror swept Natal's South Coast after a fresh shark killing yesterday, at least three families decided to pack up and leave. Some visitors said that the South Coast would become a "ghost resort" if immediate steps were not taken to make bathing safe.

The victim of the latest attack, Mr Derryet Garth Prinsloo, a forty-two-year-old farmer of Theunissen, Free State, was standing in about thirty inches of water a few yards from the shore and talking to a woman companion when he was taken by a lazy-grey shark at Scottburgh.

His frantic scream, "Help me, for God's sake help me," electrified the small crowd of early morning bathers as the shark, attacking from behind, ripped the flesh from both his legs and buttocks in a series of lightning attacks. As three rescuers pulled him from the surf on to the beach, his sixteen-year-old son, Jacques, rushed from the water and, cradling the head of his dying father in his lap, cried, "Daddy, Daddy, don't leave me. I'm with you. Please speak to me."

Mr Prinsloo was taken to Renishaw Hospital in a station wagon, but was dead on arrival. An immediate ban was imposed by order of the Town Board on further bathing.

Mr A. Laing of Boksburg and his twelve-year-old son, Neville, had been standing alongside Mr Prinsloo only minutes before the attack.

Mr Laing, feeling the debris of washed cane from the river stroking his son, "This is shark water, let's get out."

While walking out of the surf, he heard the screams for help and, looking round, saw the shark lashing its tail in a flurry of blood-stained water. He rushed back to help Mr I. Kelly of Ermelo and Mr J. A. C. Nieman of Virginia, who were pulling Mr Prinsloo by the arms away from the shark, which had knocked him on to his side. When they hauled him to the shore, both legs had been stripped of all flesh and the left leg was almost severed.

Mrs Nieman, who, with her husband and two children, had gone for an early morning bathe with Mr Prinsloo and his son, said she was standing right next to Mr Prinsloo when the attack occurred. "He was saying, 'This is what I like about the waves here – they're so beautifully even.' They were his last, words. The next thing I knew he was screaming for help."

Mr D. Stamatis of Scoftburgh, an experienced shark fisherman, sent home for a shotgun after the attack. He took up a position on the rocks, from where he saw a shark – which he believed was a five-foot, 200-pound lazy grey – make two more sorties into the shallow surf before 8.30 a.m.

Natal, South Africa, 1958

A twenty-nine-year-old bather was killed by a large shark which attacked him repeatedly yesterday while his wife and two children watched horrified at Port Edward, one hundred miles south of here. A middle-aged African dived into the surf and dragged him out of the shark's jaws after a tug-of-war.

The man, Mr Nicholas Francois Badenhorst, was dead when he was dragged to the beach by the African, Maseke, who plunged into the surf after frenzied appeals both from the victim and his brother, Andries Badenhorst, who was bathing with him.

The shark ripped off Mr Badenhorst's left arm completely and took off his right arm below the elbow. It then mauled his abdomen and one of his legs.

Mr Andries Badenhorst said last night: "My brother and I and an acquaintance were bathing a little way out – about chest-deep in the water. There were a lot of other bathers nearer the shore. Suddenly I saw this big shark. It was from ten to fifteen feet long. It attacked my brother. He yelled and I yelled. I think a line was sent out. A Native came in and pulled my brother out, but it was too late then. The water was all discoloured with blood."

Mr Nicholas Badenhorst's children, who were on the beach with their mother, are five years and twenty months old. The family was staying at a holiday camp here. Mr Badenhorst was a clerk on the South African Railways, living at Sir George Grey Avenue, Horison, Roodepoort. Arrangements were immediately made to take the family to Durban, where they boarded the train which left for the Transvaal last night.

The attack was the sixth on the South Coast since December. Before 18 December, when sixteen-year-old Bob Wherley lost a leg at Karrideene, there had been no shark attacks in Natal waters since 1954. Then in quick succession came attacks at Uvongo beach, where Alan Green, fourteen, was killed only twenty-four hours after the attack on Wherley, at Margate, where Vernon Berry, aged twenty-three, was killed on 23 December, and fourteen-year-old Julia Painting lost her left arm and was mutilated a week later, and at Scottburgh, where Mr D. G. Prinsloo, forty-two, was killed on 9 January.

The mayors of three of the South Coast's premier holiday resorts, Mr Robert Barton (Margate), Mr Arthur Howes (Amanzimtoti) and Mr Les Payn (Scottsburgh) last night appealed to holidaymakers to obey the bathing instruction of lifesavers. Mr Barton said the tragedies indicated the danger of swimming outside safe-bathing enclosures. All three mayors pointed out that resort municipalities had spent thousands of pounds and many hours of deliberation in planning the safest form of bathing.

Mackay, Australia, 1961

Doctors are fighting desperately to save the life of eighteen-year-old Margaret Hobbs, a victim of yesterday's shark attack at Mackay.

Miss Hobbs has been receiving continuous transfusions of blood and saline solutions since she was admitted to the Mater Hospital, Mackay, at 3 p.m. yesterday. She is dangerously ill. Late tonight her condition was unchanged.

Miss Hobbs, a schoolteacher of Owen's Creek, near Mackay, and a friend, Martyn Steffens, twenty-four, of Brisbane, were mauled by the shark as they stood in waist-deep water at Lambert's Beach.

Doctors in a two-hour emergency operation last night amputated

Miss Hobbs' right leg near the hip. Her right arm was torn off at the shoulder and her left arm torn off above the wrist.

Steffens had his right hand and wrist mauled. Doctors amputated his hand above the wrist. His condition tonight was serious, but doctors consider his progress satisfactory.

Graham Jorgensen, twenty-seven, who saved the couple by driving the shark away, said today the couple had entered the water to wash sand off their bodies after playing on the beach. When the attack occurred, he was sitting on the beach with the rest of the party . . .

Evidence of a growing shark menace in eastern Australian waters came with reports of shark sightings yesterday in many areas: a ten-foot shark surfaced near a fisherman while he was swimming to safety from a burning, sinking trawler off Southport, Queensland; a shark snapped a fish from a fisherman's line as he stood in shallow water near Murwillumbah; the body of a drowned man mauled by a shark was found yesterday floating in the Brisbane river; and a shark swam within ten feet of four adults and nine children at Northcliffe, south of Surfers Paradise, on Thursday.

Margaret Hobbs, eighteen, the Mackay shark victim, died at 6.30 last night. Her death ended a grim round-the-clock battle by doctors and nurses since the attack. A sister at the Mater Hospital said, "Miss Hobbs fought courageously for her life."

Miss Hobbs lost consciousness in the afternoon and her parents were called to her bedside. Friends later took them home. "They couldn't stand it any longer," a hospital sister said. A doctor was called urgently in the late afternoon, but Miss Hobbs gradually sank.

A hospital sister who was with Miss Hobbs almost continually said tonight, "There was never any real hope. Margaret just held her own for the first twenty-four hours, but her condition deteriorated overnight and it was never good at any time today. She knew her parents this morning and was able to say 'yes', 'Mum' and 'Dad' – that's all. Margaret was very brave and she was fighting until the moment she lost consciousness."

Sisters at the hospital said that Martyn Steffens had been told during the day that Margaret's condition was deteriorating. His mother and her father were with him when the news of her death was broken to him at 7.15 p.m. Friends of the couple said Steffens went to Mackay just before Christmas to meet the Hobbs family before announcing his engagement to Margaret.

More than twenty shark alarms along Queensland's central coast sent swimmers scattering from the water yesterday.

At Pacific Beach, near Surfers' Paradise, a group of fishermen digging for worms in ankle-deep water fled as a ten-foot shark cruised past in two feet of water less than ten feet away.

North Burleigh Beach lifesavers closed the beach three times in four hours when sharks nosed in close to swimmers. All lifesaving clubs from the Gold Coast to the far north maintained doubled patrols, but many swimmers stayed out of the water or remained in the shallows. A privately owned spotting aircraft will keep a tight watch for sharks at the Yeppoon to Emu Park beaches. The aircraft's pilot today saw sharks up to ten feet long cruising within three yards of swimmers.

Sydney, Australia, 1963

Miss Marcia Hathaway, a well-known Sydney actress, was fatally mauled by a shark in Middle Harbour yesterday afternoon. The shark attacked her while she was standing in murky water only thirty inches deep and twenty feet from the shore in the northern arm of Sugarloaf Bay.

Seconds before she died, while friends were hurrying her to hospital, Miss Hathaway told her fiancé, "I am not in pain. Don't worry about me, dear. God will look after me."

Miss Hathaway, thirty-two, of Greenway Flats, Milson's Point, was on a picnic trip with six friends in a motor cruiser.

When the shark attacked, her fiancé, who was beside her, fought the shark with his hands and kicked it as it twisted in the blood-stained water, trying to drag its victim into deep water.

Miss Hathaway died twenty minutes later from her terrible injuries and shock. The shark almost tore off her right leg. Miss Hathaway's fiancé and two other friends were treated at the Mater Misericordiae Hospital for shock.

Miss Hathaway and her fiancé, Frederick Knight, thirty-eight, a journalist of Cook Street, Double Bay, were in the party of seven holidaying on the twenty-eight-foot cabin cruiser *Valeeta*.

Knight said later that Miss Hathaway at first thought she had been attacked by an octopus. "I have seen men die, but I have never seen anyone so brave as Marcia," he said. "I think the last words she said to me were, 'Don't worry about me, dear, God will look after me.' When

I asked her if it hurt much, she said, 'No, I am not in pain.' She was a very religious girl. We were to announce our engagement formally on her birthday, Friday the 8th.

"I did not get a close look at the shark, I saw a fin and its girth as I straddled it. My legs were wide apart and its body touched both of them."

The *Valeeta* was anchored about twenty yards from where the shark attacked, which was close to shore. The attack occurred in a small bay with a small watercourse at its head. Several homes back on to the water about 700 yards away; they are not visible from the beach.

The other members of the party were David Mason, twenty-eight, a journalist, and Peter Cowden, twenty-seven, both of Balmain, who are joint owners of the cruiser, James Delmege, thirty-nine, of Polls Point, Alan Simpson, twenty-one, Auburn, and Sandra Hayden, nineteen, of Blacktown. Mason, Cowden and Simpson were on the *Valeeta*, Delmege and Miss Hayden were only about three or four feet from the shore gathering oysters from the rocks, while Knight and Miss Hathaway were standing in shallow water about twenty feet out.

Knight said, when the shark attacked, he was only a few feet away from Miss Hathaway. "I went to her and tried to drag her from the shark. It seemed like ten minutes to me while we struggled, but it could only have been a couple of minutes. The water was stained with blood and I never thought I would get her away from it. I think at one stage I had my foot in its mouth. It felt soft and spongy. I'm not too clear what happened. It happened so fast and I could not see much in the water. I tried to reassure her and told her that the shark had just brushed past her, but she knew a short time after that she was dying."

Delmege said he had his back to the couple when the shark attacked. Sandra Hayden was a few feet away from him. "I heard a scream, looked around and thought they were just skylarking. I continued looking for oysters," he said. "Then I heard a second scream and I turned, and saw the water bloodstained and foaming. I dashed in and helped Fred Knight to get Marcia away from the shark."

Knight said the shark apparently attacked Miss Hathaway below the calf on the right leg, then in a second lunge embedded its teeth into her upper right thigh near the hip. Her right leg was almost torn off.

Delmege and Knight carried Miss Hathaway to the sandy beach in the small cove. Mason said that, when he and Cowden saw the attack, they tore sheets off the cruiser's bunks for tourniquets, then rowed to shore in the dinghy. They applied tourniquets on the beach, lifted Miss Hathaway into the dinghy and rowed back to the *Valeeta*. They took the cruiser to a boatshed at the foot of Edinburgh Road, Castlecrag, where Knight dived overboard and swam about twenty yards to a house to get the occupants to phone for an ambulance.

He swam back to the cruiser and comforted his fiancee as they made for Mowbray Point, where they were met by ambulance officers Ray Wrightson and Robert Smith of Central District Ambulance. Miss Hathaway was unconscious. The ambulancemen used oxygen in an attempt to revive her.

They put her in an ambulance, but, because of the steep grade leading up from the water's edge and slippery surface, the ambulance clutch burnt out. Although about thirty people, including Knight, tried desperately to push the vehicle, the gradient was too steep. A reporter radioed his office and a second ambulance was sent.

Ambulance officers worked on Miss Hathaway continuously and doctors at the hospital also tried to revive her, but she was dead. Miss Hathaway's mother collapsed when told the news of her death and was taken by ambulance to a private hospital.

Mr Michael Vaux, the owner of the Castlecrag boatshed, where the *Valeeta* pulled in with Miss Hathaway, said he saw two large sharks earlier in the morning in the bay. "There were a couple of dogs taken by sharks in the area last week," he said.

Perth, Australia, 1969

A fifteen-year-old Sea Scout who was attacked by a shark in seven feet of water in the Swan River yesterday said today he had used one foot to push the shark away after it had mauled his other leg.

"After I had been bitten I was scared that the shark might strike again," Graham Cartwright of Mettam Street, Trigg, said from his bed in the Royal Perth Hospital today. "He took two chomps and that was it. I felt his rough skin with my hands and one eye as I pushed him away with my good foot.

"I called out: 'Help, help – a shark's got me' during a 400-yard swim from the other side of the river. My best friend, Greg Hams, was nearly at the shore when he heard me call. He yelled out to John, who had just reached the river's edge."

John Brockmeulen, fourteen, of Mt Lawley, called out to some boys to get an ambulance and then swam out to Graham.

"He told me to turn over on to my back and towed me ashore. I was all right in the water, but could not bear to look at my leg once I was ashore," said Graham.

Graham was bleeding profusely from a four-inch deep tear in his left thigh as he was towed 100 yards to shore.

Pathologist Graeme Shute, a scoutmaster in the 1st Mt Lawley Sea Scouts, stemmed the flow of blood. The wound extended from the knee upwards and had opened the flesh on the inside of the boy's thigh. There were one-and-a-half-inch teeth marks in a nine-inch radius.

John Brockmeulen said he thought Graham had scared the shark away by sheer luck when he touched one of its sensitive eyes. "I was confident I would not be attacked by the shark because I had read that a second person was not usually attacked," he said.

Surgeons operated on Graham's mauled leg for five hours on Saturday night. They expect him to regain the full use of it. He should be in hospital for a week.

Graham, a Balcatta High School student and keen surfer, who was to have started his end-of-term examinations today, said he did not think he would swim in the river again. "But the ocean will be OK," he said.

The three boys were among a group of twenty Sea Scouts who had spent the afternoon sailing and scouting. The attack took place thirteen miles upstream.

RODNEY FOX'S SHARK

By his own terrifying account Rodney Fox should not have been around to celebrate his sixtieth birthday this week. His disfigured hands and body bear testimony to an attack by a great white shark that crushed and ripped him so badly that only the rubber wetsuit holding him together enabled him to survive.

He understands better than anyone the horror of this week's [11 November 2000] fatal attack on a crowded Perth beach, when the surf boiled red with blood as a great white tore the leg off Ken Crew, forty-nine-year-old father-of-three swimming in the shallows. Mr Crew's death was the third fatal shark attack off the Australian coast in the past two months. Six weeks ago, two surfers were taken on successive days. Shark hunters are sharpening their harpoons, swearing vengeance on behalf of these victims.

Yet Rodney Fox – a man whose own ordeal is more blood-curdling than that of any other survivor – is begging the shark hunters to lay down their arms. "Sharks don't even like the taste of humans, with all our bones. It's just unfortunate that when they take a taste, with one or two bites, the bites can be fatal," he said.

These are forgiving words indeed from a man who has become the world's foremost authority on the great white as a result of being torn almost in half by one – and, moments after breaking free, nearly drowning when it pulled him down through the bloodstained water on the end of a tangled line.

The insurance salesman had kissed his wife Kay, who was expecting their first child, as he set out from their Adelaide home on that December morning in 1963 to take part in a spear-fishing competition off the South Australian coast. It was a bright day, but a strong wind had roughed up the sea and the water was murky. Dressed in a rubber wet suit and flippers, the young Fox swam out to a cluster of rocks and then, after taking a deep breath – he was using only a face mask – dived down.

"Ahead of me, amid some brown weed, was a twenty-pound fish which would have been the prize catch of the day," Mr Fox recalled. "It was going to be an easy shot. But then I was suddenly aware of how strangely quiet everything was. Usually, you are aware of things going on around you – small fish, reeds moving – but it was all suddenly very still. Then – bang! Something huge hit me with a tremendous force on my left side, and I found myself being propelled through the water, horizontally but face down, at breakneck speed.

"In those first seconds, I didn't even think 'shark' – I was more aware of the incredible pressure on my back and chest. It felt as if my insldes on my left were being squeezed over to the other side of my body. My face mask was gone and so was the speargun. I was still holding my breath and trying to work out what was happening. My body was clamped, like in a giant vice. And then the awful, revolting realization hit me: I was in the jaws of a shark. It was gripping me like a dog with a bone. I was going die.

"I couldn't see the shark because of the way it was holding me. Its teeth had clamped themselves around my chest and back, and my left shoulder was jammed into its throat. I was being thrust along, face down, with its body behind me. You could liken me to a rag doll caught up on the fender of a speeding train. Amazingly, I still felt no pain, but the crushing feeling on my back made me want to be sick.

"Desperately, I reached my arms out behind me, searching for the shark's head in the hope of being able to gouge its eyes and force it to let go. Then the pressure suddenly eased. For some reason the shark had relaxed its jaws. I brought my right arm around to push myself away from it – and the arm went straight back into its mouth.

"Down came the teeth – and then I felt a pain I had never endured before. I was in agony, pulling with all my strength to get my arm free. I know now that those three-inch teeth are so razor sharp and those jaws so strong that they can puncture metal and grind through bones like a knife through butter. Somehow I managed to pull my arm and hand out, shredding flesh and bones as I did so.

"Now my lungs were bursting and my first thought was to get up to the surface and breathe. At that point, I didn't realize how seriously injured I was. I just wanted air. As I burst to the surface, something told me the shark would come for me again.

"I know I have said they tend not to eat humans, but this fellow hadn't had much of a taste yet. The sea was red with blood – my blood. Then my worst fears came true. A fin brushed against my flippers. It was back. Looking down, I couldn't see it through the blood, so I kicked out and hit it on its side. I can still remember how rough it felt.

"Then it was right under me and, in a desperate attempt to stay alive, I reached down and grabbed it with both arms, wrapping my legs and arms around it in the hope this would keep me away from its jaws. As I did this, I gulped in deep breaths. But, in a flash, I was dragged under again, my arms and legs still wrapped around the shark. I was about to embark on the unimaginable – a terrifying underwater joy ride on the back of killer shark.

"We went down so deep we scraped the rocks on the bottom. It was obviously trying to shake me off. It thrashed violently from side to side, and I decided to let go as I needed air again. I kicked my way to the surface.

Suddenly, the shark was up beside me, but it seemed to be toying with me, spinning over on its side, its massive body like a rolling tree trunk. For the first time I was able to make out that great conical head, and confirm that it was a white shark. I knew that, when it came for me this time, I would have no hope. I had no strength left to fight it.

"And duly it came – one quick surge forward which filled me with terror. Thoughts of Kay and our unborn baby flashed through my mind as I prepared to die. And then, incredibly, the shark veered away and grabbed at a float that was attached to me by a long line. The float was being used as a surface storage container for the fish I was spearing, but now it had become a target for the shark.

"It swallowed the float whole and then dived – taking me with it. Down and down we went, back into its dark domain once again. But I knew I could free myself – I just had to release the line with a quick-release clip on my belt. That's when a new terror overcame me. The belt had slipped around and the clip was on my back – and my arms were so weak I couldn't reach around to it. The shark was pulling me at great speed through the water, and I realized that after all I had done to stay alive, I was going to drown.

"Suddenly the line snapped. By a remarkable piece of luck, when the shark had initially gripped me around the chest, its teeth had partially severed the line and it could not withstand the strain of pulling me through the water. It took one last supreme effort to kick my way back to the surface. Everything was a blur. There was a boat at my side, my diving friends aboard. I managed to say, 'Shark.'

"Somebody said: 'Hang on mate, it's over. Hang on.'

"I don't remember much more. I heard later they were horrified to see the gaping wound in my body. My right hand and arm were so badly slashed that the bones lay bare in several places. It was a miracle that my heart, lungs or a major artery had not been severed. I needed four hundred and sixty-two stitches, but I pulled through. I remember waking after the operation and seeing Kay beside me. She was crying, but the doctor was saying, 'He'll make it now.'"

No man would ever return to the sea again after that – would he?

Rodney Fox did. Not more than five months later, he went diving again in an effort to leave his fears where he had so terrifyingly found them. Since then he has learned everything he can about the great white, and has become such an expert that he was a consultant for the film *Jaws* and goes on lecture tours. He insists they must remain a protected creature because their numbers are waning, and they are needed to balance nature, killing diseased seals and fish. He sometimes gets calls from other shark-bite survivors – mostly surfers who have been bitten on the legs and thighs – and he says most of them agree that the great white deserves protection because swimmers must accept the risks when they venture into its territory.

CROCODILE BAPTISM IN ZAMBIA

A mass baptism of adults in Zambia was unpleasantly interrupted the other day (1970) by Leviathan himself. A twelve-foot crocodile bit a candidate in the leg.

The sect took a very tolerant view of the incident and refused to try to kill one of God's creatures for merely being hungry and seeking to assuage its hunger. They did not speculate on the possibility that the reptile favoured infant baptism – though it probably now does.

There is much to be said for this tolerance. We imagine that an early Christian in the Roman arena, when a starving lion pounced on him, reflected that the animal was a fellow sufferer rather than an enemy. Nowadays we do not hesitate to destroy a whole species in unpleasant ways if we regard it as a danger or a nuisance. Equally we are ready to destroy a species for its good qualities. The elephant is ruthlessly hunted because of the quality of its tusks and because it presents an excellent target. The dodo was exterminated because it was trustful and inoffensive. But we are inclined to think that, if the dodo had defended itself with a few well-directed pecks, it would have been denounced and exterminated as a menace to human life.

ALLIGATOR AND CROCODILE BITES

Crocodiles injure people under the following circumstances: (a) when defending their territory; (b) when defending their nest; (c) in what they perceive as self-defence; (d) when predating; (e) by accident; (f) when being handled by people. Such circumstances are not mutually exclusive, of course, and the first four generally result in the death of the creature, if it is caught.

Chief among the maneating crocodilians is the saltwater crocodile, which is large in size and is widely found throughout South-east Asia, Indonesia, and northern Australia. One of the most gruesome attacks by these crocodiles occurred on Ramree Island, off the coast of Burma (now Myanmar) during the Second World War. Approximately 1,000 Japanese troops, encircled by British forces, attempted to escape by night through a mangrove swamp. In the end, under fire from the British and as a result of predation by saltwater crocodiles, only twenty Japanese survived to be taken prisoner.

As for Australia, between 1975 and 1988, there were no fewer than twelve fatal attacks by 'salties', as they are nicknamed. In December 1985, a woman standing in ankle-deep water in the Daintree River was seized by a crocodile. The affack on thirty-two-year-old Peter Relmers at Weipa in North Queensland was rather more typical. It appears that Reimer undressed on the bank of a shallow creek and entered the water for a refreshing swim. Police investigating his death found tracks nearby on the bank that indicated a large saltie had been lying there. They reckoned it slid into the water silently as soon as it saw or heard Reimers approaching. When Reimers waded into the water he must have been seized and killed by the creature.

When a saltwater crocodile is unable to swallow its prey in one piece, it will tear it into by pieces by shaking its head and neck. The body of the victim is held above the surface of the water and literally torn to pieces. When it is a large prey such as a person, the arms, legs and sometimes even the head are parted from the torso. Then the crocodile will eat the pieces. People who are searching for the remains of a crocodile victim may have to retrieve the terrible leftovers from a surprisingly wide area, even from surrounding trees.

Reports of other attacks will be found elsewhere in this book. Meanwhile, readers with access to the internet can log on to *www.xs4all.n./-mhardema/Html/docs*, where they will see an authentic-looking photograph of hunters grouped round the body of a very large crocodile. The caption reads: "This crocodile was responsible for killing two schoolgirls at Pindi Pindi, Queensland, in 1933. They disappeared on their way to school on horseback. One girl was drowned, while the body of the other was found in the crocodile's stomach."

Attacks by salties in regions other than Australia are generally under-reported. However, in the past, Indian chronicles reported hundreds of people killed by swamp crocodiles and by river gharials (*Garialis ganteticus*) each year. Gharials in the River Ganges apparently developed a taste for human as a consequence of the custom, particularly prevalent at the burning *ghats* at Benares, of throwing cremated remains and, elsewhere, whole corpses into the river.

In the floating villages of Indonesia villagers have always had to beware of "salties". In the 1960s, a missionary working in one such village in northern Irian Jaya reported that no less than sixty-two villagers had been killed or mutilated by a solitary crocodile.

Elsewhere, in Sarawak, between 1975 and 1984, six fatal and a substantial number of non-fatal attacks took place along the Lupar river. More recently nine people were killed on the small island of Siargao, near Mindanao, in the Philippines.

Attacks by alligators in Florida and elsewhere in the USA are on the increase since they were declared a protected species. In Florida, between 1973 and 1978, alligators killed six people, though many of these were what might be regarded as "provoked", rather than "unprovoked", attacks. Among unprovoked attacks was one in 1973 by a relatively small alligator which killed and partially devoured a teenager swimming at night in the Myakka River. Alligators also took the lives of a scuba diver in Wakulla County in 1987, a child in Charlotte in 1988 and a ten-year-old boy in Palm Beach County in 1993.

The writer on the website *home.att.net/-crinaustin!Croc.htm* recounts the circumstances of an attack on a colleague on the Oklawaha River, USA, in the mid-1970s:

"While checking turtle traps in the knee-deep water of a side slough, he was surprised by a large alligator After knocking him down by striking his shin with its head, it grabbed him by his armpit and started shaking. He kept beating it on its eyes and on top of its head until it finally released him. He stated later that he never saw it approach or leave. He ran his Johnboat back to the ramp, loaded it on to the trailer and drove to the nearest hospital. His injuries included a sizeable 'goose egg' on his shin and extensive shoulder wounds that required numerous stitches in both the skin and underlying muscle. Fortunately, the alligator did not sever any major blood vessels. Considering that my colleague weighed around two hundred pounds, the alligator must have been quite large. Indeed, comparison of the distance between the shoulder punctures from the alligator's upper jaw with the corresponding distance in alligator skulls at the Florida State Museum indicated that this animal was ten to twelve feet long. This attack was probably territorial or predatory in origin."

DIVING HORROR

It happened twenty-five years ago, but the image of sharks savagely attacking his diving partner and dragging him to the hazy depths of the Caribbean is as vivid in Bret Gilliam's mind today, in 1996, as it was in the days after the attack in 1971.

Gilliam wishes he *could* forget. Telling the story in its entirety for the first time, in a chilling article written for *Scuba Times* magazine, he describes that fateful day in the Virgin Islands.

Gilliam, now editor of the *Advanced Diving Journal* and president of Technical Diving International, was with Rod Temple and Robbie McIlvaine on a scientific expedition to recover samples for a research project being conducted at Cane Bay on the island of St Croix's north shore.

The plan was to inspect and to photograph the deepest project, at 210 feet, located on the wall of a steep drop-off. Temple was the dive leader and timekeeper, in charge of the paperwork and running the decompression schedule during the ascent.

But for him there would be no ascent.

"I watched his lifeless body drift into the abyss with the sharks still hitting him," Gilliam writes. And many believe that the hurried ascent made by Gilliam – from 400 feet with practically no air in his tanks – should have killed him.

Veterans of hundreds of deep dives, Gilliam, Temple and McIlvaine made their way down the wall at Cane Bay. They eventually reached the collection project – set during a previous dive – at 210 feet. As Gilliam and McIlvaine worked, Temple looked around. He spotted two white-tip sharks, one about twelve feet long and the other a bit bigger, swimming in the distance.

"This was nothing new to us, as we dove with sharks routinely," Gilliam says. "But it was rare to see these open-ocean species so close to shore."

After finishing their work, McIlvaine started up first. He spotted the sharks again, swimming over the coral and down a sandy chute. But the sharks didn't seem to be paying attention to the divers, which in itself Gilliam thought odd because he had had 'nasty encounters' with white-tips before while diving farther offshore.

"Our plan called for Rod to be the last guy up," Gilliam writes. "I rendezvoused with Robbie at about one hundred and seventy-five feet just over a ledge, and we both rested on the coral to wait for him to join us. He was late, and Robbie fidgeted, pointing to his pressure gauge, not wanting to run low on air.

"I shrugged and gave him a 'What am I supposed to do?' look, and we continued to wait. Suddenly Robbie dropped his extra gear and catapulted himself toward the wall, pointing at a mass of bubble exhaust coming from the deeper water.

"We both figured that Rod had had some sort of air failure . . . Since my air consumption was lower, I decided to send Robbie up, and I would go see if Rod needed help. As I descended into the bubble cloud, Robbie gave me an anxious OK sign and started up.

"But when I reached Rod, things were about as bad as they could get."

A twelve-foot white-tip shark had bitten into Temple's left thigh and was tearing violently at his flesh. Clouds of blood mixed in with the bubbles. The second shark appeared and made a blinding strike, ripping into Temple's calf.

Gilliam grabbed Temple by his shoulder harness and tried to pull him free. Both divers beat at the sharks with their fists, and the sharks finally let go, but only briefly.

They returned, bypassing Gilliam and striking Temple's bleeding legs. Temple had lost lots of blood and Gilliam felt Temple's body go limp in his arms. But he held on, and the divers and the sharks tumbled downward until the sharks finally ripped Temple from Gilliam's grasp, leaving Gilliam 400 feet beneath the surface, in shock and practically out of air.

"My depth gauge was pegged at three hundred and twenty-five feet, but I knew we were far deeper than that," he recalls. "The grimness of my own situation forced itself on me through a fog of narcosis and exertion.

"That's when I ran out of air. I think that subconsciously I almost decided to stay there and die. It seemed so totally hopeless, and my strength was completely sapped. But I put my head back and put all my muscles into a wide, steady power kick for the surface.

"I forced all thoughts to maintaining that kick cycle and willed myself upward. After what seemed like an eternity, I sneaked a look at my depth gauge and it was still pegged at three hundred and twenty-five feet. I sucked hard on the regulator and got a bit of a breath – not much, but it fueled my oxygen-starved brain a bit longer, and I prayed my legs would get me up shallow enough to get another breath before hypoxia – an abnormal condition caused by a decrease in oxygen to body tissue – shut down my systems for ever.

"There's really no way to describe what it's like to slowly starve the brain of oxygen in combination with adrenaline-induced survival instincts. But I remember thinking, if I could just concentrate on kicking, I could make it. After a while the sense of urgency faded, and I remember looking for the surface through a red haze that gradually closed down into a tunnel before I passed out. The panic was gone and I went to sleep, thinking, 'Damn, I almost made it.'"

Remarkably, Gilliam did make it. The small amount of air in his safety vest floated him to the surface.

"I woke up retching and expelling huge burps of air," he recalls. "But I still had to deal with an unknown amount of omitted decompression and the certainty that I was severely bent. Swimming to shore as fast as I could, I felt my legs going numb. By the time I reached the beach I could barely stand. A couple on their honeymoon waded out and dragged me up on the sand."

(McIlvaine, presuming both of his partners were dead, had already reached the beach and had gone to notify the authorities.)

"I gasped out instructions to get the oxygen unit from our van, and then I collapsed. In an incredible burst of good fortune, it turned out the wife was an [emergency room] nurse from Florida and understood the pathology of decompression sickness."

Gilliam, airlifted to a hospital in Puerto Rico, recovered and was released two days after, still numb in the legs and arms, and nearly blind in one eye. That blindness persists to this day, but in his mind he can still see – all too vividly – the sharks ripping his partner.

GATOR CHEWS TWO

Lake Worth, Florida, 22 July 1972: One of two young boys attacked by an alligator was reported in fair condition after undergoing five hours of surgery.

The attack on Patrick Parker, aged twelve, and Jeffrey Horton, aged eleven, was the second time within a week that alligators have attacked children in South Florida.

Officials said the Horton boy escaped with foot inuries, but the alligator, estimated to be ten to fourteen feet in length, chewed the Parker youth from his right shoulder to his waist on both stomach and back".

The Horton boy told Palm Beach County Sheriff's Deputy Robert Ortiz that he and Patrick were playing in a lake west of Lake Worth when the alligator attacked.

Horton made it to the bank and ran to a nearby gasoline station and asked attendant Joseph Harrison to call for help.

Earlier this week a five-footer alligator attacked a ten-year-old girl playing on the bank of a residential canal near Fort Lauderdale.

CARIBBEAN FAMILY SHIPWRECK

A mother whose life was devastated when sharks killed two of her children during a "perfect family holiday" in the Gulf of Mexico is still struggling twenty years later to come to terms family with the tragedy.

She has not been able to stand on a beach since and her hatred of sharks has remained undiminished. Mrs Horne, an American who says she relives the appalling experience every day of her life, is, with the help of wildlife experts from the American National Wildlife Foundation, trying to overcome her hatred of sharks.

On 2 July 1974, Diane and her husband Ed set off in a forty-three-foot motor boat for a 300-mile trip with their five children – Diana, fourteen, Gerald, twelve, Billy, ten, Melissa, four, and three-year-old Tex. The weather bureau had predicted a dry night with calm seas. Yet, within two hours of leaving Florida Harbour in Panama, a sudden storm smashed their boat to pieces and they were forced to leap into rough seas in pitch darkness. They managed to rope themselves together and floated about for several hours.

Diane recalled: "We felt very alone, just out there in the water and the night seemed to go on for ever."

The family, cold and exhausted, drifting in and out of sleep, were overjoyed in the early morning by the sound of a spotter plane. In their excitement they untied the rope to spread out in the water and began shouting. It was probably their biggest mistake, because the noise and disturbance alerted the sharks.

"We saw a dorsal fin, but thought it was dolphin. All of a sudden we saw a rescue boat and were hit by the sharks at the same time," recalled Diane.

The family and screaming children thrashed the water with their legs and arms in a frantic attempt to keep the sharks at bay.

One by one the twelve-foot animals went on the attack. Their first target was Billy. Spiked teeth closed on him and the sea coloured with blood as part of his arm was torn off. Diane was pushed out of the water and the shark grazed her skin. The pilot in the aircraft reported seeing masses of sharks circling the family.

The arrival of a Coast Guard vessel saved the rest of the family from certain death. Her ten-year-old son Billy was badly savaged. Diane held him in her right arm, trying to staunch the gaping wound in his right arm, but he bled to death. Three-year-old Tex later died from exposure.

In a moving postscript Mrs Horne said: "There is not a night that I have laid my head on the pillow that I haven't thought of this, but it wasn't until I got involved with the National Wildlife Foundation, which made me understand nature more, that I've been able to accept it. They weren't really out to kill someone. They were doing their thing and I was doing my thing, and the two worlds collided."

KING OF CROCS

The crocodiles of South-east Asia have always been feared for their size and maneating ferocity, but in modern times, there has not been anything quite like the *Bulang Senang*.

In September 1984 two fishermen were at the edge of the Lupar river in Sarawak, east Malaysia, when a scaly tail flailed up from the water, stunning one of the men. His friend saw an enormous reptile emerge, seize the man and drag him screaming into the river. The "King of Crocodiles" had claimed another victim.

Sarawak's deputy police commissioner duly organized a hunt for the monster which is believed to have killed and eaten at least a dozen people. Police marksmen, professional crocodile hunters and local tribesmen patrolled the river in boats for days. Like all earlier ventures, it ended without the hunters getting even a glimpse of their supposed prey.

Others, who have joined hunts for the *Bujang Senang* include an American zoologist and a witch doctor who claimed to be able to cast a spell which would bring the creature to the surface. That was no more successful than efforts to lure it with tape recordings of sounds emitted by other crocodiles.

Few have seen the monster and survived. Those who have say it has a white patch on its back and estimate its length at about twenty-five feet. Even allowing for exaggeration, that means it is probably considerably larger than any of its much feared African cousins. It is not generally realized that the estuarine or saltwater crocodile of Southeast Asia is the most fearsome of all reptiles. Along the River Lupar, people had been disappearing for years before officials decided in 1982 that they were looking for one giant maneater. Despite the toll, the local Iban tribe has some reservations about hunting the creature. Crocodiles are believed to have spiritual powers.

No such doubts afflict Jukin Bin Tapaling, a professional crocodile hunter from the neighbouring east Malaysian state of Sabah. Mr Jukin, who is not an Iban but a Kadazan, came forward last month claiming to have killed more than twenty crocodiles, some with his bare hands. He said he could take care of matters if he was given a rifle and a boat.

The only obstacle would appear to be money. Mr Jukin says a mammoth task deserves a matching price – the equivalent of £100,000. His offer has not yet been taken up.

SEARCH FOR A SHARK

A massive hunt to track down and destroy a killer shark is due to start in Port Lincoln today [5 March 1985]. Divers in the area have described it as the biggest hunt of its kind mounted in the State.

It follows the horrific attack on Sunday on Port Lincoln housewife Shirley Ann Durdin, thirty-three, who was torn in two and devoured by a six-metre white pointer [great white] shark.

A special meeting organized last night by the Port Lincoln Skin Diving Club and attended by abalone divers as well as members of the Port Lincoln Game Fishing Club, decided on the hunt. At least five vessels, including one from Adelaide, will take part in the hunt for the killer shark. The first boat is due to begin the search at about 10.30 a.m. Others will join later today.

Two large nine-metre search vessels will stay out at sea off Wiseman's Beach, north of Port Lincoln, where Mrs Durdin was taken by the shark while diving for scallops on Sunday afternoon with her husband, Barry, and a friend. The others, smaller six-metre abalone boats, will resume the search each morning. The search vessels will fan out from a series of centre points off the coast in the Port Lincoln area in a bid to lure the giant shark into a specific area.

Whale oil and tuna blood will be poured into the sea from the search vessels to attract the shark. Special shark hooks will be baited and attached to floating drums, which will act as "positive anchors" if the shark takes the bait. The bow on each vessel will be armed with shot-guns and high-velocity weapons to kill the shark if it is hooked. The fishermen, who are concerned for the safety of abalone divers oper-ating in the area, are prepared to spend several days searching for the white pointer . . .

Kevin Bruce Wiseman has lived almost half his life in a rudimentary tin shed in the idyllically set Peake Bay on the Eyre Peninsula. The fifty-eight-year-old retired fisherman has become such a familiar figure in the area that locals now refer to that stretch of white beach about thirty-five kilometres north of Port Lincoln as Wiseman's Beach. That was until Sunday, when the serenity of the picturesque bay was shat-tered by the shark attack which brought death in the afternoon to a mother of four young children.

Mrs Durdin of Lipson Place, Port Lincoln, was snorkelling for scallops with her husband of fifteen years, Barry, and a family friend when the six-metre shark struck in two-metre deep water as her three daughters and son watched from the shore 150 metres away.

"It will never be the same again," mourned Mr Wiseman. "I loved this place for its peace and quietness, but that's changed now, hasn't it? I've seen a helluva lot of sharks in my day, but I've never seen anything as big as that one. The awful thing was I could only stand there and watch and do absolutely nothing. And what is probably even worse is that that shark will be back again."

Veteran shark catcher Neville Osborn, forty-six, said: "This one now has the taste of human flesh and he'll be back." Osborn and his friend Colin Wood, fifty-two, were fishing near Wiseman's Beach on Sunday afternoon when the great shark passed within metres of their boat. It was only hours after the shark had torn Mrs Durdin in two and devoured her. The two men are now planning to hunt the shark in what they believe is one of South Australia's few remaining long-line shark boats.

A specialist in diving medicine, Dr Carl Edmonds, said the return of the shark to the area was likely. He said the attack had been made for food or to protect the shark's territory. "The likelihood of shark attacks depends on two things: how many people are in the water and how many sharks are in the water," he said. "It is a worry when something like a white pointer, which is an open-ocean shark, comes into sheltered waters. It is certainly a cause for concern." Dr Edmonds added that sharks did not eat because they were hungry; they react to stimuli such as someone flapping around on the surface.

Mr and Mrs Durdin had only recently moved back to Port Lincoln after Mr Durdin, thirty-five, suffered a number of allergies associated with work on his farm at Karkoo. Mrs Durdin had just completed a course in farm management at Port Lincoln's TAFE College. Her distraught mother-in-law said yesterday that Shirley had loved the water since childhood.

Mr Rob Kretschmer, who watched the attack from the shore, said he had to help restrain Mr Durdin from going back into the water after his wife. "The friends they had been snorkelling with had to hold him down on the rocks to stop him going back in. He was distraught and hysterical and kept saying over and over, 'My wife, she's gone, she's gone'."

A police spokesman at Port Lincoln said that there were no immediate plans to issue a general warning to the pubhc about the shark danger. Meanwhile, police combed the shoreline in search of remains of Mrs Durdin, while a local Department of Fisheries vessel searched the waters. But all that has been found is a single flipper and police have yet to ascertain whether it belonged to Mrs Durdin.

THE CROCODILE AT CAHILL'S CROSSING

As crocodile numbers continue to rise in the north of Australia, and more and more tourists flock to the Kimberleys, there must necessarily be more crocodile-human contact. It seems logical to expect more attacks in the future, though theoretically increased public awareness as a result of publicity from attacks like those of 1987 should induce more public caution.

But there will probably still be the occasional tragedy, like the one which befell Kerry McLoughlin at Cahill's Crossing on the East Alligator River, Kakadu, in March 1987.

McLoughlin was a forty-year-old storeman who worked at Jabiru. He had been in the Northern Territory twenty years or more and knew the East Alligator well. Perhaps too well. Familiarity created the unlucky situation which led to his death.

To understand what happened it is necessary to have a mental picture picture of the location.

Cahill's Crossing – named after the old King of the Territory buffalo shooters, Paddy Cahill – traverses the East Alligator river bed at the Oenpelli side and Aboriginal Arnhem Land.

It is a concrete driveway set over big, rounded river boulders and used at low water. At high tide it is flooded. The actual crossing is about 150 metres long and is comparatively narrow – fourteen feet wide, or not much more than the width of a truck. At low tide, when it is exposed, it is plain to see. But, when the tide rises above the level of the crossing, it becomes invisible under the muddy waters. The concrete also becomes dangerously slippery. There are crocodile warning signs at each end, and these used to raise a smile from knowledgeable locals.

McLoughlin had gone to the crossing with his seventeen-year-old son on 17 March 1987 to go fishing. The crossing was a favourite fishing platform with local fishermen. The prized fish was barramundi – the fish everyone in the north wants to bring home – and a good time to catch them was on the rising tide when the water began to swirl back over the crossing from the sea. At weekends there would be a row of waving fibreglass rods as anglers cast their lines and wound in their reels hoping to hook into a fine fat 'barra'.

There were also crocodiles. They had a habit of congregating downstream from the crossing at low tide. On the rising tide some of them cruised up river.

Local fishermen knew about the crocodiles. They kept an eye on them, but did not regard them as a problem. Tourists were sometimes alarmed by the sight of the crocodile visible only a little way downstream from rod fishermen up to their knees in water. The anglers thought this a bit of a joke.

The locals would laugh when concerned tourists shouted warnings. "We know all these crocs by their first names," they would reply.

On 17 March 1987, a crocodile came who was a stranger. A big animal more than sixteen feet long. McLoughlin was unaware that it was a newcomer. He was regarded as a typical tough Territorian. A man who would dive to unsnag a barramundi lure from a sunken branch without a second thought, and who regarded crocodiles with a confident grin. He was also a friendly soul and, when he saw the big crocodile passing upstream, he told some visiting American tourists about it. He knew they would like to photograph the large reptile.

When he saw some friends across the river, he had what turned out to be a fatal impulse. He waded over to say "g'day" with his fishing rod in one hand and a stubby of beer in the other. It was a normal enough thing to do, except that maybe he had left it a little late.

Once on the Oenpelli side, McLoughlin did not stay a long time, and he did not have a lot to drink. They pointed out to him what he already knew – that the tide was rising fairly rapidly over the crossing.

So with a few parting cheery remarks he began wading back again. As he reached the centre of the crossing he found that the tide was higher and was running more strongly than he had thought. But at that point he saw it as an inconvenience rather than a danger.

Then – with a curse – he missed his footing and slipped over the edge of the concrete roadway. Now he was in a different situation. He was stumbling amongst the big rounded river boulders, difficult to walk through even at low tide. With the tide now swirling between waist and chest deep (the concrete was raised half a metre above the ordinary river-bed level), McLoughlin realized that he was in difficulties.

The tourists on the bank he was making for had started yelling. From his point of view it didn't help. He knew he had a problem, and he was furiously aware that he was making a spectacle of himself.

He tried hard to return to the crossing and regain his footing. But the surging tide pushed him farther away. There was nothing for it now but to head for the bank, wet and bedraggled. Bloody nuisance! What were all those idiots on the bank yelling about?

The group of elderly American tourists he had spoken to earlier on the bank saw McLoughlin in the water. Having no local knowledge, they couldn't understand why he was there at all. They had photographed the crocodile and knew how big it was. They could not comprehend the lack of concern of the local fishermen who said, "The crocs are always there. Don't worry, mate. They're OK."

But for once, it wasn't OK. The big crocodile, who had been causing some disturbances – "humbugging" the Aborigines called it – with the smaller crocodiles below the crossing, was new to the East Alligator system. Rangers later believed that he had been driven out from some-where else and was looking to establish himself in a new territory. He was in a cranky mood.

As McLoughlin struggled, waist-deep, toward the bank the large crocodile became alert, attracted by the splashing. It began to cruise upstream to investigate the source of the sound.

Now even the locals became concerned.

The tourists began to frantically throw sticks and stones at the crocodile. As the crocodile passed McLoughlin, people screamed and yelled. It went a little way past him, assessing the situation, then turned back purposefully towards him.

Now it became a race.

McLoughlin by this time had heard the shouts of "crocodile!" and understood the danger. As he splashed toward the bank, a man trying too hard and out of breath, it seemed to the horrified watchers to be a tragedy happening in slow motion.

"It was all so needless," said Everett Galbraith, a sixty-three-year-old American tourist. "We saw the crocodile and yelled to the man to get out of the water. But he didn't."

In fact, McLoughlin was doing his best. But with his wet clothes, the current drag and the rough bottom, it was hard to make progress.

The crocodile submerged. In what some people saw as a final gesture of defiance – but which may also have been an intelligent attempt to distract his tormentor – the hunted man hurled his stubby of beer at the spot where the crocodile had gone down.

Then, probably knowing how hopeless it was, he tried again to reach the shore. To the huge relief of the watchers he actually reached the bank by some rocks ahead of the crocodile and some distance above the crossing. Gasping for breath he began to pull himself up and out of the water by a branch.

But, just when it seemed he might be saved, the crocodile leaped, bursting through the surface. The tourists, who had been throwing stones and branches, stopped and stood appalled as the huge jaws flashed and closed across McLoughlin's head and shoulders.

"There was a hard slap," Galbraith said. "Then there was nothing. It was all quite still."

With that first bite and roll the crocodile tore his head off and decapitated McLoughlin. Then it seized the twitchiug body in the blood-stained water and swam away upstream to be lost to view around the bend.

The watchers (who included McLoughlin's seventeen-year-old son Michael, frozen with a can of soft drink in his hand) stood numbed in horror.

"It was all so fast," Galbraith said. "And yet so slow. I could just visualize what was going to happen. I had a three-metre stick and tried to get to him. But he was too far away and it all happened so fast. Afterwards, after all the yelling and shouting, it went quite still. Just nothing, as people realized what had happened. It was bizarre."

The rangers at the nearby Kakado National Parks and Wildlife were called at once and a boat was launched at a ramp just south of the crossing and sent out after the crocodile.

It was found in the mangroves a little distauce upstream, still with McLoughlm's limp body clutched triumphantly in its jaws.

The rangers fired aud scored a definite hit, the animal convulsed, dropped the body and disappeared.

"Unfortunately we were never able to tell whether we killed it or just wounded it," said ranger superintendent Clive Cook. "It was disappointing. Usually, if they're wounded, they go up on the bank and stay out of the water. If they're dead, they float after four or five days. This one was different. We kept boat patrols out, but we never saw him again. You couldn't blame the crocodile. But we felt it was necessary to preempt local vigilante groups taking the law into their own hands as happened in Queensland. It wasn't a crocodile that had been seen in the area before, and if it survived it hasn't been seen since."

"Our main role in Kakadu," he said, "is to manage the people. The crocodiles look after themselves quite well. McLoughlin was a local. He'd been in the area a long time and had become accustomed to a prior situation where crocodiles were comparatively rare and there wasn't the kind of danger we have today. He was unfortunate. He was caught by a number of related minor things which went wrong and suddenly found himself in a situation he hadn't expected. Also he was obviously very, very unlucky that there was a big crocodile strange to the area which was hungry at that moment. Most times he would have got away with it."

DOMINICAN BOAT DISASTER

Rescue workers on Wednesday, 8 October 1987, began recovering the corpses of dozens of refugees who were thrown from a capsized vessel and drowned or were torn apart by sharks, authorities said in Santo Domingo.

More than 100 of the estimated 160 Dominicans, possibly attempting illegal entry into the United States, aboard the forty-foot boat bound east toward Puerto Rico were missing and presumed dead after the Tuesday disaster, said Eugenio Cabral, Dominican civil defence director. The overcrowded vessel left Nagua, about sixty miles north of the capital on the Atlantic coast, early on Tuesday. The boat caught fire when its motor exploded and it capsized in the tumult of attempts to douse the flames.

Five civil defence boats and several fishing boats resumed a search for survivors at daybreak on Wednesday. Three bodies were recovered, and Luis Rolon, civil defence director for San Juan, said eighteen women and four men were in hospital suffering from cuts, bruises, shock and burns. The remaining thirty-five were rescued unharmed.

Rolon said a female survivor interviewed by a radio station said the vessel's captain was intoxicated during the incident, and gas canisters aboard the boat spilled at the time of the explosion, spreading the flames.

Between forty and fifty sharks attacked the survivors as they clung to the wreckage or floated after currents pulled them twenty miles off shore, said Rolon, who accompanied Cabral on his flight. Rescuers in helicopters and fishermen in small boats pulled some survivors from the water amid the shark attack, Cabral said.

Ernesto Uribe, public affairs officer at the US Embassy in Santo Domingo, said he saw pictures of the accident scene taken from a civil defence aircraft and that numerous sharks could be seen circling bodies and survivors. "It was big herd of sharks. It was an awful sight."

Many Dominicans attempt the ninety-mile crossing of the treacherous Mona Passage to Puerto Rico. One survivor told authorities that passengers had paid the boat's operators from $200 to $600 to make the trip . . .

ITALIAN JAWS

Unprovoked shark attacks in the Mediterranean – especially fatal ones – are seldom widely reported in the media because, of course, it might scare the millions of tourists who go to the region for their seaside holidays.

The shark hunt is on. In the usually peaceful waters off the coast of Tuscany a small army of amateurs and professionals are searching for a twenty-foot killer shark that last week devoured a scuba diver, Luciano Costanzo, aged forty-seven.

The shark was seen by two people as it attacked its victim. They both identified it as a white shark, of the same family as the star of the film *Jaws*. Signor Costanzo was diving to examine undersea electricity cables in the Bay of Baratti, near Piombino. On a small motor-launch was his son, Luca, and Signor Paolo Bader, a friend. They say the shark attacked several times and then dragged its victim underwater. A search later found only small pieces of the body and torn fragments of his wet suit.

The actual hunt is without spectacular heroics. A police launch is searching with an underwater television camera, but it has a range of a couple of yards only.

Yesterday a shark cage was finally obtained and frogmen of the fire brigade are being slowly towed around in it. They also hope to find further remains of Signor Costanzo. His friends and colleagues have been trying to search for the shark themselves by diving normally, but have been stopped by the police.

Signor Carlo Gasparri, an expert diver who was once world spearfishing champion, is using a giant "mousetrap" baited with a dead sheep and claims that, if the shark is still around, it will not escape. He is also using huge steel fish-hooks with live fish as bait on a vertical line chained to anchored buoys.

As the hunt continues, the waterfront of the sleepy village of Baratti is becoming crowded with visitors. At the weekend small groups and families came with sandwiches and binoculars as the weather became unseasonably warm. There was not a single scuba diver to be seen.

Some of the anchored, baited hooks placed in the sea to catch the twenty-foot great white shark being hunted off the Tuscany coast have been torn from their moorings, it was discovered yesterday. In the hunt for the shark that killed a scuba diver last week, police divers have found the victim's air-tanks, his face mask and his ballast belt. The lead weights on his belt showed clearly the shark's teeth marks.

A number of residents along the coast between Piombino and San Vicenzo have claimed sightings of the maneater before and since the attack.

The hunt for the maneating great white shark off the coast of Tuscany has developed into a confused free-for-all involving the Italian Coast Guard, the Carabinieri, the fire brigade, a number of helicopters and "avengers" who want to dive with anti-shark guns.

The normally placid waters of the Gulf of Baratti are being chopped up by hovering helicopters and cruising launches. The search for the remains of Luciano Costanzo was officially called off two days ago after recovermg only some of the victim's equipment and a few small fragments of flesh. But the search for his killer, said to be twenty-five feet long, has begun in earnest. Until yesterday only baited hooks and a kind of giant steel mousetrap, using a dead sheep as bait, had been used so as not to obstruct the search for remains.

The official co-ordinator of the hunt is Signor Carlo Gasparri, an expert diver. "There is no need for helicopters," he said. "Sharks are hunted with baited hooks and that's all. The rest is all nonsense."

Clearly, however, several would-be shark killers do not agree and, as they hunt their quarry, curious onlookers can be seen all around the bay, keeping watch with binoculars, cameras and sandwiches. The authorities receive several reports of sightings every day from different points on the coast.

It seems the whole of Italy has suddenly become shark mad. Most newspapers have reporters permanently on the spot and print interviews with shark experts around the world. Each television news bulletin has the latest report on the situation, and it is not unusual to hear housewives, barmen, barbers and taxi drivers giving impromptu conferences on the migratory and feeding habits of Carcharodon carcharias, the lethal great white.

Off the Tunisian coast fishermen reportedly caught a twenty-one-foot thresher shark on Saturday. The species has not been seen there for thirteen years. The fishermen cut open their prize to see if it might have been the wanted fish, but found no such evidence.

The only people not enthralled by the great shark hunt are the inhabitants of resort villages around Piombino. They fear the affair is being overplayed and will ruin the tourist trade this summer.

CALIFORNIA'S BAY AREA

On a quiet day at the Farallon Islands a great white shark tried to eat scuba diver LeRoy French of Concord. "I could feel his mouth around my body and then he chomped me," French said. "When his teeth bit into my metal air tank, he let me go."

Last fall, also at the Farallons, a giant shark grabbed diver Mark Tiserand of San Francisco by the leg and dragged him off, as if looking for a quiet spot for a meal. "He was swimming off with me so fast I could feel the water rushing past," Tiserand recalled.

Last week, twenty-five yards off the beach near Jenner, Rodney Orr of Santa Rosa was knocked off his paddle board, then got a close look at some pearly whites. "My head was in its mouth, I could see the teeth."

Episodes like these are making the Bay Area coast the shark attack centre of the world. A search through this paper's files reveals there have been more than fifty shark incidents recorded off the Bay Area alone, though most receive little attention in the media. French, Tiserand and Orr all survived by fighting off their attacker. French and Tiserand had their lives saved when they were airlifted by helicopters to hospitals for emergency surgery. French ended up with a scar that runs four feet down his side, Tiserand with shark teeth souvenirs that doctors removed from his leg. Orr just about had his head bitten off, but escaped with big gashes around his left eye and neck. The shark lost interest when Orr clubbed him with his spear gun.

Waters off the Bay Area coast have sharks of mind-boggling size. In one fifty-minute period at the Farallon Islands, scientist Peter Klimely of Scripps Institute chummed up and tagged three different great whites that were all seventeen feet long. A few years back, at Ano Nuevo State Reserve in San Mateo County, a shark measuring nineteen feet and weighing an estimated 5,000 lbs washed up on the beach. That is as big as the one in the movie *Jaws*.

After a career of studying sharks, scientist John McCosker of the Steinhart Aquarium in San Francisco has identified the zone where the attacks are most common. "I call it the Red Triangle," said McCosker, who has travelled throughout the world to study maneaters. The Triangle is bordered by Ano Nuevo to the south, the Farallon Islands twenty-five miles out to sea to the west and Tomales Bay to the north.

Both Ano Nuevo and the Farallons are breeding grounds for elephant seals, and the young 200-pound pups make perfect meals for the big sharks. The mouth of Tomales Bay, meanwhile, is believed to be a breeding ground for great whites.

Anywhere near the Triangle, it may be foolish to spearfish, dive for abalone, surf, swim or kayak. Yet these sports remain popular because months can go by without an incident – and also because the history of danger is unpublicized. Yet the attacks just keep happening. In January a shark knocked surfer Sean Sullivan of Pacifica off his surfboard, leaving bite marks in the board. Sullivan reportedly escaped by getting back on his board and surfing into the beach with the shark chasing him.

I never gave the idea of a shark eating me any thought until a fall day about ten years ago. I had arrived at Pigeon Point lighthouse, where there are a few secluded coves nearby that are ideal for body surfing, but this time there was a crowd at the beach. It turned out that an abalone diver had just been bitten in half and killed at the exact spot I was planning to swim that day.

Since then there have been many other episodes. While fishing at the Farallon Islands with Abe Cuanang, the boat anchored, our depth finder was reading the bottom as ninety feet deep. Suddenly it was reading sixty-five feet, then fifty feet. It made no sense.

Then, all at once, it did make sense. "It's the Big Guy," Cuanang shouted. The Big Guy in this case was a great white so large under the boat that it was registering as the bottom of the ocean on the depth finder.

The same week Ski Ratto of Pacifica was fishing in his seventeen-foot Boston Whaler when he sensed "something was looking at me". Ratto looked behind him and a great white four feet across at the head, possibly longer than the boat, was on the surface, and it was indeed looking at him. "I started the engine and got the hell out of there."

Ever since these episodes I have not been one to dangle my legs over the side of the boat or body surf, abalone dive or anything else that means being in the water with the Big Guy. As long as other people do, it is inevitable that every once in a while someone will be attacked by a shark.

BRAZIL SHUDDERS OVER KILLER CROCS

One cannot help wondering whether the fears expressed below in 1991 have proved justified over the intervening years.

Scientists with an interest in Latin America's flora and fauna are appalled, but for once their outrage has nothing to do with the felling of trees in the Amazon. The latest row to engulf the beleaguered government of Brazil is over its importation of maneating African crocodiles.

Brazilians were told when 110 Nile crocodiles were flown from Zimbabwe to a high-security compound in Osorio, in Brazil's deep south, eighteen months ago. A private company there plans to breed them to export their skins, which are of better quality than those of indigenous species. But word soon got out, and before long the government was being accused of environmental recklessness. There were dire warnings of a repeat of the killer bees catastrophe, caused when imported African bees escaped from a Brazilian breeder in São Paulo. The swarm headed north to Mexico, killing hundreds of people along the way.

Local ecologists insist that eventually some of the Nile crocodiles, which can grow to twenty-one feet in length and weigh a tonne, are bound to escape. They fear the crocodiles will find it easy to breed in the swampy land around Porto Alegre, where the farm is situated. Then, the scientists warn, they will reproduce, migrate, and eventually overwhelm rival, less ferocious South American beasts.

Nile crocodiles, made famous in Tarzan movies, are among the world's most dangerous predators, killing dozens of people in Africa each year. They have been known to stalk humans, often women washing clothes along a river bank, finally charging forward to seize their prey in powerful jaws. Scientists who met in an emergency congress in Brazil last October concluded that though the farm might be secure now, precautions could relax in future years, especially if the farm is sold or if the world price for Nile crocodile skins currently £150 drops.

Brazil's version of the crocodile, known as the caiman, of which there are seven species in South America, is a relatively timid creature and does not have a reputation as a maneater. In comparison with the

Nile crocodile, Florida's alligators and South America's caimans are "pussycats", said one crocodile expert.

Some Brazilian officials privately admit the country's Environmental Protection Agency made a mistake in granting the import licence. The body has been besieged by letters and telexes from scientists around the world. Last month, after a long crusade by locals to prevent it, the farm was also given a seal of approval by the state government. Now the campaigners say they will go to court to force the owners to send the crocodiles back.

"We have nothing against breeding in captivity, but we cannot allow the introduction of species which place Brazilian lives at risk," said Luis Felipe Kunz, vice-president of the local environmental association.

Critics of the Brazilian project include the World Wide Fund for Nature and the governments of neighbouring Paraguay, Peru and Colombia, which are fearful of invasion by the killer crocodiles.

The farm's owners, saying they do not understand what the fuss is about, have insisted that they are complying strictly with Brazilian environmental regulations. They are breeding up to 3,000 crocodiles, which are kept in a high security compound.

The owners say the farm's double-walled enclosures and other security features make escape impossible. But environmentalists point out that similar guarantees were made by the Brazilian bee-keeper who first brought the African killer bees to Brazil in 1956.

"They're going to get out," said one crocodile specialist, "and they're going to change the whole way people here relate to water."

SOUTH AUSTRALIAN WATERS

An experienced diver told yesterday [8 September 1991] how he heard a "thunderous roar" when his diving partner was taken by a shark off Aldinga Beach. Off-duty police officer Mr Dave Roberts watched in horror underwater as the shark he estimated was four metres in length careered past him thrashing its head about.

"I could not see him, but I knew the shark had my buddy," Mr Roberts said. "The thunderous noise was so loud I couldn't hear anything else."

A police spokesman said the dead man "had no warning. He was literally taken in one big grab."

The dead man, nineteen, of One Tree Hill, was a student at the University of Adelaide and was the ninth person to die in a shark attack in South Australian waters. Police have not released his name.

The shark, which Mr Roberts believes was a white pointer [great white], took the young diver about 350 metres off Snapper Point, the main look-out at Aldinga Beach, at about 3 p.m. yesterday. The man was diving with a group of other students and members of the Adelaide University Skindiving Club in eighteen metres of water at a popular skindiving spot called the Drop Off. Three other people, including Mr Roberts, were in the water in the vicinity of the tragedy, but no one else was attacked. Four others who had been part of the diving group had climbed aboard their boat minutes earlier.

By nightfall yesterday police had recovered the dead man's air tank, his diving finds and a small part of his body. The search was called off at dark, but will resume at first light today. The tank's rubber hose, which led to the mouthpiece, was severed.

Mr Roberts, a senior constable in the police prosecuting branch, said the group was on its second dive of the day and he and his "buddy" (a diving term for partner) were returning to their boat when the shark struck.

"We were heading back to the boat, which was not far ahead of us, when I looked back at him and everything was all right," Mr Roberts recalled. "I turned back and went down to have a look at this colourful rock, and then suddenly heard this thunderous noise. I turned again and saw the shark. It was close to me and it was thrashing its head around. The noise was very loud. It was like a boat crashing over waves on top of you. The whole bottom was dusted up. The shark kept thrashing from side to side. I couldn't make him out clearly, but I knew he was there. I hung around and took a defensive position behind the rock and it moved away. It came within one and a half feet of me as it went past. It didn't look at me. It just took my buddy first – just dragged him past me as I was behind the rock. It was totally unexpected – you just never see them out there. I don't know if I'll dive again – this scared the life out of me."

Yesterday's dive had lasted about twenty minutes before the attack and had followed fourteen other dives by about thirty club members who were spending the day at Aldinga Beach. Ben Petersen, eighteen Aldgate, was first back to the boat and had helped three others into it when he suddenly heard screaming. "It was Dave Roberts screaming out 'Shark', so I pulled the anchor up and we drove the boat over to him," Mr Petersen said. "A tank, fins and other diving equipment floated by. We got Dave into the boat and he was saying a four-metre shark had come up and grabbed his mate."

Veteran Mr Rodney Fox recalled last night how he was attacked in the same place in 1963: "It's an interesting place to dive – lots of fish gather there near a big drop off the reef." Mr Fox had been defending his title as SA spear fishing champion when a white pointer hurled him through the water. He escaped after gouging its eyes and snout. Once he reached the surface he realized his chest was badly mutilated. Although he needed eighty-seven stitches, Mr Fox became fascinated with white pointers and continues to research them. Mr Fox continued with his sport and became involved in the making of several shark-attack movies, including *Jaws*, the Emmy-award-winning *Mysteries of the Sea*, and the South Australian Film Corporation's *Caged in Fear* television special. He is also a consultant to the Cousteau Society.

HAWAIIAN HOLIDAY

A Vancouver doctor who was swimming with a friend while on vacation in Hawaii says that she tried to fight off a 4.5-metre Pacific tiger shark with a piece of driftwood minutes before her friend was attacked and killed.

Maui County police Sergeant Waldo Fujie said that Dr Luise Sourisseau, of West 14th Avenue, Vancouver, and her friend were swimming near Lahaina one morning last week [November 1991] when they noticed a shark which they said was the size of a car swim by. Sourisseau froze and was brushed by the shark, but her friend Martha Morrell, forty-one, of Lahaina, was attacked and killed after she panicked and started thrashing around in the water.

"When you splash in the water with any wild animal or predator, they could attack," Fujie said. He added that Sourisseau hit the shark with a piece of driftwood which she saw floating in the water, but was eventually forced to swim to safety while it was attacking Morrell.

The two women had been swimming in front of the Morrells' beach front home. A maid saw the attack and made the initial call to the emergency line.

Fujie said that sharks have been known to frequent that area for feeding during the night. Hawaiian police said that it was the first witnessed shark attack resulting in death in the last thirty-three years. "It is rare for this to happen. You could get into a car accident quicker than a shark attack."

The dead woman's body was recovered with limbs missing. Fujie said one shark was instrumental in the attack, but, since then, there have been reports of at least two or three in the area.

May Sourisseau said her daughter is still in Hawaii with friends, trying to recover from the attack. "It's been very upsetting for her." She added that her daughter, who did not want to be interviewed, said that she had initially thought the shark was a dolphin.

KILLER GATOR

A family canoe outing ended in tragedy on 20 June 1993, when a ten-year-old boy was killed by a ten-foot alligator which grabbed him while he was with his parents and kept him under water for five minutes.

Bradley Weidenhammer, of Lantana, Florida, was helping his parents pull their canoe over a log and was knee-deep in water when the alligator grabbed him and bit into the right side of his head before dragging him under water.

Jim Wardle, deputy sheriff for Martin County, said the boy's father tried to pull his son free. Bradley's body was recovered only after several adults on nearby boats began hitting the alligator with paddles. The family had been visiting the Jonathan Dickinson State Park, Florida, with a group of children. Bradley was airlifted to hospital, but was pronounced dead on arrival.

Alligators are a common sight in the park, a popular spot for weekend trips. Attacks on humans are common in Florida, although deaths are rare. When alligators begin mating in the spring they become aggressive, as males mark their territory and females later protect their young.

WELSH STINGRAY ATTACK

A man will have to undergo plastic surgery after being attacked [in July 1994] by a stingray while fishing on a Welsh beach.

Bob Dix, aged fifty-one, a fireman from Cambridge, was helping another angler to land the fish during a competition in Borth, Dyfed.

Another man kicked the stingray's wings and it spun round and lashed Mr Dix's leg with its venomous tail. It sliced through his wellington boot and clothing, inflicting an inch-deep wound.

Mr Dix was detained at a hospital in Aberystwyth for two days, and will require skin grafts.

The stingray, which was five feet long and estimated to weigh forty pounds was judged to be the largest fish of the two-day competition. It was released back into the sea.

Mr Dix said: "We decided to let it go without bringing it in to weigh it. It was a vicious attack."

Oliver Crimmen, fish curator of the Natural History Museum, said it was rare to find stingrays in shallow water, although they were fairly common further off the coast.

TANZANIAN SAURIANS

A team led by Dr A. Fazil with Shiomi Ranot, Ofer Kubi and five staff members of Clal Crocodile Farms Int. Ltd. (CCF) conducted surveys and interviews in rural Tanzania from 10 December 1994 to 14 February 1995. The aims of the mission were to clarify information on human mortality from crocodile attacks and the effect of crocodile populations in rural areas.

Working with 4 x 4 trucks and a boat, and camping along selected rivers and lakes for up to two weeks, the team interviewed local villagers, chiefs, and administrators by day and conducted spotlight surveys by night. Approximately 1,000 kilometres of rivers, swamps and lake shores were covered. including the Lower Rufiji between Mpanga and Utete, Kilombero and Kibasira swamps between Mlimba and Ifakara, the south-eastern shore of Lake Rukwa, Ruvu River from Ruvu to the sea, and sections of the Wami and Pangani rivers. Further surveys of the Ruvuma River and Lake Nyasa are planned following the rainy season.

Preliminary data analysis confirms information from previous surveys. Crocodile densities of around three kilometres were recorded in protected areas in the Rufiji, Lake Rukwa and lower Pangani. A preponderance of very large individuals up to twenty feet (six metres) were noted.

The interviews with local people indicated that previous quantification of the problems of human mortality from crocodiles are underestimates and the scope of this problem in rural areas is quite shocking. For example the village of Mpanga on the upper Kilombero river with about sixty-five families lost eight people (five of them children) last year and an additional three people were taken in the last two months!

Similar high levels were recorded from other villages and as far as we know, no other country in the world suffers similar crocodile fatalities. Detailed analysis of the data is in preparation. The causes of this appalling mortality arise in part from the widely dispersed, but dense rural population along rivers and lakes. The Government has disarmed local people and maintains extensive anti-wildlife poaching units in each region, so that the people fear the crocodiles and also fear to break the law and kill them.

CCF has reached a comprehensive agreement with the Tanzanian Wildlife Management Authority to establish a proper Management Programme for crocodiles in the country. Following this survey, recommendations have been made by CCF to the Tanzanian authorities which include improving the ranching programme in the country. Opening farming to overseas investors and the creation of a National Farmers Association will assist in the transfer of know-how to develop the industry. Egg and hatchling collection centres organized and monitored by the regional wildlife offices, and with income from egg collection returned to local communities are proposed. The existing National Parks and Game Reserves are proposed as crocodile sanctuaries with only limited and carefully supervised egg collection based on continued monitoring.

To control crocodiles outside the Parks, hunting conducted by local communities and regulated by regional wildlife wardens is proposed, but restricted to crocodiles over eight feet length. Skins resulting from the proposed harvest will be tagged and recorded at local wildlife stations before being transferred to licensed dealers . . .

MUGGERS IN NEPAL

Crocodile ranching may offer the best hope of preserving the mugger crocodile. IUCN set up such a program in 1995 in Nepal.

Once the wild populations in the country's southern zone have been stabilized by releasing captive bred muggers, local people will be allowed to collect eggs or hatchlings and sell them back to the breeding facility. When these crocs grow large enough to survive in the wild, they will be released. Other crocodiles bred and reared at the facility will be sold to private ranchers in the area.

This scheme offers a winning strategy for all: ongoing reintroductions benefit the mugger; fishermen earn money by selling eggs to the breeding facility; hatchlings sold to ranchers generate income for the facility to pay for crocodile studies and local education programs; and ranchers make money by rearing hatchlings and selling the leather.

This approach also discourages poaching, since all the hatchlings are processed through the facility, and private ranchers will be granted skin permits only for the number of animals they are known to have. Skins from wild crocodiles are generally low quality compared to those supplied by ranchers. This further discourages poachers since only quality skins can find a market. If checks reveal that a rancher has animals without ID numbers, unlogged mortalities or excess skins, a heavy punishment could result.

It would be nice to believe that the mugger could be preserved simply by leaving them alone, but the mugger's situation offers a rare opportunity to forge a new relationship. Rather than people exploiting the species to its end, a cycle of sustainable use can benefit humans, mugger populations and their habitat, as well as a plethora of economically valueless, but biologically significant, species dependent on wetlands.

THE SURF IN BRAZIL

A dramatic increase in shark attacks is threatening local surfers and the economy in Recife, a popular resort in north-east Brazil. Despite a ban on surfing, a shark claimed another life last month. International shark experts will meet in Brazil in November to study the problem.

Local surfers and fishermen say they cannot remember any shark attacks off the palm-fringed beaches of Recife before 1992. Then, suddenly, they started. In 1994 alone, there were eleven attacks along a ten-kilometre stretch of coast. The sharks go mainly for surfers, though three swimmers have also been attacked, all of them outside the coral reef which shelters most of the beaches.

Researchers believe that surfers are more susceptible to shark attacks because of the movements they make on the surface of the water while waiting for waves, and because they spend more time in deep water.

The first response of the local government was to put up signs in Portuguese and English which said: "Surfers, be cool! Respect natural boundaries. Do not go beyond the reef." But the signs neglected to mention sharks. Local oceanographer Favio Hazin accused the government of "hiding its head in the sand". Locals began spray-painting sharks on to the signs, and surfers held a protest on the beach, complete with a bloody, mauled mannequin.

When the new state government came into power in January [1995], it promptly banned surfing and bolstered Hazin's shark research efforts at the Federal Rural University of Pernambuco. Since the crisis began, Hazin's team have caught more than 200 sharks in order to study their behaviour and life cycle. The shark meat is donated to feed hungry local children. Meanwhile, police have begun patrolling the beaches, confiscating boards from surfers who defy the ban.

"What is happening in many areas of the world is that aquatic recreation is beginning to take off, and so shark attacks are more frequent," says George Burgess, director of the International Shark Attack File at the University of Florida in Gainesville, USA. The recent spate of shark attacks off popular beaches in Hong Kong supports this view. However, Brazilian surfers have been holding championships off the beaches near Recife since the 1970s, so the increase in surfing cannot entirely explain the sudden surge of shark attacks.

In a preliminary unpublished report, Hazin and his colleagues point an accusing finger at the port of Suape, built in 1989 just south of the three beaches where most of the attacks have occurred. The port may be bringing people and sharks into closer contact, they say. The researchers found a correlation between months when there are more passing ships, and months when there are shark attacks. Sharks are known to follow big ships, especially if sailors are dumping rubbish overboard. Hazin's team has found an onion, a pineapple and a can of beer in the stomachs of local sharks.

From the imprint in a bite-shaped piece of styrofoam bodyboard, the biologists have identified one of the culprits as a bull shark, although there is also evidence that tiger sharks are responsible for some attacks.

The Brazilians are now seeking advice on whether to install safety nets around the beaches of Recife . . . Educating local surfers to avoid going out at dawn and dusk, when the sharks are most active, to avoid water where there are birds diving and fish jumping, and to avoid channels where sharks tend to congregate may all help.

This type of advice, however, may simply be water off a surfer's back. "Those surfers who get bitten by sharks here wear their scars as a badge of honour," says Burgess "The more dangerous they think it is, the more attractive surfing is for some people," says Hazin. "I try to emphasize that they're not only risking their lives, they're damaging the state economy."

BENIN'S CROCODILES AND PYTHONS

During 1965–72 I operated a wildlife collection business in Dahomey (now Benin) and in this period I saw not one African slender snouted crocodile *(Crocodylus cataphractus)* despite travelling weekly up the Oeme river past the Zou branch, the Zou every other week, the Couffo and the Mono river along the Togo border about once every couple of months and the hyacinth-choked Okpara occasionally.

I collected many West African dwarf crocodiles *(Osteoleamus tetraspis),* for which I had to compete with the food market. One of the dwarfs I shipped in the 1960s died recently at the Brookfield Zoo at a recorded length of eight feet, a giant dwarf! Nile crocs were also plentiful, but less in demand for local cuisine, but I avoided collecting *niloticus* in the Mono river region.

The Mono is the centre of a small animist tribe of crocodile worshippers. Once a year a new-born baby, sired by the crocodile priest with a different young maiden each year whose high honour is to be chosen to bear the child, is sacrificed to appease a rather large *niloticus* river god, thus assuring a good catch of fish for the coming year.

I had many orders for juvenile *cataphractus* and put out the word that I would purchase these. Maurice Abelanski, the noted French crocodile hunter, based at the time in Bohicon, Dahomey, shipped hundreds of *niloticus* hides to France each year, but did not recount ever seeing any *cataphractus*. In nearly seven years of collecting in the wetlands of southern Dahomey, of which five days a week were spent in good crocodile habitat, I neither saw nor heard of any cataphractus in the region. Nor did I see any *cataphractus* skulls for sale in the local markets where there were usually *niloticus* and *Osteoleamus* parts availabe.

On an unrelated note, ball or royal python *(Python regius)* worship, whose main temple and python high priest are in Ouidah, Dahomey (the python Vatican so to speak), is an early example of sustainable use and conservation. Grain is stored by villagers in granaries raised on stilts. Rodents are a persistent problem. For at least the last 600 years pythons have been venerated as gods, with local priests exhorting villagers to bring them into the villages as sacred animals where they are kept in a kind of religious farming. No python worshipper would ever harm a ball python or think of eating one. The village python collections and their offspring keep the rodent population down and protect the village grain stores. The python cult is so strong that the Portuguese in the seventeenth century built a cathedral directly across the square from the python temple. Sustainable use may be a difficult concept for some today, but the Dahomeans in their corner of Africa have been practicing species protection through value for hundreds of years to their advantage and that of the pythons.

CROCODILE ATTACKS IN MADAGASCAR

The following information was collected through regional water and forest representatives, and there is no reason to doubt its veracity. In fact it is certainly an underestimation. The most detailed reports show that many times people are caught by crocodiles (by a foot and sometimes by the hands) while crossing a river, washing or collecting water. The accidents are reported to occur mainly between 4 p.m. and 6 p.m., "the time at which women are collecting water and people in general coming back from the fields". The attacks are happening mainly between November and March (hot season). The following summary is collected from detailed reports of individual attacks which specify year, district, locality and information on the victim.

Summary: Reported attacks and deaths due to crocodiles in Madagascar between 1990 and 1996

Year	Deaths	Reported attacks
1990	14	27
1991	7	18
1992	11	22
1993	5	16
1994	8	23
1995	12	34

The population usually try to kill the crocodile, but most of the time they fail in getting them. The comments given during the collecting of information were almost always the same:

- The local populations request the extermination of these dangerous animals;
- The local authorities request at least to bring down the numbers of crocodiles;
- The agents of the management authority facing extreme difficulties, if not impossibilities, to take any action for preservation of animals considered as nuisances, recommend the opening of legal hunting to regulate the numbers of animals.

HONG KONG SWIMMING IN BLOOD

A second man has died in a suspected shark attack in Hong Kong, sparking fears that a killer shark was stalking the annual 1995 Dragon Boat Festival which drew huge crowds to the colony's beaches on Friday.

A police spokeswoman said that the latest victim, identified as Herman Lo Cheuk-Yuet, was swimming with friends off Sheung Sze Wan beach in the New Territories when he was dragged under and mauled. "He was attacked by a giant fish about six to seven feet long," said the spokeswoman, declining to call it a shark. "The right leg was eaten by the fish. The left leg was wounded."

Lo, twenty-eight, was helped to shore by friends and rushed to hospital, but was dead on arrival. He was the second victim in two days, and shark experts think the same shark could be responsible for this and other fatal attacks in the same area this time every year.

On Thursday Tso Kam-Sun, forty-four, who once represented Hong Kong in swimining at the Asian Games, was found dead in his diving suit off nearby Sai Kung beach with his right leg cleanly severed. Police could not confirm that Tso was killed by a shark.

Australian shark expert Vic Hislop, who came to Hong Kong two years ago after a number of fatal shark attacks, said the shark was a repeat killer and warned of more attacks on the way. "Every year it's been the same," Hislop told government radio. "This time we are aware to it and we've been notified on the 1st of June of the first attack . . . so you've probably got about three weeks before that shark will be in your area. Something could be done about it."

The Government recently installed shark-proof nets at a number of key beaches.

The latest attack came as huge crowds came out to the beaches on Friday, a local holiday, many to participate in the annual Dragon Boat races, a traditional festival which celebrates a legendary sea rescue. According to the legend, a minister expelled from high office tried to commit suicide by throwing himself into a river; fishermen had to beat the water furiously with their paddles to prevent him from being eaten by fish.

ANDAMAN ISLANDS' SALTIES

The Andaman Islands off India's east coast were surveyed in 1975 and 1976 by Rom Whitaker, who estimated the population at fifteen breeding females and 100–200 crocodiles. Later studies by Choudhury and Bustard in 1979 reported thirty nests and thirty-nine crocodiles. No crocodiles have been released under restocking programmes as it was thought that this population would recover and stabilize following the ban on hunting in 1972.

During November and December 1993 a survey of North Andaman Island and the northern part of Middle Andaman was conducted using a twenty-two foot dugout canoe. Creeks and bay surveys were carried out during low tide during the day and spotlight counts made at night using a six-volt flashlight. Indirect evidence such as tracks, old nests and interview information from local inhabitants was also recorded.

Crocodile nesting habitats were surveyed on foot and assessment made of habitat disturbance such as logging, siltation, land use, fishing and boat traffic. A total of 110 main creeks were surveyed and 220 hours of daytime observations and 176 hours of night surveys were completed.

A total of forty-five *C. porosus* were observed during the two-month survey, and indirect evidence suggested another eighty individuals. The majority of the crocodiles seen were adults. Most major creeks supported one or two adult crocodiles.

Sighting of crocodiles by locals, and human-crocodile conflicts both in disturbed and undisturbed areas was more prevalent during the breeding season (May–July). This was possibly due to the movement of breeding females to nesting habitats in the limited areas freshwater marsh which are now adjacent to human habitats. Viable nesting habitat, flat wetlands with freshwater just behind the mangrove fringe, is continually being taken up for settlement and intensive agriculture. Nesting habitat and streamside timber have been destroyed and heavy siltation of the freshwater streams and mangrove creeks resulted.

The only remaining nesting habitat is tidal cane fringe close to settlements and paddy fields, which is the least preferred nesting habitat. Mechanized boat traffic and intensive fishing also result in disturbance and mortality. Small crocodiles are caught in nets and females nesting close to settlements are killed for their fat, gall bladder and eggs which are considered to have high medicinal value.

Both humans and their livestock are occasionally taken by crocodiles and the crocodile is usually killed. Such incidents are rarely reported.

The present survey gave no indication of large-scale crocodile hunting, but loss of nesting habitat, collection of eggs and killing of females are having detrimental effects on the population. The remoteness of the area and lack of staff and resources make monitoring, management and protection difficult. Recommendations are made to mitigate the negative impacts on the breeding habitat by establishing buffer zones and planting trees. An intensive environmental education programme and feasibility studies for crocodile ranching and farming as an incentive for conservation are also proposed.

HOLIDAY SNAPS IN FRENCH LAKE

There is a nasty nip in the waters of a southern French holiday spot. The Lac de la Ganguise, popular with swimmers and windsurfers, has been found to be sheltering at least two piranhas, reported *The Times* on 16 August 1996.

The first of the predatory South American fish to be landed from the lake near Castelnaudary, thirty miles south-east of Toulouse, was caught after a considerable struggle by a holidaymaker. According to witnesses, it measured an impressive fourteen inches and sported an equally impressive set of teeth.

A second, larger specimen was caught a few days later by Jean-Marc Simon, a local fisherman, who first spotted the fish near the surface. "I put some live bait on my hook. Five minutes later I brought up this thing," M. Simon said. The "thing" in question turned out to be another piranha, this time measuring eighteen-and-a-half inches.

The second catch prompted an investigation as gendarmes and fish experts went to the scene. The piranha was measured, sketched and captured on film before being sent to the Natural History Museum in Paris for tests. This is not the first time piranha have been found in France. In 1991 two were caught in the Garonne.

Serrasalmus natteri is a gregarious creature. It can grow to more than nineteen inches long and live for eight years. In France the fish cost between fifty and 100 francs (£6.35 and £12.70), and are a popular choice for collectors of tropical fish on condition that they are kept in isolation because of their natural tendency to eat the rest of the tank.

In their natural habitat, the creatures are not vicious. However, if they are forced into smaller lakes in a drought, they can become extremely predatory, even turning to cannibalism. Piranhas will also attack people. Attracted by the smell of blood, a shoal in a feeding frenzy can strip a body bare of flesh in minutes.

The local authorities say that they believe the fish were released into the lake from a local aquarium. "Bathers can continue swimming. Piranhas are dangerous only in shoals," a local official said this week. "In any case, these probably belong to the family of piranhas which are purely vegetarian."

Whether the two piranhas caught in Castelnaudary do indeed belong to the vegetarian branch of the family or to their flesh-eating cousins

will not be known until the test results come back from the Natural
History Museum. Bathers may have grown wary, but fishermen
dreaming of the catch of a lifetime are turning up in droves.

CROCODILE KILLS SCOTSWOMAN

An eighteen-year-old British student has been killed by a crocodile
while spending part of her "year out" doing charity work in Tanzania.
Laura Campbell-Preston was attacked as she swam with friends in a
waterhole that was thought to be safe. No one else was hurt.

The accident happened last Thursday and a service was held for her
yesterday a the village school in Moshi, where she had been teaching
English while waiting to go to university. The funeral will be held in
Lochawe, Strathclyde, on Friday. Her family live in Taynuilt, Argyll,
where her parents Robert, forty-six, and Rosie, forty-five, run Inverawe
Smoke House, which sells smoked salmon by mail order.

Her twenty-three-year-old sister, Clare, said: "Five of them went
swimming in a waterhole. It was known to be safe, but there had been
heavy rain and a random crocodile got in. She was attacked and killed."
She added that the family attached no blame to World Challenge, the
London-based charity under whose auspices her sister had been
working, or anyone else. "It was no one's fault and Laura was not being
reckless. It was a safe waterhole and one that was always visited."

Charles Rigby, a spokesman for World Challenge Expeditions, said:
"This was a dreadful accident that no one could have predicted."

CROCODILE IN HARARE

A giant crocodile that had been regularly jabbed by a keeper to make it
snap its jaws and lash its tail for tourists finally bit off the arm of its
tormentor. Now the owners of the reptile park in Harare face prosecution for cruelty to animals.

Witnesses at Harare Snake Park said yesterday [19 September 1996]
that Smart Bester climbed into the seventy-nine-year-old male
crocodile's pit and was jabbing it in the stomach with a stick when it
struck.

Merryl Harrison, manager of Zimbabwe's Society for the Prevention of Cruelty to Animals, said she would prosecute the park's owners for cruelty, and was considering seeking an injunction to prevent the animal's destruction. Cruelty complaints against Mr Bester go back six years.

ZAMBEZI EXPLORERS

Two British adventurers are celebrating a record-breaking kayak expedition today, 16 October 1996, from the source of the Zambezi River to the sea. They fled from a maneating crocodile and braved some of the world's most dangerous white-water rapids during their three-month journey.

Justin Matterson, thirty-three, and Rupert FitzMaurice, thirty-one, both suffered from malaria as they paddled 1,675 miles from north-west Zambia to the magnificent sand-barred river delta on the Indian Ocean coast of Mozambique.

On the trip, which involved sixty-seven days of canoeing, the pair were almost capsized by hippos, caught in a whirlpool, paddled within a few feet of the Victoria Falls and rode out Force five winds on one of the continent's largest man-made lakes. Mr Matterson, from Evanton, Ross and Cromarty, veteran of a 2,000-mile run through the Himalayas, and Mr FitzMaurice, of Forest Row, East Sussex, who runs expeditions for the charity Raleigh International, believe they are the first to conquer the river unsupported.

The Source to Sea Appeal, spawned by the canoeists's adventure, has so far raised £7,000 towards a £25,000 target for the Leukaemia Research Fund. Both men are now recuperating in Harare, Zimbabwe, and are to give a talk on their experiences at the Royal Geographical Society in January.

Their most terrifying moment came as they were negotiating a narrow passage beyond the Cabora Bassa lake in Mozambique. They had been warned by Afrikaner settlers to beware of a crocodile which they later learnt had been blamed for the deaths of five men.

"Fitz felt a bang and the back of his kayak go down," Mr Matterson said. "He thought he had hit a submerged tree, but, when he turned around, he had the shock of his life. He saw what he considered to be the biggest crocodile head he has ever seen. It was resting on the kayak at a slight angle, looking towards him so you could see his teeth. His head appeared to be grinning. Fitz was in a hell of a state."

The head slunk back into the water as Mr FitzMaurice sprinted down the river. As the two men were pulling into the side, Mr Matterson spotted the crocodile gliding up behind his partner. He screamed a warning to Mr FitzMaurice, who dashed for the bank. "I don't know why he didn't go for Fitz again. With a croc that size, you would have had no chance."

It was not until this century that the source of the 2,200-mile Zambezi was located in a Zambian swamp near the border with Angola and Zaire. For nearly forty miles the pair followed the stream on foot, then made a detour around Angola, on Foreign Office advice, and picked up the river again at the Chavuma Falls in Zambia.

"On three occasions we startled hippos on the bank," Mr Matterson said. "They hurl themselves into the river and head for deep water. It is quite an adrenalin-pumping, fear-inducing moment. Hippos munch more people than any other animal. It is like being charged by a Buick."

In Mozambique the river passed through a wildlife conservation area known as Hippo City, home to more than 300 hippos. "That was a nerve-racking experience," Mr Matterson said. "The people get taken on that stretch of the river every year. When we got to the sea we were silent for a good few hours. Basically we have kayaked through the heart of Africa."

SOUTH AFRICAN SURF

When it comes to killer sharks Andrew Carter is probably the world's leading human guinea pig. He is the only man to have survived a double attack by a great white shark, which left him seconds from death. In the horrific encounter off the coast of South Africa, Andrew's right leg was bitten to the bone from hip to knee. His best friend died from massive injuries inflicted by the same shark.

The attack was in September 1994, but in the next month Andrew will attempt to overcome his fear by returning to surf in the same waters in which he was attacked.

The memories of what happened are still vivid. "There was a fabulous clear blue sky and I'd been out surfing for about half an hour with my friend Bruce Corby," he remembers. "Suddenly, I felt this huge bang from behind. I realized straight away it was a shark. The first three seconds were the worst, sheer terror like I could never have imagined.

"I remember its power. It was the most helpless feeling because it had its jaws clamped round my leg and my surfboard, pulling me down into the water. I felt like my bones were being crushed. Its jaws alone were about four or five feet long. I looked down into its face. I think its eyes were probably closed.

"I could feel it was biting me, but I didn't feel much pain because my adrenalin was racing. It was just a crushing sensation and fear of dying because I was so far offshore, about two hundred metres, where you're totally helpless, in the shark's domain.

"The guy who was closest to me said I let out one piercing scream. He said he thought the shark was biting me in half because its jaw was right over my leg, and the water all around me just flowed red. He turned round and paddled for dear life and I can understand why. You can't help someone escape from a shark that size."

Carter thought that he was being eaten alive. "It was a feeling of such unbelievable horror. I was holding on to my surfboard with all my might. Then for some reason the shark opened its mouth, probably to get a bigger bite. It went back into the water and leapt forward again. Because I was holding my board so tight, it twisted round and jammed in the shark's mouth, and I started to swim a few strokes away.

"I kept looking back because I was terrified it would come at me from behind. And then I saw it let go of the board and disappear. I knew then that it was coming after me.

"I was too far from shore and losing an enormous amount of blood, so I knew I was minutes away from passing out. In desperation I clawed my way back to my surfboard and, as I grabbed it, I caught the luckiest wave of my life, which carried me in to shore."

He saw two girls sunbathing on the beach and started shouting for help. One girl tore off her clothes, tied them round his leg and packed them into the massive wound.

"She was holding my hand all the time. I was very cold and could feel the warmth from her body flowing into me. It was then that I thought I would die and started to see my life flowing past my eyes. My vision went, I could barely hear, but I realized I had no fear of death and was completely at ease with myself."

Andrew's friend, Bruce, was further out and had to come through Carter's blood to escape. None of the witnesses realized he was the shark's second victim until they saw him dying.

"A guy on the beach saw Bruce coming in on a wave," Carter says. "He shouted, 'Get out of the water. Andrew's been attacked.' Bruce said, 'I've been attacked too,' but apparently he seemed very normal. Only then did the guy look down at him and see that he didn't have a leg. He grabbed Bruce and pulled him out of the water, and Bruce became totally hysterical. He went into shock and within about two minutes he'd stopped breathing. They gave him artificial respiration on the beach and revived him, but he was brain dead from that moment on and died forty-eight hours later."

Carter had a five-hour operation involving around 2,000 stitches. Every muscle and tendon had to be painstakingly sewed back together.

The champion surfer who has won South African and European titles, remembers that only about two inches of flesh held his leg on to his torso. "The attack changed me a great deal," he says now. "It was a big thing to realize I have no fear of death when it comes to it. I used to get very uptight waiting for people when they were late or hanging about for a plane, whereas now I sit back and relax. I feel as though I'm living on borrowed time . . .

"Now I have to go back to the place I was attacked to overcome my fear forever. I've been surfing for twenty-two years and only been attacked once. If anything, I think I'm kind of invincible now because I can get away from the buggers.'

SNAP ATTACK

Legs were crossed in Bloomsbury, the London publishing house, when news arrived [on 12 October 1997] that one of its most prized authors had been bitten in the most intimate of places by an alligator.

Hunter S. Thompson, renowned for a temperament more acidic than the 1960s psychedelia of his books, was to have made a rare sortie across the Atlantic to promote his latest effort, *The Proud Highway: The Fear and Loathing Letters*, Vol. 1. But the tour has been cancelled while the author recovers from his brush with reptilia at his home in Woody Creek, Colorado.

"He said he had been bitten on the thigh and possibly, er, higher up," I am told. "It is most distressing." Knowing Mr Thompson, I just hope the alligator is all right.

IN THE TEETH OF SOLOMON

A female worker at a wildlife park in northern Australia was attacked by a fifteen-foot long crocodile and miraculously survived. Tourists watched in horror as Karla Bredl, who only minutes earlier had been feeding the reptile, was grabbed around the leg and then the waist after she fell.

As the crocodile, named Solomon, tried to pull her into the water, the twenty-one-year-old park attendant's father, Joe, jumped on its back and gouged its eyes. He then grabbed a rake and beat the crocodile about the head in an attempt to force it to open its jaws.

Last night [23 February 1997] Miss Bredl was in intensive care at Mackay hospital in Queensland, where she was being treated for a broken pelvis, a fractured leg and internal injuries. The hospital said her condition was stable. Doctors said Miss Bredl's injuries would have been worse had Solomon not lost most of his teeth in fights with other crocodiles and because of a calcium deficiency.

Miss Bredl, an attendant at the family's Barefoot Bushman Wildlife Park in north Queensland, had been joking about the crocodile's lack of teeth with the audience only a few seconds earlier. "If I ever get grabbed, I'd rather it be this one," she laughed.

"Then she slipped and it was on her," Rob Bredl, her uncle, said. "But she's a bright spark. As they pulled her out, she said, 'I'm bloody glad he's got no teeth'." Mr Bredl said: "When Solomon grabbed her across the pelvis, the rake was doing nothing, so my brother said, 'Bugger it.' Joe was belting it around the eyes with the rake, but it wasn't doing any good. So he jumped on its back in the water and he was wrestling it, trying to stick his thumbs in its eyes and finally it let go."

The family do not plan to destroy the crocodile, which is said to have a fairly placid nature. "He usually won't eat anything with bones in it," Mr Bredl added.

BY THE SKIN OF OUR TEETH

Karla Bredl stared death in the face this week when a sixteen-foot crocodile clamped its jaws round her legs after she fell into the water at a wildlife park in northern Queensland, Australia. The terrified twenty-one-year-old was saved by her father, who jumped on the crocodile's back and jabbed his thumbs into its eyes to make it release its hold.

The London *Daily Mail* (26 February 1997) talked to three people who were plunged into a similar nightmare . . . and lived to tell the tale.

Holidaymaker Martin Richardson nearly died last year when a shark attacked him in the sea off Egypt. The twenty-nine-year-old from Colchester, Essex, owes his life to a school of dolphins who kept the killer at bay for two vital minutes while he was snatched to safety.

Martin says:

Of course I've seen the Jaws film; but never in my wildest dreams did I expect to become a victim. I was backpacking around Egypt and decided to visit an old friend who was working on a diving boat off the Sinai Peninsula. It was the perfect opportunity to take some diving lessons.

On the third day we were heading back to port when I spotted two dolphins swimming with their baby. They've always fascinated me, so I leapt overboard to join them. Unfortunately, they vanished as soon as I jumped in, so I headed back to the boat.

Suddenly something charged into my left side and the water bubbled red with blood. I knew what it was as soon as the first bite sunk into my flesh – a shark – and the boat seemed to be miles away.

I screamed for help until I ran out of breath. By then the shark had taken three bites out of me and disappeared. I was terrified that it would come back. Moments later it did – and snatched another mouthful of flesh. As I stared through the waves, I could actually see its blueish head. I punched it on the nose; it wasn't very amused and went for me again.

"Please God, don't let me die here, surrounded by all this blood and in the middle of nowhere," I prayed to myself, as I twisted frantically around in the water to see where the next attack was coming from. I knew I'd had a good life and done everything I'd set out to accomplish. I touched my St Christopher necklace and thought: "This is it, I'm a goner." But the shark never came back for that last bite. I wondered what was keeping it away. It was only after the boat turned up that I found out what had happened.

As my friends, diving instructor Harry Hayward and boat owner Dani Hermon, hauled me out of the sea, they told me about the bottlenose dolphins who had continued to circle the boat, flapping their fins and tails, until I was safe. They gave me a chance of life, and I'll be forever grateful to them. But my battle for survival didn't stop there.

I was so badly bitten that my blood was spraying around the boat. After giving me oxygen and applying tourniquets to stem the massive bleeding, the crew sped back to shore to get me to a doctor. I just wanted to go to sleep, but they wouldn't let me – even resorting to singing to stop me from becoming unconscious.

Doctors at a military hospital fifty-miles away patched me up. The shark had bitten into my stomach, shoulder and back breaking a rib and puncturing a lung. You could see my spine. I looked like something out of a horror film. The doctor said he lost count after two hundred stitches and I needed five pints of blood. One of the nurses told me they'd expected me to die. But I'm a stubborn guy and was determined not to let some big fish get the better of me.

I felt terrible when I stood up and thought all the bones were going to fall out of my body. Since the attack, I've spent hours exercising the muscles that were ripped and sewn back together. The scars are horrendous. I have trouble moving my arm, part of my back is still numb and there are lumps of scar tissue where I was bitten.

I don't have nightmares about my close shave, although my rescuers who saw me ripped apart still do.

I've always loved travelling and am planning to set off again soon. One of my first stops will be the Barrier Reef in Australia. I'll be going diving again as soon as possible. But this time, I'm going to wear a mask, so I can spot what's coming. I won't be nervous. There's only one thing to fear in life and that is fear itself. I've been through the worst and the chances of being bitten again are pretty remote.

Onlookers watched in horror as a six-month-old tiger cub being led on a leash through Sparkwell Wildlife Park near Plymouth, suddenly grabbed a boy's head in its jaws. Exeter schoolboy and army cadet Robert Gardner, now sixteen, was just seven years old when the labrador-sized Siberian tiger called Zircon leapt at him. A keeper managed to get his hand into the eighty-pound animal's jaws and ease out Robert's ripped scalp, although it still left him in need of thirty-four stitches. Robert says:

It was such a treat to go to the wildlife park when we were little, but today there's no way I could go without feeling nervous.

I was seven years old on the day it happened. We'd just finished lunch and while my dad bought an ice-cream for my baby sister, Nicola, Mum took me and my younger brother, Paul, to see the bears. I thought they were great and ran back to tell my dad all about it.

I sped along a little path, shot round a corner and came face to face with a tiger cub on a leash being taken back to its cage. It came up higher than my waist and looked straight at me.

The next minute it jumped on me, pulled me to the ground and started tearing at my head. I think it probably just thought I wanted to play, but it ripped off my scalp and there was blood everywhere. It also sank its claws into my leg and stomach as it mauled me.

I've mentally blocked out a lot of what happened because I was so frightened, but I remember the noise of people screaming and shouting for help as the tiger held me firmly in its mouth. If a passer-by hadn't helped the keeper pull the cub off me – which took some doing, believe me – I'm sure I would have been killed.

Somebody clamped a sweatshirt to my head to try to stop the bleeding and keep the wound intact, then there was a blur of sirens as the police and ambulance arrived.

I remember my parents running towards me, both bewildered by what had happened. When my mum first heard my scream, she thought I'd just fallen over and grazed my knee. They couldn't believe what had happened. I was deathly white and in a lot of pain, but I remained conscious throughout the ordeal. I stayed quite calm, which worried my parents more than if I'd been screaming.

I was in the operating theatre for more than an hour while the doctor put in stitches from the top of my head to my neck. It was a deep wound. At school afterwards, I was treated like a hero and everyone wanted to see the scars on my head and body – which you can still see today.

I hated anything to do with tigers since. I don't even like seeing them on television, although I don't turn away when the Esso advert comes on. The wildlife park asked us if we wanted Zircon put down, but I refused. It was obeying its natural instincts. I was unlucky. I was in the wrong place at the wrong time, but I'm glad that I didn't have my eighteen-month-old sister with me. If the tiger had attacked her, she wouldn't have stood a chance.

I've never had nightmares about what happened, but I think of it every anniversary. It's silly, but I'm glad when the day's over and I get home safely. I heard that Zircon died recently, after being attacked by another tiger. I can't say I was sorry.

Snakes not only bite the hand that feeds them – some inject a deadly venom, too. And for Isle of Wight Zoo director Jack Corney, sixty-two who "milks" them for medical research, it's a risk of the job. In 1987 he was declared clinically dead after a Diamond Back rattlesnake sank its deadly fangs into his hand. Amazingly he survived. Married to Judith and with two daughters and a son, he is the only man in Britain to have survived a bite by a cobra and a rattlesnake. Jack says:

The last thing you should do when a snake bites you is panic. It's the natural reaction, but it will kill you because it makes the blood – with the poison in it – flow through your body faster. When you've got a lethal dose of venom in your bloodstream, you've got to freeze your mind. Knowing this has saved my life three times.

Nine years ago I put my hand in the reptile enclosure and plucked out a Diamond Back rattlesnake. I thought it was going to be just another normal day. It wasn't.

I've got one hundred potentially lethal snakes – including cobras and vipers – which I milk for the venom that spits from the grooves of their fangs. It's used by the Liverpool School of Tropical Medicine for medical research. I'm always very careful, because the snakes are angry and frightened when you hold their head over the collecting bucket. I was holding a rattlesnake by the back of the neck when I suddenly felt its fangs in my thumb. I probably only lost my concentration for a split second, but that was long enough for it to seize the advantage over me.

I knew exactly what was coming next – a feeling of suffocation as the poison attacks the nervous system and paralyses the lungs and throat. My arm soon swelled up to three times its normal size. I tried to stay calm. I wrapped a tight bandage around my arm, called an ambulance, noted the time and type of snake, and called the Liverpool School, so they could work out what antidote the hospital should give me. Once, after another bite, serum had to be brought eighty miles from London by relays of police motorcyclists.

The pain from being bitten was terrible. I tried to think positive, but I felt like screaming. I was sure I was going to die.

I managed to take control of my mind, thanks to the training I'd had from my RAF flying days, where I was taught not to panic in dangerous situations. I still had hold of the snake because I didn't want it slithering out of reach or biting me again – and carefully put it back in its case. But in hospital, I learned that my heart did stop. I listened to the voices of five doctors around the bed, fighting to bring me back. I felt myself floating out of my body. Everything was growing dimmer and I wanted to ask someone to switch on a light. I watched a doctor try to locate the pulse on my wrist while another stuck a needle into me. I felt really calm, it was a wonderful sensation. I thought about my wife and three children. Someone said, "We're losing him . . . he's gone." And everything went black.

The next thing I remember is looking at a clock on the wall. I'd been unconscious for three hours and, I found out later, my heart had stopped for three minutes.

For the next five days I was in a critical condition, drifting in and out of consciousness. I think I would have come out of hospital in a coffin if it hadn't been for the fantastic staff in intensive care. Almost two weeks later I was allowed home.

My arm was paralysed for weeks and the circulation in my right hand is still affected. I get arthritis there, too. But I don't blame the snake. It's an awesome creature that was just doing what comes naturally. Since then, I've been airlifted to the nearest intensive care unit twice after being bitten by the same Siamese Cobra. Every time I've been hurt it's my fault, and I'm terrified of it happening again.

Some people think I'm mad doing this job, but I get a kick out of being able to do something others can't. I've trained myself not to panic, but every time I pick up a lethal snake I know the smallest mistake could kill me.

PRINGLE BAY, SOUTH AFRICA

A great white shark with a dorsal fin said to measure about a metre is believed to have been responsible for the shark attack in which avid diver Mr Ian James Hill, aged thirty-nine, of Durban, died yesterday [December 1997].

According to witness accounts of the attack, Hill was spearfishing about 350–400 metres from the shore in about ten metres of water when the shark attacked him at about 2 p.m.

He leaves his wife Sandra and nine-year-old daughter Charlene. Mrs Hill and Charlene, who had been waiting on the beach for Hill to return to shore, were sedated by a Pringle Bay doctor last night.

People who saw the attack said they had spotted a large dorsal fin in the area earlier in the day.

"They saw Hill standing in the water, then they saw the fin and then they saw a pool of blood where he had been standing," said police spokesperson Senior Superintendent John Sterrenberg. "Another witness stopped his car when he saw what appeared to be thrashing in the water. He saw a buoy and then he saw a dorsal fin measuring about a metre."

Although the circumstances of the attack are unknown, local fishermen said they suspected Hill had speared several fish and that these were hanging from his diving buoy when he was attacked. The smell of blood attracts sharks.

Sterrenberg said the South African Police Services Coastal Patrol Unit and the John Rolfe helicopter searched the area immediately after the attack was reported. He said the wind was strong and the sea became rough and the water dirty, making the search difficult. The search was called off when it became dark.

Hill's mother, Mrs Rosemary Hill, had not yet been contacted by police or family members when a Durban reporter telephoned her last night. The *Cape Times* later put her in touch with a police spokesperson. She said her son was an electrician and an avid member of the

Wahoo Diving Club in Durban. She confirmed he was on holiday in the Cape with his family.

The family was due to leave Pringle Bay yesterday for Hermanus, she said – so it would appear her son may have been on a final dive at the small resort.

Shark expert Mr Triall Witthuhn of Struisbaai knew Hill and described him as "a top diver in South Africa". Witthuhn, who tags great white sharks for the Oceanographic Research Institute, said last night that south-east coast sea waters had been abnormally warm recently. Sharks had to eat substantially more as their gastric juices digested food far more quickly in warm water, he said.

"The shark moves around more and he eats more. If such a hungry great white saw a seal, he would eat it – and unfortunately a diver in a wetsuit looks like a seal," Witthuhn said. "But sharks are not aggressive – if they are hungry, they eat. When they are hungry again, they eat what they find – not necessarily a human being. The maneater stories are rubbish."

Divers, in particular, should be aware that warmer water brings extra dangers. "Any diver will tell you our waters are full of sharks."

A great white shark killed a diver, the latest in a wave of attacks in South Africa which has raised fears among surfers and tourists.

Mr Hill was spearfishing about 400 yards from the shore in about thirty feet of water when the shark attacked . . . Only a speargun was retrieved and a helicopter search was called off.

The death in Pringle Bay was the first in the Cape Town area in more than a decade. It comes on the heels of a recent spate of shark attacks elsewhere in the country and has fuelled safety concerns among the thousands of British and other overseas tourists and surfers who have flocked to the sunsoaked Western Cape over the holiday season.

While surfing experts insist such incidents are isolated, they are concerned by the implications of the latest tragedy. They have given a warning that shark activity has increased because of higher sea temperatures . . .

A twenty-five-year-old Australian surfer died earlier this year when he was attacked by a shark on a remote beach in the Eastern Cape.

INCREASE IN SOUTH AFRICAN ATTACKS

Shark attacks off the Cape provinces of South Africa – mostly on surfers and bodyboarders who are possibly mistaken for seals – have quadrupled this year and the growing number of cage-diving operations is being blamed.

More sharks are being attracted to the area because cage-dive operators throw chum and bait into the ocean, says Rex Hart, surfer and co-ordinator of Save Our Swimmers and Sharks. He argues that the sharks learn to associate human activity with food and is lobbying to have the practice banned.

However, researchers at the Natal Sharks Board are sceptical; Sheldon Dudley says, "This year's shark attacks have occurred over a wide area from Saldanha Bay on the west coast to East London on the east coast, which is some 650 kilometres from the nearest cage-diving site." The South African White Shark Research Institute says a more likely reason for the increase in attacks is that commercial fishing in South African waters has decimated the fish population.

International Shark Attack File, kept by the Florida Museum of Natural History, shows that the increase in shark attacks is a worldwide phenomenon, which could reflect better reporting, increasing numbers of people doing watersports or El Nino-related environmental changes affecting water temperature and fish movements.) For further information, check out these websites – White Shark Research Institute: www.whiteshark.co.za; Natal Sharks Board: http://shark.co.za; Shark Attack File: www.flmnh.ufl.edu/fish/research/ISAF/shark.htm

BOY BITES CROC BACK

Here are two news reports of the same remarkable story, each of which differs in detail, one is dated 22 September 2000 and the other 20 February 2001.

A twelve-year-old boy has survived a crocodile attack while snorkelling off Western Australia by gouging the animal's eyes.

Sam West ended up with his head in the three-metre saltwater crocodile's jaws while swimming off the Kimberley coast about 600 kilometres (370 miles) south-west of Darwin.

His father, trawler owner Bill West, said the crocodile gripped his son several times, leaving him with lacerations to the head, wrist and hands.

'It gripped his head first, released him, then gripped his hands,'' Mr West was quoted as saying. "It gripped him four or five times. He's very, very lucky to be alive. He's one very gutsy little boy."

Mr West said the attack happened about twenty metres from the shore of a remote island. "It was probably over in moments, but it seemed like ages." he added.

A plane in the area heard the trawler's distress calls and took Sam to hospital in Darwin. A hospital spokesman said the boy was in satisfactory condition.

Saltwater crocodiles are found primarily in the brackish water of tidal rivers. However, adults may venture out to sea and swim between islands. Dr Adam Britton, author of the Crocodilian web site, says individuals have been known to swim distances of over 1,000 kilometres (625 miles) in the sea. Saltwater crocodiles may live more than seventy years and reach six metres.

An Australian boy escaped the jaws of a fourteen-foot crocodile by biting its nose. The boy drove the creature away by copying a move he'd seen in the film *Deep Blue Sea*.

The crocodile released its grip after the boy bit it and gouged its eye with his fingers. In the film, a swimmer escapes from a shark by stabbing it in the eye with a cross.

Attack victim Sam West, twelve, said: "That movie saved my life. If I hadn't seen *Deep Blue Sea* and remembered the story so well, I wouldn't be alive today. There is no doubt about that."

The attack happened while Sam was snorkelling in north-west Australia. After its first attack the crocodile let go when Sam punched it, but it then attacked again.

"I was about to raise both fists. The crocodile shot forward more quickly than the blink of an eye. Excruciating pain shot through and my arms were trapped inside the crocodile's jaws. I thought I'd be drowned – I was going to die. What could I do? I bent forward and my lips were against its snout, so I opened my mouth and bit with all the strength I could muster. The crocodile had my arms inside its mouth, and my teeth were locked on to its nose.

"Then it quit. It just let go, but then came back for another go at me.

It grabbed my left arm, and into my memory flashed the scene from the movie *Deep Blue Sea*. With my right hand, I gouged its eye with my finger. The last time I kept it there for a couple of seconds. Then the crocodile jerked away. It turned, and was gone."

Australian crocodile expert Graham Webb said: "He's incredibly lucky to be alive. Within seconds the crocodile would have gone into a 'death roll' and drowned the boy before eating him."

SOUTH AFRICAN KILLER CROCODILES

A romantic midnight dip off the St Lucia estuary on South Africa's east coast ended in tragedy yesterday after a young Johannesburg woman was eaten by a crocodile.

The legs and torso of Tracy Hunt, twenty-two, were later found by fishermen at Honeymoon Bend, one mile from where the attack took place and two days after she went swimming with her boyfriend, Claudio Celestino, twenty-five, in the muddy waters of the estuary lake.

Hours after the discovery of Miss Hunt's remains, a second woman was killed by a crocodile while crossing the Enseleni River near Richards Bay, north of St Lucia. The local woman, who was using a popular crossing point, was grabbed by a crocodile which was still standing guard over its victim as officials attempted to recover the body.

The first tragedy came when the Johannesburg couple went for a late-night swim after booking into the Gwala Gwala guest lodge in the St Lucia wetlands, a popular tourist spot in Kazulu-Natal province. Wading in neck-deep waters, Miss Hunt suddenly screamed out in agony and Mr Celestino turned round to see his girlfriend disappear under the water. Unable to save her, he swam back to shore and reported the tragedy to the guest lodge, saying that he had seen crocodiles.

The couple had ignored signboards warning visitors about swimming in the estuary, where crocodiles, sharks and hippopotamuses are sighted regularly. Wildlife officials say that most of the crocodile attacks occur between November and April, when heavy rains swell local rivers, providing cover for the reptiles. The rains also coincide with the animals' breeding season. Crocodiles kill about twelve people in South Africa every year.

BOD IN A COD

A huge cod caught off Australia's Great Barrier Reef revealed a grisly secret after it was landed in Queensland at the weekend. Weighing more than forty-four kilograms (ninety-seven pounds) and measuring five feet nine inches long, the fish – a flowery cod with distinctive blotchy skin – was triumphantly lowered by trawlermen into the ship's hold.

The trawler docked in Cairns and the cod was delivered to the Fine Kettle O' Fish filleting factory. But when staff cut open its stomach yesterday a man's head rolled out.

A co-owner of the factory, Peter Monson, said the head was whole and not badly disfigured. "There was disbelief. You would never dream of it," he said.

Detective Sergeant David Miles of Cairns police added: "The fish was fairly big and the head appeared to be fairly much intact inside it."

Police removed the fish and the grisly find for forensic examination. They suspect that the head may be that of a local fisherman, Michael Edwards, thirty-nine, who disappeared on Sunday after falling from his trawler east of Slashers Reef.

Trawlermen were puzzled about how the head could have found its way into the fish's stomach so quickly. Flowery cod, also known as Morgan cod, normally suck in their prey and do not have sharp teeth.

Cod are voracious migratory fish which normally feed on other fish and invertebrates. The flowery cod is often described as a shy fish, preferring coral reefs close to shore, but frequently descending to well below thirty metres (100 feet). It is found in the Red Sea, Indian Ocean and off Australia's Pacific coast.

The Fishing Cairns' website describes the variety of cod species on offer to visiting anglers: "Humans find a great deal of affection for these seemingly gentle giants, with the game boat skippers and dive boat operators making an event of hand feeding their "pet" while on charter. The fishes' huge mouths will engulf substantial offerings"

THE PERILS OF OZ WATERS

If the red-back spiders under loo seats don't get you, the blue-ringed octopus will. People delight in spreading shock-horror stories about Aussie wildlife, and often it works. Marie Davies has been instructing prospective divers Down Under and finds that many are terrified of being eaten by sharks – or worse. In this article she put matters in perspective:

Vast, diverse, exotic and home to the largest tropical reef system in the world, Australia is a diver's dream. Each year, lured by cheap air fares and strong currencies, Brits and other tourists flock Down Under to don their scuba gear and explore its underwater technicolour paradise.

Scuba diving in Australia is still a growing sport, if PADI qualification figures are any guide, and each year more and more reports surface of the potential dangers Down Under, with horrific headlines grabbing the imaginations of the public.

It's true – by dipping your fins into the Pacific Ocean, you could conceivably become a shark snack or fall victim to a potentially lethal bite or sting. But are these fears justified?

Sharks have killed more people in Australian waters than anywhere else in the world, averaging about one fatal attack per year – until 2000, when no fewer than five people died. Three of these attacks were by great whites. Previously, there had been only nine Australian fatalities in ten years, although the deaths of three other people are also believed to have resulted from shark attacks.

Worldwide attacks peaked at seventy-nine last year, the highest forty years, according to the university of Florida's International Shark Attack File. But it is attacks on people at the surface, surfers and swimmers, which are the most common, accounting for almost four-fifths of all attacks.

Until 1994, not a single scuba diver had been killed by a shark Down Under. So can divers diverse easy? Not quite. Australia now has the second highest percentage of attacks on divers in the world after the USA. In 1999, eleven per cent of Australian shark attacks were on divers and snorkellers, and this rose to 18.4 per cent in 2000.

There are about 400 different species of shark, but only a handful have ever been known to attack humans, and most of these attacks were not fatal.

Over the past 200 years it is the grey nurse shark (known elsewhere as the sand tiger or raggedtooth) that has accounted for forty-three per cent of attacks worldwide. But the great white shark (*Carcharodon carcharia*) is the stuff of Hollywood legends, and is regarded as the most deadly shark found off Australia's coastline.

Last year, two surfers were killed off the coast of South Australia in attacks on two consecutive days, and two months later, a great white fatally bit off a swimmer's leg in waist-deep water in Perth, Western Australia. Why are such attacks on the increase? Chris McDonald, Shark Supervisor at Sydney Aquarium, says that one of the main reasons is the huge reduction in fish populations.

The amount of food available in the ocean is decreasing and sharks are now travelling further afield to feed. They are attracted to movement and sound in the water, but many experts believe that mistaken identity is the major reason for attacks on humans, especially in poor visibility such as in breaking surf. In such conditions swimmers, surfers or non-submerged divers can resemble seals at the surface, and seals are the great white's favourite snack.

"Global warming might also be a factor," says McDonald. "Changing temperatures in the water means changing patterns in shark migration." This means sharks are coming closer to shore and, with more holidaymakers taking up water pursuits such as diving and surfing, the odds of being attacked, whether mistakenly or not, increase accordingly.

Shark fans cite cage-diving as another reason for the incidence of attacks. By encouraging human interaction with sharks, they argue, we are associating ourselves with food. McDonald, however, does not believe that instigating a jaw-to-jaw encounter is one of the factors. "Contrary to what people believe, the great white isn't much of a threat to humans," he says. "The most common shark attacks are from tigers, dusky whalers and bull sharks.

Bull shark attacks are especially common, he says, as the species is attracted to people swimming in very shallow waters.

British backpacker Rob Collins was training as a PADI Dive Master in Airlee Beach, Queensland, when he had his first encounter with a potentially lethal shark. During a morning dive, a three-metre tiger shark circled the dive group while they were hanging on the descent line.

"The dive was awesome, but, just as we were coming up, I saw a large shadow out of the corner of my eye," he says. "We'd been diving with blacktips and whitetips, so I knew it was a shark. But this one scared me because it was three times as big.

"Then the sunlight just glinted off its body for a second and I realized it was a tiger. I'd heard loads of stories about them attacking divers and I felt a bit like bait just hanging there. Then I lost sight of it, which was even more scary."

Fortunately, the shark did not reappear and all the divers surfaced safely. Rob's buddy, Lisa McQuillin, was the only other diver to see the tiger. "I was really scared," she said, "and, when I told the other divers, they were a bit shocked. Some of them didn't want to go back in the water, even though we were moving to a different site."

However, like many divers, Lisa is quite nonchalant about the unexpected visitors. "You couldn't really blame the shark if it did attack. I mean, we were in its backyard, after all."

The dive began in the twilight hours of early morning, when sharks are at their most active and most hungry. Recently a man's head and limbs were found inside a tiger shark, caught off Lord Howe Island in New South Wales, which just goes to show how unpredictable these guys can be. But the fact is, only rarely do they attack divers.

If you want to dive in a statistically safe spot, choose Sydney. There are frequent sightings of sharks around the bay, but there hasn't been a fatal attack in the harbour since 1963. If you want the facts, top of the league for attacks is Queensland (37.5 per cent), with New South Wales and Western Australia coming in joint second with less than half this number. Surprisingly, there has been only one recorded attack on a diver in Victona, and attacks are rare in Northern Australia too.

However, the North has other dangers for divers – if a crocodile doesn't get you, you could be prey to an extremely toxic tentacle. Australia is host to the most venomous marine creatures in the world, but the sting from a box jellyfish, or sea wasp, is definitely one to avoid.

Box jellyfish have between ten and sixty stinging tentacles, each armed with up to 5,000 stinging cells or nematocysts. Chemicals on human skin activate the cells and contact could be fatal for an adult. Last year there were about seventy reported deaths in Northern Australia between November and April.

These creatures are more likely than sharks to come into accidental contact with humans, which earns them the "Most Dangerous" title. Ricky Chan, a marine biologist from the University of New South Wales, says this is due mainly to their transparency, which makes them difficult to see in the water.

They are not aggressive creatures, but when swimmers fail to see them and bump into the tentacles, the jellyfish release their toxic cells in defence. "They probably can't penetrate through wetsuits, but in tropical waters divers normally wear a shorty, so there will inevitably be exposed bits," says Chan. Interestingly, turtles are not affected by their sting and even eat these invisible creatures! But, because of the risk box jellyfish pose to humans, for six months of the year (October–April), as they drift close to the shore, the beaches of Northern Australia are closed.

If you should get stung by a box jellyfish, you won't get off lightly. Victims have reported excruciating pain, which can last for weeks. Experts recommend that you don't try to remove the tentacles while they are still active, as it worsens the injury and leaves scars. On all beaches in Northern Australia you'll find tubs of vinegar, which deactivates the tentacles. Ice-packs can ease the pain; basic first aid, artificial ventilation and CPP may also be needed.

Another non-aggressive creature is the tiny blue-ringed octopus, which prefers to hide away from prying dive masks in rock pools and shallow coral. The chances of a diver being bitten by one are small, and the reason it is considered one of the most deadly organisms in the world, says Ricky Chan is because it attracts attention.

"When the blue-ringed octopus feels threatened, rings on its body change from dark brown to bright neon blue and it looks very pretty," he says. "But this is just its way of advertising its toxicity and is a warning for you to stay away."

When the octopus is not angry, it displays a yellowy-brownish colour, enobling it to blend with the sand and rock. This makes it hard to see, but any divers who accidentally put a hand on one could be in for a nasty surprise.

If you mistakenly touch a blue-ringed octopus, it will inject you with lethal enzymes that cause paralysis. The bite is painless, but the toxin travels through the saliva into your bloodstream. Death can occur within thirty minutes, usually from respiratory failure brought on by the venom, rather than drowning due to the paralysis. There is no anti-venom available in Australia, so, if you do get bitten, artificial ventilation is recommended until the effects of the venom disappear.

There have been very few diver fatalities from either box jellyfish or blue-ringed octopus, mainly because both creatures favour shallow near-shore waters and divers tend to dive a little deeper and usually off boats. They also tend to be more aware of the potential dangers of marine creatures than swimmers or surfers.

In the depths of Australian waters another venomous creature lurks – the sea snake. There are approximately fifty species worldwide, and about thirty-two live in Northern Australian waters. They like warm tropical water, though sightings have been reported as far south as Sydney.

Even though nine of the 10 deadliest snakes in the world live Down Under, there are no documented fatalities from sea snakes. They are usually pretty inoffensive and over the past ten years, only three incidences of bites have been recorded.

However, these slippery critters are predators and, even though they have small mouths, they can bite. Their venom is two to ten times as toxic as a cobra's but, luckily for divers, they usually transfer only a small amount to their victims. Only a quarter of those bitten show signs of poisoning. Distinct teeth marks are left, but there isn't much pain or swelling. The bad news is that "envenomation" can paralyse the nervous system, making breathing difficult. Eventually, the victim can suffocate to death. Kidney damage and heart failure may also occur, due to muscle destruction.

Anti-venom is available, though this has some nasty side effects, including rashes, fever and joint aches and pains. To treat a bite, remove the surface venom, apply a pressure bandage, remain calm and go immediately to a hospital.

Finally, sea snakes are incredibly curious. Fascinated with my hoses and fins, I fell victim to their inquisitiveness only recently whilst diving on Ningaloo Reef in Western Australia. It's amazing how fast you can fin when a yellow-belly sea snake is chasing your tail!

The best way to eliminate the chance of being picked on by a shark or bitten or stung by a venomous marine creature is to stay clear of the water, but as that advice is worse than useless to divers, just avoid touching anything and try to look as little like a seal as possible.

Attracting considerable attention in Australia these days is the shark repellent rod or SharkPOD (Protective Oceanic Device). It emits a type of electrowave that's supposed to annoy sharks and can keep them at bay for up to ten metres. Its effectiveness varies according to species, though tests show that it's pretty convincing around great whites.

As the power has to be turned low enough to prevent the diver getting shocks, the repellent is less effective than it might be. But there is now talk of the technology being miniaturized and put into BCs and lifejackets. The Australians seem to believe in it, and used such devices during the triathlon event at the Sydney 2000 Olympic Games. It wouldn't have done for any of the swimmers to have been chomped in front of millions of people worldwide!

If you don't have the luxury of a SharkPod and find yourself in the water with the most feared of sharks, you might not know it anyway. Great whites creep up on their prey, usually attacking from underneath. If you do see one, Ricky Chan suggests you drop to the bottom, if possible, and wait for it to disappear. "Make sure you know where the shark is and don't forget to look underneath you as well," he says. Studies have shown that aggressive behaviour also deters them. "They are very defensive creatures and they don't want to hurt themselves if they can help it."

FLORIDA GATORS MUNCH

June 2001

A woman who was attacked by a twenty-five-stone alligator while she swam at a Florida nudist resort says she didn't even see the creature.

Dagmar Dow, aged forty-three, says the nine-and-a-half-foot alligator pulled her under the water before she knew what was going on.

Her husband Ray kicked the alligator repeatedly as he pulled his wife ashore. She suffered serious injuries to her leg and arm.

"I knew something had pulled me under – that's it," she said from her bed at Tampa General Hospital. "It just went down so fast. I was more in shock probably than pain."

Mr Dow said it was like "one of the scenes out of *Jaws*."

The attack happened at the Lake Como nudist resort in Pasco County on Wednesday. The alligator nearly severed Mrs Dow's left foot and left deep lacerations on her right arm. It is not yet clear whether or not her foot will have to be amputated.

July 2001

A man's decomposing body missing its right arm has been found in the same Florida canal as an arm apparently bitten off by an alligator.

Police believe both are parts of the same man, John Mark Helmreich, a homeless newspaper vendor who liked to bathe in the canal.

Police identified Mr Helmreich by taking fingerprints from the hand of the severed arm. The arm had alligator bites on it, but no jewellery or distinguishing marks. Police spokesman Jim Leljedal said the body has not yet been formally identified. He said he thinks it is likely Mr Helmreich fell into the canal and drowned, rather than being attacked by an alligator, but a post-mortem and identification checks are being carried out on the body.

June 2001

A Florida alligator has made an unsuccessful bid to eat a horse as it drank from a lake in Titusville. The alligator dragged the horse into the water and hung on to its tail during the attack.

The horse's owner, Connie Kirk, says she is afraid her children will be attacked next. "I looked out, saw my horse and there was a gator holding on to its tail," said Mrs Kirk.

The horse suffered bite wounds in the attack. Trapper Bill Robb called it an "unusually aggressive gator". He said, "I am really impressed because this is just unheard of, for them to go after livestock that size."

Mrs Kirk said the four-year-old pony, called Seminole, "went under twice and he got bit in the chest and the backside. The gator had him by the nose there for a little while, but I guess the horse was too big for him."

Mrs Kirk added, "I'm just concerned because the entire neighbourhood has children, and a lot of kids come down here to fish out of the pond. If he can pull down a horse like that, he can pull down a child pretty easily."

FATAL PENIS ATTACKS

Two Papua New Guinea fishermen bled to death after their penises were bitten off by piranha-like river fish.

The fish followed a trail of urine in the water and bit off the organs with razor sharp teeth in both of the June 2001 attacks, which have terrified villagers along the Sepik River. It's thought the fish is a relative of the piranha because they home in on urine streams to find their prey.

Authorities say the killer fish may be a food-source fish introduced from Brazil in 1994 by the United Nations Food and Agricultural Organization and the Papua New Guinea National Fisheries Authority. However, marine biologist and aquaculturist Ian Middleton said he believed they were a different species, introduced from across the Indonesia border.

He believed the fish had started biting humans because of a lack of naturally occurring food. He said: "The reason for biting people on their genitals is a result of the fish detecting a chemical change in the water, swimming up the urine trail and biting the genitals."

EIGHT-YEAR-OLD VERSUS SALTIE

An eight-year-old Australian girl has fought off an attack by a crocodile as she played in the sea.

A six-foot saltwater crocodile sank its teeth into Taleesha Fagatilli, dragging her into deeper water and began a death roll. But the reptile inexplicably released Taleesha, who is recovering in hospital from deep bite marks after the attack at Four Mile Beach, Port Douglas, in Queensland.

She has had surgery for deep cuts and slashes to her chest, leg and arm. Taleesha, who was on holiday with her family, said: "The crocodile pulled me under and was scratching me."

Screaming, she managed to stagger back to her father, Bruno, who was on the beach. He grabbed her, along with her brother and sister, and rushed to hospital.

Bruno said: 'Taleesha was covered in blood and screaming. We didn't expect to encounter a croc in a couple of feet of water."

Saltwater crocodiles are the world's largest reptile and can reach twenty-seven feet long. Twelve people have been killed by them in the past twenty years.

ANOTHER ITALIAN GREAT WHITE

A father and son have beaten off an eighteen-foot shark with a piece of wood after it started ramming their fishing boat. They were fifteen miles off the popular holiday resort off Rimini when their eighteen-foot boat was attacked.

Coastguards say they are monitoring the area in case the Great White heads for Italy's holiday beaches. A spokesman said: "It is a maneater. I would advise people in the sea to be careful and if they see a fin to get out as quickly as possible."

The men say they were lucky to escape with their lives as the shark was threatening to sink their boat. Giacomo Longhi said: "It just seemed to go on forever. He just kept hitting the boat over and over again."

His father Tersilio added: "The shark was the length of our boat. I grabbed a piece of wood and kept hitting it, then it disappeared."

MALAWI CROCODILES CLAIM 250

Malawian crocodiles have eaten or seriously maimed 250 Africans in the year 2001.

Tribal leaders have asked the government to kill the Lower Shire Valley crocodiles, which are a protected species. Ministers have sent hunters to the area to carry out a controlled cull, but they are only allowed to kill 200 a year.

Environment Minister Harry Thomson says, "We know that crocodiles are a menace here – they are eating people. But our hands are tied."

He added that the number of deaths means the Government is reviewing its policy on protecting the reptiles.

DEATH IN SHALLOW SURF

The Virginia Beach community is in a state of shock after a shark killed a ten-year-old boy in the first fatal shark attack in the US this year. Beachgoers are staying ashore and authorities patrolled waters following the tragedy, the first in the area in thirty years.

David Peltier, of Richmond, Virginia, suffered a seventeen-inch gash to his left leg and lost a huge amount of blood from a severed artery. He died in a Norfolk hospital.

"I'd rather give the shark a little time to get further down. the coast," said Debbie Morris, thirty-nine, of Virginia Beach, who refused to allow her eleven-year-old daughter into the water.

David was bitten while surfing with his father and two brothers in about four feet of water, about 150 feet from shore, off Sandbridge Beach, said Ed Brazle, division chief for the city's Emergency Medical Services.

David's father, Richard Peltier, spotted the shark and shouted to his three sons, who were in the water. Mr Peltier, a welder, hauled David on to his surfboard as the two older boys ran to shore, witnesses said. The shark brushed Mr Peltier's leg then lunged at David, who was freed from its jaws after his father hit the shark on its head. Mr Peltier then paddled to shore with his son, where witnesses and lifeguards administered first aid to the boy. Mr Peltier was treated for a hand injury.

There have been forty-nine shark attacks all over the world this year, up to 3 September 2001, with one fatal one in Brazil, said George Burgess of the International Shark Attack File in Gainesville, Florida. Twenty-eight attacks have been in Florida waters.

THIRTEEN-FOOT SNAKE

Phil Peras, aged twenty, came across the thirteen-foot snake in the Cagayan de Oro River on the island of Mindañao, in the Philippines.

Mr Peras wrestled for some time with the snake in his boat, eventually electrocuting it with a 110-volt electric rod powered by a car battery, before beheading it with his knife. The *Sun Star* reports on 3 September 2001 how Mr Peras tackled the snake, which weighed nearly twenty kilos and had brown skin, yellow spots and stripes of black – possibly an anaconda.

Despite electrocuting the snake and it falling into the water, the snake hit back, confronting Mr Peras with its mouth open, exposing its fangs. The headless snake was eventually brought ashore, still writhing. Mr Peras sold it on the roadside to a taxi driver.

Viviencio Garfin, of the Bureau of Fisheries and Aquatic Reources, said the species wrap their bodies around their victims and crush their bones.

GREAT CROCS OF OZ

In Australia in the heyday of crocodile hunting, in the early 1950s when skin prices were high, some huge saltwater crocs were shot.

Ron and Krys Pawloski hunted in the Gulf country for long years, and were Australia's first crocodile farmers, at Karumba. In 1957 Krys wrote her name in the record books by shooting an 8.7-metre (28 feet 4 inches) long estuarine crocodile in the Norman River.

In 1929 Claude Le Roy used a six-inch noble lure (gelignite) to blow up a 7.7-metre (twenty-five feet) crocodile in a hole just below the Hartley's Creek crocodile farm, north from Cairns, while George Snow shot a 6.8-metre (twenty-two feet) croc in the Albert River near Burketown in 1948.

Peter Cole bagged *the* Wyaaba Monster in the Staaten River in the mid-fifties, and that creature measured 7.5 metres (24 feet 46 inches). Hunters had been trying to shoot the Wyaaba Monster for fifty-odd years and, though wounded on a number of occasions by rifle fire, it kept coming back. Local Aborigines said that croc could not die because it was part of their dreaming.

Crocodiles ranging from 4.5 to six metres were the rule, rather than the exception, in those halcyon days of professional crocodile hunting. The reason such monsters were about was that no one had bothered too shoot them before commercial hunting began.

Big crocs over six metres are rarely seen today, but one that exceeds eight metres lives in the Goyder River swamps of northern Arnhem Land. Individuals around the 4.5- to six-metre range are not uncommon, and I have photographed such crocs in the East and South Alligator rivers of the Kakadu National Park and in some of the remote Arnhem Land and Cape York rivers and billabongs.

Early sea and land explorers Captain Philip Parker King and John Lort Stokes sailed into the Van Diemen Gulf on the ship *Beagle* and saw many crocodiles in the three rivers they named the Alligator Rivers, now part of Kakadu National Park. But there are no *alligators* in Australia.

The only other Australian crocodile is the Johnston or freshwater crocodile, *Crocodylus johnstoni*. It can reach a length of up to 3.6 metres, but no attack on humans has been recorded unless the reptile was cornered. Normally a fish eater, it will take birds, dogs and small wallabies, but bush people and Aborigines warn that small babies should not be left unattended near waterholes where "freshies" live.

The saltwater crocodile is misnamed, as it has been recorded up to 300 kilometres or more inland in fresh water, and most reptiles are probably born in the upper freshwater reaches of large rivers and never leave them. This is something to remember when travelling in the tropics! For example, crocs appear on a regular basis in Katherine's River and have been seen in the great gorge, and the township is far inland from Darwin.

Attacks on humans are rare, though it does attract media hype. Crocodiles are opportunist hunters and even when not hungry they will kill prey if it does not involve too much activity. Humans are slow, very stupid and easy to kill, so if one just happens to swim past the temptation is too much for the saurian and it may attack.

Crocodiles do not, however, hunt on land, thus it is safe to fish and walk along crocodile-inhabited pools. But do stay away from deep edges, as a crocodile can leap from the water its body length except for the section from the back legs down. When camping, do so well away from the water's edge, and vary your path to the water so you don't start a (crocodile) recognisable pattern. When fishing, remove all fish and baits from the boat as hungry crocs have been known to crawl into boats and turn them over to get to the enticing smell of dead fish and bait.

An amusing event occurred at Prince Charlotte Bay, north of Cooktown, sometime ago when a prawn-spotting float plane was forced to land close to an estuary. The two men on board were taken off by a trawler and spent the night on it.

During the night there was a lot of splashing near the plane that woke everyone up, and a spotlight showed a huge crocodile climbing on to one of the plane floats. The onlookers later swore on a stack of bibles that the croc was trying to mate with the float, and it caused the plane to flip over with only the floats left above the water. The croc was back at daylight, attempting again to make love to the floats!

The sight of your first crocodile in the wild is something you never forget, as a big one is majestic and just oozes out power and strength; some people say evil. They have an uncanny ability to remain on the water's surface without moving and sink below it without leaving a ripple, but can accelerate to an amazing speed in the blink of an eye.

Canoes have been attacked, and people in them savaged and eaten. I used to do a lot of canoeing until I got bumped twice by crocs coming up underneath the canoe, perhaps thinking that the shape gliding over them was a territorial intrusion by another crocodile. I think that is why there have been several clashes with crocs and canoes; dinghies appear to be safer but, as the following story shows not always.

I myself became the hunted when a mate and I were fishing downstream in the East Alligator, near an Arnhem Land escarpment called Turkey Dreaming. We caught some nice barramundi and had lunch in the shade of the escarpment, and waited for the tide to rise, so we could head back to the boat ramp forty kilometres upstream.

Craige fell asleep, leaning up against the bow rail, while I leaned against the motor, just resting my eyes. I must have been asleep for a few minutes because I woke with a start as the hair on the back of my neck was on edge. Without hesitation, I threw myself forward into the centre of the boat. Craige had woken at the same time as I did, his eyes the size of saucers.

"Jeeze, mate, that mongrel missed you by this much," he said with a shaky voice.

Only a metre behind the outboard lay 3.6 metres of hungry crocodile, a female who was nesting in this area and still does today. We had seen her several times in the morning, when we were fishing, but she showed no interest and kept well away from us. Once we relaxed our vigil, though, she had come up and tried for me. A fraction of a second was between me and death by the living nightmare of the tropics, only because, when she came up, she hit the motor and the back of the boat.

A mate of ours, Kerry McLaughlin, was not so lucky when he was taken by a 4.8-metre male croc on Cahill's Crossing a month earlier.

The incident was a sobering experience for both of us, and it does show how cunning a crocodile really is, because, when we were active and alert, she did not bother us; yet, once our guard was down, she came in. We will never know if she was after the two barra we had kept or after me, but it was me she had targeted.

Crocodiles are a fact of life in the tropics-and they must be treated with caution and respect, but by taking reasonable care anyone can enjoy this wonderful region. The message is, when outdoors anywhere, beware of some of Nature's not-so-nice subjects that can kill you. Some – like mosquioes – are invisible. And mosquitoes are the biggest killers of the lot.

Part 4

Killers Close to Home

PIG'S BABY SNACK

On Monday 17 August 1888, a poor woman named Kate Duane, residing in Pump Lane, near Moyderwell, in Glasgow, left her infant child in the cradle, while she went out of her cabin on some business, leaving nobody in the house to take care of the infant.

Shocking to relate, on her return she found the poor baby nearly devoured by a hungry pig – the eyes and face, with many parts of the body, having been lacerated and eaten.

The poor innocent must have suffered dreadful torture before death put an end to its agony.

IN THE DEVIL BUSH

Osei was a carpenter of the highest quality.

Carpenters have always been ten-a-penny in the African bush, and most of them are little better than adzemen. But Osei was different. He had a genuine love for his chosen vocation, and many's the hour and day he would spend on a single block of wood, methodically working on it until he had it carved to his satisfaction. The golden brown patina of the majestic African walnuts, the exquisitely rippled grain of the rich red mahoganies, the aphrodisiac fragrance of the rose-pink Guareas – only those born to be carpenters are capable of appreciating the sort of pleasure experienced by Osei as he whittled and smoothed the time away in his little lean-to workshop under the old mango tree at the foot of the village.

And there was no disputing the fact that Osei was a true carpenter. His name became synonymous with quality. His fame spread, and people came from far and wide to purchase his carvings and employ his services. As a result, his position in the village hierarchy had escalated gradually over the years, so that by now he had achieved a status second only to that of the chief himself.

With that, Osei the Carpenter was content. He had no further ambitions left in life. Except, of course, to build a house, a splendid house of mud brick and the finest of timbers, a home worthy of the name of Osei the Carpenter, for Bindu, his beautiful new wife . . .

So he toiled away happily now in the yellow heat of noon, lifting, shoving and heaving at the heavy mahogany planks he had pitsawn and stacked here on the edge of his little farm during the previous dry season, piling on one side the sizes he required and throwing to the other side those he did not. Sweat ran down the broad slopes of his shoulders to trickle in tiny rivulets down his spine to the cleft of his buttocks, staining to a dark chocolate hue the wrap of faded khaki around his loins. He sang as he worked, sporadic and sudden volleys of sound discharged into the atmosphere in an unnerving, tuneless whine that sent overhead flights of parrots sheering away sharply in squawking alarm.

Under the timber stack, death stirred suddenly, uneasily.

The dry rustling sound went through Osei the Carpenter like the thrust of a cold spear. He straightened abruptly every sense alert, his red-veined eyes wide and suspicious. A pulse throbbed on his neck as he stood motionless, listening . . . listening . . .

A large tombo fly zinged, unheeded, around his head. It settled on his neck and waited, antennae oscillating, on guard for the anticipated swipe of a hand. None came, and it focused its huge green eyes on the conduit of blood before it. Slowly and expertly, it sank its proboscis into the bulging artery.

From far up the hill the cracked call of a village rooster echoed faintly in the still air. Now the gentlest of zephyrs stirred the leaves of the young pepper plant beside him. The papery susurration reassured him and he relaxed, exhaling slowly. He slapped irritably at the fly and returned his attention to the task on hand.

Only the bottom tier of planks remained, set upon billets of wood to keep them clear of the wet African clay. Although barely half a year had elapsed since he had stacked them, the fecund humidity of these equatorial regions was such that this bottom layer was now cocooned in a tangled mat of thorny vines. He attacked the wiry tendrils with his machete, the broad blade spanging tinnily with each stroke.

Satisfied at last, he laid down his machete and reached for the nearest length of timber. He yanked at it, a short, grunting jerk. It did not even budge. Exasperated, he grasped the centre plank and wrenched at it with the full power of his sinewy old arms. The whole bottom deck came apart so easily and with such a splintery explosion of sound that he was caught completely by surprise. He stumbled backwards on to his rump with a resounding wallop.

From underneath what was left of the timber stack a long black coil of doom erupted and was upon him instantly grabbing the calf of his leg in a huge pink maw, chewing at it like a dog, as cobras will, with each bite injecting enough venom to flatten an elephant.

His first high, gurgling scream brought the villagers pell-mell down the hill, but by the time they reached him it was too late. They saw the cobra disappearing into the forest like a galleon in full sail, its carmine neck puffed out angrily and held high above the ground. They saw Osei sprawled on his back, his limbs twitching gruesomely and his teeth grinning at them in a final, terrible rictus.

But Osei the Carpenter was aware of none of these things. Nor was he aware of his new and beautiful wife weeping over him. His spirit was already winging its way over the dark and turbulent waters of the River of the Dead.

In accordance with custom for those who had died of snakebite or other unnatural causes, Osei was laid to rest in the Devil Bush. This was a tract of low-lying, swampy forest a few miles from the village. It was a silent, gloomy place, home to clouds of mosquitoes by night and voracious tsetse flies by day. Snakes of many kinds infested it, and legions of the little brown rats that they fed upon. Great hairy spiders lay in wait behind vast, sticky webs, webs that were strong enough to stop a man in his tracks. It was a singularly horrible piece of bush, forbidden to all except the witch doctor and his burial parties. It was, in any case, a place no human being in his right mind would want to venture anywhere near . . .

MANEATER IN A RAILWAY CARRIAGE

Towards the end of my stay in British East Africa, I dined one evening with Mr. Ryall, the Superintendent of the Police, in his inspection carriage on the railway. Poor Ryall! I little thought then what a terrible fate was to overtake him only a few months later in that very carriage in which we dined.

A maneating lion had taken up his quarters at a little roadside station called Kimaa, and had developed an extraordinary taste for the members of the railway staff. He was a most daring brute, quite indifferent as to whether he carried off the stationmaster, the signalman, or the pointsman; and one night, in his efforts to obtain a meal, he actually climbed up on to the roof of the station buildings and tried to tear off the corrugated-iron sheets. At this the terrified *baboo* in charge of the telegraph instrument below sent the following laconic message to the Traffic Manager: "Lion fighting with station. Send urgent succour." Fortunately he was not victorious in his "fight with the station"; but he tried so hard to get in that he cut his feet badly on the iron sheeting, leaving large bloodstains on the roof. Another night, however, he succeeded in carrying off the native driver of the pumping-engine, and soon afterwards added several other victims to his list.

On one occasion an engine-driver arranged to sit up all night in a large iron water-tank in the hope of getting a shot at him, and had a loop-hole cut in the side of the tank from which to fire. But as so often happens, the hunter became the hunted; the lion turned up in the middle of the night, overthrew the tank and actually tried to drag the driver out though the narrow circular hole in the top through which he had squeezed in. Fortunately the tank was just too deep for the brute to be able to reach the man at the bottom; but the latter was naturally half paralysed with fear and had to crouch so low down as to be unable to take anything like proper aim. He fired, however, and succeeded in frightening the lion away for the time being.

It was in a vain attempt to destroy this pest that poor Ryall met his tragic and untimely end. On 6 June 1900, he was travelling up in his inspection carriage from Makindu to Nairobi, accompanied by two friends, Mr Huebner and Mr Parenti. When they reached Kimaa, which is about two hundred and fifty miles from Mombasa, they were told that the maneater had been seen close to the station only a short time before their train arrived, so they at once made up their minds to remain there for the night and endeavour to shoot him. Ryall's carriage was accordingly detached from the train and shunted into a siding close to the station, where, owing to the unfinished state of the line, it did not stand perfectly level, but had a pronounced list to one side.

In the afternoon the three friends went out to look for the lion, but finding no traces of him whatever, they returned to the carriage for dinner. Afterwards they all sat up on guard for some time; but the only noticeable thing they saw was what they took to be two very bright and steady glow-worms. After events proved that these could have been nothing else than the eyes of the maneater steadily watching them all the time and studying their every movement. The hour now growing late, and there being apparently no sign of the lion, Ryall persuaded his two friends to lie down, while he kept the first watch. Huebner occupied the high berth over the table on the one side of the carriage, the only other berth being on the opposite side of the compartment and lower down. This Ryall offered to Parenti, who declined it, saying that he would be quite comfortable on the floor; and he accordingly lay down to sleep, with his feet towards the sliding door which gave admission to the carriage.

It is supposed that Ryall, after watching for some considerable time, must have come to the conclusion that the lion was not going to make its appearance that night, for he lay down on the lower berth and dozed off. No sooner had he done so, doubtless, than the cunning maneater began cautiously to stalk the three sleepers. In order to reach the little platform at the end of the carriage, he had to mount two very high steps from the railway line, but these he managed to negotiate successfully and in silence. The door from this platform into the carriage was a sliding one on wheels, which ran very easily on a brass runner; and as it was probably not quite shut, or at any rate not secured in any way, it was an easy matter for the lion to thrust in a paw and shove it open. But owing to the tilt of the carriage and to his great extra weight on the one side, the door slid to and snapped into the lock the moment he got his body right in, thus leaving him shut up with the three sleeping men in the compartment.

He sprang at once at Ryall, but, in order to reach him, had actually to plant his feet on Parenti, who, it will be remembered, was sleeping on the floor. At this moment Huebner was suddenly awakened by a loud cry, and on looking down from his berth was horrified to see an enormous lion standing with his hind feet on Parenti's body, while his forepaws rested on poor Ryall. Small wonder that he was panic-stricken at the sight. There was only one possible way of escape, and that was through the second sliding door communicating with the servants' quarters, which was opposite to that by which the lion had entered. But in order to reach this door Huchner had literally to jump on to the maneater's back, for its great bulk filled up all the space beneath his berth.

It sounds scarcely credible, but it appears that in the excitement and horror of the moment he actually did this, and fortunately the lion was too busily engaged with his victim to pay any attention to him. So he managed to reach the door in safety; but there, to his dismay, he found that it was held fast on the other side by the terrified coolies, who had been aroused by the disturbance caused by the lion's entrance. In utter desperation he made frantic efforts to open it, and exerting all his strength at last managed to pull it back sufficiently far to allow him to squeeze through, when the trembling coolies instantly tied it up again with their turbans. A moment afterwards a great crash was heard, and the whole carriage lurched violently to one side; the lion had broken through one of the windows, carrying off poor Ryall with him. Being now released, Parenti lost no time in jumping through the window on the opposite side of the carriage, and fled for refuge to one of the station buildings; his escape was little short of miraculous, as the lion had been actually standing on him as he lay on the floor. The carriage itself was badly shattered, and the woodwork of the window had been broken to pieces by the passage of the lion as he sprang through with his victim in his mouth.

All that can be hoped is that poor Ryall's death was instantaneous. His remains were found next morning about a quarter of a mile away in the bush, and were taken to Nairobi for burial. I am glad to be able to add that very shortly afterwards the terrible brute who was responsible for this awful tragedy was caught in an ingenious trap constructed by one of the railway staff. He was kept on view for several days, and then shot.

SOME SERIAL KILLERS

There have always been multiple killers, especially killers for gain, but the "serial killer" (a term coined only in the 1970s) is a different breed – someone who specializes in killing strangers, not for gain but for pleasure; someone who also appears to be, and often is, sane and normal in all senses but one.

In the increasingly footloose world of the nineteenth century, before the days of the telephone, when people expected to be out of touch with family and friends for weeks or months at a time, it was not difficult for the serial killer to find victims whose disappearance would not at first be remarked on and with whom no one was likely to connect him. In the later decades of the nineteenth century, his tally was believed rarely to have fallen below half a dozen and to have been more often calculable in tens or twenties. Some were held responsible for the murder of hundreds. Before the days of forensic science and computer analysis, it was impossible to be sure.

In 1871–2, Vincenz Verzeni killed "probably twelve" young women near Rome, strangling them, disembowelling them and drinking their blood. In the 1890s, Herman Webster Mudgett (alias H. H. Holmes) tortured, murdered and stripped the flesh from "at least twenty-seven" women during the Chicago Fair; contemporaries thought the true figure was nearer two hundred. Even Jack the Ripper – who carved out the genitalia of five prostitutes in London's Whitechapel in 1888 – may have had other deaths to his credit; since he was never caught (and serial killers rarely give up unless they *are* caught) it cannot be certain that his lethal career ended there. The theory has been advanced, and quite persuasively, that he emigrated to Baltimore and took up where he had left off in London . . .

After the First World War, in the hungry wastelands of Europe, there emerged – briefly – a few homicidal psychopaths who not only murdered to satisfy their sexual needs but to make an incidental profit from their labours.

In 1921–4, in what was then Münsterberg, Silesia, there was Carl Denke, landlord of a rooming house who killed an estimated thirty of his boarders, chopped them up, ate some there and then, and salted down the rest for later consumphon. In Berlin a fifty-year-old former butcher named Grossmann sold frankfurters at the main railway station made from the pickled and ground flesh of buxom country girls he picked up at that same station while he was hawking his wares. And in Hanover there was a cross between Sweeney Todd and Varney the Vampire – Fritz Haarmann, who was found guilty in 1924 of biting to death at least twenty-seven young homosexuals and making them into sausages for sale; some experts estimated that fifty victims would have been nearer the mark and there could have been more; a total of six hundred boys disappeared in Hanover in 1924 alone.

Although the years of hunger passed, memories of such cannibal killers lingered on, and not only in Europe. In Westchester County, NY in 1934, sixty-six-year-old Albert Howard Fish was found to have an extensive collection of press cuttings about Haarmann when he was arrested and tried for abducting twelve-year-old Grace Budd, strangling her and dismembering her body. Over the nine days following the murder, he later admitted, he had kept himself in a state of permanent arousal by eating strips of her flesh cooked with vegetables. Although tried for this crime alone, Fish claimed to have abducted, killed, ravished and cannibalized at least a hundred children between 1910 and the date of his trial – and since he was a housepainter who had worked or travelled in twenty-three states, there is a strong probability that he was, indeed, a serial rather than a single killer.

STARVATION DIET SOVIET STYLE

By the spring of 1921 one quarter of the peasantry in Soviet Russia was starving. Famine struck not only in the Volga region but in the Urals and Kama basins, the Don, Bashkiria, Kazakhstan, western Siberia and the southern Ukraine. The famine was accompanied by typhus and cholera which killed hundreds of thousands of people already weakened by hunger. The worst affected regions were on the Volga steppe. In Samara province nearly two million people (three-quarters of the population) were said to be dying from hunger by the autumn of 1921: 700,000 of them did in fact die by the end of the crisis. In one typical volost, Bulgakova, with a population of 16,000 in January 1921, 1,000 people had died, 2,200 had abandoned their homes and 6,500 had been paralysed by hunger or disease by the following November.

Throughout the Volga region hungry peasants resorted to eating grass, weeds, leaves, moss, tree bark, roof thatch and flour made from acorns, sawdust, clay and horse manure. They slaughtered livestock and hunted rodents, cats and dogs. In the villages there was a deathly silence. Skeletons of people, children with their bellies bloated, lay down quietly like dogs to die. "The villagers have simply given up on life," one relief worker noted in Saratov. "They are too weak even to complain." Those with enough strength boarded up their ruined farms, packed their meagre belongings on to carts, and fled to the towns in search of food. At the town markets a few loaves of bread would be exchanged for a horse. Many people did not make it but collapsed and died along the road. Huge crowds converged on the railway stations in the vain hope of catching a train to other regions – Moscow, the Don, Siberia, almost anywhere, so long as it was rumoured there was food. They did not know that all transportation from the famine region had been stopped on Moscow's orders to limit the spread of epidemics. This was the scene at the Simbirsk railway station in the summer of 1921:

Imagine a compact mass of sordid rags, among which are visible here and there lean, naked arms, faces already stamped with the seal of death. Above all one is conscious of a poisonous odour. It is impossible to pass. The waiting room, the corridor, every foot thickly covered with people, sprawling, seated, crouched in every imaginable position. If one looks closely he sees that these filthy rags are swarming with vermin. The typhus stricken grovel and shiver in their fever, their babies with them, Nursing babies have lost their voices and are no longer able to cry. Every day more than twenty dead are carried away, but it is not possible to remove all of them. Sometimes corpses remain among the living for more than five days ...

A woman tries to soothe a small child lying in her lap. The child cries, asking for food. For some time the mother goes on rocking it in her arms. Then suddenly she strikes it. The child screams anew. This seems to drive the woman mad. She begins to beat it furiously, her face distorted with rage. She rains blows with her fist on its little face, on its head and at last she throws it upon the floor and kicks it with her foot. A murmur of horror arizes around her. The child is lifted from the ground, curses are hurled at the mother, who, after her furious excitement has subsided, has again become herself utterly indifferent to everything around her. Her eyes are fixed, but are apparently sightless.

Hunger turned some people into cannibals. This was a much more common phenomenon than historians have previously assumed. In the Bashkir region and on the steppelands around Pugachev and Buzuluk, where the famine crisis was at its worst, thousands of cases were reported. It is also clear that most of the cannibalism went unreported. One man, convicted of eating several children, confessed for example: "In our village everyone eats human flesh but they hide it. There are several cafeterias in the village – and all of them serve up young children: The phenomenon really took off with the onset of winter, around November 1921, when the first snows covered the remaining food substitutes on the ground and there was nothing else to eat. Mothers, desperate to feed their children, cut off limbs from corpses and boiled the flesh in pots. People ate their own relatives – often their young children, who were usually the first to die and whose flesh was particularly sweet.

In some villages the peasants refused to bury their dead but stored the corpses, like so much meat, in their barns and stables. They often begged relief workers not to take away the corpses but to let them eat them instead. In the village of Ivanovka, near Pugachev, a woman was caught with her child eating her dead husband and when the police authorities tried to take away his remains she shouted: "We will not give him up, we need him for food, he is our own family, and no one has the right to take him away from us." The stealing of corpses from cemeteries became so common that in many regions armed guards had to be posted on their gates.

Hunting and killing people for their flesh was also a common phenomenon. In the town of Pugachev it was dangerous for children to go out after dark since there were known to be bands of cannibals and traders who killed them to eat or sell their tender flesh. In the Novouzensk region there were bands of children who killed adults for their meat. Relief workers were armed for this reason. There were even cases of parents killing their own babies – usually their daughters – in order to eat their flesh or feed it to their other children.

It is easy to say that such acts were simply a sign of moral depravity or psychosis. But it was often compassion which drove people to cannibalism. The agony of watching one's children slowly die of hunger can spur people to do anything, and in such extreme circumstances the normal rules of right and wrong can seem remote. Indeed when interviewed the flesh-eaters appeared quite rational and had often developed a new moral code to legitimize their behaviour. Many of them argued that eating human flesh could not be a crime because the living soul had already departed from the bodies, which remained "only as food for the worms in the ground". Moreover, the craving for human flesh which starving people can easily develop once they have eaten it was not peculiar to any social class. Hungry doctors often succumbed to eating it after long spells of relief work in the famine region, and they too stated that the worst part of the experience was "the insuperable and uncomfortable craving" which they acquired for human flesh.

NIGHTMARES IN THE SOVIET UNION

In the Soviet Union it was decided that the 1937 census must be suppressed because it proved a truth that Stalin and his entourage already knew. Indeed, the evidence – stories of hunger and death, official requests for guidance, handwritten, sweat-stained pleas for help; last testaments and prayers – had poured across their desks for months in the winter of 1932, the anguished spring of 1933. What it described turned out to be the greatest famine in Soviet history, and one of the most devastating of the entire twentieth century. Exactly how many people died, from the effects of the famine itself or as a result of the campaign of collectivization that preceded it, is something that will probably never be known. For while it may be possible to count the adults, the people who had names and histories and whose lives had made some impact on official records, the infants usually died before they were even given names. Demographers are still debating the disaster, and a range of mortality figures has been proposed. The most serious converge on a total of between five and seven million.

The catastrophe was without precedent. There are many ways in which the stories of starvation that people tell, from 1921–2, from 1929–33 and later from the post-war famine of 1946–7, are similar. Survivors all recount their gradual loss of sensation, the numbness, even the loss of the feeling of hunger itself, the gradual descent into a twilight life, a waking death. All describe the desperate scavenging, the diet of lime leaves, bark and carrion. There are always stories, too, of cannibalism, of infanticide, of human flesh disguized as rissoles or potted meat. But the epoch of collectivization, dekulakization and the great famine, 1929–33, was the most intense and murderous of all. Whole villages simply disappeared. "We did not have enough books in which to enter these mass deaths," a local statistical office clerk, an employee of the ZAGS, wrote to his supervisor in 1933. "Our priority was the burial of corpses."

The story of the great Soviet famine begins with the confrontation between Bolshevism and the peasantry, the mutual mistrust and misunderstanding, the Marxists' hatred of the village, the peasants' of the city. It has a pre-history in the famine of 1921–2. The revolution was never made to benefit the countryside, though Lenin claimed that his party represented the poorest peasants. In return, the peasants, though they did not want the old world back (they seldom actively supported the Whites in the Civil War), were wary of Bolshevism and often hostile to its agents. They did not like the note of obligation, the taxes, the house searches and conscription. The grain requisitions of the Civil War alienated millions from the new government. But the famine of the early 1920s would numb the spirit of resistance. It has been estimated (again, the numbers are uncertain) that about six million people died in those two years.

The fear of starvation had begun during the Imperialist War; but by 1919 it had become a reality across the whole of southern Russia. A friend wrote to Got'e from Saratov in December 1919 with rumours of "two reliable instances of cannibalism" and a story that "university laboratory assistants were eating dogs and cats". This food crisis was set to deepen: a bad harvest in 1920 was followed by an exceptionally dry spring in 1921. That summer the peasants began to sicken, then to die. It was the first great famine of the Soviet era. Even the Civil War had not prepared the witnesses for all that they would see. As Sorokin, who travelled in the famine region, later wrote, "My nervous system, accustomed to many horrors in the years of Revolution, broke down completely before the spectacle of the actual starvation of millions in my ravaged country." "Russia received the shock of famine broken not only in body, but in spirit," wrote the American relief worker H. H. Fisher. "Distrust of the government and its agents, suspicion and hatred of neighbours, left the peasants confused and hopeless and less able to withstand the shock to which unfavourable natural conditions always exposed them. When, in the summer of 1921, the signs of a greater famine became unmistakable, the peasants became panic-stricken, and fled the villages in their terror, or remained stolidly to wait for death."

On this occasion the Soviet government permitted foreign aid teams, and notably the American Relief Association (ARA) to operate within the famine zone. The idea had been controversial. Herbert Hoover, the future American President, had been pressing for a food campaign in the Soviet Union since 1919, when he brought the problem to the attention of the Allies at the Versailles Peace Conference, but the Soviet government did not allow the wagons to cross into the famine territory until 1921. Bureaucratic delays and bottlenecks were always blamed, but the underlying reason, as the Americans knew, was the Soviet fear of spies, their visceral suspicion of the foreigner. The starving were fortunate this time (there would be no relief a decade later, for officially, that second time, there was no famine to relieve). By 1922 the ARA was feeding over eight million people a day.

The scenes in villages across the Black Earth steppe would etch themselves on the Americans' memories. The famine was worst in the grain regions of the lower Volga around Saratov and Samara, in the provinces of Orenburg and Ufa, towards the Ural Mountains, and across an area to the north of these which took in the cities of Penza and Voronezh. Large parts of Ukraine, as well as the North Caucasus, were also affected. Fisher toured much of this countryside, and what he saw reduced him to near-despair. "Men and women . . . exhumed dead animals," he wrote, "and hungrily devoured cats and dogs when they could be found." When he visited the town of Ufa in late August, he saw about five hundred unburied bodies lying in the streets; Soviet doctors admitted that four-fifths of the corpses had died of hunger. By this time, too, more than fifteen thousand people in Ufa province had already died of cholera. Other diseases, including typhus and dysentery, would account for thousands more. The Cheka privately estimated that one-fifth of the population in the region of Ufa had died of famine and its consequences by the end of 1921.

'We entered the village of N. in the afternoon,' Sorokin wrote:

> This place was as though dead. Houses stood deserted and roof-less, with gaps where windows and doors had been. The straw thatch of the houses had long since been torn away and eaten. There were no animals in the village, of course, no cattle, horses, sheep, goats, dogs, cats, or even crows. All had been eaten. Dead silence lay over the snow-covered roads until, with a creak, a sledge came in sight, a sledge drawn by two men and a woman and having on it a dead body.

Reports of cannibalism now began to reach the cities. One version – for which there is a separate Russian word, *"trupoyedstvo"*, "the eating of flesh from a corpse" (as opposed to *lyudoyedstvo*, which is the killing and eating of living human beings) – might involve the butchery of dead neighbours, or of a person's own dead children, or else it might follow the robbery of a recent grave. "People spoke in the simplest manner about eating the foul impurities that passed for food," Fisher remembered. "And many would argue that the eating of human flesh was not a crime, since the living soul had departed, and the body remained only as food for worms in the ground."

The other kind of cannibalism was more systematic, though rarer, and its victims were often homeless children, orphans or friendless travellers. The stories persist even now. Adults from the famine regions will still remember – or perhaps still dream and fear – that they were lured along a side street once when they were children, and that a stranger offered them some sweets, a crust of bread. Some instinct, they will all continue, must have saved them, some extra sense of doubt or menace. They shudder. Other children died.

Such individual tales may well be fantasies, like urban myths, but the basic truth behind the fear is real. Indeed, officials in some of the worst-affected districts resorted to a ban on the sale of processed meats in the winter of 1921 in order to stop the trade in human flesh. Grisly scenes were recorded by local medical inspectors and police: Nikolai Borodin's account of one such incident, though graphic, was not unusual. The police in his district of Ukraine had discovered a cellar under one of the peasants' cottages. Their suspicions were aroused by the fact that the man and woman who lived there had been selling rissoles in the local town. What they found when they opened the door; and what Borodin claims he saw as he stretched to see over the crush of official backs, were "barrels containing parts of children's bodies, sorted and salted, and scalped heads. In the centre of the cellar stood a butcher's block and there was a knife, an axe, and some rags on the floor. Behind me,' he added, 'someone vomited loudly." He did not feel too well himself – he had bought and eaten one of the couple's rissoles the same day. Screams rang in his ears as he walked away. He looked back across the dusty square and saw the couple kneeling in a pool of their own blood while members of the crowd kicked them to death . . .

Besieged Leningrad (1941–3) was a scene of stoicism, but it was also a hunting ground for crime. "Speculators" and "parasites" offered to arrange a burial in exchange for vodka, beer or bread, they promised to obtain a coffin, they demanded advance payment in meat or ration cards. Some refused to move a body unless they were generously bribed. Local criminals also offered to help convey the bodies to the cemeteries. They would pile several on to a cart, offload them quickly, cook the books. You got a ration of vodka for each corpse, and it was easy to inflate the numbers. No one really checked, not in the cold, the twilight, the dense fog. Vodka, like bread, was money, and money, also like bread, was life.

The city tried to curb this grisly crime by checking individual documents, by issuing each corpse with papers. But this created a new problem, as the bureaucratic mania deterred some people from engaging with officialdom at all. The relatives of the dead were "afraid that they did not have the right papers", and so they stopped taking bodies to the morgue or the cemetery for themselves. Their unwillingness simply added to the scores of fresh corpses "which were dumped anonymously into streets and stairwells". The crisis was contained in the end when special blockade cemeteries (including Piskarevskoe) were designated in the suburbs. Eventually, too, an old brickworks was converted into an emergency crematorium. Miraculously, there were no major epidemics in Leningrad through all the months of siege.

The hunger, however, was murderous, and inevitably, the most desperate measure of all was cannibalism. The official record does not evade it. "The cemeteries were poorly guarded," it observed, and "bodies or parts of bodies, and especially those of children", began to disappear. One woman was arrested on her way back from a graveyard with five children's bodies in a sack. Corpses left in hospital yards were butchered so often that guards had to be posted there as well as in the graveyards and the morgues. "I went to a bread store that was not far from my home," one survivor recalled. "I would walk past people lying dead in the street and then walk past these same bodies going home again and parts of their bodies would be missing. It was an hour or so sometimes and body parts would be taken." "Even now," another survivor added, "I cannot buy meat pies from traders on the streets. I'm always afraid of what might be inside them." Every Leningrader shudders at the thought . . .

The second half of the 1940s was difficult because the hardship and, indeed, the hunger did not stop. There was a continuing need to keep in mind the lessons of survival you had learned – a flexible approach to property, for instance, and a careful husbanding of food. The two years 1946 and 1947 would see another famine.

Immediately after the war, collective farmers worked in exchange for food. The rations were always meagre. "We get two hundred grammes of bread for a work day," wrote a peasant from the Ukrainian town of Kamenets-Podolsk in the spring of 1946. "We have been getting by without bread for ages now. We don't know what is going to happen, but we cannot go on like this for long." "A lot of people are hungry," wrote another. "There aren't even any potatoes, and people are going to the fields to work without food." Stepan Ustimovich was three in 1947, but he remembers what the hunger meant. "At first we went without bread and ate potatoes," he told me. "Then we ate leaves. And then we ate the weeds."

The spring came late in 1946. The ground was still frozen, in many places, well into May But the lengthening days brought little hope. June and July were unusually hot and dry. The crop in the fields was thin, the wheat scorched and the potatoes so small, where they grew at all, that people began to talk of a real famine. "We don't want to starve to death," wrote a peasant from the Kiev region. "It is going to be like 1933." "It's still summer," another complained, "so what is it going to be like this winter? I survived the whole war, I'm still alive, but now it seems I am to die of hunger."

Just after Christmas, a woman from the Ukrainian province of Poltava wrote to her husband, who was living two days' journey from his family in Bryansk. "Please ask your bosses to give you some time off or at least to get some kind of document for me," she begged,

so that they will take the children at the orphanage. The children have already swollen up, and I don't know what's going to happen to them. My own arms have swollen . . . I cannot carry flour any more. Lena is especially swollen, but we are all ill. It's already worse at the markets than it was in 1933, everything is expensive. I beg you for the last time, find a way out for your own family . . . We are dying like dogs, cold, hungry and barefoot.

It was to be a famine which affected the industrial north as well as the agricultural regions of the south and Ukraine. It would last for eighteen months, and account for tens of thousands of lives. Although the state would play it down, denying reality once again, this famine was less brutal, in many respects, than that of 1933. The government's response to it was certainly less callous. The war, in fact, had made some local administrators more sensitive, respectful perhaps of the widows and fathers of men beside whom they had fought. Some collective-farm chairmen kept back grain and other supplies during the requisition season in 1946, and though many were arrested, the punishment they faced was often more lenient than expected. There were even attempts to secure foreign aid for the starving through the United Nations, Red Cross and other charitable organizations. But the 1947 famine was more than a mere postscript to the war. Death from starvation is always terrible, and the memory of 1933 was still fresh. Hunger inspired panic and despair. Once again, it seemed, the government was going to take its grain and butter from the villages while children swelled and died. The war had solved nothing.

By February 1947 the echoes of 1933 were everywhere: in the haunted faces of the children, in the despair of the mourners as they dragged the corpses to the pit, and always, when the last dogs and sparrows had been shot and skinned, in the unaccustomed silence. "'We ate the animals," remembered one survivor, "we cut up the horses. When they were all eaten, we hunted gophers, hares and sparrows . . . In the spring of 1947, when the swans came back, we started to eat them, we boiled them with bran and grits." The weakness followed, the dysentery and the first deaths. "A great many people are dying," a woman wrote that spring, "and now they take them to the cemeteries and leave them there. The local officials have made bigger graves, common graves, and they have started burying people in them all together."

"Grandfather died in our house, although he was not old – only sixty," remembered one old man. "But there were families in the village where everyone died. The people were too weak to bury the bodies of their relatives, and sometimes the corpses would lie for days." Stepan Ustimovich's mother died. "Most people survived it somehow," he told me. "They made porridge with husks and peelings, they ate cats even. But mostly they got through. But Mother, well, she caught a cold, and there weren't any doctors. And then there were complications, and it got worse. I think it was February, I was three, February 1947. I remember the last days, how I was still sitting on her lap, and then I remember the funeral." In some villages, mortality was a lot higher than Stepan Ustimovich remembers. The survivors left, just as their parents had done less than fifteen years before.

Yet again, but this time in a land where scientists were working on a new atomic bomb, their hunger drove some people to cannibalism. On 19 February 1947, a bag containing human remains was discovered under a bridge near Kiev. The body was identified as that of a youth of sixteen or seventeen, but all that was left was his head, and 'both his legs, from which all the meat had been cut with a sharp knife'. Three weeks later a woman was arrested for killing her seven-year-old daughter. She and the child's older sister had already eaten most of the corpse. At about the same time, it was discovered that another woman had killed, butchered and salted her seventy-year-old husband.

Beneath the euphemism and concealment, then, beyond the world of Stalin's middle class, there was a struggle going on about the basic means to live. You need no theory of long-term brutalization to explain the desperation in the villages in 1947. In public, certainly, there was a facade of decorous grief, mild envy of dead heroes, and good, solid stoicism. But the land of the censored nursery rhyme was also a place where little boys played football in the streets with the skulls of unburied soldiers. On summer nights, too, their fathers stamped on glowing cigarettes and crept out to the silent battlefields in search of necessary plunder. Even in the 1970s there were corpses with gold teeth. Their uniforms had rotted, but there might be metal crests and buttons to collect and even, on a really good night, a handgun that would work if you could get it clean.

THE SIEGE OF LENINGRAD

The sufferings of the citizens of Leningrad (now St Petersburg) during the Second World War, when the city was besieged by German forces, have become the stuff of legend. Many of the records of this period were embargoed by Stalin, and it was only within the last few years that a research team led by Dr John Barber of King's College, Cambridge, succeeded in unearthing an invaluable cache of original documents that provide first-hand accounts of what it was like for Leningraders to endure death by starvation. They detail all too clearly the full horrors of some of the most ghastly and widespread episodes of cannibalism in modern times. As Dr Barber states:

> We now have official reports as to what happened, produced at the time or very shortly afterwards, which leave no doubt that cannibalism existed and that it took place on a far from insignificant scale. In addition to that, we have access to records, diaries, reminiscences that were produced by people who lived through the siege in which they quite explicitly and as a matter of fact talk about cannibalism as a part of everyday life.

The majority of the accounts come from the period when Leningrad was worst hit, during the winter of 1941–2. Temperatures fell to below –30° C, one of the coldest winters on record, and almost no food was getting into the city. There was no public heating, light or water supply. The transport system had failed and some 600,000 people died in only a few months. The records describe in detail the extent of the human misery:

> There were corpses in people's houses, in the streets, in the rivers, in the squares and at the cemeteries themselves, where the personnel just couldn't cope with the influx of corpses; there would be hundreds and thousands of unburied corpses just lying there. At the largest cemetery, the Piskarovskaya, in February 1942, it's recorded that on some days there were up to 20,000 or 25,000 unburied bodies. So there was the opportunity for people who were in a desperate state to have access to human meat, and in many diaries and other records of the time we find people noting almost as a matter of course that they are walking along a street and they see a corpse which has had, as is written, the tender parts carved off. And quite often someone will look out of a window and see the body of a person who had fallen dead there the previous evening chopped up with only parts of it remaining.

Extracts from letters written by a starving Leningrader in January 1942 make similarly grim reading: "The city has become a morgue – the streets have become avenues of the dead. In every basement of every house there is a heap of dead bodies. There are processions of bodies through the streets, and there are piles of them in the hospitals."

In their desperation, people began to eat anything they could find. The paraffin glue used by the city's carpenters was melted down and became a local delicacy dubbed, with gallows humour, "meat in aspic". Grass and plants were uprooted from the frozen earth, and bark was stripped from the trees. People began to die in their thousands. As the body count rose, the attitude of the starving Leningraders towards their dead changed gradually from sorrow to ambivalence and, finally, to cannibalistic craving. This transition, which occurred from the winter of 1941–2 onwards, is graphically illustrated by the inability of the dty's funeral services to deal with the mass of bodies. A 1943 report from the Leningrad funeral service reads as follows:

> People began to steal parts of chopped-up bodies, particularly those of children. In one unburied coffin, the head and feet were

left but all the remaining parts of the body had been carried away. At the Serafamofski cemetery, the director and the local police inspector discovered a corpse's head that had been cut off. Tracks led to a wooden house on the boundary of the cemetery, where they discovered the inhabitants cooking human flesh. The caretaker of the Bogoslovski cemetery stopped a woman was carrying something out of the cemetery on a toboggan. In her bag were discovered the bodies of five children.

A report written by the Military Procurator of Leningrad in February 1942 and marked "Absolutely Secret" describes in detail the scale of the problem and the arrests made of people who had committed cannibalism. In December 1941, for example, twenty-six people were arrested for cannibalism. In January 1942, 366 people were arrested for cannibalism, and in the first half of the following month 494 people were arrested. By mid-1942 the rate of arrests for cannibalism was running at about 1,000 per month.

These figures tally with the Cheka's reports, which reveal that, by the summer of 1942, 2,000 people had been charged with cannibalism; almost all of them had been found guilty, and nearly 600 of them had been executed. What was also interesting about the report was that canniballism cut across all social and gender boundaries; it was neither an exclusively male activity nor something to which only the lower echelons of sodety resorted. Doctors, teachers, soldiers, males and females in equal measure – all resorted to eating human flesh, as one elderly siege survivor, Zinaida Kuznetsova, recalled:

I know that my neighbours ate their son – at the end of the war they let it slip. The boy always went around in a gas mask, collecting horse dung to eat. Then all of a sudden he disappeared. They said he'd gone away to the countryside. Then it slipped out in conversation that they'd eaten him, and they were arrested and tried for it.

There was a woman in the bread queue who was always trying to get me to go with her to her house, saying that it was nice and warm where she lived, that everything was just like it was before the war, but I didn't believe her and I didn't go. It later turned out that she'd killed and eaten twenty-two children in this way.

By December 1943, as the Red Army began to push the German armies back beyond its frontiers, Leningrad began to emerge from its collective nightmare.

Japanese soldiers killed and ate an Allied PoW [prisoner of war] a day in New Guinea in the final stages of the Second World War, according to documents discovered by a Japanese scholar in Australia.

The papers provide the first official proof of what had previously been widely rumoured: that Japanese soldiers engaged in cannibalism in the occupied territory as the war drew to a close.

The discovery was made by a Japanese who spent six months studying government archives in Canberra. Toshiyuki Tanaka, an associate professor at Melbourne University, found more than 100 documented cases of cannibalism by Imperial Japanese Army troops in New Guinea and sworn statements from Australian soldiers who recognized the remains of cannibalized colleagues. Among the documents, the first official Japanese record of cannibalism, is a memo issued on 18 November 1944 by a Japanese major-general in New Guinea expressing concern at the consumption of human flesh by Imperial Army soldiers.

"Those who have consumed human flesh (excluding that of the enemy), knowing that it is human flesh, will be sentenced to death as for the worst human crime," the memo says.

Eating one's enemies was apparently not considered a moral or criminal offence by Japanese army commanders. Among the papers are sworn statements from former Australian and Allied prisoners about how some of their colleagues were killed and eaten.

A Pakistani corporal captured in Singapore and taken to New Guinea reported that Japanese soldiers fended off starvation by killing and eating one PoW a day.

An Australian corporal said he recognized the mutilated bodies of colleagues when New Guinea was liberated. The flesh from one had been removed from chest to ankles, he said in a statement dated 20 May 1950, to a committee investigating war crimes.

SAFARI ANTS

In the early part of 1941, soon after I took over the running of the Coryndon Memorial Museum as honorary curator, Mary and I spent many of our evenings in the museum. Consequently, we moved into the wood-and-iron bungalow that had been occupied by Dr van Someren when he was curator. The building was on the land that had been made available to the museum's trustees in 1939, and it was very near the back entrance to the museum. It was one of the few remaining houses dating back to the earliest days of Nairobi.

The bungalow lay within the municipality of Nairobi, and, fortunately, the museum board of trustees had persuaded the government to grant the whole fifteen acres surrounding it to them, so that the land could not be built upon except by the museum and its associated organizations.

The outside walls and roof of the bungalow were of corrugated iron, which, in the course of time, had become badly rusted and now needed a coat of paint. The inside walls and ceilings were made of half-inch match boarding six inches wide. Over the years a number of holes had developed in the walls, some at floor level, giving rats and mice access to the rooms from the gap between the outer and inner walls. There were also holes higher up the walls, in which spiders and other insects took refuge whenever we chased them.

At the time we moved in, there were two small swarms of bees living between the inner and outer walls, in two different parts of the building. There was also a much larger swarm engaged in constructing a honeycomb under the roof, above the ceiling. The floorboards had been perforated by termites in several places, and although we succeeded in freeing these areas of the pests by spraying paraffin down the holes, nevertheless the holes were still present underneath the covering of rough rush matting.

One evening, when Mary and I were having supper, we heard a buzzing noise developing in our bedroom and went to investigate. We found that tens of thousands of biting ants, known as "safari ants", or *siafu* in Swahili, had invaded the room through the holes in the floor. They had then entered the space between the outer and inner walls and were swarming up to raid the honey and grubs in one of the bees' nests. By the time we arrived on the scene, the battle was in full swing and the noise was terrific. Hundreds of bees were flying out from the holes in the upper level of the wall, carrying with them dead safari ants, which they dropped on to the floor. Meanwhile, thousands more ants were moving up between the walls to the honeycomb. We watched for a few minutes and then left the combatants to their own devices, hoping that the contest would be over by morning. Meanwhile we slept in the spare room.

In the morning, we found thousands of dead ants lying all over the room, though we could not see a single dead bee – and the battle was still going on. We were very interested in the fact that there were no dead bees. When a human being is stung, either the bee is hastily hrushed off, leaving its sting and little poison sac behind in its victim – after which the insect quickly dies – or the bee is crushed against the body of the victim and killed. In either case, the sting remains temporarily in the victim's flesh. Even when one tries to pull the sting out with a thumb and fingernail, in the process the whole of the contents of the poison sac is squeezed farther into the body, which is very painful.

As a youth, I had spent a great deal of time with my friend Gicuru, who initiated me in the art of beekeeping. I learned from him never to try to pull out a bee sting with my fingers. The proper method, after lightly brushing the bee from the body, is to scrape the sting from the flesh with the flat side or the back of a knife blade. In this way, the sting can be pulled out without injecting additional poison into the wound.

Obviously, when the bees in our house attacked and stung the safari ants they must have quickly withdrawn their stings and then been ready to carry on with the work of stinging other ants.

The fantastic battle raged for two whole days, and in the end the safari ants gave up the unequal struggle. So far as we could tell, they got nothing for their pains – neither grubs nor honey – and suffered a very considerable loss to their armies This was the only time I have seen these ants defeated.

In early 1942, shortly after the party returned to Nairobi, our young son, Jonathan, had a lucky escape from *siafu*, or biting ants – the same insects that had attacked the bees the year before. In the interval, we had had the corrugated iron removed from the exterior walls and roof of the house and had dealt with the bees both in the walls and in the ceiling. We had also thoroughly sealed the holes in the wooden floorboards in the spare room – now used as Jonathan's bedroom – through which the siafu had come to attack the bees.

In the evenings, after we put Jonathan to bed, we left the door wide open, so that we could hear if he cried or called out to us. One evening, we heard a most awful wail from Jonathan, and we both rushed into his bedroom and switched on the light. He was sleeping in a cot under a mosquito net, and we had thought him safe from any kind of attack by insects. Unfortunately, we had overlooked the fact that siafu will climb up the legs of furniture and find a means of penetrating almost anything! We found, to our horror, that Jonathan was completely covered with hundreds of these biting ants. They were already all over his cot, and the floor was a seething mass of insects. In a matter of seconds we got him out of his cot and into another room. Following their usual habit, an army of these ants had got into his room and up to his crib and had swarmed all over him in large numbers. Only then had they launched their biting attack. (It is not known how the order to attack is given, or which member of a raiding party gives it.)

After Mary and I had carried Jonathan to safety, out of the way of the main invading army, the next frantic minutes were spent in clearing him of hundreds of *siafu*. Those clinging to his face, eyes, and other tender parts of his body had to be taken off one by one, as carefully as possible.

It was a matter of great relief to us that Jonathan survived the ordeal so well. Once we got him clean and quieted down, I and members of our African staff attacked the ant army that had invaded his bedroom. We used quantities of boiling water, paraffin, and pyrethrum powder, and in due course we routed them and succeeded in killing the vast majority.

After Jonathan's escape, we set the four legs of his cot in wide pans, which we kept filled with water and paraffin, making it impossible for the ants to get to him that way. We also made quite sure each night that neither his bedding nor the mosquito net was trailing on the floor and thus providing a means for the ants to climb up into the cot, should they invade his room again. In spite of these precautions, we had a minor attack a few years later, when the ants succeeded in getting on to the ceiling, from where they dropped down on the net of our son Richard's cot and so down the sides and into his bed. On this occasion, we happened to go into his room quite accidentally and were able to rescue him before he was actually attacked.

These ants are a real scourge to domestic animals and livestock in Africa. They attack puppies and kittens – who are relatively helpless when they are born – sitting hens, ducks, and turkeys, and even lambs and calves. The suddenness of the attack by thousands of ants all biting simultaneously makes it practically impossible for the mother to remove her young in time to save their lives.

Horses too, when confined in a stable, are often the victims of a vicious attack. On more than one occasion, Mary and I, our staff, and our children (in the days when the children were growing up and had ponies) have been awakened in the middle of the night by sounds of frenzied kicking and neighing from the stables and have gone out to find our ponies being attacked by an army of *siafu*. When this happens the poor animals get frantic with pain, and it takes several people to hold them still while others are dealing with the ants in the same way as we dealt with those on Jonathan that night.

Although *siafu* must rank as a menace as far as human beings are concerned, there is little doubt that they are one of nature's means of controlling the population of some of the smaller creatures whose young are helpless, and even of some of the larger mammals. Marching down into dens and burrows, they attack young jackals, wild cats, mongooses, and many other creatures. I suppose several thousand young animals are killed every year in this way.

It is possible that the introduction of *siafu* might have been an answer to the rabbit problem of Australia – were it not for the fact that, having once dealt with the rabbits, they would have almost certainly turned their attention to newborn lambs and other helpless creatures.

GABOON VIPER'S REVENGE

A sixteen-year-old boy who likes to play with snakes was bitten by a deadly African viper stolen from a display case at the National Zoo in Washington, DC, hospital officials said on 5 April 1983.

Five East Coast zoos rushed supplies of anti-venin to the Children's Hospital to try to save Louis Morton, who was bitten on the right shoulder shortly before midnight two days ago by a Gaboon viper, "one of the two or three most poisonous snakes in the world", Dr Murray Pollack said.

The boy remained in critical condition in the intensive care unit of the hospital but officials said, "The medical team treating him says he is responding to the anti-venin serum and making progress."

"There have been so few cases, we are not sure exactly how to treat it," said Dr Pollack. He added that fewer than ten serious cases of that type of snake's bite are on record worldwide.

Dr Muriel Wolf, one of the doctors who treated the boy, said he was "bleeding quite severely and had problems with his blood pressure when he arrived". She said "he began to stabilize" after an initial treatment with an anti-toxin, but "he's still in a life-threatening situation".

If the youngster survives, he faces charges in connection with the theft of a pair of African snakes late last Monday from a glass cage at the National Zoo, a police spokesman said.

Doctors said Louis was alive only because a bus driver and police helped rush him to the hospital after he was bitten. He got his first dose of anti-venin about two hours later. A police officer also delivered a plastic bag containing the five-foot-long vipers to show doctors what had bitten him.

Transit official said the boy Morton was carrying a plastic bag when he boarded a bus near the zoo before midnight. He left the bus in downtown Washington, slinging the bag over his shoulder – but returned almost immediately to tell the driver he had been bitten.

REVENGE OF THE VAMPIRE BATS

Attacks by rabid vampire bats in a rural town in Brazil's north-eastern Bahia state have left three people dead and have struck terror into a community now scared to go out at night and urgently seeking medical aid. Media reports claim that up to 500 people in the town of Apora have been attacked.

In a macabre echo of Hollywood horror films such as Hitchcock's *The Birds* or the more recent *Swarm*, movies where nature takes revenge on man, the bats have been attacking the residents of Apora (population 1,500) since the middle of last month, when loggers started felling trees around caves. The logging allowed light into bat colonies, forcing the nocturnal creatures to other, more wood-shrouded haunts. During their migration the bats have been swooping around the town of Apora, not normally on their flight path, biting residents, mostly at night. The bats normally feed on woodland animals around their caves or on cows and horses. In Apora they are also attacking dogs and cats, which transmit rabies more easily to humans than farm animals. The recent deaths in Apora have been from bat-transmitted rabies.

The Bahia health department has sent 3,500 doses of vaccine and hundreds of doses of oral serum to the town. Apora's mayor has asked for 500 more doses of the oral serum because of a high demand.

"Many people in Apora are taking the oral antidote and getting inoculated against these bats, even if they haven't been bitten because they have become extremely worried that they may be the next to be attacked," said Dr Eliana de Paula Santos, director of Bahia state health ministry's department of epidemiological safety. "Many people have even stopped going out at night." Doors and windows of buildings are being covered by netting.

Tony Hutson, a bat expert with the Bat Conservation Trust in London, said that similiar incidents had occured in Central and South America, where vampire bats are found. "Now and again they will enter a village and feed on people for a while. A few years ago in Peru there were attacks when people tried to reopen old gold mines," he said.

Mr Hutson said the events were unpredictable and usually short-lived. Like all warm-blooded animals, bats can carry rabies. But the creatures were responsible for very few of the 50,000 annual world-wide deaths from rabies, he added.

JEFFREY DAHMER

Konerak, a young Asian boy was only fourteen and he was running for his life. This was his only chance for escape from the foul-smelling apartment where the creepy blond guy had slipped him some kind of powerful drug. It seemed that luck was on his side when he started to come round just as the blond man left the apartment.

It took all the strength he had to stand up and walk to the door. He was so disoriented from the drug and so panicked that it made no difference that he was naked. His instincts told him he must get out of the apartment and run away as far and as fast as he could.

It was just before 2 a.m. when Sandra Smith called 911, the emergency services number, to report the boy running around "buff naked". She didn't know who he was, but she could see he was injured and terrified.

The paramedics were the first to arrive and they swiftly wrapped the dazed boy in a blanket. The blond man stood nearby. Shortly after-wards two police officers arrived and tried to find out what was going on.

Eighteen-year-old Sandra Smith and her cousin Nicole Childress, also eighteen, were standing near the boy when the Milwaukee City police arrived. The conversation became heated between the girls, the blond man and the police.

The man told the police that Konerak was his nineteen-year-old lover who had been drinking too much. Drugged and incoherent, Konerak was unable to make himself understood or contradict the smooth-talking blond Dahmer, who gave the police a picture ID.

Sandra and Nicole tried to intervene on Konerak's behalf. They had seen the terrified boy try to resist Dahmer before the police arrived. The young women were angry and upset because the police seemed to be ignoring them and listening instead to the white man.

Just to be on the safe side, the two officers went with the boy and Dahiner to his apartment. There was a horrible stench in the apartment, but it was neat and tidy. Konerak's clothes were folded in a pile on the sofa. Dahmer showed the officers a couple of photographs of Konerak wearing only a pair of black bikini briefs. The boy himself, meanwhile, sat quietly on the sofa, unable to talk intelligibly. It is not even clear that he understood the calm explanation Dahmer gave the police as he apologized for the fact that his lover had caused a disturbance and promised it would not happen again.

The police believed the blond white man. They had no reason not to. He was well spoken, intelligent and calm. The Asian was apparently drunk and incoherent. The officers, not wanting to get in the middle of a domestic dispute between homosexual lovers, left the apartment with Konerak still sitting quietly on the sofa.

What they missed in the apartment bedroom was the body of Tony Hughes, whose decomposing corpse had lain for three days on the bed.

What they missed was the blond man immediately strangling the boy and having sex with his corpse.

What they missed were the photos that the blond man took of the dead boy, the subsequent dismembering of his body and the cleaning of his skull so that it could be kept as a trophy.

What they missed was the opportunity to take the name of Jeffrey Dahmer off the ID he had given them and to run a background check, which would have told them that the calm, well-spoken man was a convicted child molester who was still on probation.

The story did not stop there. The two young women ignored by the police went home to Sandra Smith's mother, Glenda Cleveland, a thirty-six-year-old woman who lived next to the Oxford

Apartments building that Dahmer called home. Cleveland called the police to find out what had happened to Konerak; she asked how old the child was.

"It wasn't a child – it was an adult," the officer responded. When she continued to ask questions, he told her: "Ma'am, I can make it any more clear, it's all taken care of. He's with his boyfriend and in his boyfriend's apartment . . . It's as positive as I can be . . . I can't do nothing about somebody's sexual preferences in life."

A couple of days later Cleveland called the officers back after she read a newspaper article about the disappearance of a Laotian boy name Konerak Sinthasomphone, who looked like the boy who had been trying to escape from Jeffrey Dahmer. They never sent anybody to talk to her. Cleveland even tried contacting the Milwaukee office of the FBI, but nothing came of it – that is until a couple of months later, when all hell broke loose.

On Monday, 22 July 1991, two Milwaukee police officers were driving around in the very high crime area in the vicinity of Marquette University. The heat was oppressive and the humidity almost unbearable. The smell of the neighbourhood was all the more pungent in the heat: the garbage on the streets, the urine and faeces left by the homeless, the rancid stink of cooked grease . . .

Around midnight, as the two officers sat in their car, they saw a short, wiry black man with a handcuff dangling from his wrist. Assuming he had escaped from another policeman, they asked him what he was doing. The man started to pour out a tale about this "weird dude" who put cuffs on him in his apartment. The man was thirty-two-year-old Tracy Edwards.

Edward's story smacked of some homosexual encounter that normally the police would avoid, but the two officers thought they ought to check out this man who had cuffed Edwards and who lived at the Oxford Apartments at 924 North 25th Street.

The door to apartment 213 was opened by a nice-looking thirty-one-year-old blond man. Dahmer was very calm and rational. He offered to get the key to the handcuffs from the bedroom.

At this point Edwards repeated that the knife Dahiner had threatened him with was also in the bedrooom, so one of the officers decided to go look for himself. He noticed photographs lying around that shocked him: dismembered human bodies and skulls in a refrigerator. When he collected his wits, he yelled to his partner to cuff Dahmer and place him under arrest.

Suddenly Dahmer lost his cool and fought as the cop tried to cuff him. While one officer subdued Dahmer, the other went to the refrigerator and opened it. He screamed loudly and slammed the door on the face that stared out at him. "There's a fucking head in the refrigerator!"

Upon closer examination, the apartment revealed an intimate juxtaposition of the tidy and the unspeakable. While the small home was neat and clean, especially for a bachelor, and his pet fish well cared for, the stench of decomposition was overwhelming.

The box of baking soda in the refrigerator could not entirely absorb the odour of four decomposing severed heads, which were stored in plastic bags tied with plastic twisties.

The doors to the bedroom, bedroom closet and bathroom had been fitted with special deadbolt locks. In the back of the closet police discovered a metal stockpot that contained decomposed hands and a penis, and on the shelf above were two skulls. Also in the closet were containers of ethyl alcohol, chloroform and formaldehyde, along with some glass jars holding preserved male genitalia.

In due course two more skulls were found in a computer box and another three in a filing cabinet. Three headless torsos were discovered in a fifty-five-gallon drum.

The full-scale search also revealed numerous polaroid photos of his victims taken by Dahmer at various stages. One showed a man's head with the flesh still intact lying in the sink. Another displayed a victim cut open from neck to groin like a deer gutted after the kill, the cuts so clean one could clearly see the pelvic bone. Some photos showed his victims in various erotic and bondage poses before he murdered them.

The police, the county medical examiner, the media, the families of any missing young men as well as those of the victims, Dahmer's own family, and it seemed the whole city of Milwaukee, let alone the nation, were desperate to find out precisely what had happened. Gradually the findings in the apartment told much of the story of Dahmer's killings and, once in custody, he told the rest. The years of repressing his awful secrets, which he knew intellectually were wrong, gave way to a need to describe his crimes in detail.

The remains of eleven victims were found in the apartment and Dahmer volunteered information on six others. He also revealed what he did to the men once he had them at his mercy, in his home,

In all seventeen cases, Dahmer told his interviewers, his victims came with him consensually, most of them having been picked up at gay bars or in adult bookstores. Usually, he said, he put sleeping pills in their beer or coffee to knock them out; sometimes he had to use force. Then his fantasies took control.

"Once I had the opportunity and the place where I could actually make these fantasies come true," he said, "then trying to hold them back was . . . just seemed too much."

There was no obvious touchstone in Dahmer's past which can be pinpointed as the event that created a serial killer. He had a seemingly normal childhood, living with his father, mother and younger brother in an upper-middle class neighbourhood in Bath Township, Ohio.

Dahmer described his relationship with his parents as "pretty good, pretty average", but inside the household there was trouble. His mother suffered a mental illness of her own, and the marriage was not a happy one. Police were called to the house more than once, and a divorce was granted on 24 July 1978, after each of his parents charged the other with extreme cruelty and gross neglect".

"He was raised in a very sanitized, upper-middle-class environment," said Ashok Bedi, director of the Milwaukee Psychiatric Hospital, who had hoped to treat Dahmer before his death in prison. "It was the kind of environment where the darkness of the human psyche can be sanitized and repressed. They can't afford the stigma of mental illness. So his darkness just got deeper and deeper, with no outlet."

For the young Jeffrey that outlet might have been his fascination with dead animals. He dissected road kills, keeping the bones in jars of formaldehyde and starting an animal graveyard. Dahmer said there was no sexual element to it, explaining it as "morbid curiosity". But the anatomy lessons he learned as a boy would be put to use as an adult.

Dahmer said he first discovered his homosexuality when he was thirteen, a fact he kept secret from his family and friends. He told the interviewers he had one homosexual experience at fourteen with a neighbour boy – "very light sex, kissing, holding, that type of thing" – but that was it. He also called it 'a mistake.

Dahmer's father told a reporter that a neighbourhood boy had sexually assaulted Jeffrey when he was eight, but Dahmer does not mention it in the FBI interview. "There was no specific incident that triggered it," he said of his sexual orientation. "They say some people are molested by someone, that's what makes them become homo-sexual. That never was in my case."

By the time he was sixteen, Dahmer told the interviewers, he began having strong sexual fantasies. He said he dreamed of sex with a good-looking, Chippendale dancer-type. But, in his fantasies, he would have total control; he talked about one fantasy of striking someone with a blackjack and having sex with the body. The morbid nature of his thoughts troubled him, Dahmer said, and he turned to drinking in high school. Heavy drinking would soon become both his escape from and the fuel for his gruesome fantasies come true.

Dahmer graduated high school in 1978, and by that summer he was living alone in the family house after his parents moved out. One night he was driving home, he told the interviewers, and he saw a young hitchhiker. Suddenly, an opportunity presented itself.

"I never thought it would really happen," Dahmer said. "But every-thing was set up so perfectly that one time in Ohio."

He stopped and picked up the hitchhiker, who turned out to be nine-teen-year-old Steven M. Hicks, who agreed to go back to Dahmer's house "for a few beers". But things soon got out of hand.

"The guy wanted to leave," Dahmer later told police, "and I didn't want him to."

Dahmer told police he got angry and smashed Hicks in the back of the head with a barbell and later choked him to death with it. Then, he said, he had sex with Hicks' corpse, and cut the body open to examine it. Days later, when he was done with it, Dahmer cut the body into small pieces, put it into garbage bags and, at 3 a.m. loaded it into his car and headed for the dump. On the way, though, police stopped him.

Dahmer's reign of terror could have ended right there. But it didn't. The police pulled Dahmer over, ordered him out of the car and gave him a sobriety test. They shined their flashlights into the car, spotted the garbage bags, and asked what the terrible smell was.

"Scared the hell out of me," he told the interviewers.

Dahmer said the bags contained some old garbage he'd forgotten to take to the dump. The police gave him a ticket for driving left of the centreline and let him go.

"I couldn't believe it, I thought I was dreaming," Dahmer said. "So I went back home."

Dahmer ended up smashing the corpse with a sledgehammer and

scattering the remains throughout the 1.7-acre wooded lot. In 1991 Dahmer drew a map to show police where the parts were buried – "You don't forget your first one," he told them – and a search turned up more than 500 pieces of bone.

Dahmer said he didn't kill again for ten years. Instead, he tried every other way possible to satisfy his urges. When asked what kept him going, he told the interviewers: "Heavy drinking, pornography, masturbation." After high school Dahmer spent three months at Ohio State University, he told the investigators, "and drank, literally drank my way out of that."

He then enlisted in the Army, on the advice of his stepmother, who hoped he might find some discipline but that did not work out, either. Stationed in Germany, he said he discovered a more graphic type of pornography – the first he'd ever seen "with the orientation I have," he told the interviewers – and he got heavily into it. "Oh, yeah," he said, "I spent thousands of dollars on that over the years."

Drinking again was his downfall. The FBI file contains a number of army memorandums that detail occasions of insubordination including one in which a drunken Dahmer's response to a commanding officer's order was "I'm not going to [expletive] do it." He was dischared in March 1981. Because he was sent home six months early, he didn't want to go straight home, so he flew to Florida, but life didn't change much for Dahmer. He got a job at a sandwich shop, getting paid under the table as he collected unemployment insurance, and continued drinking and buying porn.

He returned home in September and moved in with his grandmother in West Allis, Wisconsin, but things got no better. His drinking continued, he had a series of low-paying jobs, and he had several run-ins with the law. He was arrested for public drunkenness in 1981; for disturbing the peace after dropping his pants in front of a crowd in 1982; and for lewd and lascivious behaviour in 1986. He began picking up men in gay bars and bathhouses in Milwaukee and Chicago, although he was eventually thrown out of one bathhouse for drugging some of his partners.

Dahmer went to great lengths to satisfy his sexual desires. "I was trying everything," he told the interviewers, "from grave robbing to actually stealing a mannequin out of a Boston store at South Ridge to placate the desire without having to hurt anybody. But it didn't ever work, and one thing led to another."

In 1987, Dahmer spent a night at Milwaukee's Ambassador Hotel with twenty-four-year-old Stephen Tuomi. He had slipped Tuomi a cocktail with the prescription drug Halcion in it, and he received a surprise the next morning.

"I woke up and the guy was dead underneath me," he told the interiewers. "I didn't know how, how I was going to handle that. Never had that happen . . ."

Thinking quickly, Dahmer went out and bought a large suitcase, stuffed the body into it and hauled it down to the street. There he hailed a cab, whose driver helped Dahmer lift the suitcase into the trunk – he even commented on the smell – and drove him back to his grandmother's house. There, Dahmer dissected and disposed of the body. Again Dahmer could have been caught, but again he escaped detection. And, although he claims not to have deliberately killed Tuomi, this incident triggered something inside him.

"After that," Dahmer said, "it all started again."

Soon the killing began in earnest. Dahmer said he killed three men at his grandmother's house, then stepped up the frequency when he moved to his own apartment in Milwaukee in 1988. "For a long time it was just once every two months," he said. "Near the end it was once every week . . . Just really got completely out of control."

Beween 1988 and his arrest in 1991 Dahmer killed fifteen men. They were all good-looking gay men, from teens to their early thirties. There were whites, blacks, Hispanics and Asians (he took exception to news stories that said he was racist for specifically targeting blacks). Each went back with Dahmer, looking for companionship and love; each met his death in Dahmer's chamber of horrors, a victim of his uncontrollable urge to possess them. Dahmer would typically pick up his victim at a gay bar or bookstore, take him home for sex – in some cases he offered money in exchange for taking photos of the man – and then drug him. Usually he used Halcion, six or seven of them, mixed in some coffee.

"And that would be it," he told the interviewers. "Within a half an hour they'd be asleep."

As long as the drug was working, Dahmer had what he most wanted: complete control of another human.

Dahmer explained his needs in this exchange during the prison interview, when he was asked to describe his fantasy:

"Dahmer: Thoughts of a good-looking, well-built young guy, having total control of him. I don't know if killing ever came into it, came into play. But if that was the only way to keep him, then that would be done.

"Q: So . . . the total domination, total . . .

"Dahmer: Right.

"Q: Love slave?

"Dahmer: Yeah."

But once the drug wore off, Dahmer would have to take other measures to keep control. Generally that meant strangling them, usually with his bare hands.

"I wasn't interested in torture," he said in the interview. "All I wanted to do was make it quick and painless for them. I know it sounds ridiculous for me to say that, but that's what my goal was. So I'd have complete control over them, so I wouldn't have to worry about them leaving in the morning and I could fulfill my fantasies."

Once he had the body he so craved, his sexual desires would be unleashed. He had sex with and masturbated on the bodies. He would keep the bodies for several days, keeping them fresh in a large freezer he bought for that purpose. And he took photos of the bodies, some half-dissected or with their internal organs exposed. But even that wasn't enough for Dahmer. He wanted to keep the men forever.

"I wanted to see if it was possible to make – again, it sounds really gross – uh, zombies, people that would not have a will of their own . . . but would follow my instructions without resistance. So after that I started using the drilling technique."

The "drilling technique" involved boring holes in their heads and pouring muriatic acid into the frontal lobes. He hoped to be able to keep them alive indefinitely, love slaves always at his beck and call. However, it never worked as well as he hoped, Dahmer told the FBI interviewers, although one victim, Jeremiah Weinberger, lived for two days before he died.

"I came back from work the second night," Dahmer said. "He had died and it kind of struck me as particularly horrifying, because he was the only one that died with his eyes, his eyes were just wide open."

Once Dahmer was done with the dead body, he would then need to dispose of it. That, too, became part of his sexual ritual.

"The first time I didn't know how to dispose of the remains, but once

I started doing it, it became sexually exciting to me." Dahmer described the process in detail to the interviewers. He would remove the internal organs and cut the remaining flesh into small pieces. He "removed the head and put that in the freezer". He said he would then put the skeleton in an eighty-gallon pot with a strong cleaning solution and boil it clean.

The skulls were generally kept, some of them painted and placed on a shelf to look like plastic skulls. Other body arts were also kept, including hands and in one case a penis, but most of the bones were placed in a powerful acid bath and then poured down the toilet. Most of the flesh was also placed in the acid bath or was wrapped tightly and tossed in the trash. But not all the flesh was disposed of.

At some point the killing, the necrophilia, the keeping of human mementos wasn't enough. Dahmer felt he needed more. It was then, with Rick Beets, perhaps his sixth or seventh victim, that Dahmer turned to cannibalism.

"It started out as experimentation," he said. "Made me feel like they were more a part of me." Dahmer said he ate the heart, liver, thighs and biceps, and would prepare it "on the skillet, just like you prepare a regular piece of meat".

The interviewers questioned him about the taste:

"Dahmer: Uhh . . . There's no way of saying without it sounding, uh, gruesome.
"Q: I don't find it offensive.
"Dahmer: Well, it . . . I, I don't know how to describe it. You've had *filet mignon*, haven't you?
"Q: Uh huh, that's one of my favourites.
"Dahmer: Yeah. Very tender."

During an earlier police interview, Dahmer reportedly said he used steak sauce.

Along the way police had many chances to catch him. Besides the 3 a.m. trip to the dump and the body in the suitcase, police questioned Dahmer four times and entered his apartment twice during his killing spree. Among those close calls:

• In 1988 police questioned Dahmer about a man's claim that

Dahmer robbed and drugged him at Dahmer's grandmother's home. Police dropped the case after Dahmer denied the allegations.

- Also in 1988 police searched his apartment after he was accused of sexually assaulting a teenage boy. Dahmer was later convicted and served nine months in jail, but the officers somehow missed the photos, skulls and other evidence of his crimes.

- In 1988 Dahmer lured a fifteen-year-old boy into his apartment with plans to kill him. He hit the boy on the back of the head with a rubber mallet, but failed to incapacitate him. The boy escaped and went to the police, but Dahmer was never questioned about it.

- In 1991 a neighbour complained to police about the stench coming from Dahmer's apartment. An officer knocked on he wrong door and never spoke to Dahmer.

- Another time there had been a murder in another apartment in his building and again police, said Dahmer, "came into my apartment and looked around and didn't see anything".

But the most infamous police failure came 27 May 1991, when two women found a naked boy, dazed and bleeding, staggering on the street outside of Dahmer's apartment. As it turned out, Konerak would be dead by the next day, and four more men would be killed before Dahmer was finally caught.

In the end, after he'd been caught and sent to prison, Dahmer did express remorse at what he'd done. He said he always knew what he was doing was wrong, but that he couldn't stop himself:

"If I could eliminate those fantasies, those overwhelming fantasies, starting when I was fifteen or sixteen, short circuited them, not think about them, not, not entertaining them . . . then that probably would have stopped everything . . . One thing . . . that's puzzled me is why I can't seem to generate more feeling. I mean, if I had been able to feel more emotion, this may not have happened. But it just seems like my emotion, my emotional side has been deadened."

Though he will go down in history as a serial killer, Dahmer did not display the hallmark signs of a serial killer, known as the "homicidal triad" – bed-wetting, fire-setting and animal abuse. The closest he came was dissecting animals, but Dahmer said he only worked on those he found dead. He spoke about that to the interviewers, which they included in their summary: "Dahmer stated that . . . on one occasion, where he found an Irish setter and brought it home and was going to kill it and then skin it, but when the dog looked at him with its eyes, Dahmer could not kill it, so he just let it go."

He never took such pity on his human victims.

ISSEI SAGAWA

Her family will never get over the death of Renée Hartevelt, a Dutch student, killed in Paris by Issei Sagawa. Freed after just four years, he has bizarre celebrity status in his native Japan. Now they face another publicity round, cruelly close to home.

There appears no chance of an end to the suffering of Johanna Hartevelt. Few mothers have had to endure such a life time of cruelty and horror. Tonight, a television programme on UK's Channel 4 will pour salt on a terrible wound.

Hartevelt was the mother of a beautiful Dutch girl, Renée. In 1980, Renée won a scholarship to Paris to study French at the Sorbonne. The following year, in a case that attracted worldwide notoriety, the twenty-five-year-old was murdered in a Parisian bedsit by a small, shy, bespectacled, thirty-one-year-old Japanese student, who sliced her body into pieces and feasted on her flesh.

Declared insane by the French courts, Issei Sagawa, the man who ate Renée was transferred in 1984 to a hospital in Japan. There, pressure exerted by his millionaire banker father secured his controversial release after a total of only four years in mental institutions in the two countries.

To the disgust of the Hartevelt family, Sagawa has turned his cannibalism into the sickest of Japanese jokes. He has written a best-selling book, appeared in pornographic films, and even become a food critic for the Japanese magazine *Spa*. He boasts in repellent detail of butchering the corpse of Renée.

For those with iron-clad stomachs, the story will make magnetic viewing. However, in Amsterdam last week, Johanna Hartevelt's oldest son, Ben Groenendijk, Renee's half-bro ther and spokesman for the family, sadly shook his head. Nobody from Channel 4 had contacted him. Once again, his family's grief has become fodder for someone else's ambition. Once again, Dutch newspapers will mine the tragedy, friends in Britain will phone.

"Making a programme on British television doesn't bother us that much, if it is done with serious intentions," he said. "But it all changes for my parents when they see other people are making fun of it, making a Dracula story out of their daughter. For our family, there have been many times like that. It happened more than ten years ago, but still we cannot hide from it."

It is difficult to think of a more terrible telephone call than the one Johanna Hartevelt received in 1981, informing her of her daughter's murder. Yet, almost incredibly, it was not the first time that the Japanese had brought tragedy to her family.

In 1941, the year of Ben Groenendijk's birth, Hartevelt was living in what is now Indonesia. She was married to a pilot in the colonial Dutch Indies Air Force. The news the following year that her husband had been shot down by Japanese fighters and was missing, presumed dead, was followed within weeks by the Japanese invasion. Hartevelt and Groenendijk were thrown into a concentration camp. They were to spend the next three years in Japanese hands, scrabbling to stay alive. When they finally returned to the Netherlands, *via* Australia, in 1947, a door in their life was closed. Johanna was later remarried to Jan Hartevelt, an army officer who joined a steel company. There would be no more excursions to the Orient, but the family had not heard the last of Japan.

A former naval pilot and former Dutch military attaché in London, Groenendijk is well-equipped for his role as family representative. Today he is the distinguished head of the Netherlands' aircraft accident investigation board. He has been trained to respond calmly to horror.

A trim, silver-haired man of fifty-two, he talked quietly and unemotionally last week of his step-sister's "happy, joyful" childhood, of her talent for French, and of her last letter home from Paris. Renée scribbled that she had taken pity on "this funny little Japanese guy, whom nobody else would talk to". However, when Groenendijk turned to the depressing sequence of events that led to Sagawa's release from a Japanese psychiatric hospital less than four years after the murder, he clenched his knuckles and raged.

"I remember about the same time there was a man who lunged at the French president, François Mitterrand. He was only carrying a rose. They sent him to jail, but the man who ate my sister went free."

Over the years, Groenendijk said, the Hartevelt family had suffered a double loss; of Renée, so talented and lovely, and, almost as painfully, of their belief in justice. "If they steal your bicycle, you're a victim," he said. "But if they steal your child, the authorities don't want to know you. The word victim isn't even written in the law. It's all about rehabilitating the criminal."

From the start, the family had suspected that Sagawa, now forty-four, might go free. The man's father was politically powerful in Japan. The Hartevelts' French lawyers warned that there might be political interference to save a big oil deal with Japan. "France wanted to do business with Japan, that was the message we got," Groenendijk said. "They didn't want a nasty problem about cannibals. They wanted the problem to disappear."

With the help of a sympathetic French lawyer, and compelling testimony from Renée's friends, the Hartevelts fought off defence attempts to indicate that their daughter was a sexually promiscuous tease who had provoked Sagawa. There was conclusive evidence that she had felt sorry for the Japanese, and had gone unsuspectingly to his flat to help him with a translation. "She was too good for this world," Groenendijk mused. "She went to help him, and he killed her."

Sagawa shot her in the back of the head, dismembered her, ate part of her and packed the remains in two suitcases. He was seen dumping them in the Bois de Boulogne and was arrested immediately, confessing freely to the crime.

With the help of disputed medical evidence purporting to show a faint scarring of brain tissue from a childhood bout of encephalitis, Sagawa's family succeeded in having him declared insane. Under an agreement with Japan at the time, he would automatically be returned to a suitable institution in his own country. "We knew from the start what would happen if he went back," said Groenendijk. "It was totally predictable that they would release him."

The family had more than one reason for wanting Sagawa locked up. From jail, he had boasted that he would repeat his crime. "If I am freed, I will eat another woman. Renée was very appetising," he told a Japanese writer. Unknown to the French authorities at the time, Sagawa had also written the Hartevelts a letter. It was smuggled out of jail by a priest. It has haunted the family ever since.

"He wrote that he wanted to come and see my parents," Groenendijk said wearily. "He wanted to present himself before them so they could punish him for his crime by killing him themselves. He wanted to die over the grave of Renée."

For the past eight years, the Hartevelts have monitored Sagawa's movements, terrified that he will turn up in Holland. Last year he paid a self-promotional visit to Germany, and Groenendijk made a quiet, ultimately futile, attempt to have him officially barred from entry to the Netherlands.

"Nobody wanted a fuss with Japan," he said. "In the event he didn't come here, but it's still terrible to know not just that crime pays, but that Sagawa is getting rich off Renée. He's really enjoying himself, reliving the murder of my sister. The law is giving this opportunity to a criminal." For Groenendijk, the issue is clear. "Either he is mad or he is not. If he is mad, people should be protected and he should be in hospital. If he is not mad, he should have stayed in jail."

Jan and Johanna Hartevelt, both in their mid-seventies, do not speak directly to the media. I asked Groenendijk how his parents had managed to bear such a distressing assault on their daughter. His response was eloquent and moving.

"My mother and stepfather, especially my mother, believe that the loss of your child is such a deep and terrible shock that you have no spare room for other thoughts. They told me years ago that parents who lose their child in a car crash share exactly the same kind of grief. The facts of what happened are more important to the outside world than to you. Your heart is too small to dwell on details. They don't think they are worse off than any other parent who has lost their child. I'm very happy they have this philosophy."

WHITE TIGER IN MIAMI

A rare white Bengal tiger, one of the star attractions at Miami's sprawling suburban zoo, fatally mauled a zookeepr on Monday, 6 June 1994, after the man entered the animal's outdoor enclosure.

Veteran zookeeper David Marshall, forty-five, was killed after he entered the moated enclosure apparently unaware that the tiger was still uncaged, said Metrozoo spokesman Ron Magill. He said that the death occurred during a time of day when the 350-pound male tiger named Lucknow was to be moved from one enclosure to another. There were no witnesses and, although the death was believed to be accidental, county homicide officers said they would investigate.

"As beautitul, as majestic, as approachable as these animals seem to be, there's the old saying, 'You can take the animal out of the wild, but you can't take the wild out of the animal,'" said Magill, a friend of Marshall, who was close to tears at a morning news conference. "Unfortunately that's been proven today."

Asked if the tiger would be destroyed, Magill answered: "Nothing happens to the tiger. The tiger was just being a tiger. To condemn the tiger would be to compound the tragedy. People have a misconception that they are pets. Nothing could be further from the truth. This is what we would expect a tiger to do."

Magill said that Marshall had to ignore or overlook several safety features at the tiger exhibit to have entered the paddock where the tiger roamed. "Everything seems to point to human error."

Marshall, a Metrozoo employee for eleven years, had no pulse when found by other zoo employees after he failed to respond to a call on the radio. He had suffered severe lacerations.

Deaths caused by zoo tigers are considered extremely rare. Tiger expert Ron Tilson of the Minnesota Zoo said that he could remember "one, maybe two such incidents in the US in the last seven years". By comparison, an average of one person a year is killed by zoo or circus elephants in the United States.

Lucknow and his sister Kampur were acquired ten years ago from the Cincinnati zoo, where they were born. Although extremely popular with zoo visitors, white tigers are controversial among many zoologists since most in captivity result from selective breeding of parents and offspring with the same genetic mutation. Tilson, tiger species co-ordinator for the American Association of Zoological Parks and Aquariums, has deplored the practice of such in-breeding.

KISS OF THE SCORPION MAN

A man was taken to hospital after he kissed his pet scorpion goodnight and it stung him on the tongue.

Jordan Lazelle, eighteen, of Hayling Island, Hampshire, UK, kissed Twiggy, a Sin Great Black Emperor scorpion, after coming home from a drink with friends.

Mr Lazelle said: "I went to kiss him on the pincer and he just grabbed my lip. I opened my mouth in shock and he jumped in and stung me on the tongue. I felt very dizzy and went outside to walk it off, and I collapsed in the road.

"I've kissed Twiggy goodnight hundreds of times without any problem. Obviously he just wasn't in the mood."

SOUTH KOREAN CANNIBAL GANG

Judges pronounced the death sentence yesterday, 31 October 1994, on six members of a cannibal murder gang who ate their victims' flesh in a grisly rite to boost their courage after killing kidnapped hostages, court authorities said.

"They deserve death sentences for their unthinkable and inhuman massacre," Lee Kwang Yul, the senior judge at the Seoul District Criminal Court said. During the trial, all three judges voiced anger at Kim Ki Hwan, twenty-six, and six other gang members, including a young bar hostess, who were arrested in September. The woman received a suspended three-year sentence.

The case shocked the South Korean nation and resulted in calls for the death penalty. Meanwhile the judges hastened through court procedures, completing them only twenty-five days after the cannibal group was charged.

The prosecution accused the seven of a grim series of kidnappings, tortures and murders, after which they practised the ritual eating of human flesh and incinerated the bodies of their victims, picked from rich clients of a fancy department store in Seoul.

The network confessed to killing five abducted victims over a period of a year, under an operating slogan of "Kill the haves and take their money".

The first victim was a twenty-three-year-old woman selected for "courage building" training near their hide-out in a remote village. There police found a cache of dynamite, air rifles and axes, along with jewellery and $75,000 (£46,000) in cash.

HUNGRY BRAZILIANS

Starving slum-dwellers in a north-eastern Brazilian city are eating human body parts, including brains, found among hospital waste at a local rubbish dump, the city's mayor said yesterday.

"I know human remains were eaten. It's a return to cannibalism," stated Germano Coelho, mayor of Olinda in Recife state. He said he had personally visited the city's main open-air rubbish dump, known as the Lixao de Peixinhos, where 1,200 families had erected shacks from refuse and were eking out a living by collecting rubbish and selling it.

These rubbish collectors sometimes came across bodies or parts of bodies. "They are either bodies of murdered people or medical refuse from hospitals . . . It's a dangerous place," Mr Coelho said.

He added the slum-dwellers told officials from the mayor's office how hunger and poverty drove them to eat the human flesh. "They even spoke of the consistency of it," he said.

Brazil's national *O Globo* newspaper said missionaries saw a widow and her family eat a portion of human brains found among the garbage. It quoted one member of the family, Adilson Soares, as saying: "I ate it because I had no choice. I had nothing else to stop the hunger."

THE WOLF INSIDE EVERY DOG

A village yesterday came to the defence of a Canadian hybrid timber wolf threatened with destruction after savaging a baby boy as he played with his brother and sister.

Jaye Coxhead, aged twenty-two months, had fourteen stitches in wounds to his head and face after Ishtar, mostly timber wolf but part husky, bit him as he played at the family home in Pentraeth, Anglesey.

The cross-bred was first "manufactured" five years ago by the South African Defence Force, which was seeking to improve the quality, stamina and aggression of its patrol dogs at the height of unrest in the townships. "They have very long fangs which would go through the toughest padding like a knife through butter," an officer in the force said at the time.

Yesterday the RSPCA called for a ban on imports of the animal, which it said was "highly dangerous with a tremendous potential for aggression". But Lynn Coxhead, the boy's mother, said that the attack was entirely out of character, and villagers described Ishtar as "the most popular dog" in the village. One said that it was "gentle and very good with kids".

Andrew Williams, who runs the village garage, said he was planning to buy a timber wolf for his own family. "Ishtar is a lovely dog. I regularly play with him on the forecourt with the children. Everybody in the village knows him and loves him, Ishtar has no enemies at all. It would be a dreadful shame if his owners were forced to put him down. From what I can make out, it wasn't his fault anyway. It all happened when the children got hold of a box of chocolates and were throwing them around. Ishtar tried to catch a piece of chocolate and Jaye was in the way."

Sybil Jones, the village postmistress, also praised the Coxhead family's pet. "He's lovely," she said. "My son plays with him regularly. We would all be very upset if he was destroyed because of this."

In South Africa the cross-bred, with yellow eyes and teeth twice the length of a domestic dog's, has struck fear in the hearts of even the most determined demonstrators. Army trainers have learnt to treat them with respect. "Once they have got their teeth through to the flesh they do not let go," one officer said.

A year after the South Africans created the breed, the genetic technology was exported to the United States, where wolf-dogs became popular among "rednecks" in the Midwest and affluent crack cocaine dealers in the inner cities.

The American Society for the Prevention of Cruelty to Animals called for government action against breeders, warning that the hybrids were "very volatile". Stephen Zawistowski, the society's science adviser, said: "When wolf hybrids attack, they do not just bite, they go for the kill. Their behaviour is very predatory."

Yesterday the RSPCA said that 123 of the hybrids were known to be kept in Britain, but the figure might be much higher. Three months ago twenty of the dogs were imported by breeders who sell puppies for up to £500 each.

"It is a wild animal of unpredictable nature and great strength," the society said. "We do not want them destroyed, though, just neutered so no more can be bred."

Mrs Coxhead, whose son is recovering at home after treatment in hospital, said that she and her husband had spent a year considering whether Ishtar was going to be "the correct dog" for the family. "He's not a vicious animal and never has been. We've had him since the day Jaye was born," she said. "Ishtar is now with an expert who is going to assess him and decide whether he is to be put down or goes to another home. He has always been marvellous with the children."

North Wales Police are investigating the incident, although the keeping of a wolf-dog does not come under either the 1991 Dangerous Dogs Act or the Wild Animals Act. "The matter is the subject of an inquiry and once all the facts have been established a decision will be taken as to what action is appropriate," a police spokesman said.

Julie Kelham, who has four hybrid wolves at her home in Newark, Nottinghamshire, said that the breed was fast gaining popularity in Britain. "My wolf-dogs are very friendly and I let my two children play with them," she said, "But like any big dogs, you have to be sensible and I do not leave them alone with the kids."

The attack on twenty-two-month-old Jaye Coxhead by the family pet, a dog with more Canadian timber wolf in him than was at first thought, has stirred ancestral fears in Britain that had lain dormant for 250 years. In 1743, a Scottish hunter named McQueen returned to his home on the River Findhorn with the body of what he claimed was the last wolf in Britain. That, as far as lycophobics were concerned, was that.

Nonetheless, the Eastern European culture of the lycanthrope, and its manifestation in werewolf movies, has perpetuated the myth of the wolf as a threat to man, and fairy stories from "Little Red Riding Hood" to the tale of the boy who cried "wolf" have ensured the animal's continued bogey reputation.

However, as sympathy began to outweigh fear in the conservationist atmosphere that has grown since the 1960s, there have been numerous projects to reintroduce the wolf to Britain. The most recent was this year [1994] at Kincraig, in the Scottish Highlands.

There are dwindling wolf populations in Spain, Scandinavia and the former Soviet Union, where unsentimental locals cull them systematically. (The only increase in Russian wolf numbers this century was during the two world wars, when men were busy killing each other.)

Even in modern society, every domestic dog has a little wolf in him. Accepted canine evolutionary history describes how wolves used to scavenge around human settlements 14,000 years ago. Gradually, men began to rely on them, and their highly developed senses, to warn of danger. Selective breeding ever since has been responsible for everything from the chihuahua to the St Bernard.

Since the 1976 Dangerous Animals Act, it has been illegal to keep a wolf in Britain without a licence, but this law does not apply to hybrids. The problem with Ishtar was that the years of breeding which have led to the even temperament, fidelity, and domesticity of most pets, had been bypassed. "There are a number of breeders producing these animals," said the RSPCA. "We are very much against it. The wolf is genetically predisposed to attack; it has none of the kinder tendencies that come with breeding. Foreign wolves are imported and coupled with domestic dogs with the result that their savage genes are at large in the canine population. We are calling for a ban on the import of wolves, a ban on breeding, and compulsory neutering of all existing hybrids."

Before the Dangerous Animals Act the relative ease of buying a wolf led to such problems as the "Devil-Face" incident of 1961, when a Canadian timber wolf of that name which had been bought from London Zoo, escaped to terrorize Clapham in south London. It died while being recaptured. In 1974, a wolf called Walter escaped from the set of Legend of the Werewolf at Pinewood studios. It, too, caused widespread panic, and was hunted down by police marksmen.

Consider, then, before turning little Towser out into the garden when the moon is full, that he may yet feel the pulsing of his forefathers' blood in his veins, and heed the ancestral voices that are calling him.

Letter to the Editor of *The Times*, London, 1994

Sir,

Wolf-dog hybrids may have been bred most recently by the South African police but the concept is far from new. Dutch dog breeders introduced wolf bloodlines into the German shepherd in the 1920s to increase the dog's resistance to distemper. Virtually all of the first generation of these wolf hybrids actually died of distemper but the hybrids live on as a recognized dog breed named the Saarloos wolf-dog.

In the 1960s Czech breeders crossed German shepherds with Carpathian wolves. This hybrid is also recognized by the International Cynological Federation, as the Czech wolf-dog.

Dog breeders go through cycles of attraction to wolves. When I worked as a veterinary assistant in San Francisco in the late 1960s the wolf-dog was the hippy's natural companion. I saw none in veterinary practice again until the early 1990s. In my experience, when wolf-dog hybrids bite, they bite seriously, rather than with the inhibition bred into most domestic breeds.

AMERICA'S RABID FOXES

Rabies is spreading throughout the eastern United States, posing a growing threat to health and safety, according to public officials in August 1997.

Doctors in the affluent country towns of Virginia and Maryland have been startled to receive cases of people attacked and bitten by foxes which later tested positive for rabies. Dr Nancy Welch, who treated a woman last month for potential infection, said: "We haven't had a rabid fox here in Chesapeake for at least ten years."

Four people were attacked last autumn by a rabid fox in the gardens of the Woodlawn Plantation at Mount Vernon, near the heavily visited residence of George Washington.

Health officials have described the "very mobile virus" as potentially "a major problem for the US". Dr Suzanne Jenkins, assistant state epidemiologist for Virginia, told the *Washington Times*: "The whole East Coast has a racoon rabies outbreak."

Racoons and foxes are blamed for spreading the disease, which has traditionally had a stronghold only in the rural, heavily wooded southeast. There have been recent reports of rabid racoons in Ohio, a state which had only ten rabid animal cases in 1995.

Rabies, carried in saliva, attacks the brain and nervous system. If a person infected with the rabies virus is not treated immediately with repeated injections of vaccine, convulsions, aversion to water and death will follow. However, doctors want to spread the message that the injections, once notoriously agonizing, are now less painful, and people should not shun the treatment if bitten by an animal acting suspiciously.

Fewer than two people on average die each year from rabies in the entire United States. But the number having rabies vaccinations after animal bites has risen from 16,000 in 1981 to more than 39,000 today. The risk is growing because rapid economic growth is pushing communities further into America's vast wooded areas.

DANGEROUS CRITTERS AT HOME

Drugged darts, a collection of steel poles and nets and a bottle of rum, as well as a pistol, would be considered as equipment for a regular cop, even in Florida.

Not so for Pat Reynolds, one of Miami's animal police or "critter-cops", as they are known, now patrolling Dade County to check on the welfare and security of exotic pets. The rum is poured over the jaws of cougars, lions, leopards, monkeys and alligators that may get a grip on Pat's anatomy. Alcohol loosens the hold.

The exotic pets market in southern Florida is on the increase, with more than half-a-million people now owning at least one. While large cats cannot be kept without a permit requiring the owner to have a year's experience of the animal, anyone can buy and keep monkeys, snakes, alligators and a host of other animals.

"I caught a girl with no permit feeding a cougar on tinned catfood," says Reynolds. "They're a status symbol, especially for the drug dealers."

Reynolds has found a mountain lion in a tool shed and a boa constrictor under a car bonnet, and has often captured monkeys from roofs of houses, especially after Hurricane Andrew in 1992, when 2,000 escaped. Many animals, detoothed and declawed by their owners, lasted only weeks after the destructive force of the storm set them free into the swamps of south Florida. Others are still loose, such as a black jaguar which has been sighted several times. Thousands of escaped alligators swam Dade County's urban canals until one of Reynolds's helpers fished them out.

He sometimes calls on his trapper friend Todd Hardwick for assistance. Miami's answer to Crocodile Dundee can trap anything, but his speciality is snakes.

Reynolds takes ill-treated animals he rescues to his pal Dirk Neugebohrn's animal refuge. "This cougar was being kept in a wooden shack with no fencing or cage," said Reynolds, pointing to a beautiful, muscular grey cat called Elsie. "The danger is to let children near them. In their natural environment they will hunt deer, hogs and raccoons. A child is about the right prey size."

Reynolds got a call to Bunche Park, near Miami, about a cayman being kept in a children's paddling pool surrounded by rickety wooden planks. Shredder, five feet long, had seventy-two teeth and ate live chickens. "Man, I know, he's deadly," agreed the owner, who was fined $40 and ordered to erect sturdy fencing.

Next on Reynolds's checklist was Elaine Bishop, owner of a Vietnamese pot-bellied pig, a wolf, a fifteen-foot python, a monkey she kept in nappies "just in case" and Dasha, a growling leopard in a ten-foot cage next to the kitchen.

I pointed out that Rudi, her monkey, needed her claws clipping. "My darling girl," cooed Bishop, "my children have hands, not claws."

UNGRATEFUL ANGOLAN TIGER

A flying ark yesterday brought thirty-one starving animals from war-torn Angola to Johannesburg, hours after a television cameraman was mauled to death by a tiger at Luanda zoo during the mission. Rick Lomba, forty-four, a cameraman who was also a producer and director of wildlife documentaries, was seized by the tiger after a safety gate was left open.

Quinton Coetzee, deputy director of Johannesburg zoo, who was co-ordinating the evacuation from Luanda, seized an AK47 from a guard and killed the animal. No one else was injured in the incident, which took place in an alleyway behind the cages.

"He was killed on the spot," said Marco Vercrysse, a Belgian photographer, who saw the attack on Mr Lomba. "One of the Angolan guys opened a gate, but forgot to close another," he said. "He didn't stand the slightest chance." Roger Ballad-Tremeer, the head of South Africa's mission in Angola, dismissed the suggestion of irony involved in the expensive evacuation of the animals from a country in which aid workers say that at least 50,000 people have been killed since the civil war flared up again in 1992. "It is a small contribution to the general plight of the Angolan people," he said. A UN aid mission yesterday reached the town of Cunje, besieged for a year by Unita.

Six relief workers in Angola with the UN World Food Programme were killed and ten injured when their twenty-truck convoy was ambushed on Sunday by Unita rebels, the Angop news agency said. The convoy had delivered food to refugees in Dondo when attacked with rockets eighty miles south-east of Luanda.

During the animal evacuation, an ostrich and a buffalo died after being tranquillized for the journey. Last night the animals, most of which are to be taken to zoos in South Africa, were recovering in quarantine quarters at Johannesburg zoo. They included tigers, lions, buffaloes, hyenas, mongooses, chimpanzees and a brown bear. The animals had been starving after money for their upkeep had dried up.

L.A. COYOTE TALES

Crime is still top of the agenda in Los Angeles. The latest manifestation is "home invasion", the domestic equivalent of carjacking, where heavily armed gangs follow their victims into their homes to ransack and rob.

But the residents of Woodland Hills, one of the city's foothill communities abutting the Santa Monica mountains, are more concerned with a four-footed menace – coyotes. "It's a situation where we are almost prisoners in our own homes," says Malvin Sumner, a retired doctor.

Coyote stories are rampant in L.A. this year. There are anecdotes of joggers pursued by roving packs, toddlers stalked, baby-sitters terrified in city parks, and coyotes crashing through cat flaps in pursuit of pets.

Angelenos are well used to the sight of *Canis latras* padding down their streets at dusk to hunt cats and small dogs. Mark Twain once wrote of "a living, breathing allegory of Want. He is always hungry. He is always poor, out of luck, friendless."

"He looks like a medium-sized Alsatian, but with a round, bushy tail and slender legs that can outrun most dogs. Shot, poisoned and reviled for decades, the coyote has nevertheless found powerful allies in the animal rights movement. "He is a gorgeous creature," says Lila Brooks, director of California Wildlife Defenders. "He fulfils an important biological function by devouring carcasses, rats and plague-carrying ground squirrels."

In 1993, Brooks and others successfully lobbied the Los Angeles Animal Regulation Commission to ban coyote trapping. A small group of homeowners have led the backlash, claiming the coyotes can now roam the streets with impunity.

The underlying issue, say wildlife experts, is that human residents of California are pushing out from cities into what was animal habitat, while the animal population has boomed as deep drought has given way to several years of healthy rainfall.

Last month a 356-pound black bear strayed from the Angeles National Forest into the nearby community of Azusa. State wildlife officers twice failed to tranquilize it, and the fleeing bear died in a fusillade of shots. Animal rights campaigners and residents were outraged. An official report last week unleashed charges of bungling on all sides.

In April 1994, marathon runner Barbara Schoener was stalked and killed in northern California by a mountain lion, which was later trailed and shot. Donations came in faster for the cougar's cub than for the woman's two young children.

Late in 1993 Michael Lazarou, a film writer and producer, watched from a kitchen window as a coyote scaled his six-foot garden wall and hungrily approached his eighteen-month-old son. He reached his son when the animal was no more than six feet away.

With the politics of animal welfare so highly charged in L.A., the city last week settled for a tortured compromise that predictably has pleased nobody. Trapping will be resumed – but residents who request it must first coyote-proof their homes, notify all other households within 300 yards, take briefings on how to coexist with coyotes and pay $200.

Already some residents have turned to shooting the animals. "It's never ending," says Alicia Goddard, a Humane Society spokeswoman, "and never will end until people move out of town and the coyotes are all gone."

BALKASH THE SIBERIAN TIGER

A tiger that killed its keeper was the descendant of one that killed two men at the same British zoo, an inquest was told yesterday. John Aspinall, the millionaire owner of Howletts Wild Animal Park near Canterbury, said the death of Trevor Smith, thirty-one, could have been the result of "bad blood".

Mr Smith of Goodneston, Kent, died instantly when he was bitten by Balkash, one of about only 120 Siberian tigers in the world, while cleaning the animal's enclosure in November 1994.

Mr Smith's widow Deborah, twenty-two, is considering suing the wildlife park, which tries to bridge the gap between man and other mammals. Unlike other zoos, keepers at Howletts are allowed, if they volunteer, to enter the enclosures to play with the big cats.

In 1980, two keepers were killed within a month by Zaya, Balkash's great-grandmother. The head keeper died when he went alone into the cage where the tigress had been nursing its cub, and another keeper was killed when Zaya leapt over a fence and savaged him as he cleaned a cage containing the cub.

Mr Aspinall, who shot Zaya fifteen years ago, told yesterday's inquest in Canterbury: "There may be a faulty gene, an abnormal gene which has crisscrossed on to him so that he has a mean streak in his genotype which surfaces. I'm not going to let anybody go back in with any descendant of Zaya." He said humans had learnt that inherited characteristics could come out eight generations later.

Mrs Smith said her husband had wanted to leave his dangerous job so they could start a family and was considering returning to his previous work as a postman.

Mr Smith volunteered to clean the closure containing Balkash, a male tiger aged two-and-a-half and Zamsan, a tigress, on a Sunday afternoon because his boss Nick Marx, the head carnivore keeper, had received a call from a farmer to put down a dying horse that could be fed to exhibits at the park. Mr Marx told the inquest it was possible the tigers could have been upset by the change in routine when Mr Smith replaced him.

Balkash and Zamsan had not eaten for three days and were due to be fed later that day. Roger Brown, a visitor to the park, told the inquest that the two tigers appeared friendly when Mr Smith entered their enclosure. They nuzzled the keeper and he tickled their ears. "When Trevor Smith was fondling the tigers, I thought I could hear them purr," Mr Brown said.

The tigers then appeared to become more animated, moving faster and getting more excited. Balkash, who weighs between 400 lb and 500 lb, suddenly drew up on its rear legs and put its front paws on Mr Smith's shoulders, facing the keeper. Mr Smith fell and Balkash ran across the enclosure, holding the keeper's dead body in its mouth.

Dr Ian Lesley, a pathologist, said Mr Smith died instantly from a fractured skull and fractured neckbone.

Mr Brown's wife Margaret said: "They were very switched on to his (the keeper's) presence. They went straight over to him. The animals did seem very pushy at a certain point. I seem to remember Trevor Smith starting to realize that they were serious. This wasn't just play."

Mr Marx, who was at his home in the grounds, heard Mr Smith

shouting and grabbed a spade to run and help. He had to hit Balkash so hard to make it drop Mr Smith that the tool snapped.

Since Mr Smith's death, keepers have been forbidden by Mr Aspinall from entering enclosures, but he hopes to lift the ban after the inquest. "I can't promise that there won't be another accident, how can I?" he told the inquest. "But we will try to reduce the odds. We will keep the ethos and spirit of the place at the same time. We don't want to abandon that. We don't want another boring zoo where the keepers just become jailers and functionaries rather than companions."

Other zoos, such as London, ban their staff from joining dangerous animals in their cages, but Howletts, which breeds endangered species, has pursued its philosophy of bridging the gap between species for thirty-seven years.

Mr Aspinall dismissed the idea that Balkash bit Mr Smith because it was hungry. "I have been to tigers' enclosures, animals that haven't been fed for eight days," he said. "They are rather nimble and active but they don't change. They are friends: other tigers that they know and humans that they know are not on the menu."

He himself had been alone with tigers many times over the years, although now he was getting older and weaker he preferred to have his head keeper with him. Mr Aspinall's daughter-in-law Louise needed stitches in her head two years ago after being attacked by Zamsan.

Mr Marx was asked by the coroner whether Balkash had become less reliable "having tasted human blood". Mr Marx replied that the tiger had not changed since Mr Smith's death. "He comes up and talks to me at the fence." He added that he had had no qualms about allowing Mr Smith to take his place cleaning the tigers' enclosure. "Obviously a stranger couldn't go in and do my job with the tigers," he said. "Perhaps the tiger would behave in a friendly fashion, perhaps he would kill him. Trevor wasn't a stranger. He was proud to go in with the tigers."

Mr Smith, who had been employed at Howletts since 1988, had known Balkash and Zamsan since they were cubs. "The animals liked him," Mr Marx said. He believed the tigers were disadvantaged by being denied close human contact since Mr Smith's death. "Their life just can't be as full," he said.

The jury returned a verdict of accidental death on Mr Smith. The coroner said: "It is tragic that someone who so obviously enjoyed his job should have met his death by a tragic accident."

STREETWALKING COUGARS

An unusual threat has come to plague the people of California, where attacks on humans by mountain lions have prompted calls for culling, writes Christopher Goodwin in Los Angeles.

A month ago Scott Fike was on an afternoon bicycle ride through a state park close to Los Angeles when a mountain lion, also known as a cougar, leapt at him. Fike was clawed and bitten on the head before fighting off the beast. A few days later park officials tracked down the animal and shot it.

Last year Iris Kenna, fifty-six, died after being savaged by a cougar on a road near San Diego, and Barbara Schoener, forty, was mauled to death by one when she was jogging near Sacramento. Between 1910 and 1986 there were no recorded cougar attacks on humans in California. In the past ten years there have been at least eight. In one particularly gruesome incident, a four-year-old girl was left partially paralysed and blind in one eye.

There have been increased sightings of cougars near schools, shopping centres and other suburban areas, resulting in calls to repeal legislation that has protected them.

The lion population has tripled to 6,000, leaving them fighting over declining numbers of deer and other wild prey. Household pets make easier kills, bringing the lions ever closer to man. At the same time, the danger of clashes between man and beast has risen, as population pressure in an increasingly crowded state has pushed the suburban sprawl towards the mountains and further into the desert. California's population has risen from twenty million to thirty million in the last 20 years.

Under a 1970 law lions are off-limits to hunters. Some conservative politicians, backed by a pressure group of victims of lion attacks, are pushing for that legislation to be lifted as a way of reducing the population. The state spends £19 million a year protecting lion habitats.

Nanse Browne, forty-two, who was charged by a lion while she was jogging in Los Angeles, has set up Lion Watch, a support group for victims. She calls the animals "serial killers" and is demanding culling. Some gun owners are itching to be allowed to kill lions for sport.

BUSTAH THE CHIMPANZEE

A volunteer zoo worker was maimed by a chimpanzee that ripped off a child's arm five years ago. Angelica Todd, twenty-five, had her thumb and finger bitten off while she was feeding Bustah, a thirty-three-year-old chimpanzee, at Port Lympne Wild Animal Park founded by John Aspinall, the millionaire casino owner, in 1973.

Miss Todd, an experienced former employee of the zoo near Folkestone, England, who is now a zoology student, is being treated at a hospital in East Grinstead, West Sussex, which specializes in micro-surgery. After a request by her parents, the hospital refused to disclose her condition or discuss whether attempts were made to reattach the thumb and index finger to her right hand.

The two zoos in Kent owned by Mr Aspinall have been dogged by a series of attacks by animals on visitors and keepers, casting a shadow over the zoos' philosophy of treating captive animals, in Mr Aspinall's words, as "honoured guests". Some think the animal-friendly ethos has led to a too relaxed approach. A young woman was attacked by wolves at Port Lympne in 1977 after entering a cage without permission. In 1980 a tigress killed two keepers at Howletts Zoo, near Canterbury. Four years later a young keeper at Port Lympne was crushed to death by an elephant. Last August Louise Aspinall, the owner's daughter-in-law, was bitten by a tiger cub.

Five years ago Matthew McDaid, aged two, lost his left arm when he put it through the bars of Bustah's cage to stroke him after getting into a private area of the zoo.

Mike Lockyer, the zoological director at Port Lympne, said that Bustah was not to blame and would not be put down. The chimpanzee is due to be exported to a wildlife centre in South Africa in the next few days to spend the rest of his life in retirement. Mr Lockyer said that male chimpanzees of Bustah's age were considered to be dangerous. "They have got to be treated with great care and respect." The zoo would now look closely at whether anything could be done to improve safety.

The Royal Society for the Prevention of Cruelty to Animals (RSPCA) said: "Chimps are deceptive. They are very, very strong and are capable of tearing flesh and pulling off limbs. When they get angry, they can do almost anything. People tend to think if chimps as cuddly little creatures in television tea adverts, but wild chimpanzees are just that – wild."

CHINESE FOETUS-EATERS

No one could accuse the Chinese of being squeamish about the things they eat – monkeys' brains, owls' eyes, bears' paws and deep-fried scorpions are all items on the menu. But most dishes revered as national favourites sound as harmless as boiled rice when compared to the latest *plat du jour* allegedly gaining favour in Shenzhen – human foetus.

Rumours that dead embryos were being used as dietary supplements started to spread early last year with reports that some doctors in Shenzhen hospitals were eating dead foetuses after carrying out abortions. The doctors allegedly defended their actions by saying the embryos were good for their skin and general health.

A trend was set and soon reports circulated that doctors in the city were promoting foetuses as a human tonic. Hospital cleaning women were seen fighting each other to take the treasured human remains home. Last month reporters from *EastWeek* – a sister publication of *Eastern Express* – went to Shenzhen to see if the rumours could be substantiated. On March 7 a reporter entered the state-run Shenzhen Heath Centre for Women and Children, feigning illness, and asked a female doctor for a foetus. The doctor said the department was out of stock but to come again.

The next day the reporter returned at lunchtime. The doctor eventually emerged from the operating theatre, holding a fist-size glass bottle stuffed with thumb-sized foetuses.

She said: "There are ten foetuses here, all aborted this morning. You can take them. We are a State hospital and don't charge anything . . . Normally we doctors take them home to eat – all free. Since you don't look well, you can take them."

Not every State hospital is as generous with its dead embryos as the Health Centre for Women and Children. At the Shenzhen People's Hospital, for example, the reporter was in for a surprise.

When a Ms Yang, the head nurse, was asked for foetuses, she looked anxious and asked other staff to leave. After closing the door, she asked the undercover buyer in a low voice: "Where did you [get to] know that we sell foetuses?"

The reporter answered: "A doctor friend in Hong Kong told me."

"What is his/her name?"

The reporter was not prepared for this line of questioning and could not come up with a name. Yang told him that foetuses were only for sale within the hospital and were not for public purchase. She added that some staff would, however, sell the foetuses on to Hong Kong buyers.

The reporter learned that the going rate for a foetus was $10 but, when the merchandize was in short supply, the price could go up to $20. But these prices are pin money compared to those set by private clinics, which are said to make a fortune selling foetuses. One chap on Bong Men Lao Street charges $300 for one foetus. The person in charge of the clinic is a man in his sixties. When he saw the ailing reporter, he offered to take an order for foetuses that had reached full term and which, it is claimed, contain the best healing properties.

When a female doctor named Yang – no relation – of Sin Hua clinic was asked whether foetuses were edible, she said emphatically: "Of course they are. They are even better than placentas. They can make your skin smoother, your body stronger and are good for kidneys. When I was in an army hospital in Jiangti province, I often brought foetuses home. They were pink, like little mice, with hands and feet. Normally, I buy some pork to make soup [with the foetuses added]. I know they are human beings, and [eating them] feels disgusting. But at that time, it was already very popular."

A Mr Cheng from Hong Kong claims he has been eating foetus soup for more than six months. To begin, the man, in his forties, would make the trip to Shenzhen frequently for business and was introduced to foetuses by friends. He says he met a number of professors and doctors in Government hospitals who helped him buy the foetuses.

"At first, I felt uncomfortable, but doctors said the substances in foetuses could help cure my asthma. I started taking them and gradually the asthma disappeared," Cheng said.

Now Chen only eats foetuses occasionally to top up his treatment, but there was a time when he made regular cross-border trips with the gruesome merchandize.

"Every time [I made the trip], I carried a Thermos flask to Shenzhen and brought the foetuses back to Hong Kong to make soup. If they gave me twenty or thirty at a time, I put them in the refrigerator. I didn't have the soup every day – it depended on the supply. Usually I washed the foetuses clean and added ginger, orange peel and pork to make soup. After taking it for a while, I felt a lot better and my asthma disappeared. I used to take placenta, but it was not so helpful."

When asked if he was concerned about the foetuses containing diseases, Cheng was dismissive.

"I bought them from Government hospitals. They would check the pregnant women before doing the operations and only sell them to me if there was no problem. Also, I always boil them over high heat, which kills any bacteria."

Although Cheng has overcome any squeamishness over eating foetus soup, he says he draws the line at consuming whole dead embryos. He also refrains from telling people of his grisly dietary habits.

Zou Qin, thirty-two, a woman from Hubei with the fine skin of a someone several years younger, attributes her well-preserved looks to a diet of foetuses. As a doctor at the Lun Hu Clinic, Zou has carried out abortions on several hundred patients. She believes foetuses are highly nutritious and claims to have eaten more than 100 in the past six months. She pulls out a foetus specimen before a reporter and explains the selection criteria.

"People normally prefer [foetuses of] young women and, even better, the first baby and a male." She adds: "They are wasted if we don't eat them. The women who receive abortions here don't want the foetuses. Also, the foetuses are already dead [when we eat them]. We don't carry out abortions just to eat the foetuses.

"Before, my sister's children were very weak. I heard that foetuses were good for your health and started taking some to my nephews," Zou says, without remorse. "I wash them with clear water until they look transparent white and then stew them. Making soup is best."

But she admits there are drawbacks to this dubious delicacy. "Foetuses are very smelly and not everybody can take the stink," she said. "You can also make meat cakes by mixing foetuses with minced meat, but you have to add more ginger and chives to get rid of the smell."

Hong Kong legislator Dr Tan Siu-tong is surprised that it could be within anyone's capability to overcome the stench of a dead foetus, even if their stomachs are lined with lead. "When all the placental tissue is dead, the smell is awful and is enough to make you feel sick. It is like having a dead mouse in the house," he said.

The foetuses allegedly eaten by the Chinese are all provided by China's extensive abortion services. Last year doctors in the People's Hospital – the biggest hospital in Shenzhen – carried out more than

7,000 terminations, 509 on Hong Kong women. The Hong Kong Family Planning Association (FPA) estimates that twenty-four per cent of all abortions on Hong Kong women are performed in the dubious surroundings of a Chinese hospital. A Ms Li from Hong Kong has had two abortions in Shenzhen, but has never heard of people eating foetuses.

"But 1 didn't want the babies, so after the abortions, I just left them with the hospital," she says. "I didn't want to look at them, and I certainly didn't want to keep them. Foetuses of two or three months are just water and blood when they come out. They are so small, how can you eat them?"

Doctors in the territory [Hong Kong] have responded with disgust and incredulity to stories of people supplementing their diets with foetuses. Many have read articles of foetal cannibalism, but none has been able to verify the reports. They are treating the issue with scepticism. Dr Margaret Kwan, a gynaecologist who until two weeks ago held the post of chief executive at the FPA, says: "This is the strangest thing I have ever heard coming out of China. I just hope it is not true."

Dr Warren Lee, President of the Hong Kong Nutrition Association, is aware of the unsavory rumours.

"Eating foetuses is a kind of traditional Chinese medicine and is deeply founded in Chinese folklore. In terms of nutrition, a foetus would be a good source of protein and fats, and there are minerals in bone. But I don't know if eating foetuses is just folklore or more than that," he says.

According to Lee, it is conceivable that foetuses are rich in certain hormones that are beneficial to the adult human body, but, should this be the case, the foetal matter would have to be converted into an injectible form for best results, as most hormones – including the hormone for diabetes, insulin – are broken down in the digestive system before they have a chance to be absorbed by the body. But Lee suggests that anyone who eats a foetus would be seeking a remedy that is far more elusive than a hormone or mineral.

"Some people may think there is also an unidentified substance or chemical that has healing powers, but there is no evidence that this is true." Lee urges people to be wary: "There are people out there who just want to make money and they will come up with all sorts of formulas or substances which, they say, will cure diseases."

As a child, Patrick Yau was fed on human placentas by his mother, who worked at a local hospital, but in his current position as a psychologist with the Social Welfare Department he is both repulsed and shocked by the notion of eating foetuses.

"As a Catholic, I object to abortions because I believe the foetus is a human life, and I certainly object to eating a dead baby after it has been aborted," he says.

Yau concedes that in China, where the one child policy has turned abortions into an acceptable remedy to an unfortunate human blunder, people may have adopted a new outlook on life before birth, such that embryos are stripped of their status as human beings.

But Tang fails to understand how anyone anywhere can convince themselves "that they are just eating an organism when they are actually eating a dead body". "It may not be a formed human being, but, when they think about it, most people would think: "Ugh! No, I can't eat that." I don't think civilized people with an education could do that sort of thing."

Dr Wong, a Hong Kong doctor who practices Western medicine, thinks only the ignorant would eat human foetuses. He explains that foetuses contain mucoploysaccharide, which is beneficial to the metabolism, but states that it can be found in a lot of other food. Chinese doctor Chu Ho-Ting agrees that there is no place for foetuses in medicine and suggests that it might even be unhealthy if the pregnant woman was infected by disease.

"Most bacteria can be killed under 100° heat but some require 400°. Some peopie believe eating foetuses can strengthen the immunity of the human body against diseases, but this is wrong. Although foetuses contain protein, they are not as nutritious as placenta, which contains different kinds of nutrients. But even placenta has to be taken with other Chinese herbs."

ELEPHANTS IN SOUTH AFRICA

A conservation debate is raging in South Africa over reports of aberrant behaviour among wild animals in local game reserves. There is speculation that it could be linked to the trade and relocation of animals in the burgeoning game reserve industry.

The debate centres on recent attacks on other animals and humans. Last week a young bull elephant at the Pilanesburg game reserve in

North-West Province charged a group of tourists and killed a warden who went to shoot it; last month a rhino fatally gored a game ranger in Botswana; and earlier this year a wounded giraffe kicked to death a conservation official in the Northern Province.

Nineteen white rhinos have been killed in Pilanesburg since March 1996 by elephant herds showing increasing signs of pathological behaviour. This has included attempts to mate with rhino cows.

"It is as though the animals are beginning to bite back," an environmentalist involved in investigations at Pilanesburg told a South African newspaper. "They are being hunted, culled, captured, transported and shunted into small and closed game reserves. We may be seeing early-warning signs that conservationists may have been playing God with the animals without anticipating the consequences."

Specialists from the Rhino and Elephant Foundation in Johannesburg, a leading research institution, suggest the anti-social behaviour could be the consequence of the increase in trade and relocation of wild animals. The bull elephant at the centre of last week's tragedy was an orphan taken either from a herd in an Eastern Cape reserve or from a herd killed during the Kruger National Park's controversial culling programme of the 1980s.

Ecologists have speculated that aggressive behaviour could be a sign of the trauma and stress that the animals have been subjected to. The practice of culling at the Kruger National Park, a reserve approximately half the size of Wales, has been used as a way of combating over-population and involves shooting adults and moving the young to other reserves. It is suggested that the orphaned elephants were traumatized by the killing that took place around them and were adversely affected by being sent to game reserves where there were no matriarchs to care for and discipline them.

Another influencing factor, it has been suggested, is the fact that most South African game reserves, with the exception of the Kruger, are small and closed systems, unlike those in East and Central Africa.

Marion Garai, an elephant specialist, has been studying the elephants at Pilanesburg. It is she who has linked the animals' aggression to the absence of matriarchal discipline in an area with a high density of rhinos. Despite their fearsome appearance, rhino bulls are vulnerable when attacked by elephant. Ms Garai says other factors have not been ruled out, including the possibility that the elephants' aggression may have been heightened by something in their diet.

CABO THE JUNGLE CAT

In legal maneuvering that would do O. J. Simpson proud, defenders have kept the law at bay to spare a jungle cat from the death penalty for mauling a two-year-old girl so severely that she needed 200 stitches. And, no matter how many times Illinois's DuPage County Judge Bonnie Wheaton orders that the exotic cat named Cabo be killed and tested for rabies, he always seems to have someone waiting to come to his rescue.

With no end in sight for this case – which so far has included emergency court action, an animal rights demonstration, a manhunt, comments from Governor Jim Edgar and a flurry of legal paperwork – it's easy to wonder what happened to everyone's sense of proportion. After all, we're talking about a cat. The DuPage County Animal Control Department already has euthanized 496 cats in 1995.

"This is a case, really, that the courts should never have been involved in," said Richard Matasar, dean of Chicago-Kent College of Law. "It should have been worked out by the people involved early on."

Added Mike Dsida, a lawyer and instructor at Loyola University, Chicago: "It's ridiculous. It's outrageous that so much energy and time are being spent on protecting a cat when there are countless people who have legitimate legal claims who are going unrepresented."

The curtain rose on the Cabo drama on 18 June, during an innocent Father's Day get-together at the Downers Grove home of Sari Mintz and her fiance, Thomas Harmon, who have both claimed to own Cabo at various points in the case. Sari's brother, Bill Mintz of Chicago, was visiting with his wife Judy and their toddler Alice. The girl and her mother were waiting in the back yard for Sari Mintz and Harmon to return from an errand when Cabo leapt on to the girl and began biting her face and head.

The bickering began almost immediately, when Mintz and Harmon returned from their errand and began to blame Judy Mintz for the attack, according to court testimony. In an effort to protect Cabo, the pair told paramedics that a dog had inflicted the wounds, Judy Mintz later testified.

Alice's mother played along with the lie, keeping the truth from doctors until her daughter's treatment for supposed dog bites was well under way. Then Alices's parents decided that they had better have

Cabo tested for rabies. Sari Mintz and Harmon refused, according to Richard Stavins, the lawyer who represents Alice and her parents, so the family turned to the DuPage County State's attorney's office.

Ever since, the threat of rabies has hung over the case, despite the fact that it is extremely uncommon for rabies to be transmitted through cat bites, according to Dr John Flaherty, an infectious disease specialist at the University of Chicago Medical Center. "Most animals that get it die from it," he said. Since Cabo remains alive and well, "I don't know why they are getting so nervous."

Indeed, Cabo has been vaccinated against rabies, although a veterinarian has testified that the rabies vaccination commonly used for house cats is not licensed for use with jungle cats. Such animals are of a different species from domestic cats and are native to Africa and Asia.

Judge Wheaton issued an emergency order on 23 June that Cabo be turned over to animal control authorities so that he could be killed and his brain tested for the disease. State law required this, Wheaton ruled. By that time, though, the cat had been transported across the state line to its veterinarian in Iowa City. Harmon had originally purchased Cabo from an Iowa City breeder.

Authorities tried to serve the court order on Mintz, but she was nowhere to be found. Several days passed. She later claimed to have been unaware of the order and away on business . . . However, her whereabouts on those days have remained a mystery.

Governor Edgar called for her employer to take action against Sari Mintz if she refused to comply with the court order. But she returned on Wednesday to Illinois, appeared in court and agreed to obey Wheaton's order. Regardless of whether she intended it, the hiatus served as a temporary reprieve for Cabo.

Harmon offered yet another reprieve when he surfaced with his lawyer and claimed that he alone owned Cabo. Through his attorney, Harmon said that Mintz has no right to decide Cabo's fate.

Johnson County health officials in Iowa had ordered that Cabo be confined at the vet's clinic for fourteen days for rabies observation. With the cat custody battle raging, the Johnson County attorney declared that Wheaton's order could not be enforced. Instead, the county opted to continue enforcing its isolation order, which expires on Monday.

Wheaton attempted to resolve the dispute on Friday by issuing yet another order, this time directed at Harmon, but so far authorities have been unable to find Harmon and serve him with the order. So, for now, Cabo is safe. But nobody knows what will happen . . . Only time will tell whether more defenders will launch additional efforts to save the jungle cat. But, for now, it remains to be seen how far authorities will be willing to go in order to bring Cabo the cat to justice. "Illinois isn't going to put itself in the position of starting a civil war with Iowa over something this silly."

[Nearly three months later, 19 September 1995] Yet another act in what a prosecutor has called a needless drama of Shakespearean proportions was played out on Monday in a DuPage County court, where Downers Grove resident Sari Mintz was ordered to pay a $500 fine for keeping a dangerous animal.

The charge – a village ordinance violation – and the fine belie the extent of the tragedy that has resulted from Mintz's ownership of Cabo the cat, a small jungle feline that Mintz and her fiance, Thomas Harmon, kept in their home.

Within the past three months a two-year-old girl has been left badly mauled, one of the cat's owners [Thomas Harmon] has committed suicide, the other has been transferred out of her job and the animal itself has been killed after a battle that crossed state borders.

"This case is disturbing and goes beyond normal ordinance violations," DuPage County Judge Roy Lawrence said as he slapped the maximum possible criminal penalty on Mintz, a former public relations worker with the Illinois State Toll Highway Authority. "This animal offered a substantial background of what you could expect from it," he said.

Monday's action lays to rest official action against Cabo and his owners, but Mintz still faces civil lawsuits relating to previous alleged attacks by the cat. Months before the toddler's tragic mauling, according to prosecutors, Mintz had already been found guilty on a previous charge of keeping a dangerous animal, fined $50 and warned by the DuPage County Animal Control Department to get rid of the cat. Mintz and Harmon ignored the warning . . .

Eventually Downers Grove police charged Mintz and Harmon for the second time with illegally keeping a dangerous animal. Harmon was also charged with obstructing a police officer when the officer came to investigate the incident.

Last month Harmon committed suicide by inhaling carbon monoxide in the garage of the couple's home, according to authorities.

"This is a Shakespearean tragedy," said Downers Grove prosecutor Linda Pieczynski, as Mintz faced the charge against her on Monday. Mintz had ample reason to know the cat was dangerous, Pieczynski said. "There are pending lawsuits in Cook and DuPage Counties from previous alleged attacks by this cat, and in 1994 Mintz was found guilty of keeping a dangerous animal and fined. I know this case and Mintz has been under intense media scrutiny, but had she taken hold of things at the beginning, none of this would have happened."

A BURMESE PYTHON IN THE BRONX

A New York teenager was crushed to death by his pet python after he had failed to keep the snake properly fed, police reported.

Grant Williams, nineteen was found unconscious in a pool of blood, the life practically squeezed out of him by a twelve-foot Burmese python named Damien, which was still wrapped over his body. The snake had been given nothing more than a single dead chicken in the past week and may have been crazed by hunger.

Mr Williams was found in the hallway. He may have been trying to escape the flat to summon help. Medical orderlies summoned the strength – of body and mind – to lift the forty-five-pound, five-inch-thick python off Mr Williams and hurl it into an adjacent room, but the snake lover died in hospital.

At the time of the attack, Mr Williams was preparing to feed Damien a live chicken. It is possible that the python, peckish, opted for the larger prey. When on the brink of a kill, the Burmese python (*Moorus bivattatus*) can move with deadly speed and there are few creatures able to escape its grasp.

Mr Williams may have suspected that his familiarity with Damien placed him above danger, but a hungry python does not quibble about such niceties. Captain Thomas Kelly, from the 46th precinct, said, "It looks accidental."

Mr Williams and his brother kept a number of snakes, many uncaged, in their Bronx flat. The dead man's mother, Carmelita Williams, said that she had tried to persuade her son to abandon his hobby. 'I begged him to get rid of the python,' she said, weeping. "I even threatened to call the police."

Damien was last night caged at an animal control centre, after being fed. Its fate is uncertain.

RUSSIAN CANNIBALISM FLOURISHES

When police in the Crimean city of Sebastopol were called to investigate a murder this week, nothing had prepared them for the grisly scene that unfolded during a routine search of a block of flats.

Entering the home of a former convict, the officers found the mutilated remains of human bodies being prepared for eating. The flat's owner, her mother and her boyfriend, had been stabbed to death by the thirty-three-year-old suspect and their bodies neatly butchered. In the kitchen investigators found the internal organs of two victims in saucepans, and nearby on a plate a freshly roasted piece of human flesh.

Although the gruesome details of the killings have stunned Sebastopol, more shocking perhaps is the growing evidence suggesting that cannibalism is not an isolated problem, but is rife in the former Soviet Union.

In the past twelve months ten people, from Siberia to St Petersburg, have been charged with killing and eating their victims. The authorities are at a loss to explain the phenomenon. Last month there were two cases of cannibalism. One man in the Siberian coal-mining town of Kemerovo was arrested after he admitted killing and cutting up a friend, and using his flesh as the filling for *pelmeni*, a Russian version of ravioli.

Twice last year convicts in overcrowded prisons killed and ate their cellmates because they claimed they were hungry and wanted to relieve overcrowding. Criminal experts said that most cases of cannibalism were part of the general rise of serial killings, which have increased because police resources are so stretched by rising crime and because of Russia's mounting economic and social problems.

Andrei Tkachenko, the director of the Serbsky Psychiatric Centre in Moscow, where serial killers are sent for observation, said that, in the 1980s, the centre received about three to five patients a year. Now, on average, at least ten serial killers are sent.

"If you were to get a complete figure, you would find that there are considerably more instances of serial murders in Russia now than anywhere else in the world," he told the *Moscow Times*.

Cannibalism, in particular, could just be the grim legacy of Russia's tortured history this century, when time and again the population has resorted to eating human flesh to survive.

The first recorded cases were during the famine of 1921, when the plight of the people in the Volga region was so great that a trade in human body parts flourished briefly. Mass outbreaks of cannibalism emerged again during the period of Stalin's collectivization in the 1930s, when millions died of starvation in Ukraine and many resorted to ambushing and eating strangers and children.

"These were people who cut up and ate corpses, who killed their own children and ate them," wrote Vasili Grossman, a Soviet writer. "I saw one. She had been brought to the district centre under convoy. Her face was human, but her eyes were those of a wolf."

NIKOLAI DZHURMONGALIEV

Cannibalism is sadly not uncommon in the former Soviet Union – perhaps it's a reflection of the poor state of the scoff.

Nikolai Dzhurmongaliev – known as "Metal Fang" because of his white metal false teeth – is the king of the Soviet cannibals, having slaughtered and served up around 100 women to his dinner guests in the former Soviet republic of Kazakhstan. He said he believed that attractive women and prostitution were the root of all evil.

After friends discovered a head and intestines in his kitchen, Dzhurmongaliev was sent to an insane asylum in Tashkent, from which, in due course, he bribed his way out. After being recaptured and put on trial, he was found guilty of only seven murders and incarcerated. But again he escaped, in 1989.

The authorities, however, never admitted that Dzhurmongaliev had escaped and, in secret, spent two years tracking him down, eventually recapturing him in Uzbekistan.

Interior Minister Colonel Yuri Dubyagin described him as "absolutely normal, but at some point he got a taste of female meat". Such an attitude may explain why there are so many high-scoring serial killers in the former Soviet Union; Dzhurmongaliev was held not responsible for his actions and is back in a loony bin.

CANNIBALISM BY RUSSIAN MILITARY

Aleksandr Lebed arrived at Nato's headquarters on 7 October 1996 to to do battle on the subject of Russia's future relations with the Alliance. The outspoken former general has, after earlier conciliatory remarks, added his gravel voice to Kremlin denunciations of Nato's planned enlargement. He may repeat the assertion last week by Yevgeni Primakov, the Foreign Minister, that Russia would consider enlargement as a provocative breach of the treaty on Conventional Forces in Europe and take "retaliatory measures".

Moscow's resistance is related to uncertainties at home, where General Lebed is engaged in his own wars on several fronts. As the negotiator responsible for halting the bloodshed in Chechnya, he faces bitter opposition to what nationalists call a capitulation. As a would-be successor to the ailing President Yeltsin, he is the target of sniping within the Kremlin and, as the man responsible for Russia's security, he has been battling to save the Russian Army from bankruptcy and mutiny.

The crisis in the Russian Armed Forces is one of the biggest threats not only to Russia itself, but to its neighbours and to the stability of Europe. What was once a trained, capable and disciplined force is now little more than a rabble – impoverished, corrupt and surly.

The Government's repeated failure to pay soldiers even their meagre wages, the plundering of the military budget by regional bosses and mafia interests, and the crippling costs of programmes started when the Soviet Union was a superpower have taken a severe toll.

The Armed Forces now have wage arrears of some 15,000 billion roubles. As a result, military units have been selling their weapons, tanks, supplies and whatever they can lay hands on simply to buy food and fuel. A worrying proportion of these weapons is reaching Afghans, dictators and criminals. Soldiers, and especially conscripts, have been left to fend for themselves and in remote garrisons in the frozen north and the Far East some units are on the brink of starvation. Ugly rumours of cannibalism, a practice not unknown in Russian military history, are again circulating.

The supply of manpower is disappearing as fast as discipline and training. On paper there should be one-and-a-half million men under arms, but Moscow admits this has fallen to one million and the true figure may be well below that. Only about ten per cent of those called up are actually drafted; school-leavers are evading conscription, which they see as virtual penal servitude. The once-pampered officer corps is being pensioned off as fast as possible, but is still far larger than warranted. Military housing is well below standard, and men with inadequate shelter and clothing have frozen to death.

Russia still has some formidable military elements; the soldiers in Bosnia are effective and disciplined, and the rocket forces are maintaining their morale. But the military collapse elsewhere is a national humiliation, and one that greatly increases the historically rooted-paranoia among Russia's leaders about military encirclement in the event of Nato expansion. Pride in the Army is a source of national cohesion in a country which badly needs such symbols of certainty. Regardless of the succession battles in the Kremlin, no Russian government can safely ignore the political dangers implicit in an army bleeding to death.

KILLER BEES IN THE USA

The elderly woman making her way down the sunny suburban street paused to flick something away from her hair, then raised her handbag as if to fend off an attacker. Within minutes, she was cowering on the ground, screaming in agony as a swarm of killer bees attacked with incredible ferocity.

More than 20,000 were all over her like a "dark cloud", in the words of one terrified witness – stinging her more than 500 times.

The seventy-seven-year-old woman staggered into the middle of Maryland Parkway in Las Vegas, bringing traffic to a standstill. Two people who rushed out of their homes to help were driven back by the bees. The first two police officers to arrive were stung and had to summon the fire department for help. But for between seven and ten minutes police, drivers and passers-by could only watch helplessly.

Fire department spokesman Tim Scymanski said: "It was a horrible, terrifying scene. The woman was sitting on a kerb thrashing at the bees. She was sobbing with pain and the bees kept coming in."

Firemen finally used their hoses to drench the victim and the insects. Thousand of bees were washed across the pavement and two firemen were stung brushing more off the woman before they could take her to hospital, where she was in a critical condition last night.

Rodney Mehring, head of BeeMaster pest control, said: "She is lucky to be alive." He tracked down the hive to the hollow of an old tree and destroyed it. He estimated that it contained up to 40,000 killer bees. Given that between fifty and sixty per cent of the hive gets involved in an attack he estimated that more than 20,000 tried to sting her.

The Nevada Division of Agriculture described the insects as "Africanized", referring to the aggressive hybrid that invades the hives of domesticated bees and then produces ferocious bees that will attack at the slightest provocation. Simply swatting one might have triggered the mass attack or they may have been attracted by something in her handbag.

Mr Mehring said: "This state is fighting an invasion of these killer bees." The bees came from a Brazilian experiment in 1957 when African bees were crossbred with the European honey bee. Several escaped, and since then an estimated 1,000 people have died in Brazil. By 1990 the bees were crossing into the US, where seven people have died.

The sting is no different from a honey bee. It is the mass attack technique that can kill.

SCOTTISH TEDDY BEAR'S PICNIC

A Scottish wildlife park has launched an inquiry into an incident in which a bear bit off and ate the arm of a boy aged ten.

The attack took place at the Camperdown Wildlife Centre, Dundee, after it had closed for the night. A spokesman said it was unlikely that Jeremy, the European brown bear, who became famous as the star of Sugar Puffs television commercials in the 1960s, would be destroyed.

A number of children, who had sneaked into the park, saw the attack on Ross Prendergast when he stuck his hand through the bars of the bear's cage. The boy's arm was severed at the elbow and he was badly mauled about the chest and shoulders.

Dundee's Royal Infirmary said the boy, of Ganton Court, Dundee, was in satisfactory condition.

The attack was the second at the wildlife park within forty-eight hours. On Saturday a man was bitten by a wolf. Yesterday a hastily penned note at the centre's reception warned visitors "Some of our animals bite".

The zoo's conservation officer, Mr George Reid, said that it was the first time in eighteen years that the bear had been involved in an incident. "He is not normally aggressive and I often let him play with me and scratch my head through the mesh."

A KHMER ROUGE CANNIBAL

There was a time when Chan Sayon, a worker at the La Paillote hotel in Phnom Penh, might have relished eating the guests. Now he just bows before showing them to their rooms.

Once a Khmer Rouge guerrilla, Sayon bayoneted and axed to death thirty-two captured government soldiers. He cannibalized five of his victims by slitting them open and eating their livers – a practice believed to bring strength and longevity to the devourer.

Now he checks in holidaymakers at the Swiss-run hotel in the capital of Cambodia; he has been rehabilitated by a government anxious to bring tourists back to the strife-torn country and heal the wounds of the past. Thanks to the unexpected success of its amnesty for Khmer Rouge guerrillas, the government is wrestling with the problem of rehabilitating hundreds of the world's most bloodthirsty fighters. Their documented atrocities include pulling out their victims' fingernails, drowning them in specially designed vats, hacking them to death with hoes, and butchering them and eating their internal organs.

"Of course this causes problems for us, because we have to teach them right from wrong," said Colonel Say Khom, forty-one, in charge of the Khmer Royal Armed Forces Reconciliation Centre, where more than half Cambodia's 6,000 former guerrillas have undergone rehabilitation. "Even if they join our own armed forces, we cannot tolerate such acts."

At the ramshackle camp the former jungle fighters listen attentively to lectures on liberal democracy and human rights given by a United Nations-sponsored instructor; they are tutored in "respect for nationality, religion and king". And they are reminded that, as Buddhists, they cannot enter heaven if they consume human flesh. They undergo military drill and community service, including making mud bricks to build the type of village houses they once ransacked. Some of the men repair dykes and harvest rice in the paddy fields where 1 million Cambodians died labouring under the Khmer Rouge tyranny from 1975 to 1979. After three months they join the army on a £13-a-month soldier's salary.

Those with a skill or rudimentary education can reintegrate into civilian life. Sayon got his job earning £40 a month thanks to the smattering of English he picked up as a child at a refugee camp in Thailand. He drifted into the Khmer Rouge in 1989, aged twenty, and learned to use a Chinese-made AK-47 rifle to hunt and ambush soldiers who, he was taught, belonged to a Vietnamese "army of occupation".

He insists the prisoners he killed were Vietnamese spies, even though they wore government uniforms and spoke Cambodian. He interrogated his victims while they were tied up and kneeling. "I knew they were enemies because they did not speak in pure Cambodian tongue," he said, though he admitted they may have been incoherent with fear.

Sayon would cut open each victim and take out the liver to share round. "Eating liver was good for the blood, like eating dog," Sayon said. The flesh was salted and dried. "The best parts were the thighs, calves, and chest and arm muscles. We fried it with chilli peppers and herbs. It tasted like beef."

He fought mainly at night, sleeping by day in a treetop hammock in the camp just inside the Thai border. Sayon left in 1992 after tiring of primitive life in the rebel camp. Now he puts his past atrocities down to the excesses of youth. His wife is expecting their first child.

Squatting in his tiny one-room home behind a dingy shop, he thumbed through photographs showing him in Khmer Rouge battle dress, an axe tucked into his belt. He admits he was probably brainwashed by the Khmer Rouge.

The government claims that, since its amnesty came into effect in July 1994, the Khmer Rouge has been reduced by desertions to less than half its former fighting strength.

Not everyone believes the Khmer Rouge can be rehabilitated. "These men are jungle fighters," said Matthew Lee, a consultant to the Red Cross in Phnom Penh. "They are not just going to settle down and farm chickens. A lot will revert to their old ways." Already there are signs that some guerrillas have become common outlaws. In January 1995 an American professor and her guide were murdered by two former Khmer Rouge soldiers who had joined a group of bandits preying on tourists.

Despite the threat to visitors, the Khmer Rouge's legacy of horrors is proving to be one of the country's biggest tourist lures. Tuol Sleng, a high school in Phnom Penh used by the Khmer Rouge as a gruesome prison and torture chamber, is today a museum. Photographs of thousands of victims, mainly "intellectuals" (doctors, teachers, Buddhist monks and anyone who wore glasses) have been archived, along with their "confessions" and notes kept in chilling detail by their torturers. "It's like visiting the Second World War concentration camps," said Wes Sturgeon, a visitor from Texas, "but in this country you can find the equivalent of real live Nazis wandering around and selling souvenirs."

MISS DAISY MAE PIGGY

While those close to Daisy Mae Manthey deny charges that she is aggressive, ill-tempered and perhaps violent, even her biggest fans have to admit one thing about her: she is a pig.

She is a Vietnamese pot-bellied pig, to be precise, who lives on a quiet street in Chicago's suburban Schiller Park. In early July 1997 Daisy's world was turned upside down, say her owners, Betty Jean and Richard Manthey, who also have a dog, two rabbits and two ducks as pets – she became embroiled in a controversy that has one side crying, "Foul," and the other saying, "Hogwash."

According to Schiller Park police, Daisy bit somebody on the hand and forearm on Wednesday night a charge the Mantheys just can't believe.

"Daisy is a sweetheart," declared Betty Jean, forty-eight, of the five-pound porker. "She has never bitten anybody."

Yet, according to a police report, at about 7.30 p.m. Wednesday a woman approached the Mantheys' yard to pet their dog. As she was petting the dog, "a pig came running up to the woman and bit her", the official police report stated.

Police seized Daisy later that night and took her to a Franklin Park animal farm. Next day, after it was determined that Daisy did not need to be quarantined, she was released to the Mantheys' custody.

Daisy spent that afternoon recovering from the previous day's drama – a most unpleasant and undignified experience, according to the

Mantheys. Daisy's owners maintain that biting would be thoroughly out of character.

"The kids in the neighborhood play with her all the time," said Betty Jean. "She is a little on the heavy side, but she is a very beautiful pig."

Looks aside, Daisy has a rap sheet as long as, well, one of her pig legs. In May 1995 she escaped from the yard and took off down the block at a stately pace, only to be apprehended soon after by police, her owners said.

Formerly of eastern Kentucky, Daisy has resided in Schiller Park for just over three years. On top of it all, Daisy may also be involved with a jewel theft.

"She [the victim] accused the pig of stealing the diamond ring off her finger," said Betty Jean Manthey, who dismisses the allegation. "I've taught Daisy a lot of tricks, but I haven't taught her to be a diamond thief."

The victim filed a police report stating that "as a result of the bite, she lost a double heart-shaped fourteen-carat gold ring". But Schiller Park Police Chief Peter Puleo said that, without further evidence of the pig's involvement in the ring's disappearance, the issue will have to be settled in a civil proceeding.

RED FIRE ANTS

Invasive fire ants, responsible in the USA for the decline of native ant species and the animals that depend on them for food, are also attacking humans – in their own beds.

A new [1999] report in the *Annals of Internal Medicine* details ten cases of fire-ant attacks on humans indoors. Of the indoor victims 3 died. Outdoor fire ant stings have caused at least eighty deaths. The report warns that infants and the bedridden elderly are most at risk from these aggressive insects.

Red fire ants, native to South America, first arrived in the USA about sixty years ago through the port of Mobile, Alabama. Since the 1930s they have spread through fourteen states, across the south-eastern US and Puerto Rico, and colonies have been found as far afield as California, Arizona, New Mexico and Virginia. The ants spread through mating flights and are also carried by agricultural vehicles which move infested plants and soil to previously uninfested areas.

The invaders have consumed or outcompeted most of the native black ant population in the south-east, threatening species like horned lizards that depend on the less aggressive black ants for food. In all, fire ants have colonized more than 310 million acres in the USA and Puerto Rico. Amazingly, some fire ant colonies have been found to have adapted to include more than one egg-laying queen per colony.

Fire ants sting and kill insects as their primary food source, but have been known to kill farm animals if other food is not available. Humans encountering the ants outdoors are often stung as the insects protect their territory. Red fire ants are the only ants which will swarm to the surface of their ant hill or mound to attack the source of any disturbance. Indeed, fire ants thrive in disturbed habitats, including construction sites. In some areas, including New Orleans, Louisiana, and San Antonio, Texas, fire ants now bite more than fifty per cent of the human population each year. One study showed that fifty-one per cent of previously unexposed medical students were stung within three weeks of arriving in San Antonio. Within five minutes fire-ant stings raise welts on a human and within twenty-four hours the victim displays a rash of inflamed pustules.

The medical complications of fire-ant stings can range from mild irritation at the sting site to death from an allergic reaction, depending on the number of stings and the physical condition of the victim.

In 1989 the first case of fire ants attacking a human inside a building was reported. Since then nine more indoor attacks on people in six states have been reported, including eight described by Dr Richard deShazo, the lead author of the article in *Annals*, director of the division of allergy and immunology, and chairman of the Department of Medicine at the University of Mississippi Medical Center.

In 1992 a five-day-old baby was attacked in its crib in Alabama. The infant went into shock and coma, but survived. In another incident a developmentally delayed two-year-old suffered damage to his cornea when fire ants selectively attacked his head and eyes.

Dr deShazo provides case histories of two fatal fire ant attacks in nursing homes.

In February 1997 a sixty-year-old man in a nursing home in Starkville, Mississippi, was found covered in fire ants when checked at 4 a.m., though no ants had been seen at midnight. A trail of ants led from the baseboard of his room on to his bed. Though the man responded well to treatment with antihistamines and corticosteroids, he developed pneumonia and suffered a heart attack; he died of complications just over a year later.

In August 1998 a sixty-seven-year-old woman in a nursing home in Brookhaven, Mississippi, was found under attack by an army of fire ants during a routine 4 a.m. bed check by staff. No ants had been seen during the previous bed check three hours earlier. The victim could not walk without help and was confined to her bed when not in a wheelchair. She suffered 500 bites and died five days later.

One week after that attack fire ants were found in the room of a ninety-nine-year-old patient in the same facility. The nursing home had been inspected and treated by a pest control company only four days before the first, fatal attack.

Any sighting of a swarm of ants indoors is a warning. Residents and caregivers of infants, children and bedridden people such as patients in health care facilities should be watched closely until the ants are eliminated, says Dr deShazo.

Eliminating fire ants is not easy, he says. The colony cannot be destroyed unless the queen ant is killed. He offers the following advice:

(a) assume that, if one fire ant is seen, an active infestation is present;
(b) investigate both interior and exterior of the building carefully;
(c) exterminate all ants found indoors with liquid pesticides as soon as possible;
(d) Treat ant activity on the perimeter or basement and in the yard with bait-based insecticides, which are most likely to reach and kill the queen ant;
(e) Since fire ants are attracted to electrical fields, examine equipment with wires, fuses and switches. Fire ants may invade electrical equipment, including computers, air conditioners and circuit breakers.

Dr deShazo says that extermination indoors should be carried out by a professional pest control service and that reinfestation is common.

RABID BATS ALERT

DuPage County, Illinois, Health Department officials are reminding area residents to exercise caution around wild animals after a bat captured in a Naperville home tested positive for rabies earlier this week [October 1998].

The positive diagnosis was the first confirmed case of rabies in DuPage County since a skunk tested positive in 1989, according to Ardith Baker, animal control manager for the county.

The wayward bat, which somehow got into a twelve-year-old Naperville boy's bedroom, bit or scratched the boy as he startled it. The bat was turned in to the DuPage County Animal Control unit and later killed. Nancy Gier, a Health Department spokeswoman, said that the boy is undergoing preventive treatment and is not expected to develop the disease.

"The child was bitten under unusual circumstances, but the bat did turn out to be rabid," said Gier. "There's not a huge threat from rabid bats, but people need to be aware that bats can carry rabies."

Rabies, which attacks the central nervous system, is caused by a virus present in the saliva of a rabid animal and can be transmitted by biting or through infected saliva that comes in contact with an open wound, but the disease is rarely found in humans. No confirmed cases of rabies in humans have been reported in Illinois since 1954, according to the Illinois Department of Public Health.

In late August a bat discovered in an Orland Park residential area straddling Cook and Will Counties also tested positive for rabies. Cook County animal control authorities noted at the time that such cases were infrequent in the area. Last year a total of sixteen bats out of 353 tested in Illinois proved to be rabid.

Rabies can be carried by a number of other wild mammals, including skunks, racoons and foxes, according to the DuPage County Health Department. Cats, dogs and livestock also can develop rabies if not vaccinated.

Gier said that one of the first signs of rabies is a change in an animal's behavior: a tame animal could suddenly become aggressive or a normally wild animal might approach a campsite or home and appear friendly. Other symptoms include drooling and difficulty in walking.

TAPIR TEETH

A large, hoglike animal called a tapir pulled a thirty-four-year-old zookeeper into its cage and bit her arm off as she tried to feed the animal.

Lisa Morehead, who also suffered facial injuries and a punctured lung, was in critical condition and underwent surgery after the attack at the Oklahoma City Zoo on 20 November 1998.

ILLINOIS BROWN BEAR MUNCH

A Chicago woman was mauled by a bear on Saturday 26 June 1999 during a visit to an exotic animal farm near Downstate Marion, police said. Nicole Damato, twenty-seven, of the South Side, was listed in fair condition in a Missouri hospital after nearly losing her right leg in the altercation, a hospital spokeswoman said.

"It's something you see on television or read about, but it never happens to you," said Damato's mother, Monica.

The bear mauled Damato after she stepped into its cage to pet it at the invitation of its owner, Bobby J. Green, fifty-eight, of Creal Springs, south of Marion, according to a statement by the Williamson County Sheriff's Department. Green had walked in first, assuring her the creature was tame.

"They have no idea what set this off," Monica Damato said. She added that the brown bear was six feet tall.

Her leg firmly planted in the bear's jaws, Damato cried out to her brother, twenty-three-year-old Dominic, for help. He and a relative, Scott Oplinger, thirty-one, had accompanied her on the outing, Monica Damato said. Oplinger jumped on the bear's back, clobbering and choking it, as Dominic tugged Damato free. As Damato lay bleeding, Dominic frantically dialed paramedics, wrapping her leg in towels and ice until help arrived.

She was taken by helicopter to the South-East Missouri Hospital in Cape Girardeau, across the Mississippi River from Illinois.

Bobby Green, the animal's owner, could not be reached for comment.

Nicole Damato, the mother of two boys aged three and five, is expected to walk again, though she will need extensive rehabilitation therapy, her mother said. "She's a very strong girl, very strong mentally. She'll take this in her stride."

BIG SNAPPER IN BIG APPLE

The nearest thing to confirming the urban myth that dangerous reptiles live below as well as above the pavements of New York emerged on 16 June 2000 when a 1.35-metre alligator was discovered living in the wild.

Tom Lloyd, a contractor out for a stroll with his four-year-old daughter, saw a long dark object that he took to be a toy among the ducks and geese in a stream on Staten Island. But, when prodded with a stick, the object came alive and snapped at him.

The closest natural habitat of the creature – *alligator mississipiensis* – is North Carolina, five states away. "Somebody probably dumped him in there," said Bill Holstrom, supervisor of Bronx Zoo's reptile department.

Two police officers, directed by the city's resident reptile rescue expert, Robert Shapiro, lassoed the sixteen-kilogram gator's jaws, pulled it from the stream and taped its mouth shut. Then they put the alligator, whose age was put at between two and five years, on the back seat of a squad car and drove it to the Manhattan T-shirt shop run by Mr Shapiro.

"He was hissing, but he wasn't darting at us or anything," said Mr Shapiro, who has hundreds of unwanted reptiles in the back of the shop and deals with about five illegally owned crocodilians – alligators, crocodiles and caymans – each year. These have been handed over by owners who have decided that they can no longer look after them.

It has long been an urban myth that beneath the streets of Manhattan live crocodiles and alligators which have been flushed down into the sewers by owners who no longer want them.

"Animals need to be basking in the sun," said Mr Shapiro before the new find was sent on its way to a registered alligator keeper in Pennsylvania.

TAIGA TIGER

A Siberian tiger raised in Lincoln Park Zoo attacked and mauled a woman during a tour at the Boise, Idaho, zoo last week [early August 2000], but will not be euthanized, a Boise zoo official said.

Taiga, a 600-lb rare Siberian tiger, came through an unlocked gate and mauled Jan Gold, forty-one, who was taking a behind-the-scenes tour during Zoo Boise's fundraiser, "Feast of the Beast".

The attack ended when a police officer at the benefit fired three shots, scaring the animal. One of the shots ricocheted and struck the woman in the thigh.

Jim Dumont, recreation superintendent for the Boise Parks and Recreation Department, said that the zoo blames the attack on human error, not on Taiga, who was born in Lincoln Park Zoo in 1997. Taiga and his brother Tundra have been in Boise since October. "As far as we're concerned, we are not recommending to put the tiger down and don't plan to do anything but make sure the tiger is able to make it through the stress," he said.

Experts said that Taiga was just being a tiger when he jumped on Gold, who suffered lacerations to the back of the head, neck and shoulder, and the bullet wound in her thigh. She was in serious but stable condition in Alphonsus Regional Medical Center in Boise.

Since the attack, tiger sympathizers from across the country – including one of Taiga's former zoo-keepers in Chicago – have called Zoo Boise concerned about the fate of the tiger, said Dumont. "They are the two finest exhibition animals we have in the zoo. The city of Boise has fallen in love with these tigers." Attendance at the park has increased twenty-five per cent since Taiga and Tundra arrived, he said.

Taiga's parents were mated at the Lincoln Park Zoo as part of an effort to bolster the population of the endangered tiger species, whose natural home is the Amur region in East Asia. Only about 230 Siberian tigers remain in the wild.

When Taiga and Tundra – then named Ben and Casey – neared their second birthday, the zoo began to think about sending them to another zoo because it was running out of room, said Mary Ann Schultz, spokeswoman for the Lincoln Park Zoo. The tigers' sister and mother remain at the park. After two independent inspectors visited Zoo Boise to make sure it could handle the tigers, they were transferred. Dumont and Schultz said neither animal has ever been a problem.

Shortly after 9 p.m. Friday 11 August 2000, sixteen Zoo Boise supporters entered the tiger house to watch the animals being lured with food from a grassy outdoor recreation area back into their cages when the attack occurred. Hearing screams, Police Sergeant Rich Schnebly, who had attended the benefit as part of a community policing program, pushed through the crowd and into the building, where he found Gold with the tiger on top of her. Fearing he would hit Gold, Schnebly fired two rounds from his .45-caliber pistol over the tiger's head.

Taiga retreated to his cage, but, when Schnebly and zoo manager David Wayne moved forward to help Gold, Taiga approached again. Schnebly fired another shot and the animal backed off long enough to close the cage door.

Gold, a board member of the Friends of Zoo Boise, suffered a broken leg from a bullet that ricocheted off the wall and severe lacerations to the back of the head. Gold is still not well enough to be interviewed, a hospital spokesman said.

BULL ELEPHANT IN THAILAND

A British trainee nurse has been gored to death by a performing elephant in Thailand after it charged at tourists during an obedience display at an animal park.

Friends and neighbours of Andrea Taylor said yesterday, 26 April 2000, they were devastated by the loss of a "lovely, friendly girl". Ms Smith, twenty-three, from Wigan, Greater Manchester, was on holiday with her father Geoffrey, fifty-three, and her sister Helen, a twenty-year-old technical manager.

The family were sitting in the front row of an obedience display in the Suan Nongnuch animal park at the resort of Pattaya, ninety miles south-east of Bangkok, on Monday when the bull elephant attacked. The Foreign Office said the animal grabbed the trainer riding the elephant with its trunk and hurled him to the ground before charging at tourists in the small stone arena.

Mr Taylor, whose leg was injured in the attack, tried to shield Andrea, but discovered yesterday that she had died from internal injuries in Pattaya hospital. Several local people were also injured as they tried to bring the elephant under control and considerable damage was done to vehicles and property.

It is believed that Helen, who suffered abdominal injuries when the elephant trampled on her, has not been told of her sister's death. Both Helen and her father are said to be in a stable condition.

Neighbour and family friend Arthur Fairhurst, seventy-two, said: "It is a terrible shock that this should happen on what was meant to be a happy family holiday. Geoffrey has been to Thailand three times before and this time he decided to take the girls with him."

Ms Smith was training to be a nurse in Huddersfield and her ambition was to work as a midwife in Canada. Her sister worked in Halifax and used to drive her home to Wigan at weekends. She was a keen musician and played the trombone in local brass bands.

Animal experts suggested yesterday that the elephant may have been in musth (ready to mate). Nick Ellerton, curator at Knowsley safari park, Merseyside, said: "I would liken an elephant in musth to a drunk at a disco – it allows bulls to win fights with other elephants because they are so high on testosterone they aren't scared of getting hurt. Its a very sad story. What has probably happened here is that either an inexperienced trainer has not realized when the animal was coming into musth, or one has decided to ignore it to make money."

According to reports, the organizers of the show have been charged by police with the reckless endangerment of life. Last month the park paid a Russian tourist 150,000 baht (£2,500) in compensation after a puma injured her arm.

SERIAL KILLER SNAKES IN NIGERIA

A snake has killed seven women in one week in a village in Nigeria. The snake has also attacked another nineteen women at the village of Rijiyar Zaki, near Kano city.

Villagers have contacted snake charmers for help. Superstitious villagers fear the snake attacks were caused by a witches' curse placed on the village.

A squad of snake charmers are using all their skill to pacify the lethal reptile.

Local officials told *The Vanguard* newspaper on 3 August that extra anti-venom has been supplied to local hospitals.

Further snake charmers have been brought in to stop the number of villagers being killed by snakes in northern Nigeria. The number of deaths from snake bites has risen to around thirty, according to local media on 6 August 2001.

Villagers near Kano city say 150 people have suffered snake bites and the survivors are being treated in hospital. On August 3 the number of fatalities stood at seven, according to reports in the national media.

MALAYSIAN KING COBRA

A boy volunteer used by a snake charmer may lose two of his fingers after being bitten.

The eleven-year-old was picked from the crowd by a medicine man giving a demonstration in the street in Malaysia. He was bitten by the charmer's king cobra, despite the man placing a supposedly protective charm around him.

Although Mohamad Zaki Mat Ghani is in a stable condition in Kota Baru Hospital, his father said his thumb and index finger may need amputating. Kelantan police are looking for the dangerous charmer.

RABID DOGS

Rabies has claimed its second victim in a month in Britain after a woman bitten by a dog during a trip to Nigeria died from the disease.

The fifty-one-year-old woman died on Wednesday night, 31 May 2001, in Lewisham hospital, south London, where staff were seeking to reassure those who had come into contact with her that the chances of catching rabies were "infinitesimal". Although there is no record of transmission of the disease between humans, hospital workers and friends of the victim have been offered a rabies vaccination and counselling.

The woman, who has not been named, is thought to have caught rabies when she was bitten by a dog during a trip to Nigeria to see relatives. She was flown back to Britain and admitted to hospital on Monday, where doctors detected symptoms of the disease, including fever, headache and vomiting.

The latest rabies case comes three weeks after a man died in a

London hospital after being bitten by a stray dog during a trip to the Philippines.

Hilary Laya, fifty-four, died in University College Hospital ten days after showing the first symptoms of the disease.

Rabies kills an estimated 35,000 per year, mostly in Africa, Asia and Latin America. Travellers to such areas are urged to have the vaccination before leaving Britain because of a shortage abroad of immunoglobulin, the blood product used to treat the disease.

The last previous death from rabies in Britain was five years ago when an eighteen-year-old London man contracted the disease in Nigeria. Since 1946 there have been twenty cases of rabies in England and Wales – all of which have been traced to infection abroad.

Rabies is an acute infectious viral disease that attacks the nervous system, leaving victims suffering from convulsions, paralysis, excessive salivation and an aversion to water. There have been fewer than five known cases where recovery has occurred.

BLACK BEARS IN NEW MEXICO

A series of attacks on humans by hungry bears during 2001 has left New Mexicans as wary of their beloved mountains as some Floridians are of their beaches following recent shark attacks.

Residents of this south-western state are taking new precautions after a black bear broke into a home on 18 August in the mountain village of Cleveland, fifty miles north-east of Santa Fe, and killed a ninety-three-year-old great-grandmother, Adelia Maestas Trujillo.

The 250-pound male bear crashed through her kitchen window, most likely in search of food, then attacked the woman. She lived alone and her mangled body was found by her son, who lived near by. The bear was tracked down and shot.

It was the first deadly bear attack in New Mexico in recent memory and the product of a desperate food shortage in the animals' natural range, officials said.

"It's terrible what happened, but the bears are starving," said Juanita Martinez, a neighbor of the elderly victim. "There's no food for the bears."

Experts said the bears, who are not usually aggressive, are coming down from the isolated mountains where they live because they have little to eat. Freezing temperatures and heavy snow in northern New Mexico on 5 May killed much of this season's fruits and berries, staples of the bears' diet. Sparse rainfall in recent years has also limited the growth of juniper berries and acorns, which are eaten by the estimated 5,000-6,000 black bears living in New Mexico, said Scott Brown, a spokesman for the New Mexico Game and Fish Department.

The situation is not expected to change until the bears go into hibernation in January [2002]. Before that, the likelihood of more bear attacks is high because the animals will go on eating binges, consuming nearly 20,000 calories a day, as they prepare for their winter rest. Another incident occurred on Tuesday, when a man in Taos, New Mexico, shot a bear that had entered a home.

Earlier this summer, near Ruidoso in southern New Mexico, a black bear chased three Texas boys and bit one on the ankle. And, in June, at Philmont Scout Ranch near Cimarron, a bear injured two Boy Scouts during a brief encounter.

Joanna Lackey, division chief for the Game Department, said game officers have shot forty-three black bears since late spring. Officers killed five bears on Monday night, said Lackey, and as many as 100 calls a day about intrusive bears are coming into her office. "I have never seen anything like this in my twenty-five years here," she said.

Baudy Martinez, who with his wife Juanita owns B'Jay's Sandwich Shop in Mora, a few miles south of Cleveland, said long-time residents of the area are accustomed to seeing bears and know they must be respected and protected. They want bears and humans to live in harmony.

"This is the path the bears have been taking for thousands of years," said Martinez. "It's their natural habitat . . . The bears are precious. We have to preserve our wildlife."

VODKA AND PEOPLE MEAT

In Semipalatinsk Prison in Kazakhstan, four convicts decided to eat the very first new guy placed in their cell. Thus, when a new prisoner by the name of Volchenkov arrived, they killed him, cut meat from his arms and back, cooked and ate it. Some pieces were fried on a hotplate and some were boiled in a kettle. They blamed their actions on newspaper reports about instances of cannibalism in prisons.

In the Kzyl Orda region of Kazakhstan, a man by the name of Zhusaly, whose job was to act as a guard for a field of marijuana plants, confessed to shooting and eating his fellow guard. Zhusaly admitted that he had salted the flesh of his buddy and had eaten most of the cadaver over the course of ten days. Along with three farmers charged with growing marijuana, Zhusaly was arrested in a drugs raid. His three colleagues were also charged with concealing the murder.

The grim discovery of cannibalism was made in Perm Oblast when a member of the public brought to the police station a package of human flesh which he had bought on the street. His wife, having studied the meat, discovered skin on it.

From police enquiries the following story emerged. F. A. Boldyshev and his friend N. V. Ostanin had got drunk on vodka with a third man, A. P. Vavilin, and had killed him. Then they dismembered his corpse, threw Vavilin's head, hands and feet into an attic, and persuaded one of their mothers to cook the choicest cuts. After happily gorging themselves, they packed up the remains and sold them on the street. In custody the lethal duo confessed they had done it in order to save money on the purchase of normal food.

Specialists say that the taste of "people meat" is a specific one and it has a distinctive smell when cooked. "The taste of a victim", it is asserted in full seriousness at the Main Criminal Investigations Administration of the Ministry of Internal Affairs, "depends on the victim himself: if he drank or smoked a lot, whether he liked sweets or salt . . ."

Like other cannibals before him, Anatoly Dolbyshev, a resident of Berezniki in the Urals region near Perm, was arrested by police when a buyer found a strip of human skin on the meat bought from him. He was charged and found guilty of stabbing to death a friend of his mother's in a fight. He was also charged with "swindling and appropriation of property through deceit", when he cut up the dead man's body and sold the flesh to unsuspecting townsfolk in exchange for vodka.

In Moscow, meanwhile, a rooming house lodger by the name of Kolpakov, from Nizhny Novgorod, was killed by the son of his landlady. The killer cut a piece of soft tissue from Kolpakov's forearm, fried it in a pan and ate it. A panel of experts later found the killer to be of diminished responsibility.

According to the popular daily paper *MoskovskyKomsomolets*, a grisly discovery was made in Moscow, in Marshal Tukhachevsky Street. A beggar rummaging through rubbish bins for food found a human foot and several other body parts. Police were called to the scene and, during a search of the garbage area, found further evidence of murder: four hands, four shoulders and three feet, all female. "It became clear to the investigating officers that they were dealing with not one, but two murders," the newspaper stated.

On 3 July 1997 the Supreme Court of Chuvash Autonomous Republic sentenced to death Vladimir Nikolayev, aged thirty-eight, for killing and cannibalizing two people in the town of Novocheboksary.

Nikolayev, denounced as a particularly dangerous criminal, was arrested in his apartment in the winter of 1996. There police found a pan of stewed human meat on the stove and another cannibal dish in the oven. In the snow on his apartment balcony officers found more body parts, which Nikolayev had stored to eat later. Investigators who questioned Nikolayev said he had jokingly asked them to prepare him a meal using his stock of human flesh.

In what he claimed was a "one-man crusade to cleanse modern Russia of the permissiveness of democracy", twenty-seven-year-old Sasha Spesivtsev killed at least nineteen homeless street children whom he regarded as the detritus of society. The unemployed black-marketeer lured his victims from the streets and railway stations of the Siberian town of Novokuznetsk to his home, where, with the help of his mother, he killed and ate them.

In a stream outside Novokuznetsk, forty-three bone fragments were found, which are believed to be the remains of six bodies – four boys, one girl and a man. Investigators believe a whole family may have been killed and possibly cannibalized. However, in order to establish the genetic identity of the deceased, it was necessary to conduct a careful analysis of the bones. The Internal Affairs Ministry official in charge of the matter stated: "These preserved bones have lain in my refrigerator for a month already, waiting for the appropriate chemicals to arrive. Special preparations are very expensive . . ."

The St Petersburg cannibal Ilshat Kuzikov liked to marinate choice cuts with onions in a plastic bag hung outside his apartment window.

When the police forced their way into his home, they found Pepsi bottles full of blood and dried ears hanging on the wall – his winter supplies, said Kuzikov. He offered the police officers some meat and vodka if they would let him go free.

On 19 March 1997 Kuzikov was found guilty of killing three of his vodka-drinking buddies and eating their internal organs. He was sent to a maximum security psychiatric hospital. The self-confessed cannibal said he killed his first victim in 1992 after inviting him to his apartment for a nightcap. Kuzikov, aged thirty-seven, said he became a cannibal because he could not buy enough to eat on his meagre monthly pension of $20. After sating his appetite, Kuzikov dismembered his friends' bodies and took them to a garbage dump.

DR DOOLITTLE AND THE LION

A circus lion has bitten a drunken Chilean man who boasted to friends that he could talk to the animals. Carlos Ferrada said he could prove his special relationship with the beasts and put his arm into a lion's cage.

He was bitten, but surgeons in Angol have saved his arm after an operation. "He is lucky we didn't have to amputate," Dr Oscar Soto said. Mr Ferrada will spend the next two weeks in hospital, said a spokesman on 13 August 2001.

When asked why he had risked losing his arm, Ferrada told medical staff: "I just wanted to talk to a lion."

The incident has been the final straw for the authorities in the southern town of Angol, who have asked the circus to move on.

"They never fed the lions and they roared all night. They were nothing but trouble," one local resident said.

Another resident, Maria Mercedes Rojas, said: "Once one of the monkeys escaped and got really violent. It even got into people's houses and we had to chase it off with sticks. I tell you, I'm glad to see the back of that circus."

LEOPARD ON THE CAMPUS

A leopard attacked three students who were trying to capture it with a volleyball net.

They found it eating a pig in an isolated part of their college campus in India. It was eventually caught by forestry officials.

The animal had strayed on to the Vidyavardhaka Engineering College campus in Mysore, where it killed a pig belonging to one of the staff. When the students tried to catch it, it attacked them and then ran into a house. A constable bolted the house from outside, and officials from a local zoo tranquilized the big cat.

Five people, including a policeman, sustained injuries and have been admitted to hospital on 21 September 2001.

M. N. Jayakumar, conservator of forests, said factories on the outskirts of the city had become safe hiding places for leopards, which often strayed into the city in search of prey.

BLACK WIDOW SPIDERS

The widow's venom is, of course, a soundly pragmatic reason for fear. People who live where the widow is common have known about its danger for centuries; from Russia to North America, folk wisdom carried warnings and remedies. However, the medical establishment was slow to accept the widow as a killer of humans. The creature seemed too small to be responsible for the things she was charged with – extravagant suffering, painful death. People bitten by the spider sometimes didn't link it with the symptoms that developed hours later; if they did, doctors assured them the spider was not the cause.

Virtually all spiders use some sort of toxin to subdue prey; the question arachnologists were still debating into the twentieth century was whether any of these toxins, in the small doses delivered by spiders, could harm people. Many doctors treated black widow bites and believed their patients surmizes about the source of the problem, but the larger scientific and medical community remained skeptical. The skeptics didn't find the anecdotal evidence sufficient. They wanted definitive laboratory evidence, the kind that could be replicated. Starting in the late nineteenth century, many workers attempted to deliver such evidence in the form of animal experiments.

Reports of such animal tests – they still go on today, as scientists try to understand how the venom works – read like H. G. Wells's *The Island of Dr. Moreau*. People have applied venom to monkey kidneys and lobster claws, to the iris of the eye of a rat and to the nerves of frogs and squid. They have poisoned rats, dissected them, liquefied heart, brain, spleen, liver, kidneys, lungs, and rump muscles separately, and injected them into other rats – all of which died except for those receiving the rump-muscle fluid. They have elicited venom from widows with electric shocks. They have given widows water laced with radioactive selenium and phosphorus and then counted the Geiger clicks in the organs of guinea pigs the widows killed. They have induced widows to bite laboratory rats on the penis, after which even the rats "appeared to become dejected and depressed." They have injected animals with the blood of human widow victims; the animals reacted as if they themselves had been bitten. In one experiment, scientists caused rats to be bitten on the ankle; then, at intervals, they amputated the bitten legs at the knee, to see how fast the venom spread. Only those who lost their legs in the first five minutes were spared the full effects of the toxin. Even those amputated in the first fifteen seconds showed some symptoms.

Such experiments revealed the peculiar reactions of different animals to the venom. Rats become more sensitive to noise, so that they're easily startled; they rub their snouts and twitch; they put their heads on the floor between their hind legs, as if expecting an air raid, before they die. Cats, those nocturnal hunters, come to fear the light. They crawl backwards, belly to the floor, howling, and then drop into a condition that in human schizophrenics is known as *waxy flexibility*. The animals remain catatonically still, holding any odd position the experimenter bends them into, before they, too, die. An early experimenter noted that cats exhibiting waxy flexibility don't react to being poked and cut. Among the animals who find widow venom especially deadly are guinea pigs, mice, horses, camels, snakes, frogs, insects, and spiders, including the widow itself. Others, like dogs, sheep, and rabbits, can often survive a bite.

The meager reactions of some animals left skeptics room for argument. The Russian government tried to resolve the question in 1899. Its experimenters couldn't provoke the spiders into biting, so they concluded the danger was mere folklore. The project's photographer apparently decided to illustrate this point by putting half a dozen widows on the naked chest of another man and taking pictures. During this stunt, the man being photographed got bitten. He was seriously sick within five minutes.

Meanwhile, at least half-a-dozen Western researchers tried to toxify themselves. They teased widows into biting them, or else injected themselves with fluid derived from the venom sacs of widows. All of these researchers reported no symptoms at all – a result that bolstered the position of the skeptics. Why weren't these men affected? Research in the decades that followed showed an enormous variation in the widow's venom according to environmental factors, especially season and temperature. The early experimenters may simply have collected spiders that were too cold or too old to produce good venom. In the cases in which the experimenter allowed himself to be bitten, rather than injecting an extract, there's another possibility. The spider chooses whether to inject venom, so she can deliver a dry, bite if she wants to. Doing so is sometimes a good strategy, since the dry bite may succeed in driving off a big animal without any waste of venom. The men who injected themselves with extracts may have been misled by some faulty chemical procedure.

In 1922 an arachnologist at the University of Arkansas, William Baerg, experimented on himself. At first he couldn't convince the widow to bite him. Eventually he did elicit a bite and was rewarded with three days of pain and delirium in the hospital. That seems like compelling evidence, but since other experimenters had gone symptomless, the skeptics held out. In the next few years the evidence mounted: a doctor compiled hundreds of case histories, and other experiments using reduced doses in the interest of safety produced slight symptoms.

The next researcher to risk the widow's bite was Allan Blair, an M.D. and a member of the faculty at the University of Alabama's medical school. Blair's wife and several others volunteered to serve as his guinea pigs in a widow bite experiment, but Blair declined their offers. Taking frequent measurements and thorough notes for the scientific article he would later write, Blair provided spectacular proof of the widow's power to harm human beings. His scientific triumph nearly killed him.

BABOONS RAMPAGE IN SAUDI ARABIA

Saudi authorities are investigating whether its baboon population is out of control after a two-year-old girl was killed.

Baboons are reported to have attacked homes and injured several people in the areas of Taif, Abha, Baha and Fifa.

A National Wildlife Protection Authority official said one snatched the two-year-old from her father. She was later found dead between rocks in a mountainous area of Taif.

Officials are also reporting panic over baboon attacks on houses and schools in Baha and the Abha Faculty for Girls.

Farmers in the southern mountainous area of Fifa have repeatedly complained, saying 15,000 baboons are running amok, attacking homes and damaging farms.

The *Khaleej News* reports that Saudi authorities are now drawing up plans to sterilize or poison some of the baboons to check their populations, following a survey by a Japanese research team.

SWAZILAND BABOONS

Starving baboons have begun attacking children in Swaziland.

The baboons grabbed, beat and bit two toddlers in separate incidents at homes in Maphungawane, eastern Swaziland. Both young victims needed medical treatment. Previously the animals had targeted goats and other small animals.

Samkele Gamedze, aged three, was playing at her house when a stray baboon attacked her. The animal tossed the girl up and down before neighbours came to her rescue.

A one-year-old toddler playing outside his mother's hut was attacked by baboons on Sunday, 10 June 2001. The boy suffered injuries to his stomach and is recovering in hospital.

"I saw a baboon lifting my child who was already bleeding from his stomach. I waved a stick to chase the animal, but it attacked me too," the boy's mother said.

Fears of persecution by the wildlife authorities are preventing threatened residents from bringing the baboons under control, reports a local newspaper.

LOUIS AND THE CHEETAH

An escaped cheetah stood menacingly over Louis Bailey, aged eight, in Jackson Zoo, Mississippi, while another visitor, Frank Senters, tried to calm the boy and tell him to keep still. The animal scratched and nipped Louis before making off with his Atlanta Braves baseball cap.

"It was wild, like it had just gone crazy," said Louis after his ordeal. "It climbed the fence and jumped. We didn't do nothing to it."

The boy was released from hospital after being treated for minor injuries to his arm.

Louis had wandered into an off-limits service area when the six-stone cheetah scaled an eight-foot fence. Within ten minutes zookeepers had caught the animal. Barbara Barrett, the zoo director, said that a higher fence would be erected to contain its six cheetahs.

SHALINI AND THE WOLF

A seven-year-old girl has been killed by a wolf in northern India. She was sleeping outside her house when she was dragged into a field and attacked.

A pack of wolves in the area has reportedly also injured eight other children. Wolves killed fifty-five children and injured forty others in the Rae Bareilly district of Uttar Pradesh state just over a year ago.

Shalini's grandmother says she was snatched from outside the house in Bhujwan Ka Purwa.

"The wolf took her at 4 a.m.," says Boodha. "We got up when we heard her screams. We searched for her everywhere. In the morning we found her body in a sugarcane field."

Bhishm Raj Singh, a forest guard, explained: "The forest department has identified six maneating wolves in this area. Five of them have been killed. We are hunting for the last one. If he is killed, wolf attacks will stop."

Wildlife experts say the villagers had caught three wolf cubs to keep as pets. They later died in the village.

WELLINGTON BOMBER SEAGULLS

A Gloucestershire, UK, car park operator who has been dive-bombed by the same seagull for the last five summers is selling a book about his experiences.

Don Weston has found fame around the world after his story appeared on a website based in Gloucestershire. Now he hopes to raise money for charity with his book, *Swoop*.

The "Wellington Bomber", as the seagull is known, has again returned to the car park in Gloucester this summer.

Mr Weston has been bemused by all the publicity he has received since the story appeared on *This is Gloucestershire*, a local television programme.

"A social worker who uses the car park went to the States and saw me on television while she was taking a bath," he said. "She said she'd hoped she'd got away from me and the seagull."

Someone else saw him in a newspaper while on a cruise in the Caribbean and he has had to turn his mobile phone off when he is at work because of the number of calls he has received from foreign film crews.

An Englishwoman says she has been driven from her East Sussex home by a vicious seagull. Grace Amos, eighty-six, is too scared to return to her home after the bird nearly knocked her over and cut her head.

The bird and its partner are said to have swooped on visitors to the house before the attack. Lewes District Council said they are "a serious public health issue".

Mrs Amos, from Seaford, told the *Brighton Evening Argus* that she was going to collect her pension when she was attacked. "It nearly knocked me over and I had to hang on to the gate to keep my balance. It felt as if someone had thrown a brick at me it was so painful."

She was helped to a doctor's surgery and needed stitches in her head, she said, and was now staying with nearby relatives. "The wound was really deep. The whole of the seagull's beak seemed to have gone in my head," Mrs Amos added.

The council consulted with the Royal Society for the Protection of Birds and the Department of the Environment, Food and Rural Affairs before deciding to hire a private contractor to "despatch" the gulls.

Killing the birds or removing them are being considered as options by the council.

A spokesman said: "We are not obliged to deal with aggressive birds, but this is an exceptional case, involving an attack on an elderly lady who is now afraid to stay alone in her home. It is a serious public health issue and we have decided to hire a private contractor to deal with the violent seagulls."

WILD INDIAN ELEPHANTS

Two rampaging Indian elephants gored and trampled two men to death.

The elephants turned on villagers in India after another animal in their herd fell down a well-hole. Villagers were chasing the animals away from crops at the time. Two elderly men were killed and two others are in hospital.

Villagers were beating drums and setting off fire crackers to scare the elephants from fields. When they ran, one elephant fell down the well. The other two became enraged and attacked the mob.

Bhusan Mahato, sixty-seven, and Sarala Mahato, sixty-two, both died from their injuries on 17th October 2001. Samjhoti Mahato, fifty-eight, and Sankar Pramanik, seventeen, are both in critical condition in hospital.

The local fire brigade were called to get the other elephant out of the well.

BEAR IN US HOME

A black bear has killed a ninety-three-year-old American woman in her New Mexico home. Adelia Maestas Trujillo died of "multiple bite injuries" in her home in Cleveland, in the north-east of the state.

The 112-kilogram adult male bear, about four years old, broke in to the woman's home through the kitchen window.

It was tracked down and killed, state Game and Fish Department officials said.

The death comes during a summer of increased encounters between humans and bears in New Mexico and other Western states. Officials have said dry weather has limited the growth of food, forcing bears into populated areas for food.

FRENZIED HORNETS

A four-year-old girl and her grandmother have been stung to death by a swarm of hornets in Cambodia. Minh Heang and her grand-daughter were attacked after a massive swarm invaded their house in Koh Santepheap.

The hornets' nest in a palm tree had been destroyed by a rainstorm. The swarm descended on the house and began stinging the girl, who was asleep in a hammock.

The grandmother tried to save the girl, but was herself overwhelmed. Both victims died a few hours after the attack. Four other members of the family were also injured and taken to hospital.

The incident comes a day after a six-year-old boy was stung to death after stepping on a hornets' nest on a Malaysian beach.

TEXAS BEE STINGS

A Texas pensioner has amazed doctors by surviving a bee attack which left her with more than 500 stings.

Medical experts say the amount of venom in Joann Froberg's body was the equivalent of being bitten by two rattlesnakes.

Police fought off the bees with fire extinguishers after the sixty-seven-year-old managed to phone for help as she was being attacked. Mrs Froberg, who is in a stable condition in hospital, told the emergency services operator: "They have been biting me a long time. They are all over me."

The pensioner was on her fruit and vegetable farm in Alvin when the attack happened. The bees live on the farm and are used to pollinate produce.

Police are not sure why the insects became agitated, but say the hive may have been infiltrated by killer African bees.

MISTAKEN SWANS

Two swans attacked a car in Shropshire, England, apparently mistaking their reflections for other birds.

David Graham-Stevenson, the owner of the black Rover 820, said they damaged the Paintwork. An RSPCA spokeswoman said the birds were just trying to protect their nearby nest in Coalport.

Mr. Graham-Stevenson said: "When I went outside they were just going at the car. No matter what I did, they were not going to move and went for me when I tried to scare them off. They have significantly damaged the paintwork.

"The swans are making a nest on the canal near by, so at the moment they are very territorial and also very aggressive."

The RSPCA spokeswoman said: "They will have wanted to protect their territory and therefore will have see their reflection as a threat."

BOLSHIE BRITISH BUZZARDS

A British jogger was mistaken for a road-crash victim after being attacked by a buzzard. Simon Harvey had blood pouring from fifteen head wounds after the bird of prey attacked three times.

The bird swooped down, attacking the back of his head. As he tried to flee it dived again with talons outstretched and gouged him with its beak and claws.

A passer-by in Kendal, Cumbria, thought Mr Harvey, who was blood-splattered and in shock, had been hit by a car.

"I felt a full-fisted blow on my head from nowhere," Mr Harvey, from Windermere, Cumbria, said. "I got a big shock when I realized it was a huge bird attacking. Blood was everywhere."

Workman James Kelly, nineteen, spotted him and called an ambulance. "I thought he'd been hit by a car," Mr Kelly said.

Doctors at a Kendal hospital told him each blow had a force of 10 lbs. The bird has a four-foot wingspan and can dive-bomb at eighty mph.

The local RSPCA representative says the bird may have escaped from a falconry and was going through its display routine.

A woman has been attacked by a buzzard three times in as many weeks as she cycled to work. She has vowed to buy a helmet after going to hospital following the latest assault.

Ann Richard, a housekeeper at Laggan House on the Carron and Laggan estate near Aberlour in Banffshire, Scotland, said she is becoming terrified of the bird of prey which attacks her head with its talons.

Mrs Richard, forty-seven, was treated for cuts to her head and received an anti-tetanus injection at Fleming Hospital in Aberlour after the bird, which appears to be nesting with a female, attacked her from behind.

She said: "The first attack was last year and now it has happened for the third time in two-and-a-half weeks.

"It always comes at me from behind, using its talons and it has drawn blood every time, but this time it was bleeding so badly I decided to go to the hospital. It probably seemed worse than it actually was, as it just needed cleaning and a tetanus jab.

"After the past few weeks I could almost say I'm terrified, I'm very frightened. I suppose you could say this time it has come to a head. I'm afraid that from now on I'll be wearing a bike helmet."

THE BELEV CANNIBAL

A case of cannibalism was registered last week [circa 21 June 2001] in the city of Belev, in the Tula region of Russia.

A single man living in a flat in a multi-storey house in Belev met, in a local depot, a young man of no fixed abode and invited him to stay at his home, to live together. After some time spent together they squabbled about whose turn it was to go out and buy some vodka.

As a result, the guest grasped a metal rod and killed his host. As he explained later to the police investigator, he did not like anybody to shout at him.

Because the young killer did not have sufficient money to buy food or to afford rent for somewhere else to live, he decided to remain in the flat of his victim and then resorted to eating the flesh of his erstwhile friend. He was in the middle of one such meal when the police entered the apartment.

People in the flat next door, who had noticed that they had not seen their neighbour for some time, called the police; they also complained about the awful smell coming from his flat. As the young killer refused to open the front door to the flat, the police were forced to gain entry through a window.

COCKEREL IN ROMANIA

A toddler has been attacked by a pet cockerel. The eighteen-month-old boy suffered multiple injuries to his face and body.

He was attacked while playing in the garden of his home in Romania.

Doctors say Raul Paraschiv is lucky to have survived and it is amazing the cockerel had not damaged his eyes during the incident in Crasna, County Gorj.

Raul's mother says she has wrung the cockerel's neck and fed it to the dogs.

CHILE HOT DOGS

Doberman guard dogs ate the lower half of a homeless man who sought shelter in the grounds of a factory in Chile.

A post mortem has been carried out on the man's body, which confirmed he'd been attacked by dogs. He was identified by his brother, who said the dogs had eaten everything below his waist leaving only the leg bones.

The dogs now [3 August 2001] face being destroyed, while the man's family have announced legal proceedings against the Santiago furniture company that owns the seven dogs.

It's thought José Manuel Urra, thirty-five, climbed the fence around the factory to shelter from the rain. His brother Carlos told reporters: "I had to go and identify his remains. I couldn't believe the state of his body. The dogs had eaten everything below his waist, only his leg bones were left."

His mother, who hasn't been named, added: "My son had nowhere to live, and he had no job or anything. Guarding a property is one thing, but eating people alive is much too much."

Veterinary scientist Luis Tello said under Chilean law the owner is responsible for the actions of his or her dog. "Dobermans are guard dogs, and in this case they saw the tramp as their legitimate prey," he said. "It is normal behaviour for them to eat their victim. These dogs were deliberately bred to be aggressive and to protect their territory."

BOAS AND PYTHONS

Large constrictors have killed people on rare occasions. The details of the deaths generally remain unknown; after all, the only witnesses are the victim and the snake. Ramona and Desmond Morris recount one exception to this in their book, *Men and Snakes*: a large python encountered a passed-out drunk and began to eat his left leg. It got as far as his torso and then simply stopped. When he woke up in the morning, he called for help and the snake was removed from his leg. Unfortunately, the leg was already partially digested and had to be amputated.

About eight more or less confirmed cases of death by constrictor have occurred in North America in the past twenty or so years. Reticulated, Burmese, and African rock pythons primarily are responsible for human deaths from constrictors. An unconfirmed case involving a green anaconda also exists.

An escaped eight-foot python smothered a seven-month-old girl in her crib in Dallas, Texas in November 1980.

A twenty-one-month-old male was found dead in his crib in 1982 in Reno, Nevada. An escaped pet python snake (*Python reticulatus*) was found near the child on a cribside shelf. Autopsy findings included *petechiae* associated with asphyxial death plus puncture wounds consistent with the reptile's teeth.

An unidentified pet python "strangled" a twenty-eight-year-old man in Brampton, Ontario in 1992.

An eleven-foot pet Burmese python by the name of Sally killed a fifteen-year-old boy in his bed in Commerce City, Colorado in 1993. The snake bit the boy on the right foot and apparently suffocated him. The fact that the boy's fingers also were punctured and bleeding suggests that he tried to remove the snake from his foot. The snake weighed much less than the boy (twenty-four vs forty-three kilograms) and showed how strong these constrictors can be.

A man died in Jefferson Parish, Louisiana in 1993 after a fight with his pet sixteen-foot reticulated python named Ebenezer. The man was not constricted, but may have died of a heart attack. He suffered from hypertension. The man had snakebites on his arm and the snake had several knife wounds. A veterinarian treated the retic, which probably went to the Audubon Zoo in New Orleans.

A thirteen-foot, twenty-kilogram Burmese python killed a nineteen-year-old man in the Bronx, New York in 1996. A neighbor found him in a hallway outside his apartment with the snake wrapped around him.

A seven-and-a-half-foot African rock python suffocated a three-year-old boy in Centralia, Illinois in 1999. The boy had compression marks around his chest and bite marks on his neck and ears. No evidence of a struggle was apparent. He was sleeping with an aunt and uncle near the snake's aquarium at the time.

In none of the above cases did the snakes attempt to eat their victims. It can be easy to underestimate the strength of large constrictors. One fact that many snake owners may not realize is that, when a constricting snake compromizes your blood circulation, any extra exertion such as simply standing up can cause one to pass out. People may first pass out before they are actually killed by constriction.

THE INTERNET CANNIBAL

There were no mourners present as a black hearse drew up in front of a half-timbered house outside the picturesque German town of Rotenburg an der Fulda.

Two men braved the icy wind as they carried out a coffin containing recently discovered body parts, which had been hidden around the house. Chunks of human flesh were found in the freezer and a skull was discovered in the garden.

Elsewhere, Christmas trees illuminated by fairy lights lit up homes in the town, and the smell of mulled wine wafted through the cosy alleys, where citizens still greet their neighbours on the street. However, the 15,000 inhabitants of Rotenburg were in shock after a fellow townsman, identified as Armin M, confessed to cannibalism.

After the gruesome discovery by German police on 11 December 2002 in Armin M's house, a spokesman for the state prosecutor in Kassel said: "There is hardly any evidence left. The accused admitted to consuming more or less everything. He only buried skin, bones and hair."

The victim apparently replied to an advertisement posted on the internet, which read: "Seeking young, well-built eighteen to thirty-year-old for slaughtering." He was a homosexual male, forty-one, from Berlin, identified as Bernd Jurgen Brandes. Like his murderer, Mr Brandes was a computer technician.

The influential German tabloid *Bild* ran the headline: "Cannibal Devours Berliner", a pun on the double meaning of the German word for a jam doughnut, a "Berliner".

Mr Brandes was apparently obsessed with being eaten alive after seeing the film *The Silence of the Lambs*, in which Anthony Hopkins plays the serial killer and cannibal Hannibal Lecter.

On 9 March 2001, having made his will, Mr Brandes left the luxury flat in Berlin he shared with his partner. Only a few neighbours remember him and describe the employee of the telecoms giant Siemens as low profile and withdrawn. A colleague said Mr Brandes was a highly qualified professional, but that, on a personal level, his behaviour was distant, impersonal and strange. He never spoke about his private life unless the subject turned to women.

Even less is known about Armin M. German police are studying fifty home videos he made. He allegedly shared a last meal of flambéed human sexual organs with his victim before carving him up and freezing the remaining body parts for later meals. "The accused supposedly first cut off the penis of the victim by mutual agreement because they wanted to eat it together," one report in the German press said.

The video material is so shocking that even a hardened local police officer had to leave the room while viewing the tapes. He was quoted as saying: "I simply had to leave. I have never seen anything like it before, and I hope I will never ever have to watch something like this again."

Police say Armin M, who occupied just three rooms of the huge house he inherited from his mother, had placed eighty other advertisements on the internet. Five males had already replied. Yesterday, only two days after the discovery, new websites appeared on the internet with inquiries about the videos. One user named "Adolf" wanted to know where he could acquire them. Another website offered graphic cooking instructions for the preparation of meals made with human flesh: "Pesto and lemon juice" was recommended.

Armin M is in police custody, and is regarded as capable of standing trial, said Kassel prosecutor Hans-Manfred Jung. *Bild* added: "For lunch he gets meat loaf and potato pancake."

REYNARD THE FOX

A fox attacked a baby as he slept beside his mother on a sitting-room sofa. Louis Day was bitten in the head by the animal, which had crept into the family's suburban home through French windows.

The fourteen-week-old boy's father Peter ran into the room when he heard screams to find Louis covered in blood and the fox sitting on the floor. Grabbing his son, Mr Day tried to chase the fox out into the garden, but it only finally fled when he threw a toy car at it.

Since the terrifying incident he and his partner Sue Eastwood say the animal, which was missing fur on its back and had an injured hind leg, has returned to their garden in Dartford, Kent, UK. They are so worried that they now keep all their doors and windows shut.

Louis suffered four puncture wounds to his head, with one of the bites just missing his eye. He was kept in hospital overnight and, though he is now recovering at home, he still bears the marks of the fox's teeth on his temple and forehead.

Mr Day is convinced the fox was trying to drag the baby, who weighs thirteen pounds, outside to eat him. But he claims he has been unable to persuade the authorities to help him catch it. "I rang the RSPCA's emergency line," said Mr Day, forty-four. "They basically told me I was talking rubbish and asked me if I knew the difference between a dog and a fox. When I said I would take matters into my own hands, they said I could be prosecuted for cruelty. If it was a dog that had done this then it would have been put down, but, because it's a fox, no one seems to care."

Louis was attacked at the family's terraced home at 9.15 p.m. on Wednesday, 26 June 2002. Mr Day was in the kitchen when he heard his thirty-six-year-old partner and their baby scream.

He said. "I ran into the front room and the fox was sitting there, just looking at me. I did not see him grab Louis, but the baby was covered in blood. I remembered in what position Louis had been lying on the sofa and he had totally twisted round – the fox had obviously dragged him by his head. I just grabbed Louis in my arms and tried to chase the fox out. But it sat by the back door just looking at me. Sue was in hysterics. It was terrifying."

Mrs Eastwood said: "I can't forget the sight of that animal, the way it just sat there on the carpet, and I can't forget the way Louis screamed."

After the fox ran off; Louis was taken by ambulance to Darent Valley Hospital, where he was given two courses of antibiotics. Nurses have confirmed that the pattern of the wounds is consistent with the bite of an animal such as a fox.

The couple, who have six other children from previous relationships, say the fox which attacked Louis came back three days later, on Saturday night.

Mr Day said: "I opened the door and he was sitting there, looking at me. I chased him through the neighbours' gardens. I'm an animal lover and have always loved foxes and badgers, but, if I see that fox, I'll kill it."

The attack is the first of its kind reported in Britain for six years. A spokesman for the RSPCA (Royal Society for the Prevention of Cruelty to Animals) said: "We would like to reassure the public that foxes generally avoid human contact. It is exceptionally rare for a fox to even enter a house let alone attack a child."

EATING BABIES IS ART

Britain's Channel 4 television has been accused of sensationalism over a decision to broadcast a programme on 2 January 2003 that will show a performance artist eating the flesh of a dead baby.

The documentary, "Beijing Swings", which covers the extreme practices of some modern artists in the Chinese capital, has been condemned by the country's embassy in London and by politicians and lobby groups in Britain. Hung Liu, third secretary at the Chinese Embassy, described the programme as "detrimental" to China. "This is a wrong image and very damaging." He did not deny that the subject matter of the documentary was true, however.

"Beijing Swings" shows stills of ZhuYu, the artist, eating what appears to be a stillborn infant. There is one shot of him washing the baby before he eats it then three of him biting into the body. Zhu Yu admits he was sick afterwards.

"What will be seen is very disturbing, but we will be making sure viewers are told what to expect," said Jess Search, the Channel 4 executive in charge of the broadcaster's forthcoming season about programmes about China. She justified the programme by saying China is "at a moment of change socially and culturally. We wanted a portrait of a young and modern China."

Zhu explains his stunt by claiming: "Our subconscious tells us that eating babies is not right. But it is not prohibited. No religion forbids cannibalism. Nor can I find any law which prevents us from eating people. So I took advantage of the space between morality and the law, and based my work on it."

Zhu, who claims to be a Christian, says his religion has a major impact on his art. "Jesus is always related to blood, death and wounds, and this is reflected in my art."

Ann Widdecombe, the Tory MP and former shadow home secretary, said she was appalled that Zhu was using his religion to justify his actions. "Jesus Christ said suffer the little ones to come unto me, not that they should be eaten for public entertainment. This stunt sounds hideous."

The programme shows photographs rather than film so some critics may say Zhu could have faked eating the baby. "I'm absolutely convinced it happened," said Waldemar Januszczak, the *Sunday Times* art critic who presents "Beijing Swings". "We'd heard about Zhu Yu and wanted to talk to him The authorities in China are worried about this type of art, yet it does happen."

RABID FOX IN MAINE

A rabid gray fox bit a two-year-old girl at the Funny Farm day-care center on Old Ocean House Road, Cape Elizabeth, late Tuesday afternoon.

The fox unexpectedly jumped out of some nearby brush and charged a group of six children, grabbing the toddler by her right arm as her day-care provider was trying to whisk her inside. The girl has begun rabies treatments.

"When I scooped her up, the fox attached itself to her arm and was biting her arm," said Lisa Rockwell, director and one of the owners of the day-care center. "It was shaking around, it was really trying to shake her. So I took the little girl and I just kept spinning her around, spinning her around to see if it would get off. It was pretty relentless, but it finally got off her and then it started to charge the other children that were out there."

None of the other children was bitten, but all of their parents have been notified and told to consult their physicians because of possible exposure to the animal's saliva.

State health officials said the attack was extremely unusual. "This was a fairly sudden and dramatic situation, and it sounds like there may have been some exposure to other kids in the area, as well as an adult or two," said Geoff Beckett, assistant state epidemiologist at the Maine Bureau of Health.

Beckett said epidemiologists are working with the children's families and their medical providers to determine whether rabies shots are needed. Rockwell said she and another teacher were immunized Tuesday night, along with the little girl who was bitten and her sister. She said she thinks that all of the children who were exposed will be taking the shots.

MAX THE FLORIDA LION

A zookeeper whose arm was bitten off by a lion at Busch Gardens, Tampa, Florida, had been feeding meat to the animal as part of a training exercise minutes before the attack, park officials said Monday, 13 May 2002.

Surgeons were unable to re-attach twenty-one-year-old Amanda Bourassa's arm following Sunday's attack, which occurred as she took her parents and boyfriend on a behind-the-scenes tour of the animal's sleeping quarters.

State wildlife investigators said witnesses indicated Bourassa may have poked part of her hand or a finger through a one-and-a-half-inch opening between the bars when the 364-lb lion grabbed her. Her right arm was severed near the elbow.

The attack occurred outside the view of tourists as Bourassa was giving a private tour available only to zookeepers' family members. The theme park suspended such tours Monday, said Glenn Young, the park's vice president of zoological operations.

Busch Gardens officials said the twelve-year-old lion named Max would not be destroyed, but said the amusement park's safety policies would be reviewed.

A spokesman for the Florida Fish and Wildlife Commission said an initial probe found no violations in how the lion was being caged.

Young said that minutes before the attack Bourassa and three other zookeepers were performing a routine training exercise with the lion to encourage good behavior during the animal's health checkups.

The lion was ordered to lie down with his tail extended through the bars, a position needed to draw blood from the animal's tail, Young said. No blood was drawn during the training and Young said the animal wasn't agitated.

Bourassa rewarded the animal by tossing him bits of meat, Young said. Max has undergone such training since he arrived at Busch Gardens in 1997 as part of its "Edge of Africa" exhibit. The park also has a lioness.

Young said the attack occurred within minutes of the feeding. "These are still wild animals, and they behave like that," said Young, noting that zookeepers are forbidden from sticking their hands into the animals' cages.

The zookeeper, along with her severed arm, was rushed to Tampa General Hospital. Surgeons couldn't re-attach the arm, hospital spokesman John Dunn said.

While by no means considered a tame animal, Max has been touched by his zookeepers before and responds to them when they call him by name.

Jack Hanna, the director emeritus of the Columbus Zoo and whose TV show, *Jack Hanna's Animal Adventures*, often originates from Busch Gardens in Tampa, said the zoo has one of the best safety records in the industry. "For the numbers of visitors and the numbers of animals they have, I would say their record is in the top two or three of all the zoological parks in the US, probably the world," Hanna said.

In 1989 an animal keeper was crushed to death by a two-ton elephant. In 1993 a rattlesnake bit a zookeeper, who survived. And, in 1999, a woman claimed a Clydesdale horse bit off the tip of her finger.

"The first thing I tell people is a wild animal is like a loaded gun. It can go off at any time," Hanna said. "This is the kind of business we are in."

MONTY'S FATAL SQUEEZE

The snake owner who died Sunday, 10 February 2002, when his pet Burmese python strangled him had been ordered by a judge three years ago to get rid of a similar snake that was too large.

Officials aren't sure whether it's the same snake that killed Richard Barber, forty-three, of Aurora, Colorado, USA.

Barber died of asphyxiation when Monty, his eleven-foot-long, forty-three-pound female snake, coiled herself around his head, neck and chest and squeezed him to death, according to an Arapahoe County Coroner's autopsy report released Monday.

Records show that Barber was found guilty in October 1998 of violating a city code that makes it illegal to keep a snake more than six feet long. He was ordered to take the snake out of the Aurora city limits, said Cheryl Conway, spokeswoman for the Aurora Animal Care Division. An anonymous caller had told division officials a large snake had been seen in Barber's backyard.

"He was given a month to relocate the reptile," Conway said. "Animal care went back out for a follow-up inspection 11 November 1998, and we found that he had removed the snake."

The division is still investigating what caused Monty to become aggressive with her owner, who had apparently raised her from a baby.

Monty, believed to be about five years old, was resting comfortably on Monday in a padlocked cage at Animal Care, her long, thick body coiled around a pink towel with a heating pad underneath to regulate her temperature. The Denver Zoo will keep the snake for a couple of days and help it find a new home, according to spokeswoman Angela Baier.

"It's doubtful that any accredited zoo would want this kind of snake," Baier said. "It's not very common in zoos because they're common in the pet trade."

Authorities said Barber had taken Monty out of her cage on Sunday afternoon and wrapped her around his neck to show his room-mates. Suddenly, Barber's face contorted and he fell to the ground, a movement that may have frightened the snake and caused her to constrict, authorities said.

It took four firefighters and at least one police officer to pry the snake off Barber with their nightsticks.

As three firefighters rushed Barber upstairs to revive him, a firefighter left holding the snake was suddenly knocked off his feet when the snake coiled around his arm and began dragging him across the floor, said Rory Chetelat, spokesman for the Aurora Fire Department. The firefighter eventually spotted a cage, and he steered the snake toward it until his colleagues came back and helped put the snake in its cage.

Conway said Burmese pythons do not make good long-term pets because they can grow up to twenty feet long and weigh 200 lbs, requiring at least one person for every four feet of snake to handle and support the reptile. But Barbara Huggins, a licensed reptile rescuer, said the issue isn't whether people should be allowed to own them.

"The people who own them have to know what they are doing," she said. "There are at least hundreds of people who own these animals and never have had any trouble."

Burmese python owner Jay Barr, twenty, of Longmont said a python can be a rewarding, social pet if cared for properly. Barr, who volunteers at Colorado Reptile Rescue, has had his female python for two years since it was an eighteen-inch hatchling. The snake is more than ten feet long and weighs about 35 lbs [sic]. Burmese pythons are generally docile. They crave regular social interaction and can become alienated, edgy and aggressive when handled if they are kept primarily for display, Barr said.

Mark Berger, twenty-three, of Colorado Springs, works with Colorado Reptile Rescue in that city. He said that in 2001, the city's organization took in 250 snakes, iguanas and other reptiles because people could no longer care for them. "You can socialize a snake. You can't tame a snake. At any time, they can turn on you. Virtually every accident is because of an error on the owner's part," Berger said.

One other person in Colorado has been squeezed to death by a pet python. Derek Romero, fifteen, of Commerce City, was killed in 1993 when his family's eleven-and-a-half-foot pet Burmese python crushed his torso.

NORWEGIAN HUSKIES

A boy aged seven was killed by sledge dogs in a Norwegian village on 1 February 2002.

The boy's body was found by neighbours in a ditch after a villager's dogs got loose and attacked in Dokka, 110 miles north of the capital Oslo.

A police spokesman said that the animals – described as large huskies – had been rounded up and would be killed. He added that a witness had seen two dogs standing over the body and two other dogs near by.

Part 5

Horror in the Uplands

EUROPEAN NEANDERTHALS

Neanderthal man was a brutal cannibal who chewed on the bones of his fellow cavemen, scientists have discovered.

Butchered human remains found scattered on a cave floor are the first strong evidence of our prehistoric relatives' grisly eating habits. The 100,000-year-old bones of at least six victims were stripped of meat and marrow before being thrown on to a pile of animal carcasses.

Dr Alban Defleur, who found the remains at Moula-Guercy, in the Ardeche region of France, said: "If we conclude that the animal remains are the leftovers from a meal, we're obliged to expand that conclusion to include humans."

The seventy-eight bones came from at least six people: two adults, two fifteen- or sixteen-year olds, and two six- or seven-year-olds. All the skulls and limb bones were broken apart, with only the hands and feet left intact.

They show that a group of Neanderthals systematically removed the flesh from skeletons and then split the bones with a stone to remove the marrow and brains. Other bones show that muscles and tendons were removed. They were mixed in with deer bones that had similar cut marks and which had also been broken into pieces.

The six victims may have been eaten for survival when other food was scarce or as part of a social ritual, but there are signs that there was plenty of other food around at the time of the meal, Dr Defleur said.

"The work at the Moula-Guercy cave allows us for the first time to demonstrate the existence of the practice of cannibalism by European Neanderthals," he added.

The discovery on the west bank of the Rhone, reported in the journal *Science* [1999] ends a long debate about the Neanderthals, a primitive offshoot of the human family tree who died out 30,000 years ago. Some scientists had argued that marks previously found on bones were left by animals or during burial preparations.

Neanderthals were stockier than human ancestors and had distinctive heavy foreheads, long noses and small chins, but they made jewellery and musical instruments. Their diet included red meat, tortoise, whale meat and shellfish along with olives, tomatoes and roast nuts, and they were probably the first Europeans to start fishing in the sea.

The graves of crippled elderly Neanderthals suggest that the old and sick were cared for in life and buried respectfully in death. Why they vanished is a mystery, but they lived alongside our own ancestors, Cro-Magnon man, for at least 10,000 years.

AZTEC BLOOD SACRIFICES

The ancient Mexicans believed in two primordial beings who were at the origin of all others, even of the gods: they were Ometecuhtli, "the Lord of the Duality", and Omeciuatl, "the Lady of the Duality"; and they lived at the summit of the world, in the thirteenth heaven, "there where the air was very cold, delicate and iced." Their unending fruitfulness produced all the gods, and from it all mankind is born. At the time with which we are concerned these two great divinities had come in some degree to resemble those kings who reign but do not govern: they had been pushed into the background by the vigorous crowd of younger and more active gods. But it was still they who were held to have the privilege of fixing the birth-date of each living being, and thus its fate.

The gods, the descendants of the supreme Duality, in their turn were the creators of the earth: the most important act in this creation was clearly the birth of the sun; and this sun was born from sacrifice and blood. It is said that the gods gathered in the twilight at Teotihuacán, and one of them, a little leprous god, covered with boils, threw himself into a huge brazier as a sacrifice. He rose from the blazing coals changed into a sun; but this new sun was motionless, it needed blood to move. So the gods immolated themselves, and the sun, drawing life from their death, began its course across the sky.

This was the beginning of the cosmic drama in which humanity took on the role of the gods. To keep the sun moving in its course, so that the darkness should not overwhelm the world for ever, it was necessary to feed it every day with its food, "the precious water" (*chalchiuatl*) – that is, with human blood. Sacrifice was a sacred duty towards the sun and a necessity for the welfare of men: without it the very life of the world would stop. Every time that a priest on the top of a pyramid held up the bleeding heart of a man and then placed it in the "vessel of the eagle of the sun" the disaster that perpetually threatened to fall upon the world was postponed once more. Human sacrifice was an alchemy by which life was made out of death; and the gods themselves had given the example on the first day of creation.

As for man, his very first duty was to provide nourishment "for our mother and our father, the earth and the sun"; and to shirk this was to betray the gods and at the same time all mankind, for what was true of the sun was also true of the earth, the rain, growth and all the forces of nature. Nothing was born, nothing would endure, except by the blood of sacrifice.

The great god-king of the Toltecs, Quetzalcoatl, "never would (offer up human victims) because he so loved his subjects, the Toltecs, and he presented only snakes in sacrifice, and birds and butterflies." But Quetzalcoatl was expelled from the city of Tula by the black magic of Tezcatlipoca; and so Mexico was delivered over to the blood-thirsty gods.

In the most usual form of the rite the victim was stretched out on his back on a slightly convex stone with his arms and legs held by four priests, while a fifth ripped him open with a flint knife and tore out his heart. The sacrifice also often took place in the manner which the Spaniards described as *gladiatorio*: the captive was tied to a huge disk of stone, the *temalacatl*, by a rope that left him free to move; he was armed with wooden weapons, and he had to fight several normally-armed Aztec warriors in turn. If, by any extraordinary chance, he did not succumb to their attacks, he was spared; but nearly always the "gladiator" fell, gravely wounded, and a few moments later he died on the stone, with his body opened by the black-robed, long-haired priests. The warriors who were set apart for this kind of death wore ornaments and clothes of a special nature, and they were crowned with white down, as a symbol of the first light of the dawn, of the still uncertain hour when the soul of the resuscitated warrior takes its flight in the greyness towards our father the sun.

But these were not the only forms of sacrifice. Women were dedicated to the goddesses of the earth, and while they danced, pretending to be unaware of their fate, their heads were struck off; children were drowned as an offering to the rain-god Tlaloc; the fire-god's victims, anaesthetized by *yauhtli* (hashish), were thrown into the blaze; and those who personified the god Xipe Totec were fastened to a kind of frame, shot with arrows and then flayed – the priests dressed themselves in the skin. In most cases, the victim was dressed, painted and ornamented so as to represent the god who was being worshipped; and thus it was the god himself who died before his own image and in his own temple, just as all the gods had accepted death in the first days for the salvation of the world. And when ritual cannibalism was practiced on certain occasions, it was the god's own flesh that the faithful ate in their bloody communion.

There is no aspect of the Mexican civilization that shocks our feelings as much as this. From the first contact between the Indians and the Europeans the horror and disgust that the newcomers felt for the human sacrifices helped them to convince themselves that the native religion came from hell and that its gods were no more than devils; from then onwards they were certain that Uitzilopochtli, Tlaloc, Tezcatlipoca and all the other gods of Mexico were, in fact, demons, and that everything that concerned them, either directly, or remotely, should be rooted out for ever. The Aztec practice of human sacrifice was a great factor in making the two religions which confronted one another totally irreconcilable, and when the war broke out between the Spaniards and the Mexicans, in giving it a bitter and remorseless character from the moment the helpless conquistadores saw from afar the death of their comrades, whose grinning skulls they later found exposed on the *tzompantli*.

Clearly, it is difficult for us to come to a true understanding of what human sacrifice meant to the sixteenth-century Aztec, but it may be observed that every culture possesses its own idea of what is and what is not cruel. At the height of their career the Romans shed more blood in their circuses and for their amusement than ever the Aztecs did before their idols. The Spaniards, so sincerely moved by the cruelty of the native priests, nevertheless massacred, burnt, mutilated and tortured with a perfectly clear conscience. We, who shudder at the tale of the bloody rites of ancient Mexico, have seen with our own eyes and in our own days civilized nations proceed systematically to the extermination of millions of human beings and to the perfection of weapons capable of annihilating in one second a hundred times more victims than the Aztecs ever sacrificed.

Human sacrifice among the Mexicans was inspired neither by cruelty nor by hatred. It was their response, and the only response that they could conceive, to the instability of a continually threatened world. Blood was necessary to save this world and the men in it; the victim was no longer an enemy who was to be killed but a messenger, arrayed in a dignity that was almost divine, who was sent to the gods. All the relevant descriptions, such as those that the Spanish missionary Father Sahagún took down from his Aztec informants, for example, convey the impression not of a dislike between the sacrificer and the victim nor of anything resembling a lust for blood, but of a strange fellow-feeling or rather – and this is vouched for by the texts – of a kind of mystical kinship.

"When a man took a prisoner he said, 'Here is my well-beloved son.' And the captive said, 'Here is my revered father.'" The warrior who had made a prisoner and who watched him die before the altar knew that sooner or later he would follow him into the hereafter by the same kind of death. "You are welcome: you know what the fortune of war is – today for you, tomorrow for me," said the emperor to a captured chief. As for the prisoner himself, he was perfectly aware of his fate and he had been prepared from his childhood to accept it; he agreed, stoically. More than that, he would refuse a clemency that crossed his destiny or the divine will, even if it were offered him.

Tlacahuepan, the Mexican leader, who was a prisoner of the *Chalca* in the reign [1440–69] of Motecuhzoma I, had distinguished himself so much by his bravery that, when he was captured, his enemies offered him a part of their territory for himself and the other Aztecs they had taken. He would not only have his life, but he would be lord of that section; they even asked him to command the troops of Chalco. Tlacahuepan's only reply was to kill himself, shouting to his fellow-prisoners, "Mexicans, I am going, and I shall wait for you."

The story of Tlahuicole, a lord of Tlaxcala, who was taken by the Mexicans, was no less famous. They admired him so much that, instead of sacrificing him, they entrusted him with the command of a body of soldiers in the war against Michoacán; but on his return, covered with honours, from this expedition, the Tlaxcaltec refused to withhold himself any longer from his fate. He insisted upon his death and died upon the sacrificial stone.

To a less extent this was also the attitude of all the other victims. It was the attitude of the young man who, having lived for a year in princely luxury, was to die at the end of it in front of the image of Tezcatlipoca; and it was that of the women who calmly danced and sang while the dark-robed priests behind them waited for the moment to make their heads fall like ears of maize when they are plucked from the stem.

The sensitivity of the Indians, moulded by a powerful and very ancient tradition, was not the same as that of the Europeans of their epoch: the Aztecs were unmoved by the scenes in their blood-soaked temples, but they were horror-struck by the tortures that the Spaniards brought with them from the land of the Inquisition.

It is only these foregoing considerations that allow one to understand the meaning of war for the ancient Mexicans, the meaning of the continual war towards which all the energies of the city were directed. Certainly it is not incorrect to interpret the history of Tenochtitlan between 1325 and 1519 as that of an imperialist state which steadily pursues its aim of expansion by conquest. But that is not all. As the Mexican dominion spread, so their very victories created a pacified zone all round them, a zone which grew wider and wider until it reached the edges of their known world. Where then were the victims to come from? For they were essential to provide the gods with their nourishment, *tlaxcaltiliztli*. Where could one find the precious blood without which the sun and the whole frame of the universe was condemned to annihilation? It was essential to remain in a state of war, and from this need arose the strange institution of the war of flowers, *xochiyaoyotl*, which seems to have come into being after the terrible famines which ravaged central Mexico in 1450.

The sovereigns of Mexico, Texcoco and Tlacopan and the lords of Tlaxcala, Uexotzinco and Cholula mutually agreed that, there being no war, they would arrange combats, so that the captives might be sacrificed to the gods for it was thought, indeed, that the calamities of 1450 were caused by too few victims having been offered, so that the gods had grown angry. Fighting was primarily a means of taking prisoners; on the battlefield the warriors did their utmost to kill as few men as possible. War was not merely a political instrument: it was above all a religious rite, a war of holiness.

At bottom the ancient Mexicans had no real confidence in the future. Their fragile world was perpetually at the mercy of some disaster – there were not only the natural cataclysms and the famines, but, more than that, on certain nights the monstrous divinities of the west appeared at the crossroads; and there were the wizards, those dark envoys from a mysterious world; and every fifty-two years there was the great fear that fell upon all the nations of the empire when the sun set on the last day of the "century" and no man could tell whether it would ever rise again.

In all the cities and throughout the countryside the fires were put out. The close-packed crowds, filled with intense anxiety, gathered on the slopes of Uixachtecatl, while on the mountain-top the priests watched the Pleiades. The constellation mounted towards the zenith, but would it go on? Or would it stop, and would the hideous monsters of the end of the world come swarming out? The astronomer priest made a sign, a prisoner was stretched out on the stone. With a dull sound the flint knife opened his chest and in the gaping wound they spun the fire-stick, the *tlequauitl*. The miracle took place and the flame sprang up, born from this shattered breast, and amid shouts of joy messengers lit their torches at it and ran to carry the sacred fire to the four corners of the central valley. And so the world had escaped its end once more. But how heavy and blood-drenched a task it was for the priests and the warriors and the emperors, century after century to repel the unceasing onslaughts of the void.

THE CHOWGARH TIGERS

It is perhaps desirable to explain why maneating tigers develop maneating tendencies.

A maneating tiger is a tiger that has been compelled, through stress of circumstances beyond its control, to adopt a diet alien to it. The stress of circumstances is, in nine cases out of ten, wounds, and in the tenth case old age. The wound that has caused a particular tiger to take to maneating might be the result of a carelessly fired shot and failure to follow up and recover the wounded animal, or be the result of the tiger having lost his temper when killing a porcupine. Human beings are not the natural prey of tigers, and it is only when tigers have been incapacitated through wounds or old age that, in order to live, they are compelled to take to a diet of human flesh.

A tiger when killing its natural prey, which it does either by stalking or lying in wait for it, depends for the success of its attack on its speed and, to a lesser extent, on the condition of its teeth and claws. When, therefore, a tiger is suffering from one or more painful wounds, or when its teeth are missing or defective and its claws worn down and it is unable to catch the animals it has been accustomed to eating, it is driven by necessity to killing human beings. The changeover from animal to human flesh is, I believe, in most cases accidental. As an illustration of what I mean by "accidental" I quote the case of the Muktesar maneating tigress. This tigress, a comparatively young animal, in an encounter with a porcupine lost an eye and got some fifty quills, varying in length from one to nine inches, embedded in the arm and under the pad of her right foreleg. Several of these quills after striking a bone had doubled back in the form of a U, the point, and the broken-off end, being quite close together. Suppurating sores formed where she endeavoured to extract the quills with her teeth, and where she was lying up in a thick patch of grass, starving and licking her wounds, a woman selected this particular patch of grass to cut as fodder for her cattle. At first the tigress took no notice, but when the woman had cut the grass right up to where she was lying the tigress struck once, the blow crushing in the woman's skull. Death was instanta-neous, for, when found the following day, she was grasping her sickle with one hand and holding a tuft of grass, which she was about to cut when struck, with the other. Leaving the woman lying where she had fallen, the tigress limped off for a distance of over a mile and took refuge in a little hollow under a fallen tree. Two days later a man came to chip firewood off this fallen tree, and the tigress who was lying on the far side killed him. The man fell across the tree, and as he had removed his coat and shirt and the tigress had clawed his back when killing him, it is possible that the smell of the blood trickling down his body as he hung across the bole of the tree first gave her the idea that he was something that she could satisfy her hunger with. However that may be, before leaving him she ate a small portion from his back. A day after she killed her third victim deliberately, and without having received any provocation. Thereafter she became an established maneater and had killed twenty-four people before she was finally accounted for.

A tiger on a fresh kill, or a wounded tiger, or a tigress with small cubs, will occasionally kill human beings who disturb them; but these tigers cannot, by any stretch of imagination, be called maneaters, though they are often so called. Personally I would give a tiger the benefit of the doubt once, and once again, before classing it as a maneater, and whenever possible I would subject the alleged victim to a post-mortem before letting the kill go down on the records as the kill of a tiger or a leopard, as the case might be. This subject of post-mortems of human beings alleged to have been killed by either tigers or leopards or, in the plains, by wolves or hyenas, is of great impor-tance, for, though I refrain from giving instances, I know of cases where deaths have wrongly been ascribed to carnivora.

It is a popular fallacy that *all* maneaters are old and mangy, the mange being attributed to the excess of salt in human flesh. I am not competent to give any opinion on the relative quantity of salt in human or animal flesh; but I can, and I do, assert that a diet of human flesh, so far from having an injurious effect on the coat of maneaters, has quite the opposite effect, for all the maneaters I have seen have had remarkably fine coats.

Another popular belief in connection with maneaters is that the cubs of these animals automatically become maneaters. This is quite a reasonable supposition; but it is not borne out by actual facts, and the reason why the cubs of a maneater do not themselves become maneaters, is that human beings are not the natural prey of tigers, or of leopards.

A cub will eat whatever its mother provides, and I have even known of tiger cubs assisting their mothers to kill human beings: but I do not know of a single instance of a cub, after it had left the protection of its parent, or after that parent had been killed, taking to killing human beings.

In the case of human beings killed by carnivora, the doubt is often expressed as to whether the animal responsible for the kill is a tiger or leopard. As a general rule – to which I have seen no exceptions – tigers are responsible for all kills that take place in daylight, and leopards are responsible for all kills that take place in the dark. Both animals are semi-nocturnal forest-dwellers, have much the same habits, employ similar methods of killing, and both are capable of carrying their human victims for long distances. It would be natural, therefore, to expect them to hunt at the same hours; and that they do not do so is due to the difference in courage of the two animals. When a tiger becomes a maneater it loses all fear of human beings and, as human beings move about more freely in the day than they do at night, it is able to secure its victims during daylight hours and there is no necessity for it to visit their habitations at night. A leopard on the other hand, even after it has killed scores of human beings, never loses its fear of man; and, as it is unwilling to face up to human beings in daylight, it secures its victims when they are moving about at night, or by breaking into their houses at night. Owing to these characteristics of the two animals, namely, that one loses its fear of human beings and kills in the daylight, while the other retains its fear and kills in the dark, maneating tigers are easier to shoot than maneating leopards.

The frequency with which a maneating tiger kills depends on (a) the supply of natural food in the area in which it is operating; (*b*) the nature of the disability which has caused it to become a maneater, and (*c*) whether it is a male or a female with cubs.

Those of us who lack the opportunity of forming our own opinion on any particular subject are apt to accept the opinions of others, and in no case is this more apparent than in the case of tigers – here I do not refer to maneaters in particular, but to tigers in general. The author who first used the words "as cruel as a tiger" and "as bloodthirsty as a tiger", when attempting to emphasize the evil character of the villain of his piece, not only showed a lamentable ignorance of the animal he defamed, but coined phrases which have come into universal circulation, and which are mainly responsible for the wrong opinion of tigers held by all except that very small proportion of the public who have the opportunity of forming their own opinions.

When I see the expression "as cruel as a tiger" and "as bloodthirsty as a tiger" in print, I think of a small boy armed with an old muzzle-loading gun – the right barrel of which was split for six inches of its length, and the stock and barrels of which were kept from falling apart by lashings of brass wire – wandering through the jungles of the terai and *bhabar* in the days when there were ten tigers to every one that now survives; sleeping anywhere he happened to be when night came on, with a small fire to give him company and warmth, wakened at intervals by the calling of tigers, sometimes in the distance, at other times near at hand; throwing another stick on the fire and turning over and continuing his interrupted sleep without one thought of unease; knowing from his own short experience and from what others, who like himself had spent their days in the jungles, had told him, that a tiger, unless molested, would do him no harm; or during daylight hours avoiding any tiger he saw, and when that was not possible, standing perfectly still until it had passed and gone, before continuing on his way. And I think of him on one occasion stalking half-a-dozen jungle fowl that were feeding in the open, and on creeping up to a plum bush and standing up to peer over, the bush heaving and a tiger walking out on the far side and, on clearing the bush, turning round and looking at the boy with an expression on its face which said as clearly as any words, "Hello, kid, what the hell are you doing here?" and, receiving no answer, turning round and walking away very slowly without once looking back. And then again I think of the tens of thousands of men, women and children who, while working in the forests or cutting grass or collecting dry sticks, pass day after day close to where tigers are lying up and who, when they return safely to their homes, do not even know that they have been under the observation of this so called "cruel" and "bloodthirsty" animal.

Half a century has rolled by since the day the tiger walked out of the plum bush, the latter thirty-two years of which have been spent in the more or less regular pursuit of maneaters, and though sights have been seen which would have caused a stone to weep, I have not seen a case where a tiger has been deliberately cruel or where it has been blood-thirsty to the extent that it has killed, without provocation, more than it has needed to satisfy its hunger or the hunger of its cubs.

A tiger's function in the scheme of things is to help maintain the balance in nature and if, on rare occasions when driven by dire neces-sity, he kills a human being or when his natural food has been ruth-lessly exterminated by man he kills two per cent of the cattle he is alleged to have killed, it is not fair that for these acts a whole species should be branded as being cruel and bloodthirsty.

Sportsmen are admittedly conservative, the reason being that it has taken them years to form their opinions, and as each individual has a different point of view, it is only natural that opinions should differ on minor, or even in some cases on major, points, and for this reason I do not flatter myself that all the opinions I have expressed will meet with universal agreement.

There is, however, one point on which I am convinced that all sportsmen – no matter whether their viewpoint has been a platform on a tree, the back of an elephant or their own feet – will agree with me, and that is, that a tiger is a large hearted gentleman with boundless courage and that when he is exterminated – as exterminated he will be unless public opinion rallies to his support – India will be the poorer by having lost the finest of her fauna.

Leopards, unlike tigers, are to a certain extent scavengers and become maneaters by acquiring a taste for human flesh when unrestricted slaughter of game has deprived them of their natural food.

The dwellers in our hills are predominantly Hindu, and as such cremate their dead. The cremation invariably takes place on the bank of a stream or river in order that the ashes may be washed down into the Ganges and eventually into the sea. As most of the villages are situated high up on the hills, while the streams or rivers are in many cases miles away down in the valleys, it will be realized that a funeral entails a considerable tax on the man-power of a small community when, in addition to the carrying party, labour has to be provided to collect and carry the fuel needed for the cremation. In normal times these rites are carried out very effectively; but when disease in epidemic form sweeps through the hills and the inhabitants die faster than they can be disposed of, a very simple rite, which consists of placing a live coal in the mouth of the deceased, is performed in the village and the body is then carried to the edge of the hill and cast into the valley below.

A leopard, in an area in which his natural food is scarce, finding these bodies very soon acquires a taste for human flesh, and when the disease dies down and normal conditions are established, the animal very naturally, on finding his food supply cut off, takes to killing human beings.

Of the two maneating leopards of Kumaon, which between them killed five hundred and twenty-five human beings, one followed on the heels of a very severe outbreak of cholera, while the other followed the mysterious disease which swept through India in 1918 and was called "war fever" . . .

The map of Eastern Kumaon that hangs on the wall before me is marked with a number of crosses, and below each cross is a date. These crosses indicate the locality, and the date, of the officially recorded human victims of the maneating tiger of Chowgarh. There are sixty-four crosses on the map. I do not claim this as being a correct tally, for the map was posted up by me for two years and during this period all kills were not reported to me; further, victims who were only mauled, and who died subsequently, have not been awarded a cross and a date.

The first cross is dated 15 December 1925, and the last, 21 March 1930. The distance between the extreme crosses, north to south, is fifty miles, and east to west, thirty miles, an area of 1,500 square miles of mountain and vale where the snow lies deep during winter, and the valleys are scorching hot in summer. Over this area the Chowgarh tiger had established a reign of terror. Villages of varying size, some with a population of hundred or more, and others with only a small family or two, are scattered throughout the area. Footpaths, beaten hard by bare feet, connect the villages. Some of these paths pass through thick forests, and when a maneater renders their passage dangerous inter-village communication is carried on by shouting.

Standing on a commanding point, maybe a big rock or the roof of a house, a man cooees to attract the attention of the people in a neighbouring village, and when the cooee is answered, the message is shouted across in a high-pitched voice. From village to village the message is tossed, and is broadcast throughout large areas in an incredibly short space of time.

It was at a District Conference in February 1929 that I found myself committed to have a try for this tiger. There were at that time three maneaters in the Kumaon Division, and as the Chowgarh tiger had done most damage I promised to go in pursuit of it first.

Human Beings Killed by the Chowgarh Man-Eater

Village	Number
Thali	1
Debgura	1
Barhon	2
Chamoli	6
Kahor	1
Am	2
Dalkania	7
Lohar	8
Aghaura	2
Paharpani	1
Padampuri	2
Tanda	1
Nesoriya	1
Jhangaon	1
Kabragaon	1
Kala Agar	8
Rikhakot	1
Matela	3
Kundal	3
Babyar	1
Khansiun	1
Gargari	1
Hairakhan	2
Ukhaldhunga	1

Pakhari	1
Dungari	2
Galni	3

TOTAL   64

Annual Totals

1926	15 killed
1927	9 killed
1928	14 killed
1929	17 killed
1930	9 killed

TOTAL   64

The map with the crosses and dates, furnished to me by Government, showed that the maneater was most active in the villages on the north and east face of the Kala Agar ridge This ridge, some forty miles in length, rises to a height of 8,500 feet and is thickly wooded along the crest. A forest road runs along the north face of the ridge, in some places passing for miles through dense forests of oak and rhododendron, and in others forming a boundary between the forest and cultivated land. In one place the road forms a loop, and in this loop is situated the Kala Agar Forest Bungalow. This bungalow was my objective, and after a four days' march, culminating in a stiff climb of 4,000 feet, I arrived at it one evening in April 1929. The last human victim in this area was a young man of twenty-two, who had been killed while out grazing cattle, and while I was having breakfast, the morning after my arrival, the grandmother of the young man came to see me.

She informed me that the maneater had, without any provocation, killed the only relative she had in the world. After giving me her grandson's history from the day he was born, and extolling his virtues, she pressed me to accept her three milch buffaloes to use as bait for the tiger, saying that if I killed the tiger with the help of her buffaloes she would have the satisfaction of feeling that she had assisted in avenging her grandson. These full-grown animals were of no use to me, but knowing that refusal to accept them would give offence, I thanked the old lady and assured her I would draw on her for bait as soon as I had used up the four young male buffaloes I had brought with me from Naini Tal. The Headmen of nearby villages had now assembled, and from them I learned that the tiger had last been seen ten days previously in a village twenty miles away, on the eastern slope of the ridge, where it had killed and eaten a man and his wife.

A trail ten days old was not worth following up, and after a long discussion with the Headmen I decided to make for Dalkania village on the eastern side of the ridge. Dalkania is ten miles from Kala Agar, and about the same distance from the village where the man and his wife had been killed.

From the number of crosses Dalkania and the villages adjoining it had earned, it appeared that the tiger had its headquarters in the vicinity of these villages.

After breakfast next morning I left Kala Agar and followed the forest road, which I was informed would take me to the end of the ridge, where I should have to leave the road and take a path two miles downhill to Dalkania. This road, running right to the end of the ridge through dense forest was very little used, and, examining it for tracks as I went along, I arrived at the point where the path took off at about 2 p.m. Here I met a number of men from Dalkania. They had heard – via the cooee method of communication – of my intention of camping at their village and had come up to the ridge to inform me that the tiger had that morning attacked a party of women, while they had been cutting their crops in a village ten miles to the north of Dalkania.

The men carrying my camp equipment had done eight miles and were quite willing to carry on, but on learning from the villagers that the path to this village, ten miles away, was very rough and ran through dense forest I decided to send my men with the villagers to Dalkania, and visit the scene of the tiger's attack alone. My servant immediately set about preparing a substantial meal for me, and at 3 p.m., having fortified myself, I set out on my ten-mile walk. Ten miles under favourable conditions is a comfortable two-and-a-half hours' walk, but here the conditions were anything but favourable. The track running along the east face of the hill wound in and out through deep ravines and was bordered alternately by rocks, dense undergrowth, and trees; and when every obstruction capable of concealing sudden death, in the form of a hungry maneater, had to be approached with caution, progress was of necessity slow. I was still several miles from my objective when the declining day warned me it was time to call a halt.

In any other area, sleeping under the stars on a bed of dry leaves would have ensured a restful night, but here, to sleep on the ground would have been to court death in a very unpleasant form. Long practice in selecting a suitable tree, and the ability to dispose myself comfortably in it, has made sleeping up aloft a simple matter. On this occasion I selected an oak tree, and, with the rifle tied securely to a branch, had been asleep for some hours when I was awakened by the rustling of several animals under the tree. The sound moved on, and presently I heard the scraping of claws on bark and realized that a family of bears were climbing some *karphal* trees I had noticed growing a little way down the hillside. Bears are very quarrelsome when feeding, and sleep was impossible until they had eaten their fill and moved on.

The sun had been up a couple of hours when I arrived at the village, which consisted of two huts and a cattle-shed, in a clearing of five acres surrounded by forest. The small community were in a state of terror and were overjoyed to see me. The wheatfield, a few yards from the huts, where the tiger, with belly to ground, had been detected only just in time, stalking the three women cutting the crop, was eagerly pointed out to me. The man who had seen the tiger, and given the alarm, told me the tiger had retreated into the jungle, where it had been joined by a second tiger, and that the two animals had gone down the hillside into the valley below. The occupants of the two huts had no sleep, for the tigers, baulked of their prey, had called at short intervals throughout the night, and had only ceased calling a little before my arrival. This statement, that there were two tigers, confirmed the reports I had already received that the maneater was accompanied by a full-grown cub.

Our hill folk are very hospitable, and when the villagers learned that I had spent the night in the jungle, and that my camp was at Dalkania, they offered to prepare a meal for me. This I knew would strain the resources of the small community, so I asked for a dish of tea, but as there was no tea in the village I was given a drink of fresh milk sweetened to excess with jaggery, a very satisfying and not unpleasant drink – when one gets used to it. At the request of my hosts I mounted guard while the remaining portion of the wheat crop was cut; and at midday, taking the good wishes of the people with me, I went down into the valley in the direction in which the tigers had been heard calling.

The valley, starting from the watershed of the three rivers Ladhya, Nandhour and Eastern Goula, runs south-west for twenty miles and is densely wooded. Tracking was impossible, and my only hope of seeing the tigers was to attract them to myself, or helped by the jungle folk to stalk them.

To those of you who may be inclined to indulge in the sport of maneater hunting on foot, it will be of interest to know that the birds and animals of the jungle, and the four winds of heaven, play a very important part in this form of sport. This is not the place to give the names of the jungle folk on whose alarm-calls the sportsman depends, to a great extent, for his safety and knowledge of his quarry's movements; for in a country in which a walk up or down hill of three or four miles might mean a difference in altitude of as many thousand feet the variation in fauna, in a well stocked area, is considerable. The wind, however, at all altitudes, remains a constant factor, and a few words relevant to its importance in connexion with maneater hunting on foot will not be out of place.

Tigers do not know that human beings have no sense of smell, and when a tiger becomes a maneater it treats human beings exactly as it treats wild animals, that is, it approaches its intended victims up-wind, or lies up in wait for them down-wind.

The significance of this will be apparent when it is realized that, while the sportsman is trying to get a sight of the tiger, the tiger in all probability is trying to stalk the sportsman, or is lying up in wait for him. The contest, owing to the tiger's height, colouring, and ability to move without making a sound, would be very unequal were it not for the wind-factor operating in favour of the sportsman.

In all cases where killing is done by stalking or stealth, the victim is approached from behind. This being so, it would be suicidal for the sportsman to enter dense jungle, in which he had every reason to believe a maneater was lurking, unless he was capable of making full use of the currents of air. For example, assuming that the sportsman has to proceed, owing to the nature of the ground, in the direction from which the wind is blowing, the danger would lie behind him, where he would be least able to deal with it, but by frequently tacking across the wind he could keep the danger alternately to right and left of him. In print this scheme may not appear very attractive, but in practice it works; and, short of walking backwards, I do not know of a better or safer method of going up-wind through dense cover in which a hungry maneater is lurking.

By evening I had reached the upper end of the valley, without having seen the tigers and without having received any indication from bird or animal of their presence in the jungle. The only habitation then in sight was a cattle-shed, high up on the north side of the valley.

I was careful in the selection of a tree on this second night, and was rewarded by an undisturbed night's rest. Not long after dark the tigers called, and a few minutes later two shots from a muzzle-loader came echoing down the valley, followed by a lot of shouting from the graziers at the cattle station. Thereafter the night was silent.

By the afternoon of the following day I had explored every bit of the valley, and I was making my way up a grassy slope intent on rejoining my men at Dalkania when I heard a long-drawn-out cooee from the direction of the cattle-shed. The cooee was repeated once and again, and on my sending back an answering call I saw a man climb on a projecting rock, and from this vantage point he shouted across the valley to ask if I was the sahib who had come from Naini Tal to shoot the maneater. On my telling him I was that sahib, he informed me that his cattle had stampeded out of a ravine on my side of the valley at about midday, and that when he counted them on arrival at the cattle station he found that one – a white cow – was missing.

He suspected that the cow had been killed by the tigers he had heard calling the previous night, half a mile to the west of where I was standing. Thanking him for his information, I set off to investigate the ravine. I had gone but a short distance along the edge of the ravine when I came on the tracks of the stampeding cattle, and following these tracks back I had no difficulty in finding the spot where the cow had been killed. After killing the cow the tigers had taken it down the steep hillside into the ravine. An approach along the drag was not advisable, so going down into the valley I made a wide detour, and approached the spot where I expected the kill to be from the other side of the ravine. This side of the ravine was less steep than the side down which the kill had been taken, and was deep in young bracken – ideal ground for stalking over. Step by step, and as silently as a shadow, I made my way through the bracken, which reached above my waist, and when I was some thirty yards from the bed of the ravine a movement in front of me caught my eye. A white leg was suddenly thrust up into the air and violently agitated, and next moment there was a deep throated growl – the tigers were on the kill and were having a difference of opinion over some toothful morsel.

For several minutes I stood perfectly still; the leg continued to be agitated, but the growl was not repeated. A nearer approach was not advisable, for even if I succeeded in covering the thirty yards without being seen, and managed to kill one of the tigers, the other, as likely as not, would blunder into me, and the ground I was on would give me no chance of defending myself. Twenty yards to my left front, and about the same distance from the tigers, there was an outcrop of rock, some ten to fifteen feet high. If I could reach this rock without being seen, I should in all probability get an easy shot at the tigers. Dropping on hands and knees, and pushing the rifle before me, I crawled through the bracken to the shelter of the rocks, paused a minute to regain my breath and make quite sure the rifle was loaded, and then climbed the rock. When my eyes were level with the top, I looked over, and saw the two tigers.

One was eating at the hindquarters of the cow, while the other was lying near by licking its paws. Both tigers appeared to be about the same size, but the one that was licking its paws was several shades lighter than the other; and concluding that her light colouring was due to age and that she was the old maneater, I aligned the sights very carefully on her, and fired. At my shot she reared up and fell backwards, while the other bounded down the ravine and was out of sight before I could press the second trigger. The tiger I had shot did not move again, and after pelting it with stones to make sure it was dead, I approached and met with a great disappointment; for a glance at close quarters showed me I had made a mistake and shot the cub – a mistake that during the ensuing twelve months cost the district fifteen lives and incidentally nearly cost me my own life.

Disappointment was to a certain extent mitigated by the thought that this young tigress, even if she had not actually killed any human beings herself, had probably assisted her old mother to kill (this assumption I later found to be corrrect), and in any case, having been nurtured on human flesh she could – to salve my feelings – be classed as a potential maneater.

Skinning a tiger with assistance on open ground and with the requisite appliances is an easy job, but here the job was anything but easy, for I was alone, surrounded by thick cover, and my only appliance was a penknife; and though there was no actual danger to be apprehended from the maneater, for tigers never kill in excess of their requirements, there was the uneasy feeling in the back of my mind that the tigress had returned and was watching my every movement.

The sun was near setting before the arduous task was completed, and as I should have to spend yet another night in the jungles I decided to remain where I was. The tigress was a very old animal, as I could see from her pug marks, and having lived all her life in a district in which there are nearly as many fire-arms as men to use them, had nothing to learn about men and their ways. Even so, there was just a chance that she might return to the kill some time during the night, and remain in the vicinity until light came in the morning.

My selection of a tree was of necessity limited, and the one I spent that night in proved, by morning, to be the most uncomfortable tree I have ever spent twelve hours in. The tigress called at intervals throughout the night, and as morning drew near the calling became fainter and fainter, and eventually died away on the ridge above me.

Cramped, and stiff, and hungry – I had been without food for sixty hours – and with my clothes clinging to me – it had rained for an hour during the night – I descended from the tree when objects were clearly visible, and, after tying the tiger's skin up in a coat, set off for Dalkania.

I have never weighed a tiger's skin when green, and if the skin, plus the head and paws, which I carried for fifteen miles that day weighed forty pounds at the start, I would have taken my oath it weighed 200 pounds before I reached my destination.

In a courtyard, flagged with great slabs of blue slate, and common to a dozen houses, I found my men in conference with a hundred or more villagers. My approach, along a yard-wide lane between two houses, had not been observed, and the welcome I received when, bedraggled and covered with blood, I staggered into the circle of squatting men will live in my memory as long as memory lasts.

My forty-pound tent had been pitched in a field of stubble a hundred yards from the village, and I had hardly reached it before tea was laid out for me on a table improvized out of a couple of suitcases and planks borrowed from the village. I was told later by the villagers that my men, who had been with me for years and had accompanied me on several similar expeditions, refusing to believe that the maneater had claimed me as a victim, had kept a kettle on the boil night and day in anticipation of my return, and, further, had stoutly opposed the Headmen of Dalkania and the adjoining villages sending a report to Almora and Naini Tal that I was missing.

A hot bath, taken of necessity in the open and in full view of the village – I was too dirty and too tired to care who saw me – was followed by an ample dinner, and I was thinking of turning in for the night when a flash of lightning succeeded by a loud peal of thunder heralded the approach of a storm. Tent-pegs are of little use in a field, so long stakes were hurriedly procured and securely driven into the ground, and to these stakes the tent-ropes were tied. For further safety all the available ropes in camp were criss-crossed over the tent and lashed to the stakes. The storm of wind and rain lasted an hour and was one of the worst the little tent had ever weathered. Several of the guy-ropes were torn from the canvas, but the stakes and criss-cross ropes held. Most of my things were soaked through, and a little stream several inches deep was running from end to end of the tent; my bed, however, was comparatively dry, and by 10 o'clock my men were safely lodged behind locked doors in the house the villagers had placed at their disposal, while I, with a loaded rifle for company, settled down to a sleep which lasted for twelve hours.

The following day was occupied in drying my kit and in cleaning and pegging out the tiger's skin. While these operations were in progress the villagers, who had taken a holiday from their field work, crowded round to hear my experiences and to tell me theirs. Every man present had lost one or more relatives, and several bore tooth and claw marks, inflicted by the maneater, which they will carry to their graves. My regret at having lost an opportunity of killing the maneater was not endorsed by the assembled men. True, there had originally been only one maneater; but, of recent months, rescue parties who had gone out to recover the remains of human victims had found two tigers on the kills, and only a fortnight previously a man and his wife had been killed simultaneously, which was proof sufficient for them that both tigers were established maneaters.

My tent was on a spur of the hill, and commanded an extensive view. Immediately below me was the valley of the Nandhour river, with a hill, devoid of any cultivation, rising to a height of 9,000 feet on the far side. As I sat on the edge of the terraced fields that evening with a pair of good binoculars in my hand and the Government map spread out beside me, the villagers pointed out the exact positions where twenty human beings had been killed during the past three years. These kills were more or less evenly distributed over an area of forty square miles.

The forests in this area were open to grazing, and on the cattle-paths leading to them I decided to tie up my four young buffaloes.

During the following ten days no news was received of the tigress, and I spent the time in visiting the buffaloes in the morning, searching the forests in the day, and tying out the buffaloes in the evening. On the eleventh day my hopes were raised by the report that a cow had been killed on a ravine on the hill above my tent. A visit to the kill, however, satisfied me the cow had been killed by an old leopard, whose pug marks I had repeatedly seen. The villagers complained that the leopard had for several years been taking heavy toll of their cattle and goats, so I decided to sit up for him. A shallow cave close to the dead cow gave me the cover I needed. I had not been long in the cave when I caught sight of the leopard coming down the opposite side of the ravine, and I was raising my rifle for a shot when I heard a very agitated voice from the direction of the village calling to me.

There could be but one reason for this urgent call, and grabbing up my hat I dashed out of the cave, much to the consternation of the leopard, who first flattened himself out on the ground, and then with an angry woof went bounding back the way he had come, while I scrambled up my side of the ravine; and, arriving at the top, shouted to the man that I was coming, and set off at top speed to join him.

The man had run all the way uphill from the village, and when he regained his breath he informed me that a woman had just been killed by the maneater, about half a mile on the far side of the village. As we ran down the hillside I saw a crowd of people collected in the courtyard already alluded to. Once again my approach through the narrow lane was not observed, and looking over the heads of the assembled men, I saw a girl sitting on the ground.

The upper part of her clothing had been torn off her young body, and with head thrown back and hands resting on the ground behind to support her, she sat without sound or movement, other than the heaving up and down of her breast, in the hollow of which the blood, that was flowing down her face and neck, was collecting in a sticky congealed mass.

My presence was soon detected and a way made for me to approach the girl. While I was examining her wounds, a score of people, all talking at the same time, informed me that the attack on the girl had been made on comparatively open ground in full view of a number of people including the girl's husband; that alarmed at their combined shouts the tiger had left the girl and gone off in the direction of the forest; that leaving the girl for dead where she had fallen her companions had run back to the village to inform me; that subsequently the girl had regained consciousness and returned to the village; that she would without doubt die of her injuries in a few minutes; and that they would then carry her back to the scene of the attack, and I could sit up over the corpse and shoot the tiger.

While this information was being imparted to me the girl's eyes never left my face and followed my every movement with the liquid pleading gaze of a wounded and frightened animal. Room to move unhampered, quiet to collect my wits, and clean air for the girl to breathe were necessary, and I am afraid the methods I employed to gain them were not as gentle as they might have been. When the last of the men had left in a hurry, I set the women, who up to now had remained in the background, to warming water and to tearing my shirt, which was comparatively clean and dry, into bandages, while one girl, who appeared to be on the point of getting hysterics, was bundled off to scour the village for a pair of scissors. The water and bandages were ready before the girl I had sent for the scissors returned with the only pair, she said, the village could produce. They had been found in the house of a tailor, long since dead, and had been used by the widow for digging up potatoes. The rusty blades, some eight inches long, could not be made to meet at any point, and after a vain attempt I decided to leave the thick coils of blood-caked hair alone.

The major wounds consisted of two claw cuts, one starting between the eyes and extending right over the head and down to the nape of the neck, leaving the scalp hanging in two halves, and the other, starting near the first, running across the forehead up to the right ear. In addition to these ugly gaping wounds there were a number of deep scratches on the right breast, right shoulder and neck, and one deep cut on the back of the right hand, evidently inflicted when the girl had put up her hand in a vain attempt to shield her head.

A doctor friend whom I had once taken out tiger-shooting on foot had, on our return after an exciting morning, presented me with a two-ounce bottle of yellow fluid which he advised me to carry whenever I went out shooting. I had carried the bottle in the inner pocket of my shooting jacket for over a year and a portion of the fluid had evaporated; but the bottle was still three-parts full, and after I had washed the girl's head and body I knocked the neck off the bottle and poured the contents, to the last drop, into the wounds. This done I bandaged the head, to try to keep the scalp in position, and then picked up the girl and carried her to her home – a single room combining living quarters, kitchen and nursery – with the women following behind.

Dependent from a rafter near the door was an open basket, the occupant of which was now clamouring to be fed. This was a complication with which I could not deal, so I left the solution of it to the assembled women. Ten days later, when on the eve of my departure I visited the girl for the last time, I found her sitting on the doorstep of her home with the baby asleep in her lap.

Her wounds, except for a sore at the nape of her neck where the tiger's claws had sunk deepest into the flesh, were all healed, and when parting her great wealth of raven-black hair to show me where the scalp had made a perfect join, she said, with a smile, that she was very glad her young sister had – quite by mistake – borrowed the wrong pair of scissors from the tailor's widow (for a shorn head here is the sign of widowhood). If these lines should ever be read by my friend the doctor I should like him to know that the little bottle of yellow fluid he so thoughtfully provided for me, saved the life of a very brave young mother.

While I had been attending to the girl my men had procured a goat. Following back the blood trail made by the girl I found the spot where the attack had taken place, and tying the goat to a bush I climbed into a stunted oak, the only tree in the vicinity, and prepared for an all-night vigil. Sleep, even in snatches, was not possible for my seat was only a few feet from the ground, and the tigress was still without her dinner. However, I neither saw nor heard anything throughout the night.

On examining the ground in the morning – I had not had time to do this the previous evening – I found that the tigress, after attacking the girl, had gone up the valley for half a mile to where a cattle track crossed the Nandhour river. This track it had followed for two miles, to its junction with the forest road on the ridge above Dalkania. Here on the hard ground I lost the tracks.

For two days the people in all the surrounding villages kept as close to their habitations as the want of sanitary conveniences permitted, and then on the third day news was brought to me by four runners that the maneater had claimed a victim at Lohali, a village five miles to the south of Dalkania. The runners stated that the distance by the forest road was ten miles, but only five by a short cut by which they proposed taking me back. My preparations were soon made, and a little after midday I set off with my four guides.

A very stiff climb of two miles brought us to the crest of the long ridge south of Dalkania and in view of the valley three miles below, where the "kill" was reported to have taken place. My guides could give me no particulars. They lived in a small village a mile on the near side of Lohali, and at 10 a.m. a message had come to them – in the manner already described – that a woman of Lohali had been killed by the maneater, and they were instructed to convey this information to me at Dalkania.

The top of the hill on which we were standing was bare of trees, and, while I regained my breath and had a smoke, my companions pointed out the landmarks. Close to where we were resting, and under the shelter of a great rock, there was a small ruined hut, with a circular thorn enclosure near by. Questioned about this hut, the men told me the following story. Four years previously a Bhutia (a man from across the border), who had all the winter been sending packages of *gur*, salt, and other commodities from the bazaars at the foothills into the interior of the district, had built the hut with the object of resting and fattening his flock of goats through the summer and rains, and getting them fit for the next winter's work. After a few weeks the goats wandered down the hill and damaged my informants' crops, and when they came up to lodge a protest, they found the hut empty, and the fierce sheep-dog these men invariably keep with them to guard their camps at night, chained to an iron stake and dead. Foul play was suspected, and next day men were collected from adjoining villages and a search organized. Pointing to an oak tree scored by lightning and distant some four hundred yards, my informants said that under it the remains of the man – his skull and a few splinters of bone – and his clothes had been found. This was the Chowgarh maneater's first human victim.

There was no way of descending the precipitous hill from where we were sitting, and the men informed me we should have to proceed half a mile along the ridge to where we should find a very steep and rough track which would take us straight down, past their village, to Lohali, which we could see in the valley below. We had covered about half the distance we had to go along the ridge, when all at once, and without being able to ascribe any reason for it, I felt we were being followed. Arguing with myself against this feeling was of no avail; there was only one maneater in all this area and she had procured a kill three miles away which she was not likely to leave. However, the uneasy feeling persisted, and as we were now at the widest part of the grassy ridge I made the men sit down, instructing them not to move until I returned, and myself set out on a tour of investigation. Retracing my steps to where we had first come out on the ridge I entered the jungle, and carefully worked round the open ground and back to where the men were sitting. No alarm-call of animal or bird indicated that a tiger was anywhere in the vicinity, but from there on I made the four men walk in front of me, while I brought up the rear, with thumb on safety-catch and a constant lookout behind.

When we arrived at the little village my companions had started from, they asked for permission to leave me. I was very glad of this request, for I had a mile of dense scrub jungle to go through, and though the feeling that I was being followed had long since left me, I felt safer and more comfortable with only my own life to guard. A little below the outlying terraced fields, and where the dense scrub started, there was a crystal-clear spring of water, from which the village drew its water-supply. Here in the soft wet ground I found the fresh pug mark of the maneater.

These pug marks coming from the direction of the village I was making for, coupled with the uneasy feeling I had experienced on the ridge above, convinced me that something had gone wrong with the "kill" and that my quest would be fruitless. As I emerged from the scrub jungle I came in view of Lohali, which consisted of five or six small houses. Near the door of one of these houses a group of people were collected.

My approach over the steep open ground and narrow terraced fields was observed, and a few men detached themselves from the group near the door and advanced to meet me. One of the number, an old man, bent down to touch my feet, and with tears streaming down his cheeks implored me to save the life of his daughter. His story was as short as it was tragic. His daughter, who was a widow and the only relative he had in the world, had gone out at about ten o'clock to collect dry sticks with which to cook their midday meal. A small stream flows through the valley, and on the far side of the stream from the village the hill goes steeply up. On the lower slope of this hill there are a few terraced fields. At the edge of the lowest field, and distant about 150 yards from the home, the woman had started to collect sticks. A little later, some women who were washing their clothes in the stream heard a scream, and on looking up saw the woman and a tiger disappearing together into the dense thorn bushes, which extended from the edge of the field right down to the stream. Dashing back to the village, the women raised an alarm. The frightened villagers made no attempt at a rescue, and a messsage for help was shouted to a village higher up the valley from where it was tossed back to the village from which the four men had set out to find me. Half an hour after the message had been sent, the wounded woman crawled home. Her story was that she had seen the tiger just as it was about to spring on her; and as there was no time to run, she had jumped down the almost perpendicular hillside and while she was in the air the tiger had caught her and they had gone down the hill together. She remembered nothing further until she regained consciousness and found herself near the stream; and being unable to call for help, she had crawled back to the village on her hands and knees.

We had reached the door of the house while this tale was being told. Making the people stand back from the door – the only opening in the four walls of the room – I drew the blood-stained sheet off the woman, whose pitiful condition I am not going to attempt to describe. Had I been a qualified doctor, armed with modern appliances, instead of just a mere man with a little permanganate of potash in his pocket, I do not think it would have been possible to have saved the woman's life; for the deep tooth and claw wounds in her face, neck, and other parts of her body had, in that hot unventilated room, already turned septic. Mercifully she was only semi-conscious. The old father had followed me into the room, and, more for his satisfaction than for any good I thought it would do, I washed the caked blood from the woman's head and body, and cleaned out the wounds as best I could with my handkerchief and a strong solution of permanganate.

It was now too late to think of returning to my camp, and a place would have to be found in which to pass the night. A little way up the stream, and not far from where the women had been washing their clothes, there was a giant pipal tree, with a foot-high masonry platform round it used by the villagers for religious ceremonies.

I undressed on the platform and bathed in the stream; and when the wind had carried out the functions of a towel, dressed again, put my back to the tree and, laying the loaded rifle by my side, prepared to see the night out. Admittedly it was an unsuitable place in which to spend the night, but any place was preferable to the village, and that dark room, with its hot fetid atmosphere and swarm of buzzing flies, where a woman in torment fought desperately for breath.

During the night the wailing of women announced that the sufferer's troubles were over, and when I passed through the village at day break preparations for the funeral were well advanced.

From the experience of this unfortunate woman, and that of the girl at Dalkania, it was now evident that the old tigress had depended, to a very great extent, on her cub to kill the human beings she attacked. Usually only one out of every hundred people attacked by maneating tigers escapes, but in the case of this maneater it was apparent that more people would be mauled than killed outright, and as the nearest hospital was fifty miles away, when I returned to Naini Tal I appealed to Government to send a supply of disinfectants and dressings to all the Headmen of villages in the area in which the maneater was operating. On my subsequent visit I was glad to learn that the request had been complied with, and that the disinfectants had saved the lives of a number of people.

I stayed at Dalkania for another week and announced on a Saturday that I would leave for home the following Monday. I had now been in the maneater's domain for close on a month, and the constant strain of sleeping in an open tent, and of walking endless miles during the day with the prospect of every step being the last, was beginning to tell on my nerves. The villagers received my announcement with consternation, and only desisted from trying to make me change my decision when I promised them I would return at the first opportunity.

After breakfast on Sunday morning the Headmen of Dalkania paid me a visit and requested me to shoot them some game before I left. The request was gladly acceded to, and half an hour later, accompanied by four villagers and one of my own men, and armed with .275 rifle and a clip of cartridges, I set off for the hill on the far side of the Nandhour river, on the upper slopes of which I had, from my camp, frequently seen ghooral feeding.

One of the villagers accompanying me was a tall gaunt man with a terribly disfigured face. He had been a constant visitor to my camp, and finding in me a good listener had told and retold his encounter with the maneater so often that I could, without effort, repeat the whole story in my sleep. The encounter had taken place four years previously and is best told in his own words.

"Do you see that pine tree, sahib, at the bottom of the grassy slope on the shoulder of the hill? Yes, the pine tree with a big white rock to the east of it. Well, it was at the upper edge of the grassy slope that the maneater attacked me. The grassy slope is as perpendicular as the wall of a house, and none but a hillman could find foothold on it. My son, who was eight years of age at the time, and I had cut grass on that slope on the day of my misfortune, carrying the grass up in armfulls to the belt of trees where the ground is level.

"I was stooping down at the very edge of the slope, tying the grass into a big bundle, when the tiger sprang at me and buried its teeth, one under my right eye, one in my chin and the other two here at the back of my neck. The tiger's mouth struck me with a great blow and I fell over on my back, while the tiger lay on top of me chest to chest, with its stomach between my legs. When falling backwards I had flung out my arms and my right hand had come in contact with an oak sapling. As my fingers grasped the sapling, an idea came to me. My legs were free, and if I could draw them up and insert my feet under and against the tiger's belly, I might be able to push the tiger off, and run away. The pain, as the tiger crushed all the bones on the right side of my face, was terrible; but I did not lose consciousness, for you see, sahib, at that time I was a young man, and in all the hills there was no one to compare with me in strength. Very slowly, so as not to anger the tiger I drew my legs up on either side of it, and gently inserted my bare feet against its belly. Then placing my left hand against its chest and pushing and kicking upwards with all my might, I lifted the tiger right off the ground and, we being on the very edge of the perpendicular hillside, the tiger went crashing down and belike would have taken me with him, had my hold on the sapling not been a good one.

"My son had been too frightened to run away, and when the tiger had gone, I took his loincloth from him and wrapped it round my head, and holding his hand I walked back to the village. Arrived at my home I told my wife to call all my friends together, for I wished to see their faces before I died. When my friends were assembled and saw my condition, they wanted to put me on a charpoy and carry me fifty miles to the Almora hospital, but this I would not consent to; for my suffering was great, and being assured that my time had come I wanted to die where I had been born, and where I had lived all my life. Water was brought, for I was thirsty and my head was on fire, but when it was poured into my mouth, it all flowed out through the holes in my neck. Thereafter, for a period beyond measure, there was great confusion in my mind, and much pain in my head and in my neck, and while I waited and longed for death to end my sufferings my wounds healed of themselves, and I became well.

"And now, sahib, I am as you see me, old and thin, and with white hair, and a face that no man can look on without repulsion. My enemy lives and continues to claim victims but do not be deceived into thinking it is a tiger, for it is no tiger but an evil spirit, who, when it craves for human flesh and blood, takes on for a little while the semblance of a tiger. But they say you are a sadhu, sahib, and the spirits that guard sadhus are more powerful than this evil spirit, as is proved by the fact that you spent three days and three nights alone in the jungle, and came out – as your men said you would – alive and unhurt."

Looking at the great frame of the man, it was easy to picture him as having been a veritable giant. And a giant in strength he must have been, for no man, unless he had been endowed with strength far above the average, could have lifted the tigress into the air, torn its hold from the side of his head, carrying away, as it did, half his face with it, and hurled it down the precipitous hill.

My gaunt friend constituted himself our guide, and with a beautifully polished axe, with long tapering handle, over his shoulder, led us by devious steep paths to the valley below. Fording the Nandhour river, we crossed several wide terraced fields, now gone out of cultivation for fear of the maneater, and on reaching the foot of the hill started what proved to be a very stiff climb, through forest, to the grass slopes above. Gaunt my friend may have been, but he lacked nothing in wind, and tough as I was it was only by calling frequent halts – to admire the view – that I was able to keep up with him.

Emerging from the tree forest, we went diagonally across the grassy slope, in the direction of a rock cliff that extended upwards for a thousand feet or more. It was on this cliff, sprinkled over with tufts of short grass, that I had seen ghooral feeding from my tent. We had covered a few hundred yards when one of these small mountain-goats started up out of a ravine, and at my shot crumpled up and slipped back out of sight. Alarmed by the report of the rifle, another ghooral, that had evidently been lying asleep at the foot of the cliff, sprang to his feet and went up the rock face, as only he or his big brother the tahr could have done. As he climbed upwards, I lay down and, putting the sight to 200 yards, waited for him to stop. This he presently did, coming out on a projecting rock to look down on us. At my shot he staggered, regained his footing, and very slowly continued his climb. At the second shot he fell, hung for a second or two on a narrow ledge, and then fell through space to the grassy slope from whence he had started.

Striking the ground he rolled over and over, passing within a hundred yards of us, and eventually came to rest on a cattle track a hundred and fifty yards below.

I have only once, in all the years I have been shooting, witnessed a similar sight to the one we saw during the next few minutes, and on that occasion the marauder was a leopard.

The ghooral had hardly come to rest when a big Himalayan bear came lumbering out of a ravine on the side of the grassy slope and, with never a pause or backward look, came at a fast trot along the cattle track. On reaching the dead goat he sat down and took it into his lap, and as he started nosing the goat, I fired. Maybe I hurried over my shot, or allowed too much for refraction; anyway the bullet went low and struck the bear in the stomach instead of in the chest. To the six of us who were intently watching, it appeared that the bear took the smack of the bullet as an assault from the ghooral, for, rearing up, he flung the animal from him and came galloping along the track, emitting angry grunts. As he passed a hundred yards below us I fired my fifth and last cartridge, the bullet, as I found later, going through the fleshy part of his hind quarters.

While the men retrieved the two ghooral I descended to examine the blood trail. The blood on the track showed the bear to be hard hit, but even so there was danger in following it up with an empty rifle, for bears are badtempered at the best of times, and are very ugly customers to deal with when wounded.

When the men rejoined me a short council of war was held. Camp was three and a half miles away, and as it was now 2 p.m. it would not be possible to fetch more ammunition, track down and kill the bear, and get back home by dark; so it was unanimously decided that we should follow up the wounded animal and try to finish it off with stones and the axe.

The hill was steep and fairly free of undergrowth, and by keeping above the bear there was a sporting chance of our being able to accomplish our task without serious mishap. We accordingly set off, I leading the way, followed by three men, the rear being brought up by two men each with a ghooral strapped to his back. Arrived at the spot where I had fired my last shot, additional blood on the track greatly encouraged us. Two hundred yards further on, the blood trail led down into a deep ravine. Here we divided up our force, two men crossing to the far side, the owner of the axe and I remaining on the near side, with the men carrying the ghooral following in our rear. On the word being given we started to advance down the hill. In the bed of the ravine, and fifty feet below us, was a dense patch of stunted bamboo, and when a stone was thrown into this thicket, the bear got up with a scream of rage; and six men, putting their best foot foremost, went straight up the hill. I was not trained to this form of exercise, and on looking back to see if the bear was gaining on us, I saw, much to my relief, that he was going as hard downhill as we were going uphill. A shout to my companions, a rapid change of direction, and we were off in full cry and rapidly gaining on our quarry. A few well-aimed shots had been registered, followed by delighted shouts from the marksmen, and angry grunts from the bear, when at a sharp bend in the ravine, which necessitated a cautious advance, we lost touch with the bear. To have followed the blood trail would have been easy, but here the ravine was full of big rocks, behind any of which the bear might have· been lurking, so while the encumbered men sat down for a rest, a cast was made on either side of the ravine. While my companion went forward to look down into the ravine, I went to the right to prospect a rocky cliff that went sheer down for some two hundred feet. Holding to a tree for support, I leaned over and saw the bear lying on a narrow ledge forty feet immediately below me. I picked up a stone, about thirty pounds in weight, and, again advancing to the edge and in imminent danger of going over myself, I raised the stone above my head with both hands and hurled it.

The stone struck the ledge a few inches from the bear's head, and scrambling to his feet he disappeared from sight, to reappear a minute later on the side of the hill. Once again the hunt was on. The ground was here more open and less encumbered with rocks, and the four of us who were running light had no difficulty in keeping up with him. For a mile or more we ran him at top speed, until we eventually cleared the forest and emerged on to the terraced fields. Rainwater had cut several deep and narrow channels across the fields, and in one of these channels the bear took cover.

The man with the distorted face was the only armed member of the party and he was unanimously elected executioner. Nothing loth, he cautiously approached the bear and, swinging his beautifully polished axe aloft, brought the square head down on the bear's skull. The result was as alarming as it was unexpected. The axe-head rebounded off the bear's skull as though it had been struck on a block of rubber, and with a scream of rage the animal reared up on his hind legs. Fortunately he did not follow up his advantage, for we were bunched together, and in trying to run got in each other's way.

The bear did not appear to like this open ground, and after going a short way down the channel again took cover. It was now my turn for the axe. The bear, however, having once been struck resented my approach, and it was only after a great deal of manoeuvring that I eventually got within striking distance. It had been my ambition when a boy to be a lumber-man in Canada, and I had attained sufficient proficiency with an axe to split a match-stick. I had no fear, therefore, as the owner had, of the axe glancing off and getting damaged on the stones, and the moment I got within reach I buried the entire blade in the bear's skull.

Himalayan bearskins are very greatly prized by our hill folk, and the owner of the axe was a very proud and envied man when I told him he could have the skin in addition to a double share of the ghooral meat. Leaving the men, whose numbers were being rapidly augmented by new arrivals from the village, to skin and divide up the bag, I climbed up to the village and paid, as already related, a last visit to the injured girl. The day had been a strenuous one, and if the maneater had paid me a visit that night she would have "caught me napping".

On the road I had taken when coming to Dalkania there were several long stiff climbs up treeless hills, and when I mentioned the discomforts of this road to the villagers they had suggested that I should go back via Haira Khan. This route would necessitate only one climb to the ridge above the village, from where it was downhill all the way to Ranibagh, whence I could complete the journey to Naini Tal by car.

I had warned my men overnight to prepare for an early start, and a little before sunrise, leaving them to pack up and follow me, I said goodbye to my friends at Dalkania and started on the two-mile climb to the forest road on the ridge above. The footpath I took was not the one by which my men, and later I, had arrived at Dalkania, but was one the villagers used when going to, and returning from, the bazaars in the foot-hills.

The path wound in and out of deep ravines, through thick oak and pine forests and dense undergrowth. There had been no news of the tigress for a week. This absence of news made me all the more careful, and an hour after leaving camp I arrived without mishap at an open glade near the top of the hill, within a hundred yards of the forest road.

The glade was pear-shaped, roughly a hundred yards long and fifty yards wide, with a stagnant pool of rain-water in the centre of it.

Sambur and other game used this pool as a drinking place and wallow and, curious to see the tracks round it, I felt the path, which skirted the left-hand side of the glade and passed close under a cliff of rock which extended up to the road. As I approached the pool I saw the pug marks of the tigress in the soft earth at the edge of the water. She had approached the pool from the same direction as I had, and, evidently disturbed by me, had crossed the water and gone into the dense tree and scrub jungle on the right-hand side of the glade. A great chance lost, for had I kept as careful a lookout in front as I had behind I should have seen her before she saw me. However, though I had missed a chance, the advantages were now all on my side and distinctly in my favour.

The tigress had seen me, or she would not have crossed the pool and hurried for shelter, as her tracks showed she had done. Having seen me she had also seen that I was alone, and watching me from cover as she undoubtedly was, she would assume I was going to the pool to drink as she had done. My movements up to this had been quite natural, and if I could continue to make her think I was unaware of her presence, she would possibly give me a second chance. Stooping down and keeping a very sharp lookout from under my hat; I coughed several times, splashed the water about, and then, moving very slowly and gathering dry sticks on the way, I went to the foot of the steep rock. Here I built a small fire, and putting my back to the rock lit a cigarette. By the time the cigarette had been smoked the fire had burnt out I then lay down, and pillowing my head on my left arm placed the rifle on the ground with my finger on the trigger.

The rock above me was too steep for any animal to find foothold on. I had therefore only my front to guard, and as the heavy cover nowhere approached to within less than twenty yards of my position I was quite safe. I had all this time neither seen nor heard anything; nevertheless, I was convinced that the tigress was watching me. The rim of my hat, while effectually shading my eyes, did not obstruct my vision and inch by inch I scanned every bit of the jungle within my range of view. There was not a breath of wind blowing, and not a leaf or blade of grass stirred. My men, whom I had instructed to keep close together and sing from the time they left camp until they joined me on the forest road, were not due for an hour and a half, and during this time it was more than likely that the tigress would break cover and try to stalk, or rush, me.

There are occasions when time drags, and others when it flies. My left arm, on which my head was pillowed, had long since ceased to prick and had gone dead, but even so the singing of the men in the valley below reached me all too soon. The voices grew louder, and presently I caught sight of the men as they rounded a sharp bend. It was possibly at this bend that the tigress had seen me as she turned round to retrace her steps after having her drink. Another failure, and the last chance on this trip gone.

After my men had rested we climbed up to the road, and set off on what proved to be a very long twenty-mile march to the Forest Rest House at Haira Khan. After going a couple of hundred yards over open ground, the road entered very thick forest, and here I made the men walk in front while I brought up the rear. We had gone about two miles in this order, when on turning a corner I saw a man sitting on the road, herding buffaloes. It was now time to call a halt for breakfast, so I asked the man where we could get water. He pointed down the hill straight in front of him, and said there was a spring down there from which his village, which was just round the shoulder of the hill, drew its water-supply. There was, however, no necessity for us to go down the hill for water, for if we continued a little further we should find a good spring on the road.

His village was at the upper end of the valley in which the woman of Lohali had been killed the previous week, and he told me that nothing had been heard of the maneater since, and added that the animal was possibly now at the other end of the district. I disabused his mind on this point by telling him about the fresh pug marks I had seen at the pool, and advised him very strongly to collect his buffaloes and return to the village. His buffaloes, some ten in number, were straggling up towards the road and he said he would leave as soon as they had grazed up to where he was sitting. Handing him a cigarette, I left him with a final warning. What occurred after I left was related to me by the men of the village, when I paid the district a second visit some months later.

When the man eventually got home that day he told the assembled villagers of our meeting, and my warning, and said that after he had watched me go round a bend in the road a hundred yards away he started to light the cigarette I had given him. A wind was blowing, and to protect the flame of the match he bent forward, and while in this position he was seized from behind by the right shoulder and pulled backwards. His first thought was of the party who had just left him, but unfortunately, his cry for help was not heard by them. Help, however, was near at hand, for as soon as the buffaloes heard his cry, mingled with the growl of the tigress, they charged on to the road and drove the tigress off. His shoulder and arm were broken, and with great difficulty he managed to climb on the back of one of his brave rescuers, and, followed by the rest of the herd, reached his home. The villagers tied up his wounds as best they could and carried him thirty miles, non-stop, to the Haldwani hospital, where he died shortly after admission.

When Atropos who snips the threads of life misses one thread she cuts another, and we who do not know why one thread is missed and another cut, call it Fate, Kismet, or what we will.

For a month I had lived in an open tent, a hundred yards from the nearest human being, and from dawn to dusk had wandered through the jungles, and on several occasions had disguized myself as a woman and cut grass in places where no local inhabitant dared to go. During this period the maneater had, quite possibly, missed many opportunities of adding me to her bag and now, when making a final effort, she had quite by chance encountered this unfortunate man and claimed him as a victim.

II

The following February I returned to Dalkania. A number of human beings had been killed, and many more wounded, over a wide area since my departure from the district the previous summer, and as the whereabouts of the tigress was not known and the chances in one place were as good as in another, I decided to return and camp on the ground with which I was now familiar.

On my arrival at Dalkania I was told that a cow had been killed the previous evening, on the hill on which the bear hunt had taken place. The men who had been herding the cattle at the time were positive that the animal they had seen killing the cow was a tiger. The kill was lying near some bushes at the edge of a deserted field, and was clearly visible from the spot where my tent was being put up. Vultures were circling over the kill, and looking through my field-glasses I saw several of these birds perched on a tree, to the left of the kill. From the fact that the kill was lying out in the open, and the vultures had not descended on it, I concluded (*a*) that the cow had been killed by a leopard, and (*b*) that the leopard was lying up close to the kill.

The ground below the field on which the cow was lying was very steep and overgrown with dense brushwood. The maneater was still at large, and an approach over this ground was therefore inadvisable.

To the right was a grassy slope, but the ground here was too open to admit of my approaching the kill without being seen. A deep heavily-wooded ravine, starting from near the crest of the hill, ran right down to the Nandhour river, passing within a short distance of the kill. The tree on which the vultures were perched was growing on the edge of this ravine. I decided on this ravine as my line of approach. While I had been planning out the stalk with the assistance of the villagers, who knew every foot of the ground, my men had prepared tea for me. The day was now on the decline but by going hard I should just have time to visit the kill and return to camp before nightfall.

Before setting off I instructed my men to be on the lookout. If, after hearing a shot, they saw me on the open ground near the kill, three or four of them were immediately to leave camp, and, keeping to the open ground, to join me. On the other hand if I did not fire, and failed to return by morning, a search party was to be organized.

The ravine was overgrown with raspberry bushes and strewn with great rocks, and as the wind was blowing downhill, my progress was slow. After a stiff climb I eventually reached the tree on which the vultures were perched, only to find that the kill was not visible from this spot. The deserted field, which through my field-glasses had appeared to be quite straight, I found to be crescent-shaped, ten yards across at its widest part and tapering to a point at both ends. The outer edge was bordered with dense undergrowth, and the hill fell steeply away from the inner edge. Only two-thirds of the field was visible from where I was standing, and in order to see the remaining one-third, on which the kill was lying, it would be necessary either to make a wide detour and approach from the far side or climb the tree on which the vultures were perched.

I decided on the latter course. The cow, as far as I could judge, was about twenty yards from the tree, and it was quite possible that the animal that had killed her was even less than that distance from me. To climb the tree without disturbing the killer would have been an impossible feat, and would not have been attempted had it not been for the vultures. There were by now some twenty of these birds on the tree and their number was being added to by new arrivals, and as the acccommodation on the upper branches was limited there was much flapping of wings and quarrelling. The tree was leaning outwards away from the hill, and about ten feet from the ground a great limb projected out over the steep hillside. Hampered with the rifle I had great difficulty in reaching this limb. Waiting until a fresh quarrel had broken out among the vultures, I stepped out along the branch – a difficult balancing feat where a slip or false step would have resulted in a fall of a hundred or more feet on to the rocks below – reached a fork, and sat down.

The kill, from which only a few pounds of flesh had been eaten, was now in full view. I had been in position about ten minutes, and was finding my perch none too comfortable, when two vultures, who had been circling round and were uncertain of their reception on the tree, alighted on the field a short distance from the cow. They had hardly come to rest when they were on the wing again, and at the same moment the bushes on my side of the kill were gently agitated and out into the open stepped a fine male leopard.

Those who have never seen a leopard under favourable conditions in his natural surroundings can have no conception of the grace of movement, and beauty of colouring, of this the most graceful and the most beautiful of all animals in our Indian jungles. Nor are his attractions limited to outward appearances, for, pound for pound, his strength is second to none, and in courage he lacks nothing. To class such an animal as VERMIN, as is done in some parts of India, is a crime which only those could perpetrate whose knowledge of the leopard is limited to the miserable, underfed, and mangy specimens seen in captivity.

But beautiful as the specimen was that stood before me, his life was forfeit, for he had taken to cattle killing, and I had promised the people of Dalkania and other villages on my last visit that I would rid them of this their minor enemy, if opportunity offered. The opportunity had now come, and I do not think the leopard heard the shot that killed him.

Of the many incomprehensible things one meets with in life, the hardest to assign any reason for is the way in which misfortune dogs an individual, or a family. Take as an example the case of the owner of the cow over which I had shot the leopard. He was a boy, eight years of age, and an only child. Two years previously his mother, while out cutting grass for the cow, had been killed and eaten by the maneater, and twelve months later his father had suffered a like fate. The few pots and pans the family possessed had been sold to pay off the small debt left by the father, and the son started life as the owner of one cow; and this particular cow the leopard had selected, out of a herd of two or three hundred head of village cattle, and killed. (I am afraid my attempt to repair a heartbreak was not very successful in this case, for though the new cow, a red one, was an animal of parts, it did not make up to the boy for the loss of his lifelong white companion.)

My young buffaloes had been well cared for by the man in whose charge I had left them, and the day after my arrival I started tying them out, though I had little hope of the tigress accepting them as bait.

Five miles down the Nandhour valley nestles a little village at the foot of a great cliff of rock, some thousand or more feet high. The maneater had, during the past few months, killed four people on the outskirts of this village. Shortly after I shot the leopard, a deputation came from this village to request me to move my camp from Dalkania to a site that had been selected for me near their village. I was told that the tiger had frequently been seen on the cliff above the village and that it appeared to have its home in one of the many caves in the cliff face. That very morning, I was informed, some women out cutting grass had seen the tiger, and the villagers were now in a state of terror, and too frightened to leave their homes. Promising the deputation I would do all I could to help them, I made a very early start next morning, climbed the hill opposite the village, and scanned the cliff for an hour or more through my field-glasses. I then crossed the valley, and by way of a very deep ravine climbed the cliff above the village. Here the going was very difficult and not at all to my liking, for added to the danger of a fall, which would have resulted in a broken neck, was the danger of an attack on ground on which it would be impossible to defend oneself.

By 2 p.m. I had seen as much of the rock cliff as I shall ever want to see again, and was making my way up the valley towards my camp and breakfast, when on looking back before starting the stiff climb to Dalkania I saw two men running towards me from the direction in which I had just come. On joining me the men informed me that a tiger had just killed a bullock in the deep ravine up which I had gone earlier in the day. Telling one of the men to go on up to my camp and instruct my servant to send tea and some food, I turned round and, accompanied by the other man, retraced my steps down the valley.

The ravine where the bullock had been killed was about two hundred feet deep and one hundred feet wide. As we approached it I saw a number of vultures rising, and when we arrived at the kill I found the vultures had cleaned it out, leaving only the skin and bones. The spot where the remains of the bullock were lying was only a hundred yards from the village but there was no way up the steep bank, so my guide took me a quarter of a mile down the ravine, to where a cattle track crossed it. This track, after gaining the high ground, wound in and out through dense scrub jungle before it finally fetched up at the village. On arrival at the village I told the Headman that the vultures had ruined the kill, and asked him to provide me with a young buffalo and a short length of stout rope; while these were being procured, two of my men arrived from Dalkania with the food I had sent for.

The sun was near setting when I re-entered the ravine, followed by several men leading a vigorous young male buffalo which the Headman had purchased for me from an adjoining village. Fifty yards from where the bullock had been killed, one end of a pine tree washed down from the hill above had been buried deep in the bed of the ravine. After tying the buffalo very securely to the exposed end of the pine, the men returned to the village. There were no trees in the vicinity, and the only possible place for a sit-up was a narrow ledge on the village side of the ravine. With great difficulty I climbed to this ledge, which was about two feet wide by five feet long, and twenty feet above the bed of the ravine. From a little below the ledge the rock shelved inwards, forming a deep recess that was not visible from the ledge. The ledge canted downwards at an uncomfortable angle, and when I had taken my seat on it, I had my back towards the direction from which I expected the tiger to come, while the tethered buffalo was to my left front, and distant about thirty yards from me.

The sun had set when the buffalo, who had been lying down, scrambled to his feet and faced up the ravine, and a moment later a stone came rolling down. It would not have been possible for me to have fired in the direction from which the sound had come, so to avoid detection I sat perfectly still. After some time the buffalo gradually turned to the left until he was facing in my direction. This showed that whatever he was frightened of – and I could see he was frightened – was in the recess below me. Presently the head of a tiger appeared directly under me. A head-shot at a tiger is only justified in an emergency, and any movement on my part might have betrayed my presence. For a long minute or two the head remained perfectly still, and then, with a quick dash forward, and one great bound, the tiger was on the buffalo. The buffalo, as I have stated, was facing the tiger, and to avoid a frontal attack with the possibility of injury from the buffalo's horns, the tiger's dash carried him to the left of the buffalo, and he made his attack at right angles. There was no fumbling for tooth-hold, no struggle, and no sound beyond the impact of the two heavy bodies, after which the buffalo lay quite still with the tiger lying partly over it and holding it by the throat. It is generally believed that tigers kill by delivering a smashing blow on the neck. This is incorrect. Tigers kill with their teeth.

The right side of the tiger was towards me and, taking careful aim with the .275 I had armed myself with when leaving camp that morning, I fired. Relinquishing its hold on the buffalo, the tiger, without making a sound, turned and bounded off up the ravine and out of sight. Clearly a miss, for which I was unable to assign any reason. If the tiger had not seen me or the flash of the rifle there was a possibility that it would return; so recharging the rifle I sat on.

The buffalo, after the tiger left him, lay without movement, and the conviction grew on me that I had shot him instead of the tiger. Ten, fifteen minutes had dragged by, when the tiger's head for a second time appeared from the recess below me. Again there was a long pause, and then, very slowly, the tiger emerged, walked up to the buffalo and stood looking down at it. With the whole length of the back as a target I was going to make no mistake the second time. Very carefully the sights were aligned, and the trigger slowly pressed; but instead of the tiger falling dead as I expected it to, it sprang to the left and went tearing up a little ravine, dislodging stones as it went up the steep hillside.

Two shots fired in comparatively good light at a range of thirty yards, and heard by anxious villagers for miles round: and all I should have to show for them would be, certainly one, and quite possibly two, bullet holes in a dead buffalo. Clearly my eyesight was failing, or in climbing the rock I had knocked the foresight out of alignment. But on focussing my eyes on small objects I found there was nothing wrong with my eyesight, and a glance along the barrel showed that the sights were all right, so the only reason I could assign for having missed the tiger twice was bad shooting.

There was no chance of the tiger returning a third time; and even if it did return, there was nothing to be gained by risking the possibility of only wounding it in bad light when I had not been able to kill it while the light had been comparatively good. Under these circumstances there was no object in my remaining any longer on the ledge.

My clothes were still damp from my exertions earlier in the day, a cold wind was blowing and promised to get colder, my shorts were of thin khaki and the rock was hard and cold, and a hot cup of tea awaited me in the village. Good as these reasons were, there was a better and a more convincing reason for my remaining where I was – the maneater. It was now quite dark. A quarter-of-mile walk, along a boulder-strewn ravine and a winding path through dense undergrowth, lay between me and the village. Beyond the suspicions of the villagers that the tiger they had seen the previous day – and that I had quite evidently just fired at – was the maneater, I had no definite knowledge of the maneater's whereabouts; and though at that moment she might have been fifty miles away, she might also have been watching me from a distance of fifty yards, so, uncomfortable as my perch was, prudence dictated that I should remain where I was. As the long hours dragged by, the conviction grew on me that maneater shooting, by night, was not a pastime that appealed to me, and that if this animal could not be shot during daylight hours she would have to be left to die of old age. This conviction was strengthened, when, cold and stiff, I started to climb down as soon as there was sufficient light to shoot by, and slipping on the dew-drenched rock completed the descent with my feet in the air. Fortunately I landed on a bed of sand, without doing myself or the rifle any injury.

Early as it was I found the village astir, and I was quickly in the middle of a small crowd. In reply to the eager questions from all sides, I was only able to say that I had been firing at an imaginary tiger with blank ammunition.

A pot of tea drunk while sitting near a roaring fire did much to restore warmth to my inner and outer man, and then, accompanied by most of the men and all the boys of the village, I went to where a rock jutted out over the ravine and directly above my overnight exploit. To the assembled throng I explained how the tiger had appeared from the recess under me and had bounded on to the buffalo, and how after I fired it had dashed off in that direction; and as I pointed up the ravine there was an excited shout of "Look, sahib, there's the tiger lying dead!" My eyes were strained with an all-night vigil, but even after looking away and back again there was no denying the fact that the tiger was lying there, dead. To the very natural question of why I had fired a second shot after a period of twenty or thirty minutes, I said that the tiger had appeared a second time from exactly the same place, and that I had fired at it while it was standing near the buffalo and that it had gone up *that* side ravine – and there were renewed shouts, in which the women and girls who had now come up joined, of "Look, sahib, there is another tiger lying dead!" Both tigers appeared to be about the same size and both were lying sixty yards from where I had fired.

Questioned on the subject of this second tiger, the villagers said that when the four human beings had been killed, and also on the previous day when the bullock had been killed, only one tiger had been seen. The mating season for tigers is an elastic one extending from November to April, and the maneater – if either of two tigers lying within view was the maneater – had evidently provided herself with a mate.

A way into the ravine, down the steep rock face, was found some two hundred yards below where I had sat up, and, followed by the entire population of the village, I went past the dead buffalo to where the first tiger was lying. As I approached it hopes rose high, for she was an old tigress. Handing the rifle to the nearest man I got down on my knees to examine her feet. On that day when the tigress had tried to stalk the women cutting wheat she had left some beautiful pug marks on the edge of the field. They were the first pug marks I had seen of the maneater, and I had examined them very carefully. They showed the tigress to be a very old animal, whose feet had splayed out with age. The pads of the forefeet were heavily rutted, one deep rut running right across the pad of the right forefoot, and the toes were elongated to a length I had never before seen in a tiger. With these distinctive feet it would have been easy to pick the maneater out of a hundred dead tigers. The animal before me was, I found to my great regret, not the maneater. When I conveyed this information to the assembled throng of people there was a murmur of strong dissent from all sides. It was asserted that I myself, on my previous visit, had declared the maneater to be an old tigress, and such an animal I had now shot a few yards from where, only a short time previously, four of their number had been killed. Against this convincing evidence, of what value was the evidence of the feet, for the feet of all tigers were alike!

The second tiger could, under the circumstances, only be a male, and while I made preparations to skin the tigress I sent a party of men to fetch him. The side ravine was steep and narrow, and after a great deal of shouting and laughter the second tiger – a fine male – was laid down alongside the tigress.

The skinning of those two tigers that had been dead fourteen hours, with the sun beating down on my back and an evergrowing crowd pressing round, was one of the most unpleasant tasks I have ever undertaken. By early afternoon the job was completed, and with the skins neatly tied up for my men to carry I was ready to start on my five-mile walk back to camp.

During the morning Headmen and others had come in from adjoining villages, and before leaving I assured them that the Chowgarh maneater was not dead and warned them that the slackening of precautions would give the tigress the opportunity she was waiting for. Had my warning been heeded, the maneater would not have claimed as many victims as she did during the succeeding months.

There was no further news of the maneater, and after a stay of a few weeks at Dalkania, I left to keep an appointment with the district officials in the terai.

III

In March 1930, Vivian, our District Commissioner, was touring through the maneater's domain, and on the 22nd of the month I received an urgent request from him to go to Kala Agar, where he said he would await my arrival. It is roughly fifty miles from Naini Tal to Kala Agar, and two days after receipt of Vivian's letter I arrived in time for breakfast at the Kala Agar Forest Bungalow, where he and Mrs Vivian were staying.

Over breakfast the Vivians told me they had arrived at the bungalow on the afternoon of the 21st, and while they were having tea on the verandah, one of six women who were cutting grass in the compound of the bungalow had been killed and carried off by the maneater. Rifles were hurriedly seized and, accompanied by some of his staff, Vivian followed up the "drag" and found the dead woman tucked away under a bush at the foot of an oak tree. On examining the ground later, I found that on the approach of Vivian's party the tigress had gone off down the hill, and throughout the subsequent proceedings had remained in a thicket of raspberry bushes, fifty yards from the kill. A machan was put up in the oak tree for Vivian, and two others in trees near the forest road which passed thirty yards above the kill, for members of his staff. The machans were occupied as soon as they were ready and the party sat up the whole night, without, however, seeing anything of the tigress.

Next morning the body of the woman was removed for cremation, and a young buffalo was tied up on the forest road about half a mile from the bungalow, and killed by the tigress the same night. The following evening the Vivians sat up over the buffalo. There was no moon, and just as daylight was fading out and nearby objects becoming indistinct, they first heard, and then saw an animal coming up to the kill, which in the uncertain light they mistook for a bear; but for this unfortunate mistake their very sporting effort would have resulted in their bagging the maneater for both the Vivians are good rifle shots.

On the 25th the Vivians left Kala Agar, and during the course of the day my four buffaloes arrived from Dalkania. As the tigress now appeared to be inclined to accept this form of bait I tied them up at intervals of a few hundred yards along the forest road. For three nights in succession the tigers passed within a few feet of the buffaloes without touching them, but on the fourth night the buffalo nearest the bungalow was killed On examining the kill in the morning I was disappointed to find that the buffalo had been killed by a pair of leopards I had heard calling the previous night above the bungalow. I did not like the idea of firing in this locality, for fear of driving away the tigress, but it was quite evident that if I did not shoot the leopards they would kill my three remaining buffaloes, so I stalked them while they were sunning themselves on some big rocks above the kill, and shot both of them.

The forest road from the Kala Agar bungalow runs for several miles due west through very beautiful forests of pine, oak and rhododendron, and in these forests there is, compared with the rest of Kumaon, quite a lot of game in the way of sambur, kakar and pig, in addition to a great wealth of bird life. On two occasions I suspected the tigress of having killed sambur in this forest, and though on both occasions I found the blood-stained spot where the animal had been killed, I failed to find either of the kills.

For the next fourteen days I spent all the daylight hours either on the forest road, on which no one but myself ever set foot, or in the jungle, and only twice during that period did I get near the tigress. On the first occasion I had been down to visit an isolated village, on the south face of Kala Agar ridge, that had been abandoned the previous year owing to the depredations of the maneater, and on the way back had taken a cattle track that went over the ridge and down the far side to the forest road, when, approaching a pile of rocks, I suddenly felt there was danger ahead. The distance from the ridge to the forest road was roughly three hundred yards. The track, after leaving the ridge, went steeply down for a few yards and then turned to the right and ran diagonally across the hill for a hundred yards; the pile of rocks was about midway on the right-hand side of this length of the track. Beyond the rocks a hairpin bend carried the track to the left, and a hundred yards further on, another sharp bend took it down to its junction with the forest road.

I had been along this track many times, and this was the first occasion on which I hesitated to pass the rocks. To avoid them I should either have had to go several hundred yards through dense under-growth, or make a wide detour round and above them; the former would have subjected me to very great danger, and there was no time for the latter, for the sun was near setting and I had still two miles to go. So, whether I liked it or not, there was nothing for it but to face the rocks. The wind was blowing up the hill so I was able to ignore the thick cover on the left of the track, and concentrate all my attention on the rocks to my right. A hundred feet would see me clear of the danger zone, and this distance I covered foot by foot, walking sideways with my face to the rocks and the rifle to my shoulder; a strange mode of progression, had there been any to see it.

Thirty yards beyond the rocks was an open glade, starting from the right-hand side of the track and extending up the hill for fifty or sixty yards, and screened from the rocks by a fringe of bushes. In this glade a kakar was grazing. I saw her before she saw me, and watched her out of the corner of my eye. On catching sight of me she threw up her head, and as I was not looking in her direction and was moving slowly on she stood stock still, as these animals have a habit of doing when they are under the impression that they have not been seen. On arrival at the hairpin bend I looked over my shoulder and saw that the kakar had lowered her head, and was once more cropping the grass.

I had walked a short distance along the track after passing the bend when the kakar went dashing up the hill, barking hysterically. In a few quick strides I was back at the bend, and was just in time to see a movement in the bushes on the lower side of the track. That the kakar had seen the tigress was quite evident, and the only place where she could have seen her was on the track. The movement I had seen might have been caused by the passage of a bird, on the other hand it might have been caused by the tigress; anyway, a little investigation was necessary before proceeding further on my way.

A trickle of water seeping out from under the rocks had damped the red clay of which the track was composed, making an ideal surface for the impression of tracks. In this damp clay I had left footprints, and over these footprints I now found the splayed-out pug marks of the tigress where she had jumped down from the rocks and followed me, until the kakar had seen her and given its alarm-call, whereon the tigress had left the track and entered the bushes where I had seen the movement. The tigress was undoubtedly familiar with every foot of the ground, and not having had an opportunity of killing me at the rocks – and her chance of bagging me at the first hairpin bend having been spoilt by the kakar – she was probably now making her way through the dense undergrowth to try to intercept me at the second bend.

Further progress along the track was now not advisable, so I followed the kakar up the glade, and turning to the left worked my way down, over open ground, to the forest road below. Had there been sufficient daylight I believe I could, that evening, have turned the tables on the tigress, for the conditions, after she left the shelter of the rocks, were all in my favour. I knew the ground as well as she did, and while she had no reason to suspect my intention towards her, I had the advantage of knowing, very clearly, her intentions towards me. However, though the conditions were in my favour, I was unable to take advantage of them owing to the lateness of the evening.

I have made mention elsewhere of the sense that warns us of impending danger, and will not labour the subject further beyond stating that this sense is a very real one and that I do not know, and therefore cannot explain, what brings it into operation. On this occasion I had neither heard nor seen the tigress, nor had I received any indication from bird or beast of her presence and yet I knew, without any shadow of doubt, that she was lying up for me among the rocks. I had been out for many hours that day and had covered many miles of jungle with unflagging caution, but without one moment's unease, and then, on cresting the ridge, and coming in sight of the rocks, I knew they held danger for me, and this knowledge was confirmed a few minutes later by the kakar's warning call to the jungle folk, and by my finding the maneater's pug marks superimposed on my footprints.

IV

To those of my readers who have had the patience to accompany me so far in my narrative, I should like to give a clear and a detailed account of my first – and last – meeting with the tigress.

The meeting took place in the early afternoon of the 11th of April

1930, nineteen days after my arrival at Kala Agar.

I had gone out that day at 2 p.m. with the intention of tying up my three buffaloes at selected places along the forest road, when at a point a mile from the bungalow, where the road crosses a ridge and goes from the north to the west face of the Kala Agar range, I came on a large party of men who had been out collecting firewood. In the party was an old man who, pointing down the hill to a thicket of young oak trees some five hundred yards from where we were standing, said it was in that thicket where the maneater, a month previously, had killed his only son, a lad eighteen years of age. I had not heard the father's version of the killing of his son, so, while we sat on the edge of the road smoking, he told his story, pointing out the spot where the lad had been killed, and where all that was left of him had been found the following day. The old man blamed the twenty-five men who had been out collecting firewood on that day for the death of his son, saying, very bitterly, that they had run away and left him to be killed by the tiger. Some of the men sitting near me had been in that party of twenty-five and they hotly repudiated responsibility for the lad's death, accusing him of having been responsible for the stampede by screaming out that he had heard the tiger growling and telling everyone to run for their lives. This did not satisfy the old man. He shook his head and said, "You are grown men and he was only a boy, and you ran away and left him to be killed." I was sorry for having asked the questions that had led to this heated discussion, and more to placate the old man than for any good it would do, I said I would tie up one of my buffaloes near the spot where he said his son had been killed. So, handing two of the buffaloes over to the party to take back to the bungalow, I set off followed by two of my men leading the remaining buffalo.

A footpath, taking off close to where we had been sitting, went down the hill to the valley below and zigzagged up the opposite pine-clad slope to join the forest road two miles further on. The path passed close to an open patch of ground which bordered the oak thicket in which the lad had been killed. On this patch of ground, which was about thirty yards square, there was a solitary pine sapling. This I cut down. I tied the buffalo to the stump, set one man to cutting a supply of grass for it, and sent the other man, Madho Singh, who served in the Garhwalis during the Great War and is now serving in the United Provinces Civil Pioneer Force, up an oak tree with instructions to strike a dry branch with the head of his axe and call at the top of his voice as hill people do when cutting leaves for their cattle. I then took up a position on a rock, about four feet high, on the lower edge of the open ground. Beyond the rock the hill fell steeply away to the valley below and was densely clothed with tree and scrub jungle.

The man on the ground had made several trips with the grass he had cut, and Madho Singh on the tree was alternately shouting and singing lustily, while I stood on the rock smoking, with the rifle in the hollow of my left arm, when, all at once, I became aware that the maneater had arrived. Beckoning urgently to the man on the ground to come to me, I whistled to attract Madho Singh's attention and signalled to him to remain quiet. The ground on three sides was comparatively open. Madho Singh on the tree was to my left front, the man cutting grass had been in front of me, while the buffalo – now showing signs of uneasiness – was to my right front. In this area the tigress could not have approached without my seeing her; and as she *had* approached, there was only one place where she could now be, and that was behind and immediately below me.

When taking up my position I had noticed that the further side of the rock was steep and smooth, that it extended down the hill for eight or ten feet, and that the lower portion of it was masked by thick undergrowth and young pine saplings. It would have been a little difficult, but quite possible, for the tigress to have climbed the rock, and I relied for my safety on hearing her in the undergrowth should she make the attempt.

I have no doubt that the tigress, attracted, as I had intended she should be, by the noise Madho Singh was making, had come to the rock, and that it was while she was looking up at me and planning her next move that I had become aware of her presence. My change of front, coupled with the silence of the men, may have made her suspicious; anyway, after a lapse of a few minutes, I heard a dry twig snap a little way down the hill; thereafter the feeling of unease left me, and the tension relaxed. An opportunity lost; but there was still a very good chance of my getting a shot, for she would undoubtedly return before long, and when she found us gone would probably content herself with killing the buffalo. There were still four or five hours of daylight, and by crossing the valley and going up the opposite slope I should be able to overlook the whole of the hillside on which the buffalo was tethered. The shot, if I did get one, would be a long one of from two to three hundred yards, but the .275 rifle I was carrying was accurate, and even if I only wounded the tigress I should have a blood trail to follow, which would be better than feeling about for her in hundreds of square miles of jungle, as I had been doing these many months.

The men were a difficulty. To have sent them back to the bungalow alone would have been nothing short of murder, so of necessity I kept them with me.

Tying the buffalo to the stump in such a manner as to make it impossible for the tigress to carry it away, I left the open ground and rejoined the path to carry out the plan I have outlined, of trying to get a shot from the opposite hill.

About a hundred yards along the path I came to a ravine. On the far side of this the path entered very heavy undergrowth, and as it was inadvisable to go into thick cover with two men following me, I decided to take to the ravine, follow it down to its junction with the valley, work up the valley and pick up the path on the far side of the undergrowth.

The ravine was about ten yards wide and four or five feet deep, and as I stepped down into it a nightjar fluttered off a rock on which I had put my hand. On looking at the spot from which the bird had risen, I saw two eggs. These eggs, straw-coloured, with rich brown markings, were of a most unusual shape, one being long and very pointed, while the other was as round as a marble; and as my collection lacked nightjar eggs I decided to add this odd clutch to it. I had no receptacle of any kind in which to carry the eggs, so cupping my left hand I placed the eggs in it and packed them round with a little moss.

As I went down the ravine the banks became higher, and sixty yards from where I had entered it I came on a deep drop of some twelve to fourteen feet. The water that rushes down all these hill ravines in the rains had worn the rock as smooth as glass, and as it was too steep to offer a foothold I handed the rifle to the men and, sitting on the edge, proceeded to slide down. My feet had hardly touched the sandy bottom when the two men, with a flying leap, landed one on either side of me, and thrusting the rifle into my hand asked in a very agitated manner if I had heard the tiger. As a matter of fact I had heard nothing, possibly due to the scraping of my clothes on the rocks, and when questioned, the men said that what they had heard was a deep-throated growl from somewhere close at hand, but exactly from which direction the sound had come, they were unable to say. Tigers do not betray their presence

by growling when looking for their dinner and the only, and very unsatisfactory, explanation I can offer is that the tigress followed us after we
left the open ground, and on seeing that we were going down the ravine
had gone ahead and taken up a position where the ravine narrowed to
half its width; and that when she was on the point of springing out on
me, I had disappeared out of sight down the slide and she had involuntarily given vent to her disappointment with a low growl. Not a satisfactory reason, unless one assumes – without any reason – that she had
selected me for her dinner, and therefore had no interest in the two
men.

Where the three of us now stood in a bunch we had the smooth steep
rock behind us, to our right a wall of rock slightly leaning over the
ravine and fifteen feet high, and to our left a tumbled bank of big rocks
thirty or forty feet high. The sandy bed of the ravine, on which we were
standing, was roughly forty feet long and ten feet wide. At the lower
end of this sandy bed a great pine tree had fallen across, damming the
ravine, and the collection of the sand was due to this dam. The wall of
overhanging rock came to an end twelve or fifteen feet from the fallen
tree, and as I approached the end of the rock, my feet making no sound
on the sand, I very fortunately noticed that the sandy bed continued
round to the back of the rock.

This rock about which I have said so much I can best describe as a
giant school slate, two feet thick at its lower end, and standing up – not
quite perpendicularly – on one of its long sides.

As I stepped clear of the giant slate, I looked behind me over my
right shoulder and looked straight into the tigress's face.

I would like you to have a clear picture of the situation.

The sandy bed behind the rock was quite flat. To the right of it was
the smooth slate fifteen feet high and leaning slightly outwards, to the
left of it was a scoured-out steep bank also some fifteen feet high overhung by a dense tangle of thorn bushes, while at the far end was a slide
similar to, but a little higher than, the one I had glissaded down. The
sandy bed, enclosed by these three natural walls, was about twenty feet
long and half as wide, and lying on it, with her fore-paws stretched out
and her hind legs well tucked under her, was the tigress. Her head,
which was raised a few inches off her paws, was eight feet (measured
later) from me, and on her face was a smile, similar to that one sees on
the face of a dog welcoming his master home after a long absence.

Two thoughts flashed through my mind, one, that it was up to me to make the first move, and the other, that the move would have to be made in such a manner as not to alarm the tigress or make her nervous.

The rifle was in my right hand held diagonally across my chest, with the safety-catch off, and in order to get it to bear on the tigress the muzzle would have to be swung round three-quarters of a circle.

The movement of swinging round the rifle, with one hand, was begun very slowly, and hardly perceptibly, and when a quarter of a circle had been made, the stock came in contact with my right side. It was now necessary to extend my arm, and as the stock cleared my side, the swing was very slowly continued. My arm was now at full stretch and the weight of the rifle was beginning to tell. Only a little further now for the muzzle to go, and the tigress – who had not once taken her eyes off mine – was still looking up at me, with the pleased expression still on her face.

How long it took the rifle to make the three-quarter circle, I am not in a position to say. To me, looking into the tigress's eyes and unable therefore to follow the movement of the barrel, it appeared that my arm was paralysed, and that the swing would never be completed. However, the movement was completed at last, and as soon as the rifle was pointing at the tigress's body, I pressed the trigger.

I heard the report, exaggerated in that restricted space, and felt the jar of the recoil, and but for these tangible proofs that the rifle had gone off, I might, for all the immediate result the shot produced, have been in the grip of one of those awful nightmares in which triggers are vainly pulled of rifles that refuse to be discharged at the critical moment.

For a perceptible fraction of time the tigress remained perfectly still, and then, very slowly, her head sank on to her outstretched paws, while at the same time a jet of blood issued from the bullet-hole. The bullet had injured her spine and shattered the upper portion of her heart.

The two men who were following a few yards behind me, and who were separated from the tigress by the thickness of the rock, came to a halt when they saw me stop and turn my head. They knew instinctively that I had seen the tigress and judged from my behaviour that she was close at hand, and Madho Singh said afterwards that he wanted to call out and tell me to drop the eggs and get both hands on the rifle. When I had fired my shot and lowered the point of the rifle on to my toes, Madho Singh, at a sign, came forward to relieve me of it, for very suddenly my legs appeared to be unable to support me, so I made for the fallen tree and sat down. Even before looking at the pads of her feet

I knew it was the Chowgarh tigress I had sent to the Happy Hunting Grounds, and that the shears that had assisted her to cut the threads of sixty-four human lives – the people of the district put the number at twice that figure – had, while the game was in her hands, turned, and cut the thread of her own life.

Three things, each of which would appear to you to have been to my disadvantage, were actually in my favour. These were (*a*) the eggs in my left hand, (*b*) the light rifle I was carrying, and (*c*) the tiger being a maneater. If I had not had the eggs in my hand I should have had both hands on the rifle, and when I looked back and saw the tiger at such close quarters I should instinctively have tried to swing round to face her, and the spring that was arrested by my lack of movement would inevitably have been launched. Again, if the rifle had not been a light one it would not have been possible for me to have moved it in the way it was imperative I should move it, and then discharge it at the full extent of my arm. And lastly, if the tiger had been just an ordinary tiger, and not a maneater, it would, on finding itself cornered, have made for the opening and wiped me out of the way; and to be wiped out of the way by a tiger usually has fatal results.

While the men made a detour and went up the hill to free the buffalo and secure the rope, which was needed for another and more pleasant purpose, I climbed over the rocks and went up the ravine to restore the eggs to their rightful owner. I plead guilty of being as superstitious as my brother sportsmen. For three long periods, extending over a whole year, I had tried – and tried hard – to get a shot at the tigress, and had failed; and now within a few minutes of having picked up the eggs my luck had changed.

The eggs, which all this time had remained safely in the hollow of my left hand, were still warm when I replaced them in the little depression in the rock that did duty as a nest, and when I again passed that way half an hour later, they had vanished under the brooding mother whose colouring so exactly matched the mottled rock that it was difficult for me, who knew the exact spot where the nest was situated, to distinguish her from her surroundings.

The buffalo, who after months of care was now so tame that it followed like a dog, came scrambling down the hill in the wake of the men, nosed the tigress and lay down on the sand to chew the cud of contentment, while we lashed the tigress to the stout pole the men had cut.

I had tried to get Madho Singh to return to the bungalow for help, but this he would not hear of doing. With no one would he and his companion share the honour of carrying in the maneater, and if I would lend a hand the task, he said, with frequent halts for rest, would not be too difficult. We were three hefty men – two accustomed from childhood to carrying heavy loads – and all three hardened by a life of exposure; but even so, the task we set ourselves was a herculean one.

The path down which we had come was too narrow and too winding for the long pole to which the tigress was lashed, so, with frequent halts to regain breath and readjust pads to prevent the pole biting too deep into shoulder muscles, we went straight up the hill through a tangle of raspberry and briar bushes, on the thorns of which we left a portion of our clothing and an amount of skin which made bathing for many days a painful operation.

The sun was still shining on the surrounding hills when three dishevelled and very happy men, followed by a buffalo, carried the tigress to the Kala Agar Forest Bungalow, and from that evening to this day no human being has been killed – or wounded – over the hundreds of square miles of mountain and vale over which the Chowgarh tigress, for a period of five years, held sway.

I have added one more cross and date to the map of Eastern Kumaon that hangs on the wall before me – the cross and the date the maneater earned. The cross is two miles west of Kala Agar, and the date under it is 11 April 1930.

The tigress's claws were broken, and bushed out, and one of her canine teeth was broken, and her front teeth were worn down to the bone. It was these defects that had made her a maneater and were the cause of her not being able to kill outright – and by her own efforts – a large proportion of the human beings she had attacked since the day she had been deprived of the assistance of the cub I had, on my first visit shot by mistake.

A GRIZZLY IN YELLOWSTONE

Yellowstone National Park, Wyoming, June 1972: A grizzly bear raiding a food cache last Sunday killed a twenty-five-year-old man camping in an unauthorized area near Old Faithful.

Park officials identified the victim as Harry B. Walker of Anniston,

Alabama. His companion, who escaped unhurt, was Philip H. Bradberry, aged twenty-five, of Oxford, Alabama.

Four people have been killed by bears in the one-hundred-year history of America's first national park. Assistant Park Superintendent Vernon Hennesay said the incident occurred in a wooded section designated as an off-limits area.

Hennesay said the two men were within one hundred feet of their campsite, which could be reached only by crossing a thermal area off the regular trail, when the bear, which had raided their food supply, attacked.

Bradberry ran to the Old Faithful Inn and reported the incident to rangers, who immediately organized a party to recover the body and search for the bear.

The last death in a bear attack at Yellowstone came in 1942, Hennesay said.

Park officials said on Tuesday that an autopsy report from Montana State University indicated human hair was found on the claws of the 400 lb grizzly bear killed in the park on Monday.

The bear was caught in a snare and shot by rangers when it returned to the site where a camper was mauled to death on Sunday morning.

Hennesay said other items were found in the bear's digestive tract to indicate the bear had been at the camp before. He said the items included aluminium foil and other scrap material from the campsite. He said the findings, coupled with the fact that the bear was trapped at the campsite, gave rangers conclusive evidence they had killed the animal which committed the fatal mauling.

THE ANDES AIR CRASH

Santiago, Chile, 22 December 1972

The Chilean Air Force today found fourteen survivors of a Uruguayan Air Force plane which vanished in the Andes ten weeks ago with forty-five people on board.

Six of the fourteen who were in poor condition were flown out by helicopter. The remaining eight were left beside the shattered aircraft 18,000 feet up in the mountains under medical care until improved weather conditions allowed them to be rescued.

The first news that anyone had survived the crash came when two survivors were found earlier today after they had trudged for ten days through snow and storms to get help. The first men they met were muleteers in the Andean foothills near San Fernando. They reported they had left the fourteen behind in the fuselage of the wrecked Fokker Friendship.

Immediately the Chilean Air Force mounted a search for the wreckage. Violent storms in the area delayed the rescue operation and ground patrols on mules were sent to the site of the wreckage following directions given by the two survivors. When the weather cleared, search planes sighted the wreckage, with the ground patrol only 600 yards away. The Air Force said that the six survivors were flown out to a field hospital set up at San Fernando. Doctors with emergency kits were also on board the helicopters.

In spite of suffering from cold and hunger, the two men who had gone for help refused to be taken to Santiago and insisted on joining the rescue operations.

The aircraft vanished while on a flight from Montevideo, the capital of Uruguay, to Santiago [the capital of Chile]. Half an hour after a stop at Mendoza, the pilot reported he was having trouble and losing height rapidly.

The two men who went to get help, identified as Roberto Canessa and Fernando Parrado, were quoted today as saying that the pilot managed to make an emergency landing in the snow after the aircraft hit a crag and plunged down into a shallow valley.

Eight people were killed on impact and others suffered injuries. An unspecified number of survivors died later under tons of snow loosened by a thunderstorm. Roberto Canessa said that the survivors had to live on chocolate bars and several other light foods and sweets the passengers carried in their luggage. They used the sun's rays to melt snow for drinking water, and stripped the covering off the seats of the wrecked plane to make blankets. The seats themselves they used as pillows and mattresses for the injured. They lived inside the fuselage and used whatever they could scavenge from the strewn wreckage to plug up holes in the fuselage to keep out the cold.

Those able to work set up a huge makeshift aerial and connected the batteries to one of the plane's radios, which they managed to repair. "After some tinkering we managed to hear radio stations. On the eighth day we heard the sad news that our search had been abandoned."

He said that the wrecked aircraft slowly sank into the snow and the survivors had watched with anguish as search planes flew over them without sighting the wreckage in the days after the crash.

Santiago, 26 December 1972

Sixteen people who lived more than two months in the Andes mountains after their aircraft crashed last October survived by eating the flesh of their dead companions, an official source confirmed today.

One of the organizers of the rescue operation launched after reports that several people had miraculously survived the crash said that Chilean press stories of cannibalism were basically correct. However, he described as sensationalism some reports that the sixteen had "devoured" their fellow passengers.

As the Uruguayan survivors left Santiago for Montevideo, the Chilean press today published two documents. One was a statement by the muleteer who was the first person to encounter the two survivors who had trudged for ten days to get help. The other consisted of photographs taken by the rescuers inside the crashed aircraft which housed the survivors.

Newspapers said that Canessa and Parrado told the muleteer that the survivors had been forced to eat the bodies of their twenty-nine dead companions in order to stay alive. The photographs show human remains in the aircraft and are said to be part of a "confidential report" given to the Chilean authorities by the rescuers. The Chile Air Rescue Organization today confirmed that a report had been submitted to the authorities.

None of the survivors would either confirm or deny the Chilean press reports. The reports were encouraged by the astonishment of Chilean doctors, who considered "unexplainable" the survival of sixteen persons for seventy days in the wreckage of an aircraft at an altitude of 12,000 feet. The doctors stated in their report: "The present state of science and medicine does not permit us to give a logical reply" as to how the sixteen survived.

Father Thomas Gonzales, a Santiago priest, said today: "In the case of the dead on board the Uruguayan aircraft, the most useful thing for these human bodies was to nourish the survivors. The dead, therefore, accomplished their mission, and there is no theological opposition in this case."

Montevideo, 29 December 1972

The survivors on the Andes air crash have admitted that they ate the flesh of their dead colleagues in order to keep alive.

The young Uruguayans, most of them members of a rugby team called the Old Christians, spent ten weeks isolated on a mountainside before being rescued last week. Ten of the sixteen survivors returned to Montevideo last night and, at a press conference, compared their means of survival to the Last Supper of Jesus Christ.

"If Jesus, in the Last Supper, offered his body and blood to all the disciples, he was giving us to understand that we must do the same," said their spokesman, Alfredo Delgado.

The meeting was attended by about 500 people including the Roman Catholic Archbishop of Montevideo, Monsignor Carlos Partelli.

In an interview with the mass circulation German newspaper *Bild Zeitung*, one of the survivors, Antonio Vizentin, aged twenty-two, a student, said: "We swallowed the little bits of flesh with the feeling that God demanded it of us. We felt like Christians."

Señor Vizentin said they had chosen as their leader a medical student, Roberto Canessa, aged nineteen. "He told us we needed protein to survive. After two days he convinced us that we would only find enough protein in the human brain. To keep our strength up, we also needed the muscle flesh of the arms and legs. There was nothing criminal about what we did. It was a communion for us, like a ritual. We Christians see the body of Christ in the host."

London, 7 May 1974

Cannibalism was on the minds of many of the survivors of the Andes air crash in 1972, but, when Fernando Parrado first quietly mentioned it to a friend, he was told he was going crazy. The next day, in sub-zero temperatures, desperate hunger had driven many people to talk about it, Señor Parrado, aged twenty-four and now a businessman, revealed yesterday.

Señor Parrado was speaking with Señor Roberto Canessa, another of the survivors, at a press conference in London to mark the publication of *Alive: The Story of the Andes Survivors*, a factual account by the novelist Piers Paul Read of this epic survival adventure.

Señor Canessa, a medical student aged twenty-one, said: "The flesh was like raw cow meat. From a biochemist's point of view the cells of a cow and a human being have very little difference. When a friend dies, he has gone, and, if I had died, I would be proud if my friends could use me and even tell in my house what happened."

Both men, looking fit and well, emphasized that a more important aspect of the story was friendship, unselfishness, great love and suffering. For some of them cannibalism had a religious significance, said Señor Canessa. "We prayed very much and we felt God was not an old man sitting up there with a long beard but a friend sitting close to you.

"The story is talked about at home now, but it's not the main subject in our lives. Sometimes it comes up in conversation and we sometimes feel we must talk about it. I never have nightmares about it. The only dream I have of this experience is of very close friends and I am speaking to them. I wake and think how sad it was only a dream. I remember my first night in a soft bed afterwards. I was very nervous when I got back to my house and I remember I couldn't sleep because the bed was too soft."

Señor Parrado recalled a friend who with two broken legs in the freezing mountains wrote before his death that life was worth living in those conditions.

"I enjoy life now," said Señor Parrado. "The real things to enjoy are inside one."

WOLVES AND WILD DOGS

There was a fatal attack on 18 April 1996 at the Haliburton Forest and Wildlife Reserve in Ontario, Canada. The victim was a twenty-four-year-old woman who had been hired to look after the wolves in a new Wolf Centre at the reserve. The animals themselves were captive wolves, although they had not been socialized to humans. They lived wild in their woodland enclosure, and usually kept clear of any humans that entered. On this occasion, five wolves attacked the young woman. Her body was found and the police informed. When two officers tried to recover her body, the wolves growled at them, as if defending a food cache, and then circled them. The policemen were understandably nervous, fired shots close to the wolves and then backed out. Later six officers entered and removed the body. The woman's clothes had been ripped off, and she had pieces of flesh torn away, as well as multiple bite wounds on her body. The local coroner ordered the wolves to be put down.

Eric Klinghammer, Director of the Institute of Ethology at Nawpf-Wolf Park, Battle Ground, Indiana, USA went to investigate and after interviewing people on the spot, he worked out a likely scenario. The woman had had concerns about the alpha male wolf, but had only shared them with her fiancé rather than the reserve officials. Being relatively new to the job, she probably entered the enclosure to familiarize herself more with the place and its occupants. Fallen trees and branches littered the ground, so she might have tripped and fallen. This would have been all the wolves needed to attack.

In September 1998, another attack occurred in Canada, this time in Algonquin Park. A wolf grabbed a nineteen-month-old boy around the rib cage, and tossed him about three feet (one metre) away. The baby needed stitches but survived. The wolf had been seen around the camp-grounds during the summer. It had rummaged through backpacks and tried to drag away a sleeping-bag in which a child was sleeping. It also attacked three dogs. Later, it was hunted down and killed. It was the fifth wolf-biting attack in the park in twelve years.

Yet, while deliberate attacks on people in most parts of the world are yet to be accepted as reality by the scientific community, the situation in India appears to be different. India is not only home to the maneating tiger and leopard, but also the maneating wolf. During recent times, the local subspecies of grey wolf – the Indian grey wolf or Asiatic wolf (*Canis lupus pallipes*) – has been recognized as the perpetrator of attacks on people, particularly children. It hunts in pairs or small family parties.

Between October 1980 and March 1981, a small group of wolves worked a territory nineteen miles (thirty kilometres) long by sixteen miles (twenty-five kilometres) wide on the Andhra Pradesh side of its border with Karnataka in the south-west part of India. The prey included humans. The pack – an adult male and two adult females, two sub-adults and three cubs – accounted for the deaths of nine children, and a further twelve were injured. It always operated in the same way, hiding in bush or crops near villages and taking children who were walking alone, usually at dawn or dusk. Children accompanied by adults were not approached. The victim was attacked from behind, pushed to the ground and bitten on the head or neck. The skull was then opened and the brain consumed first. If the alarm was not raised and rescuers failed to appear, there was time enough for the wolves to eat the rest of the body.

At about the same time, another spate of wolf attacks occurred between February and August 1981 around the town of Hazaribagh, in the eastern India district of Bihar. This pack consisted of five wolves and their hunting range was a 2.7 square miles (seven square kilometres) area around the town. They were attracted by the rich pickings at the town's rubbish dump, where livestock carcasses and human bodies unclaimed from the local mortuary were not buried properly and were dug up by wolves, hyenas, jackals and domestic dogs. On one night in June 1981, five wolves were picked out by a spotlight, and were seen to excavate and eat human bodies. Whether they acquired a taste for human flesh, we will never know, but local children began to be targeted.

One of the first attacks was on 15 February 1981, when a wolf entered a yard fenced by brushwood and attacked a young boy. Several people heard the commotion and came running. Taking wooden poles, they beat the wolf to death. During the next six months, wolves were to kill and eat thirteen children aged between four and ten, and a further thirteen had close calls but mercifully escaped injury or death. During the year four wolves were killed in the vicinity of Hazaribagh, and at the end of this period a large male, thought to have been the alpha male of the pack, was caught in ravined scrub forest and shot. The villagers thought this marked the end of the attacks, but about four months later they were to be proved wrong.

At dusk on 21 December 1981, a wolf grabbed a seven-year-old boy from a compound and ran into the scrub. His mother and a relative raised the alarm, and neighbours eventually headed off the wolf. Seeing that he was surrounded, the wolf dropped the boy and made his escape. Five days after the attack, the wolf researcher S. P. Shahi went to the site of the attack and also visited the hospital where the boy was being treated. At the attack site, the unmistakable pug marks of an animal with non-retractile claws, like those of a wolf, were found. Where the wolf had carried the boy, its large canine teeth had punctured the child's abdomen and left flank, the length of the bite marks consistent with an attack by a dog-like predator, such as a wolf, rather than a large cat, such as a leopard. Whether wolves were the actual perpetrators of the attacks is not clear. Other dog-like animals could have been responsible, such as feral dogs (*Canis lupus familiaris*) and dholes (*Cuon alpinus*).

The Indian wild dog or dhole (meaning "recklessness" or "daring") is not a true dog at all. It is more closely related to our red fox, although considerably larger and more powerful. Like the wolf, it is accused of killing and eating people, but the evidence is slim.

The accounts of children as wolf victims in India, however, have not stopped. In April 1985, newspaper reports brought news that wolves had killed three more children in eastern India. And, in June 1986, forestry officials in Bihar offered a Rs5,000 (£250) reward for the capture of wolves that had killed more children in the Hazirabagh region. Wolves, according to press reports, accounted for the deaths of a further six people by November.

In 1996, another spate of attacks occurred in a sixty-mile (ninety-seven kilometres) stretch of the Ganges river basin in Uttar Pradesh. According to police figures, between April and September, thirty-three children were taken by wolves and another twenty seriously mauled. At the village of Banbirpur, according to a report in the *New York Times*, a woman was taking her eight children to a grassy clearing which was used as a toilet when a wolf grabbed the youngest, a four-year-old boy. It carried him into the corn and elephant grass that lined the river bank. Only his head was found three days later. Claw and tooth marks indicated the assailant was a dog-like animal, probably a wolf.

Local rumours are rife. Some believe the attacks are by werewolves, others blame Pakistani infiltrators dressed as wolves. Banbirpur villagers, who live in one of the poorest and over-populated parts of India, even tell of the predator approaching on all fours like a wolf but rising up on two feet to make the attack. They describe a person in a black coat, helmet and goggles! Despite the bizarre stories, fairy tales and folklore, the local authorities are convinced the attacks are by wolves, and it would not have been the first time. In 1878, British officials reported 624 human deaths from wolf attacks in the same area. In that year, 2,600 wolves paid the ultimate price – they were shot, and the killings stopped.

Elsewhere in India, predation on humans by wolves is almost unknown. Local people living in and around the Melekote wolf sanctuary, Gujarat in the Rann of Cutch, and the Mahhuandanr Valley of Bihar – all wolf habitats – consider wolves to be an "occupational hazard". They take sheep but never children. Indeed, some communities welcome the wolves, for they keep crop-raiders, such as wild boar under control. The Indian grey wolf, however, is an endangered subspecies and, despite these localized attacks on children and the taking of domestic livestock, the general feeling in India is that it should be protected . . .

On 2 March 1989, a five-year-old girl stepped off her school bus at Upper Peninsula, Detroit, and while walking the 100 yards (100 metres) to her home was attacked, killed and partly eaten by a dog that was part malamute and part wolf. Not far away in Rothbury, to the north of Muskegon, a twelve-year-old girl was waiting at the school bus-stop when she was attacked by a cross between a wolf and a shepherd on 21 October 1996. The dog pressed home its attack for about fifteen minutes and the girl was eventually rescued by the school bus driver, but not before the dog made four deep bite wounds to her head, damaged her left hand, and removed chunks of flesh from her right arm. It took seven hours of surgery to sew her up again.

In April 1991, a wolf-dog hybrid severed the arm of a sixteen-month-old child in New Jersey. At Fort Walton Beach, Florida, a wolf-dog hybrid was advertised as "pet of the week" and within hours of it being taken home it had killed a neighbour's child. This desire for the macho image had resulted in six children being killed by wolf-dog hybrids during the previous three years in the USA.

Some people keep real wolves and the outcome is inevitably the same. In April 1999 a pet wolf in Bangor, County Down, Northern Ireland, attacked a small girl who was visiting the house. The child was on the floor playing while the wolf was sleeping. Suddenly, it leapt up and grabbed the child by the head. Apart from a few puncture wounds in the lip and scratches to the nose and forehead, the girl was safe.

Clearly, the more appropriate place for a wild dog, such as a wolf, is not in the home but in the wilderness, yet even seemingly harmless wild species have been implicated as part-time people killers. The coyote (*Canis latrans*) of North America, for example, is not whiter than white. Several cases are on record of coyotes attacking and eating babies and young children, and savaging adults.

In Yellowstone Park, in 1959 a coyote attacked a group of Boy Scouts who were out hiking near Slough Creek. One of the party had a penknife which was used effectively to see the creature off. A few years later, in 1974, a coyote attacked a television crew filming the geyser eruptions. And in 1990, a young man was skiing in the park when he was attacked. He was able to defend himself with his skis. In Canada in 1988, a coyote attacked an eighteen-month-old baby in British Columbia, and in a separate incident a coyote tried to pull a teenager out of a tent in the Banff National Park. A coyote in Griffith Park, Los Angeles, savaged three adults before it attacked and was clearly trying to eat a fifteen-month-old baby playing in the park in July 1995. The following month another coyote attacked a sixteen-month-old baby boy at Los Alamos, New Mexico, and tried to drag him into the brush. The mother ran screaming into the yard and frightened the animal away. It was the second coyote attack in the area within a month.

Attacks from coyotes have also been registered in Vermont, where in two quite separate incidents hunters were attacked in 1992; in Barnstable, Massachusetts, where a woman was bitten in 1994; and in 1995, when hikers were attacked at Mt Sunapee, New Hampshire.

In the southern half of Africa, the African hunting dog (*Lycaon pictus*) has been implicated in attacks on people in the bush, but these occasions are certainly rare. The dogs would have to be sufficiently hungry and desperate to mount such an attack, but stories exist of packs being bold enough to pull down solitary travellers.

The dingo or wild dog of Australia (*Canis dingo*) has also been implicated in attacks on people. In February 1999, for example, tourists on Frazer Island were reported to have been attacked by dingoes, the result probably of people offering titbits to the island's dingo population. The worst incident was an attack on a thirteen-month-old baby in April 1998, which provoked the government to consider a cull.

TIGER VICTIM IN INDIA

A British ornithologist who was mauled to death by a tiger in an Indian wildlife reserve was cremated in Delhi yesterday, 25 February 1985, the High Commisioner said.

Mr David Hunt, aged fifty-one, was attacked and partly devoured on Friday by a tiger in Corbett National Park after he strayed from a group of tourists to take pictures of a bird, reports reaching Delhi said.

About ninety tigers roam the park, which is in the foothills of the Sivalik mountain range in Uttar Pradesh state.

Mr Hunt was reportedly tour leader of a group of seventeen British wildlife enthusiasts.

According to the *Hindustan Times*, one of Mr Hunt's legs was eaten in the attack. Wildlife experts say the tigers normally avoid human beings. However, they say, an injured or old tiger which has lost its speed may attack humans because it has trouble catching more rapid prey.

DEREK FROM NEW GUINEA

With all the news about psychopathic cannibals, one might forget there are still those who used to eat people for their living.

Derek, a cannibal from New Guinea who gave up eating people in the 1960s, has now offered a rare insight into the practice. Far from immersing prospective dinners in a pot, the victims were cooked over hot stones while wrapped in leaves and grass.

"They were delicious," Derek reminisced in a recent interview. "Better than pig or chicken. Old ones were tough. Young men and women tasted better. And babies tasted like fish. The flesh is very soft."

CLAWED TO DEATH IN THE ROCKIES

Trevor Percy-Lancaster, one of Hampshire, UK's best-known and most popular artists, was clawed to death by a grizzly bear as he struggled to save his friend from the enraged animal.

Mr Percy-Lancaster, aged forty-six, and his companion, Cheryl Reksten, aged forty-five, had disturbed a 312-pound bear on a remote, snow-covered trail in the Canadian Rockies. As the bear turned on them, rearing on its hind legs and waving its razor-sharp claws, Miss Reksten, instead of lying motionless – which experts say is enough to prevent an attack – fled and tried to climb a tree.

The bear chased after her, pulled her to the ground by her hiking boots and tore at her scalp and back as she tried to escape. Mr Percy-Lancaster waved his arms and hit the bear in an attempt to drive it away. It turned on him, savaging his back, arms and face.

Another camper ran five miles down the trail to the nearest park warden station. Wardens, arriving by helicopter, found Miss Reksten had staggered several miles from the scene of the attack; she was taken to hospital in Edmonton, where last night she was said to be stable.

The wardens, who followed the bear's tracks in the snow, shot it dead when it suddenly loomed out of the woods to attack them. The carcass was being examined for signs of rabies.

Last night friends spoke in admiration of the quiet cycling and hiking enthusiast. Emily Farrar, who lived in the same block of flats as Mr Percy-Lancaster, in Milland Road, Winchester, said: "He was deeply in love with his girlfriend. They did everything together. He was a very kind, friendly person and it is typical of him to give up his life for her."

Gerry Israelson, a park spokesman, said that the actions of Mr Percy-Lancaster, an art lecturer, probably saved his companion's life.

"It appears that because of the noise from a nearby stream and the direction in which the wind was blowing, the couple and the bear startled each other. You shouldn't run, nor should you climb a tree. What you should do is lie down and play dead," he said.

As wardens searched for other bears which might also have moved down into the area from their normal feeding grounds, the park was closed and fifteen hikers flown to safety.

Nick Lindsay, curator of Whipsnade wild animal park, said of grizzlies last night: "They are omnivores and, although they prefer berries, fruit and roots, they will also eat fish, meat or small mammals. Most of all they are natural scavengers. Many have been fed by picnickers and they, therefore, come looking for it, then get aggressive if they don't get it."

THE BLACK BEARS OF CALIFORNIA

A century ago, even before settlers arrived with their rifles and saws, Southern California's forests were barren of black bears. The land belonged to grizzlies, the king of predators, so their smaller, less ferocious cousins from the north never ventured south.

Then, in 1933, park rangers banished twenty-seven rambunctious black bears from Yosemite National Park in the north and exported them south, where they could roam free and stay out of trouble in the then uncivilized San Gabriel and San Bernardino mountains. Today, the cinnamon-colored American black bear stands out as a rare wildlife success story in a state where, more than any other place in the nation, hundreds of animals and plants hover on the brink of extinction.

An estimated 17,000–24,000 black bears – the largest population in decades – inhabit virtually every part of California, according to state wildlife biologists. The species is thriving everywhere it roves, including Los Angeles's local mountains, which are home to several hundred descendants of those Yosemite transplants.

Because their only enemy – the California grizzly – has been extinct since the 1920s, today's population of black bears might exceed the number that roamed the state before settlers headed West. With California's forests recovering from drought and hunters facing tougher regulations, bears are delivering larger, heartier litters and gaining a healthy layer of fat to survive the winters easily. In some rural areas these solitary, territorial animals are so numerous they are squeezed together at a density of two per square mile.

"You couldn't cram many more in," said Larry Sitton, a senior biologist at the California Department of Fish and Game who conducted a statewide bear survey a decade ago. "Right now the bears are just about filling all the space there is for them."

Increasingly cramped, these highly adaptive and versatile animals are expanding their territory, occasionally popping up in the oddest places – avocado groves in Ojai, onion fields near Bakersfield, even the Mojave Desert, the Santa Ana mountains and the Laguna Mountains of San Diego.

"The black bear is one of the best examples of a large mammal that is still doing well in the face of impacts from human civilization," said Glenn Stewart, a Cal Poly Pomona zoology professor who tracked Southern California bears from 1970 through 1990. "Coyotes are the other outstanding example of a medium- to large-sized animal that is competing well with humans."

But, as more bears share the wilderness with more people, the inevitable result is more conflict. Nuisance complaints and property damage have multiplied, and in two rare unprovoked attacks this month a young, 200-pound bear mauled two boys and injured several other campers as they slept at youth camps at Barton Flats in the San Bernardino Mountains. On Friday a black bear was spotted on a golf course in Lake Elizabeth, west of Palmdale, before being chased back into the Angeles National Forest by men in golf carts and sheriff's deputies.

Normally docile and easily frightened, the animals are becoming fearless in competing for food and territory.

"We're at carrying capacity for bears, so they are roaming around trying to find a place to exist," Stewart said. "Young bears that are dispersing from their mothers and trying to find homes of their own sometimes wind up in bad places – bad places in terms of their own survival and coming in contact with people."

This year [1993] ninety-three Californians, including five in the Southland, have been granted permits to kill bears that were damaging their homes, crops or livestock, according to the Department of Fish and Game. That is nearly twice the amount at this time last year. Wildlife officials grant permission to track and kill a bear when it causes repeated damage or threatens public safety; in three-quarters of cases the bear is never found. Conflicts usually peak between July and October, when bears are prone to eat just about anything and more people camp in the mountains. Every summer bears must gain an extra 100 pounds of fat to survive their winter hibernation.

"In summer they are consuming something like 20,000 calories a day, so they have to eat a lot," Stewart said. "With more people in the forest, more garbage, more people camping out, there's probably going to be more conflict."

Still, the chances of being attacked by a bear while camping or hiking are far lower than being struck by lightning, said Bob Stafford, the state's bear project co-ordinator. Only a few cases of unprovoked attacks have been recorded in California history, including the mauling of a man at Shasta Lake in 1992 and the recent attacks in the San Bernardino National Forest.

Encounters such as these "come in spurts", said Leroy Lee, a long-time houndsman in San Bernardino who tracks problem bears. "At one time it's mountain lions and then you go a long time with no problems. Now we are getting bear complaints." Lee added that hikers and campers frequently spend weeks in the San Bernardino Mountains or Sierra Nevada without encountering bears, but whenever he takes his bloodhounds, he discovers that the forest "is crawling with them".

In the late 1970s bears probably reached record lows in California because of unrestrained hunting and poaching. In 1983 the population numbered from 12,000 to 14,000, according to the state's five-year state bear study, which tracked about 200 bears. However, conditions now are just about perfect for bears. With the state's long drought shattered in two rainy springs, in 1992 and 1993, bears are finding a plentiful supply of berries and acorns, their favourite summertime cuisine. During the drought years bears were noticeably thinner. Although the animals typically do not starve to death, a female with insufficient fat cannot reproduce for an entire year. Now, with ample food, more females are giving birth, their litters often containing two cubs instead of one, and more of their young are surviving.

Although numerous animals are in jeopardy of extinction because the lands they inhabit are being bulldozed, forty-six million acres of pine and hardwood forests and shrub lands in California provide suitable bear habitat. More than half of that land is government owned and afforded some protection, according to a 1988 report by the state Department of Forestry. Also, unlike the threatened spotted owl, the black bear is not dependent on the thick, old-growth forests coveted for timber. Instead, they live in the fringes of a forest, where they forage on shrubs.

"Black bears prefer forests, in contrast to California grizzlies, which liked the prairies and foothills that were easily developed," Stewart said. "There are impacts to the forests from timber operations and over-grazing, so they are not entirely protected. But there is enough of that kind of habitat left in California that bears can do very well."

Poaching, according to wildlife wardens, also is believed to have declined, allowing the bear population to surge. The state mounted a crackdown in the mid-1980s on poachers who killed bears to sell their parts or hunt out of season. Also some areas in the state were made off limits to bear sport-hunting.

Still, some animal rights groups, led by the Fund For Animals, are trying to provide more protection for bears. Advocating a ban on bear sport-hunting similar to a ballot measure approved for mountain lions, they call the state's population estimates questionable and assert that hunting is thinning out young male bears.

Wildlife experts say California's bear population has almost peaked and many more would strain the capacity of the forests. If the population grows much more, natural selection would take over – reproduction will slacken as food becomes hard to find and males will kill each other in wars over territory.

To biologists the expanding territory of bears is a welcome trend. Black bears and mountain lions top the food chain as the only large predators left in California, and they help keep nature in balance by preying on rodents and other mammals.

But to those who are in the path of the bears' travels, it can be alarming. Bears in search of a few square miles to claim as their own are coming across suburbs, highways, camping grounds, ski resorts and logging camps, and, on these journeys, they realize that humans provide good supermarkets.

"They can get across freeways. They can swim real well. They can open doors. Nothing really stops them," Stafford said. "They are incredibly smart and they have an ability to exploit any number of things as food – carrion and insects, avocados . . ."

In July a bear raided a refrigerator in a cabin in El Dorado County, stole a slab of bacon and carried it to an upstairs bedroom for breakfast in bed, leaving a trail of slobber marks and muddy pawprints, said Stafford. In one month bears broke into sixty-two cabins in Plumas County.

In the Sierra Nevada bears sometimes bluff hikers, frightening them into running and dropping their food-laden backpacks. One bear routinely watches for mule trains crossing a precarious part of Siskiyou County's Marble Mountains, apparently in the hope of nabbing a pack toppling down a ravine. They swim across Pyramid Lake in Angeles National Forest to root through garbage cans on tiny Chumash Island. Some cross rural highways in Ventura County to pick avocados in groves, and farther north one recently caused a car wreck on Interstate 5 in Shasta.

Kevin-Barry Brennan, a state wildlife biologist in Hemet, said bears have been sporadically reported in the San Jacinto Mountains for several years, but tracks were not confirmed until the Spring of 1993. The bears, he said, probably traversed the San Gorgonio Pass and ambled across Interstate 10 at night, which means they now range farther south in California than ever before.

CANNIBAL SNIPPETS

In ancient Mexico, where the Aztecs sacrificed and sometimes cannibalized an estimated 15,000 victims yearly, Emperor Moctezuma is said to have preferred dining on the same young boys he chose to share his bed.

Cannibal killer Albert Fish also preferred the flesh of children, while California's Edmund Kemper devoured parts of at least two victims, later describing the act as a means of "possessing" them forever.

The "Chicago Rippers", four young satanists, habitually severed and devoured the breasts of women they abducted, raped and killed.

There is at least one case on record of serial murder and cannibalism commited as acts of revenge. Embittered by the murder of his wife by members of the Native American Crow tribe, trapper John Johnston waged a ruthless vendetta in the Colorado Rockies, killing scores of Crow and devouring their still warm livers, raw, as a gesture of contempt. When Hollywood tackled this story a century later, handsome Robert Redford took the eponymous lead as *Jeremiah Johnson*, the role being that of a romantic hero. No trace of liver-eating Johnston appeared on screen.

KILLER COUGAR OF EL DORADO

Piecing it all together later, the trackers concluded that the mountain lion (also known as a cougar or puma) must have watched Barbara Schoener from above, behind a cover of rock and brush. Maybe she had startled the lion from a morning nap. Maybe it was sick with rabies or simply hungry. For whatever reason, it did something mountain lions rarely do: it dropped down to the trail and fell in behind the jogger.

Schoener, a fit forty-year-old, weighed 120 pounds. The lion weighed more. It closed fast and quietly from a distance of twenty feet. The first blow knocked Schoener down a steep slope. Footprints indicate she took two long strides before she fell. The lion pounced. Somehow Schoener picked herself up and scrambled downhill another twenty-five feet. The lion pounced again.

"Defensive wounds on Barbara's forearms and hands," El Dorado County sheriff's investigators reported later, "make it apparent she did struggle with the lion." Either of two wounds – one to the neck, the other to the skull – could have been lethal.

The lion dragged what it didn't eat 100 yards away and then covered the remains with leaves.

This was early on the morning of Sunday, 1 May 1994. Sometime later that night – again from a reading of the tracks – the lion returned to its cache. By then, however, the body had been discovered and taken away by helicopter. By then, the lion was the one being hunted.

The little town of Cool is located near Auburn, about an hour from Sacramento, California. It is name after the Reverend Aaron Cool, who travelled the hills on horseback during the Gold Rush, preaching to miners in saloons. To judge by the proliferation of real estate store fronts and billboards, the population boom rumbling through the Sierra foothills – as restless Californians take flight from city and suburb alike – has not bypassed Cool.

More than 2,000 people reside here, most of them migrants from Los Angeles and San Francisco who live within a 900-home gated community called Auburn Lake Trails. The attractions are obvious. The development is well kept, the lots large and the prices modest by city standards. Deer roam the streets. The woods are a short walk in any direction.

The attack on Barbara Schoener – believed to be the first killing of a Californian by a mountain lion in the twentieth century – occurred among a network of winding trails that borders the community. Schoener, a marathon runner and mother of two, lived thirty miles away, but she came often to train on the trails. For the Auburn Lake residents her death has been the cause of healthy reflection. "Somebody got killed and eaten," said Fred Jones, a freelance nature writer who lives close to the attack site. "This is a serious business."

This is not to suggest, however, a general panic. Schoolchildren have been advised to avoid the trails and stick together. Pets have been taken in at night. Everyone's a bit more cautious, but no one is packing to go to Los Angeles. As the manager of the property owners association put it: "They'd rather take precautions against a possible mountain lion attack than take precautions against a possible drive-by shooting."

This attitude might serve the residents well, but it does not resolve some of the stickier questions raised by the attack. Since the killing, teams of hunters and dogs have picked slowly through the hills. The operation, run by the state Department of Fish and Game, is intended to track down the mountain lion and kill it. So far the hunt has come up with nothing. In the meantime, though, the public's calls to the Department of Fish and Game have been running at about sixty–forty against killing the big cat.

"One gentleman", a state biologist recalled, "volunteered to lead the mountain lion out of the area. People think of these wild animals as soft, cuddly things. They are efficient killers."

A sheriff's investigator said he's received demands that the cat be trapped and relocated. "The answer to that one is to say: 'Fine, can I put it in your back yard?'"

Differing explanations for the attack rattle through the community. Some see it as a total aberration, the work of a rogue animal. Others blame a statewide proposition that banned mountain lion hunts, causing the unmanaged population to more than double. Still others point to newcomers who treat deer almost like pets; as deer move closer, seeking handouts, mountain lions follow, seeking deer.

Finally, there are those who subscribe to the laws of probability. The real estate boom made such a tragedy inevitable. With more people in the hills and more mountain lions, more encounters were bound to happen. This theory seems to have logic on its side. It is also the most fatalistic. For lions always will behave as lions, and developers as developers – and there seems to be no outrunning either species.

SAN DIEGO MOUNTAIN LIONS

Authorities suspect that a mountain lion (also known as a puma or cougar) killed a woman whose body was found on Saturday, 10 December 1994, by two hikers in Cuyamaca Rancho State Park in eastern San Diego County.

The woman's body was badly mauled and scratched, and showed no gun shot or other wounds, according to Greg Picard, superintendent of the 26,000-acre park in the Cleveland National Forest, about fifty miles east of downtown San Diego.

If medical authorities determine that the woman was killed by a mountain lion, it would be only the second confirmed case in California of a person being killed by one of the big cats. The first was a forty-year-old woman killed in April 1994 in El Dorado County in northern California.

There have been several cases recently where mountain lions have chased or menaced visitors at Cuyamaca Rancho State Park.

Trackers have killed five mountain lions in or near the park in the past fifteen months after declaring them a threat. In the most serious incident, two rangers chased a mountain lion deep into the woods in September 1993 and shot it to death just moments after it had bitten a ten-year-old girl and attacked her dog.

At about 11 a.m. on Saturday, two hikers saw blood on a trail in the Paso Picacho portion of the park and then discovered the body about fifty feet off the trail. A backpack was also found.

The park, popular year-round with campers, hikers and picnickers, was immediately evacuated and will remain closed. The county medical examiner was called to determine the cause of the death of the woman described only as middle aged.

On Monday, 12 December 1994, authorities confirmed that the mountain lion shot on Saturday night is the animal that killed a fifty-eight-year-old woman who was hiking and bird watching in Cuyamaca Rancho State Park. But they were at a loss to explain why the mountain lions at the park have suddenly begun behaving aggressively towards humans.

In the past, zoologists have surmized that only a diseased, rabid or crippled mountain lion attacks people and that a healthy lion flees at the sight of a human. But Cuyamaca mountain lions that have menaced or attacked visitors have been healthy.

"The lions are behaving in a way we historically did not think they would," said Laura Itogawa, supervising ranger at Cuyamaca Rancho State Park. "I've been involved with this issue for two years and I wish I had answers."

Trackers in Saturday night chased and shot the lion after the fatal attack on Iris Kenna, a career counselor at a San Diego high school. It was the fifth lion killed in the past fifteen months after stalking or menacing people in or near the sprawling park east of San Diego.

County veterinarian Dr Hubert Johnstone, who performed the necropsy, said the 116-pound mountain lion was an adult male, fully capable of hunting deer. He said human hair and scalp were found inside the stomach, along with deer remains.

Jeff Weir, assistant deputy director for the state Department of Fish and Game, told reporters that the department plans a study to determine why the Cuyamaca cougars are behaving so aggressively and what can be done to protect the public. "Cuyamaca is a hot spot for cougars," Weir said. "There are several others, but Cuyamaca is the hottest."

Weir referred to Kenna's death as "a tragedy we're not sure we can prevent from happening again" until more is known about the Cuyamaca cougars' behavior.

Dr Mark Super, deputy medical examiner for San Diego County, said Kenna died of bites and clawing to the neck, head and upper body, and was probably attacked from behind while fleeing.

Mountain lion sightings have become increasingly common in California. The state mountain lion population is estimated by biologists to have tripled to more than 6,000 since a 1971 law made it illegal to hunt the big cats.

Mark Palmer, executive director of the Mountain Lion Foundation, said that the biggest concentration of mountain lions is in northern California, where there have been fewer sightings. "Something weird is happening at Cuyamaca," he said.

Kenna's death is the fourth in California from a mountain lion attack since record-keeping began. A woman jogger was killed in April 1994 in Auburn State Recreation Area in El Dorado County, and, in 1909, two people in Santa Clara County died of rabies after being bitten by mountain lions.

Rangers believe about twenty mountain lions may live in Cuyamaca Rancho State Park. By fleeing, Kenna may have done the wrong thing. "Mountain lions prefer to take down their prey from behind," said ranger Homer Townsend.

Rangers suggest that anyone who is confronted by a mountain lion should maintain eye contact with the animal, make noise and wait for the animal to leave.

Descanso, California – Now that their community has become the cougar capital of California, the residents of this tiny mountain hamlet, not usually given to philosophical musings, are discussing the proper relationship between man and beast.

The fatal attack on hiker Iris Kenna by a cougar at nearby Cuyamaca Rancho State Park on 10 December [1994] caught few by surprise in Descanso, where the 1,500 residents have learned to mix fear with respect when they regard the magnificent, heavily muscled predator also known as a mountain lion, puma or panther.

"Mountain lions kill. That's all they're designed by nature to do," said John Elliott, who runs a general store, a video rental business and a real estate firm. "The park invites people up to look at the animals like it's a zoo, but it's a zoo without bars."

Elliott, thirty-eight, said he has been awakened many a night by the sound of mountain lions growling in the moonlight. He carries a pistol when he goes into the woods.

Bob Merrigan, forty-five, who owns a cattle and horse ranch, puts it bluntly: "We have a saying in Descanso: 'When you enter the park, you enter the food chain, and you better know the risks.'"

Nestled in a small valley of trees and rolling hills in the Cuyamaca

Mountains, Descanso is the closest human encampment of the sprawling 26,000-acre park and serves as its southern gateway. Only a surveyor could tell you where Descanso ends and the park begins. With its smattering of stores and its single intersection, Descanso is less a town than a way of life; rustic, unhurried, unburdened by graffiti and noise, with plenty of open space to ride horses and breathe the mountain air at an elevation of 3,500 feet. The biggest business is the hay and feed store. To its residents – ranchers, blue-collar families, retirees, ageing hippies and high-income professionals willing to make the eighty-mile round trip daily on Interstate 8 to San Diego – Descanso is nothing short of bliss.

Into this Brigadoonish place – where a three-bedroom, 1,200-square-foot home on a third of an acre costs around $175,000 – has come the mountain lion. It is a menace that can grow up to eight feet in length from nose to tail and to a weight of 150 pounds.

"In any civilization killers aren't allowed to run loose," said Earl Hammond, fifty-seven, who, with his wife Liz, run Holidays on Horseback, taking tourists on rides from their Descanso home along the high-ridge trails of the park. "That's what we have now – killer animals running loose."

There have been other cougar sightings and cougar attacks in California as the animal's population has soared: a couple in Mendocino County were attacked, a boy was attacked in Santa Barbara County, and Barbara Schoener was killed north of Sacramento. But, in terms of numbers, the Cuyamaca cougars have been the most aggressive and unpredictable, for reasons no one can explain. Since mid-1993 six cougars have been killed with official authorization in or near the park after being deemed dangerous.

The mauling death of Iris Kenna earlier this month prompted the state Department of Fish and Game to term the Cuyamaca area California's "hot spot" for cougars. News of the deadly attack on Kenna, a fifty-eight-year-old high school counselor, has filled broadcasts from San Diego television stations, but residents of Descanso (which in Spanish translates roughly as "place of rest") have probably not seen it. Television is available only by satellite and the small dishes rented by a San Diego cable company provide only stations from Denver.

Descanso residents are used to surviving without many conveniences. There are no sewers; septic tanks are the rule. There is electricity, but no gas; propane tanks nuzzle beside most houses. There are no sidewalks, street lights or stop signs. Water is from wells. Except for the businesses of Elliott and restaurant owner Abbamonte, most of populated Descanso is set several miles west of the nearest highway, California 79, and does not hear or see the year-round stream of cars to the park.

"This is the last example of Main Street America, a real community, centered around church and school," said Abbamonte, a former New Yorker. Until recently the Descanso library, built in 1914, was listed in the Guinness Book of Records as the smallest in America at 198 square feet. The highlight of the Christmas season is the potluck dinner at the Community Hall, complete with a reading of "Twas The Night Before Christmas" and the arrival of Santa Claus. Residents hope the temperature will drop enough for the annual dusting of winter snow.

What do people like about living in Descanso? "Everything," said Ruth D'Spain, sixty-six, a member of a local planning board that has successfully fought to keep the community from being carved up into ranchettes and second homes. In the summer, when water is scarce, mountain lions venture out at dusk to drink from the horse troughs at the home of D'Spain's daughter.

"They're delightful to watch," D'Spain said, "but you learn not to go out and run around and call attention to yourself when the lions are around."

ITALIAN BROWN BEARS

If you go down to the Alps today, be sure of a big surprise: bears have returned to northern Italy for the first time in 130 years.

The return of the bears came to light recently when three women driving up a mountain road near the chic and upmarket ski resort of Cortina crashed when they swerved to avoid a brown bear which suddenly appeared in front of them. Local naturalists admitted yesterday that they had hushed up an incident a year ago in which bears had attacked and killed sheep in a mountain village on the outskirts of Cortina.

In a similar incident in October 1996 bears killed goats in the area. "In fact, there have been twenty confirmed sightings in the Dolomites since last Easter," one naturalist told *Corriere della Sera*. "But we kept them secret so as not to arouse alarm among tourists or farmers."

Bears have been absent from Italy since 1867, shortly before the country was unified. By the mid-nineteenth century farmers in the eastern Alpine villages had hunted bears almost to extinction because they preyed on livestock. The small number of surviving bears retreated across the border to Slovenia and had not ventured back until recently.

The World Wide Fund for Nature (WWF) said it was not clear why they had returned. The Fund said the Italian Alpine bear population was small and there was a danger that the bears might be hunted again. A year ago a large brown bear was found shot dead close to the border, on the Slovenian side. The WWF said it estimated that there were no more than fifteen adult bears in the area and perhaps five cubs. "We want to stabilize the population and make them self-sufficient within ten to fifteen years," a spokesman said. Under Slovenian law farmers can still shoot bears if they threaten livestock, but this is now forbidden under Italian law.

"A mountain valley with bears is more beautiful than a valley without bears," said Grazia Francescato, president of the WWF's Italian branch. She said people in northern Italy needed educating "to appreciate the positive presence of bears rather than fearing and shooting them."

Naturalists said there was evidence that wolves were also crossing from Slovenia into Italy.

THAI TIGER

A British wildlife expert is being sought by police in Thailand after a boy aged five had his arm ripped off by a tiger that had been adopted by animal lovers in Britain.

Police in Chachoengsao, east of Bangkok, said that Timothy Redford, a representative of the charity Care for the Wild International, was wanted on a charge of negligence. The charity insisted that Mr Redford, a former safari park keeper, had no responsibility for the management of the tigers.

The police have also ordered the closure of the compound, promoted in Care for the Wild fundraising literature as Tiger Mountain 2. The tiger, called Max, is one of two animals that have been used in advertisements to raise money to help to save tigers from extinction.

Police have already arrested a Thai businessman and a young boy keeper, who have been jointly feeding the tigers, and released them on bail of the equivalent of £600 each. The police said that all parties responsible for the tigers would have to pay compensation to the boy for his injuries.

Care for the Wild International first started raising funds for the two tigers in 1995, asking the public to adopt them by sending a cheque for £14.95 each – £10 of which would go directly to tiger welfare. An advertisement in the magazine *BBC Wildlife* said: "Sheba (the other tiger) was only a few days old when she was found close to the rotting and dismembered carcass of its mother . . . the Tiger Adoption Programme provides Sheba with food, shelter and attendants to watch over her as well as financing the rescue of any other unfortunate orphans."

Chris Jordan, managing director of Care for the Wild, said yesterday that the charity had no jurisdiction over the tigers: "Responsibility rests with the landowner and the Royal Forestry Department of Thailand." Mr Redford had acted as a consultant to the charity.

PAPUA'S SCHOOL FOR CANNIBALS

Neighbourhood disputes do not last long in the highlands of Papua New Guinea. If someone irritates you, a local *sanguma* or hired assassin will kill him or her for the price of a stick of home-grown tobacco. For good measure, the victim can also be eaten.

Sangumas are more than just hired killers, however. They are medicine men, sorcerers, the keepers of dark secrets. *Sangumas* operate by stealth, poisoning or putting evil curses on their victims. They also practise cannibalism – once widespread in PNG, but now banned.

Australian Catholic missionary, Brother Jim Coucher, claims to have evidence of a "*sanguma* school" operating close to the Indonesian border, in a remote highlands village called Yapsiei. Brother Coucher believes that this school is responsible for the deaths of at least two small boys – and the disappearance of seven others, all under the age of seven. "This is not a figment of the imagination. They are being eaten by *sangumas*," he said. "In some cases, people are sacrificing, then eating their own children. That's how caught up in the whole thing they are."

According to Brother Coucher, who has worked in PNG for thirty-five years, the school is being run by a "man with diabolical powers" who is already on the run from the Indonesian authorities. "This is not the first time that I've heard of schools for *sangumas*, but normally they (the initiates) are encouraged to eat the flesh from decomposed corpses. They don't have to kill," says Brother Coucher. "If they don't vomit up the flesh they pass the test."

Cannibalism used to be common in Papua New Guinea. Despite the best efforts of both Christian missionaries and colonial administrators, the practice has survived into the twentieth century.

According to the cannibalistic rites, it was believed that it was possible to acquire the strengths and wisdom of the deceased by eating his or her vital organs. The Angas people of the Central Highlands believed, for instance, that it was right to eat the organs of loved ones. This ensured that their goodness would be passed on to successive generations. The Angas' death ritual also involved hanging the dead person's body from the rafters of the house. Smoke from the central cooking fire would then preserve the body. When fully mummified, the corpses would be put on display around the village. There is evidence that the Angas were still mummifying their relatives and eating their organs as late as the 1920s.

Villagers attribute great powers to *sangumas*. "The *sanguma* do everything," said one man in Vanimo. "He cause your child to be sick or the crop go bad." Even the recent tidal wave has been attributed to the power of *sangumas*. Despite more than a century of work by Christian missionaries on the margins of this untamed and mountainous country, the old beliefs and superstitions still run deep.

"It is hardly surprising that these people are confused," said one long-time resident in Vanimo. "They've gone from the Stone Age to helicopters in one generation. Most of them never owned a bicycle before they saw a helicopter."

The irony, however, is that the re-emergence of the traditional *sanguma* comes at a time when Papua New Guinea is besieged by foreign Christian missionaries. In recent years, the American charismatic churches have joined the fray. The ratio of one missionary for every 200 inhabitants is the highest in the world.

MAN-EATING LEOPARD OF RUDRAPRAYAG

Villagers who survived the recent earthquake in Uttar Pradesh are being terrorized by a maneating leopard.

Rudraprayag district, close to the earthquake's epicentre in Chamoli, is famous for its maneaters. In 1926, Jim Corbett, the British hunter, shot a leopard that had killed 126 people. Today the villagers in this remote Himalayan region are easy prey. Fearing another earthquake, many are not prepared to stay in their damaged homes and have taken to sleeping out at night.

Bharat Singh Bhatola, sixty-four, from Tyunkhar village, said: "If we sleep indoors, the next earthquake will kill us. If we sleep in the fields as we are doing now, then the leopard will get us."

Two girls in a village outside Rudraprayag were eaten by a leopard last week, according to unconfirmed reports. Mr Bhatola also claims that a girl was killed in Luthiar village last month.

The Wildlife Institute of India, based in the nearby hill station of Dehra Dun, has embarked on an education project to reassure villagers about leopards. V. B. Sawarkar, its director, said that maneaters were very rare; many of the reported killings were untrue.

Asked about the latest threat, however, he said: "We suspect there may be an aberrant animal around."

Leopards, like tigers, eat humans only when they cannot hunt their normal prey because of injury or old age.

BANFF'S LETHAL COUGARS

People in the Canadian resort of Banff have been warned not to go alone into the countryside after a cougar stalked and killed a woman cross-country skier. The attack, on 4 January 2001, was the third incident involving the mountain lions in a few hours.

The body of Frances Frost, thirty, an actress and dancer with a troupe called Flukes of Nature, was found about eight miles north of Banff. A cougar measuring more than six feet in length had hidden behind a tree near the trail and pounced on Ms Frost's back as she passed, killing her. Park wardens, alerted by another skier who saw the cat with the body, shot it as it stood over her.

"Indications are that the animal actually stalked the victim," Ian

Syme, chief warden of the Banff National Park in the Rocky Mountains, said. "She may not even have been aware that this was taking place."

According to Mr Syme cougars rarely attacked human beings, however about five had moved closer to the town to feed on elk because they were competing with a wolf pack that had settled near them.

Early on Tuesday morning a cougar attacked an Alaskan husky sleeping in its kennel. "I came out and the cougar had Sarah by the back of her neck," said the dog's owner, John Peck, who was woken by its barking. The cougar ran off and the dog survived.

Hours later, on the other side of town, Cheryl Hyde was walking her pet schnauzer Christy along a trail near the Banff Springs Hotel when she came on a cougar feeding on the carcass of a newly killed elk. The cat followed her and cornered her before she was rescued by a neighbour who pulled her through the gate of his home.

"It may have just been warning us off its kill," Ms Hyde said. "It seems to me if it wanted to kill me, it would have. I was backing away and screaming, and it just kept coming. It didn't touch me, but it wasn't going away."

The area boasts Canada's oldest national park in 2,600 square miles of magnificent mountain wilderness known for the best skiing snow in North America and spectacular hiking and river rafting in summer. Park wardens distributed leaflets warning residents to take precautions, such as not allowing small children to go into wooded areas unsupervized, especially at night.

Mr Syme said that if adults wanted to go skiing or hiking, they should travel in groups and not take dogs because they attracted the cougars.

Although cougar attacks remain rare in North America, they are increasing. In the 1990s there were thirty-six recorded attacks, seven of which were fatal, compared with twenty, including two fatal ones, in the 1980s, and seventeen, four of which were fatal, in the 1970s. Although there have been several fatal cougar attacks in neighbouring British Columbia, Ms Frost's death was the first recorded in Alberta.

The wardens plan to move the cougars to remoter parts of the national park after fitting them with radio-tracking collars.

THE LEOPARD OF DEHRA DUN

A leopard has attacked and eaten a four-year-old girl in the foothills of the Himalayas.

The leopard grabbed the child on 12 March 2001 from her home in Bharwakatal village, near Dehra Dun, the capital of Uttaranchal State in India. It dragged the girl into the forest, where parts of her body were later recovered. It was the second such attack this year.

Chief wildlife warden A. S. Negi, said: "We have already declared the leopard a maneater after it killed a boy on 11 January, and have hired hunters to kill the leopard.

"The number of leopards is increasing in Uttaranchal. They are found in every part of the state, barring tiger reserves and big cities, and are thus facing no danger from predators. This has resulted in their coming into contact with human habitats and becoming maneaters or getting killed."

CAMBODIAN CROCODILES

A four-year-old Cambodian girl was eaten alive by crocodiles this week, 26 April 2001, when she fell into a pond at her grandfather's farm.

Siv Hong, the grand-daughter of fifty-two-year-old Kart Lim, dropped an item of clothing into the pond from a bridge, and then slipped and fell in while trying to retrieve it, said a member of her distraught family.

The grandfather jumped into the crocodile pond to try to save the child and was also attacked by the animals. A neighbour jumped in with a stick to rescue him and he was saved, though he received some nasty bite wounds.

The pond, in Kompong Thom province, north of the capital Phnom Penh, is home to some thirty to fifty crocodiles, said a news spokesman. Some farmers in Cambodia raise crocodiles for their skins, which are used to make items such as boots and handbags to be sold in expensive shops mainly in Hong Kong, the United States and Europe.

DEADLY SNAKES IN NEPAL

The monsoon has hit Nepal with extra venom this year, with eighteen people dying of snake bites since the onset of the seasonal rains in the west of the country.

Among the latest victims are a couple who died after being bitten by a highly poisonous krait snake while they were asleep in their village.

The couple were treated with traditional medicines in their village as there was no time to take them to a hospital. Even if bite victims can reach hospital quickly, there is no guarantee that they can survive the venom of snakes like the krait and cobra, which are found in the Terai lowland region of western Nepal.

American soldiers in Vietnam used to call the krait the "Five Step". The logic was that, if you got bitten by a krait, you would take five steps and then die.

Officials at a district hospital in the area said seventeen people had been admitted with snake bites, of whom four died on Thursday.

At the Tikapur-based Primary Health Centre in south-west Nepal officials said two people died of snake bites on Wednesday. Various health centres and hospitals around the region have reported ten more deaths since the monsoon began on 3 June 2001.

NEPAL'S BIG CATS

Two tigers killed eleven people in a single week in October 2001 in Nepal. Wildlife officials say the animals also mauled four other villagers.

One of the big cats has been caught and shot, the other is still on the loose, stated a report dated 31 October.

One of the maneating tigers killed six people in several villages in Nawalparasi district after straying out of Royal Chitwan National Park. The other tiger killed five villagers near Ayodhayanagar and is still on the move.

"We have sent technicians to the area after requests to track down the second maneater. We will dart it if the animal is young and healthy to be kept in a zoo, or kill it if it is old and sick," said a wildlife official.

Twelve days later: A maneating tigress has been shot dead in Nepal after killing seven people. The animal's latest victim was a woman looking for firewood and cattle fodder near an inaccessible forest.

Hunters decided to kill the tigress instead of trying to capture it. She had escaped from the National Park before terrorizing three villages in a month, reported a local news agency.

ALASKAN STALKER

Oregon woman escaped with bite and claw wounds after a mauling by a black bear that stalked her for more than an hour along a trail in South-east Alaska.

Kristy L. Abbott, twenty-seven of Harrisburg, Oregon, returned to work at American Safari Cruises, according to her father, Ralph Abbott, speaking from his home in Harrisburg. She could not be reached for comment.

Abbott told troopers that she was jogging on Petersburg Mountain Trail about 5 p.m. Wednesday [2002] she saw a black bear ahead. She stopped and sounded a portable air horn, but the bear charged. What followed were a harrowing brawl and chase, which Abbott described to her father later that night.

"She said she was at it for an hour and a half, and she traded blows with it just straight up," Ralph Abbott said. "She would keep it away with a stick as best she could. She said she somehow got a tree between the two of them, and for fifteen minutes or so she'd go one way and it would go the other."

He said his daughter did not turn her back on the gaunt, thin animal. She fought hard and edged back toward the trail head at Kupreanof State Dock. The confrontation ended when Kristy Abbott walloped the bear over the head with a large stick. She might have hit it in the eye, she told her dad. The bear lumbered away.

She was treated at Petersburg Medical Center for scrapes and puncture wounds on the back of her legs.

South-east Alaska is densely populated with black bears, said John Hechtel, a wildlife biologist with the Alaska Department of Fish and Game. Such attacks are rare but are not unheard of; he said. Black bears are typically unaggressive and shy around humans. But in rare cases black bears become single-minded predators and target people. They can attack and chase tirelessly, unruffled by loud noises or pepper sprays, encouraged by someone who runs away or plays dead.

"What you have to do is fend it off, try to fight back with all you've got, make yourself seem as big as possible, use a chunk of wood, a rock, whatever you can and concentrate your attack on the bear's face and nose," Hechtel said. "It sounds like this woman did the right thing."

SLOVAKIA'S BEARS

A group of passing mushroom pickers have saved a man who was almost killed by a large bear in Slovakia.

The thirty-year-old was attacked 3 August 2002 in a forest near Tatranska Strba He was airlifted to hospital in critical condition, but is recovering.

The group had heard his screams and ran to help. The bear fled when it saw the other people approach.

The bear attack is the most serious of a series which have happened in Slovakia's Tatra mountains this year. Daily newspaper *Novy Cas* reports that local ecologists say hungry bears have been woken early from hibernation due to record warm weather and a lack of forest food is forcing them to wander closer to villages and towns.

KILLER IN THE CATSKILLS

A 155-pound black bear killed a five-month-old girl on Monday, 29 August 2002, in the Catskills region, knocking her out of her stroller and carrying her into nearby woods, authorities said.

The baby was sleeping in her carriage by the porch of a bungalow, near her mother and two siblings, at around 2 p.m., said Fallsburg Police Chief Brent Lawrence. Witnesses told police that someone yelled, "Bear, bear, bear," he said. The mother shuttled her four- and two-year-old children inside the house, and, moments later, when she went outside again, the infant was gone.

Witnesses reported seeing the young bear with the baby, Esther Schwimmer, in its mouth as it ambled into dense woods twenty feet from the bungalow.

"It may be the first season that it may have been on its own, and it may very well have perceived this infant as a food source," said Lawrence. "I wouldn't categorize it as an attack – as far as a running, snarling attack."

Summer residents of the Machne Ohel Feige colony tried to scare the bear off. Isaac Abraham, a community leader from Williamsburg in Brooklyn, said people desperately tried to save the girl. "People started chasing the bear, throwing rocks at it," he said.

The bear dropped the infant, but she had severe injuries to her head and neck, and was pronounced dead at Ellenville Hospital, said Lawrence.

Department of Environmental Conservation and police officers pursued the young black bear into the woods. Fallsburg officer David Decker shot it once. "It was just standing there – it wasn't scared," Decker said. "As I walked toward the bear, the bear climbed up a tree. And that's when I shot the bear."

The bear had first appeared on the other side of the colony and several men chased it away. It circled to the other side and approached the bungalow near the woods, said a man standing outside the gate on Monday evening with several others. The man, who said he was a rabbi staying at a nearby camp, but declined to be identified, said bears were common in the area, but this was the first time one had been seen in Machne Ohel Feige. The child's parents left the camp on Monday evening to make funeral arrangements, he said.

"Everybody's paranoid," camper Toby Tessler said on Monday night. A second bear had been seen, he said. "The whole camp packed up."

Ward Stone, state wildlife pathologist, said it was the first time he could remember a black bear killing a human. Initial test results showed the young adult male wasn't rabid. Its stomach contained ants, seeds, vegetation, small plastic bags and fruit labels, showing it was familiar with people and their garbage, he said.

"In all my many years, thirty-four summers, we've had them eat birdseed, get into trouble eating dog food in people's yards, but black bears are just not noted for attacking humans," he said.

Four bullets were retrieved from the bear, two each from its head and neck. One bullet passed through his right forelimb, said Stone.

Black bears are common in that area of the Catskills region, Lawrence said. Fallsburg police get up to a dozen reports weekly of bears pawing through garbage cans or bird feeders.

The attack happened about seventy miles north-west of New York City, in the heart of what is known as the Borscht Belt. Big hotels and bungalows attract thousands of visitors each summer, many of them Jewish families from New York City. Scattered bungalow colonies remain. The town of Fallsburg swells from a permanent population of about 13,000 to 60,000 in the summer.

The Williamsburg community in Brooklyn, where many of the campers are from, was in shock on Monday, said Abraham. He said later that the child's father is Shmaya Schwimmer. The funeral and burial was held on Monday night in New Brunswick, New Jersey, in accordance with Jewish tradition. Many campers, he added, had cut short their stays and headed home.

The baby's grandfather is Mendel Schwimmer, who is active in the ultra-Orthodox Jewish community of Kiryas Joel. "The Governor knows the man," said Michael McKeon, Governor George Pataki's chief spokesman. "At the appropriate moment the Governor will be reaching out to call him to express his condolences."

THE TIGER AND SUBEDAR ALI

This is the story of Subedar Ali, who hit a man-eating tiger on the nose and has lived to tell the tale.

A man who fights bare-handed with a finally grown and hungry tiger could hardly expect to survive. Subedar felt the tiger begin to eat him and saw his own scalp in its mouth.

Doctors remark that he has a very strong will to live. In Delhi, the capital of India, for the eighth operation to repair his torn body, Subedar described his extraordinary encounter and escape.

Subedar is aged twenty-six and works as a *mahout* in Corbett Park, a range of jungle, river and scrub in the Himalayan foothills of northern India, where tiger, leopard and elephant roam wild. He and a fellow *mahout* rode their elephants into the jungle to cut fodder from the trees. They separated, and Subedar chained his elephant to a tree and climbed another to cut its branches with an axe.

He was about twelve feet above the ground when the tiger, which earlier had killed a man in Corbett Park, sprang at him, sank its claws into his legs and pulled him to the ground.

"I am a Muslim and I prayed to God," Subedar said. "I also prayed to the Hindu gods because I knew I needed much help."

He had the presence of mind to roll on to his front to prevent the tiger tearing at his abdomen and throat. The tiger sank its teeth into his shoulders and neck, bit off his left ear and lacerated his back from neck to thighs. Then it scalped him.

Holding Subedar's shoulder in its mouth, the tiger dragged him about ten feet into the bushes. As is usual in tiger attacks, his clothes had been pulled off Then the tiger rolled him over and straddled him. As the tiger went for his throat, the desperate man thrust his hand into its jaws and grasped its tongue and then hit its nose. The tiger bit his hand, leaving two fingers almost severed. Then it slashed at Subedar's face, slicing his lower lip in half and cutting his eyelids.

All the time Subedar was conscious and yelling at the top of his voice to his fellow mahout, Qutub, for help. His own elephant was trumpeting loudly.

Qutub emerged from the trees and the tiger backed off – tigers and elephants have a mutual dislike. Qutub placed his elephant between the tiger and Subedar, and the badly injured man rolled himself towards his own elephant and unfastened the leg chain. Weak from his wounds, he was unable to get up, so the elephant hoisted him with its trunk and placed him on its neck. Then, with the growling tiger padding closely behind, the two elephants walked for two miles back to the park offices.

Subedar was put into a truck and taken to a small hospital, where a doctor, using ordinary sewing thread, closed the bite wounds and claw slashes with 170 stitches.

Subsequently, Brijendra Singh, a warden at Corbett Park, had him taken 200 miles to hospital in Delhi. A series of painful repair operations was started. Over the following months skin from his legs was grafted on to his head to make a new scalp. His fingers and eyelids were mended.

Two weeks after the mauling, Brijendra Singh identified the tiger by its footprints, tracked it and finally lured it into a trap with a trail of meat. It is now in Kampur zoo. Subedar went to see it recently and marvelled at it size: nine feet long and 670 pounds in weight.

Subedar does bear a grudge. Indeed, he asked that the tiger should be captured, not killed. He will soon be back on full-time duty in Corbett Park and hopes to see many more tigers. "To be a *mahout* is the joy of my life," he said.

Acknowledgments
and Sources

The editor would like to thank Rosemary Cottrell, Barbara and Charles Jennings, and the staffs of Battersea Library and The British Library Newspaper Library in London for all their kind help and encouragement.

The editor and publisher are grateful to the publishers for granting permission to reproduce copyright material detailed below. While every effort has been made to locate all persons having any rights, the editor apologizes in advance for any errors or omissions inadvertently made.

Part 1 – Predators Among the Trees
Travels in West Africa, Mary Kingsley, Macmillan, 1897.
"A Devilish Cunning Panther", from *Tales from the Outposts*, Pardesi, Blackwood, 1933. Copyright © 1933 by William Blackwood & Sons.
"Headhunting" (World), *Collier's Encyclopedia*, no details.
"Among New Guinea's Head-Hunters", from *Pearls and Savages*, Frank Hurley, G. P. Putnam's Sons, 1924. Copyright © 1924 Frank Hurley. Reprinted by permission.
"The Wily Tiger of Mundachipallam", from *Nine Man-Eaters and One Rogue*, Kenneth Anderson, Allen & Unwin, 1954. Copyright © George Allen & Unwin Ltd, 1954. Reprinted by kind permission.
"The Rogue Elephant of Aberdare Forest," from *Hunter*, J. A. Hunter, HarperCollins, 1952. Copyright © 1952 by J. A. Hunter, renewed © 1980 by Hilda Hunter. Reprinted by permission.
"Vietnam Tigers", *www.lairweb.org.nz*, 2001.
"Cannibalism in Latin America", from *Encyclopaedia of Latin*

American History and Culture, Barbara A. Tennenbaum, Charles Scribner's Sons, no date. Reprinted by permission.

"The Black Bear of Mysore", from *Man-Eaters and Jungle Killers*, Kenneth Anderson, Allen & Unwin, 1957. Copyright © 1957 by Allen & Unwin. Reprinted by permission.

"The Rostov Ripper", *Sunday Telegraph*, London, 19 April 1992, *Independent*, London, 15 October 1992, and *The Times*, London, 15 October 1992.

"Wolves in Uttar Pradesh", *Daily Telegraph*, London, 26 March 1997.

"Secret Societies in West Africa", from *Travels in the White Man's Grave*, Donald MacIntosh, Neil Wilson Publishing; Abacus, 1998. Copyright © 1998 Donald MacIntosh. Reprinted by permission.

"Fly River, New Guinea", from *Four Corners*, Kira Salak, Counterpoint Press, 2001. Copyright © Kira Salak, 2001. Reprinted by permission.

"Sierra Leone Eating Habits", *The Times*, London, 10 May 2000; *Sunday Times*, London, 21 May 2000; *The Times*, London, 13 May 2000.

Part 2 – Blood on the Lowlands

"Issedones and Indians", from *The Histories*, Book 3, Herodotus, 3rd century BC.

"Celts in England", *www.bris ac uk*, 2001.

"The First Crusade", *Sunday Telegraph*, London, 11 July 1999.

"Sheriff Broth", *Sunday Times*, London, 25 October 1998.

"European Steak", from *Flesh and Blood*, Reay Tannahill, Hamish Hamilton, 1975; Abacus, 1996. Copyright © Reay Tannahill, 1975. Reprinted by permission.

"Mexican Meals", from *Cannibal*, Daniel Korn, Mark Radice and Charlie Hawes, Macmillan, 2001. Copyright © Daniel Korn, Mark Radice and Charlie Hawes, 2001. Reprinted by permission.

"Native American Cannibalism", from *The Tricksters' Epic*, Jake Page, Free Press, 2003. Copyright © Jake Page, 2003. Reprinted by permission.

"Napoleon's Retreat from Moscow", from *Flesh and Blood*, Reay Tannahill, Hamish Hamilton, 1975; Abacus, 1996. Copyright © Reay Tannahill, 1975. Reprinted by permission.

"A Ferocious French Wolf", *The Times*, London, 8 February 1838.

"The Franklin Arctic Expedition", compiled from various sources.

"Antipodean Cannibalism", from *Flesh and Blood*, Reay Tannahill, Hamish Hamilton, 1975; Abacus, 1996. Copyright © Reay Tannahill, 1975. Reprinted by permission.

"Fiji Cannibals", a missionary appeal on behalf of Fijians, 1836.

"Cannibalism in New Zealand", from *Christianity among the New Zealanders*, Right Rev. William Williams, Bishop of Waiapu, privately printed, New Zealand, 1867.

"Aborigine Recipe", from *Cooksland*, Rev. Dr Lang, Australia, 1842.

"Fiji Fancies", from *Cannibal*, Daniel Korn, Mark Radice and Charlie Hawes, Macmillan, 2001. Copyright © Daniel Korn, Mark Radice and Charlie Hawes, 2001. Reprinted by permission.

"Easter Islanders", from *Easter Island*, Alfred Metraux, OUP, 1957.

"Horror in the Sahara", article entitled "A Strange Tale of Cannibalism", Lafcadio Hearn *The Times-Democrat*, USA, 1882.

"Anasazi Man Corn", *Japan Times*, 12 July 1999, and *The Times*, London, 14 September 2000.

"South Sea Savages", from *Wanderings among South Sea Savages*, H. W. Walker, 1902.

"Russia 1918", from *On the Russians*, Maxim Gorky, no details.

"African Lions with an Appetite", from *Man-Eaters*, Michael Bright, Robson Books, 2000. Copyright © 2000 by Michael Bright. Reprinted by permission.

"Stalin's Terror Famine", source as in text.

"He Was a Good Lion", from *West with the Night*, Beryl Markham, Harrap, 1943. Copyright © Beryl Markham, 1943. Reprinted by permission.

"Spotted Hyenas Hunt in Packs", from *By The Evidence*, L. S. B. Leakey, Harcourt Brace Jovanovich, 1974. Copyright © L. S. B. Leakey, 1974. Reprinted by permission.

"White Fury on the Barrens", from *Danger!*, Ben East, E. P. Dutton, 1970. Copyright © by Ben East. Reprinted by permission.

"Tigers in the Sunderbans", *The Times*, London, 19 December 1984.

"Vampire Bites", *The Times*, London, 23 January 1986.

"A Dingo Took the Baby", *The Times*, London, 26 May 1992.

"Polar Bear Invader", *Chicago Tribune*, USA, 2 December 1993.

"China's Tradition of Cannibalism", *Cannibal*, Daniel Korn, Mark Radice and Charlie Hawes, Macmillan, 2001. Copyright © 2001 Daniel Korn, Mark Radice and Charlie Hawes. Reprinted by permission.

"Venomous Snakes", from *Snakes in Fact and Fiction*, James A. Oliver, Scribner, 1958. Copyright © 1958 by James A. Oliver, renewed 1987 by Ruth N. Oliver. Reprinted by permission of Scribner, a division of Simon & Schuster Inc.

"Bobcat Attack in South Georgia", *Atlanta Journal-Constitution*, USA, 14 February 1998.

"Cubans Turned Cannibal", *The Times*, London, 17 April 1998.

"Plane Crash in the Arctic", compiled from various sources.

"Trampling Elephants", *The Times*, London, 24 August 1991.

"A Leopard in Botswana", *The Times*, London, 17 July 1995.

"Death by White Rhino", *The Times*, London, 14 June 1996.

"Kenyan Devil Worshipers", *Daily Telegraph*, London, 21 September 1996.

"Bokassa of the Central African Republic", *The Times*, London, 5 November 1996; John Simpson, *Sunday Telegraph*, London, 10 November 1996.

"Polar Bear Charge", BBC Radio, August 2001.

"Cannibalism in Cambodia", Jon Swain, *Sunday Times*, London, 26 July 1998.

"Killer Lions of Zimbabwe", *Daily Mail*, London, 2 August 1999.

"Elephant Safari Death", *Sunday Times*, London, 6 August 2000.

"Chances with Wolves", *The Times*, London, 30 September 2000.

"Owl Attacks Human Love Rival", *Sun*, London, 8 March 2001.

"One Dark Night in Ethiopia", *Metro*, London, 30 October 2000.

"Fraser Island Kookaburras", *Morning Herald*, Sydney, 31 July 2001.

"Kenyan Killer Elephant", Ananova, 10 August 2001.

"Honey Bee Horror", Ananova, 13 August 2001.

"Angry African Aardvark", *Evening Times*, Glasgow, 10 October 2001.

"Scotch Steak on the Hoof", *Daily Record*, Scotland, 18 October 2001.

"Michigan Deer Devil", *www.Michiganlive.com*, 2 November 2001.

"Venom versus Septic Bite", from *The Red Hourglass*, Gordon Grice, Allen Lane, 1998. Copyright © Gordon Grice, 1998. Reprinted by permission.

"Panda Power", BBC World Service, 17 August 2001.

"Elephants in South Africa", Sapa, 24 January 2002.

"In the Tigers' Den", Reuters, 11 March 2002.

"Enraged Hippo in South Africa", Independent News Network, 12 April 2002.

"Canadian Cougars Pounce", Bell Globemedia Interactive Inc., 25 June 2002.

"He Ate It, Dr Lecter", Appendix to Report from the Select Committee on Transportation (1838) quoted in *Mrs Fraser on the Fatal Shore*, Michael Alexander, Phoenix Press, 2001.

Part 3 – Death in the Water

"Bold African Crocodiles", from *Eyelids of Morning*, Alistair Graham and Peter Beard, New York Graphical Society, 1973; Chronicle Books, 1990. Text copyright © 1973 by Alistair Graham. Reprinted by permission.

"The Sufferings of the Crew of the *Essex*", from *In the Heart of the Sea*, Nathaniel Philbrick, HarperCollins, 2000. Copyright © 2000 by Nathaniel Philbrick. Reprinted by kind permission.

"Dreadful Shipwreck of the *George*", *The Times*, London, 26 November 1822.

"Men Who Rivaled Jonah", from *Sea Mysteries and Adventures*, Edward Rowe Snow, Alvin Redman, 1964. Copyright © 1964 by Edward Rowe Snow. Reprinted by permission.

"The Burning of the *Cospatrick*", *The Times*, London, 31 December 1874, etc.

"Matawan Creek Shark Attacks", *New York Times*, 13 July 1916.

"Who's Who of Crocodilians", various sources.

"Around Lake Rudolf, Africa", from *Eyelids of Morning*, Alistair Graham and Peter Beard, New York Graphical Society, 1973; Chronicle Books, 1990. Copyright © Alistair Graham 1973. Reprinted by permission.

"A Cunning Crocodile", *By the Evidence*, L. S. B. Leakey, Harcourt Brace Jovanovich, 1974. Copyright © 1974, L. S. B. Leakey. Reprinted by permission.

"Bull Sharks", from *Man-Eaters*, Michael Bright, Robson, 2000. Copyright © 2000, Michael Bright. Reprinted by permission.

"Sharks in the Shallows", from *Shark Attacks*, Alex MacCormick, Constable & Robinson, UK, 1996, 2003; St Martin's Press, USA, 1997, 2003. Copyright © Alex MacCormick, 1996, 2003. Reprinted by permission.

"Rodney Fox's Shark", *Daily Mail*, London, 11 November 2000.

"Crocodile Baptism in Zambia", *Jamaica Daily Gleaner*, 1970.

"Alligator and Crocodile Bites", various sources.

"Diving Horror", *Los Angeles Times*, 20 November 1996.

"Gator Chews Two", *Los Angeles Times*, 22 July 1972.

"Caribbean Family Shipwreck", *Evening Standard*, London, 6 September 1995.

"King of Crocs", *The Times*, London, 8 February 1985.

"Search for a Shark", *Adelaide Advertiser*, 5 March 1985.

"The Crocodile at Cahill's Crossing", from *Crocodile Attack*, Hugh Edwards, HarperCollins, 1989. Copyright © 1989 by Hugh Edwards. Reprinted by permission.

"Dominican Boat Disaster", *Atlanta Journal-Constitution*, 8 October 1987.

"Italian Jaws", *The Times*, London, 6, 7 and 8 February 1989.

"California's Bay Area", *San Francisco Chronicle*, 16 September 1990.

"Brazil Shudders over Killer Crocs", *The Times*, London, 21 April 1991.

"South Australian Waters", *Adelaide Advertiser*, 8 September 1991.

"Hawaiian Holiday", *Vancouver Sun*, 3 December 1991.

"Killer Gator", *The Times*, London, 21 June 1993.

"Welsh Stingray Attack", source unknown, July 1994.

"Tanzanian Saurians", *www.flmnh.ufl.edu/natsci/herpetology/ newsletter*.

"Muggers in Nepal", *www.flmnh.ufl.edu/natsci/herpetology/ newsletter*.

"The Surf in Brazil", *New Scientist*, 19August 1995.

"Benin's Crocodiles and Pythons", *www.flmnh.ufl.edu/natsci/ herpetology/newsletter*.

"Crocodile Attacks in Madagascar", *www.flmnh.ufl.edu/natsci/ herpetology/newsletter*.

"Hong Kong Swimming in Blood", from *Shark Attacks*, Alex MacCormick, Constable & Robinson, UK, 1996, 2003; St Martin's Press, USA, 1997, 2003. Copyright © Alex MacCormick, 1996, 2003. Reprinted by permission.

"Andaman Islands' Salties", *www.flmnh.ufl.edu/natsci/herpetology/ newsletter*.

"Holiday Snaps in French Lake", *The Times*, London, 16 August 1996.

"Zambezi Explorers", *The Times*, London, 16 October 1996.

"South African Surf", from *Shark Attacks*, Alex MacCormick, Constable & Robinson, UK, 1996, 2003; St Martin's Press, USA,

1997, 2003. Copyright © Alex MacCormick, 1996, 2003. Reprinted by permission.

"Snap Snack", *The Times*, London, 13 October 1997.

"In the Teeth of Solomon", *The Times*, London, 24 February 1997.

"By the Skin of our Teeth", *Daily Mail*, London, 26 February 1997.

"Pringle Bay, South Africa", *Cape Times*, South Africa, and *The Times*, London, December 1997.

"Increase in South African Attacks", *Sunday Times*, London, 6 December 1998.

"Boy Bites Croc Back", Australian Press, 22 September 2000, 20 February 2001.

"South African Killer Crocodiles", *The Times*, London, 13 December 2001.

"Bod in a Cod", *Guardian*, London, 30 August 2000.

"The Perils of Oz Waters", *www.divernet.com/travel*, 2002.

"Florida Alligators Munch", news reports, no further details.

"Fatal Penis Attacks", *Melbourne Age*, 6 July 2001.

"Eight-year-old versus Saltie", *Sun*, London, 2 October 2001.

"Another Italian Great White", *Daily Mail*, London, 4 August 2001.

"Malawi Crocodiles Claim 250", BBC Online report, 7 February 2001.

"Death in Shallow Surf", *www.ananova.com*, 3 September 2001.

"Thirteen-Foot Snake", *Sun Star*, Philippines, 3 September 2001.

"Great Crocs of Oz", *www.ontheroad.net.au*, no date.

Part 4 – Killers Close to Home

"Pig's Baby Snack", *Glasgow Courier*, Scotland, 24 August 1888.

"In the Devil Bush", from *Travels in the White Man's Grave*, Donald MacIntosh, Abacus, 1998. Copyright © 1998 by Donald MacIntosh. Reprinted by kind permission.

"Man-Eater in a Railway Carriage", from *The Man-Eaters of Tsavo*, J. H. Patterson, Macmillan, 1907; St Martin's Press, 1985. Copyright 1907 by J. H. Patterson. Reproduced by permission.

"Some Serial Killers", from *Flesh and Blood*, Reay Tannahill, Abacus, 1996. Copyright © Reay Tannahill, 1975, 1996. Reprinted by permission.

"Starvation Diet Soviet Style", from *A People's Tragedy*, Orlando Figes, Pimlico, 1997. Copyright © 1996 by Orlando Figes. Reprinted by kind permission.

"Nightmares in the Soviet Union", from *Night of Stone*, Catherine

Merridale, Granta, 2000. Copyright © 2000 by Catherine Merridale. Reprinted by permission.

"The Siege of Leningrad", compiled from various sources.

"Japanese Soldiers Ate Prisoners", *Daily Telegraph*, London, 12 August 1992.

"Safari Ants", from *By the Evidence*, L. S. B. Leakey.

"Gaboon Viper's Revenge", *San Francisco Chronicle*, 6 April 1983.

"Revenge of the Vampire Bats", *The Times*, London, 25 July 1991.

"Jeffrey Dahmer", *www.apbonline.com*, 2002.

"Issei Sagawa", *Sunday Times*, London, 21 November 1993.

"White Tiger in Miami", *Los Angeles Times*, 7 June 1994.

"Kiss of the Scorpion Man", *The Times*, London, July 1994.

"South Korean Cannibal Gang", *The Times*, London, 1 November 1994.

"Hungry Brazilians", *Guardian*, London, 16 April 1994.

"The Wolf Inside Every Dog", *The Times*, London, 16 November 1994.

"America's Rabid Foxes", *Washington Times*, 6 August 1997.

"Dangerous Critters at Home", *Observer*, London, 11 September 1994.

"Ungrateful Angolan Tiger", *The Times*, London, 17 March 1994.

"L.A. Coyote Tales", *Observer*, London, 5 June 1994.

"Balkash the Siberian Tiger", *The Times*, London, 17 February 1995.

"Streetwalking Cougars", *Sunday Times*, London, 14 May 1995.

"Bustah the Chimpanzee", *The Times*, London, April 1994.

"Chinese Foetus-Eaters", *Eastern Express*, Hong Kong, 12 April 1995.

"Elephants in South Africa", *The Times*, London, 6 July 1996.

"Cabo the Jungle Cat", *Chicago Tribune*, 2 July, 19 September 1995.

"A Burmese Python in the Bronx", *The Times*, London, 11 October 1996.

"Russian Cannibalism Flourishes" *The Times*, London, 28 March 1996.

"Nikolai Dzhurmongaliev" *www.escapee.fsnet.co.uk*, 2002.

"Cannibalism by Russian Military", *The Times*, London, 7 October 1996.

"Killer Bees in the USA", *Daily Mail*, London, no date.

"Scottish Teddy Bear's Picnic", *The Times*, London, no date.

"A Khmer Rouge Cannibal", *Sunday Times*, London, 23 April 1995.

"Miss Daisy Mae Piggy", *Chicago Tribune*, 4 July 1997.

"Red Fire Ants", *ens.lycos.com*, Copyright © Lycos, Inc. 1999. Carnegie Mellon University. Reprinted by permission.

"Rabid Bats Alert", *Chicago Tribune*, 29 October 1998.

"Tapir Teeth", *Atlanta Journal-Constitution*, 21 November 1998.

"Illinois Brown Bear Munch", *Chicago Tribune*, 30 June 1999.

"Big Snapper in the Big Apple", *Guardian*, London, 16 June 2000.

"Taiga Tiger", *Chicago Tribune*, 16 August 2000.

"Bull Elephant in Thailand", *Guardian*, London, 26 April 2000.

"Serial Killer Snakes in Nigeria", *The Vanguard*, Nigeria, 3 and 6 August 2001.

"Malaysian King Cobra", *Straits Times*, 22 October 2001.

"Rabid Dogs", *Independent*, London, 1 June 2001.

"Black Bears in New Mexico", *www.leopard@bigcats.com/ www.bears.org*, 2001.

"Vodka and People Meat", internet, 2001.

"Dr Doolittle and the Lion", *Las Ultimas Noticias*, Chile, 13 August 2001.

"Leopard on the Campus", *Times of India*, 22 September 2001.

"Black Widow Spiders", from *The Red Hourglass*, Gordon Grice, Allen Lane, 1998. Copyright © Gordon Grice, 1998. Reprinted by kind permission.

"Baboons Rampage in Saudi Arabia", *Khaleej News*, Saudia Arabia, 14 August 2001.

"Swaziland Baboons", *Swaziland Star*, South Africa, 13 June 2001.

"Louis and the Cheetah", *The Times*, London, no date.

"Shalini and the Wolf", Star TV News, India, 18 September 2001.

"Wellington Bomber Seagulls", *This Is Gloucestershire*, UK TV, 18 July 2001; *Evening Argus*, Brighton, England, 3 July 2001.

"Elephants' Fatal Attraction", *Independent*, London, 22 March 2002.

"Wild Indian Elephants", *Times of India*, 18 October 2001.

"Bear in US Home", Ananova, 21 August 2001.

"Frenzied Hornets", *South China Morning Post*, 2 July 2001.

"Texas Bee Stings", *www.Click2Houston.com*, 24 April 2001.

"Mistaken Swans", *Shropshire Star*, UK, 28 March 2001.

"Boishie British Buzzards", *Star*, London, 6 July 2001; Ananova, 21 June 2001.

"The Belev Cannibal", *Pravda*, Moscow, 28 June 2001.

"Cockerel in Romania", Romanian press, 15 February 2001.

"Chile Hot Dogs", *Las Ultimas Noticias*, Chile, 3 August 2001.

"Boas and Pythons", various sources, August 2001.

"The Internet Cannibal", *Independent*, London, 14 December 2002.

"Reynard the Fox", *Daily Mail*, London, 2 July 2002.

"Eating Babies Is Art", *Sunday Times*, London, 29 December 2002.

"Rabid Fox in Maine", Blethen Maine Newspapers Inc., 8 August 2002.

"Max the Florida Lion", Associated Press, 13 May 2002.

"Monty's Fatal Squeeze", *Denver Post*, 10 February 2002.

"Norwegian Huskies", *Independent*, London, 1 February 2002.

Part 5 – Horror in the Uplands

"European Neanderthals", *Daily Mail*, London, 16 October 1999.

"Aztec Blood Sacrifices", from *Daily Life of the Aztecs*, Jacques Soustelle, Hachette, 1955; Weidenfeld & Nicolson, 1961. Copyright © Hachette, Paris, 1955, 1995; English translation copyright © 1961 by Weidenfeld & Nicolson. Reprinted by permission.

"The Chowgarh Tigers", from *The Maneaters of Kumaon* in *The Jim Corbett Omnibus*, Jim Corbett, OUP India 1991. Copyright © Oxford University Press, 1991. Reprinted by permission.

"A Grizzly in Yellowstone", *Los Angeles Times*, 26, 28 June 1972.

"The Andes Air Crash", *The Times*, London, 1972, 1974.

"Wolves and Wild Dogs", from *Man-Eaters*, Michael Bright, Robson Books, 2000. Copyright © 2000 Michael Bright. Reprinted by permission.

"Tiger Victim in India", *The Times*, London, February 1985.

"Bear Encounters in North America", from *Bear Attacks*, Stephen Herrero, Airlife Publishing Ltd, 1985, copyright © 1985 by Stephen Herrero, reproduced by kind permission of Lyons & Burford; and from *Alaska Bear Tales*, Larry Kaniut, Alaska Northwest Publishing, 1983; and from sources cited in text.

"Derek from New Guinea", *Sunday Times*, London, 17 May 1992.

"Clawed to Death in the Rockies", *The Times*, London, 18 September 1992.

"The Black Bears of California", no details.

"Cannibal Snippets", gathered by the editor.

"Killer Cougar of El Dorado", *Los Angeles Times*, 1 May 1994.

"San Diego Mountain Lions", *Los Angeles Times*, 19 December 1994.

"Italian Brown Bears", *The Times*, London, 31 March 1997.

"Thai Tiger", *The Times*, London, 22 April 1998.

"Papua's School for Cannibals", *Sunday Telegraph*, London, 23 August 1998.

"Man-Eating Leopard of Rudraprayag", *Daily Telegraph*, London, 6 April 1999.

"Banff's Lethal Cougars", *The Times*, London, 5 January 2001.

"The Leopard of Dehra Dun", Ananova, 14 March 2001.

"Cambodian Crocodiles", *The Times*, London, 26 April 2001.

"Deadly Snakes in Nepal", *Kathmandu Post*, 29 June 2001.

"Nepal's Big Cats", Nepal news agency website, 31 October 2001.

"Alaskan Stalker", Associated Press, 12 July 2002.

"Slovakia's Bears", *Novy Cas*, Slovakia, 5 August 2002.

"Killer in the Catskills", *The Times,* London, 30 August 2002.

"The Tiger and Subedar Ali", Trevor Fishlock, *Guardian*, London, no date.